HISTORICAL DICTIONARIES
OF WAR, REVOLUTION, AND CIVIL UNREST
Edited by Jon Woronoff

Historical Dictionary of World War II

The War Against Japan

Anne Sharp Wells

Historical Dictionaries of War,
Revolution, and Civil Unrest, No. 13

The Scarecrow Press, Inc.
Lanham, Maryland, and London
1999

SCARECROW PRESS, INC.

Published in the United States of America
by Scarecrow Press, Inc.
4720 Boston Way
Lanham, Maryland 20706
http://www.scarecrowpress.com

4 Pleydell Gardens, Folkestone
Kent CT20 2DN, England

British Library Cataloguing in Publication Information Available

Library of Congress Cataloging-in-Publication Data

Wells, Anne Sharp.
   Historical dictionary of World War II: the war against Japan / Anne Sharp Wells.
      p.   cm. — (Historical dictionaries of war, revolution, and civil unrest ; no. 13)
   Includes bibliographical references.
   ISBN 0-8108-3638-6 (cloth : alk. paper)
      1. World War, 1939–1945—Pacific Area—Dictionaries.   2. World War,
   1939–1945—Japan—Dictionaries.   3. Sino-Japanese Conflict, 1937–1945—
   Dictionaries.   I. Title.   II. Series.
   D767.9.W43   1999   99-10674
   940.54′25—dc21   CIP

To Chris and Becky

Contents

Maps

Photographs

Editor's Foreword

No other war can compare with World War II when it comes to the number of countries involved, combatants and civilians affected, and battles and other engagements fought. Nor can any other war compare in terms of those killed or maimed, taken prisoner, and afflicted by hunger and suffering amid the destruction of whole cities and vast countrysides. World War II was a war that changed the worldwide power structure, marking the relative decline of Germany, Japan, and the United Kingdom and the rise to superpower status of the United States and (temporarily) the Union of Soviet Socialist Republics. It also changed the face of war, with carriers replacing battleships and submarines wreaking havoc for all shipping, aircraft of all sorts gaining an edge over both land and sea forces, and increasingly lethal weapons placed at the disposal of all forces. Yet, out of this hecatomb emerged more positive currents, the move toward independence of colonial peoples, a gradual spread of democracy, and the rise of worldwide organizations such as the United Nations.

Although it was one war, there were substantial differences between the war against Japan and the war against Germany and Italy. In the Pacific, the role of the United States was clearly preponderant, with the other Allies playing relatively lesser parts. Because of its location, war in the Pacific involved naval forces much more than the war against Germany and Italy, and naval strategy played a more critical role. It was also against Japan that the most devastating weapon yet, the atomic bomb, was used and finally terminated the conflict. The postwar sequel bore similarities, with the Iron Curtain descending in Korea, China, and Indochina but not Japan. Indeed, several decades later, Japan would seem to have achieved most of its goals—aside from territorial aggrandizement—through peaceful means by trading with the very same countries it had fought against. This showed the futility of a war it stood little chance of winning.

World War II was also characterized by incredible complexity, the complexities of keeping alliances together, coordinating different branches of the armed forces, and attempting to restore peace and create a new world order. This makes World War II harder to describe than World War I, let alone more traditional wars. That is one of the main challenges, and also one of the main achievements, of this *Historical Dictionary of World War II: The War Against Japan,* soon to be joined by a second volume on the war against Germany and Italy. It includes entries on most of the countries involved, the major military units, and military commanders of note as well as the civilians in charge on both sides. Other entries present numerous battles and campaigns, new types of ships, aircraft, and weapons, improvements in logistics and medicine, advances in intelligence, basic strategies and tactics, and crucial bodies and conferences. To keep track of the many events, the chronology is most helpful, and the introduction affords a broader view. Because two volumes (or even ten) can hardly do justice to this war, the bibliography should be particularly welcome, with its abundance of further sources of information.

The author of both volumes on World War II is Anne Sharp Wells, who was educated at Mississippi State University and the University of Alabama, among others. She is presently a member of the staff of the George C. Marshall Foundation and serves as assistant editor of the *Journal of Military History.* From 1988 to 1997, she was on the administrative faculty of the Virginia Military Institute. But she has also been a librarian, archivist, and research assistant in the Douglas MacArthur Biographical Project, all of which were useful for this project. More notably, she has coauthored several books (with D. Clayton James), two of them on the Second World War: *A Time for Giants: Politics of the American High Command in World War II* and *From Pearl Harbor to V-J Day: The American Armed Forces in World War II.* This experience has resulted in a historical dictionary characterized by conciseness and precision, precious virtues when writing about such a complex and momentous war.

Jon Woronoff
Series Editor

Preface

Because of the enormity of World War II and the numerous geographic areas and belligerents involved, this study has been divided into two volumes. The first examines the war between Japan and the Allied powers, which took place primarily in Asia and the Pacific. Chronologically, it covers the conflict in Asia beginning with the Japanese seizure of Manchuria in September 1931, the expansion of the war following Japan's far-ranging attacks on Western-held areas in December 1941, the formal Japanese surrender in September 1945, and the immediate postwar years in Asia and the Pacific. Although this book includes references to numerous people and nations also involved in the hostilities with the European Axis powers, the entries focus on their relationship to the war against Japan. The second volume will address the war against Germany and Italy.

Japanese personal names appear in the text in Western style, with the surname last. The names of military figures carry their highest wartime ranks except for references to specific events or time periods, when contemporary ranks are substituted. Geographic locations are identified by their wartime English names. Within the dictionary section, (q.v.) and (qq.v.) refer the reader to additional entries.

This work relies heavily on the extensive and varied literature on World War II. Fortunately for this project, the staffs of the George C. Marshall Research Library, the Preston Library of the Virginia Military Institute, and the Leyburn Library of the Washington and Lee University have shared with me their splendid holdings on the war, including additionally, in the case of the Marshall Library, its excellent photographic collection. The series editor, Jon Woronoff, has provided me with valuable guidance and support. My special thanks go to Erlene and D. Clayton James for their encouragement and assistance with this project.

Acronyms and Abbreviations

AA	Antiaircraft
AAF	Army Air Forces (U.S.)
ABC	American-British Conversations
ABDACOM	American-British-Dutch-Australian Command
AFPAC	Army Forces, Pacific (U.S.)
AGF	Army Ground Forces (U.S.)
Alcan	Military highway between Alaska and Canada
Amtrac	Amphibious tractor
ANZAC	Allied command to defend the waters between Australia, New Zealand, and New Caledonia
ASF	Army Service Forces (U.S.)
ASW	Antisubmarine warfare
ATC	Air Transport Command (U.S.)
ATIS	Allied Translator and Interpretation Section, Southwest Pacific Area
AVG	American Volunteer Group
BAR	Browning automatic rifle
BCOF	British Commonwealth Occupation Force
BCOS	British Chiefs of Staff Committee
BJSM	British Joint Staff Mission
CATF	Chinese Air Task Force
CBI	China-Burma-India theater (U.S.)
CCS	Combined Chiefs of Staff (Anglo-American)
CENPAC	Central Pacific Area (Allied)
CIC	Combat Information Center
CIGS	Chief of Imperial General Staff (British Army)
CNO	Chief of naval operations (U.S.)
COMINCH	Commander in chief, U.S. Navy
CV	Aircraft carrier
CVE	Aircraft carrier escort

DDT	Dichloro-diphenyl-trichloroethane
DE	Destroyer escort
FBI	Federal Bureau of Investigation (U.S.)
FDR	Franklin D. Roosevelt
FEAF	Far East Air Force(s) (U.S.)
FMF	Fleet Marine Force
G-1	Personnel section (U.S. Army)
G-2	Intelligence section (U.S. Army)
G-3	Operations and training section (U.S. Army)
G-4	Supply and logistics section (U.S. Army)
G-5	Civil affairs section (U.S. Army)
GHQ	General headquarters
GPO	Government Printing Office (U.S.)
HMSO	His (or Her) Majesty's Stationery Office
ICRC	International Committee of the Red Cross
IGH	Imperial General Headquarters (Japan)
IJA	Imperial Japanese Army
IJN	Imperial Japanese Navy
IMTFE	International Military Tribunal for the Far East (Allied)
IRAA	Imperial Rule Assistance Association (Japan)
JCS	Joint Chiefs of Staff (U.S.)
LCI (L)	Landing craft, infantry (large)
LCI (R)	Landing craft, infantry (rocket)
LCM	Landing craft, mechanized
LCP (R)	Landing craft, personnel (ramp)
LCT	Landing craft, tank
LCV	Landing craft, vehicle
LCVP	Landing craft, vehicle and personnel
LORAN	Long-range navigation system
LSD	Landing ship, dock
LSM	Landing ship, medium
LST	Landing ship, tank
LVT	Landing vehicle, tracked
MID	Military Intelligence Division (U.S. Army)
MIS	Military Intelligence Service (U.S. Army)
NDRC	National Defense Research Committee (U.S.)
OCMH	Office of the Chief of Military History (U.S. Army)
OFS	Office of Field Service (OSRD)
ONI	Office of Naval Intelligence (U.S.)

OPD	Operations Division (U.S. Army)
OSRD	Office of Scientific Research and Development (U.S.)
OSS	Office of Strategic Services (U.S.)
OWI	Office of War Information (U.S.)
POA	Pacific Ocean Areas (Allied)
POW	Prisoner of war
PT	Patrol torpedo (boat)
RAAF	Royal Australian Air Force
RAF	Royal Air Force
RAN	Royal Australian Navy
RCAF	Royal Canadian Air Force
RCN	Royal Canadian Navy
RN	Royal Navy
RNN	Royal Netherlands Navy
RNZAF	Royal New Zealand Air Force
SACO	Sino-American Cooperative Association
SCAP	Supreme commander for the Allied Powers
SEABEE	U.S. Navy Construction Force
SEAC	Southeast Asia Command (Allied)
SOA	Special Operations Australia
SOE	Special Operations Executive (U.K.)
SOPAC	South Pacific Area (Allied)
SOS	Service of Supply (U.S. Army)
SPAR	Coast Guard women's reserve (U.S.)
SWNCC	State-War-Navy Coordinating Committee (U.S.)
SWPA	Southwest Pacific Area (Allied)
TF	Task force
U.K.	United Kingdom of Great Britain and Northern Ireland
UN	United Nations
U.S.	United States of America
USAAF	U.S. Army Air Forces
USAWWII	The U.S. Army in World War II
USCG	U.S. Coast Guard
USMC	U.S. Marine Corps
USN	U.S. Navy
USSBS	U.S. Strategic Bombing Survey
U.S.S.R.	Union of Soviet Socialist Republics
V-J	Victory over Japan
VLR	Very long range
WAAC	Women's Auxiliary Army Corps (U.S.)

WAC	Women's Army Corps (U.S.)
WASP	Women's Airforce Service Pilots (U.S.)
WAVE	Women Accepted for Volunteer Emergency Service (U.S. Navy)
WPD	War Plans Division (U.S. Army)
WSA	War Shipping Administration (U.S.)

Chronology

1931

Sept. 18–19   The Japanese Kwantung Army begins its seizure of Manchuria from China.

1932

Jan. 7   U.S. Secretary of State Henry L. Stimson announces that the United States will not recognize territorial changes acquired through aggression.

Jan. 28–May 5   Japanese troops take control of Shanghai, China, withdrawing after a truce with the Chinese government.

Feb.18   Japan proclaims the independence of Manchukuo (formerly Manchuria) and sets up a puppet government.

Nov. 8   Franklin D. Roosevelt is elected president of the United States.

1933

Mar. 27   Japan announces that it will withdraw from the League of Nations.

May 31   Japan and China conclude the Tangku Truce, after Japan's seizure of Chinese territory.

1935

June   China yields to Japanese territorial demands in the Ho-Umezu agreement.

1936

Nov. 25   Japan and Germany sign the Anti-Comintern Pact.

Dec. 12–25   Chang Hsüeh-liang forces Chiang Kai-shek to agree to cooperate with the Chinese Communists against Japan.

1937

July 7	The Sino-Japanese War begins with clashes between Japanese and Chinese soldiers at the Marco Polo Bridge near Peking, China.
July 28	Japanese troops occupy Peking, China.
July 29	Japanese forces move into Tientsin, China.
Aug. 8–Nov. 8	Shanghai, China, falls to Japanese control.
Aug. 21	The Union of Soviet Socialist Republics (U.S.S.R.) and China sign a nonaggression pact.
Dec. 12	Japanese planes sink the U.S. gunboat *Panay* in the Yangtze River in China.
Dec. 13	Japanese troops capture Nanking, China, and commit atrocities during the "rape of Nanking."

1938

Apr.	Chinese troops defeat Japanese forces in the Battle of Taierchwang.
May 20	Japanese soldiers capture Hsuchow, China.
July 11–Aug. 10	Japanese and Russian forces clash at Changkufeng near the Soviet, Korean, and Manchurian borders.
Oct. 21	Japan captures Canton, China's last open seaport.
Oct. 25	Japanese forces move into Hankow, China.
Nov. 3	Prime Minister Fumimaro Konoye announces Japan's concept of a New Order in East Asia.

1939

May 11–Sept. 16	Japanese and Soviet troops fight between Khalkhin Gol and Nomonhan on the Manchurian-Mongolian border.
Aug. 23	Germany and the U.S.S.R. sign a nonaggression pact.
Sept. 1	Germany invades Poland in the start of World War II in Europe.
Sept. 1	General George C. Marshall becomes chief of staff, U.S. Army.

1940

Apr.–May	The headquarters of the U.S. Fleet moves from California to Pearl Harbor in the Hawaiian Islands.
May 10	In Europe, Germany begins its invasion of the Netherlands, Belgium, Luxembourg, and France; Winston S.

	Churchill becomes prime minister of the United Kingdom.
June 22	France surrenders to Germany and establishes a government at Vichy allied with Germany.
July 18–Oct. 18	The British close the Burma Road to China in response to Japanese demands.
Aug. 20–Nov. 30	Chinese Communist troops carry out the Hundred Regiments Offensive against Japanese forces in northern China.
Sept. 23	Japan sends troops into northern French Indochina after pressuring Vichy France for permission.
Sept. 26	President Roosevelt prohibits exports of scrap iron and steel except to the United Kingdom.
Sept. 27	Italy, Germany, and Japan sign the Tripartite Pact, forming the Rome-Berlin-Tokyo Axis.
Oct. 12	The Imperial Rule Assistance Association replaces all political parties in Japan.
Oct. 21	The U.S. Asiatic Fleet moves its headquarters from China to the Philippine Islands.
Nov. 5	President Roosevelt is elected to a third term as U.S. president.
Nov. 12	U.S. Admiral Harold R. Stark submits his Plan Dog Memorandum regarding U.S. strategy in event of war.

1941

Jan. 10	Thailand invades French Indochina.
Jan. 27–Mar. 29	American-British Conversations in Washington produce the ABC-1 strategic document.
Jan. 31	Japan mediates the conflict between Thailand and French Indochina.
Feb. 1	Admiral Husband E. Kimmel is named commander in chief, U.S. Fleet, at Pearl Harbor.
Mar. 11	U.S. Congress passes the Lend-Lease Act.
Apr. 13	Japan and the U.S.S.R. sign a neutrality treaty.
June 22	Germany invades the U.S.S.R.
June 28	The United States establishes the Office of Scientific Research and Development.
July 25	Japan sends troops into southern French Indochina.
July 26	In response to the Japanese move into Indochina, President Roosevelt freezes Japanese assets in the United States, imposes an oil embargo on Japan, and national-

	izes the Philippine Army under the command of Major General Douglas MacArthur.
Aug. 9–12	President Roosevelt, Prime Minister Churchill, and their military advisers meet secretly in the Atlantic Conference.
Aug. 14	President Roosevelt and Prime Minister Churchill announce the Atlantic Charter.
Oct. 7	John Curtin becomes prime minister of Australia.
Oct. 18	General Hideki Tojo succeeds Konoye as prime minister of Japan.
Nov. 1	President Roosevelt places the Coast Guard under the control of the navy.
Nov. 17	The U.S. authorizes the arming of merchant ships.
Nov. 26	A Japanese task force under Vice Admiral Chuichi Nagumo departs for Pearl Harbor.
Nov. 27	U.S. officials in Washington warn commanders in the Pacific that war may be imminent.
Dec. 7	Japan attacks the U.S. Pacific Fleet at Pearl Harbor, other U.S. military installations in Hawaii, and U.S. bases on Midway Island.
Dec. 8	Japan invades Malaya and Thailand, while also attacking Hong Kong, the Philippine Islands, Guam (Mariana Islands), Wake Island, and the Nauru and Ocean Islands. Japan also occupies the International Settlement at Shanghai, China. (Because of the International Date Line, many of these attacks occur during the same time period as those of Dec. 7.)
Dec. 8	The Netherlands, the United Kingdom, and the United States declare war on Japan.
Dec. 9	Japanese troops land in the Gilbert Islands.
Dec. 9	China declares war on Japan, Germany, and Italy.
Dec. 10	Japan sinks the British ships *Prince of Wales* and *Repulse* off the Malay coast in the South China Sea.
Dec. 10	Japan seizes Guam (Mariana Islands).
Dec. 10	Japan lands two task forces on Luzon (Philippine Islands).
Dec. 11	Germany and Italy declare war on the United States, which then goes to war against them.
Dec. 11	Japanese troops move from Thailand into Burma.
Dec. 16	Japan invades Sarawak and Brunei on Borneo (East Indies).

Dec. 16	Japanese troops occupy Victoria Point in southern Burma.
Dec. 18	Japanese forces begin their invasion of Hong Kong.
Dec. 20	Admiral Ernest J. King is appointed commander in chief, U.S. Fleet.
Dec. 20	The American Volunteer Group (the "Flying Tigers") goes into combat near Kunming, China.
Dec. 22	Japan lands large numbers of troops at Lingayen Gulf on Luzon (Philippine Islands).
Dec. 22–Jan. 14	British and U.S. leaders meet in the First Washington Conference.
Dec. 23	Japan captures Wake Island.
Dec. 25	British forces surrender Hong Kong to Japan.
Dec. 26	On Luzon (Philippine Islands), U.S. forces evacuate Manila and declare it an open city.
Dec. 29	The China theater is established under Chiang Kaishek, with an Allied staff.
Dec. 31	The Allies create ABDACOM, the unified command of American-British-Dutch-Australian forces in the Far East.
Dec. 31	Admiral Chester W. Nimitz, the new commander of the U.S. Pacific Fleet, assumes his duties at Pearl Harbor.

1942

Jan. 1–2	The Declaration of the United Nations is signed in Washington.
Jan. 2	Japanese troops take control of Manila (Philippine Islands).
Jan. 7	As U.S. and Filipino troops complete their withdrawal to Bataan on Luzon (Philippine Islands), Japanese forces begin their siege of the peninsula.
Jan. 11	Japan invades Celebes and Tarakan (East Indies).
Jan. 15	ABDACOM formally commences its operations in Java (East Indies).
Jan. 15–28	Representatives of American republics attend the Rio de Janeiro Conference.
Jan. 20	Japan launches a major offensive in Burma.
Jan. 21	Japanese troops land at Balikpapan, Borneo (East Indies).
Jan. 23	Japanese forces move into Rabaul on New Britain, New Ireland in the Bismarck Archipelago, and Bougainville in the Solomon Islands.

Jan. 23	The Anglo-American Combined Chiefs of Staff hold their first official meeting.
Jan. 24–26	Allied and Japanese forces fight the naval Battle of Makassar Strait off Balikpapan, Borneo (East Indies).
Jan. 25	Thailand, allied with Japan, declares war on the United States.
Jan. 29–Apr. 22	The ANZAC command assumes the defense of the waters between Australia, New Zealand, and New Caledonia.
Jan. 17–31	British forces withdraw from the Malay peninsula to Singapore.
Feb. 1	American naval forces raid Japanese bases in the Marshall and Gilbert Islands.
Feb. 2	U.S. Major General Joseph W. Stilwell is named chief of staff to the supreme commander, China theater.
Feb. 4	Japan fights Allied naval forces in the Battle of Madoera Strait off Borneo (East Indies).
Feb. 8–9	During the night, Japanese troops land on Singapore.
Feb. 9	The Pacific War Council in London meets for the first time.
Feb. 13	Canada and the United States agree to build the Alaska Highway from Canada to Alaska.
Feb. 14	Japan invades Sumatra (East Indies).
Feb. 15	British Lieutenant General Arthur E. Percival surrenders Singapore to Japan.
Feb. 19	Japanese planes attack Darwin, Australia, damaging ships and airfields.
Feb. 19	President Roosevelt signs the executive order authorizing the removal of Japanese-Americans from the U.S. West Coast.
Feb. 19–20	Allied and Japanese naval forces fight in the Battle of Badoeng (Lombok) Strait, near Bali (East Indies).
Feb. 20	Japanese forces invade Timor (East Indies).
Feb. 23	A Japanese submarine fires on an oil refinery in California.
Feb. 25	The Allies dissolve ABDACOM.
Feb. 27–Mar. 1	Japan defeats the Allies in the naval Battle of the Java Sea (East Indies) and lands invasion forces on eastern Java.
Feb. 28–Mar. 1	A Japanese invasion force traveling to western Java

	battles Allied cruisers in the Battle of the Sunda Strait (East Indies).
Feb. 28–Mar. 9	Japan captures Java (East Indies).
Mar. 7–8	In New Guinea, Japanese troops land at Salamaua and Lae on the Huon Gulf.
Mar. 9	Japan completes its capture of most of the East Indies.
Mar. 9	Admiral King is named U.S. chief of naval operations in addition to his other duties.
Mar. 11–17	On President Roosevelt's orders, General MacArthur travels from the Philippines to Australia to set up a new command.
Mar. 19	In Burma, British Lieutenant General William J. Slim assumes command of British troops.
Mar. 22	The United States begins the large-scale evacuation of Japanese and Japanese-American citizens from the West Coast.
Mar. 22–Apr. 12	Representing the British government, Richard Stafford Cripps holds unsuccessful talks in India with Mahandas Gandhi and Jawaharal Nehru.
Mar. 23	Japan occupies the Andaman Islands in the Bay of Bengal.
Mar. 24	The Combined Chiefs of Staff designate the Pacific to be the responsibility of the U.S. Joint Chiefs of Staff (JCS).
Mar. 25–Apr. 9	Japanese Vice Admiral Chuichi Nagumo's forces raid British bases and ships in the Indian Ocean.
Mar. 30	The JCS divide the Pacific into two theaters of operation: the Southwest Pacific Area under General MacArthur and the Pacific Ocean Areas under Admiral Nimitz.
Apr. 1	The Pacific War Council in Washington holds its first meeting.
Apr. 9	American and Filipino forces on Bataan (Philippine Islands) surrender to Japanese troops, who then lead their prisoners on the Bataan Death March.
Apr. 18	The United States bombs Tokyo in the Doolittle Raid.
May 4–8	In the naval Battle of the Coral Sea, the first all-carrier engagement of the war, Allied forces stop Japan's invasion of Port Moresby, New Guinea.
May 5–7	British forces seize the port of Diego Suarez on the island of Madagascar from Vichy France.

May 6	Lieutenant General Jonathan M. Wainwright surrenders his forces on Corregidor and orders all U.S. forces in the Philippines to capitulate to the Japanese.
May 15	General Stilwell arrives in India after leading his forces in an overland retreat from Burma; British General Harold R. Alexander establishes his headquarters in Imphal, India.
May 20	Japan completes its conquest of Burma.
June 3	Japan attacks Dutch Harbor in the Aleutian Islands to divert attention from its major offensive at Midway.
June 3–6	U.S. forces defeat a massive Japanese naval force in the Battle of Midway.
June 5–7	Japanese troops land on Attu and Kiska in the Aleutians.
June 9	The last organized American-Filipino forces in the Philippines surrender to the Japanese, with guerrilla operations continuing.
June 13	The U.S. Office of Strategic Services is established under the JCS.
June 19–25	U.S. and British leaders hold the Second Washington Conference.
June 20–22	Japanese submarines shell Vancouver Island, Canada, and fire on the Fort Stevens military reservation in Oregon.
July 20	President Roosevelt recalls Admiral William D. Leahy to active duty to serve as his chief of staff and as chairman of the JCS.
July 22	Japanese forces land at Buna on the northern coast of New Guinea and begin an offensive by land to Port Moresby.
Aug. 7	U.S. forces land on Guadalcanal, Tulagi, and Florida islands in the Solomon Islands.
Aug. 8–9	As the Guadalcanal campaign gets under way, Japanese forces cause severe Allied losses in the naval Battle of Savo Island.
Aug. 17–18	Carlson's Raiders, a U.S. Marine battalion, assault Japanese forces in the Gilbert Islands.
Aug. 24–25	Japanese and Allied forces fight the naval Battle of the Eastern Solomons.

Aug. 25–Sept. 6	Allied forces turn back a Japanese invasion of Milne Bay in New Guinea.
Sept. 9	A Japanese plane launched from a submarine drops an incendiary bomb in Oregon.
Sept. 17	The Japanese ground offensive for Port Moresby halts.
Sept. 25	The Allied counteroffensive begins in Papua, New Guinea.
Oct. 11–12	Japanese and Allied forces fight the naval Battle of Cape Esperance (Solomon Islands).
Oct. 18	Vice Admiral William F. Halsey succeeds Vice Admiral Robert L. Ghormley as commander, South Pacific Area.
Oct. 26–27	Japanese and Allied carriers fight the naval Battle of the Santa Cruz Islands (Solomon Islands).
Nov. 5	British forces capture the rest of Madagascar from Vichy France.
Nov. 12–15	The Allies defeat the Japanese in the Naval Battle of Guadalcanal (Solomon Islands).
Nov. 30–Dec. 1	Japanese and Allied forces fight the naval Battle of Tassafaronga (Solomon Islands).
Dec. 2	Enrico Fermi directs the first controlled nuclear chain reaction at the University of Chicago.

1943

Jan. 14–24	British and U.S. leaders meet in the Casablanca Conference.
Jan. 22	The Allies complete the capture of Papua, New Guinea.
Jan. 29–30	Japanese and Allied forces fight the naval Battle of Rennell's Island (Solomon Islands).
Feb. 8	Brigadier General Orde C. Wingate's Chindit forces begin operations in Burma.
Feb. 9	The Guadalcanal campaign ends in an Allied victory as Japan evacuates its troops from the island.
Mar. 1–4	In the Battle of the Bismarck Sea, Allied air forces destroy a Japanese convoy carrying troops to Lae, New Guinea.
Mar. 26	In the naval Battle of Komandorski Islands, the Allies prevent the Japanese from reinforcing troops in the Aleutian Islands.
Apr. 18	U.S. planes kill Japanese Admiral Isoruku Yamamoto

	by shooting down his plane near Bougainville (Solomon Islands).
May 11–30	The Allies recapture Attu (Aleutian Islands).
May 12–25	British and American leaders hold the Third Washington Conference.
June 30	The Allied Southwest Pacific and South Pacific Areas launch Operation Cartwheel.
July 2–Aug. 25	Allied forces capture New Georgia (Solomon Islands).
July 5–6	In the naval Battle of Kula Gulf, Allied forces prevent Japanese ships from reinforcing Kolombangara (Solomon Islands).
July 10	U.S. planes based in Attu (Aleutian Islands) bomb the Kurile Islands for the first time.
July 12–13	Allied and Japanese forces fight in the naval Battle of Kolombangara (Solomon Islands).
Aug. 6–7	In the naval Battle of Vella Gulf, Allied forces prevent Japanese reinforcements from reaching the central Solomon Islands.
Aug. 12–15	British, Soviet, and U.S. representatives meet in Moscow to discuss the Soviet demand for a second front in Europe.
Aug. 14–24	British and U.S. leaders meet in the First Quebec Conference.
Aug. 15	Allied troops invade Kiska (Aleutian Islands), which the Japanese have secretly evacuated.
Aug. 15	Allied troops land on Vella Lavella (Solomon Islands).
Sept. 5–6	In the first significant U.S. airborne operation of the Pacific war, paratroopers land at Nadzab (New Guinea).
Sept. 8	Italy surrenders to the Allies.
Sept. 16	Allied forces occupy Lae (New Guinea).
Oct. 2	Australian troops seize Finschhafen (New Guinea).
Oct. 6	Allied and Japanese forces fight in the naval Battle of Vella Lavella (Solomon Islands).
Oct. 6	Allied operations in the central Solomons conclude with a landing on Kolombangara.
Oct. 18–30	Representatives of the United States, the United Kingdom, and the U.S.S.R. attend the Moscow Conference of Foreign Ministers.
Oct. 30	China, the United Kingdom, the United States, and the

U.S.S.R. announce the Four-Power, or Moscow, Declaration.

Nov. 1   Allied forces land at Empress Augusta Bay on Bougainville (Solomon Islands).

Nov. 1–2   In the naval Battle of Empress Augusta Bay, Allied forces stop the Japanese from reinforcing Bougainville (Solomon Islands).

Nov. 16   The Allies activate the Southeast Asia Command under British Admiral Louis Mountbatten.

Nov. 20–23   The United States begins its Central Pacific operations with invasions of the Gilbert Islands.

Nov. 22–26   Generalissimo Chiang Kai-shek, President Roosevelt, and Prime Minister Churchill meet in the First Cairo Conference.

Nov. 23–Dec. 9 Chinese forces halt the Japanese in the Battle of Changteh (China).

Nov. 25–26   The Allies fight the Japanese in the naval Battle of Cape St. George (Solomon Islands).

Nov. 28–30   At the Teheran Conference, the "Big Three" meet together for the first time: President Roosevelt, Prime Minister Churchill, and Soviet Premier Joseph Stalin.

Dec. 3–7   British and U.S. leaders meet in the Second Cairo Conference.

Dec. 15   Allied forces invade the Arawe peninsula (New Britain).

Dec. 26   Allied troops assault Cape Gloucester (New Britain).

1944

Jan. 2   Allied forces land at Saidor (New Guinea).

Jan. 31–Feb. 7 Allied forces take the Kwajalein atoll (Marshall Islands).

Feb. 4   Japanese troops launch an offensive on the Arakan front in Burma.

Feb. 10   The Allies complete campaigns for the Huon peninsula (New Guinea) and New Britain.

Feb. 15–20   Allied troops invade the Green Islands (Solomon Islands).

Feb. 17–22   Allied forces capture the Eniwetok atoll (Marshall Islands).

Feb. 17–18	The Allies attack Japanese bases at Truk (Caroline Islands).
Feb. 29–Mar. 24	Allied troops capture Los Negros (Admiralty Islands).
Mar. 8	Japan begins a major offensive from Burma toward Imphal and Kohima, India.
Mar. 15–25	Allied forces take Manus (Admiralty Islands).
Mar. 20	Allied troops land on Emirau (Bismarck Islands).
Apr. 18	The Japanese launch their major Ichigo offensive in China.
Apr. 22	Allied forces make amphibious landings at Hollandia and Aitape (New Guinea).
May 17	The Allies land at Sarmi (New Guinea).
May 18	Allied troops invade Wakde Island (New Guinea).
May 27–Aug. 20	Allied troops capture Biak Island (off the New Guinea coast).
June 15–July 9	U.S. forces capture Saipan (Mariana Islands).
June 15	U.S. Boeing B-29 bombers based in China attack the Japanese home islands for the first time, beginning the strategic air campaign against Japan.
June 19–20	In the naval Battle of the Philippine Sea, Japan sustains heavy losses of pilots and planes.
June 22	Japan's offensive against Imphal, India, is halted.
July 1–15	The United Nations Monetary and Financial Conference meets at Bretton Woods in the United States.
July 2	Allied troops capture Noemfoor Island (New Guinea).
July 10–Aug. 25	Allied forces defeat a Japanese army in the Battle of the Driniumor River (New Guinea).
July 18	General Kuniaki Koiso succeeds Tojo as prime minister of Japan.
July 21–Aug. 10	Allied forces capture Guam (Mariana Islands), the first U.S. territory to be retaken from Japan.
July 24–Aug. 1	From bases in nearby Saipan, Allied troops invade Tinian (Mariana Islands).
July 26	President Roosevelt meets with General MacArthur and Admirals Leahy and Nimitz at Pearl Harbor.
July 30	U.S. troops capture Sansapor (New Guinea).
Aug. 3	The Allies take Myitkyina (Burma).
Aug. 5	Prime Minister Koiso establishes the Supreme War Direction Council.

Aug. 8	Japanese forces capture Heng Yang (China).
Aug. 21–29	Representatives from China, the Union of Soviet Socialist Republics, the United Kingdom, and the United States meet at Dumbarton Oaks to discuss the formation of the United Nations organization.
Sept. 12–16	British and U.S. leaders hold the Second Quebec Conference.
Sept. 15	Allied troops land on Morotai (Molucca Islands).
Sept. 15–Nov. 27	Allied forces capture Peleliu (Palau Islands).
Sept. 17–30	Allied troops occupy Angaur (Palau Islands).
Sept. 22–24	Allied forces move into the unoccupied Ulithi atoll (Caroline Islands).
Sept. 28	Allied forces begin a major offensive against the Japanese in the Arakan area of Burma.
Oct. 15	Allied troops under General Stilwell start an offensive in northern Burma.
Oct. 18	On the demand of Chiang Kai-shek, General Stilwell is relieved of his duties and recalled to Washington.
Oct. 20	Allied forces begin the recapture of the Philippine Islands with landings on the island of Leyte.
Oct. 23–26	The Battle for Leyte Gulf, the largest naval engagement in history, occurs as the Japanese try to prevent the Allied capture of Leyte.
Oct. 24	The U.S. China-Burma-India theater is split into two theaters: China and India-Burma.
Nov. 7	President Roosevelt is elected to a fourth term.
Nov. 24	U.S. Boeing B-29 bombers attack Japan for the first time from bases in the Marianas.
Dec. 15	Allied troops capture Mindoro (Philippine Islands).

1945

Jan. 3	Allied forces capture Akyab (Burma).
Jan. 9	Allied troops invade Luzon (Philippine Islands).
Jan. 27	The Burma Road reopens as it is linked with the Stilwell Road.
Jan. 30–Feb. 2	British and U.S. leaders meet in the Malta Conference prior to the Yalta meeting.
Feb. 3–Mar. 4	Allied forces retake Manila (Philippine Islands).
Feb. 4–11	British, Soviet, and U.S. leaders meet in the Yalta Conference.

Feb. 19–Mar. 26	Allied forces capture Iwo Jima (Volcano Islands).
Mar. 3	Allied troops retake Meiktila (Burma).
Mar. 9–10	The United States launches a highly destruction air attack on Tokyo, using incendiary bombs.
Mar. 10	Allied troops land on Mindanao (southern Philippine Islands).
Mar. 20	The Allies take control of Mandalay (Burma).
Apr. 1–July 2	Allied forces capture Okinawa (Ryukyu Islands).
Apr. 3	In an administrative shift, the JCS place all U.S. Army forces in the Pacific under General MacArthur and all U.S. Navy forces under Admiral Nimitz.
Apr. 5	Admiral Kantaro Suzuki succeeds Koiso as prime minister of Japan.
Apr. 7	Allied forces sink the Japanese superbattleship *Yamato* in the East China Sea.
Apr. 12	President Roosevelt dies and is succeeded by Harry S. Truman.
Apr. 25–June 26	Nations represented at the San Francisco Conference approve the United Nations charter.
May 1	Allied troops land on Tarakan off the coast of Borneo (East Indies).
May 3	The Allies recapture Rangoon (Burma).
May 8	The war in Europe ends with the defeat of Germany.
May 10	Australian soldiers capture the Japanese stronghold of Wewak (New Guinea).
June 10	Allied forces invade Borneo (East Indies) at Brunei Bay.
July 1	Allied troops land at Balikpapan, Borneo (East Indies).
July 14	U.S. ships conduct the first naval gunfire bombardment of the Japanese home islands.
July 14	Italy declares war on Japan.
July 16	The United States successfully tests an atomic bomb near Alamogordo, New Mexico.
July 16–Aug. 2	British, U.S., and Soviet representatives hold their last wartime meeting in the Potsdam Conference.
July 26	In the Potsdam Proclamation, China, the United Kingdom, and the United States demand the unconditional surrender of Japan.
July 26	Clement Attlee replaces Churchill as British prime minister during the Potsdam Conference.
July 30	The USS *Indianapolis* sinks with heavy loss of life.

Aug. 6	The United States drops an atomic bomb on the Japanese city of Hiroshima.
Aug. 8	The U.S.S.R. declares war on Japan, effective on August 9.
Aug. 9	Shortly after midnight, Soviet troops invade Manchuria.
Aug. 9	The United States drops its second atomic bomb on the Japanese city of Nagasaki.
Aug. 14	Japan notifies the Allies that it surrenders.
Aug. 14	The U.S.S.R. and China sign a treaty of friendship.
Aug. 15	Emperor Hirohito broadcasts the announcement of the surrender to the Japanese people; the Suzuki cabinet resigns.
Aug. 17	Achmad Sukarno and Mohammed Hatta proclaim the independence of the Republic of Indonesia from the Netherlands.
Aug. 18–Sept. 4	The U.S.S.R. occupies the Kurile Islands.
Aug. 20	The Japanese Kwantung Army surrenders to Soviet forces in Manchuria.
Aug. 28	The first Allied occupation forces land in Japan.
Sept. 2	Japan surrenders to the Allies in a formal ceremony on the USS *Missouri* in Tokyo Bay; the Allied occupation of Japan officially begins.
Sept. 2	Ho Chi Minh and the Viet Minh proclaim the independence of the Democratic Republic of Vietnam.
Sept. 3	General Tomoyuki Yamashita surrenders Japanese forces in the Philippine Islands to the Allies.
Sept. 4	U.S. forces assume control of Wake Island from the Japanese.
Sept. 9	U.S. officials receive the Japanese surrender in southern Korea.
Sept. 9	Japanese forces surrender to Nationalist forces in China.
Sept. 9	Chinese forces occupy northern French Indochina.
Sept. 12	British Admiral Louis Mountbatten accepts the Japanese surrender in Singapore.
Sept. 13	British and Indian troops move into southern French Indochina.
Sept. 16	The Japanese command in Hong Kong transfers power to the British.

1946

May	The International Military Tribunal for the Far East convenes its war crimes trials.
July 4	The Republic of the Philippines achieves independence.

1947

May 3	The new Japanese constitution renouncing war takes effect.
Aug. 15	British India is partitioned into two independent nations: India and Pakistan.

1948

Jan. 4	Burma becomes independent.
Feb. 4	Ceylon becomes independent.
Aug. 15	The Republic of Korea is established in southern Korea.
Sept. 9	The Democratic People's Republic of Korea is formed in northern Korea.

1949

Oct. 1	Mao Tse-tung announces the establishment of the People's Republic of China.
Dec. 27	The Netherlands recognizes the independence of Indonesia (the former Netherlands East Indies).

1950

June 25	The Korean War begins.

1951

Sept. 1	Australia, New Zealand, and the United States sign a security treaty.
Sept. 4–8	The Allies meet in San Francisco and conclude a peace treaty with Japan, to take effect April 28, 1952; the United States and Japan sign a security pact.

1952

Apr. 28	The Allied occupation of Japan officially ends.
Apr. 29	The Republic of China signs a peace treaty with Japan.
June 6	India and Japan conclude a peace treaty.

1954
Nov. 5   Burma and Japan sign a peace treaty.

1956
Oct. 19   The state of war between Japan and the U.S.S.R offi-
                          cially ends, although the two countries do not reach
                          agreement on a peace treaty.

1978
Aug. 12   Japan concludes a peace treaty with the People's Re-
                          public of China.

Introduction

World War II was the largest and most costly conflict in history, the first true global war. Fought on land, on sea, and in the air, it involved numerous countries and killed, maimed, or displaced millions of people, both civilian and military, around the world. In spite of the alliances that bound many of the same participants, the war was essentially two separate but simultaneous conflicts: one involved Japan as the major antagonist and took place mostly in Asia and the Pacific; and the other, initiated by Germany and Italy, was contested mainly in Europe, North Africa, the Mediterranean, and the Atlantic.

Although authorities differ over the starting date of the war in Asia, many consider its beginning to be September 18–19, 1931, when the Japanese Kwantung Army began its seizure of Manchuria from China; indeed, some Japanese scholars refer to the conflict on the Asian mainland as the "Fifteen-Year War," lasting from 1931 to 1945. A number of historians judge the war's start to be July 7, 1937, when heavy fighting broke out in northern China between Japanese and Chinese forces. Others use the dates of December 7–8, 1941, when Japan's attacks on British, Dutch, and United States territories in Asia and the Pacific brought the West into the conflict. Many of the countries opposing Japan also fought Germany and Italy in hostilities that formally started when Germany invaded Poland in September 1939 and ended with Germany's defeat in May 1945, Italy having surrendered in September 1943. The war with Japan continued until the Japanese capitulation in August 1945 and formal surrender in September.

Belligerents and Coalitions

Nine of the Allied nations that had declared war against Japan signed the Japanese surrender document in Tokyo Bay on September 2, 1945: Australia, Canada, China, France, the Netherlands, New Zealand, the Union of Soviet Socialist Republics (U.S.S.R), the United Kingdom, and the United States. Two other important Allies were India and the Philippines, which became independent countries after the war's end. Of these 11 nations, all but China and the Philippines were also deeply involved in the war against Germany. The last to enter the conflict with Japan, the Soviet Union, invaded Japanese-held Manchuria early on August 9, 1945. The principal peace treaty with Japan was concluded in September 1951 and signed by 48 countries.

Of immense value to the Allied side was the extremely effective wartime alliance developed between the United States and the United Kingdom, closely bound by economic and historical ties. U.S. President Franklin D. Roosevelt and British Prime Minister Winston S. Churchill had established the basis for the coalition before the United States entered the war and developed their close friendship during a number of wartime strategic conferences. Following the Japanese attacks in December 1941, the American and British military heads formed the Combined Chiefs of Staff to coordinate global strategy and share resources. Some of the other Allied powers, such as Australia, resented their exclusion from the highest levels of decision making but participated fully in and made essential contributions to the war effort.

As a member of the Axis powers, Japan was allied with Germany and Italy but did not collaborate strategically with the European Axis members. German leaders did not advise Japanese officials of their plan to invade the Soviet Union in June 1941. Similarly, Japan did not inform its allies in advance about its attack on U.S. forces at Pearl Harbor in December 1941, although in its aftermath, both Germany and Italy declared war against the United States, which had not been officially involved in the war in Europe up to that time. The Axis countries maintained diplomatic relations and traded strategic raw materials and technology in a limited way, but they did not coordinate their separate wars. In spite of Germany's declaration of war against the Soviet Union, Japan continued to adhere to its neutrality pact with the U.S.S.R. until the Soviet attack near the end of the war. The U.S.S.R., in turn, resisted American and British pressure to go to war against Japan until the summer of 1945.

In addition to the Axis members, Japan formed alliances with the puppet governments established in its occupied areas. In early 1942, Thailand's pro-Japanese government declared war against the United States and the United Kingdom; the United States declined to recognize Thailand as a belligerent, although the United Kingdom did. Additionally, Japan sought to promote and exploit the anti-Western and anticolonialism sentiments of many Asians, including nationalist groups that had worked for independence before the outbreak of war. Using the slogan "East Asia for the Asiatics," Japan tried to raise support for its Greater East Asia Co-prosperity Sphere. None of Japan's Asian partners contributed substantially to the Japanese military cause.

Beginning of the War in Asia

For several centuries Japan successfully avoided contacts with the West, as the major European colonial powers gained access to China's ports and strategic resources. In the 1850s, Japan's leaders chose to cope with the Western incursion in Asia by bringing the nation to world-power status through industrialization, military modernization, and colonization. During the final half of the 19th century, Japan not only underwent a remarkable transformation economically and militarily but also developed ambitions to dominate the colonization of East Asia and the West Pacific. Japan's growing power and audacity astonished most Westerners when it defeated China and Russia in 1895 and 1905, annexed Korea in 1910, and four years later grabbed Germany's colonies in the Central Pacific and on China's Shantung Peninsula. The conquest of all of China and further continental expansion became priorities in Japanese strategic planning. By the late 1920s, Tokyo focused its attention on Manchuria, which both China and the U.S.S.R. claimed. Rich in mineral and agricultural resources, it appeared an ideal solution to Japan's serious overpopulation problems. In a short but ominous war beginning in September 1931, Japan's Kwantung Army routed Chinese forces in Manchuria and renamed it Manchukuo. Neither the Soviet Union nor the West responded militarily. When the League of Nations condemned the aggression in Manchuria, Japan withdrew from the organization.

Encouraged by earlier expansionism and by reports exaggerating the disunity in China, Japan provoked war in July 1937. At the Marco Polo Bridge near Peking on the night of July 7, Japanese troops conducting army maneuvers exchanged fire with Chinese soldiers. As each side increased the size of its forces in the area, the original minor incident escalated into general warfare. In Tokyo, the militarists in control of Japan's foreign and military policy anticipated a three-month campaign to force China's capitulation. Instead, the Japanese armed forces made disappointing progress inland, although after heavy fighting, they captured the port city of Shanghai in November and Nanking 150 miles to the northwest in December. In the wake of Nanking's fall, Japanese soldiers turned

Asia

to rape, murder, pillage, and other atrocities, killing many civilians. The Chinese moved the capital from Nanking to Chungking, and both Chinese Nationalist and Communist leaders vowed to suspend their civil war and fight the Japanese until they left China. The Japanese gradually gained control of much of the coast and northeastern China, but Chinese defenses largely held in the mountainous interior.

By September 1939, when Germany's invasion of Poland set off the European phase of World War II, the indecisive conflict in China had worn down Japan's armed forces and military supplies. Still committed to its continental conquest, Japan's leaders deliberated about a move into Southeast Asia, especially the Netherlands East Indies, where they could obtain the rubber, oil, and other raw materials essential to maintaining their war machine in China. Such a decision would mean war with the British and Dutch governments, which were the colonial overlords of the targeted areas, but their ability to stop Japan would be hampered enormously by the war in Europe. Much of the Japanese high command, especially army officers, preferred to seize the holdings of the U.S.S.R. across the Sea of Japan, which they had long coveted; the Kwantung Army in 1938 and 1939 had engaged in border skirmishes with Soviet troops at Changkufeng and Nomonhan. With its soldiers in China bogged down in a stalemate, Japan decided in favor of a strike in Southeast Asia and postponed indefinitely plans to seize Soviet territories in Northeast Asia. In April 1941, Japan signed a nonaggression pact with the U.S.S.R., which would ostensibly protect Japan's northern flank if it launched a strike southward. The two countries remained at peace until the final days of the war, when the Soviets made a massive, surprise attack on Japanese forces in Manchuria.

Japan's ambitions put it on a collision course with the strategic interests of the United States. Since the turn of the century, the linchpin of American foreign policy in the Far East had been to maintain the Open Door policy, which supported China's territorial and administrative integrity, sovereignty, and independence. The policy also pledged the United States to protect equal trade and commercial conditions for all nations dealing with China. By its bold, aggressive moves, especially since 1931, Japan obviously intended to make China a part of the Japanese Empire, in direct conflict with American policy. From February to December 1941, talks between the U.S. secretary of state and the Japanese ambassador repeatedly broke down over Japan's refusal to remove its troops from China and to endorse the Open Door principles. Although deeply involved in a struggle for survival against the European Axis, the United Kingdom gave the United States moral backing in its no-compromise stand on China. In April 1941, President Roosevelt announced that the United States would send to China lend-lease aid in the form of ground, sea, and air weapons as well as foodstuffs and other war relief as long as the conflict continued. "The arsenal of democracy," as the immense American war production was called, would play a pivotal role in the ultimate defeat of Japan. In its initial impact, however, it inextricably entangled the United States in the mounting wars in Asia and Europe.

In addition to its China policy, Japanese plans clashed with other fundamental American strategic interests. The United States considered American access to Southeast Asia's strategic raw materials to be essential in supplying the nation's industry and in time of war its military establishment. Japan's expansion into French Indochina in 1940 and 1941 posed a potential threat to that access as well as demonstrating continuing aggression; the United States responded by embargoing petroleum and other materials critical to Japan. Another basic premise of American policy in the Far East was its protection of the Philippine Islands, which it had acquired after the Spanish-American War of 1898. As the United States prepared the Philippines for independence in 1945, it continued to station American ground, sea, and air forces at bases in the archipelago. When tensions with Japan rose in the summer of 1941, the United States reinforced its military presence and nationalized the Philippine army.

As Japan's high command planned its seizure of Southeast Asia, Admiral Isoruku Yamamoto, head of the Japanese Combined Fleet, insisted that the initial offensive should include a preemptive attack on the U.S. Fleet, which was stationed at Pearl Harbor in the Hawaiian Islands, another American possession. Japan had no intention of occupying Hawaii, but by devastating the fleet it sought to prevent the U.S. Navy from interfering with its conquests in Southeast Asia. Japan also decided to capture the Philippine Islands not to acquire raw materials but to deny its important strategic location and bases to the United States. The Japanese targeted the British bases at Singapore and Hong Kong for similar reasons and chose other sites to establish a defense perimeter around Japan's holdings.

War with the West

On the morning of December 7, 1941, Japanese planes raided Pearl Harbor, sank much of the U.S. Fleet, and killed 2,400 Americans. Within a few hours, Japanese forces also attacked the Malay peninsula, Midway, Hong Kong, and the Philippines. The United States and the United Kingdom formally went to war with Japan the next day. On December 11, Germany and Italy, which were allied with Japan through the Tripartite Pact, declared war on the United States and presented the American military with a two-ocean war. American isolationist sentiment vanished immediately as the country began to mobilize.

During the initial six months of Japan's war with the West, Japan ap-

Japan's Conquests in the Pacific

peared almost invincible as its forces moved rapidly through the Far East and inflicted one defeat after another on the Allies. From the British it seized Hong Kong, Malaya, Singapore, Burma, and British Borneo, and one of its fleets raided the Indian Ocean, normally a British preserve. It captured the Philippines, Guam, and Wake Island from the United States. The Japanese overwhelmed the Allied forces helping the Dutch defend the

Netherlands East Indies and also moved into the Bismarcks, the Gilberts, and parts of New Guinea. In its rapid acquisition of territory, Japan took prisoner thousands of Allied civilians and military personnel, including especially large numbers of captives from Singapore, the Philippines, and the East Indies. As it advanced, Japan appeared poised to threaten India and Australia, where Japanese planes had already raided Darwin.

During the same period, Japan initiated no major operations in China except for the seizure of several airfields, but it advanced its cause by closing the Burma Road, the route used by the Allies to send military supplies to the Chinese Nationalist leader Chiang Kai-shek. The Allies could mount no effective response to the widespread Japanese expansion, although the United States made several carrier attacks against Japanese-held islands and launched the morale-building Doolittle Raid against Tokyo. By the late spring of 1942, Japan had greatly overextended its imperial boundaries, as its quick conquest of the Western colonies created a situation that it could neither exploit nor defend.

In early May 1942, a Japanese armada carrying a large invasion force moved toward Port Moresby in Papua, New Guinea, a location from which Australia could be isolated or attacked. In the Battle of the Coral Sea an Allied force intercepted the armada and fought the first all-carrier engagement of the war. While both sides sustained significant losses, the Japanese force retreated to its base at Rabaul instead of continuing its mission, marking the first time during the war that a Japanese advance had been halted. The next month, after landing troops in the Aleutian Islands, the Japanese received their first important defeat in the Battle of Midway, where American naval forces destroyed many of the Japanese Combined Fleet's vessels and veteran pilots and caused the fleet to withdraw.

Midway marked an important turning point in the Pacific War, after which Japan was unable to expand further its defensive perimeter and the Allies began to assume the offensive. While Japan had committed its main ground forces to China, the Allies chose to aid China with materials of war but not much Western manpower. Deciding against a continental axis of advance, the United States struck back at Japan through the Pacific, thus exploiting the great American advantages in carriers, submarines, amphibious assault craft, enormous land-based air power, and maximum assistance from Australia and New Zealand.

The first major Allied offensives began in August 1942 in the southern and southwestern Pacific with attempts to capture Guadalcanal in the Solomon Islands and the Papuan peninsula of New Guinea. Both campaigns were hard-fought and lengthy, lasting until early 1943 and demonstrating to the Allies the tenacity of the Japanese soldiers, even when fighting in situations they could not win. As would be the case throughout most of the island campaigns, few, if any, of the Japanese soldiers surrendered. In June 1943, also in the same Pacific regions, the Allies launched Operation Cartwheel to neutralize the important Japanese bases at Rabaul, northeast of New Guinea. Involving one approach through the central and northern Solomons and a second route along the northern New Guinea coast, the operation ended in the spring of 1944 with Rabaul effectively isolated and rendered ineffective.

Elsewhere in the Pacific, Allied forces in the north recaptured the Aleutian Islands in May and August 1943. While Cartwheel was still under way in November 1943, the Allies opened the second part of their dual advance toward Japan with an offensive to take the Gilbert Islands. Beginning with this campaign, U.S. forces would invade a series of island chains in their drive through the central Pacific toward Japan, while forces farther south would continue to move west along the New Guinea coast to the Philippines. On the continent, Allied soldiers launched offensives into Burma in late 1943 and early 1944.

Once the Allies had penetrated the long outer line of Japanese defenses from Burma and the East Indies to the Aleutians, the rest of the war was characterized by relatively free advances between large but disconnected enemy strongholds in the Pacific. The Allies bypassed isolated garrisons and focused on strategic Japanese bases that in Allied hands could become stepping stones for leaps farther along the axis to Tokyo. Japanese troops continued to resist fiercely, resulting in extremely bloody battles with heavy casualties on both sides. In late January 1944, the offensive in the central Pacific resumed with the Allied assault on the Marshall Islands, the first important territory retaken that Japan had controlled prior to the Second World War. Following the capture of the Marshalls, Allied forces in the central Pacific invaded the Marianas (June–August 1944), the Palaus (September–November 1944), Iwo Jima (February–March 1945), and Okinawa (April–June 1945). In the Battle of the Philippine Sea (June 1944), the Japanese task force sustained heavy damage and lost many of its planes and pilots.

In the southwestern Pacific, Allied forces in New Guinea bypassed large Japanese garrisons and advanced to the northwestern end of the island by the end of August 1944. While Australian troops remained in New Guinea to eliminate the remaining Japanese forces, American troops took the island of Morotai the next month and began the recapture of the Philippine Islands with an assault on Leyte in October. The landing in the Philippines set off the Battle for Leyte Gulf, the largest naval engagement in history, in which the Japanese Combined Fleet suffered such heavy losses that it could not effectively fight another surface engagement. During the Leyte landings, the Japanese first used kamikazes in organized attacks, a type of warfare they would increasingly employ during the rest of the war in place of their declining naval forces. The invasion of Luzon, the Philippines' largest and most important island, started in January 1945 and continued until the end of the war. During the spring and summer of 1945, American troops began the liberation of the southern Philippine Islands, while Australian forces assaulted Japanese-held areas previously bypassed and captured several sites on Borneo.

On the Burma front, Allied troops blocked Japanese counteroffensives toward British bases in India and continued their own movement into Burma. In January 1945, the land route from northern Burma into China reopened with 'the completion of the Stilwell (Ledo) Road from India. The Allies completed their recapture of Burma that May. In China, the Japanese launched Operation Ichigo, their most important ground offensive during the last stage of the war. Beginning in April 1944, the Japanese operation successfully captured air bases used by American bombers and advanced rapidly through eastern and central China, meeting little resistance from the Chinese Nationalist troops. In the spring of 1945, Japanese units began to withdraw to northern China, where the high command feared the Soviet Union might attack.

In addition to seizing territory from Japan, Allied forces blockaded the home islands and increasingly used long-range submarines and bombers to intercept Japanese ships carrying troops and supplies between Tokyo and its garrisons across the Pacific and Asia. In the summer of 1944, the Americans instituted their strategic air campaign against Japan. At first, American B-29 bombers traveled from India to bases in China, from which they attacked Japan and its holdings. In late November 1944, after the United States had built airfields on the newly captured Mariana Islands, the air campaign escalated; eventually all of the B-29s were based in the Marianas. The strategic bombing of the Japanese home islands caused widespread destruction of lives and homes, especially after the Americans began to use incendiary bombs against Japanese cities.

Although Japan's position appeared untenable as Allied forces moved closer to the home islands, destroyed the bulk of its navy, blockaded the country, and bombed its cities and industries, Japanese soldiers fighting the Allies showed no increased willingness to surrender. The last major campaigns in the Pacific—Okinawa, Luzon, Iwo Jima, and Leyte—were also the most costly in Allied lives. Many American strategists became convinced that a ground invasion of Japan would ultimately be required to force the country to surrender, although they anticipated that such an assault would result in many deaths on both sides. When the war in Europe ended with Germany's collapse in May 1945, Allied countries began to shift their air, ground, and naval forces to the Pacific War in preparation for a ground assault on Japan's home islands. Preliminary plans called for the invasion of Kyushu in the autumn of 1945 and Honshu in the spring of 1946.

The ground invasion of Japan became unnecessary, as the war underwent radical changes in August 1945. On August 6 and 9, American planes based in the Marianas dropped atomic bombs on the Japanese cities of Hiroshima and Nagasaki. Late on August 8, the Soviet Union declared war on Japan and the next morning moved its forces into Manchuria, overwhelming the defending Japanese troops. With the Japanese leadership in Tokyo divided on the question of surrender, Emperor Hirohito personally intervened to decide the country's capitulation. Japan formally surrendered on September 2, 1945, in a ceremony on the USS *Missouri* in Tokyo Bay. The debate continues as to whether the two atomic bombs or the Soviet entry into the war against Japan had the greater influence on Japan's decision to surrender.

Military Picture

Before the Japanese attacks of December 1941, Anglo-American leaders had already formulated the "Europe First" strategy to be followed if the United States fought against both Japan and Germany at the same time. They agreed that the United States and the United Kingdom would maintain the defensive in Asia and the Pacific until achieving victory in Europe; they would then shift their primary focus to Japan. In reality, although the Americans did indeed place the priority on the war in Europe, they also initiated offensives against Japan in the Pacific, which the British had agreed to consider an American strategic responsibility. Until the end of 1943, when the United States began to ship tremendous resources to Europe in preparation for the invasion of France, the numbers of American troops, planes, and ships in Asia and the Pacific roughly equaled those deployed against Germany. Thereafter, although Europe remained the most important combat theater, the American mobilization of troops and production grew large enough to support massive Allied offensives in the Pacific at the same time. Allied operations on the Asian mainland continued to receive a lower priority.

In addition to modifying the Europe First strategy during the course of the war, the United States also amended its prewar concepts about a war with Japan. For many years, American strategic planners had recognized the possibility of an American-Japanese clash in the Pacific and had anticipated that it would be essentially a naval war, relying on a series of amphibious assaults to capture Pacific island sites for naval bases closer to Japan. Although prewar plans called for a single advance of American forces from island to island across the central Pacific toward the Japanese home islands, the strategy adopted during the war consisted of a dual advance of Allied forces: one originating in August 1942 in the southern and southwestern Pacific and the other, initiated in late 1943, using the central Pacific route. The islands seized by amphibious assaults provided not only naval bases but also airfields for the strategic air campaign and staging grounds for the projected invasion of Japan. The Allies bypassed and neutralized Japanese strongholds such as Truk and Rabaul.

Prior to the war, both American and Japanese naval leaders shared the belief that battleships would mainly determine the outcome of any conflict between the two and gave little attention to the potential roles of aircraft carriers and submarines. After the war began, the carrier quickly superseded the battleship as the most important American surface warship, a process hastened by the Japanese sinking of most of the U.S. battleships on the first day of the war. Submarines also became extremely important to the United States, which, like Japan, initially considered their primary function to be supporting the surface fleet and attacking enemy warships. The American change of the submarine's main target from Japanese warships to merchant shipping proved highly successful, aided by improved torpedoes, Japan's failure to employ antisubmarine measures to protect its ships, and the Allied breaking of Japanese shipping codes. Japan, in contrast, employed its submarines piecemeal against warships and increasingly used them for transporting men and supplies in areas where the Allies controlled the air and the surface waters, instead of attacking the Allied lines of communication.

After the war with the West began, Japan continued to follow its continental strategy, focusing primarily on Asia in spite of the unanticipated course of the hostilities in the Pacific. Japanese planners had expected that Japan's sudden immobilization of the U.S. Fleet in December 1941 and its rapid seizure of Southeast Asia would result in a quick negotiated peace that would leave Japan in control of the strategic raw materials it sought. When the Allies showed no signs of capitulating and defeated the Japanese navy in the Battle of Midway in 1942, Japan had no feasible plan for winning the war in the Pacific, where it was unprepared to fight a lengthy battle of attrition. Until the last days of the war, Japan continued to station the majority of its army troops in China rather than deploy them to the Pacific, where Allied drives increasingly threatened the home islands. The commitment of large Japanese forces on the continent was a principal factor in the United States's effort to keep China in the war and preclude the transfer of more Japanese forces to the Pacific.

Exacerbating Japan's situation were the intense rivalry and lack of coordination between its army and navy, which often had conflicting strategic goals and were not subject to a strong governing body. In 1937, Japan created the Imperial General Headquarters to direct the army and navy in the war effort, but its structure was too weak to resolve the differences between the two services. Additionally, Japan could not afford to waste its scarce resources on an inefficient command system. While the American effort in the Pacific suffered from interservice problems to a lesser degree, the oversight and coordination by the U.S. government and the Joint Chiefs of Staff prevented an adverse impact on the course of the war.

Although in December 1941 the Allies had few resources in the Pacific, the mobilization of the U.S. economy eventually produced overwhelming quantities of tools of war for the forces fighting Japan. Nevertheless, until nearly the end of the Asian-Pacific conflict, both civilian and military Japanese remained convinced that Japan's Bushido code that emphasized honor, courage, and commitment to the emperor would give Japanese soldiers a spiritual edge in battle against the West's material superiority, regardless of the vast American production in arms for ground, air, and sea warfare. In combat, Japanese troops fought tenaciously and refused to surrender, choosing instead to make banzai charges when overwhelmed by the enemy. Through the last major Allied offensives in the Pacific, which produced the heaviest casualties on both sides, Japanese soldiers showed no decrease in morale or willingness to fight to the death. During the same period, the Japanese further demonstrated their commitment through volunteering for formally organized kamikaze missions, inflicting substantial casualties and damage to Allied ships. Plans for the defense of the Japanese home islands included suicidal attacks by both soldiers and citizens.

Because critical shortages in men and matériel often dictated where and when military actions were undertaken in the Asian and Pacific combat zones, Allied strategy and logistics remained vitally linked until the final stage of the war against Japan. The conflict was a huge logistical enterprise for both sides, intensified by the hostile terrain and climate, widespread disease, the lack of roads and ports, and the enormous distances involved in transporting and supplying the war machine. Ultimately, the superior Allied logistical system proved crucial in the victory over Japan.

Allied logistical advantages included the Japanese failure to challenge enemy shipping, the huge production capacity of the U.S. economy, the employment of large numbers of cargo ships and transport planes, and the prewar attention given by the U.S. military to logistics, such as the at-sea refueling and resupply systems developed by the navy. Hindering the effort against Japan was the allocation of scarce resources to the war against Germany and Italy, in accordance with the Allied strategic priority on that conflict. The continuing shortages of shipping and landing craft, in particular, limited plans for offensive actions against Japan. The Japanese military leaders placed much less emphasis on logistics than did the Allies and were unprepared for the logistical problems accompanying the rapid expansion of the Japanese empire through much of Southeast Asia and the Pacific in late 1941 and early 1942. Although Japan had achieved its goal of capturing strategic raw materials, it could not fully exploit its acquisitions because of insufficient shipping, which also restricted its ability to resupply its widely deployed troops. As the war progressed, Allied attacks destroyed the bulk of Japan's merchant ships, prevented food and raw materials from reaching the home islands, and further isolated Japanese garrisons throughout the Pacific.

During the war, a number of new weapons emerged, as well as scientific and technological advances that affected the conduct of the fighting. These ultimately proved beneficial to the Allies, whose cooperative research, access to raw materials, and enormous production capabilities enabled them to take advantage of new developments. Although in December 1941 Japanese fighter aircraft, destroyers, and torpedoes were vastly superior to those of the Allies, Japan later lacked the resources to produce its new designs and to match the wartime improvements introduced by the Allies. During the last year of the war, Japan's situation was so desperate that it focused on the development of kamikaze and other special attack weapons.

One area of immeasurable importance was signal intelligence, or the ability to intercept and read enciphered messages transmitted by radio. By the time of the Pearl Harbor attack, the Allies had the capability to obtain "Magic" intelligence from the reading of high-level Japanese diplomatic codes. Eventually, they also acquired "Ultra" intelligence by breaking the main Japanese naval, army, and merchant shipping codes. Because of the enormous distances involved in the Pacific War, the Japanese relied especially heavily on radio to convey messages, giving the Allied code breakers a wide variety of information. Like the Germans, the Japanese did not know that their codes had been compromised and continued to use them throughout the war, while incorporating regular changes. Signal intelligence significantly aided the U.S. submarine war against Japanese merchant vessels and warships, as well as contributing enormously to the Allied victories in the Battles of Midway, the Bismarck Sea, and the Driniumor River. During the last months of the war, the intercepts revealed Japanese diplomatic attempts to end the war, as well as the extensive preparations for the defense of the home islands. Japan's greatest achievements in signal intelligence involved Chinese codes.

Improvements in military medicine were especially significant in the battlegrounds of Asia and the Pacific, where troops of all nationalities suffered high rates of malaria and other diseases. The Allies instituted a strong anti-malarial campaign, including the use of atabrine as a preventive drug, and, during the last part of the war, widely applied the insecticide dichloro-diphenyl-trichloroethane (DDT). Two important Allied developments in the Pacific in 1943 were the introduction of penicillin and the institution of blood banks. Japan's poor logistical system limited the provision of adequate medical care, as well as food, to its troops.

Among other important Allied advantages was radar, placed on U.S. aircraft carriers and newer submarines by December 1941 and added to other warships by the end of 1942. In contrast, Japan did not use it widely on surface vessels until late 1943 and on submarines until the following year. In the period before most Japanese warships carried radar, the technology helped the Allies significantly in the Battles of the Coral Sea and Midway, as well as during the Solomons naval campaigns. In ground and airborne radar also, the Allied employment was more advanced than Japan's. The best airborne radar was installed on the Boeing B-29 Superfortress, a very long-range bomber designed for the strategic air campaign against Japan and first used in June 1944. Vital to the success of Allied amphibious assaults was the development and production of immense numbers and types of landing craft and ships.

Introduced by the Allies during the conflict were the proximity fuze, which enabled artillery shells, bombs, and rockets to explode on or close to targets; napalm, widely used in incendiary bombs and deployed by flamethrowers during the last year of the war; and the most famous new weapon, the atomic bomb, dropped on two Japanese cities shortly before the surrender. Under the auspices of the U.S. government, a massive secret wartime program known as the Manhattan Project designed and constructed the first atomic weapons. After the successful testing of the bomb in July 1945, President Harry S. Truman ordered the use of the weapon against Japan.

Costs of the War

The estimated human costs of all of World War II are beyond comprehension: military dead and missing, 15 to 20 million; civilian dead and missing, 40 to 60 million; military wounded, 25 million; civilian wounded, 10 to 20 million; homeless, 28 million; prisoners of war, 15 million; civilian prisoners, 20 million. Disease, malnutrition, poor living conditions, and inadequate medical care caused the deaths of millions more. Military operations and occupations created countless refugees, while other civilians were transported long distances to work as forced laborers.

Precise statistics are unavailable for the casualties in Asia and the Pacific; however, by any evaluation, the costs of the war with Japan were tremendous. The estimates for two of the countries invaded by Japan are indicative of the war's impact. According to the Chinese Nationalist government, its military battle deaths from 1937 to 1945 were 1.3 million, while other sources place the total of Chinese civilian and military deaths as high as 15 million. The government of the Philippines, which Japan occupied in whole or part from 1941 to 1945, claimed that more than one million of its citizens were killed by enemy action, with 100,000 civilians dying during the Battle of Manila alone.

The figures concerning the armed forces of Australia, Canada, New Zealand, the United Kingdom, and the United States are among the most reliable statistics, although each country, and often each of its service branches, used different criteria for its counts. During the war against Japan, nearly 150,000 military personnel from these countries were killed in action or died as prisoners of war. The U.S.S.R., in its 1945 campaign in Manchuria, sustained 8,000 battle deaths. Of the other Allied belligerents, India and the Netherlands also suffered heavy losses, including large numbers of prisoners captured in the first months of the war. Most of the surviving Allied prisoners spent more than three years in captivity.

Japanese sources estimate that 2.3 million Japanese military and civilian personnel working for the military were killed in combat from 1937 to 1945. Soviet forces invading Manchuria in August 1945 captured from one to two million Japanese; the U.S.S.R. delayed their repatriation for years and never accounted for 300,000 people to the satisfaction of the Japanese government. According to the U.S. Strategic Bombing Survey, 330,000 Japanese civilians in the home islands died between late 1944 and the end of the war as a result of the Allied strategic air campaign, including the use of two atomic bombs.

In addition to the deaths, the physical devastation in East and Southeast Asia and the western Pacific was immense, including not only the sites of military operations but also many of the areas occupied by Japan during the war. The ruined economies throughout the region could neither feed nor house the inhabitants. In Japan itself, the strategic bombing caused enormous material destruction and dislocation. The U.S. Strategic Bombing Survey reported that the air campaign's attacks on 66 Japanese cities had destroyed 40 percent of their most densely built areas. The bombs and the resulting firestorms ruined 2,510,000 buildings and left homeless 30 percent of the urban population. Before the war ended, 8.5 million Japanese had moved from the cities to the countryside to avoid the bombing. Six million Japanese, including both military and civilian, were overseas at the time of the surrender, in addition to massive numbers of Korean and Chinese laborers forced to work for the Japanese.

Consequences of the War

Within five years of the war's end, a number of new nations had been created, and others were in the throes of armed conflict, as the political and military administration of much of Asia and the Pacific underwent sharp changes. At the time of the surrender, Japan still controlled vast territories outside the home islands. As Allied forces began to reoccupy the areas administered before the war by European nations, they encountered resistance—sometimes violent—to the reimposition of colonial control. In some areas, the nationalist movements had been well established before the war, while others originated as opponents to Japanese control during the conflict. Japan's encouragement of anticolonialism as part of its "Asia for the Asiatics" campaign led to collaboration with nationalistic groups in such areas as the Netherlands East Indies, where Japanese forces turned their arms over to the Indonesians rather than the Allies at the end of the war.

The new nations achieved independence through a variety of means. The United Kingdom, which had incurred massive debt during the war and could no longer afford its vast empire, responded to nationalist movements and granted independence to India (1947), Pakistan (1947), Burma (1948), and Ceylon (1948). In Malaya, the federation created by the British in 1948 became independent years later after the defeat of communist insurgents, mostly ethnic Chinese, who had led the resistance during the Japanese occupation. The Netherlands reluctantly recognized the statehood of Indonesia in 1949, after sustaining heavy casualties in an especially violent conflict over the Dutch attempt to reassert their authority. In Indochina, France became involved in a lengthy, ultimately unsuccessful attempt to retain its colony. In a peaceful process instituted by the United States before the war, the Republic of the Philippines became a new country in 1946.

Following the liberation of Korea from decades of harsh Japanese rule, two new countries were established on the peninsula: the Republic of Korea in the south, sponsored by the United States; and the Democratic People's Republic of Korea in the north, whose communist government was backed by the U.S.S.R. In the Pacific, the United States became the trustee for a number of archipelagos formerly controlled by Japan: the Ryukyus (including Okinawa), the Volcanoes (including Iwo Jima), the northern Marianas, the Carolines, and the Marshalls; the Ryukyus and Volcanoes were later returned to Japan.

In a political shift of enormous proportions, the Chinese Communists won their lengthy civil war and ousted the Nationalists from power in 1949. The Nationalists moved to the island of Formosa and continued to use the name "Republic of China." On the mainland, Mao Tse-tung proclaimed the formation of the People's Republic of China. The Western Allies, especially the United States, judged the Communist victory in China an immense blow to the stability of the region, especially considered in conjunction with Communist strength in areas such as North Korea, Indochina, Malaya, and the Philippines. With the cold war between the U.S.S.R. and the United States and their allies already well under way, U.S. policy changed from the wartime encouragement of decolonization, as enunciated by President Roosevelt, to the support of colonial powers, such as France in Indochina, to halt the spread of communism. Strategically, the United States gave the priority to Europe in continuation of its wartime policy, but American involvement in Asia increasingly deepened. When war broke out in Korea in the summer of 1950, the United States became heavily involved.

The rise of communism in Asia strongly impacted the course of the military occupation of Japan. In accordance with the surrender agreement, Allied military forces occupied Japan at the close of the war and remained there until the Japanese peace treaty took effect in the spring of 1952. Although the occupation was nominally an Allied effort, it was dominated totally by the United States. Presiding over the occupation as

Supreme Allied Commander for the Allied Powers was U.S. General of the Army Douglas MacArthur. During the first two years, the occupation was basically punitive and reformist, working to demilitarize and democratize Japan, while conducting war crimes trials, overseeing the repatriation of millions of Japanese nationals and foreign workers, and purging militaristic and ultranationalistic officials from the government. During this phase, Japan adopted a liberal, democratic constitution written by MacArthur's staff. As the cold war intensified and the Chinese Communists made significant gains in 1947–1948, the U.S. government decided to reverse its course regarding the occupation and attempt to build up Japan as an economically strong state that could serve as a "bulwark for democracy" in Asia. In September 1951, as the end of the occupation neared with agreement concerning the terms of the peace treaty, the United States concluded a military alliance with Japan. During the same month, the United States also signed a defense treaty with Australia and New Zealand.

In an attempt to maintain global peace, the Allied countries in 1945 established the United Nations (UN) organization as a successor to the League of Nations, which had for a variety of reasons totally failed to deter the aggression in the 1930s that culminated in World War II. Prior to the U.S. entry into the war, President Roosevelt had joined Prime Minister Churchill in issuing the Atlantic Charter, which enunciated the principles that formed the basis for the UN. The charter advocated self-government, economic collaboration, and access to trade and raw materials for all nations, as well as renouncing territorial gains. In January 1942, 24 countries joined the United States and United Kingdom in signing the Declaration of the United Nations, which affirmed the Atlantic Charter and pledged to defeat the Axis powers. The concept of an international body was further developed at wartime conferences held in Moscow, Dumbarton Oaks, and Yalta. In April 1945, the signers of the Declaration of the United Nations, now grown to 50 countries, met in San Francisco to consider the United Nations charter, which they adopted on June 26, 1945.

In spite of the massive Allied effort to defeat Japan, Japan's surrender did not immediately end the political, economic, and social turmoil in Asia and the Pacific. Although Japan renounced war in its 1947 constitution, conflict continued across Asia, as former colonies fought for independence and civil war engulfed other areas. Further overshadowing the rehabilitation of devastated economies and landscapes were the developing cold war and the prospect of nuclear warfare.

The Dictionary

-A-

ABC-1. British and American policy agreement in January–March 1941, regarding the strategy to be followed if the United States (q.v.) entered the war. From January 27 to March 29, top military officials of the two countries met secretly in Washington, D.C., in a series of sessions called the American-British Conversations, which produced the ABC-1 document. It stated that if global war broke out, with the United States participating in wars against both Japan and Germany (qq.v.), the United States would follow the policy of "Europe First," collaborating with the United Kingdom (q.v.) to win the war in Europe while conducting defensive operations in the Pacific. After the defeat of Germany and Italy (q.v.), the priority would shift to the war against Japan. The strategy enunciated in ABC-1 affirmed the recommendations of the Plan Dog Memorandum (q.v.) written by Admiral Harold R. Stark (q.v.) in November 1940. The First Washington Conference (q.v.), held after the beginning of the war with Japan, agreed to continue the Europe First policy.

ABDACOM. American-British-Dutch-Australian Command, the first Allied theater created in the war against Japan (q.v.). During the First Washington Conference (q.v.) in December 1941–January 1942, Allied leaders established ABDACOM to try to prevent the Japanese from capturing Burma, Malaya, Singapore, the East Indies, the Philippines, and Australia (qq.v.). Formed from the limited forces available in the area, ABDACOM was headed by British Lieutenant General Archibald P. Wavell (q.v.) and briefly headquartered on Java (q.v.), beginning January 15, 1942. U.S. Lieutenant General George H. Brett served as Wavell's deputy. Dutch Lieutenant General H. ter Poorten commanded the land forces. Initially commanding the naval forces was U.S. Admiral Thomas C. Hart (q.v.), who was succeeded by Dutch Vice Admiral Conrad E. L. Helfrich in mid-February. British Air Marshal Richard Peirse headed the air forces. The command's resources were totally inadequate to stop the powerful enemy advance, and it was dissolved on February 25, as the Japanese approached Java. Many of the remaining naval forces were destroyed in the Battles of the Java Sea and Sunda Strait (qq.v.); other ships escaped to Australia or Ceylon (q.v.). *See also* Badoeng Strait, Battle of; Borneo; Madoera Strait, Battle of; Makassar Strait, Battle of; Netherlands; United Kingdom.

ADACHI, HATAZO (1884–1947). Japanese general; chief of staff, North China Area Army, 1941–1942; commander, Eighteenth Army, 1942–1945. After serving with the North China Area Army, Adachi commanded the Japanese Eighteenth Army from late 1942 to the end of the war. The army was established in Rabaul (q.v.) on New Britain on November 9, 1942, as part of the Eighth Area Army, headed by Lieutenant General Hitoshi Imamura (q.v.). Adachi's assignment was to defeat Allied counteroffensives in New Guinea (q.v.) with the eventual goal of mounting a new assault on Port Moresby (q.v.). Unable to take the offensive, the Eighteenth Army fought a series of lengthy, costly battles against the forces of the Allied Southwest Pacific Area (q.v.). In March 1944, Adachi's forces were transferred from the Eighth Area Army to the Second Area Army, under General Korechika Anami (q.v.), based in the Netherlands East Indies (q.v.). The Allied landings at Hollandia and Aitape in April 1944 isolated Adachi's army, which was nearly decimated in the Battle of the Driniumor River (q.v.) in the summer of 1944. After the fall of Wewak to Australian soldiers in May 1945, Adachi moved his remaining forces to the hills, surrendering on September 13, 1945. He committed suicide after being charged with war crimes (q.v.) involving prisoners of war (q.v.) at Rabaul. *See also* New Guinea Campaign.

ADMIRALTY ISLANDS. *See* CARTWHEEL, OPERATION; MANDATES, PACIFIC.

AIRBORNE OPERATIONS. Used most frequently in the war with Japan (q.v.) for transport and supply of Allied troops. The first airborne assaults in the Pacific occurred during Japan's conquest of the East Indies (q.v.) in early 1942. In January, Japanese paratroopers landed successfully on Celebes and Sumatra (q.v.), followed the next month by an airborne assault on Timor (q.v.). In December 1944, Japanese forces attempted a risky airborne attack on Allied airfields on Leyte in the Philippines (qq.v.), but the paratroopers were ultimately wiped out.

In the Pacific, Allied airborne assaults were relatively rare compared with amphibious assaults (q.v.). In the Southwest Pacific Area (q.v.), U.S. paratroopers made their first major landing at Nadzab, near Lae in Northeast New Guinea, on September 5, 1943. Their next airborne assault took place on July 3, 1944, on the island of Noemfoor, off the coast of New Guinea (q.v.). During the reconquest of the Philippines (q.v.) in 1944–1945, paratroopers from the U.S. 11th Airborne Division made several drops on Luzon (q.v.), where they fought mainly as ground forces. The island of Corregidor was recaptured in a combined airborne and amphibious assault that began on February 16, 1945.

In Southeast Asia, the Allies (q.v.) transported the Chindits, Merrill's Marauders (qq.v.), other forces, and massive amounts of equipment into Burma (q.v.) in airborne operations, which often included the use of gliders (q.v.). Paratroopers were dropped during the recapture of Rangoon in May 1945. The Allies also resupplied by air many of their troops, including those besieged by the Japanese at Imphal (q.v.). Throughout the region, the Office of Strategic Services, the Special Operations Executive (qq.v.), and other intelligence groups parachuted agents into enemy territory and used air drops for supplies. The shortage of transport planes (q.v.) contributed to the delay of several operations planned by the Southeast Asia Command (q.v.).

After the Japanese surrender (q.v.), Allied forces parachuted into such areas as the Netherlands East Indies to assume control from the Japanese. Throughout the Pacific and Asia, they also made air drops of food and medical supplies to internment and prisoner of war (q.v.) camps that could not be reached immediately by Allied troops.

AIRCRAFT. *See* BOMBER; BOMBER, DIVE; BOMBER, TORPEDO; FIGHTER AND FIGHTER-BOMBER; FLYING BOAT; GLIDER; HELICOPTER; TRANSPORT PLANE.

AIRCRAFT CARRIER. *See* CARRIER, AIRCRAFT.

AIR FORCE. *See* UNITED STATES ARMY AIR FORCES.

AITAPE. *See* NEW GUINEA CAMPAIGN.

ALASKA HIGHWAY. Military highway, also known as the Alcan Highway, running 1,500 miles from Dawson Creek, British Columbia, to Fairbanks, Alaska. Built in 1942 by U.S. and Canadian servicemen and civilians, the road allowed military supplies to be transported overland from the continental United States (q.v.) through Canada (q.v.) to Alaska, where large numbers of troops were stationed after the U.S. entry into the war. The highway's construction was a difficult engineering accomplishment.

ALEUTIAN ISLANDS. U.S.-owned islands west of Alaska, included in the North Pacific Area (q.v.) subtheater of the Pacific Ocean Areas (q.v.). In September 1940, the United States (q.v.) began to construct a naval base at Dutch Harbor, as well as building other bases and fortifications in the Aleutians and Alaska. These efforts accelerated after the United States entered the war, although they were hampered by shortages of manpower and shipping, the inhospitable climate, and the relatively low priority of the area. As part of the Japanese attempt to surprise the U.S. Pacific Fleet in the Battle of Midway (q.v.) in June 1942, Admiral Isoruku Yamamoto (q.v.) planned a diversionary attack on the Aleutian Islands. Admiral Chester W. Nimitz (q.v.), knowing from intelligence reports that the Aleutians attack was a secondary campaign, retained his main forces at Midway, while Japan bombed Dutch Harbor (June 3) and invaded the islands of Attu (June 5) and Kiska (June 7). The United States then evacuated the Aleuts, the native inhabitants, from the rest of the sparsely populated islands. On August 30, U.S. troops moved into Adak Island to build air bases and occupied Amchitka, between Kiska and Attu, for the same purpose on January 11, 1943. Under Vice Admiral Thomas C. Kinkaid (q.v.), who took command of the North Pacific Area in January 1943, U.S. forces turned back Japanese attempts to reinforce their garrisons on Attu and Kiska in the naval Battle of the Komandorski Islands on March 26, 1943. U.S. troops retook Attu in a hard-fought battle lasting May 11–30, 1943, which ended with the suicide of most of the remaining Japanese soldiers. On August 15 American and Canadian forces invaded Kiska, from which the Japanese forces had been secretly evacuated.

ALEXANDER, HAROLD RUPERT LEOFRIC GEORGE (1891–1969). British field marshal; general officer commanding Burma (q.v.), 1942. In March 1942, Prime Minister Winston S. Churchill (q.v.) assigned Alexander to hold Rangoon, Burma, against the rapidly advancing Japanese. Soon after his arrival, Alexander was forced to withdraw to India (q.v.) but kept his army intact. In August he was transferred to the Middle East and thereafter commanded army groups in North Africa, Sicily, and Italy in the war against Germany and Italy (qq.v.). His final wartime appointment was Supreme Allied Commander, Mediterranean Forces.

ALLIED CONFERENCES. *See* CONFERENCES, ALLIED.

ALLIED POWERS (ALLIES). Countries opposing the Axis powers (q.v.) in World War II. The Allied powers, or Allies, were also known as the United Nations after the signing of the Declaration of the United Nations (q.v.) by 26 countries in January 1942. Nineteen other nations agreed to the Declaration before the end of the war. The Allied powers represented at the formal Japanese surrender (q.v.) in Tokyo Bay on September 2, 1945, were Australia, Canada, China, France, the Netherlands, New Zealand, the Union of Soviet Socialist Republics, the United Kingdom, and the United States (qq.v.). The Allies formed the core of the postwar United Nations organization (q.v.).

ALSOS MISSION. *See* INTELLIGENCE, ALLIED.

AMERICAN VOLUNTEER GROUP (AVG). American airmen in China (q.v.) known as the "Flying Tigers." In 1937, American aviator Claire L. Chennault (q.v.), who had retired from the United States Army Air Corps, began to work for Chiang Kai-shek (q.v.) to help China in its war against Japan (q.v.). In 1941, Chennault recruited American pilots and mechanics to form an air force for China, with the knowledge of the Roosevelt (q.v.) administration. The AVG participated in combat for the first time in December 1941 when the Japanese invaded Burma (q.v.), where they were training on British fields. The AVG moved to China in the spring of 1942 as Allied troops were driven out of Burma and the Burma Road (q.v.) to China was closed. In April Chennault was recalled to active duty with the rank of brigadier general to head the China Air Task Force (CATF), which included the AVG members who wished to join the United States Army Air Forces (q.v.). The China Air Task Force formed part of the U.S. Tenth Air Force until March 1943, when it was absorbed by the newly created U.S. Fourteenth Air Force under Chennault's command.

AMPHIBIOUS ASSAULTS. Landings on enemy-held shores; they formed an essential element in most U.S. ground offensives against Japan (q.v.). In August 1942, the Pacific Ocean Areas (POA) (q.v.) theater began its major operations with a landing on Guadalcanal (q.v.) in the Solomon Islands (q.v.) and thereafter staged a series of amphibious assaults in the South Pacific Area (q.v.) as Allied forces moved north toward Rabaul (q.v.). In the North Pacific Area (q.v.), the main offensives were landings on Attu and Kiska in the Aleutian Islands (q.v.). Central Pacific Area (q.v.) forces waged amphibious warfare against Japanese soldiers in the Gilberts, Marshalls, Marianas, and Palaus and on Iwo Jima and Okinawa (qq.v.). The Southwest Pacific Area (SWPA) (q.v.) conducted amphibious operations on the New Guinea (q.v.) coast, the Trobriands, the Admiralties, the Bismarcks, Morotai, the Philippines, and Borneo (qq.v.). When the war ended, Allied strategists were preparing for a massive invasion of Japan. Amphibious operations in the Southeast Asia Command (q.v.) had been postponed, partly because of shortages in landing craft and ships (q.v.).

The American admirals in charge of amphibious operations in the Pacific were Richmond K. Turner (q.v.), V Amphibious Force and Amphibious Forces, Pacific; Theodore S. Wilkinson (q.v.), III Amphibious Force; and Daniel E. Barbey (q.v.), VII Amphibious Force. The Marine generals holding major amphibious commands were A. A. Vandegrift (q.v.), I Marine Amphibious Corps; Roy S. Geiger (q.v.), I Marine Amphibious Corps and III Amphibious Corps; and Holland M. Smith (q.v.), V Amphibious Corps. Prior to the war, the marines had specialized in amphibious doctrine and had sponsored the development of landing craft. Most of the amphibious landings conducted by marines took place in the South and Central Pacific Areas, where army troops also participated in assaults. The POA amphibious landings were usually preceded by intense naval and air bombardment and involved a wide range of naval vessels (q.v.), including carriers (q.v.). The SWPA naval forces were less well equipped and relied heavily on surprise for most amphibious operations, which were executed primarily by army forces. Critical to all of the amphibious operations were various types of landing craft, landing ships, and amphibious vehicles.

Although Japan conducted a number of amphibious assaults on hostile shores, beginning in China (q.v.), most of its landings were relatively unopposed. The Japanese army preferred to make surprise landings, frequently conducting its operations at night and at locations removed from high numbers of enemy forces. During the 1920s and

1930s, Japan developed a number of landing craft, such as the *daihatsu*, to facilitate its operations. The Soviet invasion of Manchuria in August 1945 included a series of amphibious assaults across the Amur and Sungari rivers by the Second Far Eastern Front. *See also* Japan, Invasion of; Manchuria Campaign (1945).

AMPHIBIOUS VEHICLES. *See* LANDING CRAFT AND SHIPS.

ANAMI, KORECHIKA (1887–1945). Japanese general; army vice minister, 1939–1941; commander, Eleventh Army, 1941–1942; commander, Second Area Army, 1942–1944; inspector general of army aviation, 1945; army minister, 1945. After serving as army vice minister from 1939 to 1941, Anami commanded the Eleventh Army in central China (q.v.) from April 1941 to July 1942. Highly regarded in the army, he strongly supported the formation of Hideki Tojo's (q.v.) government in October 1941. From the Eleventh Army, Anami moved to head the Second Area Army in Manchuria. He remained there from July 1942 to October 1943, when the Second Area Army headquarters, still under his command, was transferred to the Netherlands East Indies (q.v.) to direct Japanese resistance to Allied offensives in the Southwest Pacific Area (q.v.). The western part of New Guinea (q.v.) was put under his command, including the Eighteenth Army of Lieutenant General Hatazo Adachi (q.v.) beginning in March 1944. At the end of the year, Anami returned to Japan as inspector general of army aviation.

In April 1945, Anami joined the new cabinet of Admiral Kantaro Suzuki (q.v.) as army minister, also serving on the Supreme War Direction Council (q.v.). In high-level discussions during the final months of the war, Anami opposed the peace terms acceptable to Suzuki, Foreign Minister Shigenori Togo (q.v.), and Navy Minister Admiral Mitsumasa Yonai (q.v.). After the decision to surrender was made, Anami learned about a military rebellion to stop Emperor Hirohito's (q.v.) broadcast of the Japanese surrender (q.v.). He moved neither to help nor to stop the action, but after its failure, he committed suicide on August 15, 1945.

ANDAMAN ISLANDS. Islands in the Bay of Bengal, south and west of Burma (q.v.); under prewar British control. Having decided they could not defend the Andamans, the British withdrew their troops on March 12, 1942. Japanese forces took control of the islands on March 23. At the First and Second Cairo Conferences (qq.v.), the Allies (q.v.)

considered plans to assault the Andamans as part of Buccaneer, a campaign to recapture Burma, but delayed the proposed operations due to shortages of landing craft (q.v.) and higher strategic priorities. Unchallenged except by Allied air attacks, Japanese forces occupied the Andamans throughout the war.

ANGAUR. *See* PALAU ISLANDS.

ANTIAIRCRAFT WEAPONS. Directed against aircraft from the ground or naval vessels. The variety of weapons employed by Japan and the Allies (qq.v.) against aircraft ranged widely from machine guns to large antiaircraft guns. After initial losses to the Japanese, Allied antiaircraft efforts benefited enormously from the introduction of the proximity fuze (q.v.), improvements in radar (q.v.), and the development of fire direction controls.

In addition to machine guns, U.S. ground forces relied mainly on 3-inch, 37-mm, 40-mm, and 90-mm antiaircraft guns. Except for the 90-mm guns, U.S. naval vessels used the same weapons as well as 20-mm and 5-inch guns. Both the United States and the United Kingdom (qq.v.) depended heavily on the Bofors 40-mm antiaircraft gun, a Swedish weapon licensed to numerous countries. Although the United States did not begin to produce the Bofors in large numbers until mid-war, the gun was employed widely on the ground and on naval vessels (q.v.) of all sizes.

Throughout much of the war, Japan's basic antiaircraft gun was a 75-mm, in addition to machine guns and several Bofors guns captured from the Allies. During the latter part of the war, Japan added more powerful 88- and 150-mm guns, first using the latter in Tokyo (q.v.) in the spring of 1945. *See also* Bombers; Fighters; Small Arms.

ANTI-COMINTERN PACT. Treaty signed by Japan and Germany (qq.v.) on November 25, 1936, in which they agreed to cooperate against international communism sponsored by the Union of Soviet Socialist Republics (q.v.). The next year Italy (q.v.) joined the pact, followed in 1939 by Hungary, Spain, and Manchukuo (q.v.). Additional countries participated when the pact was renewed in November 1941.

ANZAC. Allied command created to defend the waters between Australia, New Zealand, and New Caledonia (qq.v.). Headed by U.S. Vice

Admiral Herbert F. Leary, ANZAC existed from January 29 to April 22, 1942, when it was incorporated into the Southwest Pacific and Pacific Ocean Areas (qq.v.).

ARCADIA. *See* WASHINGTON CONFERENCE, FIRST.

ARGENTIA. *See* ATLANTIC CONFERENCE.

ARGONAUT. *See* YALTA CONFERENCE.

ARMY AIR CORPS. *See* UNITED STATES ARMY AIR FORCES.

ARMY AIR FORCES. *See* UNITED STATES ARMY AIR FORCES.

ARNOLD, HENRY HARLEY (1886–1950). U.S. General of the Army and General of the Air Force; commander, United States Army Air Corps, 1938–1941; commanding general, United States Army Air Forces (q.v.), 1941–1945. During World War II, Arnold strongly advocated the value of strategic air power in winning the war and campaigned tirelessly for the ultimate independence of the American air forces from the army, which occurred after the war. Although subordinate to General of the Army George C. Marshall (q.v.), the army chief of staff, Arnold was a full member of the United States Joint Chiefs of Staff and the Combined Chiefs of Staff (qq.v.).

Early in the war against Japan, Arnold worked with Admiral Ernest J. King (q.v.) and the United States Navy (q.v.) to arrange Lieutenant Colonel James H. Doolittle's (q.v.) bombing raid on Tokyo (q.v.). While he believed in the priority on the European theater, Arnold also developed the air forces in the Pacific, promoting the importance of the strategic air campaign (q.v.) as he did in Europe. In 1939, he had initiated the development of a very long-range bomber, which eventually became the Boeing B-29 Superfortress (q.v.). When the new planes were produced in 1944, Arnold assigned them exclusively to the war against Japan. To the dismay of the theater commanders, who were eager to exploit the new bombers, he placed all of the B-29s in the Twentieth Air Force under his direct command and, with few exceptions, reserved the planes for the strategic air campaign. As he did in the European War, Arnold heavily pressured his subordinates to achieve specific results. He assigned Major General Curtis E. LeMay (q.v.) to improve the performance of the B-29s.

In spite of poor health, Arnold effectively represented the interests of air power through the end of the war. Beginning in December 1944, he held the five-star rank of General of the Army. Retiring as head of the Army Air Forces soon after the Japanese surrender (q.v.), Arnold received the title of General of the Air Force when the United States Air Force was created in 1947.

ARTILLERY. Included field, coastal, and antiaircraft artillery. Throughout many Pacific battles, the Japanese employed field artillery piecemeal in direct support of infantry forces rather than using the massed formations of the Allies (q.v.). In some defensive situations such as in the Palaus (q.v.), the Japanese positioned most of their artillery in caves or heavily fortified emplacements. By the time of the Luzon and Okinawa campaigns (qq.v.) in 1945, U.S. commanders considered the Japanese tactical use of artillery much more effective than earlier in the war. Japan primarily used 70-, 75-, 105-, and 155-mm howitzers and guns. The basic Japanese 105-mm howitzer could fire a 35-pound shell 12,000 yards, while the range of the 155-mm was 13,000 yards with a 68-pound shell. During the capture of the Philippines (q.v.) in 1942, the Japanese used 240-mm howitzers, their largest, to fire on Corregidor and other islands in Manila Bay.

In the Pacific, U.S. ground forces mainly used 75-, 105-, and 155-mm howitzers and guns in the field. The marines, especially, depended heavily on the 75-mm pack howitzer, which could be broken down and transported through difficult terrain or brought ashore by landing craft (q.v.) during amphibious assaults (q.v.). It had a range of 10,000 yards and fired a 16-pound shell. The 105-mm howitzer, with a 12,500-yard range, became the standard field artillery piece. Its shell weighed 33 pounds. More powerful was the 155-mm howitzer, which could fire a 95-pound shell as far as 16,000 yards. Also used in massive operations such as Luzon and Okinawa was the 8-inch howitzer, capable of reaching 18,500 yards with a 200-pound shell. The effectiveness of U.S. artillery was greatly enhanced by the proximity fuze (q.v.), developments in radar (q.v.), and improvements in direction of fire. Against Japan, the Allies also used the British 3.7-inch pack howitzer (19.5-inch shell and 6,000-yard range), the 4.5-inch howitzer (34.5-pound shell and 6,000-yard range), and the 25-pounder Mark I gun/howitzer (25-pound shell and 12,000-yard range).

In December 1941, U.S. coastal artillery in the Philippines included guns ranging from 3-inch to 14-inch, many of which dated to World

War I. These weapons delayed the Japanese capture of Manila Bay in 1942 but could not withstand the heavy air and artillery bombardment directed against them. In Singapore (q.v.), coastal guns did not deter the Japanese seizure of that city the same year, because the guns were aimed toward the sea and could not be moved to fire against attackers on the Malay peninsula (q.v.). Throughout the war, the Japanese incorporated coastal artillery and naval guns salvaged from ships (such as in Manila Bay) in defenses of areas considered targets of Allied offensives and in heavy fortifications on the Japanese home islands (q.v.). *See also* Antiaircraft Weapons.

ATLANTIC CHARTER. Declaration of principles made on August 14, 1941, by U.S. President Franklin D. Roosevelt and British Prime Minister Winston S. Churchill (qq.v.). Prior to the public announcement of the charter, the leaders and their top military advisers had met for five days in the Atlantic Conference (q.v.). According to the charter, the two countries renounced any territorial gains and opposed any such changes without the consent of the people involved. They also supported self-government for all peoples, endorsed equal access to trade and raw materials (q.v.) for all nations, and advocated international economic collaboration to improve labor standards and social security. After the defeat of the Nazis (q.v.), they wanted the world to have peace and freedom from fear, to include free passage of the seas. Finally, they endorsed the disarmament of aggressive nations. The Atlantic Charter formed the basis for the Declaration of the United Nations (q.v.), which was signed on January 1, 1942.

ATLANTIC CONFERENCE, AUGUST 9–12, 1941. Allied conference held secretly aboard ships in Placentia Bay, near Argentia, Newfoundland. U.S. President Franklin D. Roosevelt, British Prime Minister Winston S. Churchill (qq.v.), and their advisers met to discuss the war in Europe, the international situation, and common strategy, although the United States was not officially a belligerent in the conflict. Although the conferees devoted more attention to Europe than the Far East, they agreed to warn Japan against further aggression. The meeting's most visible accomplishment was the Atlantic Charter (q.v.).

ATOMIC BOMB. Developed by the Manhattan Project (q.v.); first used operationally by the United States (q.v.) against Hiroshima and Nagasaki, Japan (qq.v.), in August 1945. The German discovery of nuclear fission in the late 1930s led to the inauguration of nuclear research programs by the United States, the United Kingdom, Germany, Japan, and the Union of Soviet Socialist Republics (qq.v.). Allied collaboration resulted in the successful development of an atomic weapon in 1945.

In 1940, the British established the Maud Committee to study nuclear energy, under the direction of physicist G. P. Thomson. The following year, after the committee reported that an atomic bomb was possible, the British government assigned the study of nuclear research to the new agency code-named the Directorate of Tube Alloys, which became part of the Department of Scientific and Industrial Research. The British also collaborated with Canadian and French scientists in a project based in Canada (q.v.).

In the fall of 1939, after physicist Albert Einstein wrote President Franklin D. Roosevelt (q.v.) about the potential military importance of the fission discovery, the United States initiated a study of nuclear energy and assigned it to the new Advisory Committee on Uranium. The National Defense Research Committee and its successor, the Office of Scientific Research and Development (OSRD) (q.v.), then absorbed the uranium committee and assumed responsibility for the study. The OSRD, led by Vannevar Bush (q.v.) and his deputy James B. Conant, decided in 1942 that the development of an atomic bomb was feasible but would require a massive governmental effort. To handle the program and build the necessary facilities, the United States Army (q.v.) created the Manhattan Engineering District under the command of Brigadier General Leslie R. Groves (q.v.). In addition to American, British, and Canadian scientists, the Manhattan Project, as it was called, included emigrés from Europe.

The United States and the United Kingdom began to exchange information about nuclear energy in 1940 but had virtually suspended cooperation by late 1942. During the First Quebec Conference (q.v.) in August 1943, Roosevelt and British Prime Minister Winston S. Churchill (q.v.) agreed to resume their close collaboration and to get the other's concurrence before employing an atomic weapon against another country. They also created the Combined Policy Committee to oversee the cooperative efforts of the United States, the United Kingdom, and Canada. Chaired by U.S. Secretary of War Henry L. Stimson (q.v.), the committee's members included Bush and Conant of the OSRD; Field Marshal John Dill (q.v.) (later succeeded by Field Marshal Henry Maitland Wilson [q.v.]) and Colonel J. J. Llewellin of the United Kingdom; and Clarence D. Howe, Canadian minister of munitions and supply. Established to assist the committee and implement its decisions was a technical committee representing all three countries. In September 1944, after the Second Quebec Conference (q.v.), Roosevelt and Churchill pledged to maintain the secrecy of the atomic bomb and to continue the Anglo-American collaboration on the project after the war ended. They also acknowledged Japan as a future possible target.

After Roosevelt's death in April 1945, Stimson informed President Harry S. Truman (q.v.) about the Manhattan Project, which was so highly classified that he had not known of its existence. To advise him about the use of the atomic bomb, Truman appointed the Interim Committee, headed by Stimson and including, among others, Bush, General of the Army George C. Marshall (q.v.), and the president's own representative, James F. Byrnes (q.v.). The committee recommended that the bomb be used against Japan without a prior, specific warning. On July 4, 1945, during a meeting of the Combined Policy Committee, the British representative conveyed his government's agreement with the use of the bomb. After receiving word at the Potsdam Conference (q.v.) that the Manhattan Project had successfully tested the bomb, Truman directed that it be employed against Japan. Stimson transmitted his order to General Carl A. Spaatz (q.v.), in charge of the U.S. Strategic Air Forces in the Pacific. After the Japanese rejected the Potsdam Proclamation (q.v.) to surrender or risk destruction, the United States dropped atomic bombs over Hiroshima and Nagasaki on August 6 and 9, 1945. Had Japan not surrendered on August 14, another bomb would have been ready to use within a few days, with as many as 15 more scheduled for completion during the fall of 1945.

The decision to employ atomic weapons against Japan has been the focus of much debate. Among the factors cited in support of Truman's action were the need to shock the Japanese to force a quick, decisive end to the war; the escalating Japanese resistance to surrender, as demonstrated by the suicidal kamikaze (q.v.) attacks and the massive losses incurred by both sides during the capture of Okinawa (q.v.); the enormous casualty projections if an Allied invasion of the Japanese home islands (q.v.) became necessary; the deteriorating situation of the prisoners of war (q.v.) in Japanese custody; and intelligence (q.v.) reports indicating continuing opposition to surrender at high levels of the Japanese government. Some opponents of the decision considered the use of the bomb unnecessary, contending that Japan would have surrendered if the Allies (q.v.) had agreed publicly to the retention of the emperor or that the strategic air campaign (q.v.) and naval blockade would have soon forced Japan's capitulation. Other critics charged that the estimated casualty totals for an invasion of Japan were greatly inflated; that the bomb's employment solely against Japan was racist; or that the bomb was dropped primarily for postwar reasons, including the intimidation of the Soviet Union. Another argument supported the use of the first bomb but claimed the second was unnecessary because it was dropped before the Japanese government had time to evaluate the situation in Hiroshima.

Throughout much of the war, the United States and the United Kingdom feared that Germany (q.v.) would develop an atomic weapon and use it against the Allies or share the technology with Japan. One of the main goals of the U.S.-sponsored Alsos (q.v.) intelligence mission to Europe was to determine the status of German nuclear research. Under the direction of Werner Heisenberg, the Germans had made relatively little progress as a result of scientific miscalculations, Allied sabotage of critical supplies, and the low priority assigned the project by the German government. Japan's nuclear program, led by Yoshio Yoshino, included at least five cyclotrons usable for research but was severely slowed by shortages of resources. In August 1945, the Japanese government dispatched members of its atomic team to Hiroshima to analyze the nature of the new Allied weapon. Also conducting nuclear research during the war were French scientists working in collaboration with the Canadians and British in Canada. Although they were not part of the Manhattan Project, the French learned about it through a complex agreement with the British that involved postwar commercial use of their research. Upon the liberation of France (q.v.) in 1944, some of the scientists traveled to Paris, briefed Charles de Gaulle (q.v.) about the atomic bomb project, and claimed a role for France in the postwar development of nuclear fission. U.S. officials considered their actions a threat to the wartime secrecy of the project.

In 1942, the U.S.S.R. established a nuclear program headed by Igor Kurchatov. Although excluded from the Anglo-American cooperative effort, the Soviets received detailed information about its progress from an extensive espionage network that included spies within the Manhattan Project. The U.S.S.R. exploded its first atomic bomb in 1949. *See also* Intelligence, Soviet; Japanese Surrender; Science and Technology.

ATTLEE, CLEMENT RICHARD (1883–1967). British deputy prime minister, 1940–1945; prime minister, 1945–1951. As leader of the

Labour Party, Attlee served in the wartime coalition government headed by Prime Minister Winston S. Churchill (q.v.) and represented the United Kingdom (q.v.) at the San Francisco Conference (q.v.) to form the United Nations organization (q.v.). During the Potsdam Conference (q.v.) in July 1945, the Labour Party won the British elections, and Attlee replaced Churchill as prime minister. He endorsed the Potsdam Proclamation (q.v.) for the unconditional Japanese surrender (q.v.).

ATTU. *See* ALEUTIAN ISLANDS.

AUCHINLECK, CLAUDE JOHN EYRE (1884–1981). British field marshal; commander in chief, India, 1940–1941 and 1943–1947. Before the United Kingdom (q.v.) entered World War II, Auchinleck spent most of his army career in India (q.v.), where he returned in 1940 after heading forces in the Norwegian campaign and in the United Kingdom. During his two periods as commander in chief, India, he encountered difficulties with Prime Minister Winston S. Churchill (q.v.) but worked well with Admiral Louis Mountbatten (q.v.), whose Southeast Asia Command (q.v.) overlapped Auchinleck's duties during his second command in India. Auchinleck also served as commander in chief, Middle East, from 1941 to 1942.

AUNG SAN (1916–1947). Burmese nationalist leader. In pursuing his goal of independence for Burma (q.v.), Aung San opposed first the British and then the Japanese during World War II. Leaving his homeland in 1940, Aung San received military training in Japan (q.v.) as one of the Burmese "Thirty Comrades." He returned to Burma as a Japanese general leading the Burma National Army to fight the Allies (q.v.). After Japan declared the independence of Burma in 1943, Aung San served in the new Japanese-controlled government but began secretly to work against Japan. He helped to found the Anti-Fascist Organization and opened communications with the headquarters of British Admiral Louis Mountbatten (q.v.) in the Southeast Asia Command (q.v.). In March 1945, Aung San openly transferred the allegiance of his army to the Allies for the reoccupation of the country. After the war Mountbatten protected him from British and Burmese officials who charged him with treason for his earlier work with the Japanese. Aung San was assassinated by a political rival in 1947, the year before Burma officially became independent. *See also* Burma Campaigns.

AUSTRALIA. British dominion and member of the Allied powers (q.v.). When the United Kingdom (q.v.) declared war against Germany (q.v.) in September 1939, Australia also entered the war and contributed troops, many of whom served as part of the British force in the Middle East. After the Japanese attacks of December 7–8, 1941, Australia declared war against Japan (q.v.) and immediately asked that the United Kingdom release the Australian troops to defend their home country. British Prime Minister Winston S. Churchill (q.v.) and his military leaders were reluctant to detach the experienced Australian soldiers from their service in Libya and Egypt, where the British were battling German and Italian troops. As the Japanese took Singapore (q.v.) in February 1942, capturing thousands of Australian prisoners of war (q.v.), and advanced toward Australia through the Netherlands East Indies (q.v.), Australian Prime Minister John Curtin (q.v.) insisted on the return of the veteran troops. Most of the Australian forces came home under the command of Australian General Thomas A. Blamey (q.v.). Curtin declared publicly that Australia would thereafter rely primarily on the United States (q.v.) for its defense. Australian-British relations remained badly strained through the rest of the war.

Although Japan made destructive bombing raids against Australian ports, such as the major attack on Darwin on February 19, 1942, it did

Australia

not try to seize the country. The situation might have been different if Japanese troops had been successful in their attempts to capture Port Moresby on Papua, New Guinea (qq.v.), putting Japan in a position to isolate and possibly invade Australia. The Southwest Pacific Area (SWPA) (q.v.) theater, established on March 30, 1942, included Australia. Curtin collaborated with the new theater commander, U.S. General Douglas MacArthur (q.v.), in pressing the British and American governments to place a higher strategic priority on the theater and to give it more resources. Blamey served as commander of the SWPA Allied Land Forces, which consisted mainly of Australian troops during the operations in Papua and many subsequent New Guinea campaigns. Australia also contributed air, naval, and intelligence forces to SWPA. Because of the Australian government's decree that no Australian ground troops be sent above the equator, they did not participate in the recapture of the Philippines (q.v.).

During the last year of the war, Australian troops were involved in operations to eliminate Japanese troops in areas of New Guinea, New Britain, and Bougainville (q.v.) that had earlier been isolated and bypassed. In the summer of 1945, they also began the recapture of oil facilities in Borneo (q.v.), which the Japanese had held since early 1942. In July 1945, Joseph Benedict Chifley (q.v.) became prime minister when Curtin died. Blamey attended the formal Japanese surrender (q.v.) in Tokyo Bay on September 2, 1945, on behalf of his country. During the next month, Australian officers accepted numerous Japanese surrenders in the East Indies, New Guinea, and other Pacific islands.

Australia played a vital role in the Allied victory over Japan. In addition to the troops it committed to battle, the country served as a massive base of operations in the Pacific. The prime minister ordered total mobilization of Australia in February 1942 and provided the United States with more reverse lend-lease aid (q.v.) than it received. Although the country participated in the Pacific War councils (q.v.) in the United States and United Kingdom, Australians such as Foreign Minister Herbert V. Evatt (q.v.) complained that the Anglo-American coalition gave them insufficient voice in strategic decisions. In the formation of the United Nations organization (q.v.) in 1945, Australia challenged the concept that the five major Allied countries should have more power than the smaller nations. On September 1, 1951, Australia, New Zealand (q.v.), and the United States concluded the Tripartite Security Treaty. *See also* Submarine, Midget.

AXIS POWERS. Coalition that fought the Allied powers (q.v.) during World War II. Its main members were Germany, Italy, and Japan (qq.v.), which were later joined by Bulgaria, Croatia, Hungary, Rumania, and Slovakia. The name "Axis" originated from a statement by Italian leader Benito Mussolini (q.v.) regarding the Rome-Berlin axis established in 1936 through his alliance with Adolf Hitler (q.v.) of Germany. *See also* Anti-Comintern Pact; Tripartite Pact.

-B-

BA MAW (1893–1977). Burmese nationalist leader. Under British rule, Ba Maw headed the Sinyetha Party and served as prime minister of Burma (q.v.) from 1937 to 1939. The following year his opposition to the war in Europe and his collaboration with Japan (q.v.) led to his temporary imprisonment by the British. When the Japanese occupied the country in 1942, they installed Ba Maw as head of the civil government. He escaped to Japan as British forces retook control of Burma and was jailed by the Allies (q.v.) at the end of the war, returning to Burma in 1946.

BADOENG STRAIT, BATTLE OF. Naval engagement between Allied and Japanese forces near Bali in the Netherlands East Indies (q.v.) on February 19–20, 1942, with both sides sustaining losses. The Allies (q.v.) were considered the victors in the battle, but Japan (q.v.) occupied the island on February 20 and retained control throughout the war. The action is also called the Battle of Lombok Strait.

BAKA. *See* BOMBERS; *TOKKO*.

BALIKPAPAN. *See* BORNEO; MAKASSAR STRAIT, BATTLE OF.

BALLOON BOMB. Launched in Operation Fu-go by Japan and carried by the jet stream across the Pacific to North America, between November 1944 and July 1945. Most of the 9,000 Japanese balloons landed in the western United States or Canada (qq.v.), although one was discovered as far east as the U.S. state of Michigan. Made of paper and filled with hydrogen, the balloons were equipped with antipersonnel or incendiary bombs (q.v.) intended to set cities and forests on fire. In the only fatalities associated with the operation, one bomb killed six people on a picnic in Oregon in May 1945. The U.S. and Canadian governments prohibited press reports about the balloons to deny confirmation of the landings to the Japanese. Analysis of the sand carried as ballast led American scientists to identify the probable launching sites in Japan, which were then targeted in Allied air strikes. U.S. forces in the North Pacific Area (q.v.) shot down several of the balloons as they floated over the Aleutian Islands (q.v.). Reportedly, the Japanese also considered using the balloons for biological warfare (q.v.).

BANZAI. Suicidal assault by a group of Japanese troops, who often shouted, *"Tenno heika banzai,"* or "Long live the emperor" while attacking. Banzai charges occurred frequently during the Pacific War, often in situations where the Japanese forces were outnumbered or near defeat. Their willingness to die rather than consider surrender was part of the Bushido (q.v.) code.

BARBEY, DANIEL EDWARD (1889–1969). U.S. admiral; commander, VII Amphibious Force, Southwest Pacific Area, 1942–1945; commander, Seventh Fleet, 1945–1946. From 1940 to 1941, Barbey worked with amphibious exercises conducted by the Atlantic Fleet. After the Pearl Harbor attack (q.v.), Admiral Ernest J. King (q.v.) ordered Barbey to establish an amphibious warfare section in the navy, where one of his principal duties was the development and procurement of landing craft (q.v.). In December 1942, he was assigned to the Southwest Pacific Area (SWPA) (q.v.) to form an amphibious force, which was designated VII Amphibious Force in March 1943. He remained in SWPA for the rest of the war, directing 56 amphibious assault operations in the Trobriands, New Guinea, the Admiralties, Morotai, the Philippines, and Borneo (qq.v.). Using army troops for the landings, Barbey often improvised to compensate for the shortages of landing craft and naval vessels in SWPA. In the largest SWPA operations, Barbey headed the Northern Attack Force on Leyte (q.v.) and the San Fabian Attack Force on Luzon (q.v.). After the war ended, the VII Amphibious Force moved army troops to southern Korea (q.v.), where Barbey participated in the Japanese surrender (q.v.). Barbey's force then transported United States Marines (q.v.) and three Chinese Nationalist armies to North China (q.v.), as well as repatriating Japanese troops from China to the home islands.

BATAAN DEATH MARCH. Forced journey of American and Filipino prisoners of war (q.v.) in April 1942, during which many atrocities were committed by Japanese troops. On April 9, 1942, Japanese forces

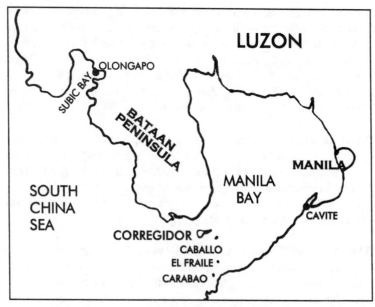

Bataan Peninsula and Manila Bay, Luzon, Philippine Islands

under the command of Lieutenant General Masaharu Homma (q.v.) captured the Bataan peninsula of Luzon (q.v.) during the campaign to conquer the Philippines (q.v.). Surrendering to the Japanese were more than 70,000 American and Filipino soldiers, many of whom were ill and weak from inadequate rations and the hostile climate during the long siege of Bataan. The Japanese guards marched the unexpectedly large number of prisoners over 50 miles in six days, providing little water and few provisions. Many died from disease or the difficult trip; others were killed by their guards.

News of the atrocities of the "Bataan Death March" eventually reached the United States and further inflamed a public already furious with the Japanese. The large number of American prisoners and the conditions they suffered in the march were factors in the decision to retake the Philippines in 1944. After the war, Homma was convicted of war crimes (q.v.) connected with the march and was executed. *See also* Philippine Islands Campaign (1941–1942).

BATTLESHIP. Massive warship with heavy armor and large naval guns. Arms limitation treaties of the 1920s and 1930s focused on battleships as the premier vessels in a nation's navy. Considering American battleships to be a potential obstacle to its plans for conquering Southeast Asia, Japan moved to eliminate the threat by striking the American fleet at Pearl Harbor (q.v.) in December 1941; within a few days, Japanese planes also sank the British battleship *Prince of Wales* and heavy cruiser *Repulse* in the South China Sea. Although the United States eventually returned to service all but three of its damaged battleships and assigned newly commissioned vessels to the Pacific, the aircraft carrier (q.v.) replaced the battleship as the most important surface ship in the war with Japan.

Thereafter, American battleships generally sailed with carrier task forces, providing antiaircraft (q.v.) protection. Their large guns bombarded coastlines prior to amphibious assaults (q.v.) of such islands as the Marianas (q.v.) and also shelled the Japanese home islands (q.v.) during the last part of the war. The ships played important roles in the Battles of the Philippine Sea and Leyte Gulf (qq.v.). The *Iowa* class of U.S. battleships was completed during the war, displaced 45,000 tons, contained 16-inch guns with a range of 23 miles, and could travel at 33 knots. The last commissioned *Iowa*-class ship, the *Missouri,* served as the site of the Japanese surrender (q.v.) in Tokyo Bay.

After the Battle of Midway (q.v.) in June 1942, Japan held back most of its battleships until the critical battles of the Philippine Sea and Leyte Gulf in 1944, which virtually destroyed the Japanese fleet. To augment its regular ships, Japan constructed two superbattleships—the *Musashi* and the *Yamato* (q.v.)—each of which displaced 72,000 tons and was armed with 18-inch guns. The *Musashi* was lost during the Battle for Leyte Gulf. In April 1945, U.S. aircraft sank the *Yamato,* en route to engage the Allied invasion of Okinawa (q.v.).

After losing the *Prince of Wales,* their primary warship in the Far East, British naval forces were too weak to challenge Japan directly. In the spring of 1942, the obsolete battleships of the British Eastern Fleet were so vulnerable that they retreated to the coast of Africa when Japanese carrier forces raided the Indian Ocean (q.v.). Gradually the British strengthened their naval forces in the war against Japan and were joined in April 1944 by one French battleship. Most of the ships remained in the Indian Ocean until the last year of the war, when several battleships joined Allied forces in the Pacific. There they aided the Okinawa campaign, shelled the Japanese home islands, and carried out operations in the southwestern Pacific. *See also* Naval Vessels.

BAZOOKA. *See* ROCKETS AND ROCKET LAUNCHERS.

BIOLOGICAL WARFARE. Focus of the Japanese army's secret Unit 731, headquartered in Harbin, Manchuria, 1932–1945. Officially known as the 731st Epidemic Prevention and Potable Water Supply Unit, it produced bacteria for anthrax, bubonic plague, cholera, dysentery, tetanus, typhoid, typhus, and other diseases, while also developing methods of using the germs in warfare. To test their results, unit personnel infected prisoners of war (POWs) (q.v.) with the bacteria, as well as subjecting them to grisly, often fatal experiments involving frostbite, gangrene, and medical procedures such as transfusions of horse blood. The 3,000 prisoners killed by Unit 731 were mostly Chinese, Korean, and Soviet; they possibly included American, Australian, and British POWs also.

The Japanese army reportedly employed biological weapons against several Chinese villages during the war, and, according to some accounts, against Soviet troops in 1939. Near the end of the war, U.S. and Canadian officials feared that the Japanese would use balloon bombs (q.v.), which they had previously armed with incendiary weapons, to spread biological warfare to North America. When the Soviet army invaded Manchuria in August 1945, Unit 731's director, Lieutenant General Shiro Ishii, and other officials escaped to Japan, leaving their laboratory equipment behind. After the war, the Union of Soviet Socialist Republics (q.v.) conducted public war crimes trials (q.v.) of Japanese soldiers who were associated with the unit.

Neither the United Kingdom nor the United States (qq.v.) used biological warfare during the war, although research programs in both countries experimented with diseases and potential applications. They also developed stockpiles of vaccines to protect Allied soldiers faced with biological agents.

BISMARCK ARCHIPELAGO. *See* CARTWHEEL, OPERATION; MANDATES, PACIFIC; RABAUL.

BISMARCK SEA, BATTLE OF THE. Allied destruction of a Japanese troop convoy, March 1–4, 1943. Lieutenant General George C. Kenney (q.v.), commander of Allied Air Forces in the Southwest Pacific Area (SWPA) (q.v.), learned from signal intelligence (q.v.) of the movement of a large Japanese naval force carrying reinforcements from Rabaul (q.v.) on New Britain to Lae in New Guinea (q.v.). Kenney ordered his American and Australian planes, all land based, to attack the convoy from low altitudes, using skip bombing (q.v.) and other tactics. The Allied planes sank most of the Japanese ships and then, assisted by patrol torpedo boats (q.v.) and other surface vessels, strafed the wreckage and men in the water, killing most of them. The overwhelming dominance of the SWPA air forces severely restricted further Japanese attempts to reinforce its garrisons on New Guinea.

BLACKLIST, OPERATION. *See* JAPAN, INVASION OF.

BLAMEY, THOMAS ALBERT (1884–1951). Australian field marshal; commander, Australian Military Forces, and Allied Land Forces, Southwest Pacific Area, 1942–1945. After Australia (q.v.) entered the war against Germany and Italy (qq.v.) in 1939, Blamey commanded Australian army troops in Greece and the Middle East until called home in March 1942 to defend Australia against the Japanese threat. In addition to heading the Australian Military Forces, Blamey was appointed to command Allied ground troops in the Southwest Pacific Area (q.v.) theater under U.S. General Douglas MacArthur (q.v.). In reality, MacArthur later bypassed Blamey much of the time through his use of the Alamo Force (actually the U.S. Sixth Army), which reported directly to him. The majority of Blamey's campaigns during the war were in New Guinea (q.v.) and New Britain, because the Australian government did not permit its forces to go north of the equator. During the last few months of the war, he led his troops to Borneo (q.v.). On September 2, 1945, Blamey represented his country at the formal Japanese surrender (q.v.) in Tokyo Bay.

BOEING B-29 SUPERFORTRESS. Very long-range, very heavy bomber (q.v.) used in the strategic air campaign (q.v.) against Japan (q.v.), 1944–1945. Much heavier and faster than the B-17 and B-24 heavy bombers, the four-engined B-29 had a top speed of 357 miles per hour and a range of 3,250 miles. It was designed to fly at 36,000 feet, with its 10- to 14-man-crew in a pressurized cabin. Its fully loaded weight of 141,000 pounds was twice that of the B-17. Armed with one cannon and 10 machine guns, it carried up to 10 tons of bombs. To accommodate its weight and size, the B-29 required specially constructed runways of 8,500 by 200 feet compared with the 6,000 by 150 feet needed for the B-17. The B-29's wing span was 141 feet; the B-17's was 104 feet.

Beginning in 1939, U.S. Major General Henry H. Arnold (q.v.)

promoted the development and production of the B-29, in accordance with his confidence in the value of strategic bombing. When the planes became available for combat in 1944, he assigned them exclusively to the war against Japan and placed all the B-29s in the Twentieth Air Force under his direct command, where they played the major role in Allied strategic bombing. Adapted versions of the B-29 dropped atomic bombs (q.v.) on Japan in August 1945.

BOMB. Included primarily general-purpose, incendiary, fragmentation, smoke, and atomic (q.v.) bombs. Among the innovations introduced by the Allies (q.v.) during the war was the proximity fuze (q.v.), which detonated the bomb when it sensed its target. In the strategic air campaign (q.v.) against Japan (q.v.), the United States (q.v.) increasingly mixed general-purpose bombs, incendiary bombs composed of magnesium, thermite, or napalm (q.v.), and oil canisters to burn Japanese cities. Also used by Allied forces, especially in the Southwest Pacific Area (q.v.), was the parafrag, a small fragmentation bomb aimed particularly at Japanese airfields; a parachute slowed the bomb, allowing the low-flying planes to avoid the explosion. Airmen in the same theater increased the effectiveness of bombs against surface ships by implementing skip bombing (q.v.) tactics. In Burma (q.v.), the United States destroyed bridges using the VB-1 azon bomb, a controlled vertical bomb directed partially by radio from the aircraft. In August 1945, U.S. bombers (q.v.) dropped atomic bombs on Hiroshima and Nagasaki (qq.v.) in Japan.

Japan experimented with bombs against the United States in 1942 when one of its submarine-based planes dropped incendiaries on Oregon forests, and in 1944–1945 when Japanese balloon bombs (q.v.) delivered antipersonnel and incendiary weapons to the United States and Canada (q.v.). In the last year of the war, Japan created the *oka* or Baka bomb, one of its suicidal, or *tokko* (q.v.), weapons.

BOMBER. Designed by British and American air strategists primarily for strategic bombing; used basically by the Japanese to support regular military operations. Like the United States (q.v.), Japan (q.v.) had no independent air force, with the army and navy having separate air resources. The Japanese bombers included a variety of land-based, twin-engined planes, as well as both land- and carrier-based dive bombers and torpedo bombers (qq.v.). The Japanese first employed their bombers in the war with China (q.v.), using both aircraft carriers (q.v.) and land bases in Japan and Formosa (q.v.) to launch repeated, heavy attacks on the capital of Chungking (q.v.) and other sites. The success of the raids increased with the introduction of effective fighters (q.v.) to protect the bombers.

Among the best-known larger Japanese bombers were the planes the Allies (q.v.) code-named Nell, Betty, Sally, and Peggy. All were land-based, twin-engined aircraft. One of the Japanese navy's long-range bombers was the Mitsubishi G3M Nell, which could attack Chinese targets from bases in Japan and Formosa. It carried a crew of five to seven, had two engines, reached a top speed of 259 miles per hour, and could carry 1,760 pounds in either bombs or a torpedo (qq.v.). Its loaded weight was 17,000 pounds. From airfields in French Indochina (q.v.), the Nell participated in the sinking of the *Prince of Wales* and the *Repulse* off the coast of Malaya in December 1941. It also struck Allied targets in the Philippines (q.v.) and Southeast Asia during the early part of the war. Later it was used as a trainer and transport plane (q.v.).

Also used by the navy was the Mitsubishi G4M Betty. A heavily produced plane, the Betty gradually replaced the Nell, which it joined during the sinkings of the *Prince of Wales* and the *Repulse*. It had a maximum speed of 272 miles per hour and a loaded weight of 27,500. It could carry 2,414 pounds in bombs or a torpedo. Its major liability was its lack of armor, which endangered its crew of seven. During the last year of the war, the Betty carried the Baka suicide bomb.

Until 1943, the Japanese army's main bomber was the Mitsubishi Ki-21 Sally, which had a loaded weight of 23,000 pounds and a top speed of 302 miles per hour. It carried a crew of seven and up to 2,205 pounds of bombs. Introduced in 1944, the Mitsubishi Ki-67 Hiryu Peggy was employed by both the army and navy from the Battle of the Philippine Sea (q.v.) to the end of the war. The navy used it as a torpedo bomber. The Peggy had a crew of six to eight, a maximum speed of 334 miles per hour and a loaded weight of 30,347 pounds. Its capacity was 2,360 pounds of bombs or one torpedo.

The most advanced bomber in the war was the U.S. Boeing B-29 Superfortress (q.v.), the very long-range, very heavy bomber introduced in 1944 and assigned to the strategic air campaign (q.v.). Throughout the war, the most-used U.S. heavy bombers were the four-engined Boeing B-17 Flying Fortress and Consolidated Vultee B-24 Liberator. As with most planes, the heavy bombers underwent improvements during the war. Although the B-17 and the B-24 were used in all theaters, greater numbers of B-24s were assigned to the Pacific because of their longer range, especially in the earlier part of the war. When fully loaded, the B-17 weighed 64,000 pounds, including 6,000 pounds of bombs. Its top speed was 287 miles. The B-24 had a top weight of 65,000 pounds and a maximum speed of 290 miles per hour. Its bomb load was 8,800 pounds. The B-17 had a crew of 6 to 10; the B-24 had 10.

The major U.S. medium bombers were the twin-engined, land-based North American B-25 Mitchell, Martin B-26 Marauder, Douglas A-20 Havoc, and Douglas A-26 Invader. Produced in great numbers, the B-25 weighed 35,000 pounds when loaded, including a four- to six-man crew and 6,000 pounds of bombs. It had a top speed of 272 miles per hour. Modifications allowed the B-25 to be launched from a carrier in the Doolittle raid on Tokyo (qq.v.) in April 1942, while later changes to it and other bombers facilitated low-level strafing and skip bombing (q.v.) in the Pacific. Less popular with pilots was the B-26, which could travel at 282 miles per hour and had a five- to seven-man crew. It carried a 3,000-pound bomb load and had a loaded weight of 34,200 pounds. The A-20, designated the Boston by the British, was lighter (27,000 pounds loaded) and faster (339 miles per hour) than the B-25 and B-26. It carried from two to three men and a bomb load of 2,600 pounds. Introduced in 1944, the A-26 had a top speed of 355 miles per hour and a crew of three. Its loaded weight was 35,000 pounds, including 4,000 pounds of bombs.

In addition to flying American-made planes in the war against Japan, the British relied especially on the twin-engined Vickers Wellington, Bristol Blenheim, and de Havilland Mosquito. The Wellington was a medium bomber with a top speed of 255 miles per hour. It carried a crew of six, weighed 34,000 pounds at capacity, and could handle a bomb load of 4,500 pounds. The much lighter Blenheim had a three-man crew, a top speed of 266 miles per hour, and a loaded weight of 14,400 pounds, including 1,000 pounds of bombs. The role of bomber was only one function of the fast, versatile Mosquito, which also served as a fighter. Fully loaded with 4,000 pounds of bombs, the Mosquito weighed 23,000 pounds, but it could travel at 415 miles per hour. Made primarily of wood, it did not carry heavy arms.

Allied bombers also sowed naval mines (q.v.) throughout Asia and the Pacific. *See also* Flying Boat; *Tokko*.

BOMBER, DIVE. Aircraft designed to dive sharply before releasing its bombs at low altitudes. The main Japanese dive bomber during the early part of the war was the single-engined Aichi D3A Val. Its top speed was 242 miles per hour, and it was armed with two machine guns and 680 pounds of bombs. Experienced in bombing attacks on Chungking and other sites in China (qq.v.), the Val was extremely effective during the Japanese attack on Pearl Harbor (q.v.) and thereafter saw extensive service in the Pacific. Gradually replaced by the single-engined Yokosuka D4Y Suisei Judy, the Val was used as a kamikaze (q.v.) plane in 1944–1945.

During the first part of the war, the most important U.S. dive bomber was the single-engined Douglas Dauntless, designated SBD for carrier-based and A-24 for land-based. The Dauntless was especially valuable in the Battles of Coral Sea and Midway (qq.v.) and during the operations in the Solomon Islands (q.v.). It had a top speed of 252 miles per hour, mounted from two to four machine guns, and carried bomb loads up to 1,000 pounds. Beginning in late 1943, the Curtiss Helldiver, another single-engined dive bomber, played a significant role in the Pacific. Armed with four machine guns, it had a maximum speed of 281 miles per hour and a bomb load of 1,000 pounds.

Used mostly by the British and Australians in Southeast Asia was the single-engined Vultee Vengeance, manufactured in the United States. It had a maximum speed of 279 miles per hour, was equipped with from five to six machine guns, and carried up to 2,000 pounds of bombs.

BOMBER, TORPEDO. Aircraft developed to launch torpedoes (q.v.), although many could also carry bombs (q.v.). Among the most important Japanese torpedo bombers was the single-engined Nakajima B5N Kate, which was armed with one machine gun, carried either one torpedo or a bomb load of 1,760 pounds, and had a top speed of 235 miles per hour. First employed in battle in China (q.v.) in 1937, it was escorted by Zero fighters (q.v.) beginning in 1940. In the Pacific War, the Kate caused much destruction at Pearl Harbor, Coral Sea, and Midway (qq.v.) and remained in use through Leyte Gulf (q.v.). It was eventually replaced by the Nakajima B6N *Tenzan* Jill, a single-engined plane that traveled at speeds up to 299 miles per hour. Except for an additional machine gun, the Jill carried the same weapons as the Kate. Both planes were converted to kamikaze (q.v.) planes in the last year of the war. Japan also equipped many of its larger bombers (q.v.) with torpedoes.

The primary U.S. torpedo bomber was the single-engined Grumman TBF Avenger, first used in combat during the Battle of Midway (q.v.).

Its top speed was 259 miles per hour. Equipped with four machine guns, its bomb capacity was 2,000 pounds or one 1,921-pound torpedo.

Also used in the Pacific and Asia was the twin-engined Bristol Beaufort, which was manufactured in the United Kingdom and in Australia (qq.v.). The Beaufort carried a crew of four and had a bomb load of 2,000 pounds or one torpedo. Its top speed was 260 miles per hour.

BORNEO. Large, oil-rich island in the East Indies, divided before the war into areas controlled by the British (Brunei, Sarawak, and North Borneo) and Netherlands Borneo, which formed part of the Netherlands East Indies (q.v.). Japanese forces invaded British Borneo at Sarawak and Brunei on December 16, 1941, and four days later landed in Dutch Borneo. By mid-February 1942, the Japanese controlled the important coastal areas of the island, although some interior areas were not conquered until October 1942. A large uprising led by the Chinese population against the Japanese occupation in October 1943 was crushed.

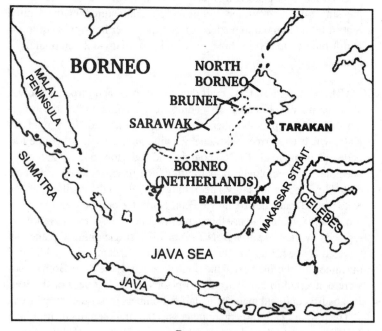

Borneo

In the spring of 1945, General of the Army Douglas MacArthur (q.v.) ordered Australian troops in the Southwest Pacific Area (SWPA) (q.v.) theater to seize three oil centers on and off the coast of Borneo. Their amphibious landings, which were supported by air and naval forces, occurred on Tarakan (May 1), Brunei Bay (June 10), and Balikpapan (July 1). Most of Borneo remained under Japanese control until the end of the war. *See also* ABDACOM; Badoeng Strait, Battle of; Madoera Strait, Battle of; Makassar Strait, Battle of.

BOSE, SUBHAS CHANDRA (1897–1945). Indian nationalist leader. Working against British colonial rule in India (q.v.), Bose was imprisoned and exiled several times in the 1920s and 1930s. When war began in Europe in 1939, he headed the Indian National Congress and pressed for immediate independence for India. The British authorities arrested him but he fled to Germany and later to Japan (qq.v.). Unlike Indian leader Mahandas K. Gandhi (q.v.), Bose supported armed methods to achieve his goals. In northern Africa, he organized a force of Indian prisoners of war (q.v.) under German command to fight the Allies (q.v.). In Asia, Bose then helped to rebuild the Japanese-supported Indian National Army (q.v.), which he led in Burma (q.v.) with the slogan "On to Delhi." Also under Japanese sponsorship, Bose headed a provisional government for India, declared war on the United Kingdom and the United States (qq.v.), and broadcast appeals to Indians for support. As the Allies recaptured Burma, Bose withdrew to Thailand and French Indochina (qq.v.). On August 18, 1945, he died in an airplane crash.

BOUGAINVILLE. *See* CARTWHEEL, OPERATION; SOLOMON ISLANDS.

BRERETON, LEWIS H. *See* PHILIPPINE ISLANDS; UNITED STATES ARMY AIR FORCES.

BRETT, GEORGE H. *See* ABDACOM; SOUTHWEST PACIFIC AREA.

BRETTON WOODS CONFERENCE, JULY 1–22, 1944. United Nations Monetary and Financial Conference, held at Bretton Woods, New Hampshire. Attended by representatives from 44 countries, the meeting addressed postwar financial issues. The participants agreed to form two new organizations: the International Bank for Reconstruction and Development (later known as the World Bank) and the International Monetary Fund.

BRITAIN. *See* UNITED KINGDOM.

BRITISH CHIEFS OF STAFF COMMITTEE (BCOS). Top military leaders of the British army, navy, and air force, who joined with the United States Joint Chiefs of Staff (q.v.) to form the Combined Chiefs of Staff (CCS) (q.v.) during the war. Throughout the British struggle against Japan, the army was represented by the chief of the Imperial General Staff, Field Marshal Alan F. Brooke (q.v.), who chaired the BCOS beginning in March 1942. The air force chief of staff was Marshal of the Royal Air Force Charles Portal (q.v.), who held that position from 1940 to 1945. Two men served as first sea lord (naval chief) during the war: Admirals of the Fleet Dudley Pound (q.v.), who died in 1943, and Andrew B. Cunningham (q.v.), his successor. Serving as the prime minister's liaison with the BCOS was Lieutenant General Hastings L. Ismay (q.v.). Representing the BCOS in regular meetings of the CCS in Washington, D.C., were the service chiefs of the British Joint Staff Mission (q.v.) and its heads, Field Marshals John Dill and Henry Maitland Wilson (qq.v.).

BRITISH JOINT STAFF MISSION (BJSM). British military delegation headquartered in Washington, D.C., to act as a liaison between the United States Joint Chiefs of Staff (JCS) and the British Chiefs of Staff Committee (qq.v.), which together formed the Combined Chiefs of Staff (CCS) (q.v.). Except during international conferences (q.v.), the CCS held its regular meetings in Washington, where the BJSM represented the British chiefs. During most of the war, the leader of the BJSM was Field Marshal John Dill (q.v.), a former head of the British army who was an especially close friend of General George C. Marshall (q.v.), chief of staff of the United States Army (q.v.) and a member of the JCS. After Dill's death in the fall of 1944, the BJSM was headed by Field Marshal Henry Maitland Wilson (q.v.).

BRITISH PACIFIC FLEET. British naval fleet in the war against Japan (q.v.); formerly the British Eastern Fleet, 1941–1944. On December 2, 1941, Admiral Tom S. V. Phillips (q.v.) took command of the new Eastern Fleet at Singapore (q.v.); he died eight days later during the sinking of the *Prince of Wales*. The remainder of the fleet moved to Trincomalee, Ceylon (q.v.), in February 1942, as Japanese troops approached Singapore. Admiral James F. Somerville (q.v.) assumed command in March and moved the fleet the following month when the Japanese sent their superior carrier (q.v.) forces on raids in the Indian Ocean (q.v.). To protect his limited forces, Somerville established the Eastern Fleet headquarters at Kilindini Harbor on Mombasa Island, off the coast of Kenya. The fleet participated in the British seizure of Madagascar (q.v.), grew smaller as most of its ships and landing craft (q.v.) were shifted to operations in other theaters, and returned its headquarters to Ceylon in September 1943, as it began to receive reinforcements, including submarines (q.v.). In the Indian Ocean, the fleet protected Allied ships from Japanese and German submarines, while attacking Japanese shipping. In August 1944, Admiral Bruce A. Fraser (q.v.) replaced Somerville as commander. After a reorganization in November, the Eastern Fleet was renamed the Pacific Fleet and eventually grew into the largest British fleet in the war. Serving with it were various British Commonwealth forces, one French battleship, and a few Dutch ships and submarines.

At the Second Quebec Conference (q.v.) in September 1944, the Allies (q.v.) discussed the British request that the fleet play an expanded role in the war against Japan, a position strongly advocated by Prime Minister Winston S. Churchill and Admiral of the Fleet Andrew B. Cunningham (qq.v.). Although U.S. Admiral Ernest J. King (q.v.) opposed the change, President Franklin D. Roosevelt (q.v.) approved it. During the last part of the war, the British Pacific Fleet joined the U.S. Pacific Fleet in the western Pacific, participated in the campaign for Okinawa (q.v.), and carried out attacks on Formosa (q.v.), the Japanese home islands (q.v.), and Southeast Asia. The fleet bore the designation Task Force 57 when it operated with the U.S. Fifth Fleet, changing to Task Force 37 when attached to the U.S. Third Fleet.

BROOKE, ALAN FRANCIS (1883–1963). British field marshal; chief of the Imperial General Staff (CIGS), 1941–1946. As CIGS, Brooke headed the army and served on the British Chiefs of Staff committee (q.v.), which he chaired beginning in March 1942. He worked closely with Prime Minister Winston S. Churchill (q.v.) and the cabinet throughout the war. Brooke attended the Allied wartime conferences (q.v.) as a member of the Combined Chiefs of Staff (CCS) (q.v.) and alternated with U.S. Fleet Admiral William D. Leahy (q.v.) as chairman of its sessions. Under Brooke's leadership, the British members of the CCS were highly organized and unified when meeting with the Americans, who frequently expressed disparate views. Brooke strongly advocated the policy of conducting only defensive operations in the Pacific until Germany (q.v.) had been defeated, a subject on which he clashed strongly with U.S. Fleet Admiral Ernest J. King (q.v.).

BRUNEI. *See* BORNEO.

BUCKNER, SIMON BOLIVAR, JR. (1886–1945). United States Army general; commander, Alaska Defense Command, 1940–1944; commander, Tenth Army, 1944–1945. As chief of the Alaska Defense Command, based at Fort Richardson, Alaska, Buckner participated in the Aleutian Islands (q.v.) campaigns in 1942 and 1943. He strongly advocated the use of the North Pacific Area (q.v.) for an invasion of Japan (q.v.), although U.S. strategists chose other routes. The next year he was transferred to the Central Pacific Area (q.v.) and appointed to head the ground forces in the forthcoming assault on Okinawa (q.v.). Beginning on April 1, 1945, Buckner's Tenth Army, including both United States Army and United States Marine forces (qq.v.), invaded Okinawa, the last major amphibious assault of the Central Pacific drive toward Japan. Buckner directed the hard-fought and bloody campaign until June 18, when he was killed by a Japanese shell. Lieutenant General Roy S. Geiger (q.v.) assumed command of the rest of the operation. Nakagusuku Bay, the large harbor in eastern Okinawa, was renamed Buckner Bay in honor of the general, who was the highest-ranking U.S. field commander to be killed in action during the war.

BUNA. *See* NEW GUINEA CAMPAIGN.

BURMA. British colony in Southeast Asia whose strategic location was fought over by Japan and the Allies (qq.v.) throughout the war. Bordering India, China, and Thailand (qq.v.), Burma was important to various groups for different reasons during the war. The British, in addition to preserving one of their colonies, saw control of Burma as vital to protecting their larger possession India from the Japanese advance across Asia. China, with its coastal ports, northern territories, and routes into Indochina controlled by the Japanese, depended on the Burma Road (q.v.) to receive military supplies for its defense against Japan. In the United States' (q.v.) view, China's continuation of its

Burma

struggle against Japan was vital to a successful outcome of the larger war, and the existence of overland routes through Burma was essential to aiding the Chinese logistically. Japan wanted to occupy Burma to close the Burma Road to China and to extend its control over Southeast Asia, denying the Allies bases of operation and positioning itself to consider India as a future objective.

Also concerned with Burma were its inhabitants, including some who collaborated with Japan to achieve independence from the British and others who supported the Allies' efforts to oust the Japanese. Among those cooperating with the Japanese were Ba Maw and U Saw (qq.v.); working first with the Japanese and then with the Allies was Aung San (q.v.). Participating in later stages of the war in Burma was the Indian National Army (q.v.), fighting on the side of the Japanese to end British control in India as well as Burma. The British granted independence to Burma in 1948.

BURMA CAMPAIGNS. Efforts by Japan and the Allies (qq.v.) to take control of Burma (q.v.), beginning in December 1941 and lasting until May 1945. Japanese troops crossed into Burma from Thailand (q.v.) on December 11, 1941, captured Victoria Point in the south on December 16, 1941, and advanced rapidly through the country. In command of Japan's forces was Lieutenant General Shojiro Iida. Opposing the Japanese was a small force of British, Indian, and Burmese troops, aided by planes flown by the American Volunteer Group (q.v.). Later added were Indian reinforcements and Chinese troops sent by Chiang Kai-shek (q.v.), who was eager to protect the Burma Road (q.v.) leading to China (q.v.). In March 1942, British Prime Minister Winston S. Churchill (q.v.) sent Lieutenant General Harold R. Alexander (q.v.) to Burma with the assignment of holding Rangoon. Also transferred to Burma in March was British Lieutenant General William J. Slim (q.v.), commander of the I Burma Corps. Brought in to direct the Chinese soldiers and a small group of U.S. troops was U.S. Lieutenant General Joseph W. Stilwell (q.v.), head of the U.S. China-Burma-India (CBI) (q.v.) theater.

The Allied reinforcements and new commanders could not stop the progress of Japan's forces, which occupied Burma by the end of May 1942 while the Allies withdrew to India (q.v.) and China. Japan also controlled the seas around Burma, having captured the Andaman (q.v.) and Nicobar Islands in the Bay of Bengal. During the following months, British responsibility for Burma passed to General Archibald P. Wavell (q.v.), whose limited offensive to take Akyab on the southwest coast in

November 1942 was turned back in May 1943. From February to June 1943, Brigadier General Orde C. Wingate's Chindits (qq.v.) conducted sabotage and guerrilla operations behind Japanese lines in Burma but suffered heavy casualties. The Allied campaign for Burma was strongly hampered by the priority placed on other theaters of the war.

In August 1943 at the First Quebec (Quadrant) Conference (q.v.), the British and Americans agreed to form the Allied Southeast Asia Command (SEAC) (q.v.) under the direction of British Admiral Louis Mountbatten (q.v.), which would direct operations in Burma. The theater formally began operations in November 1943, with Stilwell as deputy commander and Slim as head of the new British Fourteenth Army.

In early 1944 Stilwell, commanding Chinese and U.S. forces, including Merrill's Marauders (q.v.), an elite American army regiment, advanced from Ledo, India, toward Myitkyina (q.v.) in northern Burma. Japanese resistance was intense, and only after a long siege did Stilwell's forces take Myitkyina on August 3.

In central and southern Burma, Allied offensive plans in 1944 coincided with Japanese drives in the Arakan coastal area and across the Indian border to the British bases at Imphal and Kohima (qq.v.). Fighting on the side of the Japanese were elements of the Indian National Army (q.v.). The Japanese offensives were directed by Lieutenant General Masakazu Kawabe (q.v.), Burma Area Army commander. His Arakan attack in February 1944 was thrown back by Slim's army, which had moved toward the area in November 1943 and continued to advance. During the offensive toward Imphal, begun in March 1944, a Japanese army under Lieutenant General Renya Mutaguchi (q.v.) besieged the forces at Imphal and Kohima. Enormous Allied airlifts resupplied the defending soldiers at both locations until Allied ground troops ended the sieges. Mutaguchi's forces, weakened by the poor Japanese logistical system and reduced by heavy casualites, retreated in July.

In northern Burma in the fall of 1944, Lieutenant General Daniel I. Sultan (q.v.) took command of the troops formerly under Stilwell and also assumed charge of the new U.S. India-Burma theater, created after Stilwell's recall to the United States. Sultan's forces moved slowly south from Myitkyina and completed the link between the Stilwell (Ledo) Road (q.v.) and the Burma Road, which reopened in January 1945. Farther south in Burma, Slim's forces steadily advanced, occupying Akyab (January 3), Meiktila (March 3), Mandalay (March 20), and Rangoon (May 3). During the spring, the Burma National Army, which had been fighting on the side of the Japanese, joined the Allied campaign at the direction of its leader Aung San (q.v.). The recapture of Burma was completed in May, except for the elimination of Japanese forces in isolated pockets.

BURMA ROAD. Highway from Lashio, Burma (q.v.), to Kunming, China (q.v.). Chiang Kai-shek's (q.v.) Nationalist forces built the 700-mile road in 1937–1938 as a route for military supplies to reach China. It became increasingly vital as Japan (q.v.) captured Chinese seaports and closed off other avenues to the country. In 1940 Japan coerced the British into closing the Burmese end of the road to isolate China; it reopened three months later with the support of the United States (q.v.), which backed Chiang in his war against Japan. Invading Burma in December 1941, Japanese forces seized control of the road in April 1942 and denied its use to the Allies (q.v.) until January 1945. During the three years the Burma Road was closed, the Allies used a dangerous air route over the Himalayas known as the Hump (q.v.) to fly war matériel from India (q.v.) to China. They also constructed the Stilwell Road (q.v.), or Ledo Road, from India to link up with the Burma Road in northern Burma, bypassing the parts of the road still controlled by Japan. *See also* Logistics.

BURMA-THAILAND RAILWAY. Railway built by forced laborers and Allied prisoners of war (q.v.), many of whom called it the "Death Railway." As the Japanese overran Burma (q.v.), they needed improved routes to supply their troops. In a difficult engineering achievement, the railway was constructed through nearly 300 miles of jungles, mountains, and rivers (including the Kwai River) from Thailand (q.v.) to a point in Burma connecting with other railroads. In addition to 250,000 local laborers, the Japanese forced 60,000 prisoners of war (q.v.), including many Australian, British, Dutch, and American soldiers captured in Malaya, Singapore, and the East Indies (qq.v.), to build the railway. An estimated fifth of the prisoners, who worked under arduous conditions and were fed poorly, died during the construction from July 1942 to October 1943. Approximately 85,000 native workers also perished. *See also* Logistics; War Crimes Trials.

BUSH, VANNEVAR (1890–1974). U.S. engineer; dean of engineering and vice president, Massachusetts Institute of Technology, 1932–1938; president, Carnegie Institution, 1939–1955; chairman, National Advisory Committee for Aeronautics, 1939–1941; chairman, National Defense Research Committee (NDRC), 1940–1941; director, Office of

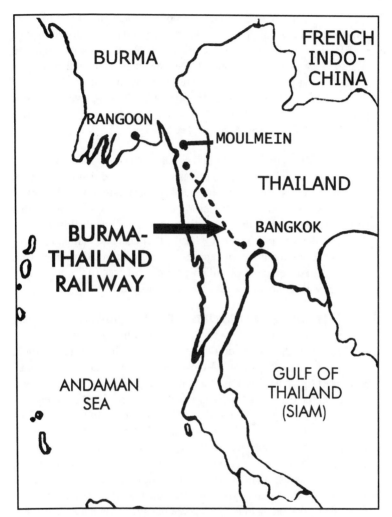

Burma-Thailand Railway

Scientific Research and Development (OSRD) (q.v.), 1941–1946. As the head of the NDRC and the OSRD, which he urged President Franklin D. Roosevelt (q.v.) to form, Bush played a vital role in the mobilization and incorporation of civilian scientists into the war effort. His access to Roosevelt and Secretary of War Henry L. Stimson (q.v.) strengthened his position immensely. In 1942, Bush recommended that the United States undertake the enormous Manhattan Project (q.v.) to build an atomic bomb (q.v.), a program he helped to administer through OSRD and several high-level committees. As the close of the war neared, Bush proposed the establishment of a permanent federal agency to continue in peacetime the relationship between civilian science and the military. Although the OSRD ended with the war, five years later Congress created the National Science Foundation to accomplish Bush's goal. *See also* Science and Technology.

BUSHIDO. The code of beliefs and conduct, "the way of the warrior," instilled in the military forces of Japan. Associated historically with the samurai class, its precepts included personal honor, total loyalty to one's superiors and to the emperor, and willingness to die in combat or by suicide rather than to surrender. In World War II, Bushido was demonstrated through suicidal banzai (q.v.) charges, kamikaze (q.v.) attacks, the small number of Japanese troops captured during the war, and the harsh treatment of Allied prisoners of war (q.v.), who were considered dishonored because they surrendered.

BYRNES, JAMES FRANCIS (1879–1972). U.S. governmental official; Supreme Court justice, 1941–1942; director, Office of Economic Stabilization, 1942–1943; director, Office of War Mobilization, 1943–1945; secretary of state, 1945–1947. A close associate of President Franklin D. Roosevelt (q.v.), Byrnes played an important role in the wartime mobilization of the United States. He also advised the president on foreign affairs and traveled with him to the Yalta Conference (q.v.). After Roosevelt's death in 1945, President Harry S. Truman (q.v.) appointed Byrnes to represent him on the Interim Committee, an advisory body concerning the use of the atomic bomb (q.v.). Truman shortly named Byrnes, who shared his distrust of Soviet leaders, to succeed Edward R. Stettinius, Jr., as secretary of state. Byrnes attended the Potsdam Conference (q.v.) in his new position. During the negotiations regarding the Japanese surrender (q.v.), Byrnes signed the messages to Japan (q.v.) refusing to guarantee the retention of the emperor, a view held also by Truman.

-C-

CAIRO CONFERENCE, FIRST (SEXTANT), NOVEMBER 23–27, 1943. Allied meeting followed immediately by the Teheran and Second Cairo conferences (qq.v.). Chinese Generalissimo Chiang

Kai-shek joined British Prime Minister Winston S. Churchill and U.S. President Franklin D. Roosevelt (qq.v.), at the latter's invitation, to discuss Allied strategy in the war against Japan (q.v.). They agreed to the Cairo Declaration, issued publicly on December 1, which enunciated "Allied aims in the far east." After Japan's unconditional surrender, China (q.v.) was to take control of Manchuria, Formosa, and the Pescadores Islands (qq.v.), and Korea (q.v.) was to become independent "in due course." Japan would also lose control of the islands it had seized or received as mandates (q.v.) after 1914.

The CCS approved future Allied operations in the Central Pacific (the Marshalls, Ponape and Truk in the Carolines, and the Marianas) and in the Southwest Pacific (the New Guinea coast to the Vogelkop peninsula, as well as the Admiralties) (qq.v.), while continuing to debate offensives to recapture Burma (q.v.). Reluctant to divert resources from Europe, the British especially opposed the part of the operation to seize the Andaman Islands (q.v.) in the Bay of Bengal in an amphibious assault, code-named Buccaneer. The United States (q.v.) and China supported the plan presented by Admiral Louis Mountbatten (q.v.), while the British Chiefs of Staff (q.v.) preferred to use amphibious resources in the Mediterranean or, in the case of Churchill, even in Sumatra (q.v.). The CCS also discussed the future use of British naval forces in the Pacific War, an idea initiated by the British chiefs and received unenthusiastically by the United States Joint Chiefs of Staff (q.v.). General Henry H. Arnold (q.v.) announced plans for a strategic air campaign (q.v.) against Japan, to be launched in mid-1944 when the Boeing B-29 (q.v.) very long-range bomber became available.

CAIRO CONFERENCE, SECOND, DECEMBER 2–7, 1943. Allied meeting following the Teheran Conference (q.v.). Concerning the war against Germany (q.v.), U.S. President Franklin D. Roosevelt (q.v.) announced that General Dwight D. Eisenhower would command the cross-channel invasion of France (q.v.); Roosevelt joined British Prime Minister Winston S. Churchill (q.v.) in trying unsuccessfully to persuade Turkey to enter the war at once. The disagreements at the First Cairo Conference (q.v.) regarding strategy in the war against Japan (q.v.) continued, with the British reiterating their opposition to Buccaneer, the amphibious landings in the Andaman Islands (q.v.) to facilitate the recapture of Burma (q.v.). Roosevelt finally overruled his military chiefs, who supported the operations because of Burma's significance as a supply route to China (q.v.), and canceled Buccaneer.

CAIRO DECLARATION. *See* CAIRO CONFERENCE, FIRST.

CANADA. British dominion and member of the Allied powers (q.v.). Led by Prime Minister W. L. Mackenzie King, Canada declared war against Germany (q.v.) on September 10, 1939, and became heavily involved in that war, especially after France (q.v.) fell in June 1940. The day after the Pearl Harbor attack (q.v.), Canada entered the war in the Pacific, where nearly 2,000 Canadian forces were stationed in Hong Kong (q.v.). During the Japanese attack on Hong Kong later in December, the Canadians suffered high casualties and the survivors remained prisoners of war (q.v.) until the Japanese surrender (q.v.).

Although most of its forces were engaged in the war against Germany, Canadian air and ground units assisted in the recapture of the Aleutian Islands (q.v.) in 1943. Canadian naval vessels accompanied the British Pacific Fleet (q.v.) and the U.S. Pacific Fleet at Okinawa (q.v.) and in other operations during the last stages of the war. Air units flew missions in the Southeast Asia Command (q.v.). At the time of the Japanese surrender, Canada was preparing to deploy substantial ground, air, and naval forces to participate in the planned invasion of Japan. Canada sent representatives to the surrender ceremony in Tokyo Bay but declined to contribute forces to the Japanese occupation (q.v.).

In 1940, Canada and the United States (q.v.) established the Permanent Joint Board of Defense to handle military coordination between the countries. Two years later, they worked together to construct the Alaska Highway (q.v.), which ran partly through Canadian territory. Throughout the war, Canada collaborated closely with the United States and the United Kingdom (q.v.), although it resented its exclusion from the highest decision-making levels. Canadian representatives belonged to the British and American Pacific War councils (q.v.), served on selective subcommittees of the Combined Chiefs of Staff (q.v.), and attended some sessions of the Anglo-American wartime conferences, including the two meetings held in Quebec (q.v.). In Allied industrial and scientific endeavors, including the development of the atomic bomb (q.v.), Canada played important roles and provided crucial materials, such as uranium.

In early 1942, as a security measure, the government evacuated Japanese Canadians (q.v.) from areas close to the Pacific coast, in much the same way as the United States handled Japanese Americans (q.v.). On June 20, 1942, a submarine (q.v.) fired on Vancouver Island in the only Japanese attack on Canadian territory until late 1944 and early

1945, when Japanese balloon bombs (q.v.) reached the western part of the country. *See also* Japan, Invasion of; Science and Technology.

CAPE ESPERANCE, BATTLE OF. *See* GUADALCANAL CAMPAIGN: NAVAL BATTLES.

CAPE GLOUCESTER. *See* CARTWHEEL, OPERATION.

CARLSON'S RAIDERS. United States Marine 2d Raider Battalion, which operated in the Gilbert Islands and on Guadalcanal (qq.v.) in 1942. When the marines formed raider units in 1941, Lieutenant Colonel Evans Fordyce Carlson assumed command of the 2d Raider Battalion. In training his men, Carlson modeled his tactics on the Chinese Communist guerrilla operations he had observed while stationed in China and adopted the Chinese slogan "gung ho," meaning "work together." On August 17–18, 1942, the 2d Raider Battalion assaulted the Makin atoll in the Gilbert Islands in a move intended to divert Japanese attention from Guadalcanal, where the 1st Marine Division had already landed. The raiders took the atoll and killed the Japanese garrison before departing. Although the operation cost U.S. lives and failed to deceive the Japanese about Guadalcanal, it boosted American morale. The raid also led the Japanese to reinforce heavily the Gilberts, which U.S. troops took in a costly invasion later in the war. In November and December 1942, Carlson's Raiders conducted a legendary 30-day operation in the jungles of Guadalcanal, where they fought and killed numerous Japanese soldiers. Carlson left the unit for medical treatment, and it was disbanded in 1944.

CAROLINE ISLANDS. Island chain in the western Pacific, occupied in 1914 by Japan (q.v.) and assigned to it as a mandate (q.v.) by the League of Nations in 1919. Among the most important islands and island groups were Truk (q.v.), Yap, Ponape, and the Palaus (q.v.). In accordance with prewar American strategic plans, which considered the Carolines to be an essential part of a drive across the central Pacific, the Combined Chiefs of Staff (q.v.) approved operations to capture Truk and Ponape before assaulting the Mariana Islands (q.v.). After the successful capture of the Marshall Islands (q.v.) in early 1944, however, they decided instead to neutralize and bypass most of the Carolines. The major exception was the Palau Islands, captured by U.S. ground forces in a costly campaign from September 15 to November 27, 1944. During the same campaign, U.S. troops on September 22–24 easily took the Ulithi atoll, which became an important base for the U.S. Pacific Fleet. Beginning in early 1944, Allied forces heavily bombed and shelled Truk, Ponape, and other parts of the Carolines, destroying their potential to threaten Allied operations. In March, U.S. planes dropped the first napalm (q.v.) bombs of the Pacific War on Ponape.

CARRIER, AIRCRAFT. Large ship that served as a floating airfield, on which planes could take off, land, and be stored. The aircraft usually included torpedo bombers (q.v.), dive bombers (q.v.), patrol aircraft, and fighters (q.v.). From carriers, planes could strike at targets 200 to 300 miles away, far greater than the 23-mile range of a battleship's (q.v.) large guns. After carrier-based planes severely damaged the American fleet of battleships at Pearl Harbor (q.v.), the carrier swiftly eclipsed the battleship as the crucial warship in the Pacific War. U.S. carriers generally operated in task forces, in which battleships, cruisers, and destroyers (qq.v.) formed a protective circle around the carriers.

The Japanese, Americans, and British built three types of carriers during the war: fleet, light, and escort. Within each category, each country used a variety of vessels, a few of which are mentioned here. The Japanese fleet carrier of the *Shokaku* class displaced 25,000 tons, traveled at 34 knots, and carried 84 aircraft. The U.S. *Essex* fleet class, which entered service in the fall of 1943, had a displacement of 27,500 tons, speed of 33 knots, and capacity for 100 aircraft. The British *Illustrious*-class fleet carriers, which were first assigned to the Indian Ocean (q.v.) in early 1944, displaced 23,000 tons and reached 31 knots, but they could handle only 40 planes. The British emphasis on heavy armor and steel decks, unlike the Japanese and Americans, protected their carriers from damage during air attacks but limited the number of aircraft that they could accommodate. The wooden decks of the U.S. carriers were especially vulnerable to Japanese kamikaze (q.v.) attacks in 1944 and 1945.

Japan's *Chiyoda* class of light carriers displaced 11,190 tons, traveled at 29 knots, and bore 30 aircraft. In September 1943, the United States introduced the *Independence* class of light carriers, which displaced 11,000 tons, had a speed of 32 knots, and carried 40 aircraft. The British *Colossus* class of light carriers, also completed during the war, displaced 30,000 tons, moved at 25 knots, and had 40 aircraft.

Escort carriers, developed by the British and Americans to protect convoys in the northern Atlantic, performed the same function in the

Pacific, as well as providing close air support during amphibious assaults (q.v.), attacking enemy submarines (q.v.), and transporting aircraft. The United States used the designation escort carriers (CVE), beginning in mid-1943; previous names were aircraft escort vessel (AVG), 1941–1942, and auxiliary aircraft carrier (ACV), 1942–1943. Its most numerous type was the *Casablanca* class, which displaced 7,800 tons, traveled at 19 knots, and carried 28 aircraft.

At the time of the Pearl Harbor strike, Japan had 10 carriers, while the United States had 3 assigned to the Pacific. Fortunately for the United States, its carriers were at sea instead of at port during the attack. Japan's advantages in December 1941 included its well-trained carrier pilots, its powerful and reliable torpedoes (q.v.), and its excellent aircraft, especially the highly maneuverable Mitsubishi Zero fighter. Japanese naval aviators were especially skilled in night fighting, unlike their American counterparts. Japan's inability to replace the experienced pilots lost in such battles as Midway (q.v.) crippled it badly during the rest of the war. Proving of immense benefit to the United States were signal intelligence and radar (qq.v.), the latter installed on American carriers in 1940–1941 but not widely used on Japanese ships until late 1943.

In the months immediately after Pearl Harbor, Vice Admiral Chuichi Nagumo (q.v.) and his carrier force chased the British Eastern Fleet in the Indian Ocean, while the United States Navy (q.v.), incapable of any stronger offensive action, conducted carrier raids on Japanese-held islands in the central Pacific. The United States also used a carrier to mount the Doolittle raid (q.v.) on the Japanese home islands (q.v.). In May 1942, Japanese and U.S. carriers met in the Battle of the Coral Sea (q.v.), the first naval action in which the surface ships never saw each other. The next month, the carriers fought in the Battle of Midway (q.v.), a severe defeat of Japanese carrier planes and pilots. Carriers again battled each other in two of the naval battles accompanying the campaign for Guadalcanal (q.v.): the Battles of the Eastern Solomons (August 24–25, 1942) and the Santa Cruz Islands (October 26–27, 1942). The carriers did not engage each other in a full-scale fight again until the Battle of the Philippine Sea (q.v.) on June 19–20, 1944, when Japan lost the bulk of its planes and crews. In the Battle for Leyte Gulf (q.v.) in October 1944, Japan used its empty carriers primarily as decoys.

As Japan's carrier forces shrank, U.S. production dramatically swelled the quality and quantity of U.S. carriers, which numbered more than 100 of all types by the end of the war. The addition of the *Essex* and *Independence* classes in the fall of 1943 enabled the United States to form a carrier task force, which raided Japanese strongholds and assisted with Central Pacific Area operations beginning with the invasion of the Gilbert Islands (q.v.). In January 1944, Rear Admiral Marc A. Mitscher (q.v.) assumed command of the Fast Carrier Task Force (q.v.), which was designated Task Force 58 when attached to the U.S. Fifth Fleet and Task Force 38 when part of the U.S. Third Fleet. Mitscher later alternated command with Vice Admiral John S. McCain (q.v.). All U.S. carriers remained under the control of the Pacific Ocean Areas (q.v.) theater, which loaned their services to the Southwest Pacific Area (q.v.) theater for the landings at Hollandia (New Guinea), on Morotai, and in the Philippines (qq.v.). In 1944 and 1945, British carriers, part of the British Pacific Fleet (q.v.) used previously in the Indian Ocean, joined the U.S. forces in the Pacific. When operating with the U.S. Fifth Fleet, they used the designation Task Force 57, changing to Task Force 37 when working with the U.S. Third Fleet. During the campaign for Okinawa, the primary targets of the Japanese kamikazes (q.v.) were the American and British carriers. In the last months of the war, Allied carriers struck at the Japanese home islands and Formosa (q.v.). *See also* Naval Vessels.

CARTON DE WIART, ADRIAN (1880–1963). British general; prime minister's personal representative to Chiang Kai-shek (q.v.), 1943–1946. After a long and colorful career in the Boer War and World War I, Carton de Wiart commanded British forces in Norway in 1940. Ordered to Yugoslavia in 1941, he was captured by the Italians and spent two years in prison, during which time he helped to negotiate Italy's (q.v.) surrender to the Allies (q.v.). After his release in 1943, Prime Minister Winston S. Churchill (q.v.) appointed him to serve as personal representative to Generalissimo Chiang Kai-shek (q.v.) in Chungking, China (qq.v.), whom Carton de Wiart greatly admired. In November 1943, he participated in the First Cairo Conference (q.v.), which included Chiang. In his dealings with Chiang, he also represented Admiral Louis Mountbatten (q.v.), head of the Southeast Asia Command (q.v.). At the close of the war, Carton de Wiart participated in the acrimonious British-Chinese negotiations regarding the Japanese surrender (q.v.) in Hong Kong (q.v.). He remained at his post after Churchill was succeeded by Clement R. Attlee (q.v.) in 1945 and left China the following year. Injuries from an accident prevented him from accepting Chiang's offer to hire him as a personal adviser.

CARTWHEEL, OPERATION. Allied campaign in 1943–1944 to isolate the Japanese stronghold of Rabaul (q.v.) on New Britain in the Bismarck Archipelago, carried out by forces of the Southwest Pacific Area (SWPA) and the South Pacific Area (SOPAC) (qq.v.). General Douglas MacArthur and Admiral William F. Halsey (qq.v.), heads of SWPA and SOPAC, respectively, planned Cartwheel with the goal of capturing Rabaul. The SWPA targets included Northeast New Guinea (q.v.), the Admiralty Islands, and New Britain. The SOPAC forces planned to move north from Guadalcanal (q.v.) through the Solomon Islands (q.v.) toward Rabaul. Altogether, 13 major amphibious landings were involved. The United States Joint Chiefs of Staff (q.v.) approved the operation but later changed the objective to the envelopment and isolation of Rabaul rather than the direct assault of it.

Two events preceding Cartwheel affected the Japanese response to the campaign: the Battle of the Bismarck Sea (q.v.), in which Allied air forces in March 1943 prevented Japanese reinforcements from reaching Lae on the New Guinea coast, and the assassination of Admiral Isoruku Yamamoto (q.v.) over Bougainville in April 1943. Operation Cartwheel began on June 30, 1943, with SWPA assaults on the Trobriand Islands off Papua, New Guinea (q.v.), and SOPAC operations in the central Solomons. After the capture of the Trobriands, SWPA forces in Northeast New Guinea captured Salamaua, Lae, Finschhafen, and Saidor, completing their conquest of the Huon peninsula in January 1944. The operations at Lae included the dropping of American paratroopers at Nadzab, the first major Allied airborne operation (q.v.) of the Pacific War. In December 1943, the 1st Cavalry and 1st Marine divisions of SWPA landed at Arawe and Cape Gloucester on New Britain. Other SWPA actions included the seizures of Los Negros and Manus in the Admiralty Islands in February and March 1944 and the capture of Madang in New Guinea in April 1944.

In the central Solomons, Halsey's SOPAC forces fought their severest battle on New Georgia at Munda Point, which they secured on August 5, 1943. In October, they assaulted Choiseul and the Treasury Islands. The next major invasion began in the northern Solomons on November 1, with landings on Empress Augusta Bay on Bougainville. There, the SOPAC forces built an air base and established a strong defensive perimeter, from which they successfully fought off charges by Japanese troops. The last large Japanese counterattack on Bougainville occurred in March 1944, after which the perimeter was considered secure and the rest of the island was bypassed by the Allies (q.v.) until late in the war, when Australian troops undertook mopping-up operations. The last SOPAC amphibious actions in Cartwheel were the capture of the Green Islands and Emirau in February–March 1944.

A number of naval battles occurred during the SOPAC offensives in the Solomons. On July 6, 1943, in the Battle of Kula Gulf, Japanese ships reinforcing the garrison on Kolombangara were challenged by Allied ships, which destroyed several Japanese vessels but did not prevent the troop reinforcement. The following week, in the Battle of Kolombangara, the Japanese accomplished another reinforcement mission with heavier Allied losses. SOPAC forces were victorious in the Battle of Vella Gulf, on August 6–7, in which Japanese troop ships sank or turned back. In the Battle of Vella Lavella, October 6–7, Japanese ships successfully evacuated Kolombangara and Vella Lavella while inflicting severe losses on Allied naval forces. During the Allied assault on Bougainville, naval battles occurred soon after the first landing and on November 24, 1943, when Allied naval forces decisively stopped the Japanese transport of reinforcements to the Solomons.

Following Operation Cartwheel, SWPA forces continued their advances along the northern part of New Guinea. SOPAC was deactivated, with its army and army air forces transferred to SWPA, which also assumed responsibility for areas bypassed by SOPAC. Most of the marine and naval forces in SOPAC were moved to the Central Pacific Area. *See also* Hyakutake, Haruyoshi; Imamura, Hitoshi.

CASABLANCA CONFERENCE (SYMBOL), JANUARY 14–24, 1943. Allied meeting of U.S. President Franklin D. Roosevelt, British Prime Minister Winston S. Churchill (qq.v.), and their advisers in French Morocco. Convened primarily to consider the next Allied target after the liberation of Northwest Africa, the conferees also discussed the war against Japan (q.v.), approving offensives to seize the Japanese stronghold at Rabaul (q.v.) in the Bismarck Archipelago, to recapture Burma (q.v.) through Operation Anakim, and to retake the Aleutian Islands (q.v.). After the Rabaul operations, the Allies (q.v.) would begin offensive actions in the Central Pacific Area by invading the Gilbert and Marshall Islands (qq.v.). The American chiefs argued strongly but futilely for a higher priority on the Pacific War. Also discussed was atomic bomb (q.v.) research. In a press conference on the final day, Roosevelt issued the demand for "unconditional surrender by Germany, Italy, and Japan" (qq.v.) to assure "future world peace."

CELEBES. *See* NETHERLANDS EAST INDIES.

CENTRAL PACIFIC AREA (CENPAC). Subdivision of the Allied Pacific Ocean Areas (POA) theater. Admiral Chester W. Nimitz (q.v.), commander of POA, also personally commanded CENPAC for the first part of the war and then delegated its direction to Admiral Raymond A. Spruance (q.v.). CENPAC's major offensive operations started in November 1943 with the invasion of the Gilbert Islands (q.v.), which was followed by campaigns in the Marshall Islands, the Mariana Islands, the Palau Islands, Iwo Jima, and Okinawa (qq.v.) After the deactivation of the South Pacific Area (q.v.) in June 1944, most of its naval and marine forces were added to the already formidable forces in CENPAC.

CEYLON. British-held island off the southeast tip of India (q.v.). After the fall of Singapore to Japan (qq.v.) in February 1942, the British Eastern Fleet moved to Trincomalee, a naval base on Ceylon which the British considered essential for controlling the Indian Ocean (q.v.) and protecting India (q.v.). Trincomalee and Colombo, the capital of Ceylon, were

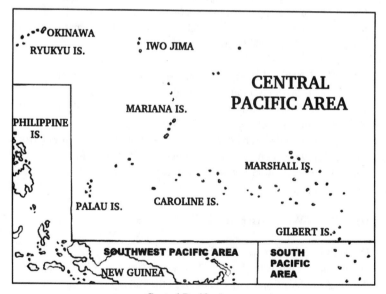

Central Pacific Area

attacked in March–April 1942 as part of the Japanese raids in the Indian Ocean led by Vice Admiral Chuichi Nagumo (q.v.), but the British retained control of the island throughout the war. On April 15, 1944, Admiral Louis Mountbatten (q.v.) moved the headquarters of his Southeast Asia Command (q.v.) to Kandy on Ceylon. The island became independent in 1948; it was renamed Sri Lanka.

CHANG HSÜEH-LIANG (1898–). Chinese warlord who controlled forces in Manchuria (q.v.) following the assassination of his father, Chang Tso-lin, by the Japanese in 1928. In Manchuria, Chang Hsüeh-liang supported the claims of Chiang Kai-shek (q.v.) against Japan (q.v.). Forced to flee southward as the Japanese advanced, Chang's troops fought alongside Chiang's soldiers. After concluding that Chiang's Nationalists and the Chinese Communists should join forces to fight the Japanese instead of each other, Chang took Chiang into custody in December 1936 and forced him to negotiate with the Communists, represented by Chou En-lai (q.v.). While held in Chang's headquarters in Sian, Chiang agreed to cooperate with the Communists against the Japanese, although the actual implementation of the United Front did not occur until September 1937. After releasing Chiang, Chang traveled to the Nationalist capital of Nanking (q.v.), where Chiang had him arrested. Chang remained a captive of the Nationalists through the end of the war with Japan, the conclusion of the Chinese civil war, and many years in Formosa (q.v.). In 1986 he moved to Hawaii.

CHANGKUFENG. Hill on the Tumen river near the borders of Korea, the Union of Soviet Socialist Republics, and Manchuria (qq.v.), where Japanese and Soviet troops battled in July–August 1938. In a fight known to the Soviets as Lake Khasan, the outnumbered Japanese seized the disputed territory but later withdrew upon orders from Tokyo. Casualties on both sides totaled 2,500. The following year, a serious border conflict between the Japanese and Soviets occurred at Nomonhan (q.v.).

CHEMICAL WARFARE. *See* POISON GAS.

CHENGTU. Site of main B-29 bomber base in China (q.v.), which was abandoned in early 1945 as the Japanese advanced. When the United States Army Air Forces (q.v.) acquired the Boeing B-29 Superfortress (q.v.) bomber, it needed bases on mainland China from which to launch its strategic air campaign (q.v.) against Japan (q.v.). The principal B-29 bases in China were built at Chengtu, a location northwest of the capital of Chungking (q.v.) chosen by Lieutenant General Joseph W. Stilwell (q.v.) because he considered it more secure than other suggested sites. The first B-29 missions flew out of Chengtu in June 1944. As the Japanese Operation Ichigo (q.v.) swept through China targeting U.S. airfields and meeting ineffective Chinese resistance, Chengtu was evacuated in January 1945. By then the United States (q.v.) had built B-29 bases in the Mariana Islands (q.v.), which then supported the B-29 strategic air campaign against Japan.

CHENNAULT, CLAIRE LEE (1890–1958). United States Army general; commander, American Volunteer Group and Fourteenth Air Force, China, 1941–1945. After his retirement as a captain from the United States Army Air Corps in 1937, Chennault worked for Chiang Kai-shek's (q.v.) government to defend China against Japan (qq.v.). With the knowledge and tacit approval of the U.S. government, in 1941 he recruited American airmen for the American Volunteer Group (AVG) (q.v.) in China, also known as the "Flying Tigers." Beginning in December 1941 he led the AVG in combat against the Japanese. In early 1942, Chennault was recalled to active duty as a brigadier general with the United States Army Air Forces (q.v.) to command the China Air Task Force, which included the AVG; he later headed the U.S. Fourteenth Air Force. Chennault used his influence with Chiang to undercut General Joseph W. Stilwell (q.v.), the China-Burma-India (q.v.) theater commander, with whom he feuded. Chiang agreed with Chennault's argument to put the priority on air power rather than on Stilwell's attempts to train the Chinese ground forces and to reopen a land route into China; Chiang eventually insisted that Stilwell be recalled. In the summer of 1945, Chennault left his position in China under pressure from U.S. military leaders. After the conclusion of the war and his retirement from the army, he returned to China to work for Chiang's government.

CHIANG KAI-SHEK (1887–1975). Leader, Chinese Nationalist government, 1928–1949; president, Republic of China, 1943–1949, 1950–1975; commander, China theater of operations (q.v.), 1941–1945. Through the intervention of Chinese warlord Chang Hsüeh-liang (q.v.) in late 1936, Chiang agreed to suspend his civil war with the Chinese Communists to form a United Front against Japan (q.v.). The promised coalition did not actually occur until after full-scale war with Japan began in mid-1937. Relations between Chiang's Nationalists and Mao Tse-tung's Communists remained tenuous; during periods of the Sino-Japanese War, especially from 1937 to early 1941, the rival Chinese groups cooperated to fight the Japanese, but through much of the war they opposed each other also. In August 1937, Chiang signed a nonaggression pact with the Union of Soviet Socialist Republics (q.v.), which provided military assistance until the Soviets concluded an agreement with Japan in April 1941. Japanese victories in 1937 forced Chiang to leave his capital of Nanking (q.v.). The next spring, he established his headquarters in Chungking (q.v.), which remained the Nationalist capital throughout the war.

After Chiang officially declared war on Japan on December 9, 1941, the Allies (q.v.) named him to command the China theater. U.S. President Franklin D. Roosevelt (q.v.), who considered China's continued participation to be crucial in the defeat of Japan, recognized Chiang as the legitimate head of China (q.v.), furnished him with military and economic assistance, and invited him to the First Cairo Conference (q.v.) in 1943. Bolstering Chiang's position with the president was the strong political support he enjoyed in the United States (q.v.). Also popular and influential in the United States were Chiang's wife, Mei-ling Soong, who used her fluent English to promote the Nationalist cause, and her brother, T. V. Soong (q.v.), who served as foreign minister during the war and traveled frequently to the United States.

In early 1942, the United States Army assigned Lieutenant General Joseph W. Stilwell (q.v.) to serve as Chiang's chief of staff, a position he held until October 1944 when Chiang demanded his recall. Major General Albert C. Wedemeyer (q.v.) succeeded Stilwell as Chiang's chief of staff. U.S. officers favored by Chiang included Major General Claire L. Chennault (q.v.); Rear Admiral Milton E. Miles, who headed the American part of the Sino-American Cooperative Organization (q.v.); and Brigadier General Patrick J. Hurley (q.v.), ambassador to China, 1944–1946. Also supportive of Chiang was British General Adrian Carton de Wiart (q.v.), Prime Minister Winston S. Churchill's (q.v.) personal representative in China. Chiang vehemently opposed the Dixie Mission (q.v.), the small U.S. delegation sent to Mao Tse-tung's (q.v.) headquarters in 1944.

In July 1945, Chiang joined the United States and the United Kingdom (q.v.) in issuing the Potsdam Proclamation (q.v.) to Japan, which called for unconditional surrender. On August 14, 1945, he agreed to a treaty of friendship with the U.S.S.R., in which he accepted changes affecting Chinese territory that the Soviets had demanded at the Yalta Conference (q.v.). In accordance with the Cairo Declaration, China regained control of much Japanese-held territory at the end of the war.

Critics accused Chiang's government of widespread corruption and charged that he used his Nationalist forces and his lend-lease (q.v.) assistance from the United States to position himself for victory over the Chinese Communists, instead of concentrating his efforts against the Japanese. In 1946, civil war broke out again, culminating in the move of Chiang and the Nationalists to Formosa, where they based the Republic of China. *See also* China, Japanese Operations in; Ho Ying-chin; Kuomintang.

CHIFLEY, JOSEPH BENEDICT (1885–1951). Australian prime minister, 1945. During the administration of John Curtin (1941–1945) (q.v.), Chifley served as treasurer and worked on plans for the postwar period. In April 1945, he was named acting prime minister because of Curtin's illness, and he became prime minister on July 12, 1945, when Curtin died.

CHINA. Asian country ruled variously by Chinese Nationalists, Chinese Communists, Chinese warlords, Japanese puppet regimes, and Japanese armies throughout the 1930s and 1940s. Chiang Kai-shek's (q.v.) Nationalist government, established in Nanking (q.v.) in 1928 and later moved to Chungking (q.v.), was recognized by the governments of the United States (q.v.) and many other countries while it fought a civil war with the Chinese Communists, led by Mao Tse-tung (q.v.), who based his headquarters in Yenan in 1935. The Nationalists and Communists announced the formation of the anti-Japanese United Front in 1937 and partially suspended the civil war until January 1941, when their military forces clashed openly. Thereafter, although Chou En-lai (q.v.) continued to act as the Communists' liaison with the Nationalists, they generally fought the Japanese on separate fronts. The two groups also vied with each other for control of the rest of the country, leading U.S. General Joseph W. Stilwell (q.v.) and others to claim that Chiang was more concerned with defeating the Communists than fighting the Japanese. In 1944, the United States sent a small delegation called the Dixie Mission (q.v.) to Yenan to discuss possible military cooperation with the Communists.

As the Japanese gained control of Chinese territory, they established

China

several puppet governments headed by Chinese. Manchuria became Manchukuo (q.v.), under former Chinese Emperor Pu-Yi (q.v.) in 1932. Following the outbreak of full-scale war in China in 1937, the Provisional Government of the Republic of China was formed in northern China with Wang K'o-min as head. Also in 1937, the Japanese created a federation called Meng-chiang, or Mongolian Borderlands. The next year the Reformed Government of the Republic of China was organized in Nanking. In 1940, the regional governments except for Manchukuo were incorporated into the Reorganized National Government of the Republic of China, headquartered in Nanking. Its leader was Wang Ching-wei (q.v.), a former high-ranking Nationalist leader who wanted China to make a separate peace with Japan (q.v.). Beginning in 1943,

Japan allowed Wang to build and control his own armed forces, which consisted mostly of defectors from the Nationalist army; he declared war against the Allies (q.v.) the same year.

With the Japanese surrender (q.v.) in August 1945, the Nationalists and Communists competed to take control of areas formerly held by the Japanese and puppet governments. U.S. forces transported two Marine divisions and several Chinese Nationalist armies to northern China, the site of much conflict. In spite of U.S.-sponsored mediation led by Brigadier General Patrick J. Hurley and General of the Army George C. Marshall (qq.v.), the civil war broke out on a large scale in mid-1946. In 1949 the Communists achieved control of the mainland and established the People's Republic of China. The Nationalists moved the government of the Republic of China to Formosa (Taiwan) (q.v.) the same year. *See also* China, Japanese Operations in; Intelligence, Allied.

CHINA-BURMA-INDIA THEATER (CBI). U.S. theater of operations headed by General Joseph W. Stilwell (q.v.), 1942–1944. Stilwell arrived in China (q.v.) in early March 1942 to assume command of the CBI theater and a number of other posts, including chief of staff to Chiang Kai-shek (q.v.). Chinese troops under Stilwell's command participated in the unsuccessful Allied attempt to defend Burma and the Burma Road (qq.v.) against the Japanese in the spring of 1942. U.S. officers then trained Chinese troops in India (q.v.) and southern China, returning to northern Burma in late 1943 to recapture territory and build a land route into China, which was opened in January 1945. Also included in CBI were Major General Claire L. Chennault's (q.v.) U.S. Fourteenth Air Force in China and the U.S. Tenth Air Force in India. To move military supplies into China while the Burma Road was closed, transport planes flew the Hump (q.v.) route from Assam, India, to Kunming (q.v.), China.

After Stilwell's recall in October 1944, CBI was split into the China theater under Major General Albert C. Wedemeyer (q.v.) and the India-Burma theater under Lieutenant General Daniel I. Sultan (q.v.). See also *Intelligence, Allied.*

CHINA INCIDENT. Term used by Japan (q.v.) to describe the Sino-Japanese War that began in July 1937.

CHINA, JAPANESE OPERATIONS IN. Conducted from 1931 to 1945. On September 18–19, 1931, the Japanese Kwantung Army (q.v.)

began its military conquest of Manchuria (q.v.), an area of northeastern China (q.v.), in spite of contrary orders from the Japanese government. By early 1932, Japan (q.v.) controlled the area and renamed it Manchukuo (q.v.). Also in early 1932, Japanese and Chinese troops fought in Shanghai (q.v.) on the eastern coast of China, where Chinese anger over the Japanese seizure of Manchuria had resulted in a boycott of Japanese goods. A truce ended the conflict, the boycott, and the presence of the Japanese army in Shanghai.

From late 1932 to mid-1937, Japanese and Chinese soldiers clashed intermittently. In 1933, Japan invaded Jehol province and jeopardized Chinese control of north China. The same year Chinese Nationalist leader Chiang Kai-shek (q.v.) agreed to the Tangku Truce providing for a demilitarized zone and the removal of Japanese troops from the immediate Peking area. In June 1935, Chinese General Ho Ying-chin and Japanese Lieutenant General Yoshijiro Umezu (qq.v.) negotiated the secret Ho-Umezu Agreement, in which the Chinese pledged to withdraw all Nationalist troops and party offices from Hopeh (including Peking) and to end anti-Japanese activities in China. By virtually conceding northern China to the Japanese, Chiang hoped to gain time to concentrate his efforts against Mao Tse-tung's (q.v.) Chinese Communist forces. He later suspended the civil war and formed a coalition with the Communists against Japan.

After the Marco Polo Bridge (q.v.) incident near Peking on July 7, 1937, the Sino-Japanese War began on a large scale, with Japan focusing on heavily populated areas and transportation centers. After taking Peking (July 28) and Tientsin (July 29) in the north, Japanese forces moved south, capturing Shanghai on November 8 and the former Nationalist capital of Nanking (q.v.) on December 13. The atrocities that accompanied the assault on Nanking shocked the world, as did the sinking of the U.S. gunboat *Panay* (q.v.) in the Yangtze River the day before the Nanking attack began. On December 27, the Japanese took Tsinan, capital of Shantung. Also in 1937, the Japanese suffered a rare defeat on September 25 at Pingsingkuan, where elements of the Chinese Communist Eighth Route Army under Chu Teh (q.v.) ambushed and destroyed a Japanese division.

In 1938, the Chinese defeated the Japanese at Taierchwang (April) and Chengchow (July), but the Japanese also continued their conquests, taking Hsuchow (May 20), Kaifeng (June 6), China's last open seaport at Canton (October 21), and the Nationalists' temporary capital of Hankow (October 25). Chiang then moved his capital to Chungking (q.v.)

for the duration of the war. By the end of the year, having taken the eastern seaports, major cities, and important railways, Japan halted major land offensives and strengthened its control of the captured areas, while bombing Chinese-held areas and trying to wear down China by attrition. With access into China ended from the north and from the seaports, the Japanese attempted to cut off the flow of military supplies from Southeast Asia by forcing the British to close the Burma Road (q.v.) for part of 1940 and by occupying northern French Indochina (q.v.) in 1940.

In northern China, the Chinese Communists carried out the Hundred Regiments offensive from August 20 to November 30, 1940, against Japanese forces. After achieving initial successes, the Chinese were subjected to Japanese punitive raids from 1941 to 1943.

On December 9, 1941, after Japanese strikes throughout Southeast Asia and the Pacific, Chiang formally declared war on Japan, Germany, and Italy (qq.v.). From March to May 1942, following the Japanese invasion of Burma (q.v.), Chiang sent Chinese troops to try to keep the Burma Road from capture. They were forced to leave when Japan took control of the country and closed the road. The United States then sent supplies to Chiang by transport planes (q.v.) flying the Hump (q.v.) from India over the Himalaya Mountains to China, but the planes delivered much smaller loads than could be carried on the overland route. During 1942, the main ground action in China followed the Doolittle Raid (q.v.) on Japan in April. Knowing that the U.S. bombers (q.v.) had crash-landed in China after attacking Tokyo, Japan retaliated by seizing Chinese airfields.

Throughout the rest of 1942 and 1943, neither the Chinese nor the Japanese made large advances on the ground in China. In 1943, the Japanese launched limited offensives to capture Chinese rice crops; they were mostly successful but in November were stopped at Changteh in Hunan. In late 1943, Chinese troops under U.S. Lieutenant General Joseph W. Stilwell (q.v.) began operations in northern Burma to reopen a land route into China. The U.S. Fourteenth Air Force under Claire L. Chennault (q.v.) controlled most of the air over China and bombed Japanese-held areas such as Formosa (q.v.) in addition to attacking Japanese supply routes and troops in China.

In 1944, the Japanese ended their raids against Chinese Communist forces in northwest China and moved some of their forces farther south. In April, Lieutenant General Yasuji Okamura's (q.v.) Chinese Expeditionary Army began the massive Operation Ichigo (q.v.), intended to capture airfields used by U.S. bombers and to extend the

Japanese transportation system from northern to southern China. The Japanese seized most of their objectives and an enormous amount of territory. Chinese defenses strengthened under U.S. Lieutenant General Albert C. Wedemeyer (q.v.) and in the spring of 1945 began to counterattack as the Japanese withdrew from some areas to strengthen the defenses in northern China and Manchuria, where they considered a Soviet attack increasingly likely.

On August 9, 1945, the Union of Soviet Socialist Republics (q.v.) invaded Manchuria in enormous numbers. By the time the Kwantung Army capitulated on August 20, 1945, Soviet troops had occupied most of Manchuria and northern Korea (q.v.) and had linked up with Chinese Communist forces in northern China.

Okamura formally surrendered Japanese forces to Chinese Nationalist General Ho Ying-chin on September 9, 1945. Many of the Japanese-held areas in China were turned over to Nationalist rather than Communist forces. Japan signed a peace treaty with Chiang's Republic of China on April 29, 1952. The People's Republic of China under Mao Tse-tung concluded a peace treaty with Japan on August 12, 1978.

CHINA THEATER. Allied theater established on January 29, 1941, with Chiang Kai-shek (q.v.) as head. In addition to China, the theater included parts of Thailand and French Indochina (qq.v.). Near the end of the war, the Allies (q.v.) decided to transfer southern Indochina to the Allied Southeast Asia Command (q.v.), a change that occurred on September 2, 1945. Throughout the war, Chiang's chief of staff was a United States Army general: General Joseph W. Stilwell (1942–1944) and Lieutenant General Albert C. Wedemeyer (1944–1945) (qq.v.).

The term *China Theater* also refers to the U.S. theater of operations created on October 24, 1944, when the U.S. China-Burma-India (q.v.) theater was split into two parts. General Wedemeyer commanded the U.S. China Theater.

CHINDITS. Long-range penetration groups operating behind Japanese lines in Burma (q.v.) under the command of British Brigadier General Orde Wingate (q.v.). Authorized by General Archibald P. Wavell (q.v.), Wingate first organized the 77th Infantry Brigade from British, Indian, and Burmese soldiers. From February to May 1943, the Chindits, supplied solely by air, conducted guerrilla operations against Japanese troops and railroads in Burma. Although their casualties were heavy and the value of their efforts was questionable, they captured the interest of the public and were honored by Prime Minister Winston S. Churchill (q.v.). Wingate received additional resources and was allowed to train larger numbers of Chindits, which he sent into Burma in February 1944. After his death the next month in a plane crash, the Chindits continued their operations and helped to destroy communication lines that affected the Japanese offensive at Imphal (q.v.). Some came under the command of U.S. Lieutenant General Joseph W. Stilwell (q.v.). The surviving Chindits, many weak and ill from tropical diseases, were evacuated to India (q.v.) later in 1944.

CHINESE COMMUNISTS. *See* CHINA; CHINA, JAPANESE OPERATIONS IN; CHOU EN-LAI; CHU TEH; DIXIE MISSION; MAO TSE-TUNG.

CHOU EN-LAI (1898–1976). Chinese Communist political leader and liaison with Chiang Kai-shek (q.v.), 1936–1946. One of the founders of the Chinese Communist party, Chou worked closely with Mao Tse-tung (q.v.) and accompanied him on the Long March in 1934–1935. Chou negotiated with Chiang's Nationalists and other Chinese leaders such as Chang Hsüeh-liang (q.v.) to suspend the civil war in order to combine efforts against Japanese aggression in China (q.v.). The United Front was finalized in September 1937. Chou moved to Chungking (q.v.), the Nationalists' wartime capital, in 1940 and continued to represent the Chinese Communists while holding an advisory position in Chiang's government. After a bloody clash between Nationalist and Communist forces in early 1941, Chou divided his time between Chungking and Mao's headquarters in Yenan. He participated in U.S.-sponsored efforts to end the civil war in 1945 and 1946. After the Communist victory in 1949, Chou became premier and foreign minister of the People's Republic of China.

CHU TEH (1886–1976). Chinese Communist marshal; commander, Chinese Eighth Route Army, 1937–1945. An early member of the Chinese Communist party, Chu accompanied Mao Tse-tung (q.v.) on the Long March in 1934–1945 and led the Communist military forces, which he continued to do throughout the war with Japan (q.v.). In 1937, when the Chinese Nationalists and Communists formed the United Front against Japan, Chu became commander of the Eighth Route Army, which was nominally under the Nationalist government but was actually directed by Chu. During the war with Japan, the Chinese Communists executed mostly guerrilla operations against the Japanese in northern China (q.v.). Their major offensive, the Hundred Regiments campaign in 1940, was followed by Japanese reprisal raids lasting until 1943. After the Japanese surrender (q.v.), Chu became commander of the People's Liberation Army and led the successful campaign to win the civil war.

CHUNGKING. Wartime capital of Chiang Kai-shek's (q.v.) Chinese Nationalist government, 1938–1945. Japanese advances in the fall of 1937 led Chiang to abandon Nanking (q.v.) as his capital and move up the Yangtze River to Hankow. Before the Japanese captured that city in April 1938, the Nationalists retreated farther inland to the river port of Chungking, where they based their government for the rest of the war. Chungking's remote, mountainous location deterred an enemy ground assault for a number of years, although Japan's Operation Ichigo (q.v.) in 1944–1945 captured nearby sites before withdrawing. Japanese planes bombed Chungking heavily during the war, especially from 1939 to 1942.

CHURCHILL, WINSTON SPENCER (1874–1965). British prime minister and defense minister, 1940–1945; prime minister, 1951–1955. Churchill, a prominent British political figure for more than half of the 20th century, served as first lord of the admiralty during the early years of World War I and reassumed that post in 1939. A member of the Conservative Party, Churchill became prime minister of the wartime coalition government on May 10, 1940, as German troops moved into the Netherlands (q.v.) and Belgium. Churchill served as his own defense minister, personally directing much of the British war effort through the British Chiefs of Staff Committee (q.v.). His dynamic speeches both boosted public morale and helped to build support for the British position in other countries, especially the United States (q.v.). Regarding a strong Anglo-American alliance as an essential element of British survival, Churchill developed a close relationship with President Franklin D. Roosevelt (q.v.) to secure and keep American assistance in the war effort. The two men met numerous times at Allied wartime conferences (q.v.) and corresponded often. Churchill also talked frequently to Harry R. Hopkins and W. Averell Harriman (qq.v.) in their roles as Roosevelt's representatives.

While believing firmly in the strategy of defeating Germany before Japan (qq.v.), Churchill nevertheless was concerned about the recovery and postwar retention of British colonial possessions in Asia and the Pacific, where he also supported most French and Dutch plans to reestablish control of their colonies. He maintained his own personal representative, General Adrian Carton de Wiart (q.v.), at Chiang Kai-shek's (q.v.) headquarters in Chungking, China (qq.v.). Churchill's liaison officer to the Southwest Pacific Area (q.v.) was Lieutenant General Herbert Lumsden, who was killed by a kamikaze (q.v.) attack in 1945 during the invasion of the Philippines (q.v.). During the last year of the war, Churchill pushed for a more visible role for the British Pacific Fleet (q.v.) and the inclusion of British ground forces in the projected invasion of the Japanese home islands (q.v.).

In elections held after the conclusion of the war in Europe, British voters turned Churchill's party out of office. While attending the Potsdam Conference (q.v.) in July 1945, Churchill was replaced as prime minister by Clement R. Attlee (q.v.), who had served as deputy prime minister in the coalition government. Churchill later served another term as prime minister. *See also* United Kingdom.

COASTWATCHERS. Allied network of individuals and small groups stationed mainly in the Solomon (q.v.) and Bismarck Islands and along the coast of New Guinea (q.v.), who provided intelligence about weather and movements of Japanese military forces. Begun by the Royal Australian Navy before the war, the system involved mostly Australians, New Zealanders, and Europeans who already lived on the islands. In mid-1942, the coastwatchers came under the jurisdiction of the Allied Intelligence Bureau in the Southwest Pacific Area (q.v.). In addition to transmitting information by radio, the coastwatchers rescued stranded airmen and sailors, including future U.S. President John F. Kennedy. Their efforts were especially important from the landing on Guadalcanal (q.v.) in August 1942 until the fall of 1944, when the Allies (q.v.) had captured most of the areas served by the coastwatchers. In the Philippine Islands (q.v.), members of the guerilla resistance also performed as coastwatchers, although they were not part of the same system. *See also* Intelligence, Allied.

COLLINS, JOSEPH LAWTON (1896–1987). United States Army general; chief of staff, Hawaiian Department, 1941–1942; commander, 25th Division, 1942–1943; commander, VII Corps, 1944–1945. Collins became chief of staff of the Hawaiian Department shortly after the Pearl Harbor attack (q.v.), and in May 1942 he assumed command of the 25th Division, which was assigned to defend Hawaii. At the end of November, the United States Joint Chiefs of Staff (q.v.) decided to send the 25th Division to Guadalcanal (q.v.), where U.S. forces had been fighting for control of the island since August 1942. Upon his arrival, Collins reported to Major General Alexander M. Patch (q.v.), who had taken command of the forces on Guadalcanal in early December. Collins directed a major offensive beginning on January 10, 1943. The Guadalcanal campaign concluded with an Allied victory in early February.

Following Guadalcanal, Collins participated in campaigns in the central Solomon Islands (q.v.) until his transfer to the European theater, where his VII Corps landed in Normandy on June 6, 1944, as part of Operation Overlord. Collins led the corps through the rest of the war in Europe. He later held a number of high-ranking positions, culminating with his service as army chief of staff (1949–1953).

COMBINED CHIEFS OF STAFF (CCS). Organization created to direct the strategic policy of the British and American coalition in the wars against the Axis powers (q.v.). Established during the First Washington Conference (q.v.) in December 1941–January 1942, the CCS included the members of the British Chiefs of Staff Committee and the United States Joint Chiefs of Staff (JCS) (qq.v.). In addition to conferring at major Allied conferences, the CCS met regularly in Washington, D.C., where the British were represented by the British Joint Staff Mission, headed by Field Marshal John Dill (qq.v.) throughout most of the war. While waging coalition war, the CCS also shared information about intelligence (q.v.) and special projects such as the development of the atomic bomb (q.v.).

For much of the first two years of American participation in the war, the British strategic views prevailed, in part because of their strong organization. During the latter part of the war, when American resources overwhelmed those of the British, the U.S. positions carried more weight. The CCS basically adhered to the policy of using its resources to defeat Germany before Japan (qq.v.), although U.S. Fleet Admiral Ernest J. King (q.v.) frequently advocated more resources for the Pacific. In the war against Japan, the CCS delegated responsibility for the Pacific (excluding Southeast Asia) to the JCS, which created two Allied theaters (the Pacific Ocean Areas and Southwest Pacific Area [qq.v.]) to conduct operations. The British Chiefs of Staff directed efforts in the Asian parts of the British Empire and administered the Southeast Asia Command (q.v.), the Allied theater created in the fall of 1943. The CCS acknowledged Chiang Kai-shek (q.v.) as head of the China theater (not to be confused with the U.S. China-Burma-India and China [qq.v.]) theaters and Joseph V. Stalin (q.v.) as head of the Union of Soviet Socialist Republics (q.v.) theater. There was little direct contact between the CCS and these two autonomous theaters.

During the last year of the war against Japan, the CCS disagreed about the role of the British Pacific Fleet (q.v.). The British wanted it to participate fully in the final campaigns against Japan, including the ground invasion if that occurred. King resisted its addition to the U.S. naval campaigns, claiming that the British fleet would pose a logistical burden that would outweigh its contributions. He was overruled. A related source of tension was the postwar goals of the two countries, with U.S. leaders reluctant to undertake operations that they considered more beneficial to the retention of the British Empire than to immediate military objectives in the war. In spite of differences among its members, the CCS performed an essential function in the successful collaboration of the United States and the United Kingdom (qq.v.).

COMFORT WOMEN. Prostitutes supplied by Japan (q.v.) to its military forces during World War II. From 1932 to 1945, approximately 200,000 women and teenage girls worked in brothels operated by the Japanese military, which used the system to provide sex to its troops and to prevent the spread of venereal disease. Most of the comfort women, as they were called, were forced to work against their will, with many living in virtual slavery throughout the conflict. The largest number of women were Korean, with others drawn from areas also occupied by Japan: China, Formosa, the Netherlands East Indies, and the Philippines (qq.v.). Included were a group of Dutch colonists, on whose behalf the Dutch government prosecuted Japanese officers for war crimes (q.v.) after the war.

COMPUTERS. *See* SCIENCE AND TECHNOLOGY.

CONANT, JAMES B. *See* ATOMIC BOMB; MANHATTAN PROJECT; OFFICE OF SCIENTIFIC RESEARCH AND DEVELOPMENT.

CONFERENCES, ALLIED. *See* ATLANTIC CONFERENCE, AUGUST 9–12, 1941; BRETTON WOODS CONFERENCE, JULY 1–22, 1944; CAIRO CONFERENCE, FIRST (SEXTANT), NOVEMBER

23–27, 1943; CAIRO CONFERENCE, SECOND, DECEMBER 2–7, 1943; CASABLANCA CONFERENCE (SYMBOL), JANUARY 14–24, 1943; DUMBARTON OAKS CONFERENCE, AUGUST 21–OCTOBER 7, 1944; MALTA CONFERENCE, JANUARY 30–FEBRUARY 2, 1945; MOSCOW CONFERENCE (TOLSTOY), OCTOBER 9–20, 1944; MOSCOW FOREIGN MINISTERS CONFERENCE, OCTOBER 18–30, 1943; PEARL HARBOR CONFERENCE, JULY 26–29, 1944; POTSDAM CONFERENCE (TERMINAL), JULY 16–AUGUST 1, 1945; QUEBEC CONFERENCE, FIRST (QUADRANT), AUGUST 11–24, 1943; QUEBEC CONFERENCE, SECOND (OCTAGON), SEPTEMBER 12–16, 1944; RIO DE JANEIRO CONFERENCE, JANUARY 15–28, 1942; SAN FRANCISCO CONFERENCE, 1945; TEHERAN CONFERENCE (EUREKA), NOVEMBER 28–DECEMBER 1, 1943; WASHINGTON CONFERENCE, FIRST (ARCADIA), DECEMBER 22, 1941–JANUARY 14, 1942; WASHINGTON CONFERENCE, SECOND, JUNE 19–25, 1942; WASHINGTON CONFERENCE, THIRD (TRIDENT), MAY 12–25, 1943; YALTA CONFERENCE (ARGONAUT), FEBRUARY 4–11, 1945.

CORAL SEA, BATTLE OF THE. Naval battle of May 4–8, 1942, in which Allied forces halted a Japanese offensive to take Port Moresby (q.v.) in Papua, New Guinea (qq.v.). In April, Japanese officials decided to expand their defensive perimeter by moving into the southern Solomon Islands (q.v.) and capturing Port Moresby in Papua. With the conquest of these areas, Japan could pose a threat to Australia (qq.v.) and interfere with supply lines between Australia and the United States. (q.v.). Alerted by intelligence about the Japanese plans, Admiral Chester W. Nimitz (q.v.) sent a task force under Rear Admiral Frank Jack Fletcher (q.v.) to the area. The smaller Japanese naval force landed troops on Tulagi in the Solomons on May 3 and then joined the larger Japanese invasion armada heading for Port Moresby. The Allied and Japanese forces engaged in a fierce fight on May 7–8, the first major battle in which carriers (q.v.) conducted the action without the surface ships sighting each other. Both sides lost ships and planes, making the battle a tactical draw. Strategically, it was an Allied victory, because the Japanese force returned to its base on Rabaul (q.v.) without accomplishing its mission, marking the first time in the war that a Japanese advance had been halted.

CORONET. *See* JAPAN, INVASION OF.

CORREGIDOR. *See* PHILIPPINE ISLANDS CAMPAIGN (1941–1942); PHILIPPINE ISLANDS CAMPAIGN (1944–1945).

CRIPPS, RICHARD STAFFORD (1889–1952). British politician; ambassador to the Union of Soviet Socialist Republics (q.v.), 1940–1942; member, war cabinet, and head, Cripps mission to India (q.v.), 1942; minister of aircraft production, 1942–1945. After the United Kingdom (q.v.) went to war with Japan (q.v.) in late 1941, the British government tried to obtain support of the war effort from the Indian nationalists by sending Cripps to India. From March 22 to April 12, 1942, Cripps negotiated with Indian leaders, promising postwar self-rule for India in exchange for cooperation during the war. Mohandas K. Gandhi and Jawaharlal Nehru (qq.v.) rejected the Cripps proposal, and Gandhi began his "Quit India" campaign, arguing that if the British withdrew from India, the Japanese would have less reason to invade it. Cripps served as minister of aircraft production for the rest of the war, after a brief period as a member of the war cabinet. In 1946, Prime Minister Clement R. Attlee (q.v.) appointed him to a three-man mission to plan the transition to self-rule for India.

CRUISER. Warship generally smaller, faster, and more lightly armored than a battleship (q.v.) but equipped with heavy guns. The two classes, as described in a naval treaty of 1930, were heavy cruisers, with gun sizes ranging from 6.1 to 8 inches, and light cruisers, with guns up to 6.1 inches; these categories had wide variations. Cruisers patrolled shipping routes, used their heavy guns to assist amphibious assaults (q.v.), and protected fleets with antiaircraft weapons (q.v.). Both carrier (q.v.) and amphibious task forces included cruisers.

Japan's *Nachi* class of heavy cruisers displaced 10,000 tons and carried 10 8-inch guns. Its *Sendai* class of light cruisers displaced 5,600 tons and had 7 5.5-inch guns. Japan (q.v.) armed both its heavy and light cruisers with torpedo tubes, its excellent Long Lance torpedoes (q.v.), and heavy armament. Its sailors were well trained in night fighting and the use of torpedoes, which they employed to great effect in the campaigns for the Netherlands East Indies and the Solomon Islands (qq.v.).

The United States (q.v.) equipped its *New Orleans* class of heavy cruisers, which displaced 9,950 tons, with nine 8-inch guns. Its *St. Louis* class of light cruisers displaced 10,000 tons and carried eight 5-inch guns. Hampering the performance of U.S. cruisers during the first part of the war were the inexperience of its crews in night tactics, defective torpedoes, and the lack of torpedo tubes on its heavy cruisers. The use of radar and signal intelligence (qq.v.) gradually helped American cruisers to overcome the early Japanese advantages. In one of the worst cruiser disasters, nearly 800 men died when a Japanese submarine sank the U.S. heavy cruiser *Indianapolis* (q.v.) during the last weeks of the war.

CUNNINGHAM, ANDREW BROWNE (1883–1963). British Admiral of the Fleet; first sea lord, 1943–1946. Prior to becoming first sea lord (the military head of the Royal Navy), Cunningham earned distinction in the war against Germany and Italy (qq.v.), serving as naval commander for the invasions of North Africa, Sicily, and Salerno. In October 1943, Cunningham succeeded Admiral of the Fleet Dudley Pound (q.v.) as first sea lord, member of the British Chiefs of Staff Committee (q.v.), and member of the Combined Chiefs of Staff (q.v.). In addition to overseeing the naval aspects of the invasion of France (q.v.) in June 1944, Cunningham was deeply involved in the building of the British Pacific Fleet (q.v.) during the latter part of the war. Both Prime Minister Winston S. Churchill (q.v.) and Cunningham wanted the British naval force to play an important role in the war against Japan (q.v.), leading to protests from U.S. Admiral Ernest J. King (q.v.). Cunningham retired the year after the war ended.

CURTIN, JOHN (1885–1945). Prime minister of Australia (q.v.), 1941–1945. As head of the Labor Party, Curtin became prime minister when Australia was already at war with Germany and Italy (qq.v.). After Japan launched its wide-ranging attacks of December 7–8, 1941, Curtin immediately demanded that the Australian soldiers be returned from the Middle East to defend their homeland. British reluctance and slowness in releasing them made many Australians furious, and Curtin announced that Australia would depend on the United States (q.v.) for its defense. He worked closely with General Douglas MacArthur (q.v.), commander of the Southwest Pacific Area (q.v.), the Allied theater that included Australia, to obtain more resources for the region. Partly at his insistence that Australia be given a voice in the fight against Japan, both the United States and the United Kingdom (q.v.) formed Pacific War councils (q.v.). He died shortly before the war ended and was succeeded by Joseph Benedict Chifley (q.v.).

-D-

DE GAULLE, CHARLES. *See* FRANCE.

DEPTH CHARGE. *See* SUBMARINE.

DEREVYANKO, KUZMA N. *See* JAPANESE OCCUPATION; UNION OF SOVIET SOCIALIST REPUBLICS.

DESTROYER. Naval vessel (q.v.) valued for its speed and capabilities for maneuverability and quick attack; used primarily to protect fleets and convoys from enemy air and submarine (q.v.) strikes and to assault enemy ships. Destroyers formed an integral part of amphibious and carrier (qq.v.) task forces. In December 1941, Japanese destroyers were superior to Allied vessels in design, accuracy and range of torpedoes (q.v.), and skill of crews, who had trained extensively at night and during poor weather. Although the guns of American destroyers were effective, the range and reliability of their torpedoes were poor at first. Additionally, their crews lacked experience in the night tactics employed successfully by the Japanese. In later stages of the war, radar (q.v.), signal intelligence (q.v.), and improved torpedoes shifted the advantage to the Allies. The Japanese *Kagero*-class destroyer displaced 2,000 tons, traveled at 35 knots, and was equipped with 6.5-inch guns and eight torpedo tubes. The U.S. *Fletcher* class, introduced during the war in great numbers, had a displacement of 2,100 tons, speed of 35 knots, 5.5-inch guns, and 10 torpedo tubes. Both countries also built smaller versions called destroyer escorts, used mostly for convoy duty.

In early 1942, Japanese destroyers were instrumental in the Allied defeat in the Netherlands East Indies (q.v.). They also inflicted enormous damage during the campaigns in Guadalcanal and other islands in the Solomons (qq.v.), excelling particularly in night actions. Both sides converted some of their destroyers to transports, which, in the case of Japan, constituted a major part of the "Tokyo Express" supply route between Rabaul (q.v.) and the Solomons. Participating in other naval actions of the war, Allied destroyers sustained their heaviest damage in the campaign for Okinawa (q.v.), where they formed a radar picket line to draw Japanese kamikaze (q.v.) attacks.

DEWITT, JOHN L. *See* JAPANESE AMERICANS.

DIEGO SUAREZ. *See* MADAGASCAR.

DILL, JOHN GREER (1881–1944). British field marshal; chief of the Imperial General Staff (CIGS), 1940–1941; head, British Joint Staff Mission (q.v.), 1941–1944. Immediately after Japan launched its attacks in December 1941, British Prime Minister Winston S. Churchill (q.v.) traveled to Washington, D.C., to meet with U.S. President Franklin D. Roosevelt (q.v.). Among Churchill's military advisers was Dill, who had just resigned as CIGS. One of the decisions reached at the First Washington Conference (q.v.) was the formation of the Combined Chiefs of Staff (CCS) (q.v.), which was charged with the strategic direction of the war. To meet regularly with the American members of the CCS, the British left in Washington the British Joint Staff Mission, a high-level delegation under Dill's direction.

As head of the British Joint Staff Mission, Dill represented the views of the British Chiefs (q.v.) to the United States Joint Chiefs of Staff (q.v.), while working to achieve consensus and maintain a strong Anglo-American coalition. He served as a member of the Combined Policy Committee to direct Anglo-American-Canadian collaboration on the development of the atomic bomb (q.v.). Dill's close personal friendship with General George C. Marshall (q.v.) added immeasurably to the functioning of the alliance. When Dill died in the fall of 1944, Marshall arranged for him to be buried in Arlington National Cemetery in Virginia.

DIXIE MISSION. U.S. government delegation to the Chinese Communist headquarters in Yenan, China (q.v.), from July 1944 to March 1947. Formally known as the United States Army Observer Group, the Dixie Mission included military officials, diplomats, and members of the Office of Strategic Services (OSS) (q.v.). Colonel David D. Barrett, previously a military attaché in China, served as the first head of the group, which reached its maximum size of 45 in August 1945. Conceived as an American liaison with the Chinese Communists, the Dixie Mission initially met with Mao Tse-tung, Chou En-lai, and Chu Teh (qq.v.) to discuss United States–Chinese cooperation in the war with Japan (q.v.). The poor record of the Chinese Nationalist military against Japanese forces had encouraged American representatives to regard the Communists as a potential military ally, especially in northern China. Also discussed were the possibilities of U.S. lend-lease (q.v.) aid and a military coalition between the Communists and Nationalists. In the early stages, the Communist leaders tended to credit the mission's members, who were relatively low ranking, with more influence than they actually held.

Chiang Kai-shek (q.v.) viewed the Dixie Mission as a threat to his support from the U.S. government and refused to allow its members to travel to Yenan until President Franklin D. Roosevelt (q.v.) pressured him. Also opposing the mission were the U.S. Naval Group, China and the Sino-American Cooperative Organization (q.v.). Within a few months of the delegation's first meetings in July 1944, Chiang forced the recall of General Joseph W. Stilwell (q.v.), whose headquarters had favored the contacts with the Chinese Communists. Major General Albert C. Wedemeyer, Stilwell's successor, and Brigadier General Patrick J. Hurley (qq.v.), presidential envoy and ambassador, strongly backed Chiang and shifted the Dixie Mission's emphasis from cooperation to the collection of intelligence. Later renamed the Yenan Liaison Group, the mission ended in March 1947.

Although the efforts of the Dixie Mission did not result in a coordinated military effort against the Japanese, the Chinese Communists did assist the American air campaign by helping airmen downed in Japanese-held areas, providing information about potential targets for air strikes, and relaying weather reports. They also shared intelligence (q.v.) about the Japanese army and prisoners of war (q.v.).

DONOVAN, WILLIAM JOSEPH (1883–1959). U.S. attorney and United States Army general; director, Office of Coordinator of Information, 1941–1942; director, Office of Strategic Services (q.v.), 1942–1945. Donovan, a highly decorated World War I veteran and prominent attorney, was appointed by his old friend President Franklin D. Roosevelt (q.v.) to head the new Office of Coordinator of Information in 1941 and its successor, the Office of Strategic Services (OSS) the following year. Nicknamed "Wild Bill," Donovan became a brigadier general in 1943 and was promoted to major general the following year. As the director of the OSS, he reported to the United States Joint Chiefs of Staff (q.v.). In addition to gathering intelligence information, the OSS worked with resistance groups and carried out various covert operations. In the war against Japan (q.v.), most of its activities were in the China-Burma-India (q.v.) theater.

DOOLITTLE, JAMES HAROLD (1896–1993). United States Army and Air Force general. An early army aviation pioneer, Doolittle left the service during the 1930s to work in private industry and returned to active duty in 1940. In April 1942, he led the Doolittle Raid (q.v.), a dangerous mission to bomb the Japanese capital of Tokyo (q.v.), for which he received the Congressional Medal of Honor. Beginning in mid-1942, Doolittle held major positions in the war against Germany and Italy (qq.v.). When the war in Europe concluded in May 1945, Doolittle and his Eighth Air Force were scheduled for transfer from the United Kingdom (q.v.) to the Mariana Islands (q.v.) in the Pacific to join the strategic air campaign (q.v.) against Japan. The war ended, however, before the Eighth could began its operations in the Pacific, although Doolittle had already arrived on Okinawa (q.v.). Doolittle returned to industry in 1946 while remaining an adviser on various air force projects.

DOOLITTLE RAID. U.S. bombing raid on Tokyo, Japan (qq.v.), April 18, 1942. Soon after the devastating attack on Pearl Harbor (q.v.) and the widespread Japanese successes throughout the Pacific and Asia, American military leaders began to plan a dramatic raid on Japan in lieu of a major offensive the United States (q.v.) could not yet mount. They chose James H. Doolittle (q.v.), an aviation pioneer and lieutenant colonel, to head it. For the mission, the military modified B-25 medium bombers (q.v.), which normally used land bases, to fly from an aircraft carrier (q.v.). On April 18, 1942, 16 B-25s took off from the *Hornet* to bomb Tokyo, continuing on to the Asian continent where 15 crash-landed in China (q.v.) and one in the Union of Soviet Socialist Republics (q.v.). Physical damage to Japan was relatively minor, but the psychological impact on Japanese military leaders was enormous, influencing them to attempt to expand their Pacific defense perimeter for better protection. Not realizing that the attack came from a carrier, they suspected the use of airfields in the Aleutian Islands or in China (qq.v.), where they killed a number of Chinese in retaliation. For the United States, the raid boosted morale and made heroes of Doolittle and his airmen. Most of the group survived, but several were caught by the Japanese and executed. The fliers who landed in the U.S.S.R. were interned and later returned to the United States.

DRINIUMOR RIVER CAMPAIGN. Costly engagements near Aitape in Northeast New Guinea (q.v.), July 10–August 25, 1944. After capturing Aitape on April 22, 1944, Allied forces of the Southwest Pacific Area (SWPA) (q.v.) moved in additional forces and carefully prepared defenses around the airfields and along the Driniumor River 15 miles to the east, where signal intelligence (q.v.) indicated the Japanese

Eighteenth Army under Lieutenant General Hatazo Adachi (q.v.) planned to attack. Defending the area was the XI Corps under Major General Charles P. Hall. A massive night charge by the Japanese began the action, which lasted for six weeks in the jungles and marshes along the river. Both sides suffered heavy casualties, but the Japanese losses were especially severe, costing 10,000 dead. Adachi's ability to threaten the Aitape area ended, as his army was trapped between American and Australian forces.

DUMBARTON OAKS CONFERENCE, August 21–October 7, 1944. Meeting concerning the formation of the United Nations organization (q.v.), held in Washington, D.C. Delegations from China, the Union of Soviet Socialist Republics, the United Kingdom, and the United States (qq.v.) met to discuss the formation of an international organization to guarantee postwar peace. Their proposals were used at the San Francisco Conference (q.v.) in 1945 to develop the charter of the United Nations. Issues left unresolved at Dumbarton Oaks concerned the number of seats allotted to the U.S.S.R. and the scope of the veto that could be exercised by permanent members of the Security Council.

DUTCH EAST INDIES. See NETHERLANDS EAST INDIES.

DUTCH HARBOR. See ALEUTIAN ISLANDS.

-E-

EAST INDIES. See BORNEO; JAVA; NETHERLANDS EAST INDIES; SUMATRA; TIMOR.

EASTERN SOLOMONS, BATTLE OF. See GUADALCANAL CAMPAIGN: NAVAL BATTLES.

EDEN, ANTHONY (1897–1977). British foreign minister, 1935–1938, 1940–1945, 1951–1955; secretary of state for war, 1940; prime minister, 1955–1957. As foreign minister in Prime Minister Winston S. Churchill's (q.v.) wartime government, Eden participated in most of the major international conferences and attended several meetings in the Union of Soviet Socialist Republics (q.v.), including the Moscow Foreign Ministers Conference (q.v.). A strong advocate of the formation of the United Nations organization (q.v.), Eden also supported the claims of Free French leader Charles de Gaulle as the representative of France (q.v.) and backed his efforts to reclaim French Indochina (q.v.).

EICHELBERGER, ROBERT LAWRENCE (1886–1961). United States Army general; commander, I Corps, 1942–1944; commander, Eighth Army, 1944–1948. From the summer of 1942 until the Japanese surrender (q.v.), Eichelberger conducted operations in the Southwest Pacific Area (q.v.). In one of his earliest assignments, he took command of American troops stalled in the jungles of New Guinea (q.v.), reorganized his forces, and led them in the capture of Buna in January 1943. Also in the campaign for New Guinea, Eichelberger directed successful offensives at Hollandia and on the island of Biak. His newly created Eighth Army played an instrumental role in the liberation of the Philippines (q.v.), mainly in operations south of Luzon (q.v.), and was scheduled to invade Japan (q.v.), had it not surrendered. Until 1948, Eichelberger continued to command the Eighth Army, which served as the principal force in the Japanese occupation (q.v.).

EMPRESS AUGUSTA BAY. *See* CARTWHEEL, OPERATION.

ENIWETOK. *See* MARSHALL ISLANDS.

EUROPE FIRST POLICY. *See* ABC-1; PLAN DOG MEMORANDUM; WASHINGTON CONFERENCE, FIRST.

EVATT, HERBERT VERE (1894–1965). Australian attorney general and minister for external affairs, 1941–1945. As minister for external affairs, Evatt represented Australia effectively in meetings of the Allies (such as the Pacific War councils [q.v.]) and expanded his country's formal relationships with other nations. He attended the San Francisco Conference (q.v.) in 1945 and helped to found the United Nations organization (q.v.), which he served as president of the General Assembly in 1948–1949.

-**F**-

FAST CARRIER FORCE. Task force of aircraft carriers, battleships, cruisers, and destroyers (qq.v.), which operated as part of the U.S. Pacific

Fleet. In January 1944, Rear Admiral Marc A. Mitscher (q.v.) took command of the Fast Carrier Force, which became Task Force 58 (TF 58) under Admiral Raymond A. Spruance's (q.v.) Fifth Fleet and Task Force 38 (TF 38) when part of Admiral William F. Halsey's (q.v.) Third Fleet. Although it belonged to the Pacific Ocean Areas (q.v.) theater, where it participated in all major Central Pacific (q.v.) operations, the Fast Carrier Force also assisted in Southwest Pacific Area (q.v.) theater operations at Hollandia (New Guinea), Morotai, Leyte, and Luzon (qq.v.). From late October 1944 to January 1945, Vice Admiral John S. McCain (q.v.) headed the Fast Carrier Force as TF 38. Mitscher resumed command of TF 58 from January to May 1945, when McCain again took over TF 38 until the end of the war. *See also* United States Navy.

FIGHTER AND FIGHTER-BOMBER. Aircraft employed to attack enemy planes, to escort bombers (q.v.), and to strike targets on the ground or sea. By the time of the Pearl Harbor attack (q.v.), Japan's fighters were superior to comparable Allied planes, while its pilots were experienced in combat and well trained in night tactics.

During much of the Sino-Japanese War and at Nomonhan (q.v.) in 1939, the Japanese navy relied heavily on the Mitsubishi A5M Claude fighter. The single-engined Claude had a top speed of 273 miles per hour. Armed with two machine guns, it carried 130 pounds of bombs (q.v.). The Claude performed well against Soviet planes at Nomonhan and against a variety of aircraft used by the Chinese. During the same period, the main fighter of the Japanese army was the Nakajima Ki-27 Nate. A highly maneuverable and lightly armored plane, the Nate had a maximum speed of 286 miles per hour. It carried two machine guns and 220 pounds of bombs. Like the Claude, the Nate excelled at Nomonhan and in China (q.v.).

In 1940, the Japanese navy introduced the most famous Japanese fighter of the war, the Mitsubishi A6M Zero-sen Zeke, commonly called the Zero. From 1940 until 1943, the Zero's maneuverability, speed, ability to climb quickly, and range made it superior to Allied planes. The single-engined Zero traveled at speeds up to 344 miles per hour. It carried two machine guns, two cannon, and bombs weighing 130 pounds. The Japanese first used the Zero in 1940 as an escort for dive bombers and torpedo bombers (qq.v.) in raids on Chungking, China (qq.v.), where it defeated the defending planes. It participated in the strikes against Pearl Harbor and other Allied forces in December 1941. In the first years of the Pacific War, the Zero outperformed all

Allied fighters, both land and carrier based. While the Allies (q.v.) began to produce planes more competitive with the Zero, Japanese alterations did not markedly improve its performance, which was eventually surpassed. In the last year of the war, the Zero became one of the first aircraft to be converted to kamikaze (q.v.) use. The Zero was the most numerous of Japanese warplanes.

The Japanese army's smaller and lighter counterpart to the Zero was the Nakajima Ki-43 Hayabusa Oscar, which entered combat in 1942. The Oscar achieved a top speed of 363 miles per hour and carried two guns or cannon and a bomb load of 1,100 pounds. Like its predecessor Nate, the Oscar was extremely maneuverable but constructed and armored so lightly that it was very vulnerable to enemy fire. In numbers of planes produced by Japan, the Oscar was second to the Zero.

In December 1941, the main U.S.-produced fighters in the Pacific were the single-engined Brewster F2A Buffalo, Grumman F4F Wildcat, Curtiss P-40 Warhawk, and Bell P-39 Airacobra. All were inferior to the Japanese Zero, which was eventually outperformed by the Lockheed P-38 Lightning, the Chance Vought F4U Corsair, the Grumman F6F Hellcat, the Republic P-47 Thunderbolt, the North American P-51 Mustang, and the Northrop P-61 Black Widow. The Lightning, available to the United States Army Air Forces (AAF) (q.v.) in very small numbers when the United States entered the war, reached the Pacific in force in late 1942. It had two engines and a top speed of 414 miles per hour. Equipped with four machine guns and one cannon, it carried 3,200 pounds of bombs. Although the Zero was more maneuverable, the Lightning was faster and better armed. The Corsair, first used by the Marines in the Pacific in early 1943, was a single-engined plane with a top speed of 462 miles per hour. It carried six machine guns and a bomb load of 2,000 pounds.

The Hellcat, one of the navy's main fighters beginning in 1943, had one engine and a top speed of 376 miles per hour. Armed with six machine guns, it carried six rockets (q.v.) and a 2,000-pound bomb load. It could fly and climb faster than the Zero. The single-engined Thunderbolt, which entered service with the AAF in 1943, could fly at 460 miles per hour. In addition to six machine guns, it carried six rockets and 2,000 pounds of bombs.

Beginning in the spring of 1945, the long-range version of the North American P-51 Mustang was stationed on Iwo Jima (q.v.) to escort Boeing B-29 Superfortress (q.v.) bombers on raids to Japan. Previously used heavily in Europe, the single-engined Mustang could reach

487 miles per hour. Its arms included six machine guns and 2,000 pounds of bombs or rockets.

The Black Widow, a twin-engined night fighter designed specifically for that purpose, carried extensive radar (q.v.) equipment. Larger than the Lightning, its top speed was 360 miles per hour. Its usual armament was four machine guns, four cannon, and 3,200 pounds of bombs. The Black Widow operated in the Pacific during the last year of the war.

At the start of the war with Japan, the British Hawker Hurricane was outfought by the Zero below 10,000 feet but was superior at altitudes above 20,000 feet. The single-engined Hurricane could fly at 342 miles per hour. Equipped with 12 machine guns or four cannon, it carried 1,000 pounds of bombs or rockets. The Hurricane remained in service throughout the war.

In late 1943, the British allocated significant numbers of the Supermarine Spitfire to the Southeast Asia Command (q.v.), where it was effective in countering Japanese bombing raids and reconnaissance flights over India (q.v.). One heavily produced model of the single-engined Spitfire had a top speed of 408 miles per hour and carried two cannon, two machine guns, and a bomb load of 1,000 pounds.

Another fighter important in Asia and the Pacific was the Bristol Beaufighter, a twin-engined plane designed for night action and equipped with radar. The Beaufighter could achieve a speed of 330 miles per hour. In addition to four machine guns, it carried one torpedo, a bomb load of 2,500 pounds, or a combination of bombs and rockets.

During the war, Australia produced the single-engined Commonwealth Boomerang, which flew extensively in the Southwest Pacific (q.v.) beginning in August 1942. The Boomerang could reach 296 miles per hour and was armed with four machine guns and two cannon.

At Nomonhan, the Union of Soviet Socialist Republics (q.v.) used the single-engined Polikarpov I-15, I-153, and I-16 fighters. The highly maneuverable I-15 had a top speed of 230 miles per hour. Armed with four machine guns, it carried 220 pounds of bombs or six rockets. The I-153, another version of the I-15, was slightly faster and had retractable landing gear. The I-16 could reach 326 miles per hour, was equipped with two machine guns and two cannon, and carried 220 pounds of bombs or rockets.

Among the fighters employed by the Soviets in their conquest of Manchuria (q.v.) in August 1945 was the Yakovlev Yak-9. It had one engine and a top speed of 435 miles per hour. Armed with two machine guns and one cannon, the Yak-9 had a bomb load of 440 pounds.

FLETCHER, FRANK JACK (1885–1973). U.S. admiral; carrier task force commander in the Pacific, 1942; commander, Northwestern Sea Frontier and 13th Naval District, 1942–1943; commander, North Pacific Area, 1943–1945. At the time the United States (q.v.) entered the war, Fletcher headed a cruiser division in the Pacific Fleet; he subsequently took part in the important Pacific naval operations during the first year of the war. His expedition to relieve the forces on Wake Island (q.v.) was canceled after the island's capture by Japan (q.v.). Early in 1942, his carrier task forces raided Japanese bases and ships in the Gilbert and Marshall Islands and on New Guinea (qq.v.). Fletcher headed U.S. naval forces in the major Battles of the Coral Sea and Midway (qq.v.), turning over command to Rear Admiral Raymond A. Spruance (q.v.) during the latter operation when his flagship *Yorktown* was hit. During the Guadalcanal invasion (q.v.) in August 1942, Fletcher commanded the carrier task forces during the landings and early naval battles. He was wounded on August 31 and returned to the United States.

After Fletcher recovered from his wounds, he headed the Northwestern Sea Frontier and 13th Naval District through late 1943. He then commanded the North Pacific Area (q.v.) until the end of the war, when he directed the occupation of northern Japan. After the war, he chaired the navy's General Board.

FLYING BOAT. Used for patrols, antisubmarine warfare, bombing, reconnaissance, rescues, and evacuation of casualties. A widely used Japanese flying boat was the four-engined Kawanishi H8K Emily, which carried 4,400 pounds of bombs (q.v.) or two torpedoes (q.v.). The Emily operated with a 10-man crew and could achieve a speed of 270 miles per hour.

The best-known U.S. flying boat was the Consolidated Vultee PBY Catalina. A twin-engined plane with a crew of nine, it had a top speed of 177 miles per hour. Its maximum bomb load was 2,000 pounds. Also widely used was the twin-engined Martin PBM Mariner, which could carry twice the bomb load of the Catalina. It had a nine-man crew and a maximum speed of 205 miles per hour. Used extensively in Southeast Asia and the Indian Ocean (q.v.) was the British-produced Short Sunderland, a four-engined craft capable of flying 212 miles per hour. It had a 10-man crew and a bomb capacity of 1,900 pounds.

FLYING TIGERS. *See* AMERICAN VOLUNTEER GROUP.

FORMOSA. Island off the southeastern coast of China (q.v.), also known as Taiwan. In 1895, China (q.v.) ceded Formosa to Japan (q.v.), which heavily fortified it. During the war, Japan used it as a base of operations, sending bombing raids to China and attacking the Philippines (q.v.) on December 8, 1941, with planes from Formosan airfields. In addition to the value of its bases, the island's strategic location protected the shipment of men and raw materials (q.v.) between Japan and Southeast Asia. In the Luzon versus Formosa debate (q.v.) among U.S. military leaders in 1944, Admiral Ernest J. King (q.v.) argued that Formosa should be captured as part of the drive across the Central Pacific (q.v.). After the decision was made to assault Luzon (q.v.) in the Philippines (q.v.) instead, the Allies (q.v.) did not invade Formosa during the war, although they bombed it heavily during 1944 and 1945.

After the Japanese surrender (q.v.), Nationalist China took possession of Formosa in accordance with the Cairo Declaration (q.v.) made during the war. When Chiang Kai-shek's (q.v.) army was defeated and ousted from the mainland by Mao Tse-tung's (q.v.) Chinese Communist troops in 1949, the Nationalist army remnants and Chiang's government moved to Formosa and established the Republic of China.

FORRESTAL, JAMES V. *See* UNITED STATES; UNITED STATES NAVY.

FRANCE. Allied country invaded by Germany (q.v.) in May 1940. After the French surrender the following month, Germany stationed its troops in the northern and central parts of the country and permitted the puppet Vichy France (q.v.) government to administer the unoccupied part of France and the colonies. French Indochina (q.v.) remained under the control of the Vichy French, as did Madagascar (q.v.) until captured in 1942 by the British. In 1940, New Caledonia (q.v.), Tahiti, and other French islands in the southern Pacific declared their allegiance to the Free French, the movement to liberate France from German and Vichy control. Beginning in 1940, British Prime Minister Winston S. Churchill and Foreign Minister Anthony Eden (qq.v.) favored Charles de Gaulle's claims to represent the Free French, although U.S. President Franklin D. Roosevelt (q.v.) withheld his support for much of the war. The Allies (q.v.) mounted a major amphibious assault (q.v.) across the English Channel to France on June 6, 1944, and began to retake control of the country from German forces. De Gaulle announced the formation of a new French government in September 1944, after the liberation of Paris.

Long before the Free French returned to France, their leaders were eager to participate in the war against Japan (q.v.) and to reestablish control over the French colonies. In the fall of 1943, the Free French National Defense Committee developed plans to send an expeditionary corps to the Far East the following year and expressed interest in joining the Pacific War councils (q.v.). Dependent on Allied aid to rearm, build, and transport their military forces, the French received encouragement and limited aid for their Far East plans from the British, who basically supported the restoration of the French empire. In contrast, the Roosevelt administration, which publicly opposed colonialism, deferred the repeated French requests to participate in Asia and the Pacific, using the reason that such actions would hinder the war in Europe. In May 1945, the French offered four air squadrons and two divisions of ground troops for use against Japan. On July 19, the Combined Chiefs of Staff (q.v.) rejected the air forces and accepted the ground divisions, with the provisions that they would operate under strict British or American control and could not be used until July 1946, when sufficient shipping would be available.

Although the French military was unable to play a significant role in the war against Japan, a French battleship (q.v.) joined the British naval forces in the Far East in April 1944 and took part in operations in the Indian (q.v.) and Pacific Oceans. Additionally, French agents operated in occupied Indochina, supported by the British. French representatives participated in the formal Japanese surrender (q.v.) ceremonies in Tokyo Bay on September 2, 1945. *See also* Atomic Bomb.

FRANCE, VICHY. Collaborationist French regime formed after the surrender of much of France to Germany (qq.v.) in June 1940. Headed by Marshal Philippe Pétain, it was allowed by the Germans to govern the French colonies and the part of France not under German military occupation. In Asia, Japan (q.v.) pressured the weak Vichy government to grant it special rights in French Indochina (q.v.), moving Japanese troops into the northern part of the country in 1940 and into the south the following year. The French colony of Madagascar (q.v.) off the east coast of Africa was seized in 1942 by British forces, who feared the Vichy French would permit Japan to use the island as a base for controlling the Indian Ocean (q.v.) and threatening India (q.v.). The Vichy government's limited powers were drastically curtailed in November 1942 when the German army occupied the entire country in response to the Allied invasion of French colonies in Northwest Africa.

In September 1944, Charles de Gaulle announced that his Free French government had assumed power in France.

FRASER, BRUCE AUSTIN (1888–1981). British admiral; commander, British Eastern Fleet, 1944; commander, British Pacific Fleet (q.v.), 1944–1945. During the first part of the war, Fraser worked with and eventually headed the Home Fleet, which defended the waters around the United Kingdom (q.v.). In August 1944, he assumed command of the British Eastern Fleet in the Indian Ocean (q.v.) and, in November 1944, of the newly created British Pacific Fleet. In 1945 Fraser's force joined the U.S. Pacific Fleet in the campaign for Okinawa (q.v.) and carried out attacks on Formosa and Japan (qq.v.). On September 2, 1945, he represented the United Kingdom in the Japanese surrender (q.v.) ceremony in Tokyo Bay. After the war, Fraser served as first sea lord, 1948–1951.

FRASER, PETER (1884–1950). New Zealand (q.v.) prime minister, 1940–1949. As a member of the British Commonwealth, New Zealand was already at war with Germany (q.v.) when Fraser took office. After Japan (q.v.) began its massive Pacific attacks in early December 1941, New Zealand declared war and participated in the Allied effort to defeat Japan, contributing armed forces, food, and war matériel. In 1945, Fraser participated in the San Francisco Conference (q.v.) to form the United Nations organization (q.v.).

FRENCH INDOCHINA. French protectorate in Southeast Asia, composed of Cambodia, Laos, Annam, Cochin China, and Tonkin. After the German conquest of France (q.v.) in June 1940 and the establishment of the pro-German Vichy France (q.v.) government, Japan (q.v.) successfully pressured the new regime to grant it special privileges in Indochina. In 1940, Japanese troops established bases in northern Indochina, allowing them access to new routes for attacking and further isolating China (q.v.). Early the next year, Thailand (q.v.) invaded Indochina to seize border areas; when the military action proved inconclusive, Japan agreed to mediate and awarded the disputed territories to the Thais, whose leaders were sympathetic to Japan. In the summer of 1941, Japan moved forces into southern Indochina, which positioned them for strikes against other parts of Southeast Asia. As a result of the Japanese action in southern Indochina, U.S. President Franklin D. Roosevelt (q.v.) froze Japanese assets in the United States (q.v.) and escalated efforts to strengthen the defenses of the Philippines (q.v.). The British and the Dutch took similar actions regarding Japanese holdings.

When Japan launched its multiple military strikes in December 1941, it used Indochina as a staging base for attacks on the Malay peninsula (q.v.) and other areas. Japan dominated Indochina throughout the war, but it permitted Vichy French officials, led by Governor-General Jean Decoux, to administer local areas until March 9, 1945. Japan then ousted Decoux and his Vichy government, which it accused of working with the new, Allied government in France. Japan then promoted the ostensible independence of the parts of Indochina and imprisoned French civilians and military forces. On March 23, 1945, the French government announced its postwar plans for Indochina, which it proposed would receive more autonomy but remain under French control.

During the latter part of the war, the British, who supported the French intention to reclaim Indochina, parachuted French agents and supplies behind Japanese lines. Also fighting the Japanese, especially in northern Indochina, was the Viet Minh (q.v.) organization, a nationalist group under the direction of Ho Chi Minh (q.v.). The Viet Minh carried out guerrilla activities with the help of the U.S. Office of Strategic Services (q.v.) and declared the independence of Vietnam after Japan's capitulation.

At the Potsdam Conference (q.v.), the Combined Chiefs of Staff (q.v.) decided to assign Allied jurisdiction of Indochina south of the 16th parallel to the Southeast Asia Command (q.v.) instead of the China Theater (q.v.). The change took effect on September 2. One week later, Chinese forces accepted the surrender of Japanese troops north of the parallel, while British and Indian soldiers assumed control south of the parallel on September 13. By late 1945, the British had turned over the administration of the southern area to the French. The Chinese withdrew from the north in early 1946, after the French agreed to grant them more privileges in Indochina. The same year, the French and the Viet Minh reached a temporary accommodation, but by December, the two were engaged in war.

FRIEDMAN, WILLIAM F. *See* INTELLIGENCE, ALLIED SIGNAL.

-G-

GANDHI, MOHANDAS KARAMCHAND (1869–1948). Indian nationalist leader. During World War II, Gandhi continued the campaign for Indian independence that he had conducted for many years. In early 1942, British representative Richard Stafford Cripps (q.v.) offered to grant postwar self-rule to India (q.v.) in exchange for its cooperation until the defeat of the Axis powers (q.v.). Gandhi rejected any delay in autonomy and launched the "Quit India" movement, which demanded that the British leave India immediately so the Japanese would not attack it. He further advocated civil disobedience rather than armed resistance in the event that Japan (q.v.) did invade. The British authorities arrested Gandhi and other members of his Indian Congress Party in 1942, releasing Gandhi two years later because of his poor health.

GEIGER, ROY STANLEY (1885–1947). United States Marine general; commander, 1st Marine Air Wing, Fleet Marine Force, 1941–1943; director, Division of Marine Aviation, 1943; commander, I Marine Amphibious Corps, 1943–1944; commander, III Amphibious Corps, 1944–1945; commander, Tenth Army, 1945; commander, Fleet Marine Force, 1945–1946. Geiger, an airman and later a corps commander, took part in a number of major campaigns against the Japanese. From September 1942 to February 1943, he directed the Cactus Air Force, composed of 1st Marine Air Wing and other available planes, in support of the Guadalcanal ground and naval campaigns (q.v.), using Henderson Field (q.v.) as his base. After working with marine aviation in Washington, D.C., he returned to the Pacific in November 1943 to succeed Lieutenant General A. A. Vandegrift (q.v.) as head of the I Marine Amphibious Corps on Bougainville during Operation Cartwheel (q.v.). In 1944, his command was renamed the III Amphibious Corps, which assaulted Guam in the Marianas (qq.v.), Peleliu in the Palaus (q.v.), and Okinawa (q.v.). After Lieutenant General Simon B. Buckner (q.v.) was killed on Okinawa in June 1945, Geiger assumed command of the Tenth Army until a permanent replacement arrived, becoming the first marine general to command a field army. The next month he became head of Fleet Marine Force, Pacific.

GERMAN-SOVIET NONAGGRESSION PACT. Agreement signed on August 23, 1939, which preceded by one week the German invasion of Poland that marked the beginning of World War II in Europe. The accord between the two opposing nations shocked the world, including Germany's ally Japan (qq.v.), whose forces were fighting Soviet troops at Nomonhan (q.v.) at the time of the agreement. Negotiated by Foreign Ministers Vyacheslav M. Molotov (q.v.) of the Union of Soviet Socialist Republics (q.v.) and Joachim von Ribbentrop of Germany (q.v.), it was also known as the Molotov-Ribbentrop Pact. Its secret protocols concerning the control of Eastern Europe were not acknowledged by the U.S.S.R. for many years.

GERMANY. Axis power (q.v.) involved in World War II, September 1, 1939–May 8, 1945. Beginning in the mid-19th century, Germany had a strong influence in Japan (q.v.), particularly in the areas of industry, law, medicine, education, and the armed forces. The Japanese modeled their general staff partly on the German system. Under its leader Adolf Hitler (q.v.), Germany formed an alliance with Japan through the Anti-Comintern (1936) and the Tripartite (1940) Pacts (qq.v.), although the signing of the German-Soviet Nonaggression Pact (q.v.) in 1939 severely strained relations with Japan for a time. In accordance with the Tripartite Pact, Germany declared war on the United States (q.v.) on December 11, 1941, after the United States and Japan had gone to war, but otherwise the two countries did not collaborate strategically. Germany, for example, did not tell Japan of its intention to invade the Union of Soviet Socialist Republics (q.v.) in June 1941; Japan did not inform Germany about its planned attack on Pearl Harbor (q.v.). Japan, instead of joining its ally in declaring war on the U.S.S.R. in 1941, adhered to its neutrality agreement with the Soviets until August 1945, when the Soviets attacked Japanese forces.

The most tangible way in which Germany and Japan cooperated during the war was the *Yanagi* operations (q.v.), in which surface ships and submarines (q.v.) attempted to run the Allied blockades to trade crucial raw materials (q.v.) and technology. Many of the vessels, including German and Japanese submarines in the Atlantic and Indian Oceans (q.v.), were located and sunk by the Allies (q.v.) using signal intelligence (q.v.). Germany also assigned several U-boats to a Japanese base in the Indian Ocean, where they attacked Allied shipping.

Although Germany and Japan did not formally share high-level intelligence to the degree that the United States and the United Kingdom (q.v.) did, they did trade limited information about Allied merchant ships and the U.S.S.R. The presence of their diplomats in each other's capitals provided for some exchange of information. Japanese Ambassador Hiroshi Oshima (q.v.) was close to both Hitler and Foreign Minister Joachim von Ribbentrop. The detailed reports Oshima sent to Tokyo from Berlin inadvertently benefited the Allies, who could read the Japanese diplomatic codes.

Japan closed the German embassy in Tokyo in late May 1945, after Germany's surrender to the Allies. Japan resumed full diplomatic relations with the Federal Republic of Germany in 1955 and with the German Democratic Republic in 1973. *See also* Atomic Bomb; Intelligence, Japanese; Science and Technology.

GHORMLEY, ROBERT LEE (1883–1958). U.S. admiral; naval observer, United Kingdom (q.v.), 1940–1942; commander, South Pacific Area (SOPAC) (q.v.), 1942; commander, Hawaiian Sea Frontier and 14th Naval District, 1943–1944; commander, U.S. naval forces in Germany (q.v.), 1945. When the United States (q.v.) entered the war, Ghormley was serving as a naval observer in London, working closely with British officials. He remained in that post until his appointment in 1942 to head the South Pacific Area. Soon after assuming his command, Ghormley was ordered to launch a major U.S. offensive against Japan (q.v.) in the southern Solomon Islands (q.v.). Although Ghormley had little time to plan, the invasions of Guadalcanal (q.v.) and Tulagi took place on August 7, 1942. The ground campaign grew extremely bloody as both the United States and Japan sent massive reinforcements to the island, while costly naval battles occurred in the surrounding waters. On October 18, 1942, Pacific Ocean Areas (q.v.) theater commander Admiral Chester W. Nimitz (q.v.) replaced Ghormley with the more aggressive Vice Admiral William F. Halsey (q.v.). The Guadalcanal campaign continued until February 1943.

Ghormley then headed the Hawaiian Frontier and 14th Naval District until 1944, when he was transferred to Europe to work with Admiral Harold R. Stark (q.v.), commander of U.S. Naval Forces in Europe, and to supervise the demobilization of German naval forces at the end of the war. He retired in 1946.

GIAP. *See* VO NGUYEN GIAP.

GILBERT ISLANDS. Island group in the west central Pacific Ocean seized by U.S. forces in 1943 as part of the Central Pacific (q.v.) drive toward Japan (q.v.). Owned by the British before the war, the Gilbert Islands were occupied in December 1941 by the Japanese, who were attacked in August 1942 by Carlson's Raiders (q.v.), a small American marine force. After the raiders' withdrawal, the Japanese increased their defenses on the islands. U.S. Admiral Chester W. Nimitz (q.v.), commander of the Pacific Ocean Areas (q.v.) theater, and some of his planners considered the capture of the Gilberts to be a vital part of their island-hopping drive from Hawaii to Japan. They needed airfields in the Gilbert Islands to provide land-based air support for their next, more important target, the Marshall Islands (q.v.).

Nimitz appointed Vice Admiral Raymond A. Spruance (q.v.) to direct the operation. Under him were Rear Admiral Richmond Kelly Turner (q.v.), in command of the V Amphibious Force, and marine Major General Holland M. Smith (q.v.), head of the V Amphibious Corps. The same team would direct other operations in the Central Pacific Area (CENPAC).

On November 20, 1943, CENPAC forces assaulted the coral reefs of the atolls of Makin and Tarawa. The Japanese troops on Makin were small in number and inflicted relatively few casualties on the invading 27th Infantry Division. In the Tarawa atoll, however, where the 2d Marine Division went ashore on the island of Betio, the high casualties made it one of the costliest American battles in history in terms of the proportion of casualties to the troops involved. The capture of the atolls was completed on November 23. As was the case with many battles of the Pacific War, almost all of the Japanese soldiers died, many in suicidal banzai (q.v.) charges.

GLIDER. Employed against Japan (q.v.) mostly to transport troops and equipment. Two types of Allied gliders were the U.S. Waco CG-4A Haig (designated Hadrian by the British) and the British Horsa. Made of wood and steel, the CG-4A could carry 15 fully armed troops or 3,710 pounds of cargo. The glider's nose was hinged to facilitate unloading of equipment. The larger Horsa, constructed entirely of wood, held from 20 to 30 armed troops. The gliders were usually towed by transport planes (q.v.) such as the C-46 and the C-47.

GREATER EAST ASIA CO-PROSPERITY SPHERE. Japanese concept regarding its relationship with the Asian continent. Using the propaganda slogan "East Asia for Asiatics," Japan urged the nations to unite in one economic sphere, ousting the colonial powers so that Asians would enjoy prosperity together. In reality Japan used the idea to justify its seizure of raw materials (q.v.) from Southeast Asia to further its own economic, political, and military domination of East Asia.

Japan intended the Co-prosperity Sphere to include Japan, China (q.v.), Manchukuo (q.v.), and Southeast Asia, as well as the Pacific mandates (q.v.) islands. During the war, Japan held only one meeting of the Sphere, sponsoring the Greater East Asia Conference in Tokyo in November 1943. Attending were Wang Ching-wei (q.v.), head of the Reformed Government of the Republic of China; Chang Chung-hui of Manchukuo; Wan Waithayakon of Thailand (q.v.); Jose Paciano Laurel of the Philippines (qq.v.); and Ba Maw of Burma (qq.v.).

GREW, JOSEPH CLARK (1880–1965). U.S. diplomat; ambassador to Japan (q.v.), 1932–1941; undersecretary of state, 1945. A career diplomat, Grew served in Germany (q.v.), Denmark, Switzerland (q.v.), and Turkey before his assignment to Japan in 1932. In his early years in Japan, he advised conciliation and acceptance of Japanese expansion on the Asian mainland unless the United States was willing to go to war to stop it. He later recommended economic pressure on Japan to halt its aggression. In the summer of 1941, Grew unsuccessfully urged that President Franklin D. Roosevelt (q.v.) meet with Japanese Prime Minister Fumimaro Konoye (q.v.). After the Pearl Harbor attack (q.v.), Grew was interned in Japan until his exchange in August 1942. During the rest of the war, he served in the State Department, rising to undersecretary of state. He consistently counseled that Emperor Hirohito (q.v.) be retained on the throne as part of any settlement of the war.

GROVES, LESLIE RICHARD (1896–1970). United States Army general; commander, Manhattan Project (q.v.), 1942–1946. A member of the United States Army Corps of Engineers, Groves oversaw the construction of the Pentagon, the massive building to accommodate the U.S. defense headquarters. In September 1942, he received the assignment to head the Manhattan Project, the secret government program to develop an atomic bomb (q.v.). The first successful explosion of an atomic bomb occurred on July 16, 1945, near Alamogordo, New Mexico; atomic weapons were dropped on Hiroshima and Nagasaki in Japan (qq.v.) the following month.

GUADALCANAL CAMPAIGN. Allied offensive in the Solomon Islands (q.v.), August 7, 1942–February 9, 1943. In the summer of 1942, the U.S. high command decided to mount major offensives in Papua, New Guinea (q.v.), and the Solomon Islands, with the objectives of protecting the lines of communication between the United States and Australia and New Zealand(qq.v.) and eventually assaulting the large Japanese base at Rabaul (q.v.), New Britain. Theater boundaries were adjusted to facilitate the operation for the southern Solomons; it came

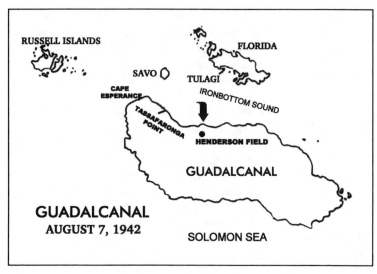

Guadalcanal, August 7, 1942

under the command of Vice Admiral Robert L. Ghormley (q.v.), who headed the South Pacific Area (SOPAC) (q.v.) subtheater and reported to Admiral Chester W. Nimitz (q.v.). Guadalcanal in particular was targeted because Japanese forces were constructing an airfield on it.

The Japanese high command wanted to control the Solomon Islands to cut the Allied communications. The Japanese Combined Fleet, under Admiral Isoruku Yamamoto (q.v.), and the Seventeenth Army, under Lieutenant General Haruyoshi Hyakutake (q.v.), were responsible for the area. After the U.S. invasion of Guadalcanal, the Imperial General Staff ordered Hyakutake to mount a massive effort to retake the island.

On August 7, 1942, the U.S. 1st Marine Division landed on the Solomon islands of Tulagi, Florida, and Guadalcanal, which together had 3,700 Japanese troops. Although there was little initial resistance, the capture of Guadalcanal soon turned into a lengthy, bloody campaign during which thousands of Japanese and U.S. reinforcements were added and costly naval battles were fought in the surrounding waters. Soon after landing, the U.S. ground forces captured the unfinished airfield, completed it, and named it Henderson Field (q.v.). Early in September, marine Brigadier General Roy S. Geiger (q.v.) arrived to direct the air units, known as the Cactus Air Force. From their perimeter around the airfield, the marines launched and defended against major attacks, such as the Battle of Bloody Ridge.

As the losses mounted in October, Vice Admiral William F. Halsey (q.v.) succeeded Ghormley as SOPAC commander. In late October and early November, the American forces repulsed a major Japanese offensive and then began to enlarge the perimeter, while Carlson's Raiders (q.v.) moved into the jungle to seek Japanese troops. Major General A. A. Vandegrift's (q.v.) 1st Marine Division, suffering from disease and injuries, was replaced in December by army and marine troops under Major General Alexander M. Patch (q.v.). Among the replacements was the 25th Division commanded by Major General Joseph Lawton Collins (q.v.).

At the end of 1942, the Japanese high command decided to abandon Guadalcanal and concentrate on the defense of the other Solomons. As Collins led a major offensive in January 1943, Japan began to evacuate its troops, with most removed from the island by early February. Guadalcanal was declared secured on February 9, 1943. SOPAC's next major campaign targeted the central Solomons, which it launched on June 30 as part of Operation Cartwheel (q.v.). The 1st Marine Division went to Australia for a long recovery period; it would next take part in actions on New Britain. *See also* Guadalcanal Campaign: Naval Battles.

GUADALCANAL CAMPAIGN: NAVAL BATTLES. Series of naval battles between Allied and Japanese forces in the Solomon Islands (q.v.) during the fight for Guadalcanal, August 1942–February 1943. Control of Guadalcanal was contested on the sea as well as on the land, with the waters north of the island becoming known as the Ironbottom Sound because of all the sunken vessels. The Japanese continuously sent reinforcements and supplies from their bases in Rabaul (q.v.), New Britain, traveling the waters of the "Slot" in a movement called the "Tokyo Express" by Americans. Allied ships, as well, transported additional personnel and matériel to the island.

The Japanese naval strength affected operations from the beginning, when the Allied naval forces, fearing attack, withdrew from the landing areas after most of the men but few provisions and equipment had been unloaded. The first major engagement was the Battle of Savo Island on the night of August 8–9, which was disastrous for the Allied forces caught by surprise. In the Battle of the Eastern Solomons, August 24–25, opposing carriers (q.v.) fought as Japanese reinforcements tried to reach Guadalcanal, with losses on each side. On October

11–12, Japanese and Allied transport forces carrying troops for the campaign met in the Battle of Cape Esperance. The Japanese lost several vessels, but the soldiers of both sides were delivered safely. The Battle of the Santa Cruz Islands, October 26–27, a Japanese offensive to affect the course of the campaign on the ground, was primarily a carrier fight, in which the Japanese inflicted severe damage on American vessels but lost more pilots.

On November 12–15, the Japanese made another major attempt to oust the Americans from the island, especially the airfield; the result was the decisive Naval Battle of Guadalcanal. Over four days, different battles raged, with numerous vessels sunk, troop transports lost, and other casualties including two American admirals. It ended in a clear American victory, for after this battle, Allied forces held control of the seas around Guadalcanal. In the Battle of Tassafaronga, November 30–December 1, American ships challenged Japanese destroyers trying to resupply the troops on the island, but the Americans suffered heavy damage and casualties. The last major naval engagement of the campaign was the Battle of Rennell's Island, January 29–30, 1943, in which Japanese land-based planes successfully bombed Allied ships. During the next few days, the Japanese secretly evacuated their troops from Guadalcanal.

GUAM. Island in the Marianas (q.v.) chain, occupied by Japan (q.v.) on December 10, 1941, and recaptured by the United States (q.v.), July 21–August 10, 1944. Guam, owned by the United States since 1898, was seized by Japan soon after the Pearl Harbor (q.v.) attack and fortified in 1944 against an expected invasion. U.S. troops landed on July 21, 1944, as part of the Central Pacific (q.v.) drive to acquire the Marianas, under the command of Admiral Raymond A. Spruance (q.v.). The invading troops encountered heavy opposition from the Japanese troops, under the command first of Lieutenant General Takeshi Takashima and then, after his death, of Lieutenant General Hideyoshi Obata, who was also killed in action. Some of the heaviest fighting occurred during banzai (q.v.) charges on the Orote Peninsula. By the conclusion of the action on August 10, most of the defending soldiers had died. After the recapture of Guam, Allied forces built major air and naval bases on the island, which were used to support the invasions of Iwo Jima and Okinawa (qq.v.) and to carry out the strategic air campaign (q.v.) against Japan. Guam was the first U.S. territory liberated from Japanese control during the Pacific War.

-H-

HALSEY, WILLIAM FREDERICK (1882–1959). U.S. Fleet Admiral; commander, Aircraft Battle Force, Pacific Fleet, 1940–1942; commander, South Pacific Area (q.v.), 1942–1944; and commander, Third Fleet, 1943–1945. On December 7, 1941, Halsey's aircraft carriers (q.v.) were based at Pearl Harbor (q.v.), but at the time the Japanese struck the rest of the fleet, the carriers were at sea and escaped damage. During the first months of the war, Halsey led raids on Japanese-held islands in the Central Pacific and, more dramatically, collaborated with the United States Army Air Forces (q.v.) in launching the Doolittle Raid (q.v.) on Tokyo (q.v.) on April 18, 1942. Illness prevented Halsey's participation in the Battle of Midway (q.v.).

In October 1942, Admiral Chester W. Nimitz (q.v.), commander of the Pacific Ocean Areas (q.v.) theater, appointed Halsey to head the South Pacific Area (SOPAC) subtheater, where the fight for Guadalcanal (q.v.) was progressing poorly. Halsey's aggressiveness and energy bolstered the morale of the American forces and helped to bring the campaign to a successful close. He then worked closely with General Douglas MacArthur (q.v.), commander of the Southwest Pacific Area (q.v.) theater, to conduct Operation Cartwheel (q.v.), designed to neutralize the Japanese stronghold of Rabaul (q.v.), New Britain.

Upon the deactivation of the SOPAC theater in June 1944, Halsey's naval and marine units were integrated with the Central Pacific Area (q.v.) forces. During the last year of the war, he alternated command of the Pacific Fleet with Admiral Raymond A. Spruance (q.v.). Under Halsey its title was the Third Fleet; with Spruance in command, it became the Fifth Fleet. The Third Fleet assisted in the landings on Leyte and Luzon in the Philippines (qq.v.), leading to Halsey's controversial participation in the Battle for Leyte Gulf (q.v.). During the summer of 1945, Halsey directed carrier attacks on Japan.

Halsey's boldness and charisma made him a popular figure in the U.S. Congress and press, although he drew criticism for his actions at Leyte Gulf and the severe damage inflicted on his forces by typhoons. In December 1945 he was promoted to Fleet Admiral.

HANSELL, HAYWOOD S., JR. *See* STRATEGIC AIR CAMPAIGN.

HARRIMAN, W. AVERELL (1891–1986). U.S. diplomat; lend-lease (q.v.) representative, 1941–1943; ambassador to the Union of Soviet

Socialist Republics (q.v.), 1943–1946; ambassador to the United Kingdom (q.v.), 1946; governor of New York, 1956–1958. As the special emissary of U.S. President Franklin D. Roosevelt (q.v.), Harriman coordinated lend-lease aid to the United Kingdom and the U.S.S.R. In this role and as ambassador to the U.S.S.R., Harriman worked to strengthen the Allied coalition and met frequently with British Prime Minister Winston S. Churchill, Soviet Premier Joseph V. Stalin (qq.v.), and other British and Soviet officials. He represented the United States at the Moscow conferences of 1941, 1942, and 1944 (q.v.) and attended other major Allied conferences (q.v.).

HART, THOMAS CHARLES (1877–1971). U.S. admiral; commander, U.S. Asiatic Fleet (q.v.), 1939–1942. When Hart assumed command of the Asiatic Fleet on July 25, 1939, most of its forces were in China or the Philippine Islands (qq.v.). Amid rising tensions between the United States and Japan (qq.v.), Hart moved his headquarters to the Philippine capital of Manila (q.v.) on October 21, 1940, where he conducted training exercises for his forces. On November 20, 1941, the Navy Department told him to move his fleet south to Singapore or the Netherlands East Indies (qq.v.) if Japan attacked the Philippines, recognizing that U.S. forces in the Philippines could not withstand a major enemy attack. In early December, Hart conferred with British Eastern Fleet commander Admiral Tom S. V. Phillips (q.v.) regarding the need for cooperation by their navies if Japan moved southward.

In the hours and days following Japan's assault on Pearl Harbor (q.v.) on December 7, 1941, Japanese air attacks in the Philippines destroyed the Cavite Navy Yard, and Hart ordered most of his fleet to leave the islands. With Japanese ground troops moving rapidly toward Manila, Hart departed by submarine (q.v.) on December 26 and moved his headquarters to the Dutch naval base at Surabaja, Java (q.v.), in the Netherlands East Indies instead of to Singapore, which was in danger of capture. Upon his arrival in Java, he became the naval commander of the newly formed ABDACOM theater (q.v.), the first combined Allied attempt to counter the Japanese advance. With ABDACOM's weak position further complicated by command problems, Hart was ordered to return to the United States on February 14, 1942. Dutch Vice Admiral Conrad E. L. Helfrich took over his ABDACOM position.

Upon his return to the United States, Hart retired but was recalled to active duty as a member of the navy's General Board. He served in the

U.S. Senate from 1945 to 1946, having been appointed to fill an unexpired term.

HATTA, MOHAMMAD (1902–1980). Indonesian nationalist leader. Because of his involvement in a nationalistic student organization, Hatta was arrested by authorities of the Netherlands East Indies (q.v.) in 1934 and remained a prisoner until Japan (q.v.) captured the islands and released him. Hatta and Achmad Sukarno (q.v.), another nationalist leader, collaborated with the Japanese during their occupation and, under Japanese sponsorship, organized the national defense force called the Peta Army. Following the Japanese pledge in 1944 to grant independence at a later date, Hatta worked on committees to plan the transition. On August 17, 1945, Hatta and Sukarno announced the formation of the Republic of Indonesia. Hatta served as vice president (1945–1956) and prime minister (1948–1950) of the new nation, which the Dutch did not recognize until 1949.

HAWAII. *See* JAPANESE AMERICANS; PEARL HARBOR, ATTACK ON.

HELICOPTER. First used by the Allies (q.v.) in the Pacific War in 1943, but never in large numbers. The United States Army (q.v.) operated the U.S.-produced Sikorsky R-4 helicopter, while the United States Coast Guard and the British flew other versions. The R-4 carried a crew of two, could achieve speeds of 75 miles per hour, and had a range of 130 miles. In the Pacific and Southeast Asia, its primary uses were rescue missions and the evacuation of casualties, as in the invasion of Luzon (q.v.) in January 1945. Also during the war, the Japanese developed and used the Kayaba Ka-1 autogiro for antisubmarine warfare.

HENDERSON FIELD. Airfield on the island of Guadalcanal (q.v.), which was begun by the Japanese and finished by U.S. forces in 1942. The airfield was a primary target of the U.S. invasion that began on August 7, 1942. American forces quickly seized the partially built field and completed it, naming it in memory of Major Lofton R. Henderson, a marine pilot who had died in the Battle of Midway (q.v.). Much of the subsequent ground action was set off by Japanese attacks on the U.S. defense perimeter around the air base.

HIGASHIKUNI, NARUHIKO (1887–1990). Japanese general; commander, General Defense Command; 1941–1945; prime minister, 1945. An imperial prince and uncle-in-law of Emperor Hirohito (q.v.), Higashikuni took charge of the General Defense Command shortly after the Pearl Harbor attack (q.v.). In this post he was charged with the air and land defense of Kyushu, Honshu, Shikoku, and the Izu Islands near Honshu. He shared responsibility for long-range air operations with the Combined Fleet (q.v.), which protected the Japanese home islands (q.v.) by sea.

After the emperor broadcast the news of the Japanese surrender (q.v.), the government of Prime Minister Kantaro Suzuki (q.v.) resigned. Because he could represent both the imperial family and the armed forces during a period of instability, Higashikuni was asked to form a government to oversee the official surrender and the beginning of the Allied occupation. He served as prime minister from August 17 to October 6, 1945, the only member of the imperial family to hold the position.

HIGGINS, ANDREW JACKSON (1886–1952). U.S. shipbuilder. From his facilities in New Orleans, Higgins developed the Eureka, a small boat with a protected propeller, which could operate in shallow waters and beach easily. Higgins worked with the United States Marine Corps (q.v.) in the 1930s to develop landing craft and ships (q.v.) suitable for amphibious assaults (q.v.). Among his products were the LCVP (landing craft, vehicle, personnel) and the LCM (landing craft, medium), both known as "Higgins boats." Higgins Industries also built a popular model of the patrol torpedo (PT) boat (q.v.).

HIROHITO (1901–1989). Emperor Showa of Japan, 1926–1989. As the head of state of a constitutional monarchy, Hirohito was regarded as divine and played a vital symbolic role in Japanese nationalism and religion. His closest adviser from 1940 to 1945 was Koichi Kido (q.v.), lord keeper of the privy seal; he also relied on the advice of the *jushin* (q.v.), or senior statesmen. Hirohito's actual influence on the course of World War II has been the focus of much debate since the war began. Although authorities differ about his participation in the decision to attack in 1941, they generally agree that his actions in August 1945 facilitated the Japanese surrender (q.v.).

During negotiations earlier that summer, Japanese representatives insisted that the emperor be retained if Japan were to surrender. This the Allies (q.v.) refused to promise, but they subsequently allowed Hirohito to continue as emperor and declined to try him for war crimes (q.v.) as some had demanded. Forced to renounce his divinity, Hirohito cooperated with the Allied occupation and helped to set its peaceful tone.

HIROSHIMA. Japanese port city targeted in the first atomic bomb (q.v.) attack by the United States (q.v.). Located on the island of Honshu, Hiroshima had remained relatively intact in comparison with other Japanese cities heavily damaged by the strategic air campaign (q.v.). On August 6, 1945, the Boeing B-29 entitled the *Enola Gay,* part of the 509th Composite Group of the United States Army Air Forces (q.v.), flew from Tinian (q.v.) to Hiroshima to drop the uranium bomb called "Little Boy." The explosion and resulting fires destroyed almost five square miles of the city and initially killed 80,000 people; later the same year, 60,000 more died from their injuries and exposure to radiation. The heavy damage to communications and transportation systems delayed the government's ability to assess the type of weapon and the extent of destruction, although it dispatched its leading atomic scientist to the area. On August 9, a second atomic attack struck Nagasaki (q.v.).

HITLER, ADOLF (1889–1945). German chancellor, 1933–1945, and head of state, 1934–1945. Also leader of the Nazi Party (q.v.), Hitler ruled Germany (q.v.) as a dictator and aggressively seized control of much territory in Europe. When his forces invaded Poland on September 1, 1939, Polish allies France and the United Kingdom (qq.v.) went to war against Germany, marking the formal beginning of World War II in Europe. Aligned with Japan as an Axis power (q.v.), Hitler declared war on the United States (q.v.) four days after the Japanese attack on Pearl Harbor (q.v.). Hitler died on April 30, 1945, as Allied forces approached his headquarters in Berlin.

HO CHI MINH (1890–1969). Vietnamese nationalist leader. An early member of the Communist Party, Ho advocated the independence of French Indochina (q.v.) and subsequently opposed the move of Japanese forces into Indochina with French permission. In 1941, he helped to found the Viet Minh (q.v.), a nationalist organization, and continued his efforts from South China until he was imprisoned by Chiang Kai-shek's (q.v.) government in 1942. Upon his release the next year, Ho worked with the Viet Minh to undermine the Japanese in Indochina. He received some aid from the U.S. Office of Strategic Services (q.v.).

On September 2, 1945, Ho declared the independence of Vietnam from France (q.v.). Warfare ensued the following year with the French, who were unwilling to grant Vietnamese autonomy. After a peace accord in 1954, Ho held the presidency of North Vietnam and carried on a war against South Vietnam.

HO YING-CHIN (1889–1987). Chinese Nationalist general; minister of war, 1930–1944; army chief of staff, 1938–1944; commander in chief, Chinese army, 1944–1946. A longtime associate and supporter of Chiang Kai-shek (q.v.), Ho represented Chiang in signing the Tangku Truce (1933) and the Ho-Umezu Agreement (1935), which in effect yielded control of northern China to Japan (qq.v.) in exchange for peace. Both Chiang and Ho wanted to focus on consolidation of Chiang's power over the Chinese Communists without having to face the Japanese at the same time.

As chief of staff of the Chinese army, Ho clashed with U.S. Lieutenant General Joseph W. Stilwell (q.v.), who was appointed chief of staff to Chiang in early 1942. Ho led Chinese soldiers in Burma (q.v.) under Stilwell's command in the spring of 1942, but thereafter he opposed sending substantial Chinese forces to Burma. During the Japanese Operation Ichigo (q.v.) in 1944, the Chinese army performed so poorly that Stilwell pressed his superiors in Washington to put him in command of the army and to replace Ho. Instead, Chiang requested and won Stilwell's recall in October 1944. Ho was forced to resign as war minister the next month, but Chiang then named him commander in chief of the Chinese army, contrary to the recommendation of Major General Albert C. Wedemeyer (q.v.), Stilwell's successor in China. In September 1945, Ho accepted the formal Japanese surrender (q.v.) in China and worked closely with Japanese commanders to ensure that control of Japanese-held areas be transferred to the Nationalists instead of the Communists. In 1949, Ho served briefly as premier of the Republic of China before moving to Formosa (q.v.) with other Nationalists.

HODGE, JOHN R. *See* KOREA.

HODGES, COURTNEY H. *See* JAPAN, INVASION OF.

HOKKAIDO. *See* JAPANESE HOME ISLANDS.

HOLCOMB, THOMAS. *See* UNITED STATES MARINE CORPS.

HOLLANDIA. *See* CARRIER, AIRCRAFT; INTELLIGENCE, ALLIED SIGNAL; NEW GUINEA.

HOMMA, MASAHARU (1887–1946). Japanese army general; commander, Japanese Fourteenth Army, 1941–1942. Homma's Fourteenth Army led the Japanese invasion of Luzon (q.v.) in the northern Philippines (q.v.) in late December 1941 and rapidly advanced toward the peninsula of Bataan (q.v.), to which the bulk of the American and Filipino troops had withdrawn. The forces on Bataan surrendered on April 9, 1942, and the U.S.-Filipino command in the rest of the archipelago capitulated in early May after the capture of the U.S. headquarters on Corregidor (q.v.). Although Homma achieved his assignment of conquering the Philippines, the campaign took much longer than planned, and he was removed from command in the summer of 1942. He held no responsible position for the rest of the war. In 1946, Homma was executed for war crimes (q.v.) involving the Bataan Death March (q.v.), a forced march of American and Filipino prisoners of war (q.v.) during which many prisoners died from atrocities.

HONG KONG. British colony in southern China (q.v.) that surrendered to Japan (q.v.) on December 25, 1941. The British government had considered Hong Kong a probable target if Japan went to war but knew it could not adequately defend the colony. Attacked early on December 8, 1941, Hong Kong's garrison resisted but was unable to hold off the invading troops and capitulated on December 25. Japan occupied the area throughout the war, returning it to the British in a formal ceremony on September 16, 1945. Preceding the event were negotiations between the British and the Chinese Nationalists regarding which government would accept the Japanese surrender (q.v.).

HONSHU. *See* HIROSHIMA; JAPAN, INVASION OF; JAPANESE HOME ISLANDS; TOKYO.

HOPKINS, HARRY R. *See* UNITED STATES.

HULL, CORDELL (1871–1955). U.S. secretary of state, 1933–1944. Prior to the entry of the United States (q.v.) into the war, Hull worked against Japanese aggression in Asia and held a series of negotiations with Japanese Ambassador Kichisaburo Nomura and Special Envoy Saburo Kurusu (qq.v.) that continued in late 1941 even as the Japanese fleet sailed for Pearl Harbor (q.v.). By the time Nomura officially informed Hull of Japan's declaration of war on the afternoon of December 7, 1941, Hull had already received word of the Pearl Harbor attack.

Hull's promotion of the "Good Neighbor" policy toward Latin America (q.v.) during the 1930s contributed significantly to the cooperation of the American republics with the U.S. war effort. In addition to continuing efforts regarding Latin America, Hull played prominent roles in the wartime Moscow Foreign Ministers Conference and the Dumbarton Oaks Conference (qq.v.). President Franklin D. Roosevelt (q.v.) often bypassed Hull when conducting foreign policy, as shown in the many wartime Allied conferences (q.v.) Roosevelt held with British Prime Minister Winston S. Churchill (q.v.), where Hull was not included. After Roosevelt's election to a fourth presidential term, Hull resigned on November 21, 1944, and was succeeded by Edward R. Stettinius, Jr. In 1945 Hull received the Nobel Peace Prize for his work in forming the United Nations organization (q.v.).

HUMP. Hazardous air route over the Himalaya Mountains used by Allied planes flying mainly between Assam, India, and Kunming, China (qq.v.). In April 1942, the Allies (q.v.) began to send transport planes (q.v.) over the Hump to deliver military supplies to the Chinese, after the main land route into China, the Burma Road (q.v.), was closed by Japan (q.v.). The Hump served as the primary avenue between the Western Allies and the Chinese until the overland route into China reopened in January 1945. The airlift continued until the war's end, transporting 650,000 tons throughout the war. From mid-1944 to early 1945, U.S. Boeing B-29 Superfortress (q.v.) bombers based in India also traveled the Hump to Chinese airfields, from which they carried out a strategic air campaign (q.v.) against Japan and the areas it occupied.

HURLEY, PATRICK JAY (1880–1941). United States Army general and diplomat; special envoy to China (q.v.), 1944; ambassador to China, 1944–1945. After the United States entered the war, Hurley, a former secretary of war (1929–1933), was recalled to active duty as a general officer and assigned the difficult task of sending supplies to the blockaded Philippines (q.v.). He next served as minister to New Zealand (q.v.) for several months and then carried out a number of special missions for President Franklin D. Roosevelt (q.v.), meeting with Soviet Premier Joseph V. Stalin (q.v.) in Moscow and with Generalissimo Chiang Kai-shek (q.v.) in Chungking (q.v.). In 1944, Roosevelt appointed Hurley as his special representative and later ambassador to China, where one of his tasks was to mediate between the factions led by Chiang and Mao Tse-tung (q.v.). Close to Chiang, Hurley supported the relief of U.S. General Joseph W. Stilwell (q.v.) as Chiang's chief of staff and as head of the China-Burma-India (q.v.) theater. After an unsuccessful trip to Mao's headquarters in Yenan in November 1944, Hurley actively opposed cooperation with the Communists, which the American Dixie Mission (q.v.) was then discussing. At the close of the war with Japan, Hurley continued to work with the different Chinese forces, resigning in November 1945 to protest what he identified as U.S. State Department interference on behalf of the Chinese Communists.

HYAKUTAKE, HARUYOSHI (1888–1947). Japanese general; commander, Seventeenth Army, 1942–1945. In May 1942, Hyakutake's Seventeenth Army was activated and sent to bases at Rabaul and Truk (qq.v.) as part of the Japanese campaign to cut the United States' (q.v.) communication lines with Australia and New Zealand (qq.v.). Some of Hyakutake's forces were sent to New Guinea (q.v.) to conduct an overland invasion of Port Moresby (q.v.) in the summer of 1942. In August he faced another major operation when U.S. forces invaded the island of Guadalcanal (q.v.) in the Solomon Islands (q.v.), where a small number of Japanese workers were building an airfield. The fight for control of the island became extremely bloody as both sides sent in massive reinforcements, and Hyakutake eventually moved to the island to personally direct the campaign. In November 1942, his Seventeenth Army was placed under the jurisdiction of the new Eighth Area Army, established in Rabaul and headed by General Hitoshi Imamura (q.v.), who also assumed responsibility for New Guinea. At the end of 1942, the Japanese high command decided that Hyakutake should concentrate on defending other islands in the Solomons and should withdraw from Guadalcanal, which he did in January and February 1943. During the Allied Operation Cartwheel (q.v.), Hyakutake's forces fought fiercely in the Solomons. In October, Imamura told Hyakutake that his main mission was to defend Bougainville (q.v.) against a U.S. invasion, which occurred in November. After an unsuccessful counteroffensive in March 1944, Hyakutake received orders to defend his position but undertake no more attacks. He and his men strengthened their control over part of the island, which the Allies bypassed until Australian forces began a new campaign in 1945. Hyakutuke remained on Bougainville until the end of the war.

-I-

ICHIGO, OPERATION. Operation Number One, a major Japanese ground offensive in China (q.v.), April 18, 1944–May 1945. In early 1944, the Japanese high command decided to launch a massive attack in eastern and central China, with the dual goals of eliminating air bases used by U.S. bombers (q.v.) and opening a complete land route from northern China and Manchuria (q.v.) south to French Indochina (q.v.). The U.S. Fourteenth Air Force under Major General Claire L. Chennault (q.v.) had been attacking Japanese forces and supply lines from Chinese bases, some of which were being expanded to accommodate the new Boeing B-29 Superfortress (q.v.) bombers with the range to attack the Japanese home islands (q.v.). Allied submarines (q.v.) had damaged the Japanese merchant marine (q.v.) so badly that Japan desperately needed new land routes for men and raw materials (q.v.).

Ichigo began on April 18, 1944, under the direction of Lieutenant General Yasuji Okamura (q.v.), commander of Japan's Chinese Expeditionary Army. First targeted was Honan province in central China, where Chiang Kai-shek's (q.v.) Nationalist forces offered little resistance. The Japanese then moved into Hunan province, capturing Changsha and attacking Heng Yang, the first site strongly defended by the Chinese, who were aided by U.S. airmen. Chinese Major General Fong Hsien-Chueh directed the six-week Chinese fight before Heng Yang fell on August 8. As the Japanese approached southeastern China, most of Chennault's airfields had to be abandoned, with extensive loss of equipment and supplies. In the face of the Japanese advances, Chiang wanted to withdraw the limited Chinese forces he had sent to northern Burma (q.v.), where Lieutenant General Joseph W. Stilwell (q.v.) was in a critical phase of his operations to open an Allied land route to China. Stilwell's resistance to Chiang during Ichigo and his attempt to oust Chiang's army chief Ho Ying-Chin (q.v.) ultimately culminated in Stilwell's recall in October 1944. By year's end, the United States considered China much less important strategically because of the weakness of the Chinese armies against the Japanese, Chiang's demands during the Stilwell crisis, and most importantly, the U.S. acquisition of the Mariana Islands (q.v.) for B-29 bases.

In southwest China the Japanese captured the cities of Kweilin (November 10, 1944) and Liuchow (November 11), putting them in position to threaten Chiang's capital of Chungking as well as Kunming (qq.v.), the end point of the soon-to-be-reopened Burma Road (q.v.).

In early January 1945, the B-29 base at Chengtu (q.v.) was abandoned to the Japanese. Lieutenant General Albert C. Wedemeyer (q.v.), who had assumed Stilwell's duties in China, organized the Chinese defense. Operation Ichigo came to an end in May 1945, as Okamura withdrew some of his forces north, where the Japanese increasingly anticipated an attack by the Union of Soviet Socialist Republics (q.v.).

IMAMURA, HITOSHI (1886–1968). Japanese general; commander, Sixteenth Army, 1941–1942; commander, Eighth Area Army, 1942–1945. As commander of the Sixteenth Army, Imamura accepted the surrender of the Allied forces in the Netherlands East Indies (q.v.) in March 1942. In November 1942, he moved to Rabaul (q.v.), New Britain, to assume command of the new Eighth Area Army, which was created to counter Allied offensives in the South Pacific and Southwest Pacific Areas (qq.v.). Under his command were the new Eighteenth Army under General Hatazo Adachi (q.v.), which would be assigned to New Guinea (q.v.), and the Seventeenth Army under Lieutenant General Haruyoshi Hyakutake (q.v.), which was engaged in heavy combat on Guadalcanal in the Solomon Islands (qq.v.) when Imamura arrived in Rabaul. His initial orders were to recapture the Solomons and reinforce New Guinea, with the eventual goal of seizing Port Moresby (q.v.). By early January 1943, Imamura was told to evacuate Guadalcanal and Buna, New Guinea, while focusing on the rest of the Solomons and preparing for new offensives in New Guinea. Instead, during Operation Cartwheel (q.v.) in 1943–1944, Rabaul (including Imamura's headquarters) was isolated, the remainder of Hyakutake's force was entrenched on one end of Bougainville in the Solomons, and Adachi's army was transferred to the jurisdiction of the Second Area Army. At the close of the war, Imamura surrendered his forces in Rabaul. He was imprisoned for war crimes (q.v.) until 1954.

IMPERIAL GENERAL HEADQUARTERS (IGH). Japanese military organization that directed the conduct of the war. Established after the start of the war with China (q.v.) in 1937, the IGH was intended to unify the highly independent commands of the army and navy. Included were the chiefs of staff of the two services, the army and navy ministers, and selected members of important bureaus. (There was no separate Japanese air force.) The IGH was divided into two sections headed by the army and navy chiefs of staff, but it had no mechanism to settle disputes between the sections. Actual coordination between the army and navy was limited, unlike that in the United States Joint Chiefs of Staff (q.v.) and the British Chiefs of Staff Committee (q.v.).

Responsible ultimately only to Emperor Hirohito (q.v.), the IGH was independent of the prime minister and political units of the government. The army and navy ministers, to whom the chiefs of staff reported in peacetime, served as members of the cabinet, but the prime minister was forced to choose them from the active lists of the army and navy. Consequently, the high commands of the services could veto men they did not like, further lessening civilian influence on the military. The prime minister found it difficult to get military information from the IGH, much less to exert control over the course of the war.

The position of army chief of staff was held successively by General Hajime Sugiyama (1940–1944), Prime Minister Hideki Tojo (1944) (q.v.), and General Yoshijiro Umezu (1944–1945). Navy chiefs of staff included Admiral Osami Nagano (1941–1944) (q.v.), Admiral Higeru Shimada (1944), Admiral Koshiro Oikawa (1944–1945), and Admiral Soemu Toyoda (1945) (q.v.).

The Liaison Conference was created to provide coordination between the political and military authorities during the war. Including representatives from the cabinet and the IGH, the conference debated strategy and made recommendations to the emperor. When Kuniaki Koiso (q.v.) became prime minister in July 1944, he replaced the Liaison Conference with the Supreme War Direction Council (q.v.), which continued until the end of the war.

IMPERIAL RULE ASSISTANCE ASSOCIATION (IRAA). *Taisei Yokusan Kai,* the organization that replaced political parties in Japan (q.v.), 1940–1945. Formally established on October 12, 1940, the IRAA was promoted by Prime Minister Fumimaro Konoye (q.v.), who had taken office in July 1940. He intended it to mobilize spiritual unity throughout the country in support of the government and to replace the existing system of competitive, corrupt political parties. Each Japanese automatically became a member of the IRAA, which established a number of administrative levels, ranging from the national headquarters to small neighborhood groups. Through its extensive organization, the IRAA concentrated on building and maintaining popular morale and support for the war. It promoted conservation, increased production, and civil defense among citizens.

In May 1942, the IRAA created the Imperial Rule Assistance Political Society (IRAPS) to serve as a mechanism for nominating candidates to serve in the Diet; until the end of the war, nearly all Diet members belonged to the IRAPS. On March 30, 1945, the IRAPS was succeeded by the Political Association of Great Japan. The IRAA was dissolved on June 13, 1945. During the postwar Japanese occupation (q.v.), many elected and community leaders active in the IRAA were purged from their public positions by Allied authorities.

IMPHAL. Site of a major Allied base in northeastern India (q.v.), which the Japanese tried and failed to take in a critical offensive, March–July 1944. The overall Japanese commander in Burma (q.v.), Lieutenant General Masakazu Kawabe (q.v.), and his Fifteenth Army commander, Lieutenant General Renya Mutaguchi (q.v.), planned the offensive across the Indian border toward Imphal and Kohima (q.v.) to destroy the supply bases of British Lieutenant General William J. Slim (q.v.), who was planning a major attack into Burma. By seizing Imphal, the Japanese also hoped to sever Allied lines of communication, impede the Hump (q.v.) airlift to China (qq.v.), and provoke an anti-British uprising in India, assisted by the elements of the Indian National Army (q.v.) fighting on the side of the Japanese in Burma.

On March 8, the Japanese offensive toward Imphal began. Japanese troops cut the vital Imphal-Kohima road on March 29 and soon surrounded the British and Indian forces in each location. To relieve the forces in Imphal, the Allies (q.v.) mounted a massive air supply operation by diverting transport planes (q.v.) from the Hump airlift to send in reinforcements and supplies, as well as evacuate casualties. Not until June 22 did Allied ground forces break through to end the siege of Imphal. The Japanese logistical system was incapable of sustaining a lengthy operation without the capture of enemy supplies, and in July Mutaguchi withdrew his remaining forces into Burma, pursued by Slim's army. The Japanese sustained extremely heavy losses: 53,000 casualties, including 30,000 killed. Many of the remaining forces were ill, and most equipment was lost. *See also* Burma Campaigns.

INDIA. British territory and member of the Allied powers (q.v.). When the United Kingdom (q.v.) declared war against Germany in 1939, it announced that India (q.v.) was also at war, infuriating Indian nationalists who had not been consulted and who began openly to oppose the war effort. After entering the war against Japan, the British sent Richard Stafford Cripps (q.v.) to India to persuade the nationalists to support the war in exchange for the promise of postwar self-rule. Nationalist leaders Mohandas K. Gandhi and Jawaharlal Nehru (qq.v.) demanded immediate independence and rejected the British proposals. In his "Quit India" movement, Gandhi urged the British to leave India so the Japanese would have less reason to attack it; in the event of a Japanese invasion, he encouraged civil disobedience rather than armed resistance. The British imprisoned Gandhi, Nehru, and many other nationalists for their work against the war and British rule. Food shortages, transportation difficulties, and Japanese bombing raids throughout the war further exacerbated tensions with the British.

Actively working with the Axis powers (q.v.) was Indian nationalist leader Subhas Chandra Bose (q.v.), who headed the Japanese-supported provisional Indian government. Bose also led the Indian National Army (q.v.), recruited mostly from Indian prisoners of war (q.v.) captured during the Japanese conquests of the Malay peninsula and Singapore (qq.v.). Another force of former Indian prisoners fought the Allies under German command in northern Africa.

In spite of sentiment to end British rule, India contributed significantly to the Allied coalition, signing the Declaration of the United Nations (q.v.), sending delegates to the Pacific War councils (q.v.), and joining the new United Nations organization (q.v.). Large numbers of Indian troops served with Allied forces in Africa, the Middle East, Italy, and Southeast Asia, where they played an essential role in the recapture of Burma (q.v.). From bases in India, the Allies conducted operations against Burma and sent supplies into China (q.v.), using the Hump air route and later the Stilwell Road (qq.v.). Indian airfields were also used in the strategic air campaign (q.v.). During the war, British Generals Archibald P. Wavell and Claude J. E. Auchinleck (qq.v.) served as commander in chief, India; Wavell also became viceroy of India. The U.S. China-Burma-India (q.v.) and India-Burma theaters also involved forces in India.

In 1942, as Japanese soldiers overran Burma, Allied forces retreated to India and China. Japanese troops crossed the Indian border in 1944 in attempts to capture Imphal and Kohima (qq.v.), withdrawing after several months. Throughout much of the war, Japanese planes attacked Allied bases in India, as well as such cities as Calcutta.

At the end of the war, Indian forces participated in the Allied occupation of Japan (q.v.) and formerly Japanese-held territories. India declined to sign the main Japanese peace treaty (q.v.), concluding a separate accord with Japan on June 6, 1952. With Louis Mountbatten (q.v.) as the last viceroy of India, the British in 1947 agreed to Indian independence and partitioned the area into India and Pakistan.

INDIA-BURMA THEATER. *See* BURMA CAMPAIGNS; SULTAN, DANIEL ISOM.

INDIAN NATIONAL ARMY. Military force allied with Japan (q.v.), composed primarily of Indian prisoners of war (q.v.) captured during the Japanese seizure of the Malay peninsula and Singapore (qq.v.). Originally formed in February 1942 by appeals to the nationalist and anti-British sentiments of the prisoners, the Indian National Army was reorganized in 1943 by Subhas Chandra Bose (q.v.), the revolutionary Indian leader who had escaped India for Germany (qq.v.) and then Japan. Under Bose, the army fought in Burma (q.v.) and India in 1944, participating in the battles at Imphal (q.v.), Meiktila, and Rangoon. The army's performance did not substantially help the Japanese or provoke the support in India that Bose wanted. After the war, the British put the army's members on trial for their wartime activities.

INDIAN OCEAN, JAPANESE RAIDS IN. Under the command of Vice Admiral Chuichi Nagumo (q.v.), the Japanese First Air Fleet traveled by carrier (q.v.) throughout the Indian Ocean from March 25 to April 9, 1942, striking bases on Ceylon (q.v.) at Colombo and Trincomalee, which was the main British naval base in the Far East after the loss of Singapore (q.v.), and engaging in battles with British vessels, resulting in several sinkings. British Admiral James F. Somerville (q.v.), commander in chief of the British Eastern Fleet, sent his old battleships (q.v.) to safety near the coast of Africa when he learned of the arrival of Nagumo, whose superior force had been so successful at Pearl Harbor (q.v.). Working with Nagumo, Vice Admiral Jisaburo Ozawa's (q.v.) forces destroyed merchant ships in the Bay of Bengal and attacked two Indian towns, while the submarines (q.v.) sank additional Allied ships. After incurring few losses, Nagumo's fleet departed from the Indian Ocean on April 9, leaving the British so wary of further Japanese moves that they decided to capture Madagascar (q.v.) to protect their control of the ocean. The headquarters of the British Eastern Fleet did not return to Ceylon until September 1943. Throughout the war, Japanese and German submarines (q.v.) attacked Allied ships in the Indian Ocean.

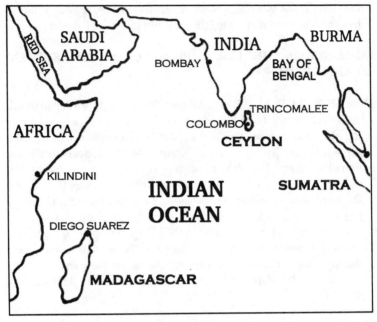

Indian Ocean

INDIANAPOLIS. U.S. heavy cruiser sunk in the Pacific with severe loss of life, July 30, 1945. The USS *Indianapolis* was at Pearl Harbor (q.v.) during the original Japanese attack and subsequently participated in campaigns in the Aleutians, Gilberts, Marshalls, Marianas, Palaus, and Iwo Jima (qq.v.), as well as the Battle of the Philippine Sea (q.v.) and carrier (q.v.) attacks on Japan. Near Okinawa (q.v.) in 1945, the ship was damaged by a kamikaze (q.v.) attack, repaired, and subsequently returned to sea. After delivering components of atomic weapons to U.S. facilities on Tinian (q.v.) in the Mariana Islands in late July 1945, the *Indianapolis* began its trip west from Guam to the Philippine Islands (qq.v.). Torpedoed by a Japanese submarine (q.v.) on the night of July 29–30, the ship sank in 12 minutes, with some crewmen trapped inside but with a substantial number escaping to open waters. Because of communication problems and lack of coordination between theaters, the ship was not missed and the survivors were not found until August 2, by which time many men had drowned, died from exposure, or been attacked by sharks. Some 316 men of the original 1,199 survived. The high number of deaths occurring so close to the end of the war spurred intensive investigations. In a controversial action, the ship's captain was court-martialed for failing to zigzag to avoid torpedo (q.v.) attacks.

INDOCHINA. *See* FRENCH INDOCHINA.

INDONESIA. *See* NETHERLANDS EAST INDIES.

INTELLIGENCE, ALLIED. Included signal intelligence (q.v.), espionage, sabotage, reconnaissance, mapmaking, translation of enemy documents, interrogation of prisoners of war (q.v.), and support of resistance and guerrilla operations. Joining the intelligence components of the armed forces in the war with Japan were the British Special Operations Executive (SOE) and the U.S. Office of Strategic Services (OSS) (qq.v.). Among the resources of the U.S. military were Japanese Americans (q.v.) who served as translators and interrogators, and Navajo code talkers (q.v.). Japanese Canadians (q.v.) also participated in the Allied effort.

The responsibilities for nonsignal intelligence varied according to geographic area. Fleet Admiral Chester W. Nimitz (q.v.) relied on his Joint Intelligence Center and barred the OSS from operating in his Pacific Ocean Areas (q.v.) theater. General of the Army Douglas MacArthur (q.v.) also excluded the OSS from the Southwest Pacific Area (q.v.) theater, where the Allied Translator and Interpreter Section, the Allied Geographical Section, and the Allied Intelligence Bureau (AIB) included American, Australian, British, Dutch, and New Zealand representatives. Among the AIB's responsibilities were information collection, clandestine operations, and the coastwatcher (q.v.) service. The AIB maintained especially close relations with the resistance movement in the Philippines (q.v.).

The complexity of the Allied command arrangements in Asia was reflected in the variety of intelligence agencies active on the continent. In China (q.v.), U.S. General Joseph W. Stilwell's (q.v.) headquarters did not control all American intelligence activities in the theater, such as the U.S. Naval Group, China, and the Sino-American Cooperative Association (SACO) (q.v.), which was affiliated with the Chinese Nationalist government. Not until 1945 did the OSS and the American part of SACO report directly to the U.S. theater commander. The U.S. Dixie Mission (q.v.) to the Chinese Communists, which operated as part of the theater organization, also included an intelligence function.

In spite of an American-British agreement to the contrary, the SOE also conducted operations in China, especially in Communist-held territory. Adding to the confusion, both the Chinese Nationalists and Communists collected extensive intelligence and shared selective information with the Western Allies (q.v.).

British, American, and Dutch military agencies undertook intelligence operations, sometimes with conflicting postwar goals, in Burma, French Indochina, Malaya, Sumatra, and Thailand (qq.v.). Both the SOE and the OSS were active in the same areas. Also working with resistance and guerrilla groups in Burma were the Chindits and Merrill's Marauders (qq.v.).

Outside the war zone, the Allied effort against Japan was supported by intelligence operations in numerous countries. In Latin America (q.v.), the U.S. Federal Bureau of Investigation (FBI) held the Allied responsibility for intelligence and banned the OSS from working in the area. SOE agents in Latin America operated secretly to avoid conflict with the FBI. Allied agents were active in neutral countries such as Portugal and Switzerland (q.v.) and in some belligerent countries. In Europe, the U.S. Alsos mission sought information about the discoveries of German scientists; one of its chief goals was to determine whether Germany had developed an atomic bomb (q.v.), a proximity fuze (q.v.), and other technology that could be shared with Japan as well as employed against the Allies in Europe. *See also* Intelligence, Soviet.

INTELLIGENCE, ALLIED SIGNAL. Also called special intelligence. One of the most important advantages of the Allies (q.v.) in World War II was signal intelligence, or the ability to intercept and read many of the enciphered radio messages transmitted by Axis (q.v.) officials. In an agreement reached in the fall of 1940, the United States and the United Kingdom (qq.v.) agreed to share signal intelligence.

In 1940, U.S. cryptanalysts led by William F. Friedman broke the system used to encipher Japanese diplomatic communications on "Purple" machines. The intelligence gained from reading the high-level diplomatic messages was called "Magic" and proved extremely important, although its value was limited by the information that the embassies transmitted; for example, diplomats using the Purple system did not discuss plans to attack Pearl Harbor (q.v.) but did address Japanese attempts to negotiate an end to the war. One of the most useful sources of Magic intelligence was the Japanese ambassador in Berlin, Lieutenant General Hiroshi Oshima (q.v.), whose reports to Tokyo relayed valuable information about the German high command and the German-Soviet war. The United States provided the British with a Purple machine before they entered the war with Japan (q.v.).

The Allies could also read some of the Japanese army and navy cryptologic systems during parts of the war, although changes in these codes and the immense volume of the messages complicated their use. In 1940, the Allies broke aspects of the main Japanese navy code, JN-25, but the code was significantly altered in December 1941. Japanese army codes could not be read until September 1943, the same year that the merchant code was broken. Signal intelligence originating from Japanese military sources is sometimes called "Japanese Ultra" or "Ultra-J" by Americans, to distinguish it from the "Ultra" intelligence obtained from German messages enciphered on "Enigma" machines. The British and some Americans use the term *Ultra* to encompass all high-level signal intelligence from Germany (q.v.) and Japan.

In the war against Japan, Ultra-J was particularly instrumental in the Allied victories at Midway (q.v.) in June 1942 and in the Bismarck Sea (q.v.) in March 1943. The next month, it enabled American pilots to kill Admiral Isoruku Yamamoto (q.v.) by shooting down his plane in the Solomon Islands (q.v.). In New Guinea (q.v.), Ultra-J facilitated the invasion of Hollandia in April 1944 and helped Allied forces to win the Battle of the Driniumor River (q.v.) in July–August 1944. It provided important information about Japanese plans to mount a massive defense of the home islands in the summer of 1945. One of the most valuable applications of Ultra-J involved the highly effective American submarine (q.v.) war against Japanese merchant and military vessels. Signal intelligence also allowed the Allies to attack the *Yanagi* operations in which German and Japanese vessels exchanged raw materials (q.v.) and technology. *See also* Intelligence, Allied; Intelligence, Japanese; Intelligence, Soviet; Science and Technology.

INTELLIGENCE, JAPANESE. Included signal intelligence, espionage, sabotage, reconnaissance, mapmaking, translation of enemy documents, interrogation of prisoners of war (q.v.), and support of resistance and guerrilla operations. The Japanese army, navy, and foreign office all carried out intelligence operations. In the army, the *Kempei,* or military police, held the responsibility for counterespionage, army security, guerrilla operations, and intelligence collection.

The *Kempei* increased its size dramatically during the war and operated extensively in each army command, maintaining control over both army forces and the occupied population. Appealing to anticolonialist sentiments, the *Kempei* organized such groups as the Indian National Army (q.v.) to assist Japan's cause.

Japan's extremely detailed intelligence regarding China (q.v.) was backed up by an extensive network, which continued to operate efficiently throughout the war. By the time the war with the West began, Japan had accumulated extensive knowledge about its first targeted areas: Hawaii, the Philippines, the Malay peninsula, and Singapore (qq.v.). Through the skillful use of aerial reconnaissance (conducted at times by commercial aircraft), analysis of published sources, contacts with anti-Western groups, and human agents, Japan had obtained accurate information about Allied military forces, installations, and orders of battle, which aided its offensives in December 1941. Later in the war, as Allied advances increasingly restricted the movements of Japanese aircraft and ships, the effectiveness of Japanese intelligence declined dramatically.

In the area of signal intelligence, or the interception and deciphering of radio transmissions, Allied accomplishments substantially exceeded those of Japan. The greatest successes of Japanese code breakers involved China; reportedly, Japan could read more than 90 percent of China's encoded messages. Also penetrated were some codes of the United States Army Air Forces (q.v.) in China and Burma (q.v.). At different times, Japan deciphered certain transmission signals of other American agencies, as well as those of the United Kingdom and the Union of Soviet Socialist Republics (qq.v).

Japan's Axis partners, Germany and Italy (qq.v.), shared intelligence information with Japan on a limited basis. Although Germany and Japan exchanged some signal intelligence concerning the Soviet Union and Allied merchant shipping, the two did not collaborate in the way the Western Allies (q.v.) did. Germany, for example, did not reveal to Japan its knowledge about British codes. Japan collected information from its diplomatic officers and military attachés around the world. The Japanese ambassador to Germany, Hiroshi Oshima (q.v.), enjoyed high-level access to German military officials and sent to Tokyo detailed reports; unknown to Oshima, the Allies could read his coded messages. In addition to Germany and Italy, Japan's offices in Sweden, Switzerland (q.v.), and Portugal were especially important for intelligence gathering. Japan also worked closely with Polish intelligence agents, both before and during the European War, to gain information about the Soviet Union.

INTELLIGENCE, SOVIET. Regarding the war against Japan (q.v.), consisted mostly of espionage. Although the Union of Soviet Socialist Republics (q.v.) and Japan stayed neutral until August 1945, each country was uncertain about the other's ultimate intentions and continued intelligence operations. The Soviets and Japanese collected some information through their maintenance of diplomatic relations. Additionally, Soviet agents operated around the world, including Richard Sorge (q.v.), a Soviet spy based in Tokyo (q.v.) until his capture in 1941. The U.S.S.R. also conducted espionage against its allies, experiencing particular success in placing agents within the British government and intelligence services. The Soviets penetrated the Manhattan Project (q.v.) and acquired detailed information about the development of the atomic bomb (q.v.). By the time President Harry S. Truman (q.v.) told Premier Joseph V. Stalin (q.v.) about the bomb at the Potsdam Conference (q.v.) in July 1945, Stalin had read intelligence reports about the project for years. Top U.S. officials learned during the war that the U.S.S.R. knew about the project, but the United States (q.v.) did not begin to comprehend the extent of Soviet wartime espionage until the late 1940s, when American intelligence analysts working in Operation Venona first learned to decrypt Soviet diplomatic messages intercepted in the United States during the war.

The U.S. and British governments also shared intelligence with the U.S.S.R., although Stalin ignored their warnings about Germany's (q.v.) plan to invade in June 1941. At Prime Minister Winston S. Churchill's (q.v.) insistence, Stalin received selected signal intelligence concerning German strategy during the war. The British attempted to protect their code-breaking ability by disguising the source of the information, but the Soviets knew from their spies that the British had broken German codes.

INTERNATIONAL MILITARY TRIBUNAL FOR THE FAR EAST. *See* WAR CRIMES TRIALS.

INTERNEES. *See* JAPANESE AMERICANS; JAPANESE CANADIANS; PRISONERS OF WAR HELD BY ALLIES; PRISONERS OF WAR HELD BY JAPAN.

ISHII, SHIRO. *See* BIOLOGICAL WARFARE.

ISMAY, HASTINGS LIONEL (1887–1965). British army general; chief of staff to minister of defense, 1940–1945. In May 1940, Ismay became chief of staff to Prime Minister Winston S. Churchill (q.v.) in his capacity as the minister of defense, a position held throughout the war. Ismay, nicknamed "Pug," acted as a liaison between the British Chiefs of Staff (q.v.) and Churchill, who involved himself personally with all aspects of the war effort. Ismay also attended the wartime Allied conferences (q.v.). After the war Ismay served as the first secretary general of the North Atlantic Treaty Organization (1952–1957).

ITALY. Axis power (q.v.) until 1943, when it negotiated with and joined the Allies (q.v.). Under its fascist leader Benito Mussolini (q.v.), Italy formed alliances with Germany and Japan (qq.v.), signing the Anti-Comintern Pact (q.v.) in 1937 and the Tripartite Pact (q.v.) in September 1940. Although Germany and Italy cooperated militarily to some extent in World War II, they did not have a similar relationship with Japan. During the late 1930s and during the war, Italy and Japan carried out limited educational and cultural exchanges.

On July 25, 1943, Mussolini was replaced by Field Marshal Pietro Badoglio. Early in September the Italian government surrendered to the Allies, but German troops remained in Italy to fight Allied forces until May 1945. Switching to the Allied side, Italy declared war on Germany on October 13, 1943, and on Japan on July 14, 1945.

IWABUCHI, SANJI (1893–1945). Japanese admiral. After Iwabuchi participated in the naval battles of Midway and the Solomons Islands (qq.v.), he became the commander of the naval forces in Manila Bay. When Allied forces invaded Luzon in the Philippine Islands (qq.v.) in early 1945, Iwabuchi led the defense of Manila (q.v.) against the orders of General Tomoyuki Yamashita (q.v.), the top army commander in the archipelago, who had ordered the city evacuated. During the fierce month-long battle for Manila, large numbers of civilians were killed, many as the victims of Japanese atrocities. Iwabuchi and most of his men also died during the battle. War crimes trials (q.v.) after the war held Yamashita responsible for the actions of Iwabuchi's troops.

IWANE, MATSUI. *See* NANKING.

IWO JIMA. Small island in the Volcano Islands, 700 miles from Tokyo (q.v.) and heavily fortified by Japan (q.v.) before the United States

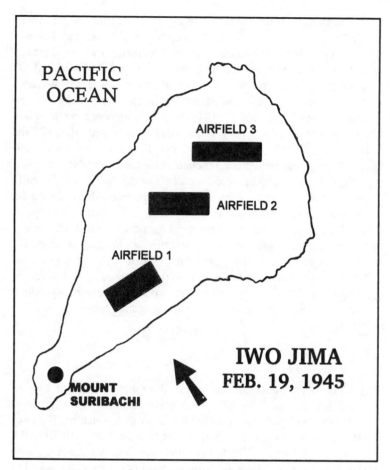

Iwo Jima, February 19, 1945

(q.v.) invaded, February 19–March 26, 1945. The U.S. high command wanted the eight-square-mile island of Iwo Jima for air bases to provide fighter (q.v.) support for Boeing B-29 Superfortress (q.v.) bombers flying from the Mariana Islands (q.v.) to bomb Japan; they also wanted to eliminate the Japanese radar (q.v.) facilities on the island. The capture of Iwo Jima would also provide facilities for repairing planes damaged in raids on Japan and the staging of air-sea rescue missions for downed pilots. Anticipating the U.S. invasion, Japan's military leaders sent reinforcements under Lieutenant General Tadamichi Kuribayashi, bringing the garrison to 21,000 men.

The assault of Iwo Jima was part of the Central Pacific Area's (CENPAC) (q.v.) operations. The Pacific Ocean Areas (q.v.) theater commander, Fleet Admiral Chester W. Nimitz (q.v.), assigned the operation to Admiral Raymond A. Spruance (q.v.), head of the CENPAC subtheater and commander of the U.S. Fifth Fleet. After intense naval and air bombardment of the island, the United States Marines (q.v.) went ashore on February 19, 1945, beginning an operation that planners thought would take one week. Instead, it lasted until March 26 and cost nearly 26,000 U.S. casualties. Iwo Jima's volcanic ash, well-placed guns, and underground shelters made the assault extremely difficult, combined with the suicidal charges of the defenders. One early objective of the invading forces was the capture of Mount Suribachi, climaxed by the raising of a U.S. flag on top; a famous photograph of the flag raising became the basis for a memorial statue in Arlington, Virginia, in the United States. As was the case in many other Pacific invasions, nearly all of the Japanese forces died. Although the fight for Iwo Jima was longer and costlier than projected, air bases and rescue facilities on the island did result in the saving of about 22,000 Allied airmen in the strategic air campaign (q.v.) against Japan.

-J-

JAPAN. Constitutional monarchy headed throughout the war by Emperor Hirohito (q.v.). The position of prime minister was held successively by Fumimaro Konoye (1937–1939) (q.v.), Kiichiro Hiranuma (1939), Nobuyuki Abe (1939–1940), Mitsumasa Yonai (1940) (q.v.), Konoye (1940–1941), Hideki Tojo (1941–1944) (q.v.), Kuniaki Koiso (1944–1945) (q.v.), Kantaro Suzuki (1945) (q.v.), and Naruhiko Higashikuni (1945) (q.v.). Directing Japan's military effort was the Imperial General Headquarters (q.v.), composed of army and navy leaders. Created to join the political and military aspects of the war was the Liaison Conference, succeeded in 1944 by the Supreme War Direction Council (q.v.). From 1940 to 1945, the Imperial Rule Assistance Association (q.v.) replaced all political parties and worked to unify all citizens behind the government and the war effort. Following the Japanese surrender (q.v.) in 1945, the government operated under the supervision of the Supreme Commander for the Allied Powers (q.v.) until April 1952, when the Japanese peace treaty (q.v.) ended the Japanese occupation (q.v.). *See also* Intelligence, Japanese.

Japan

JAPAN, INVASION OF. Peaceful entry of U.S. troops in late August 1945, preceded by the development of war plans for massive assaults had Japan (q.v.) not surrendered. In the fall of 1944, U.S. military planners began to formulate arrangements for the invasion of the Japanese home islands (q.v.), code-named Downfall. They envisioned two major operations: the first, Olympic, an assault on the island of Kyushu, would be followed several months later by Coronet, an invasion of the island of Honshu. The unexpected length of the Leyte, Luzon, Iwo Jima, and Okinawa campaigns (qq.v.) postponed detailed preparations. On May 25, 1945, the United States Joint Chiefs of Staff (q.v.)

issued plans for Olympic, which was scheduled to begin on November 1, 1945, under the overall command of General of the Army Douglas MacArthur (q.v.), with the naval and amphibious phases to be directed by Fleet Admiral Chester W. Nimitz (q.v.). Following intensive air bombardment, the U.S. Sixth Army under General Walter Krueger (q.v.) was to land on Kyushu, where bases would be developed to support the Coronet operation in March 1946. To lead the ground invasion of Honshu that spring, the planners designated the U.S. Eighth Army under Lieutenant General Robert L. Eichelberger (q.v.) and the U.S. First Army under General Courtney H. Hodges, which was being redeployed from Europe to the Pacific. Reserve forces for later stages of the operation would be drawn from Australia, Canada, France, New Zealand, and the United Kingdom (qq.v.). Many aspects of the plans were incomplete at the time the war ended.

Although the Allied program to build an atomic bomb (q.v.) was well under way during the invasion planning, the JCS considered the weapon's completion, detonation, and impact on the war to be extremely uncertain. Some officials believed that naval and air power could force Japan's capitulation; others believed that a ground invasion would ultimately be necessary. Many involved in the planning process did not know about the atomic program or, like MacArthur and Nimitz, learned about its existence in July.

In early July, the JCS requested MacArthur and Nimitz to prepare contingency plans for a postsurrender invasion of Japan. MacArthur's plan, named Blacklist, was implemented in August 1945 following the Japanese surrender (q.v.).

JAPANESE AMERICANS. *Issei* (born in Japan) and *Nisei* (born in the United States [q.v.]). Following the attack on Pearl Harbor (q.v.), some members of the U.S. public and government regarded Japanese Americans, especially those living on the West Coast, as potential enemy agents and saboteurs. Executive Order 9066, which President Franklin D. Roosevelt (q.v.) signed on February 19, 1942, authorized the exclusion of selected persons from certain military areas in the United States. Subsequently, Lieutenant General John L. DeWitt, commander of the Western Defense Area, directed the evacuation of 120,000 Japanese Americans from their homes in California, Oregon, Washington, and Arizona. Leaving behind their businesses and other property, the Japanese Americans were transported to relocation centers and camps built in remote areas in Arizona, Arkansas, California,

Colorado, Idaho, Utah, and Wyoming. The most famous camp, Manzamar, was in California. Overseeing the resettlement process was the War Relocation Authority, which allowed some Japanese Americans to leave the camps for temporary agricultural work and others to move to locations in the eastern and midwestern parts of the country. At the end of the war, 44,000 Japanese Americans remained in the camps; the last were released in 1946.

In Hawaii, where one-third of the population had Japanese ancestors, Japanese Americans were not interned, with the exception of 1,000 *Issei,* who were transferred to the United States. In Canada, Mexico, and other parts of Latin America (qq.v.), people of Japanese descent came under varying degrees of governmental restrictions. At Japan's (q.v.) request, Spain represented Japanese interests in the United States, sending officials to inspect internment camps and investigate complaints by Japanese nationals. Sweden assumed the same responsibility for Japanese concerns in Hawaii, where Spain had no consulate. Under the auspices of Spain and Switzerland (q.v.), which protected U.S. citizens and property in Japan, the United States exchanged 4,700 internees with Japan during the war.

Many Japanese Americans served with distinction in the U.S. armed forces. Highly decorated units fought in North Africa and Europe, most notably the 442d Regimental Combat Team. In the war against Japan, Japanese Americans served mostly in the Military Intelligence Service, where they worked with signal intelligence (q.v.), interrogated prisoners of war (q.v.), translated captured documents, and issued propaganda. They participated in all major campaigns in the Pacific, serving also with the Dixie Mission in China (qq.v.) and with Detachment 101 of the Office of Strategic Services in Burma (qq.v.). *See also* Japanese Canadians.

JAPANESE CANADIANS. Relocated by the Canadian government during the war. In December 1941, 23,000 people of Japanese ancestry lived in Canada (q.v.), mostly in British Columbia. The government began to move Japanese men of military age to inland work camps in January 1942. The following month, the rest of the Japanese Canadians in British Columbia were relocated to camps farther east, where they lived under stark conditions. Most of their property was confiscated. Canada repatriated 4,000 internees to Japan (q.v.); the others remained in detention during the rest of the war. They were allowed to return to British Columbia in 1947.

JAPANESE COMBINED FLEET. Main combat organization of the Japanese navy. The fleet's commanders included Admiral Isoruku Yamamoto (1939–1943), Admiral Mineichi Koga (1943–1944), Admiral Soemu Toyoda (1944–1945), and Admiral Jisaburo Ozawa (1945) (qq.v.). *See also* Leyte Gulf, Battle of; Midway, Battle of; *Tokko.*

JAPANESE HOME ISLANDS. The four main islands of Hokkaido (the northernmost), Honshu, Shikoku, and Kyushu (the southernmost). Tokyo (q.v.), the capital, is on the largest and most heavily populated island of Honshu. The Inland Sea lies between Honshu, Shikoku, and Kyushu. To the south and west of Kyushu is the East China Sea. West of the home islands is the Sea of Japan, which also borders Korea and the Union of Soviet Socialist Republics (qq.v.). To the north, the Sea of Okhotsk separates Hokkaido from the Kurile Islands (q.v.), Sakhalin (q.v.), and the Soviet mainland. The terms of the Japanese surrender (q.v.) in 1945 restricted Japan's sovereignty to the four main islands and smaller adjacent ones. The Allied military occupation of the home islands lasted from August 1945 to April 1952. The following year, the United States (q.v.) returned to Japan part of the Ryukyu Islands, which had belonged to Japan since 1879. The rest of the Ryukyus, including Okinawa (q.v.) reverted to Japanese control in 1972. *See also* Japan, Invasion of; Japanese Occupation; Japanese Peace Treaty.

JAPANESE INTERNMENT. *See* JAPANESE AMERICANS; JAPANESE CANADIANS; LATIN AMERICA; MEXICO; PRISONERS OF WAR HELD BY ALLIES.

JAPANESE OCCUPATION. U.S.-dominated military occupation of the Japanese home islands (q.v.), August 1945–April 1952. Heading the occupation was the Supreme Commander for the Allied Powers (SCAP) (q.v.), a position held by General of the Army Douglas MacArthur (1945–1951) (q.v.) and Lieutenant General Matthew B. Ridgway (1951–1952). U.S. government directives, originated by the State-War-Navy Coordinating Committee and other agencies, were relayed to SCAP by the United States Joint Chiefs of Staff (q.v.). Providing limited advice from Washington was the Far Eastern Commission, composed of delegates from Australia, Canada, China, France, India, the Netherlands, New Zealand, the Philippines, the Union of Soviet Socialist Republics, the United Kingdom, and the United States. (qq.v.). In Tokyo, representatives of the British Commonwealth, China, the United States, and the U.S.S.R. comprised the Allied Council for Japan, an advisory body with marginal authority. The Soviet mission in Japan, headed by Lieutenant General Kuzma N. Derevyanko, repeatedly but futilely complained about its exclusion from power in the occupation. In contrast to the postwar situation in Germany, the United States tightly controlled Allied participation in Japan, both diplomatically and militarily.

In late August 1945, U.S. forces began to move into Japan, in accordance with the Blacklist invasion plan designed by MacArthur. The primary responsibility for the military occupation was assigned to the U.S. Eighth Army, commanded by Lieutenant General Robert L. Eichelberger (q.v.) until 1948. During the first months of the occupation, General Walter Krueger's (q.v.) U.S. Sixth Army also served in Japan. From 1946 to 1950, Australia, India, New Zealand, and the United Kingdom contributed soldiers and airmen to the British Commonwealth Occupation Force in Japan. The United States denied Soviet demands to station large numbers of Soviet soldiers in Japan.

At the conclusion of the war, civilians in the Japanese home islands faced severe food shortages, rampant inflation, and public health crises. Fifteen million people were homeless due to the strategic air campaign (q.v.). Allied forces entering the country had to deal immediately with these problems, as well as releasing and sending home the Allied internees and prisoners of war (q.v.). They sought to return Korean and Chinese laborers in Japan to their home countries and to repatriate the millions of Japanese civilians and military personnel in locations throughout Asia and the Pacific. Lack of shipping delayed many of these transfers, as well as the Allied need for labor and Soviet refusal to permit prompt repatriation of the Japanese it captured in Manchuria (q.v.). The military forces also disarmed the Japanese, destroyed caches of weapons and poison gas (q.v.), and cleared mines (q.v.) from the waters around the country.

From 1945 to 1947, the occupation focused on the demilitarization, democratization, and reform of Japan. As much as possible, SCAP used the existing Japanese governmental structure to execute his orders, while purging numerous officials due to their past ultranationalist or militarist associations. The most visible Japanese public official during the occupation was Shigeru Yoshida (q.v.), who served several terms as prime minister. Emperor Hirohito (q.v.) remained on the throne, although he was forced to renounce his divinity. Under American guidance, the Japanese adopted a constitution renouncing war, effective May 3, 1947. Among other reforms undertaken by SCAP were the disbanding of the armed forces, the dissolution of the *zaibatsu* (key families dominating industry and transportation), the proscription of militarism and ultranationalism in the schools, the decentralization of education, changes in land distribution and ownership, the extension of the vote to women, and the elimination of state Shinto as Japan's official religion. During the same period, the Allies (q.v.) began their prosecution of war crimes (q.v.) and imposed reparations on Japan.

In 1947–1948, the occupation underwent a "reverse course," changing its emphasis from reform to rehabilitation, especially in the economic sphere. With the cold war under way and communist groups gaining increased influence in China and throughout Asia, the United States decided to halt its more disruptive occupation reforms, restrain the growth of the Japanese communist party, assist the country economically, and rebuild Japan into a capitalistic, democratic ally in Asia. Japan's economy received an enormous boost during the Korean War (1950–1953), when Allied forces used Japanese bases, industries, and personnel to support the war effort. In September 1951, when the Japanese peace treaty (q.v.) was concluded, the United States and Japan signed a security pact. The peace treaty went into effect on April 28, 1952, officially ending the occupation.

JAPANESE PEACE TREATY. Agreement formally ending the war between the Allied powers and Japan (qq.v.) on April 28, 1952. Following the formal Japanese surrender (q.v.) on September 2, 1945, Allied military forces occupied the Japanese home islands (q.v.). Although nominally an Allied endeavor, the Japanese occupation (q.v.) was largely directed by the U.S. government through the Supreme Commander for the Allied Powers (SCAP), U.S. General of the Army Douglas MacArthur (qq.v.). In 1947, the United States (q.v.) began to work on a peace treaty and hosted the San Francisco Conference on September 4–8, 1951. Representatives of 48 countries signed the treaty, and the occupation of Japan ended on April 28, 1952. In the accord, Japan relinquished claims to Korea, Formosa, the Pescadores Islands, the Kurile Islands, southern Sakhalin, and the Pacific mandates (qq.v.) from World War I. Japan also pledged to follow the charter of the United Nations organization (q.v.). On the day the peace treaty was signed, the United States and Japan concluded a security pact to provide for the continued stationing of U.S. troops in Japan. At the same time, the United States also entered into security agreements with Australia, New Zealand, and the Philippines (qq.v.).

Not invited to the San Francisco Conference was the Chinese government headed by Mao Tse-tung (q.v.), which the United States did not recognize as the legitimate government of China (q.v.). India, Burma (qq.v.), and Yugoslavia refused to attend the conference. India, which protested the Chinese exclusion, negotiated a separate treaty with Japan, signing it on June 6, 1952. Burma based its nonparticipation on the continued presence of U.S. troops in Japan; it reached a peace agreement with Japan on November 5, 1954, which provided for Japanese reparations to Burma. The countries that sent representatives to the San Francisco Conference but did not sign the treaty were the Union of Soviet Socialist Republics (q.v.), Czechoslovakia, and Poland. On April 29, 1952, Japan signed a peace treaty with Chiang Kai-shek's (q.v.) Republic of China. It concluded a treaty with the People's Republic of China on August 12, 1978.

In 1955, Japan and the U.S.S.R. began negotiations regarding a peace treaty. Among the issues dividing them were territorial disputes, the Soviet refusal to repatriate or account for Japanese prisoners of war (q.v.), including many soldiers and workers captured at the close of the war, the suppression of the Japanese communist party, and Japan's recognition of Chiang Kai-shek's government rather than Mao's Chinese government. Japan wanted the Soviets to return southern Sakhalin, the southern Kuriles, the Hobomai Islands, and Shikotan, but the U.S.S.R. would not discuss Sakhalin and the Kuriles. The two countries agreed to normalize relations in 1956 but did not sign a peace treaty. Following the Soviet agreement, Japan was allowed to become a member of the United Nations.

JAPANESE PERUVIANS. *See* LATIN AMERICA.

JAPANESE SURRENDER. Formally signed by the Japanese government on September 2, 1945. At the First Cairo Conference (q.v.) in November 1943, the Allies (q.v.) called for Japan's unconditional surrender in the Cairo Declaration, which also detailed plans to divest Japan of most of its territorial acquisitions. Following the Japanese loss of Saipan (q.v.) and the fall of the Hideki Tojo (q.v.) government in July 1944, a number of Japanese officials increasingly believed that Japan should negotiate an end to the war to ensure the retention of the emperor and significant parts of the empire. Beginning in early 1945,

Emperor Hirohito (q.v.) consulted with the *jushin* (q.v.), or senior statesmen, regarding the end of the war. During 1944 and 1945, the governments of Kuniaki Koiso and Kantaro Suzuki (qq.v.) tried unsuccessfully to conclude the conflict in China (q.v.), while they initiated abortive peace feelers toward the Allies (q.v.) through Swedish, Swiss, and Soviet channels. Japanese diplomatic efforts in the summer of 1945 focused on the Union of Soviet Socialist Republics (q.v.), where Ambassador Naotake Sato (q.v.) futilely attempted to obtain the cooperation of Foreign Minister Vyacheslav M. Molotov (q.v.) to mediate a settlement, in which former Prime Minister Fumimaro Konoye (q.v.) would represent Emperor Hirohito. During the same period, the U.S.S.R. was secretly transferring huge numbers of men and equipment from Europe to the Manchurian border in preparation for war against Japan.

During the last months of the war, much of the Japanese government and high command remained committed to continuing the war, even as the Allied strategic air campaign (q.v.), naval gun bombardment, mining of Japanese waters, and blockade of the home islands intensified. The United States, the United Kingdom (qq.v.), and China issued the Potsdam Proclamation (q.v.) on July 26, 1945, calling for Japan to surrender unconditionally or face destruction. On August 6 and 9, 1945, the United States dropped atomic bombs (q.v.) on the Japanese cities of Hiroshima and Nagasaki (qq.v.). The U.S.S.R. notified Japan on August 8 of its declaration of war, which took effect on August 9; early that morning, an enormous Soviet military force attacked the Kwantung Army (q.v.) in Manchuria. The U.S. strategic bombing of Japan continued.

Japanese leaders remained divided on the question of surrender as exemplified in the deadlocked Supreme War Direction Council (q.v.). On the night of August 9–10, Emperor Hirohito stated during an imperial conference that he wished Japan to end the war. Later on August 10, the Japanese transmitted their first surrender offer, conditioned on the retention of the emperor, to the United States and China through the Swiss government and to the United Kingdom and the U.S.S.R. through the Swedish government. In response, U.S. Secretary of State James F. Byrnes (q.v.) refused to guarantee the position of the emperor, who would be compelled to submit to the authority of the Supreme Commander for the Allied Powers (q.v.). With many officials still opposed, the emperor again urged compliance with the terms. The Japanese government then notified the Allies of its agreement on August 14, although an unsuccessful military coup tried to abrogate the decision. On August 15, the emperor announced the news of the surrender to the Japanese people in a radio broadcast.

In late August, American military forces began to arrive in Japan. The official surrender ceremony took place on September 2, 1945, aboard the battleship USS *Missouri* in Tokyo Bay. Accepting the surrender on behalf of the Allied powers was U.S. General of the Army Douglas MacArthur (q.v.). Representing the United States was Fleet Admiral Chester W. Nimitz (q.v.). Other Allied countries signing the document were Australia, Canada (qq.v.), China, France, the Netherlands, New Zealand (qq.v.), the United Kingdom, and the U.S.S.R. Also present were U.S. General Jonathan M. Wainwright and British Lieutenant General Arthur E. Percival (qq.v.), who had been prisoners of war (q.v.) since 1942. Attending for Japan were Foreign Minister Mamoru Shigemitsu (q.v.), who signed on behalf of the government and the emperor, and General Yoshijiro Umezu (q.v.), who represented the Imperial General Headquarters (q.v.).

Ceremonies took place in a number of other locations. Members of the Japanese imperial family had traveled to some of these places to convince the local commanders to surrender. The Kwantung Army in Manchuria surrendered to the U.S.S.R. on August 20. On September 3, General Tomoyuki Yamashita (q.v.) surrendered his Shobu forces in the Philippines (q.v.). The next day, the United States occupied Wake Island (q.v.). On September 9, Japanese forces in Korea (q.v.) south of the 38th parallel surrendered to the United States. Lieutenant General Yasuji Okamura (q.v.) relinquished control of Japanese forces in China to Nationalist General Ho Ying-chin (q.v.) on the same day; elsewhere in China, Nationalist and Communist troops competed, even battling each other, to assume control of Japanese-held areas. Also on September 9, Chinese military forces occupied Hanoi, in northern French Indochina (q.v.). Admiral Louis Mountbatten (q.v.) accepted the transfer of power in Singapore (q.v.) on September 12. On the following day, British and Indian occupation forces arrived in Saigon, in southern French Indochina. On September 16, Hong Kong (q.v.) was returned to the British, after negotiations with Chiang Kai-shek's (q.v.) government concerning which country would assume control. Australian and British forces accepted surrenders in other locations throughout Southeast Asia and the southern Pacific. Logistical difficulties and nationalistic movements prevented the prompt replacement of Japanese control by Allied forces in such areas as the

Netherlands East Indies (q.v.). In some cases, individual Japanese soldiers in isolated locations did not surrender for years. *See also* Manchurian Campaign (1945); Switzerland.

JAVA. Large central island in the Netherlands East Indies (q.v.), which the Japanese captured from the Allies (q.v.) in ground operations lasting from February 28 to March 9, 1942. The Netherlands (q.v.) administered its Indies territory from the capital of Batavia on Java, the area's most densely populated island, where they stationed most of their ground and naval forces. The new Allied ABDACOM (q.v.) theater also placed its headquarters on Java from January 15, 1942, until the theater's dissolution on February 25, when the Dutch reassumed the responsibility for the island's defense against the approaching Japanese. As the Allies lost the battles of the Java Sea and Sunda Strait (qq.v.), Japan landed its first troops on Java on February 28 and completed the capture of the island on March 9. Japan considered Java extremely important not only for its strategic location but also for its oil deposits, oil refineries, and other industries. The island remained under Japanese control throughout the war, as Dutch guerrilla missions to the island were unsuccessful. In September 1945, British forces encountered violent resistance when they arrived on Java to reestablish control on behalf of the Dutch.

JAVA SEA, BATTLE OF. Naval battle lasting from February 27 to March 1, 1942, in which Japanese forces defeated Allied ships attempting to stop the Japanese invasion of Java (q.v.). Learning that a massive Japanese armada was sailing to Java, where landings would occur on both the eastern and western sides, the Allied naval force in Java attempted to find and attack the transports. Commanded by Dutch Rear Admiral Karel Doorman, the Allied ships encountered the invasion force for eastern Java, and in actions spanning three days, they suffered severe losses (including the ship on which Doorman died) and delayed but failed to halt the Japanese landings that resulted in the rapid capture of the island. Two Allied ships that participated in much of the action then fought in the Battle of Sunda Strait (q.v.), which involved the Japanese force traveling to western Java. The remnants of ABDACOM's naval forces escaped to Australia and Ceylon (qq.v.).

JUSHIN. Japanese senior statesmen, who acted as an unofficial advisory council to Emperor Hirohito (q.v.) from the 1930s to 1945. Composed of former prime ministers, the lord keeper of the privy seal, and the president of the privy council, the *jushin* recommended new prime ministers and conferred with the emperor about major issues, such as the termination of the war. Although Japan (q.v.) did not surrender until August 1945, the emperor began to confer individually with the *jushin* in early 1945 to discuss the war situation. Several of the *jushin*, including former Prime Minister Fumimaro Konoye (q.v.), had been meeting separately since 1943 to try to engineer an end to the war. Most conferences of the *jushin* with the emperor were called by Koichi Kido (q.v.), the lord keeper of the privy seal from 1940 to 1945.

-K-

KAITEN. See TOKKO.

KAMIKAZE. Japanese suicidal air missions, used as an organized strategy from October 1944 to the end of the war. In kamikaze or "divine wind" attacks, the pilots usually tried to crash their bomb-laden planes into the decks of Allied ships. In accordance with the Bushido (q.v.) code, the kamikaze airmen were willing to die for the emperor and the defense of Japan (q.v.). The first coordinated kamikaze attacks occurred during the Allied invasion of Leyte in the Philippines (qq.v.) in October 1944. To defend against kamikazes during the Okinawa operation (q.v.) in the spring of 1945, the Allies (q.v.) instituted a system of radar (q.v.) picket ships to spot and try to destroy the Japanese planes before they could hit their principal targets, but kamikaze attacks still inflicted heavy casualties on the Allied naval forces. Kamikazes were the most effective of the *tokko* (q.v.), or "special attacks" used by the Japanese during the last part of the war.

KAWABE, MASAKAZU (1886–1965). Japanese general; chief of staff, China Expeditionary Army, 1938–1939, 1942–1943; commander, Burma Area Army, 1943–1944; commander of Army Air Forces, 1945. As overall commander of Japanese troops in Burma (q.v.), Kawabe authorized the offensive into India at Imphal (qq.v.) in March–July 1944. With this attack he intended to delay the planned British move into Burma by destroying Allied supplies at Imphal, but the operation was unsuccessful, resulting in huge casualties and failing to stop the British. After the disastrous Imphal offensive, Kawabe was recalled to Japan for the remainder of the war.

KEMPEI. *See* INTELLIGENCE, JAPANESE.

KENNEY, GEORGE CHURCHILL (1889–1977). United States Army general; commander, Allied Air Forces, Southwest Pacific Area, 1942–1945; commander, U.S. Fifth Air Force, 1942–1944; commander, U.S. Far East Air Forces, 1944–1945. From August 1942 to the end of the war, Kenney commanded American, Australian, New Zealand, and Dutch air forces under General Douglas MacArthur (q.v.) in the Southwest Pacific Area (q.v.), participating in the campaigns for New Guinea, the Solomon Islands, the Bismarcks, Morotai, and the Philippine Islands (qq.v.). In the Battle of the Bismarck Sea (q.v.), Kenney's forces destroyed a major Japanese convoy carrying reinforcements to New Guinea. Throughout the fight for New Guinea, his planes transported troops, supported landings, and performed a number of actions normally carried out by naval forces, which the theater lacked. In 1945, Kenney's aircraft also joined in the assault on Okinawa (q.v.) and the strategic air campaign (q.v.) against Japan (q.v.). Kenney's U.S. Far East Air Forces eventually included the Fifth, Seventh, and Thirteenth air forces. An aggressive and innovative commander, Kenney excelled in adapting his forces to the needs of the Pacific War. He is credited with the introduction of skip bombing (q.v.) and the parafrag bomb (q.v.) to the Pacific.

KHALKHIN-GOL. *See* NOMONHAN.

KIDO, KOICHI (1889–1977). Lord keeper of the privy seal, 1940–1945. After serving as minister of education and home minister, in 1940 Kido became lord keeper of the privy seal. In this position he functioned as Emperor Hirohito's (q.v.) closest adviser, meeting with him daily. Holders of his position were supposed to remain removed from politics, although Kido worked with the *jushin* (q.v.) to recommend new prime ministers. In July and August 1945, Kido favored a surrender in accordance with the Potsdam Proclamation (q.v.). After the resignation of Kantaro Suzuki's (q.v.) cabinet on August 15, 1945, Kido personally recommended that Naruhiko Higashikuni (q.v.) form a transition government to execute the surrender. Kido was imprisoned for war crimes (q.v.) by the Allies (q.v.) and released in 1955. *See also* Japanese Surrender.

KIMMEL, HUSBAND EDWARD (1881–1968). U.S. admiral; commander in chief, U.S. Pacific Fleet and U.S. Fleet, 1941. In February

1941, Kimmel assumed his command at Pearl Harbor on the island of Oahu in Hawaii. In the aftermath of the devastating Japanese attack on Pearl Harbor (q.v.) on December 7, 1941, he was removed from his post and accused of dereliction of duty. During and after the war, numerous civilian and military committees investigated the causes of the American losses at Pearl Harbor, with the U.S. Senate voting in May 1999 to clear him of all charges. He retired in early 1942.

KING, ERNEST JOSEPH (1878–1956). U.S. Fleet Admiral; commander in chief, Atlantic Fleet, 1941; commander in chief, U.S. Fleet, 1941–1945; chief of naval operations, 1942–1945. When the United States (q.v.) entered World War II, King headed the Atlantic Fleet, which was heavily engaged in undeclared warfare with German submarines (q.v.) trying to prevent American aid from reaching the United Kingdom (q.v.). In the aftermath of the Japanese attack on Pearl Harbor (q.v.), King was promoted to replace Admiral Husband E. Kimmel (q.v.) as commander in chief, U.S. Fleet, with headquarters in Washington instead of Hawaii, where Kimmel had been based. The position of chief of naval operations was added to his duties in March 1942, making him the only man to hold these posts concurrently. King also served as a member of the United States Joint Chiefs of Staff (JCS) and the Combined Chiefs of Staff (CCS) (qq.v.).

A firm believer in the importance of the war against Japan (q.v.) and the United States Navy's (q.v.) preeminent role in that conflict, King constantly pushed for more resources for the Pacific, in spite of the U.S. policy of "Europe First." His forcefulness and abrasiveness often led to conflicts with the British members of the CCS, especially during the wartime conferences (q.v.). Partly through King's efforts, the United States had more military personnel in the Pacific than in the war against Germany until December 1943, when the massive buildup for the invasion of France caused a rapid shift in the proportion of troops. He served as executive agent for the JCS in directing the Pacific Ocean Areas (q.v.) theater and worked closely with its commander, Fleet Admiral Chester W. Nimitz (q.v.). King strongly advocated the Guadalcanal operation (q.v.) in August 1942 and fought successfully for the Central Pacific (q.v.) drive toward the Japanese home islands (q.v.) in 1943–1945. During the last year of the war, he unsuccessfully opposed the addition of the British Pacific Fleet (q.v.) to the American naval forces approaching Japan.

In December 1944 King received five-star rank as Fleet Admiral. Shortly after the war he retired from active duty.

KING, W. L. MACKENZIE. *See* CANADA.

KINKAID, THOMAS CASSIN (1888–1972). U.S. admiral; commander, North Pacific Area (q.v.), 1943; commander, Seventh Fleet,
1943–1945. Arriving in Pearl Harbor (q.v.) several days after the
Japanese attack, Kinkaid participated in the Battles of the Coral Sea
and Midway and in the Solomons campaign (qq.v.). In January 1943,
he took command of the North Pacific Area (q.v.), where he directed
the successful recapture of Attu and Kiska in the Aleutian Islands
(q.v.) and advocated the use of the northern route to invade Japan
(q.v.). Kinkaid's next assignment, beginning in November 1943, was
to head the Allied Naval Forces in the Southwest Pacific Area (q.v.).
The main force under his command was the U.S. Seventh Fleet. After supporting operations in the Admiralty Islands, New Guinea, and
Morotai (qq.v.), Kinkaid's fleet landed ground forces on Leyte and
Luzon in the Philippines (qq.v.). As the Leyte operation got underway
in October 1944, Kinkaid's Seventh Fleet participated with Admiral
William F. Halsey's (q.v.) Third Fleet in the massive Battle for Leyte
Gulf (q.v.). When the war ended, Kinkaid was involved in naval plan-
ning for the projected invasion of Japan (q.v.). He represented the
United States Navy (q.v.) at the surrender of Japanese forces in south-
ern Korea (q.v.).

KISKA. *See* ALEUTIAN ISLANDS.

KNOX, WILLIAM FRANKLIN (1874–1944). U.S. secretary of the
navy, 1940–1944. A longtime newspaperman and influential Republican, Knox ran unsuccessfully for vice president on the Republican
ticket in 1936. Four years later, he agreed to Democratic President
Franklin D. Roosevelt's (q.v.) request that he serve as secretary of the
navy. At the same time, the president appointed Henry L. Stimson
(q.v.), another well-known Republican, as secretary of war, strength-
ening bipartisan support for his administration. Before the United
States (q.v.) entered the war, Knox strongly supported greater U.S. assistance to the Allies (q.v.). After the Pearl Harbor attack (q.v.) in December 1941, Knox traveled to Hawaii, where he decided to relieve
Admiral Husband E. Kimmel (q.v.) as head of the U.S. Fleet. He promoted Admirals Ernest J. King and Chester W. Nimitz (qq.v.) to take
over Kimmel's restructured commands. Knox died in April 1944 and
was succeeded by his deputy, James V. Forrestal.

KOGA, MINEICHI (1885–1944). Japanese admiral; commander in chief, Combined Fleet, 1943–1944. After U.S. pilots killed Admiral Isoruku Yamamoto (q.v.) in April 1943 by shooting down his plane, Koga was named to succeed him as commander of the Japanese Combined Fleet (q.v.). In keeping with policy, he wanted to use the Combined Fleet in a decisive battle but was unable to attempt such an action during his tenure. As Allied naval forces advanced, Koga tried to move his headquarters to the southern Philippines (q.v.), but his plane was lost in a storm on March 31, 1944. Admiral Soemu Toyoda (q.v.) then took over command of the fleet.

KOHIMA. Location of a small British base on an important supply route north of Imphal, India (qq.v.), attacked by the Japanese in March–June 1944. As part of a major offensive to take Imphal, the Japanese cut the critical road between Kohima and Imphal on March 29 and encircled Kohima, where a small garrison held out against a Japanese force that eventually included an entire division. Transport planes (q.v.) resupplied the Allied troops at Kohima until ground reinforcements broke through the Japanese lines on April 20. The Japanese retained control of the road to Imphal until June 5, when the major threat to Kohima ended.

KOISO, KUNIAKI (1880–1950). Japanese army general; governor general of Korea (q.v.), 1942–1944; prime minister, 1944–1945. Following the Allied capture of Saipan (q.v.) in July 1944, Koiso joined in the move to oust Hideki Tojo (q.v.) as prime minister. He succeeded Tojo in office and served until the following spring. Under his direction the Supreme War Direction Council (q.v.) was formed to coordinate the civilian and military parts of the government, which remained divided about the course of the war. Koiso wanted to extricate Japan (q.v.) from the war on acceptable terms, but his attempts to reach a settlement of the China (q.v.) war with Chiang Kai-shek (q.v.) were unsuccessful. Koiso also hoped to win a decisive military victory over the Allies and then to negotiate peace with the United States (q.v.), using the Union of Soviet Socialist Republics (q.v.) as an intermediary, but instead, during his tenure the Allies invaded the Palaus, the Philippine Islands, and Iwo Jima (qq.v.). Following the Allied landings on Okinawa (q.v.) on April 1, 1945, Koiso and the army disagreed about the appointment of the new army minister. When Koiso's attempt to add the position to his duties failed, he resigned. After the war Koiso was imprisoned by the Allies (q.v.) for war crimes (q.v.); he died in prison.

KOLOMBANGARA, BATTLE OF. *See* CARTWHEEL, OPERATION.

KOMANDORSKI ISLANDS, BATTLE OF. *See* ALEUTIAN ISLANDS.

KONOYE, FUMIMARO (1891–1945). Japanese prince and statesman; prime minister, 1937–1939, 1940–1941. Under Konoye as prime minister, Japan engaged in war with China (q.v.), proclaimed the New Order in East Asia, joined the Axis powers (q.v.) in the Tripartite Pact (q.v.), signed a nonaggression treaty with the Union of Soviet Socialist Republics (q.v.), and established the Imperial Rule Assistance Association (q.v.) to unify and mobilize the Japanese people in support of the government. Konoye's government also negotiated futilely with the United States (q.v.) about mutual grievances. In July 1941, the U.S. government froze Japanese assets because of Japan's move into the southern part of French Indochina (q.v.). In October 1941, with his cabinet divided about the advisability of war with the United States, Konoye resigned and was succeeded by Hideki Tojo (q.v.). Although holding no formal position during the rest of the war, he increasingly advised negotiations with the Allies (q.v.) to end the conflict and influenced the selection of Kantaro Suzuki (q.v.) as prime minister in April 1945. Konoye agreed in the summer of 1945 to travel to the U.S.S.R. as Emperor Hirohito's (q.v.) special envoy to negotiate peace terms, with the U.S.S.R. acting as intermediary with the Allies; the Soviets, however, delayed their cooperation and then declared war on Japan. In December 1945, after his arrest on a possible charge of war crimes (q.v.), Konoye committed suicide. *See also* Japanese Surrender.

KOREA. Peninsula on the Asian mainland across the Sea of Japan from Japan (q.v.), which annexed it in 1910. At Changkufeng (q.v.) near the northeastern border of Korea, Japanese and Soviet troops fought a territorial dispute in the summer of 1938. No other battles, except for domestic resistance to the Japanese occupation, were fought in Korea until August 1945, when Soviet troops invaded. Throughout its occupation of Korea, Japan exploited the country economically and used many of its people as forced laborers in Korea, in Japan, and overseas. During the war, Japan also sent many Korean women to its occupied areas as "comfort women" (q.v.), or forced prostitutes, for Japanese troops. A number of Koreans also served in the armed forces of Japan, Nationalist China, and Communist China.

After the Union of Soviet Socialist Republics (q.v.) went to war against Japan on August 9, 1945, its troops swept into Manchuria, southern Sakhalin (qq.v.), and northern Korea, taking the ports of Rashin and Yuki on August 12. In moving southward along the Korean peninsula, Soviet forces advanced south of the 38th parallel, the dividing line agreed to by the Soviet Union and the United States (q.v.). The Soviet troops soon withdrew from the area south of the parallel, which U.S. troops were to occupy after Japan's capitulation. On September 9, the governor-general of Korea, former prime minister Nobuyuki Abe, formally surrendered all Japanese forces south of the 38th parallel to the United States, represented by Lieutenant General John R. Hodge, Admiral Thomas C. Kinkaid (q.v.), and Vice Admiral Daniel E. Barbey (q.v.). Hodge's XXIV Corps served as the occupation force.

Although the Allies had agreed to Korea's eventual independence at the First Cairo Conference (q.v.), the onset of the cold war led to the proclamation of two Korean nations: a communist country in the north, which Soviet troops had occupied at the close of the war; and a capitalist country in the south, sponsored by the United States. The establishment of the different countries, far from resolving Korea's problems, was followed by the Korean War (1950–1953) and an armed truce.

KRUEGER, WALTER (1881–1967). United States Army general; commander, Sixth Army, 1943–1945. An expert in training military forces, Krueger arrived in the Southwest Pacific Area (q.v.) theater in early 1943 to command the new U.S. Sixth Army. Theater commander General Douglas MacArthur (q.v.) bypassed Australian General Thomas A. Blamey (q.v.), his Allied Land Forces commander, by creating the Alamo Force to report directly to him. He named Krueger to lead Alamo Force, which consisted basically of the Sixth Army. Beginning with Operation Cartwheel (q.v.) in June 1943, Krueger commanded major offensives in New Guinea, New Britain, the Admiralty Islands, Morotai, and the Philippine Islands (qq.v.), where his Sixth Army was the major force in the recapture of Leyte and Luzon (qq.v.). Plans for the projected ground invasion of Japan scheduled the Sixth Army under Krueger's command to spearhead the assault. After the war, Krueger held occupation responsibilities in Japan and retired in 1946. *See also* Japan, Invasion of.

KULA GULF, BATTLE OF. *See* CARTWHEEL, OPERATION.

KUNMING. Chief city in Yunnan province in southern China (q.v.) and terminal point of the Burma Road (q.v.). Important as a training and transportation center, Kunming was also the destination of the Allied airlift over the Hump (q.v.), which transferred vital supplies from India into China when the overland route of the Burma Road was closed. During Japan's Operation Ichigo (q.v.) offensive in 1944–1945, Kunming was considered vulnerable but was protected by the efforts of Lieutenant General Albert C. Wedemeyer (q.v.), head of the China theater (q.v.).

KUOMINTANG. Chinese Nationalist political party headed by Chiang Kai-shek (q.v.). From 1928 to 1949, the Nationalists controlled parts of China (q.v.), while they were challenged by Chinese Communists, regional warlords, and the Japanese army. The civil war between the Nationalists and the Communists intensified after Japan's (q.v.) defeat and ended in 1949–1950, when Chiang and many of his followers moved the Nationalist government to Formosa (q.v.).

KURILE ISLANDS. Archipelago bounded by the Union of Soviet Socialist Republic's (q.v.) Kamchatka peninsula to the north and the Japanese island of Hokkaido to the south. In 1855, Japan (q.v.) occupied the southernmost islands and 20 years later acquired the northern part of the chain. Japanese used air and naval bases in the Kuriles to support various wartime operations, such as the Pearl Harbor attack (q.v.) and the occupation of Attu and Kiska in the Aleutian Islands (q.v.). From July 1943 to 1945, U.S. forces of the Northern Pacific Area (q.v.) carried out air and naval attacks against the Kuriles bases.

Soviet forces invaded the Kuriles on August 18, 1945, and took control of the islands by September 4. The Kuriles were officially transferred to the U.S.S.R. in accordance with Premier Joseph V. Stalin's demand at the Yalta Conference (qq.v.). Japan repeatedly but futilely requested that the southern islands in the Kuriles, where its claims were strongest, be returned to Japanese sovereignty. The U.S.S.R. did not sign the main Japanese peace treaty (q.v.) in 1951 or conclude a separate agreement with Japan; ownership of the Kuriles remained one of the issues in dispute between the countries.

KURUSU, SABURO (1888–1954). Japanese diplomat. As Japan's (q.v.) ambassador to Germany (q.v.), Kurusu helped to negotiate the

Tripartite Pact (q.v.) in 1940. In November 1941, he joined Ambassador Kichisaburo Nomura (q.v.) in Washington, D.C., to conduct peace negotiations with Secretary of State Cordell Hull (q.v.). Interned after the Pearl Harbor attack (q.v.) in December, he was repatriated to Japan and soon retired.

KWAI RIVER. *See* BURMA-THAILAND RAILWAY.

KWAJALEIN. *See* MARSHALL ISLANDS.

KWANTUNG ARMY. Japanese army stationed in Manchuria. From its original mission to protect the Japanese-owned South Manchurian Railway, the Kwantung Army evolved into a highly political force almost independent of the government in Tokyo (q.v.). Believing that Japan should expand aggressively on the continent, some of its members provoked the "Mukden Incident" of 1931 that resulted in the war that separated Manchuria from China (q.v.); the province then became a Japanese puppet state named Manchukuo (q.v.). Officers of the Kwantung Army, notably Hideki Tojo (q.v.), its chief of staff, were involved in the beginning of the full-scale Sino-Japanese War in July 1937. The army also fought the Union of Soviet Socialist Republics (q.v.) in border disputes at Changkufeng (q.v.) in 1938 and near Nomonhan (q.v.) in 1939. During the war of 1941–1945, Japan tried to keep large forces in Manchuria to deter a Soviet attack, but when the U.S.S.R. declared war on Japan in August 1945, the invading Soviet forces totally overwhelmed the Kwantung Army under General Otozo Yamada (q.v.). Although the Kwantung Army was still large when the Soviet offensives began, its veteran troops and commanders had been transferred to reinforce Pacific areas and to defend the Japanese home islands (q.v.). The Soviet forces defeated the Japanese decisively and caused extremely high casualties. The Kwantung Army surrendered on August 20, 1945. Many of its members were subsequently held for many years by the U.S.S.R., which refused to repatriate the soldiers while using them as forced labor and trying some of them for war crimes (q.v.). *See also* Manchuria Campaign (1931–1932); Manchuria Campaign (1945).

KYUSHU. *See* JAPAN, INVASION OF; JAPANESE HOME ISLANDS; NAGASAKI.

-L-

LANDING CRAFT AND SHIPS. Vessels designed to transport men and equipment to a beach during an amphibious operation. Prior to the entry of the United States (q.v.) into the war, the Japanese had developed and used landing craft in some of its Chinese operations. After their swift expansion throughout Southeast Asia and the Pacific in late 1941 and 1942, the Japanese employed many landing craft to resupply their forces in coastal areas where Allied planes were dominant. They also converted some of the vessels to serve as gunboats, torpedo boats, and patrol boats for anti-submarine warfare. One of the best-known types was the *daihatsu,* which was 48 feet long, traveled at 7 knots, and could carry 70 men, 10 tons of cargo, or 1 light tank (q.v.). Its steel hull had a hinged ramp at the bow to deposit troops and equipment directly on the shore. Craft with similar designs ranged from 35 to 58 feet in length.

Before the United States entered the war, the United States Marines (q.v.) had worked with Andrew J. Higgins (q.v.) and his shipbuilding company to design experimental landing craft. The British had requested American factories to build landing ships that could transport tanks to European shores and landing craft suitable for short operations in the English Channel. Some developmental work had also been done with amphibious vehicles. In December 1941, however, the United States possessed very few landing craft. Soon after the Pearl Harbor (q.v.) attack, the United States dramatically escalated its production, both for itself and the Allies (q.v.). Although other Allied countries also manufactured such vessels, shortages in landing craft and ships throughout the war limited a number of Allied offensives.

The smaller landing craft used to transport men and equipment to the shore were generally carried to the landing area by larger vessels. The landing craft, vehicle and personnel (LCVP), was a shallow-draft boat designed primarily to bring infantry forces to the beach, where it could operate in three or four feet of water, and then to repeat the trip to carry additional troops. Also known as the "Higgins boat," the standard LCVP was developed prior to U.S. entry into the war and underwent improvements during the conflict. The LCVP was 36 feet in length and could transport 8,100 pounds of cargo or 36 troops. Its maximum speed was 9 knots. Similar in size and speed were the landing craft, vehicle (LCV), which could carry 36 people, 1 truck, or 10,000 pounds of cargo; and the landing craft, personnel (ramp), or LCP (R). The landing craft, mechanized (LCM), like the LCVP called a "Higgins boat," was 50 feet long, could achieve a speed of 11 knots, and could accommodate one medium tank, 60 men, or 60,000 pounds of equipment. The landing craft, tank (LCT), was 118 feet long, had a speed of 6 knots, and could haul 150 tons of cargo, including medium tanks. The landing craft, infantry (large), or LCI (L), could travel longer distances than the smaller craft, reaching a top speed of 14 knots. It was 158 feet long and conveyed 188 troops (in addition to its crew) to the shore, where it used two ramps to unload the men. Some LCIs were converted to rocket ships, or LCI (R)s, which shot rockets (q.v.), set up smoke screens, and fought fires on ships and land.

Larger ships transported landing craft to the assault area and could move men and equipment directly between two shores. Among the oceangoing vessels was the widely used landing ship, tank (LST), considered by some to be the most important amphibious vessel. Based on a British design, the LST transported both people and equipment, as well as smaller landing craft and amphibious vehicles, directly to the beach. It was 328 feet in length, traveled at 10 knots, and held 160 troops. Some LSTs were converted to serve as repair or hospital ships. The landing ship, medium (LSM), was 203 feet long, carried 60 men, and transported tanks and amphibious vehicles to the shore.

Also facilitating amphibious landings was the landing ship, dock (LSD), which did not actually travel to the beach. It delivered landing craft, amphibious vehicles, and troops to the assault area, from which the craft or vehicles proceeded to the shore. The LSD was 457 feet long, carried 240 men, and traveled at 15 knots. Also employed to convey landing craft and men to the assault area were ships converted for the purpose, such as the APD, or high-speed transport. Originally a destroyer, the APD was 314 feet long and could hold LCP (R)s and 200 men. Its top speed was 23 knots. Other converted designs were the APA, or attack transport, and the AKA, or attack cargo ship.

Highly important in amphibious assaults (q.v.) was the landing vehicle, tracked (LVT), an amphibian tractor commonly known as an amtrac. During the 1930s, Donald Roebling developed an amphibious vessel called the alligator; a later version was named the buffalo. The LVT entered production in July 1941. Valued for its ability to travel across coral reefs, its original role was to carry troops and equipment, but after the Gilbert Islands (q.v.) campaign, LVTs were given heavy armor, equipped with guns or howitzers, and often used as tanks during amphibious assaults. An LVT normally carried 30 troops and was frequently carried to the assault area by an LST. Also widely used in the war against Japan was the army-sponsored amphibious truck called the Dukw or Duck. It transported supplies and equipment, especially ammunition; evacuated casualties directly from the field to the hospital ship; and, beginning in late 1943, often carried rocket launchers during amphibious assaults. LVTs and Dukws were conveyed to the assault area by LSTs, LSDs, LCVPs, and other vessels.

LATIN AMERICA. Prior to December 1941, Japan traded extensively with Latin American countries, especially Argentina, Brazil, Chile, Mexico (q.v.), and Peru. As its prewar tensions with the United States (q.v.) grew, Japan increased its diplomatic presence in Latin America, where many people of Japanese descent lived. Latin American nations, especially Argentina and Chile, also had significant economic and political ties with Germany and Italy (qq.v.), which also had sent numerous emigrants to the region.

The United States considered the security of the Western Hemisphere to be an essential element in its national defense and sought to counter the potential Axis (q.v.) threat by negotiating prewar agreements with Latin American countries regarding military bases and security. With congressional authorization, the U.S. Federal Bureau of Investigation (FBI), through its Special Intelligence Service, began to operate in Latin America in 1940 and continued its intelligence (q.v.) work during the war. U.S. relations with Latin America benefited enormously from the "Good Neighbor" policy inaugurated by Secretary of State Cordell Hull (q.v.) in the 1930s. Another important figure was Nelson A. Rockefeller, who served as coordinator of the Office of Inter-American Affairs (1940–1944) and assistant secretary of state for Latin America (1944–1945). In these positions, Rockefeller handled propaganda, humanitarian assistance, and economic aid.

Upon U.S. entry into the war, the U.S. State Department called the Rio de Janiero Conference (q.v.) of the American republics, which agreed to break diplomatic relations with the Axis countries and to establish the Inter-American Defense Board. Within a short time after the conference, all nations had severed relations except for Argentina and Chile, which did so much later. From February 21 to March 8, 1945, representatives of all American countries but Argentina met in the Inter-American Conference on Problems of War and Peace at the Chapultepec Castle, Mexico City. They agreed to the Act of Chapultepec, a mutual security pact to last throughout the war. On March 27, 1945, Argentina became the last Latin American country to declare war against the Axis powers.

In addition to providing a secure flank for the United States during the war, Latin America also contributed vital raw materials (q.v.) to the war effort. Two countries sent armed forces overseas: Brazil to Europe and Mexico to the Philippines (q.v.). The network of air and naval bases in Latin America arranged by the United States proved more significant to the war against Germany and Italy than to the Pacific War. In return for their cooperation, Latin American nations received lend-lease (q.v.) aid from the United States, with the largest share going to Brazil.

As was the case in the United States and Canada (q.v.), people of Japanese ancestry became the focus of suspicion and fears about espionage after the Pearl Harbor attack (q.v.). Mexico removed its Japanese residents from the west coast and the U.S. border. In South America, the largest Japanese population was in Brazil, which confined some Japanese in internment camps. Peru, with the second-largest number of Japanese residents, treated them harshly, closing Japanese schools, canceling land leases, and imposing severe economic restrictions. As a further measure, in cooperation with the U.S. government, Peru deported about 1,700 Japanese Peruvians to U.S. internment camps. The deported internees ranged from Japanese diplomats to longtime community leaders and their families, who had been born in Peru. Some of their names appeared as potentially dangerous aliens on prewar lists compiled by Peruvian officials and the FBI. Eleven other nations also sent Japanese inhabitants to the United States, which received in all approximately 2,100 Latin American Japanese. The United States exchanged some of the Latin American Japanese for Americans who had been interned by Japan in Asia and the Pacific; others resisted repatriation to Japan. At the close of the war, the United States sent additional internees to Japan and tried to return the others to Latin America. Peru in particular refused to accept some of its deportees, who remained in the United States after the war.

LAUREL, JOSÉ PACIANO (1891–1959). President of the Philippines (q.v.), 1943–1945. After the Japanese invasion of the Philippines in December 1941, President Manuel Quezon and Vice President Sergio Osmeña (qq.v.) moved to the island of Corregidor in Manila Bay and later fled to the United States (q.v.), where they set up a government in exile. Laurel, a supreme court justice, remained in the Philippines and collaborated with the Japanese occupation. In a government set up by the Japanese, Laurel held the title of president from 1943 to 1945.

After a postwar amnesty policy cleared him of treason charges, he became active in politics and served in the Philippine Senate.

LEAHY, WILLIAM DANIEL (1875–1959). U.S. Fleet Admiral; chief of naval operations, 1937–1939; ambassador to Vichy France (q.v.), 1941–1942; chief of staff to U.S. president and chairman, United States Joint Chiefs of Staff (JCS) (q.v.), 1942–1949. After a distinguished naval career including a term as chief of naval operations, Leahy retired in 1939. The next year President Franklin D. Roosevelt (q.v.), a longtime friend, appointed him to the politically sensitive position of ambassador to Vichy France, which he began in January 1941. After the deterioration of relations between the United States (q.v.) and the Vichy regime, Roosevelt called Leahy home to hold the new positions of chief of staff to the president and chairman of the JCS, which he assumed in July 1942. He also served as a member of the Combined Chiefs of Staff (CCS) (q.v.) and attended the major Allied conferences (q.v.), serving as alternate chairman of the CCS meetings. Throughout the war Leahy functioned as a liaison between the other JCS members and Roosevelt, whom he worked with daily and advised on military matters. After Roosevelt's death in April 1945, Leahy continued in his posts under President Harry S. Truman (q.v.), retiring in 1949.

LEDO ROAD. *See* STILWELL ROAD.

LEMAY, CURTIS EMERSON (1906–1990). United States Army and Air Force general; commander, XX Bomber Command, 1944–1945; commander, XXI Bomber Command, 1945. Before his transfer to Asia in the fall of 1944, LeMay won praise for his innovative leadership in the strategic air war against Germany and Italy (q.v.). In his Asian posts, LeMay commanded the Boeing B-29 Superfortresses (q.v.) used in the strategic air campaign (q.v.) against the Japanese home islands (q.v.) and Japanese-held areas. First based in India and China (qq.v.) with the XX Bomber Command, LeMay in early 1945 assumed command of the XXI Bomber Command in the Marianas (q.v.), where the United States (q.v.) had built B-29 bases after capturing the islands in 1944. LeMay worked to improve the impact of the bombing attacks against Japan, where the high-level daylight bombing methods used by the B-29s were hampered by poor visibility and proved highly inaccurate. The techniques LeMay developed for low-level incendiary bombing proved devastating to the Japanese cities constructed of wood. The most destructive raid occurred on the night of March 9–10, 1945, when much of Tokyo (q.v.) burned. After the war LeMay headed the Strategic Air Command and later served as chief of staff, U.S. Air Force. *See also* Strategic Air Campaign.

LEND-LEASE ACT. U.S. legislation sponsored by the Franklin D. Roosevelt (q.v.) administration and passed March 11, 1941, to provide aid to countries fighting the Axis powers (q.v.). The act authorized the U.S. government to accept any type of repayment it wished in exchange for aid, in contrast to previous laws requiring foreign countries to pay cash for their purchases. Created with the intention of helping the United Kingdom (q.v.), the program later included China, the Union of Soviet Socialist Republics, and other Allied powers (qq.v.), for a total of more than 40 countries. Continuing after the United States (q.v.) became a belligerent, lend-lease allowed the United States to use its vast production capabilities to serve as "the arsenal of democracy," according to Roosevelt. Among the materials covered were ammunition, aircraft, ships, trucks, tanks (q.v.), and food. U.S. lend-lease aid to the Allies totaled $50 billion. Many of the Allies provided reverse lend-lease to the United States in the form of raw materials (q.v.), labor, and food for U.S. troops abroad, with Australia providing more than it received. Reverse lend-lease equaled $7.8 billion.

LEYTE CAMPAIGN. Capture of the island of Leyte in the central Philippine Islands (q.v.) by U.S. forces of the Southwest Pacific Area (SWPA) (q.v.) theater, October 1944–May 1945. Under General Douglas MacArthur (q.v.), SWPA planned to capture Leyte and build airfields on it to support the more critical invasion of Luzon (q.v.). The Japanese forces on Leyte were led by Lieutenant General Sosaku Suzuki and reinforced by troops from Luzon, where General Tomoyuki Yamashita's (q.v.) Fourteenth Area Army was in charge of defending the Philippines. Yamashita preferred to yield control of Leyte and make his strongest defense on Luzon, but his superior, Field Marshal Hisaichi Terauchi (q.v.), ordered him to send additional troops to Leyte and challenge the invaders there. The Japanese navy also sent major forces to contest the invasion.

The fight for the island began with landings on October 20, 1944, which set off the enormous naval Battle for Leyte Gulf (q.v.) and the destruction of the Japanese fleet. From October until December, the U.S. Sixth Army under Lieutenant General Walter Krueger (q.v.) conducted offensive actions in Leyte. The U.S. Eighth Army then relieved the Sixth, which was scheduled to invade Luzon the next month.

Lieutenant General Robert L. Eichelberger (q.v.), commander of the Eighth Army, directed the rest of the campaign, which lasted until May and left most Japanese defenders dead. Suzuki had died the previous month when the ship evacuating him was sunk. Leyte's soil proved unsuitable for air bases, so U.S. forces captured the island of Mindoro on December 15, 1944, to provide air cover for the Luzon operation.

LEYTE GULF, BATTLE FOR. Largest naval engagement in history, occurring in the waters of the Philippine Islands (q.v.), October 23–26, 1944. As the forces of the Southwest Pacific Area (SWPA) (q.v.) theater began the reconquest of the Philippines with landings on Leyte (q.v.), the Japanese launched a major naval offensive to drive them away. SWPA's main naval force was the U.S. Seventh Fleet, under Vice Admiral Thomas C. Kinkaid (q.v.). To assist with the Philippine landings, Admiral Chester W. Nimitz (q.v.), head of the Pacific Ocean Areas (q.v.) theater, had loaned the U.S. Third Fleet commanded by Admiral William F. Halsey (q.v.). In a situation that caused communication and command problems during the Battle for Leyte Gulf, Halsey continued to report to Nimitz instead of to SWPA head Douglas MacArthur (q.v.), as Kinkaid did.

The Japanese high command designated the bulk of its surface fleet, arranged in four groups, to attack the invading forces. The Northern Force, under Vice Admiral Jisaburo Ozawa (q.v.), consisted largely of carriers (q.v.) with no aircraft, because of the severe Japanese losses sustained during the Battle of the Philippine Sea (q.v.). Acting as a decoy, Ozawa's force successfully drew Halsey's fleet away from Leyte and was severely damaged off Cape Engaño on October 25–26. During the time Halsey chased Ozawa, however, he was not in communication with Kinkaid, who was contending with other powerful Japanese forces. On October 24–25, Kinkaid's fleet nearly destroyed the Japanese Southern Force and Fifth Fleet in the Surigao Strait. Vice Admiral Takeo Kurita's Central Force, the most powerful of the Japanese fleets, encountered a small Allied force off Samar near the vulnerable Allied ships landing forces and equipment on Leyte. At a critical point, Kurita broke off the action and withdrew, while suffering further losses. As a result of the Japanese losses in the Leyte Gulf action—four carriers, three battleships, 10 cruisers, and nine destroyers (qq.v.)—the Japanese Combined Fleet (q.v.) could not mount another surface battle in the war. Among the lost ships was the superbattleship *Musashi*. One new element introduced during the Leyte action was Japanese kamikaze

Battle for Leyte Gulf, October 23–26, 1944

(q.v.) attacks on Allied ships, which became increasingly frequent and destructive during the rest of the war.

LIBERTY SHIPS. *See* MERCHANT MARINE.

LINDBERGH, CHARLES AUGUSTUS (1902–1974). U.S. aviator. Before the Japanese attack on Pearl Harbor (q.v.), Lindbergh opposed American involvement in the European War, spoke at isolationist rallies sponsored by the America First Committee, and resigned his commission as a colonel in the United States Army Air Corps Reserve. After the United States (q.v.) entered the war, President Franklin D. Roosevelt (q.v.), whom Lindbergh had challenged and criticized in his speeches, blocked his attempt to return to active duty in the armed forces. He then served as an adviser to various aircraft manufacturers. In 1944, he traveled as a civilian consultant to the Southwest Pacific Area (q.v.), where he worked with the air forces under Lieutenant General George C. Kenney (q.v.). There he tested fighter planes (q.v.) (especially the Lockheed P-38 Lightning), trained pilots to use fuel more effectively, and flew 50 combat missions before returning to the United States. In 1954, Lindbergh received the rank of brigadier general in the U.S. Air Force Reserve.

LOCKWOOD, CHARLES ANDREWS, JR. (1890–1967). U.S. admiral; commander, Submarines, Southwest Pacific, 1942–1943; commander, Submarines, Pacific Fleet, 1943–1945. Early in the war, Lockwood identified a major problem with American torpedoes (q.v.) and personally forced a correction of its defects. Under his leadership, American submarines (q.v.) in the Pacific effectively targeted Japanese merchant ships as well as combat vessels, sinking more than 1,300 during the war. The success of the submarine campaign crippled Japan's ability to supply its far-flung garrisons and to bring essential raw materials (q.v.) to the Japanese home islands (q.v.). *See also* Logistics; Merchant Marine.

LOGISTICS. Systems for supporting and supplying military forces, including transportation of men and matériel; provision of food, fuel, equipment, and ammunition; construction of bases and other facilities; communications; and care of personnel, including medical treatment. The war in Asia and the Pacific was an enormous logistical undertaking for both Japan and the Allied powers (qq.v.). It involved immense distances, difficult climates and types of terrain, and poorly charted areas. As the war progressed, the superiority of Allied logistics became a major advantage.

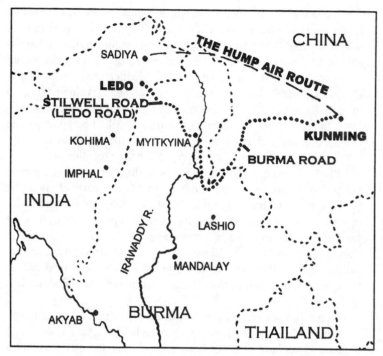

Stilwell (Ledo) Road and the Hump Air Route

Factors favoring the Allies included the huge production capability of the U.S. economy, when it became fully mobilized; the lend-lease (q.v.) system, which shared U.S. production with a number of Allied countries; the enormous reverse lend-lease provided by Australia and New Zealand (qq.v.); the relative security enjoyed by Allied shipping lanes in the Pacific, where Japan focused its main attacks on warships instead of cargo vessels; the merchant marine (q.v.); the transport planes (q.v.) that made possible such operations as the Hump airlift to China (qq.v.); and advances in medicine (q.v.). Also important was the vast U.S. military logistical system. Its largest element was the United States Army Services of Supply (later Army Service Forces), headed by Lieutenant General Brehon B. Somervell (q.v.). The United States Navy's (q.v.) systems for at-sea refueling and resupply enabled fleets to operate away from ports for extended periods of time. Throughout the war zone, the Army Corps of Engineers and the Navy Seabees constructed vital facilities and served in combat.

In Asia and the Pacific, the Allied logistical effort was hampered by the strategic priority on the war against Germany and Italy (qq.v.), which affected the weapons, shipping, and landing craft (q.v.) available to the forces opposing Japan. In many cases, newer weapons and technology went first to Europe and the Mediterranean, while agencies such as the Office of Scientific Research and Development (q.v.) initially focused their resources on solving problems in the same theaters. In spite of the increased production of Allied cargo ships, the demands of the global war always exceeded the available shipping, with landing craft also in short supply. With the exception of the Central Pacific (q.v.) offensives, shortages in shipping and landing craft affected plans for many operations against Japan, particularly in the Southeast Asia Command (q.v.). Logistics in the China-Burma-India (q.v.) theater suffered both from its low Allied priority as well as the Japanese successes in seizing the major railways and highways in Burma (q.v.) and much of China. At the time of the Japanese surrender (q.v.), the Allies were involved in the massive logistical task of shifting enormous forces from Europe, where the war ended in May, to the Pacific.

When Japan seized much of Southeast Asia and the Pacific in late 1941 and early 1942, it seriously overextended its logistic system. Not only did Japan have to resupply its widely separated garrisons, but it also had to maintain and increase the imports of food and raw materials (q.v.) that enabled the Japanese war industries to function. Although Japan had accomplished a major objective in capturing Southeast Asia's strategic raw materials, it could not fully exploit its acquisitions because of insufficient shipping. Prior to the war with the West, Japan had emphasized the building of warships rather than cargo ships, and its situation worsened when the Allies began to attack Japanese shipping. Although Japan attempted to substitute submarines (q.v.) and other vessels for cargo ships, it became unable to supply its military forces and industries. By the middle of the war, the Allies could replace lost pilots, planes, or ships; Japan could not. *See also* Alaska Highway; Burma Road; Science and Technology; Stilwell Road; United States Army; United States Navy.

LOMBOK STRAIT, BATTLE OF. *See* BADOENG STRAIT, BATTLE OF.

LOS NEGROS. *See* CARTWHEEL, OPERATION.

LUZON CAMPAIGN (1945). Allied operations to recapture the largest and northernmost island in the Philippine Islands (q.v.) from Japan (q.v.), January 9, 1945–August 1945. Prior to attacking Luzon, forces of the Southwest Pacific Area (SWPA) (q.v.) theater assaulted the Philippine islands of Leyte (q.v.) and Mindoro. On January 9, 1945, the U.S. Sixth Army under Lieutenant General Walter Krueger (q.v.) and elements of the U.S. Eighth Army began the invasion of Luzon. Transporting and covering the troops were 1,000 ships, which sustained damage and significant casualties from kamikaze (q.v.) attacks.

Opposing them was the Japanese Fourteenth Area Army under the

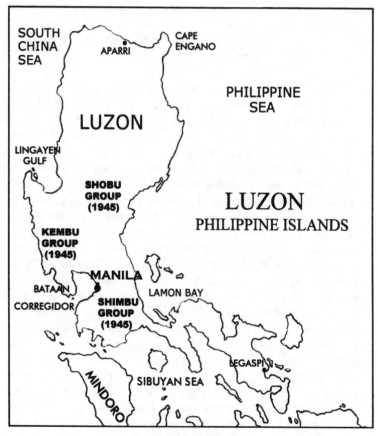

Luzon, Philippine Islands

command of General Tomoyuki Yamashita (q.v.), the conqueror of Malaya and Singapore (qq.v.) who intended to defend the island primarily from the mountainous areas. He divided his forces into three armies: Shimbu Group, east of Manila (q.v.); Kembu Group, Clark Field and west of Manila; and Shobu Group, north of the Luzon Central Plain. He personally commanded the largest, Shobu Group, in the northern mountains. Yamashita ordered the evacuation of Manila, but his orders were ignored by the city's naval commander, Rear Admiral Sanji Iwabuchi (q.v.), whose elite naval ground forces fought a savage month-long defense of the city. U.S. forces slowly made progress against Yamashita's forces: the Kembu Group was largely defeated by early March, most of the Shimbu Group was destroyed by early June, and the Shobu Group was pushed into the mountains of northwestern Luzon but was still a strong force of more than 50,000 when the war ended. Yamashita's Shobu group surrendered formally on September 3, 1945, after the capitulation of Japan.

LUZON VERSUS FORMOSA DEBATE. Strategic debate among U.S. military leaders in 1944 regarding the direction of the war in the Pacific. As the course of the war turned against Japan (q.v.) and U.S. strategists began to consider an eventual ground invasion of the Japanese home islands (q.v.), they recognized the need to acquire a large land area from which to mount the operation. Admiral Ernest J. King (q.v.) favored the seizure of the southern half of the island of Formosa (q.v.) or Fukien province on the eastern coast of China (q.v.), which lay opposite Formosa. The most vocal opponent of King's views, General Douglas MacArthur (q.v.), pushed instead for the recapture of Luzon (q.v.), the northernmost and largest island in the Philippine Islands (q.v.). In the spring and summer of 1944, Japanese advances in China during Operation Ichigo (q.v.) made the selection of Fukien province unlikely. King then argued for an invasion of southern Formosa as part of the Central Pacific (q.v.) drive, while MacArthur promoted the strategic value of the Philippines and the moral obligation of the United States (q.v.) to liberate its prisoners of war (q.v.), internees, and loyal Filipinos. At the Pearl Harbor conference (q.v.) in July 1944, Admiral Chester W. Nimitz (q.v.) and MacArthur discussed the issue with President Franklin D. Roosevelt and Admiral William D. Leahy (qq.v.). In the fall of 1944, the United States Joint Chiefs of Staff (q.v.) approved MacArthur's proposal to retake the Philippines. The island of Leyte (q.v.) was invaded in October 1944 in preparation for the assault of Luzon in January 1945.

-M-

MACARTHUR, DOUGLAS (1880–1964). U.S. General of the Army; commander, United States Army Forces in the Far East, 1941–1951; commander, Southwest Pacific Area, 1942–1945; commander in chief, United States Army Forces, Pacific, 1945; Supreme Commander for the Allied Powers in Japan, 1945–1951. After serving as army chief of staff, 1930–1935, MacArthur moved to the Philippine Islands (q.v.) to organize and advise the armed forces of the new commonwealth. He retired from the United States Army (q.v.) in 1937 while continuing to act as military adviser to the government of President Manuel Quezon (q.v.). In the summer of 1941, as tensions with Japan (q.v.) rose, President Franklin D. Roosevelt (q.v.) recalled MacArthur to active duty to command the United States Army Forces in the Far East, which included the nationalized Filipino troops. After the Japanese invaded the Philippines in December 1941, MacArthur directed the defense until March 1942, when he left the islands for Australia (q.v.) on Roosevelt's orders.

MacArthur remained in the Pacific during the rest of the war, commanding the Southwest Pacific Area (q.v.) theater and directing campaigns in New Guinea (q.v.), the Bismarcks, Morotai (q.v.), and the Philippines. The largest U.S. operation of the war with Japan was his recapture of the island of Luzon (q.v.) in the Philippines, which began in January 1945 and continued until the end of the war. In December 1944, MacArthur was elevated to General of the Army, a five-star rank. In an administrative reorganization in April 1945, MacArthur became commanding general of United States Army Forces in the Pacific and was designated to lead the projected ground invasion of Japan in November. When Japan capitulated in August 1945, MacArthur was named Supreme Commander for the Allied Powers in Japan (q.v.); in this capacity, he accepted the Japanese surrender (q.v.) on behalf of the Allied powers (q.v.) in a formal ceremony on the battleship USS *Missouri,* September 2, 1945.

From 1945 to 1951, MacArthur directed the Allied occupation of Japan; he also commanded the U.S. Far East Command, 1947–1951. When the Korean War broke out in 1950, he was given the additional job of heading the United Nations Command in defending South Korea. In 1951, President Harry S. Truman (q.v.) relieved MacArthur of all his commands, and he returned to the United States for the first time since 1937. *See also* Japan, Invasion of; Japanese Occupation.

MCCAIN, JOHN SIDNEY (1884–1945). U.S. admiral; commander of land-based aircraft, South Pacific, 1942; chief, Navy Bureau of Aeronautics, 1942–1943; deputy chief of naval operations for air, 1943–1944; commander, carrier forces, 1944; commander, Task Force 38 (Fast Carrier Force), 1944–1945. During the opening months of the campaign for Guadalcanal (q.v.), McCain directed naval air operations in the South Pacific Area (q.v.). After service in Washington, he returned to the Pacific in August 1944 to lead a carrier (q.v.) group under Vice Admiral Marc A. Mitscher's (q.v.) Fast Carrier Force, participating in the invasions of Morotai (q.v.) and of Leyte in the Philippines (qq.v.). Beginning on October 30, McCain and Mitscher alternated as commander of the Fast Carrier Force, which thereafter was called Task Force 38 under McCain and Task Force 58 under Mitscher. McCain headed the carrier force from October 30, 1944, to January 1945, and from May 28 to September 2, 1945, the periods when Admiral William F. Halsey commanded the Third Fleet. His major operations during these times were the invasion of Luzon (q.v.), the second half of the Okinawa campaign (q.v.), and the strategic air campaign (q.v.) against the Japanese home islands (q.v.) in the summer of 1945. McCain attended the Japanese surrender (q.v.) ceremony on September 2, 1945, and died four days later while traveling to the United States.

MCNAIR, LESLEY J. *See* UNITED STATES ARMY.

MADAGASCAR. French-owned island in the Indian Ocean (q.v.) off the eastern coast of Africa, which was seized by the British in 1942. After Vice Admiral Chuichi Nagumo (q.v.) and his First Air Fleet raided the Indian Ocean in March and April 1942, British leaders worried that the Japanese would return and threaten British control of the seas. They especially feared that the Japanese would coerce the government of Vichy France (q.v.) into allowing them access to bases in the French colony of Madagascar as they had done with French Indochina (q.v.), a possibility further substantiated by intelligence information. On May 5–7, 1942, British forces made an amphibious assault (q.v.) and captured the port of Diego Suarez. Beginning in September, they landed on other parts of the island, and the Vichy French representatives surrendered on November 5. The British later shifted control of the island to the Free French. *See also* Submarine, Midget.

MADOERA STRAIT, BATTLE OF. Naval battle in the Netherlands East Indies (q.v.) during which American and Dutch forces from Java attempted to reach Borneo (q.v.) to attack Japanese ships on February 4, 1942. A Japanese air attack damaged several vessels and forced the Allied ships to retreat.

MAGIC. *See* INTELLIGENCE, ALLIED SIGNAL.

MAKASSAR STRAIT, BATTLE OF. Naval battle of January 24, 1942, in which U.S. forces sank Japanese ships off the coast of the valuable oil center of Balikpapan, Borneo (q.v.), in the Netherlands East Indies (q.v.). Also known as the Battle of Balikpapan, it was the first surface engagement by U.S. vessels in the Pacific War. Four American destroyers sank at least five Japanese vessels, including troop transports, in a night battle.

MAKIN. *See* GILBERT ISLANDS.

MALACCA STRAIT. *See* SUMATRA.

MALAY PENINSULA. British protectorate in Southeast Asia, captured by Japanese forces in December 1941–January 1942. On December 8, 1941, Japan's Fifteenth Army, commanded by Lieutenant General Tomoyuki Yamashita (q.v.), landed on the northern Malay peninsula and southern Thailand (q.v.) under the protection of Vice Admiral Jisaburo Ozawa's (q.v.) fleet. Opposing them on the ground was the command of British Lieutenant General Arthur Percival (q.v.), whose troops were Australian, British, Indian, and Malay. Early British losses included the battleship *Prince of Wales* and cruiser *Repulse,* which were sunk on December 10 while trying to slow the Japanese invasion. With Japan in control of the seas and the air, Yamashita moved rapidly southward toward his main goal, the massive British base on the island of Singapore (q.v.). Japan effectively used equipment ranging from tanks (q.v.) to bicycles to collapsible boats to pursue and outflank the defenders. Percival's forces, which had no tanks, fought with little success as they withdrew through the heavy jungles of the peninsula toward Singapore, completing their movement to the island on January 31, 1942. Singapore surrendered on February 15, concluding a well-executed campaign by Yamashita, since called the "Tiger of Malaya." The peninsula and Singapore remained under Japanese control throughout the war.

Malay Peninsula and Singapore

MALINOVSKY, RODION YAKOVLEVICH (1898–1967). Marshal

of the Soviet Union; commander, Trans-Baikal Front, 1945. Throughout most of the war, Malinovsky commanded forces on the European
front, where he captured Bucharest and received the rank of marshal.
With the defeat of Germany (q.v.), he was appointed to head the Trans-
Baikal Front (equal to an army group) along the Manchurian border.
Early in the morning of August 9, 1945, after the Union of Soviet Socialist Republics' (q.v.) declaration of war against Japan (q.v.), Malinovsky's massive forces moved east into western Manchuria (q.v.) toward Hsinking and Mukden, inflicting heavy casualties on the Japanese
Kwantung Army (q.v.) and achieving overwhelming, rapid success in
the area where the Japanese least expected an attack. By August 18, organized resistance had ended. In the immediate postwar years, Malinovsky continued to command Soviet troops in the region, rising to

commander of the Far East Military District in 1956. The next year he served as minister of defense.

MALTA CONFERENCE, JANUARY 30–FEBRUARY 2, 1945. Allied conference between British and U.S. delegations prior to the Yalta Conference (q.v.). Most of the sessions focused on the war against Germany (q.v.) and the need to coordinate the Anglo-American strategic positions before meeting the Soviets in Yalta. The Combined Chiefs of Staff (q.v.) also discussed the progress of the war against Japan (q.v.), approving offensive operations against Iwo Jima and Okinawa (qq.v.). Additionally, they considered future operations in Southeast Asia and Japan itself. In response to the question of British participation in the strategic air campaign (q.v.) against Japan, first raised at the Second Quebec Conference (q.v.), the United States (q.v.) agreed to provide the British with bases but stipulated that they would not be located in the Mariana Islands (q.v.), which were reserved for Boeing B-29 Superfortress (q.v.) missions.

MANCHUKUO. Japanese puppet state in Manchuria, created on February 18, 1932, after Japan's Kwantung Army (qq.v.) seized the area from China (q.v.). Japan chose the name "Manchukuo" to link the new state with the Chinese Manchu dynasty (overthrown in 1911), and installed the last Manchu emperor, Henry Pu-Yi (q.v.), as the titular head. The League of Nations, the international organization established after World War I to maintain world order, refused to recognize the legitimacy of Manchukuo, in line with the position of the United States (q.v.) announced by Secretary of State Henry L. Stimson (q.v.). After the League's Lytton Commission found the Japanese guilty of aggression in Manchuria, Japan announced its withdrawal from the League. Until August 1945, Japan administered the area, exploited its natural resources to support the Japanese war effort, and resettled many Japanese there. Under Soviet control in August 1945 it again became known as Manchuria. *See also* Manchuria Campaign (1931–1932); Manchuria Campaign (1945).

MANCHURIA CAMPAIGN (1931–1932). Japanese seizure of area in northeastern China (q.v.), whose rich natural resources attracted Japan and the Union of Soviet Socialist Republics (qq.v.). Through its South Manchurian Railway and Kwantung Army (q.v.), Japan increasingly dominated Manchuria's economy in the 1920s. On the night of

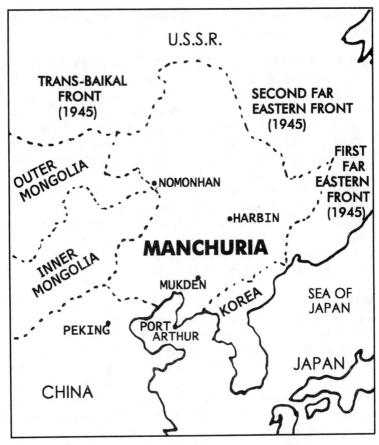

Manchuria

September 18–19, 1931, militant members of the Kwantung Army set off an explosion on the South Manchurian Railway near Mukden and accused the Chinese of sabotage. In retaliation for the "Mukden Incident," the Japanese army seized Mukden and then invaded the rest of Manchuria, with the authorities in Tokyo (q.v.) trying but failing to restrain their progress. Chiang Kai-shek (q.v.) ordered his Chinese Nationalist forces in Manchuria to withdraw, facilitating the Japanese occupation.

In 1932, Japan proclaimed the area to be the independent state of Manchukuo (q.v.), but most countries refused to accept it as such.

Japanese control ended in August 1945, when the U.S.S.R. invaded and defeated the Kwantung Army.

MANCHURIA CAMPAIGN (1945). Rapid Soviet capture of Manchuria in August 1945, after the Union of Soviet Socialist Republics (q.v.) declared war on Japan (q.v.). While the two countries were still officially at peace in March 1945, Soviet leaders began to plan the attack on Manchuria. The next month they began to transfer men and equipment from eastern Europe to the Far East in enormous numbers, concealing the magnitude of the shift from the Japanese. In the summer of 1945, Marshal Alexander M. Vasilevsky (q.v.) became the commander of Soviet forces in the Far East, which were divided into three fronts, or army groups: Marshal Rodion Y. Malinovsky's (q.v.) Trans-Baikal Front; the First Far Eastern Front under Marshal Kirill A. Meretskov (q.v.); and General Maksim A. Purkayev's (q.v.) Second Far Eastern Front. The more than 80 divisions and 1.5 million men included many veteran soldiers and commanders of the war in Europe. Soviet plans called for an invasion of Manchuria in mid-August, which was advanced by a week because the American use of atomic bombs (q.v.) against Japan seemed likely to produce a quick capitulation.

Defending Manchuria was the Japanese Kwantung Army (q.v.), headed by General Otozo Yamada (q.v.). The Kwantung Army included approximately 700,000 soldiers in 40 divisions, but it had been weakened by the transfers of experienced commanders and troops to other armies. Beginning in 1944, Japanese strategists planned to defend Manchuria by delaying invading troops at the borders and then withdrawing successively to a series of defensive lines and finally to a stronghold in the area surrounding Tunghua, near the border with Korea (q.v.). Japanese intelligence (q.v.) believed that the Soviets would not attack until the fall of 1945 or the spring of 1946. In August 1945, Japanese defensive fortifications were incomplete and their troops unprepared.

On the evening of August 8, 1945, Vyacheslav M. Molotov (q.v.), Soviet people's commissar for foreign affairs, informed Japanese Ambassador Naotake Sato (q.v.) in Moscow that the U.S.S.R. had declared war on Japan. Shortly after midnight on August 9, before the news had reached Tokyo, Soviet troops swept rapidly across the Manchurian borders. From Mongolia (q.v.), the Trans-Baikal Front advanced into western Manchuria, totally surprising the Japanese. In the second major offensive, the First Far East Front simultaneously invaded eastern Manchuria. At the same time, the Second Far East Front conducted a support operation by assaulting Japanese forces in northern Manchuria, preventing them from redeploying to assist other areas. The swift, massive attacks overwhelmed the Japanese, and all Soviet fronts met their objectives, with the Second Far East Front encountering the stiffest opposition. By August 16, most of the Kwantung Army had been defeated, although some resistance continued days longer. On the night of August 14, the Japanese had received cease-fire orders from Tokyo, which Yamada then overruled. The Soviet armies stopped and then resumed their advances. After much confusion, the Kwantung Army formally surrendered on August 20. The Japanese suffered extremely heavy casualties, in contrast to relatively light Soviet losses.

As part of the Manchurian campaign, the First Far East Front occupied the northern part of Korea. In related operations, Soviet forces completed their captures of southern Sakhalin (q.v.) and the Kurile Islands (q.v.). After the war, the U.S.S.R. transferred control of Manchuria to the Chinese Communists.

MANDATES, PACIFIC. Territories in the Pacific held by Germany (q.v.) prior to World War I and administered after the war under a system authorized by the League of Nations. In 1919, the League gave Japan (q.v.) the mandate for the former German-owned islands north of the equator, primarily the Carolines, Marshalls, and Marianas (excluding U.S.-owned Guam) (qq.v.). These islands had been seized by Japan upon the outbreak of war in 1914. Among other mandated areas were Northeast New Guinea, Bougainville, New Britain, and the Admiralty Islands, all assigned to Australia (qq.v.).

MANHATTAN PROJECT, 1942–1945. U.S. government project to develop an atomic bomb (q.v.). In the summer of 1942, the Office of Scientific Research and Development (OSRD) (q.v.) recommended that the U.S. military assume the responsibility for the design and construction of an atomic weapon. To conceal the enormous, highly classified program, the United States Army (q.v.) established the Manhattan Engineering District in June 1942 and appointed as head Brigadier General Leslie R. Groves (q.v.), an engineer. The Manhattan Project, also known as the S-1 project (Section 1 of the OSRD), ultimately employed 129,000 people in many different locations and cost $2 billion.

Overseeing Groves's direction of the project was the three-man Military Policy Committee chaired by Vannevar Bush (q.v.), the OSRD director, and including representatives of the United States Army and

Navy (qq.v.). Bush's deputy in the OSRD, James B. Conant, worked closely with Groves concerning the research aspects of the project, which involved numerous civilian scientists. The Military Policy Committee reported to the Top Policy Group appointed by President Franklin D. Roosevelt (q.v.). In addition to Bush, its members included Secretary of War Henry L. Stimson (q.v.), Army Chief of Staff George C. Marshall (q.v.), and Vice President Henry A. Wallace, whom Roosevelt later excluded from the group. Beginning in the fall of 1943, the Combined Policy Committee governed Anglo-American-Canadian collaboration on the atomic bomb project.

One of the early significant events in the Manhattan Project occurred at the University of Chicago on December 2, 1942, when Enrico Fermi directed the first controlled nuclear chain reaction. In addition to using existing research universities, the project built vast facilities at three classified locations: Los Alamos, New Mexico, where the design and construction of the bomb occurred; Oak Ridge, Tennessee, built primarily to produce uranium in a grade suitable for the bomb; and Hanford, Washington, assigned to create usable plutonium for the bomb. In charge of the Los Alamos site was physicist J. Robert Oppenheimer. The Manhattan Project's personnel included a considerable number of European emigrés and, beginning in late 1943, British and Canadian scientists.

Researchers eventually built different types of bombs using uranium and plutonium. On July 16, 1945, the project successfully exploded a plutonium-based bomb near Alamogordo, New Mexico. After President Harry S. Truman (q.v.) ordered the use of atomic bombs against Japan (q.v.), components of the weapons were transported on the USS *Indianapolis* (q.v.) to the island of Tinian in the Marianas (qq.v.), where facilities had been prepared for the assembly of the weapons. Specially trained crews flying modified Boeing B-29 bombers (q.v.) dropped the first weapon, a uranium bomb named "Little Boy," on Hiroshima (q.v.), Honshu, on August 6, and the second, a heavier plutonium bomb called "Fat Man," on Nagasaki (q.v.), Kyushu, on August 9. Other bombs were under production at the time of the Japanese surrender (q.v.).

In 1946, the United States (q.v.) tested additional atomic bombs in the Marshall Islands (q.v.). On January 1, 1947, the Atomic Energy Commission assumed responsibility for the atomic program from the Manhattan Project. *See also* Intelligence, Soviet; Strategic Air Campaign.

MANILA. Capital of the Philippine Islands (q.v.), located on the largest island of Luzon (q.v.). As the invading Japanese forces approached Manila in late December 1941, General Douglas MacArthur (q.v.) ordered it vacated by U.S. and Filipino troops to spare its destruction. Japanese troops occupied it on January 2, 1942. In early 1945, as U.S. forces invaded Luzon, Japanese General Tomoyuki Yamashita (q.v.) ordered his Fourteenth Area Army to yield control of Manila and conduct the defense from designated mountainous areas. The head of the Manila Naval Defense Force, Rear Admiral Sanji Iwabuchi (q.v.), refused to recognize Yamashita's authority and decided to fight for Manila. The battle for the city was the largest urban engagement in the war against Japan (q.v.) and lasted from February 3 to March 3. The trapped Japanese forces committed numerous atrocities against the civilian population, especially in the final days. Additional civilian casualties resulted from the heavy artillery (q.v.) fire by both sides. Total civilian deaths were estimated at 100,000. The Japanese defenders, including Iwabuchi, died in the battle. After the war, Yamashita was executed for war crimes (q.v.) including the atrocities committed by Iwabuchi's men.

MANUS. *See* CARTWHEEL, OPERATION.

MAO TSE-TUNG (1893–1976). Chinese Communist leader; chairman of the People's Republic of China, 1949–1976. After traveling to northwest China (q.v.) with other Communist members and armed forces in the Long March (1934–1935), Mao established his headquarters in Yenan, where he remained throughout the war with Japan (q.v.). The Chinese civil war between the Communist forces and the Nationalist soldiers of Chiang Kai-shek (q.v.) began in the late 1920s and lasted until Mao's triumph in 1949.

During the Japanese war in China, the civil conflict continued to a lesser degree, although the two sides formed the United Front in September 1937 and cooperated for a time in fighting the Japanese. Chou En-lai (q.v.) represented Mao in Chungking (q.v.), the Nationalist wartime capital. Although the United States (q.v.) recognized Chiang as China's official leader, it sent a small liaison group, the Dixie Mission (q.v.), to Mao's base in Yenan in mid-1944.

With the Japanese surrender (q.v.), Mao's forces controlled much of China's territory. The civil war resumed full-scale in 1946 and eventually resulted in a Communist victory. In 1949, Mao was named chairman of the People's Republic of China. *See also* China, Japanese Operations in.

MARCO POLO BRIDGE. At Lukouchiao, 12 miles from Peking, China (q.v.); site of firefight in 1937, which marked the start of the Sino-Japanese War. On the night of July 7, 1937, Japanese troops legally stationed in the area exchanged fire with Chinese troops in a minor incident, which was followed by more fighting and a cease-fire on July 11. Both sides sent heavy reinforcements to the area, fighting resumed, and the Japanese captured Peking on July 28. The Japanese then moved farther south into China and attacked Chinese ports. The Sino-Japanese War continued until the Japanese surrender (q.v.) to the Allies (q.v.) in August 1945. *See also* China, Japanese Operations in.

MARIANA ISLANDS. Islands in the western Pacific captured from Japan (q.v.) by U.S. forces in 1944 and used as bases for attacks on Japan. The three main islands targeted by the Central Pacific Area (CENPAC) (q.v.) forces in 1944 were Saipan, Tinian, and Guam (qq.v.). Japan had administered Saipan and Tinian as mandates (q.v.) since World War I and had seized Guam, a U.S. territory, on December 10, 1941. The invasion of the Marianas followed the capture of the Gilbert and Marshall Islands (qq.v.). Members of the U.S. high command, especially Admiral Ernest J. King (q.v.), regarded the seizure of the Marianas as the most indispensable operation in the Pacific.

To lead the operation, Admiral Chester W. Nimitz (q.v.) chose Admiral Raymond A. Spruance (q.v.), commander of CENPAC and the U.S. Fifth Fleet. Reporting to him were Vice Admiral Richmond Kelly Turner (q.v.) over the Marianas Joint Expeditionary Force, Lieutenant General Holland M. Smith (q.v.) over all ground operations and personally in command of the Saipan assault, and Vice Admiral Marc A. Mitscher (q.v.) over the Fast Carrier Force. One amphibious force invaded Saipan and then Tinian; the other assaulted Guam.

The islands were heavily fortified and fiercely defended. The capture of Saipan took from June 15 to July 9; its loss was considered so serious by Japan that the government of Hideki Tojo (q.v.) fell. A Japanese attempt to disrupt the landings and destroy the U.S. fleet resulted in the Battle of the Philippine Sea (q.v.), which occurred on June 19–20 and devastated the Japanese naval forces. The next objective was Guam, where the fighting occurred from July 21 to August 10. The invasion of Tinian, mounted from nearby Saipan, began on July 24 and

SAIPAN

JUNE 15
JULY 24

TINIAN

MARIANA
ISLANDS
1944

ROTA

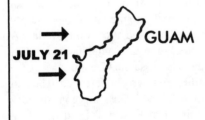

JULY 21

GUAM

Mariana Islands, 1944

ended August 1. During the rest of the war, the Marianas were used for Allied naval and air bases, from which Boeing B-29 Superfortress (q.v.) bombers attacked the Japanese home islands (q.v.).

MARSHALL, GEORGE CATLETT (1880–1959). U.S. General of the Army; army chief of staff, 1939–1945. Assuming his duties of chief of staff on September 1, 1939, as the war in Europe began, Marshall oversaw the mobilization and massive expansion of the United States Army (q.v.), which eventually numbered more than eight million people. In 1942, he reorganized the army into air, ground, and service forces.

As a member of the United States Joint Chiefs of Staff and the Combined Chiefs of Staff (qq.v.), Marshall attended the wartime Allied conferences (q.v.) and played an essential role in developing and executing the global Allied strategy for winning the war. He advocated the policy of defeating Germany before Japan (qq.v.) and pushed strongly for a cross-channel invasion of Europe as early as possible. In the war against Japan, he acted as the agent for the Joint Chiefs in directing the Southwest Pacific Area theater (SWPA) headed by General Douglas MacArthur (q.v.), whom he visited in December 1943 during a tour of the Pacific. Early in the war, Marshall recommended the appointment of Major General Joseph W. Stilwell (q.v.) to head the China-Burma-India (q.v.) theater and strongly backed him until President Franklin D. Roosevelt (q.v.) ordered his relief. From the beginning of the U.S. program to develop an atomic bomb (q.v.), Marshall served on high-level advisory committees regarding nuclear energy and its use.

In December 1944 Marshall was promoted to the five-star rank of General of the Army. After the war, he headed a presidential mission to China (q.v.), served as secretary of state (1947–1949), held the post of secretary of defense (1950–1951) during part of the Korean War, and received the Nobel Peace Prize (1953).

MARSHALL ISLANDS. Island chain in the central Pacific, which was administered by Japan (q.v.) from 1914 until its seizure by U.S. troops in 1944. The capture of the Marshall Islands was an essential part of Admiral Chester W. Nimitz's (q.v.) plan to drive across the Central Pacific from Hawaii to Japan. Prior to invading the Marshalls, he ordered the acquisition of the Gilbert Islands (q.v.) to the east, so that planes based there could conduct preinvasion bombardment of the Marshalls. Because Japan had controlled the latter islands for so long, U.S.

planners believed them to be extremely well fortified. For the Marshalls operation, Nimitz appointed the same team he had used in the Gilberts: Vice Admiral Raymond A. Spruance (q.v.), fleet commander; Rear Admiral Richmond Kelly Turner, head of V Amphibious Force; and Marine Major General Holland M. Smith (q.v.), head of V Amphibious Corps.

After days of heavy bombardment, forces of the Central Pacific Area (CENPAC) (q.v.) assaulted the Kwajalein atoll on February 1, 1944, completing its capture on February 7. U.S. troops next attacked Eniwetok from February 17–23. Although the Marshalls were defended fiercely, U.S. losses were relatively light and, as was the case in the Gilberts, nearly all of the Japanese defenders died. During the Eniwetok invasion, U.S. carriers (q.v.) attacked the large Japanese naval base at Truk (q.v.) in the Caroline Islands (q.v.). Throughout the rest of the war, the Allies (q.v.) used the Marshall Islands for naval and air bases.

MATSUOKA, YOSUKE (1880–1946). Japanese diplomat; foreign minister, 1940–1941. In 1933, Matsuoka, Japan's representative to the League of Nations, led the withdrawal of his country from the League after it criticized Japanese aggression in Manchuria (q.v.). He then headed the South Manchuria Railway Company, which was deeply involved in the expansion of Japanese influence in Manchuria. Matsuoka served as foreign minister in Prime Minister Fumimaro Konoye's (q.v.) government from July 1940 to July 1941. During his tenure, he negotiated the Tripartite Pact (q.v.) with Germany and Italy (qq.v.) and the neutrality treaty with the Union of Soviet Socialist Republics (q.v.), forced the British to close temporarily the Burma Road (q.v.) in 1940, pressed Vichy France (q.v.) to allow Japanese troops in French Indochina (q.v.) in 1940–1941, and opposed negotiations with the United States (q.v.). Matsuoka was forced to resign in the summer of 1941. After the war he was charged with war crimes (q.v.) but died before he came to trial.

MEDICINE. Armed forces in the war with Japan (q.v.) faced hostile climates, rugged terrain, and a variety of diseases, in situations further complicated by the logistic difficulties of supplying the troops with food and medical care. Soldiers suffered from beri-beri, cholera, dengue, diphtheria, dysentery, malaria, tetanus, typhoid, typhus, and other diseases. At various times, malnutrition affected both Japanese and Allied forces as well as prisoners of war (q.v.) held by the Japanese.

Allied officials instituted a preventive medicine campaign against malaria, the primary disease afflicting soldiers in some regions of Asia and the Pacific. Because Japan had captured the world's main source of quinine (q.v.), the basic drug used against malaria, the Allies (q.v.) increased the production of atabrine, an artificial substitute, and required soldiers to take it on a preventive basis. They also enforced the use of mosquito nets, drained swamps, and, during the final months of the war, widely employed the insecticide dichloro-diphenyl-trichloroethane (DDT).

As the war progressed, the Allies significantly improved the treatment of ill and wounded troops. One of the most important changes was the introduction of penicillin, which the United States first produced in 1941 after British scientists successfully tested the drug. In the spring of 1943, Allied military physicians in North Africa began to use penicillin to prevent and treat infections. It became available in the Southwest Pacific (q.v.) in the fall of 1943 and was used widely beginning in 1944. Both sulfa drugs, already in use when the war began, and penicillin saved many lives.

In another major development, Allied physicians discovered that, although the use of blood plasma could benefit wounded soldiers until they reached more advanced medical facilities, the transfusion of whole blood was then necessary to improve the chances of recovery. Following the British example, in 1943 the United States (q.v.) established a blood bank system, which during the last part of the war enabled the extensive shipment of whole blood to combat zones in the Pacific. Medical officials developed a series of graduated facilities to treat injured troops, ranging from stations close to the battlefield to fully equipped hospitals, both on land and on specially designated ships. The earlier treatment of wounds increased survival rates, as did vast improvements in evacuating the casualties by landing craft, transport planes, and helicopters (qq.v.). Following treatment in hospitals close to the war zone, the severely injured were sent to rehabilitation facilities in their home countries.

In comparison with the Allies, Japan's medical care of its troops was much less advanced and was severely hampered by the deficiencies of its supply system, which failed to provide many of its soldiers with adequate food, much less medicine. Japan had no preventive medicine program comparable to the Allied campaign against malaria, although its troops did receive some antimalarial drugs. The Japanese military was particularly unprepared for the medical problems it encountered in tropical areas, having conducted its operations prior to 1941 in colder climates. Additionally, after enjoying initial successes, Japanese troops in Pacific combat were basically on the defensive, forced to withdraw before the Allied advance. When unable to evacuate casualties during a retreat, Japanese troops sometimes killed their wounded rather than allow them to be captured. Other injured soldiers, in keeping with the Bushido (q.v.) code, committed suicide as Allied forces approached.

After the war, Allied officials overseeing the occupation of Japan and its former territories confronted numerous public health problems evolving from malnutrition, epidemics, housing shortages, and injuries caused by the strategic air campaign (q.v.). In addition to handling immediate civilian relief, they instituted extensive public health programs, including the liberal use of DDT. Also requiring medical care were the liberated Allied prisoners of war. *See also* Logistics; Office of Scientific Research and Development; Science and Technology.

MERCHANT MARINE. Commercial ships and crews; an area in which the Allies (q.v.) had an enormous advantage over Japan (q.v.). As a nation with insufficient agricultural and strategic raw materials (q.v.) in the Japanese home islands (q.v.) and a widespread military presence, Japan depended heavily on its merchant shipping to connect the parts of its empire, although it focused on the prewar production of warships rather than merchant vessels. In early December 1941, Japan's shipping capacity was barely adequate, and by the following May, it could not meet the needs of either the economy or the Japanese military forces stationed throughout much of Southeast Asia and the Pacific. Allied submarines (q.v.), surface vessels, and aircraft focused their attacks on the Japanese lines of communication, sinking much shipping and laying mines (q.v.) to close ports and waterways. In 1943, Japan's increased use of armed escorts and convoys to protect its merchant fleet was nullified by the breaking of the Japanese merchant code by Allied signal intelligence (q.v.). While Japanese industry tried unsuccessfully to produce replacements for the lost ships, the military modified captured ships, requisitioned merchant vessels from French Indochina (q.v.), and expanded the use of submarines and a variety of fishing boats, barges, and small craft for transport. Japan also tried to develop additional overland supply routes in Asia through the building of the Burma-Thailand Railway (q.v.) and the capture of additional Chinese territory in Operation Ichigo (q.v.).

The size of Japan's merchant shipping decreased from more than 6 million tons in December 1941 to 1.5 million tons in August 1945. Before the United States (q.v.) entered the war, the Roosevelt (q.v.) administration began to expand the country's merchant marine and to commission ships for its allies. The urgent need for cargo ships that could be produced quickly in large numbers resulted in the design of the Liberty ship; the first, named the *Patrick Henry,* was completed in September 1941. More than 2,700 were produced, including one ship assembled in the record time of four days and 15 hours. The Liberty ship was 441 feet long, carried 9,100 tons of cargo, and operated with a 42-man crew. Its speed was 11 knots. The later Victory ship was faster, traveling at 15 knots. Of the more than 100 Victory ships built, nearly all were assigned to the Pacific War because of the longer distances involved. Liberty and Victory ships formed an essential part of the Allied logistical system, operating throughout the Pacific to deliver troops, equipment, and other cargo to Allied theaters.

In November 1941, the United States authorized the arming of its merchant ships and the stationing of navy gunners on some of them. When the U.S. government assumed wartime control of the country's privately owned merchant ships, its crews remained civilians, but they were subject to the authority of the U.S. Coast Guard and overseas U.S. military commanders. Many seamen died during the war; others became prisoners of war (q.v.). In 1988, the United States granted veteran's status to merchant mariners who had served on oceangoing ships during World War II. *See also* Logistics.

MERETSKOV, KIRILL AFANES'EVICH (1897–1968). Marshal of the Soviet Union; commander, Maritime Army (Far East), 1945; commander, First Far Eastern Front, 1945. Meretskov commanded forces in the wars with Finland and Germany (q.v.) before his appointment in April 1945 to head the Maritime Army in the Far East. In the Union of Soviet Socialist Republic's (q.v.) attack in Manchuria (q.v.) in August of the same year, he commanded the First Far Eastern Front. Meretskov's forces drove into eastern Manchuria at the same time that the Trans-Baikal Front under Marshal Rodion Y. Malinovsky (q.v.) advanced into western Manchuria. Although it faced strong fortifications and stormy weather, the First Far Eastern Front surprised and crushed the Japanese defenders, capturing Mutanchiang and Wangching and moving into northern Korea (q.v.). The last organized resistance against Meretskov's forces occurred on August 26.

MERRILL'S MARAUDERS. U.S. 5307th Composite Unit (Provisional), composed of volunteers who fought in Burma (q.v.) in 1944, under the command of Brigadier General Frank D. Merrill. Trained in the long-range deep penetration methods of the British Chindits (q.v.), the group was code-named Galahad and referred to as Merrill's Marauders by the U.S. press. Like the Chindits, the Marauders used guerrilla tactics to fight behind Japanese lines, where they received their supplies by air. They were instrumental in General Joseph W. Stilwell's (q.v.) campaign to capture Myitkyina (q.v.) in northern Burma, from February to August 1944. The unit, weakened by casualties and tropical disease from months in the jungles, was then disbanded.

MEXICO. Member of the Allies (q.v.) and the only Latin American (q.v.) nation to send a military force to fight in the war against Japan (q.v.). Mexico broke diplomatic relations with Japan immediately after the Pearl Harbor attack (q.v.) and declared war on the Axis powers (q.v.) in May 1942, following German attacks on Mexican ships. Prior to the war, officials of the United States (q.v.) and Mexico met extensively to settle past disputes and to discuss the use of Mexican airfields and naval bases by the U.S. military. Throughout the war, Mexico provided the United States with important raw materials (q.v.) and cooperated in defense arrangements, such as the installation of radar stations in Baja California. To lessen the danger of espionage, the Mexican government moved people of Japanese ancestry from the Pacific coast and the U.S. border to other areas of the country, but handled them less restrictively than did the United States and Canada (q.v.). Thousands of Mexican nationals joined the U.S. military; others helped to fill the manpower shortage in U.S. industries and agriculture. In 1945, the Mexican military sent an air squadron to assist the Allied effort in the Philippines (q.v.).

MIDGET SUBMARINE. See SUBMARINE, MIDGET.

MIDWAY, BATTLE OF. Naval battle between the Japanese Combined Fleet (q.v.) and the U.S. Pacific Fleet near the island of Midway, June 3–6, 1942, in which the Japanese suffered a decisive defeat. Admiral Isoruku Yamamoto (q.v.), commander of the Combined Fleet, planned the offensive to invade U.S.-held Midway Island with the major goal of drawing out and destroying the Pacific Fleet, including the carriers (q.v.) that had escaped damage at Pearl Harbor (q.v.). By capturing

Midway, Japan would also extend its western defensive perimeter, a particular concern since the Doolittle Raid (q.v.) on Tokyo in April. Yamamoto's plan included a diversionary attack on the Aleutian Islands (q.v.), which began on June 3 with an air raid on Dutch Harbor. The next day his forces began their bombing of Midway Island and prepared to wait for the Pacific Fleet to arrive from Pearl Harbor to defend Midway. Unknown to Yamamoto, Pearl Harbor code breakers had warned Admiral Chester W. Nimitz (q.v.) about the Japanese plans, and Nimitz had sent a large force under Rear Admiral Frank Jack Fletcher (q.v.) to the Midway area before the Japanese arrived. When Yamamoto's forces assaulted Midway, land-based planes from Midway and carrier-based planes from the fleet surprised the Japanese by attacking them in force. On the second day, when his flagship was damaged, Fletcher turned over tactical command to Rear Admiral Raymond A. Spruance (q.v.). Yamamoto lost four carriers and 3,500 men, including trained pilots who could not be replaced, and had to withdraw without directly challenging the U.S. battleships (q.v.) as he had planned. The Battle of Midway is considered by many to be a major turning point in the war in the Pacific.

MILES, MILTON E. *See* SINO-AMERICAN COOPERATIVE ORGANIZATION.

MILNE BAY. Site of Allied bases on the southeastern tip of Papua, New Guinea (q.v.); objective of failed Japanese assault, August 25–September 6, 1942. Allied troops moved into the Milne Bay area in late June 1942 to build airfields and naval bases, needed to protect Port Moresby (q.v.) and to support future operations in New Guinea. By August, nearly 10,000 Allied air, combat, and service forces were stationed at Milne Bay. As the Japanese conducted an overland offensive to capture Port Moresby, Japanese troops on August 25 made an amphibious landing several miles from the Allied bases at Milne Bay. Heavily outnumbered but equipped with tanks (q.v.), the Japanese attacked the airfields and sustained substantial casualties before withdrawing; most of the survivors were evacuated. Bad weather hindered the actions of all forces.

MINDORO. *See* PHILIPPINE ISLANDS CAMPAIGN (1944–1945).

MINE. Used on land or in water. The Allies and Japan (qq.v.) each employed land mines against enemy personnel and tanks (q.v.). The

Japanese set the explosives both in small numbers and in large mine-fields, such as in the Philippine, Iwo Jima, and Okinawa (qq.v.) campaigns in 1945. Both land and naval mines formed an important part of the beach defenses against Allied amphibious assaults (q.v.) throughout the Pacific. The Japanese also employed naval mines, usually less advanced than the Allied types, to protect important shipping lanes from Allied submarines (q.v.). Early in the war they planted mines in the waters between Hokkaido and Sakhalin and in the Yellow Sea between China and Korea (qq.v.), although several Allied submarines managed to penetrate the defenses. Allied minesweepers preceded most landings in the Pacific to clear both Allied and Japanese naval mines from the assault areas.

The Allies used acoustic, magnetic, and hydraulic naval mines against Japan, laying them by aircraft, submarines, and surface vessels such as minelayers and patrol torpedo boats (q.v.). Allied bombers (q.v.) planted the greatest number of mines, targeting rivers and harbors throughout Japanese-held areas of Asia and the Pacific. In addition to sinking ships, the mines paralyzed shipping in some ports for extensive periods, while the Japanese attempted to clear the harbors with minesweepers and other vessels converted for the purpose. During the final months of the war, Boeing B-29 Superfortress (q.v.) bombers participating in Operation Starvation planted thousands of mines around the Japanese home islands (q.v.), sowing them in such enormous quantities that sea traffic in some areas was virtually halted. During the postwar period, Allied and Japanese minesweepers spent years clearing away mines deposited during the war.

MITSCHER, MARC ANDREW (1887–1947). U.S. admiral; carrier (q.v.) commander in the Pacific, 1942–1943; commander, Fleet Air, U.S. West Coast, 1943; commander, Fast Carrier Task Force, Pacific Fleet, 1944–1945; deputy chief of naval operations for air, 1945–1946. Ordered to the Pacific early in 1942, Mitscher commanded the carrier *Hornet* in the Doolittle Raid against Tokyo (April 1942) and in the Battle of Midway (June 1942) (qq.v.). From late 1942 to mid-August 1943, he directed air campaigns in the Solomon Islands (q.v.). After a brief term in the United States (q.v.), Mitscher in January 1944 became the commander of the Fast Carrier Force, Pacific Fleet, which played an integral role in the defeat of Japan (q.v.). His task force was instrumental in the invasions of the Marshalls, the Marianas, Iwo Jima, and Okinawa (qq.v.), as well as the landings at Hollandia on New Guinea (q.v.). Mitscher participated in the victories in the Philippine Sea and Leyte Gulf (qq.v.). His force also raided Truk, the Palaus, and the Japanese home islands (qq.v.) and sank the superbattleship *Yamato* (q.v.). When Mitscher served under Admiral William F. Halsey (q.v.) as head of the Third Fleet, his carrier force was designated Task Force 38; it bore the title of Task Force 58 when Admiral Raymond A. Spruance commanded the Fifth Fleet. Beginning in late October 1944, Mitscher alternated with Vice Admiral John S. McCain (q.v.) as chief of the Fast Carrier Force, which Mitscher headed as Task Force 58. Relieved by McCain in late May 1945, Mitscher served as deputy chief of naval operations for air.

MOLOTOV, VYACHESLAV MIKHAILOVICH (1890–1986). Soviet people's commissar of foreign affairs, 1939–1949. As one of his first actions in office, Molotov led the negotiations in August 1939 for the German-Soviet Nonaggression Pact (q.v.) that preceded the invasions of Poland in September 1939. He also approved the Union of Soviet Socialist Republics's (q.v.) neutrality treaty with Japan (q.v.) in April 1941. In May 1942, Molotov signed an agreement for a 20-year Anglo-Soviet alliance. He attended the wartime conferences in Teheran, Yalta, Potsdam, and San Francisco (qq.v). In 1945, Molotov told Japanese Ambassador Naotake Sato (q.v.) that the U.S.S.R. would not renew its neutrality treaty with Japan when it expired in 1946. In other dealings with Sato the same year, Molotov misled him about Soviet war intentions and delayed meeting with him until August 8, when the Soviet Union declared its intention to enter the war against Japan.

MOLUCCA ISLANDS. *See* MOROTAI; NETHERLANDS EAST INDIES.

MONGOLIA, INNER. Area of China (q.v.), which Japan (q.v.) began to occupy in the 1930s, seizing the Jehol province in early 1933. Japan incorporated Jehol into Manchukuo (q.v.) and combined two eastern provinces into the puppet government of Mongolian Borderlands, or Meng Chiang, headed by Teh Wang. In 1949, Inner Mongolia became an autonomous area of the People's Republic of China.

MONGOLIA, OUTER. Nation named Mongolian People's Republic in 1924; closely allied with the Union of Soviet Socialist Republics (q.v.). In 1936, Mongolia signed a mutual assistance treaty with the

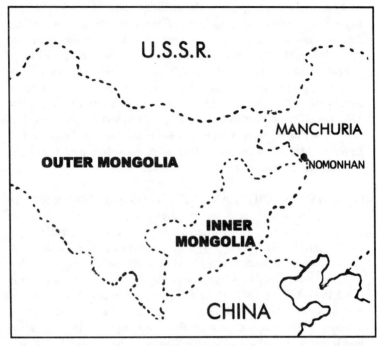

Mongolia

U.S.S.R., which sent troops into the country two years later. In May 1939, Mongolian soldiers clashed near Nomonhan (q.v.) with troops from neighboring Manchuria, where Japan had established the puppet country of Manchukuo (q.v.). The border skirmishes escalated into heavy combat between Soviet troops and the Japanese Kwantung Army (q.v.), continuing until September 1939. Thereafter, both sides retained substantial forces in the area. In August 1945, Mongolian troops participated in the massive Soviet invasion of Manchuria, which was staged partly from Mongolian territory. At the instigation of the Soviets, an agreement reached at the Yalta Conference (q.v.) in February 1945 recognized the status quo in Outer Mongolia.

MORGENTHAU, HENRY T., JR. *See* UNITED STATES.

MOROTAI. Small island in the Molucca Islands of the Netherlands East Indies (q.v.), recaptured by the Allies (q.v.) from September 15 to

October 4, 1944. In planning for the Allied advance into the Philippine Islands (q.v.) in 1944, Southwest Pacific Area (SWPA) (q.v.) strategists selected Morotai as the preferred site for air bases to assist the upcoming invasion. Known to have few Japanese troops, Morotai was chosen over nearby Halmahera, which had a sizable Japanese presence. Following the capture of major objectives in New Guinea (q.v.), Allied troops under the command of Lieutenant General Walter Krueger (q.v.) landed on Morotai on September 15, the same day Central Pacific (q.v.) forces assaulted the Palaus (q.v.). The Pacific Ocean Areas (q.v.) sent one carrier (q.v.) group from its Fast Carrier Force (q.v.) to assist the SWPA operation. On Morotai, the troops encountered difficult terrain but little Japanese resistance. After Allied ships prevented significant Japanese reinforcement from Halmahera, Krueger announced the end of the operation on October 4. Later the same month, Allied bases on Morotai were used in the invasion of the Philippines. Morotai's airfields also supported raids on Japanese shipping and bases in the East Indies.

MOSCOW CONFERENCE (TOLSTOY), OCTOBER 9–20, 1944. Meeting of Soviet Premier Joseph V. Stalin, British Prime Minister Winston S. Churchill (qq.v.), and their advisers, with U.S. Ambassador W. Averell Harriman (q.v.) present as an observer. The participants conferred about the scale and timing of the Soviet entry into the war against Japan (q.v.). Stalin and Churchill also discussed postwar boundaries for Poland and agreed to a division of British and Soviet influence in the Balkans, actions later renounced by U.S. President Franklin D. Roosevelt (q.v.).

MOSCOW FOREIGN MINISTERS CONFERENCE, OCTOBER 18–30, 1943. Meeting of U.S. Secretary of State Cordell Hull, British Foreign Secretary Anthony Eden, and Soviet People's Commissar of Foreign Affairs Vyacheslav M. Molotov (qq.v.). In addition to the Soviet demands for a second front in the war in Europe, the diplomats discussed the possibility (never realized) of establishing weather stations in Siberia to aid U.S. planes attacking Japan. Most important for the Far East, Soviet Premier Joseph V. Stalin (q.v.) told Hull in private that the Union of Soviet Socialist Republics (q.v.) would enter the war against Japan (q.v.) after Germany's (q.v.) defeat. On October 30, the conferees, joined by a Chinese representative, issued the Four-Power Declaration, or Moscow Declaration, which called for unconditional surrender and the formation of an international organization to maintain peace after the war.

MOUNTBATTEN, LOUIS (1900–1979). British admiral; chief, Combined Operations, 1942–1943; supreme allied commander, Southeast Asia Command, 1943–1946. As head of British Combined Operations, Mountbatten directed commando operations, including the disastrous raid on Dieppe, France, in 1942, and conducted initial planning for the later Normandy invasion. During the First Quebec Conference (q.v.) in August 1943, the Allies (q.v.) created Southeast Asia Command (SEAC) (q.v.) with Mountbatten as supreme allied commander. Basing his headquarters in India (q.v.) and later in Ceylon (q.v.), he oversaw a complicated command comprised of Allied forces throughout Southeast Asia. The main military actions under his leadership occurred in Burma (q.v.), which was recaptured from the Japanese in 1945. In a formal ceremony in Singapore (q.v.) on September 12, 1945, Mountbatten accepted the Japanese surrender (q.v.) of forces in the region.

Mountbatten's postwar career included service as India's last viceroy and first governor-general, first sea lord, and chairman of the British Chiefs of Staff Committee (q.v.).

MUKDEN INCIDENT. *See* MANCHURIA CAMPAIGN (1931–1932).

MUSSOLINI, BENITO (1883–1945). Italian premier and dictator, 1922–1943. Called "Duce" or "Leader" by his supporters, Mussolini organized the Fascist Party in 1919 and took control of the government in 1922. Under Mussolini, Italy (q.v.) formed alliances with Germany and Japan (qq.v.). Like Germany, Italy declared war on the United States (q.v.) on December 11, 1941. Mussolini was forced out of office and arrested in July 1943, as Italy negotiated its surrender to the Allies (q.v.). Rescued by a German commando mission, Mussolini lived in northern Italy under German protection until April 1945, when he was killed by Italian partisans during the recapture of the country.

MUTAGUCHI, RENYA (1888–1966). Japanese general; commander, 18th Division, 1940–1943; commander, Fifteenth Army, 1943–1944. As an army officer in China (q.v.), Mutaguchi participated in the beginning of the Sino-Japanese War in 1937. He led the 18th Division in the successful campaign for the Malay peninsula (q.v.), December

1941–February 1942. Beginning in 1943, he commanded the Fifteenth Army under the direction of Lieutenant General Masakazu Kawabe (q.v.), head of the Burma Area Army. An aggressive commander, he repelled Allied actions in Burma (q.v.), including the efforts of the Chindits (q.v.) in 1943. He is best known for the Imphal (q.v.) offensive in 1944, which he urged Kawabe to authorize. Crossing the Indian border to attack the British base at Imphal, Mutaguchi believed the operation would take less than one month; instead, it lasted more than four, killed at least one-third of his force, and ended in a disastrous withdrawal into Burma. After the failure at Imphal, Mutaguchi was replaced and retired after the war ended.

MYITKYINA. Town in northern Burma (q.v.), occupied by Japanese soldiers on May 8, 1942, and recaptured on August 3, 1944, by Allied forces under U.S. General Joseph W. Stilwell (q.v.). Myitkyina was a vital point in Stilwell's campaign to build a supply road (later called the Stilwell Road [q.v.]) from India to connect with the Burma Road (q.v.) to China (q.v.). Allied troops including Merrill's Marauders (q.v.) took the airfield near Myitkyina on May 17, 1944, and besieged the city, which the Japanese strongly defended before evacuating it on August 3.

-N-

NADZAB. See AIRBORNE OPERATIONS; CARTWHEEL, OPERATION; NEW GUINEA CAMPAIGN.

NAGANO, OSAMI (1880–1947). Japanese Fleet Admiral; navy chief of staff, 1941–1944. Prior to becoming part of the high command, Nagano attended the international naval disarmament conferences in Washington (1920) and London (1930 and 1935–1936). He became the navy chief of staff in April 1941. In the fall of 1941, he supported the Japanese decision to seize resources in Southeast Asia by force if diplomatic negotiations failed. While criticizing the army's strategic proposals, Nagano hesitated to endorse Admiral Isoruku Yamamoto's (q.v.) plan to destroy the U.S. Fleet at Pearl Harbor (q.v.) in conjunction with Japanese assaults in Malaya, the Philippines, and the East Indies (qq.v.). After Yamamoto threatened to resign in October 1941 as commander of the Combined Fleet, Nagano reluctantly approved the Pearl Harbor plan. In early 1944, as Japan's strategic position weakened, Prime Minister Hideki Tojo (q.v.) forced Nagano to resign. When Japan decided to surrender in August 1945, Emperor Hirohito (q.v.) requested Nagano's help in preventing disruptions of the peace process by navy officers. During the Allied occupation, Nagano was charged with war crimes (q.v.) but died before the end of the trial.

NAGASAKI. Japanese port and shipbuilding center on Kyushu, attacked by the U.S. in its second use of an atomic bomb (q.v.), August 9, 1945. Nagasaki, the alternate choice for the bombing, was hit after bad weather prevented the crew of the *Bockscar,* a Boeing B-29 Superfortress (q.v.) based on Tinian (q.v.), from striking the city of Kokura, its original target. The bomb "Fat Man" destroyed two square miles of the city and killed 25,000 people, with 45,000 others dying from their injuries and radiation exposure by the end of the year. The attack on Nagasaki followed three days after the atomic bombing of Hiroshima (q.v.).

NAGUMO, CHUICHI (1887–1944). Japanese admiral; commander, First Air Fleet, 1941–1942. Nagumo led the carrier attacks on Pearl Harbor (q.v.) on December 7, 1941, which devastated the Pacific Fleet and shocked the United States (q.v.). In the following months, Nagumo led successful raids on Australia, the East Indies, and the Indian Ocean (qq.v.). The long distances covered by his forces as well as the damage they inflicted further astounded and alarmed the Allies (q.v.) during the early part of the Pacific War. Nagumo also participated in the Battle of Midway (q.v.) and in naval battles during the Guadalcanal campaign (q.v.). In 1942, he was replaced as head of the First Air Fleet and was stationed in the Japanese home islands and then in the Mariana Islands (qq.v.), where he committed suicide on Saipan (q.v.) after the U.S. invasion in July 1944.

NANKING. Capital of China (q.v.) from 1928 to 1937, which was captured by the Japanese on December 13, 1937, in a bloody battle that deteriorated into the infamous "Rape of Nanking." After the lengthy fight for Shanghai (q.v.) ended in November, the Japanese Central China Front Army under General Matsui Iwane moved toward Nanking, 150 miles to the northwest. As the Japanese advanced, the Chinese Nationalist government moved its capital, eventually settling in Chungking (q.v.). On December 12, Japanese planes attacked Allied ships in the Yangtze River, sinking the American gunboat *Panay* (q.v.) and provoking international complaints. The next day, the Japanese reached

Nanking and destroyed much of the city while looting, raping, and killing many of its inhabitants, atrocities for which Iwane was executed after the war. Estimates for the mostly civilian Chinese deaths in the "Rape of Nanking" range from 110,000 to 300,000. In 1940, Japan established in Nanking a puppet government under Wang Ching-wei (q.v.). After the war, the Chinese Nationalists again used Nanking as their capital until their ouster from the mainland in 1949. *See also* China, Japanese Operations in; War Crimes Trials.

NAPALM. Jellied gasoline used in incendiary bombs (q.v.) and flamethrowers. Invented by a U.S. chemist in 1943, napalm adhered to its targets, where it burned longer and at higher temperatures than gasoline. In the Pacific, the United States (q.v.) dropped its first napalm bombs in March 1944 against Ponape in the Caroline Islands (q.v.). The earliest employment during ground operations occurred on Tinian (q.v.) in July 1944, followed by wide use in later Allied operations. In the strategic air campaign (q.v.), Boeing B-29 (q.v.) bombers first dropped incendiary bombs containing napalm during raids against Japanese-held Hankow, China (q.v.), in late 1944, and against the Japanese home islands (q.v.) in January 1945.

NATIONAL DEFENSE RESEARCH COMMITTEE (NDRC). *See* OFFICE OF SCIENTIFIC RESEARCH AND DEVELOPMENT (OSRD).

NATIONALISTS, CHINESE. *See* CHIANG KAI-SHEK; CHINA, JAPANESE OPERATIONS IN; HO YING-CHIN; KUOMINTANG.

NAVAJO CODE TALKERS. Navajo Indians who transmitted encoded messages for the United States Marines (q.v.) during the Pacific War. In 1942, the marines recruited a small number of Navajos to develop a code based on their complex, unwritten language, which few non-Navajos spoke. Approximately 400 Navajos served as code talkers with the marines during their major campaigns in the Pacific from 1942 to 1945. Speaking in code, Navajo marines rapidly relayed information by telephone or radio under difficult combat conditions. Marine officers considered their performance at Iwo Jima (q.v.) to be especially outstanding and vital to the battle. The Japanese never broke the Navajo code, which the United States (q.v.) kept classified for many years after the war.

NAVAL VESSELS. Included battleships, aircraft carriers, cruisers, destroyers, submarines, motor torpedo or patrol torpedo boats (qq.v.), and other types. Prior to December 1941, strategists of both Japan and the United States (qq.v.) envisioned any future war between the two countries as a naval war, to be fought and decided primarily by their capital ships, the battleships. The perceived importance of the battleship was Admiral Isoruku Yamamoto's (q.v.) major reason for attacking the U.S. Fleet at Pearl Harbor (q.v.). Ironically, the success of his carrier-based planes in sinking U.S. battleships contributed to the carrier's replacement of the battleship as the most important surface warship of the Pacific War.

Japanese naval advantages included well-trained crews, the development and mastery of night tactics, the quality of its planes (especially the Mitsubishi Zero fighter [q.v.]), its torpedoes (q.v.), and its powerful destroyers and cruisers. Its liabilities were the failure to use radar (q.v.) extensively until later 1943, the neglect of antisubmarine warfare practices such as the use of convoys and escorts, its strategy of attacking Allied warships rather than lines of communication, and its inability to replace its losses in trained naval pilots. The Allied blockade increasingly limited the supply of fuel for naval operations. During the last 10 months of the war, when its fleet had been virtually destroyed, Japan's desperate resort to kamikaze (q.v.) attacks sank or seriously damaged many Allied ships, although failing to halt the Allied advances.

Favoring the Allies were the widespread use of radar, installed on U.S. carriers before Pearl Harbor and placed on all American warships by late 1942; achievements in signal intelligence (q.v.); technological advances such as the proximity fuze (q.v.) and improved torpedoes; and the immense production capabilities of U.S industry. Amphibious assaults (q.v.) were facilitated by the development of a variety of landing craft and ships (q.v.). Supporting U.S. naval forces was an enormous logistical system, which resupplied and refueled the ships at sea, rapidly constructed bases on captured territory, provided floating docks and repair facilities, and cared for the wounded on hospital ships. Although shipping shortages continued throughout the war, the U.S.-produced Liberty and Victory ships carried enormous amounts of cargo. The British Pacific Fleet (q.v.) was the largest non-U.S. force; other Allies also contributed to the naval war against Japan. *See also* Aircraft; Merchant Marine.

NAZI PARTY. Shortened name for the National Socialist German Workers' Party, which ruled Germany (q.v.) from 1933 to 1945 under the leadership of Adolf Hitler (q.v.).

NAZI-SOVIET PACT. *See* GERMAN-SOVIET NONAGGRESSION PACT.

NEHRU, JAWAHARLAL (1889–1964). Indian nationalist; president, Indian Congress Party; prime minister, India (q.v.), 1947–1964. A leading nationalist, Nehru opposed the British government's decision to involve India in the war against Germany (q.v.) without Indian consent and joined other members of the Indian Congress Party in protest activities. The British imprisoned him from 1940 to 1941 for his participation in Mohandas K. Gandhi's (q.v.) civil disobedience campaign. Soon after the United Kingdom entered the war against Japan (qq.v.), Nehru and Gandhi met with Richard Stafford Cripps (q.v.) to discuss the British offer to grant self-rule to India after the war if Indian nationalists would not oppose the British war effort. After rejecting the Cripps mission, Gandhi urged the British to "quit India" to keep the Japanese from attacking the country. The leaders of the Congress Party supported Gandhi and were arrested by British authorities. Nehru remained in jail from August 1942 to June 1945. When India gained independence in 1947, Nehru became its first prime minister.

NETHERLANDS, THE. Allied nation, whose government escaped to the United Kingdom (q.v.) when Germany (q.v.) invaded the country in May 1940. From its London base, the government under Queen Wilhelmina retained control of the Netherlands East Indies (q.v.), halted the sale of oil to Japan (q.v.) in August 1941, declared war on Japan on December 8, 1941, and participated in ABDACOM (q.v.), the futile Allied effort to stop the Japanese advance in early 1942. When Japan captured the islands in March 1942, Lieutenant Governor Hubertus J. van Mook and a few other officials escaped to Australia (q.v.); van Mook held the title "Minister of Colonies" throughout the war. The numerous Dutch residents of the Indies were interned by the Japanese under harsh conditions.

The Dutch aircraft in the Far East were virtually destroyed in the defense of Singapore (q.v.), while most of the naval vessels were lost during ABDACOM operations and the ground forces, a poorly equipped colonial army of 85,000, were captured. Because the Netherlands East Indies then came under the jurisdiction of two Allied theaters, Vice Admiral Conrad E. L. Helfrich, the commander of Dutch armed forces in the East, split the surviving forces between Ceylon (q.v.), where his ships and submarines served with the British Eastern Fleet (later the

British Pacific Fleet [q.v.]), and Australia (q.v.), where the Dutch contributed planes and other resources to the Southwest Pacific Area (SWPA) (q.v.) theater. Members of the Dutch intelligence (q.v.) service functioned in both locations, with the greater number based in Australia. Their attempts to conduct guerrilla operations behind Japanese lines were mostly unsuccessful, especially in Java and Sumatra (qq.v.), where their agents were consistently betrayed. Dutch merchant ships also participated in the war against Japan. At the time of the Japanese surrender (q.v.), the Combined Chiefs of Staff (q.v.) were considering Dutch offers to send additional forces to the Pacific, where they proposed to participate in the recapture of the Netherlands East Indies.

NETHERLANDS EAST INDIES. Dutch colony that included Bali, part of Borneo (q.v.), Celebes, Java (q.v.), the Moluccas, Sumatra (q.v.), western Timor (q.v.), and western New Guinea (q.v.). Rich in oil and other strategic raw materials (q.v.), its acquisition was a primary objective of Japan's Greater East Asia Co-prosperity Sphere (q.v.) and one of the reasons Japan decided to go to war in December 1941. Although the Netherlands (q.v.) had been occupied by Germany (q.v.) since May 1940, its government in exile continued to administer the colony. Dutch forces stationed in the Netherlands East Indies joined the short-lived ABDACOM (q.v.) attempt to stop the enemy, but by March 9, 1942, the Japanese controlled most of the colony.

To administer the archipelago, the Japanese assigned Sumatra, Java, and Madura to the army and the remaining areas to the navy. They released political activists imprisoned by the Dutch, including Achmad Sukarno and Mohammad Hatta (qq.v.), who encouraged cooperation with the occupation in exchange for eventual independence. The Japanese campaign to gain the support of nationalists was aided by Queen Wilhelmina's promise in late 1942 to consider a postwar commonwealth instead of independence for the Indies. The Japanese also permitted the creation of the Peta Army, a home defense force numbering 100,000. On August 11, 1945, Sukarno and Hatta conferred in Saigon with Japanese Field Marshal Hisaichi Terauchi (q.v.), who appointed them to head the Indonesian Independence Preparatory Committee.

Allied forces from the Southwest Pacific Area (q.v.) theater took control of much of Netherlands New Guinea in 1944 and 1945, Morotai (q.v.) in the Moluccas in 1944, and parts of Borneo in 1945, but

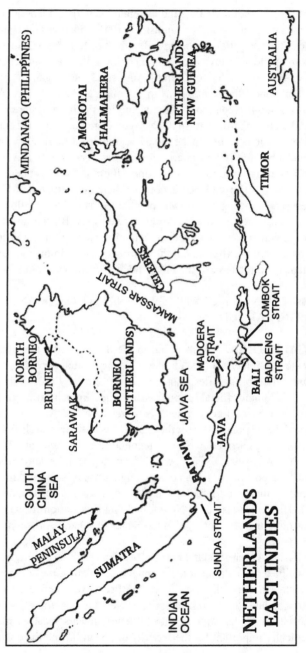

Netherlands East Indies

most of the Netherlands East Indies remained under Japanese control until the end of the war. On August 17, 1945, Sukarno and Hatta announced the formation of the new Republic of Indonesia. The Japanese commanders on Java and Sumatra delayed their announcement of the Japanese surrender (q.v.) until August 22 and began to transfer their arms and other equipment to nationalist groups before Allied troops arrived in September. First occupying the islands were British and Indian troops from the Southeast Asia Command (q.v.). Their immediate missions to disarm the Japanese soldiers, establish law and order, and liberate civilian internees and prisoners of war (q.v.) were complicated by strong nationalist opposition to the reinstatement of Dutch control. The violence encountered by the British and Indians was especially strong on Java and heightened when Dutch colonial officials tried to resume their administrative posts. By the late fall of 1946, the Dutch had assembled enough military forces in the Pacific to take over from the British, but they ultimately could not suppress the resistance and recognized the independence of Indonesia in 1949.

NEW BRITAIN. *See* CARTWHEEL, OPERATION; MANDATES, PACIFIC; RABAUL.

NEW CALEDONIA. French island in the South Pacific that supplied strategic raw materials (q.v.) to the Allies (q.v.) and served as an important Allied base. After France's fall to Germany (qq.v.) in 1940, New Caledonian officials supported the Free French rather than the Vichy France (q.v.) government. New Zealand and Australia (qq.v.) assumed the responsibility for the island's defense. In March 1942, the first U.S. troops arrived in New Caledonia; some of them later became part of the Americal Division, which derived part of its name from the island. The port of Noumea became an important base for Allied operations in the South Pacific, such as the campaign for Guadalcanal (q.v.). The Allies also used New Caledonia as a station for ships and planes traveling between the United States (q.v.) and Australia.

NEW GUINEA. Large island north of Australia (q.v.). Before the war, New Guinea was administered in three parts: Papua, the southeastern peninsula, an Australian territory; Northeast New Guinea, an Australian mandate (q.v.); and Netherlands New Guinea, the western part of the island, under Dutch control. New Guinea's location made it strategically important for the security of Australia and the control of

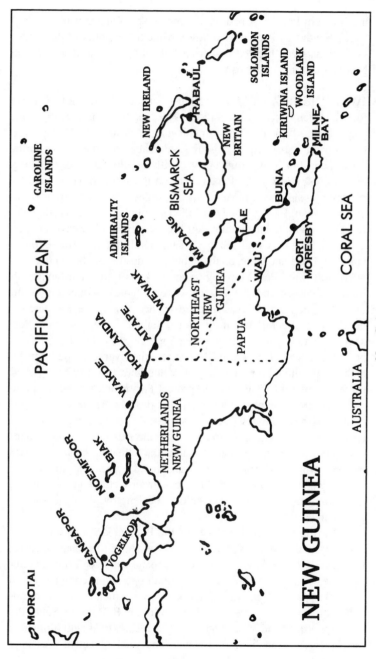

New Guinea

the southern Pacific. Allied operations in New Guinea were handled by the Southwest Pacific Area (q.v.), while the majority of the Japanese actions were directed first from Rabaul (q.v.) and then from the Netherlands East Indies (q.v.).

NEW GUINEA CAMPAIGN. Contest between Allied and Japanese forces, which lasted from 1942 to 1945. The first phase of the campaign focused on the Papuan peninsula. In March 1942, Japanese forces from Rabaul (q.v.) captured Salamaua and Lae on the northeastern coast of New Guinea (q.v.), with the ultimate goal of taking Port Moresby (q.v.), the Papuan city on the southern coast held by Australian soldiers. If Japan (q.v.) controlled Port Moresby, it could threaten Australia (q.v.) and cut Allied supply lines. In early May, the Japanese attempted to capture Port Moresby by sea but were stopped in the Battle of the Coral Sea (q.v). Two months later, Japanese forces landed at Buna and Gona on the Papuan peninsula and began to move overland toward Port Moresby on the Kokoda trail, an arduous path through jungles and the rugged Owen Stanley Mountains. With overextended lines and Australian resistance, the Japanese forces, under Major General Tomitoro Horii, halted 30 miles from Port Moresby and began to withdraw on September 17. During the same period, Japanese forces tried to support the overland operation by making an amphibious landing at Milne Bay (q.v.), where Allied forces were building airfields to protect Port Moresby; the Japanese withdrew by September 6. General Douglas MacArthur (q.v.), commander of the Southwest Pacific Area (SWPA) (q.v.), ordered a counteroffensive to begin on October 1, with the Australians, under General Thomas A. Blamey (q.v.), pursuing the retreating Japanese troops on land, while U.S. forces were transported by sea and air to other points. The Australian and American troops converged on Buna, where they fought for weeks before the lengthy, costly battle for Papua ended on January 22, 1943.

Occurring next was the Battle of the Bismarck Sea (q.v.), March 1–4, 1943, in which the Allied Air Forces under Lieutenant General George C. Kenney (q.v.) annihilated a Japanese convoy bringing reinforcements to the Lae area. Major ground operations commenced on June 30 as part of Operation Cartwheel (q.v.), which involved coordinated offensives by forces of Admiral William F. Halsey's South Pacific Area (q.v.) and MacArthur's SWPA theater to assault ultimately the Japanese stronghold of Rabaul. The final objective was later changed to the isolation of Rabaul rather than its capture. By the start of Cartwheel, the SWPA forces also included for the first time the U.S. Sixth Army under Lieutenant General Walter Krueger (q.v.). The main SWPA targets were Wau and Salamaua, taken by Australian soldiers in heavy fighting, and Lae and Finschhafen, captured by American troops in actions that included a major airborne operation (q.v.) at Nadzab. Opposing them was the Japanese Eighteenth Army under Lieutenant General Hatazo Adachi (q.v.), which was gradually pushed farther to the west. In March 1944, Adachi's army was transferred from the administration of the Eighth Area Army on Rabaul to the Second Area Army under General Korechika Anami (q.v.) in the Netherlands East Indies (q.v.).

In April 1944, Australian troops moving overland seized Madang, previously Adachi's headquarters. At the same time, in a massive operation bypassing the bulk of Japanese forces, American soldiers were transported nearly 600 miles to the west, where they made three amphibious landings at Hollandia and Aitape on April 22 and immediately began to build airfields. Carriers (q.v.) loaned by the Pacific Ocean Areas (q.v.) assisted with the Hollandia/Aitape operations. Landings at Sarmi (May 17) and the nearby island of Wakde (May 18) followed, involving heavy combat to secure the area. The next target was Biak Island, desired for its airfields and its strategic location on Geelvink Bay. The Allied troops invading on May 27 soon faced such heavy resistance, even after reinforcement, that MacArthur sent Lieutenant General Robert L. Eichelberger (q.v.) to direct the operation personally. Biak was secured in mid-July. In the meantime, Allied troops acquired additional airfields by capturing Noemfoor Island 60 miles west of Biak on July 2.

On July 10, Adachi's army mounted an offensive on the eastern side of Aitape, engaging Allied forces at the Driniumor River (q.v.). In bloody operations lasting until August 25, the Japanese were forced to withdraw and thereafter were unable to threaten Aitape and areas to the west, where the Allies (q.v.) built bases to support the upcoming Philippines campaigns (q.v.). In other operations, SWPA forces captured Sansapor on July 30 and completed the conquest of the Vogelkop peninsula on August 31. As American troops invaded the Philippines, beginning in October 1944, the Australian army remained on New Guinea, capturing the Japanese stronghold at Wewak on May 10, 1945. Adachi eventually took his remaining 13,000 troops to the hills, surrendering after the Japanese government capitulated.

NEW ZEALAND. British dominion and member of the Allies (q.v.). In September 1939, New Zealand entered the war against Germany (q.v.), subsequently sending armed forces to participate in actions against Germany and Italy (q.v.). After Japan's (q.v.) attacks of December 7–8, 1941, New Zealand declared war, signed the Declaration of the United Nations, and joined the Pacific War Councils (qq.v.). Throughout the war with Japan, New Zealand's prime minister was Peter Fraser (q.v.).

From January to April 1942, New Zealand came under the Allied ANZAC (q.v.) command; it was then included in the South Pacific subtheater of the Pacific Ocean Areas (qq.v.). While many of New Zealand's military forces continued to battle Germany and Italy, other ground, sea, and air forces participated in campaigns in the Pacific under American direction and also served with the British Pacific Fleet (q.v.). New Zealanders also served as coastwatchers (q.v.).

One of New Zealand's major contributions to the Allied war effort was its provision of agricultural and manufacturing products, especially its exports of food to the United Kingdom (q.v.) and to U.S. forces in the Pacific. The country suffered shortages of manpower for production and consequently moved personnel from the military to the labor force during the latter part of the war. New Zealand also served as a base for U.S. troops during much of the war. New Zealand joined with Australia (q.v.) in protesting the inferior position accorded the smaller powers in the formation of the United Nations organization (q.v.). New Zealanders served with the Allied occupation forces in Japan. On September 1, 1951, New Zealand signed a security pact with Australia and the United States (q.v.).

NIMITZ, CHESTER WILLIAM (1885–1966). U.S. Fleet Admiral; commander, Pacific Ocean Areas (POA) (q.v.), 1941–1945. Nimitz headed the Bureau of Navigation (actually the navy's personnel department) from 1939 to 1941. Appointed after the Pearl Harbor attack (q.v.) to succeed Admiral Husband E. Kimmel (q.v.) as commander of the Pacific Fleet, Nimitz assumed his post at Pearl Harbor on December 31, 1941. During his first months of command, he focused on rebuilding the fleet and executing limited carrier (q.v.) attacks on Japanese-held islands until American forces became strong enough for major offensive action.

On March 30, 1942, the United States Joint Chiefs of Staff (JCS) (q.v.) partitioned the Pacific into two theaters of operation: POA, under Nimitz, and the Southwest Pacific Area (SWPA) (q.v.), headed by General Douglas MacArthur (q.v.). Nimitz's command, which was dominated by American naval and marine forces, was divided into three subtheaters: North Pacific, Central Pacific, and South Pacific (qq.v.). He worked closely with Admiral Ernest J. King (q.v.), who acted as the executive agent for the JCS in communicating with the theater. Among the major operations completed during Nimitz's tenure were the Battles of the Coral Sea and Midway and campaigns in the Solomons, the Aleutians, the Gilberts, the Marshalls, the Marianas, the Palaus, Iwo Jima, and Okinawa (qq.v.). His forces also attacked Japanese merchant shipping, assaulted the Japanese home islands (q.v.), and assisted SWPA campaigns in New Guinea and the Philippines (qq.v.).

At the formal ceremony on September 2, 1945, Nimitz accepted the Japanese surrender (q.v.) on behalf of the United States (q.v.). Promoted to Fleet Admiral in December 1944, he succeeded King as chief of naval operations after the war.

NISEI. *See* JAPANESE AMERICANS.

NOEMFOOR. *See* AIRBORNE OPERATIONS; ASSAULTS; NEW GUINEA CAMPAIGN.

NOMONHAN. Site of fighting between Japanese and Soviet troops on the Manchurian-Mongolian border, May 11–September 16, 1939. The battle was named Khalkhin-Gol by the Union of Soviet Socialist Republics (q.v.) and Nomonhan by Japan (q.v.). Since 1938, the U.S.S.R. had stationed troops in Outer Mongolia (q.v.), its close ally, while the Japanese Kwantung Army (q.v.) occupied Manchukuo (q.v.), the Japanese puppet state in Manchuria (q.v.). Following border clashes between soldiers of Mongolia and Manchukuo in May 1939, Soviet and Japanese forces engaged in intense combat throughout the summer. Heavily reinforced Soviet troops, led by General Georgi K. Zhukov (q.v.) and using an enormous number of tanks (q.v.), inflicted substantial losses on the less heavily equipped Japanese infantry forces, whose doctrine held that the superior Japanese spirit would prevail over enemy armor. Significant air attacks also took place. Both sides agreed to a cease-fire on September 16, influenced in part by the start of war in Europe and the German-Soviet Nonaggression Pact (q.v.), which was signed during Zhukov's offensive at Nomonhan.

NOMURA, KICHISABURO (1887–1964). Japanese foreign minister, 1939–1940; ambassador to the United States (q.v.), 1940–1942. A distinguished naval officer, Nomura served in the Russo-Japanese War and represented Japan (q.v.) at the Paris Peace Conference after World War I. Throughout most of 1941, Nomura conducted lengthy negotiations with U.S. Secretary of State Cordell Hull (q.v.) as tensions between the two countries escalated, although the Japanese government did not fully inform Nomura of its intentions regarding war. He was joined during the last month of talks by Saburo Kurusu (q.v.). Because of communications difficulties, Nomura delivered Japan's declaration of war to Hull after the secretary had received word of the Pearl Harbor (q.v.) attack on December 7, 1941. Nomura was interned in the United States and resigned soon after his repatriation to Japan in 1942.

NORTH PACIFIC AREA. Subtheater of the Allied Pacific Ocean Areas (POA) (q.v.) theater, under the command of Admiral Chester W. Nimitz (q.v.). It included regions north of the 42d parallel, primarily the U.S.-owned Aleutian Islands (q.v.). The North Pacific Area was headed successively by three naval officers: Rear Admiral Robert A. Theobald, May 1942–January 1943; Rear Admiral Thomas C. Kinkaid (q.v.), January–November 1943; and Vice Admiral Frank Jack Fletcher (q.v.), November 1943–August 1945. For much of the war, the chief army officer in the area was Lieutenant General Simon B. Buckner (q.v.), head of the Alaskan Department.

In early June 1942, in conjunction with the Battle of Midway (q.v.), Japanese naval forces in the northern Pacific attacked U.S. facilities at Dutch Harbor and seized the islands of Attu and Kiska. U.S. forces occupied Adak (August 30, 1942) and Amchitka (January 11, 1943), where they constructed bases. U.S. surface vessels, submarines, and aircraft (including the Eleventh Air Force) repeatedly attacked the Japanese garrisons and the ships and submarines (q.v.) that resupplied them, stopping an entire convoy in the Battle of the Komandorski Islands (March 26, 1943). U.S. forces recaptured Attu (May 11–30, 1943) in a costly battle, followed by an unopposed American-Canadian landing on Kiska (August 15, 1943), which the Japanese had secretly abandoned. Throughout the rest of the war, the main military activities in the North Pacific were offensive actions conducted by U.S. aircraft, submarines, and ships against the Kurile Islands (q.v.) and Japanese shipping. Planes also conducted reconnaissance and mapping missions, mostly over the Kuriles. More than 200 American air-

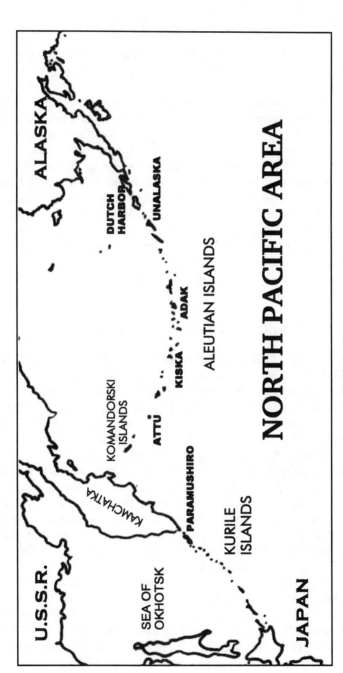

North Pacific Area

men made emergency landings in the Union of Soviet Socialist Republics (q.v.), where they were interned, some until the end of the war. U.S. forces also destroyed several Japanese balloon bombs (q.v.) passing over the Aleutians.

Although the main Allied Pacific offensives were conducted farther south, U.S. strategists considered the North Pacific as a potential route for the invasion of Japan (q.v.). They also explored potential cooperative military ventures with the U.S.S.R., involving North Pacific forces and bases. The United States Army Air Forces (q.v.) made plans to build Boeing B-29 (q.v.) airfields in the Aleutians, although the capture of the Marianas (q.v.) provided preferable sites for the strategic air campaign (q.v.). In addition to protecting the Canadian and American coasts from major Japanese attacks, the forces of the North Pacific Area also guarded convoy routes for lend-lease (q.v.) aid going to the U.S.S.R.

-O-

OCTAGON. *See* QUEBEC CONFERENCE, SECOND.

OFFICE OF SCIENTIFIC RESEARCH AND DEVELOPMENT (OSRD). Agency created by an executive order of U.S. President Franklin D. Roosevelt (q.v.) in June 1941 to coordinate the efforts of civilian scientists with the military in providing for national defense. The OSRD superseded the National Defense Research Committee (NDRC) (formed in June 1940), which then became its advisory council. The key men overseeing OSRD's success were Vannevar Bush (q.v.), its director from 1941 to 1946, and his deputy James B. Conant, a chemist and the president of Harvard University. Both men enjoyed direct access to Roosevelt. Much of the OSRD's work was accomplished through research contracts awarded to more than 50 universities and production by large defense corporations. It also exchanged information with other Allied programs, especially the British, and maintained an office in London.

During the first part of the war, in accordance with U.S. policy, the OSRD concentrated on the effort against Germany and Italy (qq.v.) and placed a lower priority on the vastly different needs of the conflict with Japan (q.v.). In October 1943, it established the Office of Field Service (OFS), headed by Karl T. Compton, to increase support of the Pacific War. The OFS opened offices at the theater headquarters of the

Japanese attack on U.S. bases at Pearl Harbor on Oahu in the Hawaiian Islands, December 7, 1941. U.S. Navy. Courtesy of the George C. Marshall Research Library.

Japanese soldiers on the Bataan Peninsula of Luzon in the Philippine Islands. Captured Japanese photograph, U.S. Army Signal Corps. Courtesy of the George C. Marshall Research Library.

From the deck of the U.S. aircraft carrier *Hornet,* a B-25 bomber takes off as part of the Doolittle Raid on the Japanese home islands, April 18, 1942. U.S. Navy. Courtesy of the George C. Marshall Research Library.

Chinese Generalissimo Chiang Kai-shek and U.S. Lieutenant General Joseph W. Stilwell, April 1942. U.S. Army.

Japanese soldiers in combat, 1942. Captured Japanese photograph, U.S. Army Signal Corps. Courtesy of the George C. Marshall Research Library.

Meeting of the Anglo-American leaders during the Casablanca Conference, January 14–24, 1943. From left to right: (seated) President Franklin D. Roosevelt and Prime Minister Winston S. Churchill; (standing) General Henry H. Arnold, Admiral Ernest J. King, General George C. Marshall, Admiral of the Fleet Dudley Pound, General Alan F. Brooke, and Field Marshal John Dill; (second row, visible between Pound and Brooke) Air Chief Marshal Charles Portal. U.S. Army Signal Corps. Courtesy of the Frank McCarthy Collection, George C. Marshall Research Library.

Construction of the Ledo Road (later renamed the Stilwell Road), 1943. Beginning in the town of Ledo in Assam, India, the Allies built a 500-mile road through the jungles and mountains of northern Burma in order to open a land route to China. U.S. Army Signal Corps. Courtesy of the George C. Marshall Research Library.

U.S. Marines in combat on Bougainville in the Solomon Islands, late 1943 or early 1944. U.S. Marine Corps. Courtesy of the George C. Marshall Research Library.

Antiaircraft guns shoot down a Japanese torpedo plane during a U.S. carrier raid on the Japanese-held Marshall Islands, December 4, 1943. U.S. Office of War Information. Courtesy of the George C. Marshall Research Library.

An LST (landing ship, tank) transports Allied soldiers to a beach in New Guinea. U.S. Army Signal Corps. Courtesy of the George C. Marshall Research Library.

American leaders discuss future strategy in the Pacific War during the Pearl Harbor Conference, July 26–28, 1944. From left to right: General Douglas MacArthur, President Franklin D. Roosevelt, Admiral Chester W. Nimitz, and Admiral William D. Leahy. U.S. Navy.

U.S. Marines advance on Iwo Jima, February 19, 1945. U.S. Marine Corps. Courtesy of the George C. Marshall Research Library.

The U.S. cruiser *Biloxi* in the Pacific, April 1945. U.S. Navy. Courtesy of the
George C. Marshall Research Library.

Boeing B-29 Superfortresses drop incendiary bombs on the Japanese city of Yokohama, May 29, 1945. U.S. Office of War Information. Courtesy of the George C. Marshall Research Library.

The Manhattan Project successfully tests the first atomic bomb near Alamogordo, New Mexico, July 16, 1945. Courtesy of the George C. Marshall Research Library.

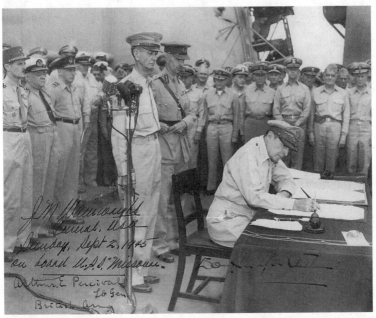

During the Japanese surrender ceremony on the U.S. battleship *Missouri* on September 2, 1945, General of the Army Douglas MacArthur signs the document on behalf of the Allied powers. Standing behind him are U.S. General Jonathan M. Wainwright and British Lieutenant General Arthur E. Percival, who were captured by the Japanese in 1942 and remained prisoners until the end of the war. The photograph bears the signatures of all three men. U.S. Army Signal Corps.

Southwest Pacific and Pacific Ocean Areas (qq.v.) and was in the process of establishing its Pacific Branch in Manila when the war ended. The OFS also worked closely with Australian and British Commonwealth scientific agencies.

In its selection of projects, the OSRD focused primarily on areas that promised to be useful to the wartime effort and also undertook specific assignments at the request of the military, which continued to maintain separate research programs. It also held the responsibility for the improvement of military medicine (q.v.). In addition to addressing new problems, the OSRD devoted considerable resources to the development and production of innovations that originated elsewhere. Among the many subjects of OSRD research were radar (q.v.), the proximity fuze (q.v.), bombs (q.v.), rockets and rocket launchers (q.v.) (including the bazooka), the mapping and charting of the Pacific, napalm (q.v.), flamethrowers, penicillin, antimalarial programs, DDT, and amphibious vehicles (q.v.) such as the Dukw. OSRD personnel provided advice on targets for the strategic air campaign (q.v.) against Japan, analyzed bomb damage, and studied the problem of kamikaze (q.v.) attacks. The Office of Strategic Services (q.v.) also relied on the OSRD for the development of special equipment for its operations.

The development of the atomic bomb (q.v.) fell under OSRD's jurisdiction until its transfer in 1942 to the U.S. military's Manhattan Project (q.v.), although Bush and other top OSRD leaders retained oversight over the scientific aspect of the program. The OSRD participated in the Alsos (q.v.) intelligence mission to Europe to determine the status of German progress on the atomic bomb, the proximity fuze, and other weapons. After the war, the Truman (q.v.) administration dismantled the OSRD. *See also* Landing Craft and Ships; Science and Technology.

OFFICE OF STRATEGIC SERVICES (OSS). U.S. wartime intelligence (q.v.) agency. By an executive order in July 1941, President Franklin D. Roosevelt created the Office of the Coordinator of Information (COI), a civilian organization reporting directly to him regarding national security. As its director, Roosevelt appointed attorney William J. Donovan (q.v.), who had undertaken numerous foreign missions for the president and had recommended the formation of the COI.

In a reorganization effective July 13, 1942, Roosevelt established two new agencies to succeed the COI: the Office of War Information, which assumed the COI's propaganda function, and the OSS. Still headed by Donovan, the OSS now came under the jurisdiction of the United States Joint Chiefs of Staff (q.v.). Among its assignments were sabotage, guerrilla operations, and the collection and analysis of information. The OSS's program for subversive warfare was patterned after the British Special Operations Executive (SOE) (q.v.), which helped the new OSS by training agents and sharing special equipment. Although not without differences, the OSS and the SOE worked closely together in Europe. They often clashed in Asia.

The independence and unorthodox nature of the OSS leadership, agents, and practices evoked suspicion in the American army and naval intelligence agencies, the Federal Bureau of Investigation (FBI), and the State Department. The FBI insisted that the OSS be banned from working in Latin America (q.v.) and collecting domestic information in the United States (q.v.). Similarly, the objections of theater commanders prevented its operation in the Pacific Ocean Areas and the Southwest Pacific Area (qq.v.). In the war against Japan, the OSS focused on China (q.v.) and parts of Southeast Asia.

In China, the OSS initially served under the U.S. Naval Group, China, and the Sino-American Cooperative Organization (SACO) (q.v.), later reporting through the U.S. Fourteenth Air Force. SACO and its Chinese Nationalist head, General Tai Li, greatly hampered OSS activities throughout the country. After February 1945, when the OSS came directly under the command of theater head Lieutenant General Albert C. Wedemeyer (q.v.), OSS operations expanded significantly. The OSS worked to counter Japanese authority in occupied areas, rescue downed Allied airmen, and provide target information for the air war. Its agents also formed an important part of the Dixie Mission (q.v.) to the Chinese Communists and engaged in limited guerrilla training with them.

From Chinese bases, the OSS supported guerrillas opposing the Japanese in French Indochina (q.v.), including the Viet Minh and Ho Chi Minh (qq.v.). Their assistance to the Viet Minh, who wanted independence for the country, directly contradicted the SOE's intention to restore French rule after the defeat of the Japanese. In Thailand (q.v.), the OSS helped the Free Thai forces. On the Malay Peninsula (q.v.), the OSS maintained contact with the Malayan People's Anti-Japanese Army, as the SOE did separately. The OSS also attempted several unsuccessful expeditions to Sumatra (q.v.).

In Burma (q.v.), OSS Detachment 101 operated behind enemy lines in support of efforts to reopen the Burma Road (q.v.). Relying on parachute drops for the placement of agents and for resupply, the OSS sabotaged Japanese installations, saved airmen, and collected information. The detachment worked mainly with members of the Kachin tribe, eventually arming 10,000 of them to harass and demoralize the Japanese troops. President Harry S. Truman (q.v.) abolished the OSS in October 1945. Many OSS members joined the brief-lived Central Intelligence Group and then its permanent successor, the Central Intelligence Agency, which was created in 1947. See also Intelligence, Allied.

OKAMURA, YASUJI (1884–1966). Japanese general; commander, North China Area Army, 1941–1944; commander, Chinese Expeditionary Army, 1944–1945. As an army officer, Okamura participated in the invasion of Manchuria (q.v.) in 1931–1932 and in the start of the Sino-Japanese War in 1937. After heading the North China Area Army from 1941 to 1944, he became the commander of the Chinese Expeditionary Army. His major action in this post was his direction of the enormous Ichigo (q.v.) offensive beginning in April 1944, which seized U.S. bomber (q.v.) airfields in eastern China (q.v.) and a number of vital military and transportation centers in central and southern China. In May 1945, Okamura halted the drive to move forces north, where Japan feared the Union of Soviet Socialist Republics (q.v.) would enter the war. After the Japanese surrender (q.v.) and a brief stay in a Chinese prison, Okamura provided advice to Chiang Kai-shek (q.v.) during the Chinese civil war. He returned to Japan in 1949.

OKINAWA. Largest island of the Ryukyu Archipelago and site of one of the bloodiest battles of the war, April 1–July 2, 1945. Located 350 miles south of Kyushu, one of the main Japanese islands, Okinawa was defended by the Japanese Thirty-second Army under Lieutenant General Mitsuru Ushijima, with well-positioned heavy weapons and air support from other Japanese-controlled areas. The Japanese high command believed that Allied forces would target Okinawa, which Ushijima planned to defend primarily from the rugged area around Shuri Castle in the southern part of the island.

Fleet Admiral Chester W. Nimitz (q.v.) and his planners in the Pacific Ocean Areas (POA) (q.v.) theater considered the Okinawa operation to be the last vital amphibious landing in the Central Pacific Area (CENPAC) (q.v.) drive prior to the invasion of Japan (q.v.) itself. Nimitz placed in charge Admiral Raymond A. Spruance (q.v.), commander of the CENPAC subtheater and the Fifth Fleet, who most

Okinawa, April 1, 1945

recently had overseen the capture of Iwo Jima (q.v.). The U.S. Tenth Army, headed by Lieutenant General Simon B. Buckner, Jr. (q.v.) and containing both army and marine (qq.v.) forces, was by far the largest ground force used in the Central Pacific. The formidable armada of ships accompanying the invasion included vessels from the British Pacific Fleet (q.v.) and other Allied navies.

After intense preassault bombardment, U.S. forces moved ashore on April 1, 1945, encountering relatively light resistance on the ground until they moved toward the well-fortified lines around Shuri Castle, where horrendous casualties on both sides occurred. As the armies battled on the island, nearly 2,000 kamikazes (q.v.) attacked the beach-head and the vast fleet offshore, causing the greatest ship losses suffered by the United States Navy (q.v.) during the war. Japan (q.v.) attempted to send its superbattleship, the *Yamato* (q.v.), on a suicide mission to attack the Okinawa naval forces, but Allied forces sank it far from its objective. Before the island was declared secure on July 2, Buckner was killed in action (June 18) and Ushijima and his chief of staff committed suicide (June 22), as did many other Japanese soldiers. Marine Lieutenant General Roy S. Geiger (q.v.), as senior commander, directed the Okinawa operation after Buckner's death. Later, General Joseph W. Stilwell (q.v.) assumed command of the Tenth Army, which was being considered for use in an invasion of Japan. During the latter half of the campaign, Admiral William F. Halsey (q.v.) and the Third Fleet command replaced Spruance and the Fifth Fleet.

The human cost of Okinawa was enormous. The total number of Americans killed on the ground and sea was the highest of any Pacific operation. The United States (q.v.) suffered 36,000 wounded and 12,500 dead, including many deaths in the fleet. Japan lost 110,000 killed and 7,400 captured. Approximately 42,000 civilians on Okinawa also died. The huge losses and the pattern of Japanese resistance to the last man seemed to indicate that an even fiercer fight and much higher casualties would occur during a ground invasion of Japan. The Okinawa operation was one of the factors considered when the U.S. leadership decided to use atomic bombs (q.v.) against Japan in August 1945.

After the war, the United States continued to administer the Ryukyu Islands, which had been part of Japan since 1879. The United States returned part of the Ryukyus to Japan in 1953 and turned over control of the rest, including Okinawa, in 1972.

OLYMPIC. *See* JAPAN, INVASION OF.

OSHIMA, HIROSHI (1886–1975). Japanese army officer and diplomat; military attaché in Germany (q.v.), 1934–1938; ambassador to Germany, 1938–1939, 1941–1945. Oshima, one of the leading Japanese advocates of close ties to Germany, helped to negotiate the Anti-Comintern and Tripartite Pacts (qq.v.) between Germany and Japan (q.v.). As ambassador in Berlin, he met personally with Adolf Hitler (q.v.), had direct access to Foreign Minister Joachim von Ribbentrop, and read German battle reports. Oshima reported frequently and at length to his superiors in Tokyo (q.v.) about Germany's conduct of the war, his conversations with officials in Berlin, and gossip he had heard about the German high command. Unknown to the Japanese, American intelligence could intercept and read the high-level Japanese diplomatic code (Purple) used by their embassies. Oshima's long, detailed messages provided a rich body of information to the Allies (q.v.), especially about the progress of the war between Germany and the Union of Soviet Socialist Republics (q.v.).

After the war, Oshima was convicted by the Allied war crimes trials (q.v.), sentenced to a life sentence, and paroled in 1955. *See also* Intelligence, Allied Signal.

OSMEÑA, SERGIO (1898–1961). Vice president, 1941–1944, and president, 1944–1946, Philippine Commonwealth. After Japan (q.v.) invaded the Philippine Islands (q.v.) in December 1941, Osmeña was evacuated with other high government officials. For most of the 1942–1944 period he worked with President Manuel Quezon (q.v.) and the rest of the Philippine government in exile in Washington, D.C., becoming president upon Quezon's death in 1944. When American troops invaded the Philippine island of Leyte (q.v.) on October 20, 1944, Osmeña accompanied General Douglas MacArthur (q.v.) to the shore, where the two men broadcast announcements of the landing to the Philippine people. In 1946, Osmeña was defeated by Manuel Roxas for the presidency of the newly independent Philippines.

OZAWA, JISABURO (1886–1966). Japanese admiral; commander, Southern Expeditionary Fleet, 1941–1942; commander, First Mobile Fleet, 1941–1944; commander, Third Fleet, 1944; vice chief of naval general staff, 1944–1945; commander, Combined Fleet, 1945. In December 1941, Ozawa's command protected the Japanese landings in Thailand and the northern Malay peninsula (qq.v.). During the following months, his naval forces participated in the conquest of the Malay peninsula, Singapore, and the East Indies (qq.v.), in addition to engaging in raids against British ships and bases in the Indian Ocean (q.v.). He later commanded two fleets in the Battle of the Philippine Sea (June 1944) (q.v.), an overwhelming American victory in which the bulk of Japanese pilots and planes were lost, and participated in the Battle for Leyte Gulf (q.v.), where he successfully used his forces to draw Admiral William F. Halsey's (q.v.) Third Fleet away from the main Japanese action. During the closing months of the war, Ozawa served as the last commander of the Japanese Combined Fleet (q.v.). He retired after the end of the war.

PACIFIC FLEET. *See* BRITISH PACIFIC FLEET; UNITED STATES NAVY.

PACIFIC OCEAN AREAS (POA). Allied theater of operations commanded by U.S. Admiral Chester W. Nimitz (q.v.), who reported to Admiral Ernest J. King (q.v.) as executive agent for the United States Joint Chiefs of Staff (q.v.). On March 30, 1942, the Joint Chiefs divided the Pacific into POA and the Southwest Pacific Area (SWPA) (q.v.). POA covered the Pacific with the exceptions of Southeast Asia and the areas assigned to SWPA. POA was subdivided into three parts: North Pacific Area (q.v.), including Alaska and the Aleutian Islands (q.v.); Central Pacific Area (q.v.), the most active subtheater during the last part of the war; and South Pacific Area (q.v.), where POA's first major offensive occurred on Guadalcanal (q.v.). Nimitz's command consisted primarily of U.S. naval and marine forces. During most of the war his principal fleet commanders were Admiral Raymond F. Spruance and Admiral William A. Halsey (qq.v.). POA headquarters was at Pearl Harbor (q.v.) until late 1944, when Nimitz shifted his offices to Guam in the Mariana Islands (qq.v.).

PACIFIC WAR COUNCILS. Advisory organizations formed by the United Kingdom and the United States (qq.v.) to allow other Allied countries to discuss the direction of the war in the Pacific. The Pacific War Council in the United Kingdom met for the first time on February 9, 1942, and included representatives from the United Kingdom, Australia, India, the Netherlands, and New Zealand (qq.v.); Canada (q.v.) joined later. The U.S. organization with the same name held its first meeting on April 1, 1942, with members from Australia, Canada, China (q.v.), India, the Netherlands, New Zealand, the Philippine Commonwealth (q.v.), and the United Kingdom. British Prime Minister Winston S. Churchill and U.S. President Franklin D. Roosevelt (qq.v.) created the groups to address charges that the Anglo-American alliance was determining strategy for the war against Japan (q.v.) without considering the views of other countries involved. The councils permitted the expression of ideas; however, the members had no power to enforce their opinions.

PALAU ISLANDS. Island group in the Caroline Islands (q.v.) in the western Pacific, including the islands of Peleliu and Angaur, which U.S. troops invaded in September 1944. By the time of the Palaus operation,

Allied Theaters in the Pacific

Allied forces held the Mariana Islands (q.v.) and were planning next to capture the Philippines (q.v.). Because the Palaus were located between those two island groups, some military planners believed the islands should be captured to protect the flanks of Allied forces attempting to invade the Philippines. One of the strongest advocates of the Palaus operations was Admiral Chester W. Nimitz (q.v.), in whose theater the Palaus lay and whose Third Fleet was to be loaned to the Philippine campaign to cover the initial landings. Other planners, anticipating the strong resistance that most invasions of Japanese-held islands encountered, believed the Palaus could be bypassed. The United States Joint Chiefs of Staff (q.v.) approved the operation on Nimitz's recommendation. Assigned to the operation was the III Amphibious Corps under Lieutenant General Roy S. Geiger (q.v.).

The first island assaulted was Peleliu, invaded on September 15, 1944, and secured on November 27. The Japanese forces did not try to defend the beaches, as was the case in many previous invasions, but attacked the invaders from an elaborate interior system of caves and tunnels. Peleliu's lengthy capture involved extremely fierce fighting, resulting in high American casualties and the death of almost all of the Japanese garrison. Its original invasion force, the 1st Marine Division, was assisted in late September by army units and relieved in mid-October by the 81st Infantry Division, the army force that had captured the island of Angaur, September 17–30, where resistance was much lighter. On September 22–24, army units took control of the Ulithi atoll in the Caroline Islands, which was unoccupied; its harbor proved much more valuable than bases constructed on Peleliu and Angaur.

PANAY. U.S. gunboat that was attacked and sunk in the Yangtze River in China (q.v.) by Japanese planes on December 12, 1937. The Japanese government described the event as an accident, formally apologized to the United States (q.v.), and paid an indemnity. The administration of President Franklin D. Roosevelt (q.v.) accepted the Japanese explanation, although witnesses differed over whether the incident was intentional. Coinciding with the Japanese atrocities in Nanking (q.v.), the bombing of the *Panay* angered the American public and contributed to the anti-Japanese feeling in the United States.

PAPUA. *See* MILNE BAY; NEW GUINEA; PORT MORESBY.

PATCH, ALEXANDER MCCARRELL, JR. (1889–1945). United States Army general; commander, Americal Division, 1942–1943; commander, IV Corps and Desert Training Center, 1943–1944; commander, Seventh Army, 1944–1945. In the spring of 1942, he was sent to the South Pacific Area (q.v.) to organize and train the new Americal Division, named because it was composed mostly of American troops on New Caledonia (q.v.). The division went into combat for the first time on Guadalcanal (q.v.), where Patch in early December 1942 relieved Major General A. A. Vandegrift (q.v.) and the 1st Marine Division, most of whom were ill and exhausted after months of jungle combat. The next month Patch became the commander of the XIV Corps, including both army and marine (qq.v.) reinforcements on Guadalcanal, where he oversaw the successful conclusion of the campaign on February 9, 1943.

In April 1943, Patch was transferred from the Pacific. He held a training assignment in the United States (q.v.) until named in March 1944 to head the Seventh Army in Sicily. In August of that year, his army invaded southern France and advanced toward Germany as part of the Sixth Army Group. At the conclusion of the war in Europe he returned to the United States, where he trained troops until his death in late 1945.

PATROL TORPEDO (PT) BOAT. U.S. name for motor torpedo boats, used primarily in the Pacific War to attack Japanese shipping, particularly in coastal areas. PT boats also laid mines (q.v.), generated smoke screens, conducted intelligence missions, and carried out rescues. In March 1942, PT boats evacuated General Douglas MacArthur (q.v.), his family, and his main staff from the Philippines (q.v.). The vessels played a prominent role in the campaigns for the Solomon Islands and New Guinea, including the Battle of the Bismarck Sea (qq.v.). During the Allied recapture of the Philippines in 1944–1945, PT boats destroyed Japanese suicide craft.

Made with wooden hulls, PT boats were 77 to 80 feet in length, displaced 56 tons, operated with crews of 12 to 14, and could travel at speeds of 41 knots. They were armed with torpedoes (q.v.), depth charges, and a variety of guns. Three American companies built PT boats: the Electric Boat Company (Elco boats), Higgins Industries (Higgins boats), and the Huckins Yacht Company.

PEARL HARBOR, ATTACK ON. Surprise Japanese bombing of the U.S. Pacific Fleet at its main bases on Oahu, Hawaii, on December 7, 1941. When Japan decided to expand into Southeast Asia and the East Indies (q.v.), Admiral Isoruku Yamamoto (q.v.), commander of the Japanese Combined Fleet (q.v.), insisted that the U.S. Pacific Fleet had to be disabled before Japan could achieve its goals. He planned a preemptive air strike on Pearl Harbor, where the main U.S. Fleet had been based since May 1940. The attack force, led by Vice Admiral Chuichi Nagumo (q.v.), left the Kurile Islands (q.v.) on November 26, 1941, and launched its aircraft carrier (q.v.) attacks on Sunday, December 7. The Japanese achieved complete surprise, losing 100 men while killing 2,400 Americans, sinking much of the fleet, and destroying many aircraft. The strike severely damaged all eight U.S. battleships (q.v.), although only two were lost permanently. The three U.S. carriers based in the Pacific escaped damage because all were at sea when the attack occurred. Also left intact were the oil storage and naval repair facilities on Oahu.

On December 8, 1941, President Franklin D. Roosevelt (q.v.) asked Congress to declare war on Japan, calling December 7 "a day which will live in infamy," and the United States (q.v.) entered the war. By attacking Pearl Harbor, the Japanese won a tactical victory but lost strategically, because the U.S. population, including many former isolationists, united in outrage against their action. Yamamoto had hoped that the destruction of the U.S. Fleet would enable Japan to make quick territorial gains and then negotiate a peace with the United States, but the attitude of the American public made that impossible.

As a result of the attack, Admiral Husband E. Kimmel (q.v.), commander of the Pacific Fleet and the U.S. Fleet, and Major General Walter C. Short, head of army forces on Oahu, were relieved of duty. Numerous investigations by the military and by Congress have tried to determine responsibility for the heavy losses and the lack of readiness, with special attention devoted to the availability and accuracy of intelligence (q.v.) information, and in May 1999 the U.S. Senate voted to clear both Kimmel and Short of charges. Controversy about the attack continues, however.

PEARL HARBOR CONFERENCE, JULY 26–28, 1944. Meeting of U.S. President Franklin D. Roosevelt, Admiral William D. Leahy, General Douglas MacArthur, and Admiral Chester W. Nimitz (qq.v.) to discuss the Pacific War. The main topic of discussion was the next major strategic decision in the war against Japan (q.v.): the assault of Luzon in the Philippines (qq.v.), which MacArthur advocated, or the island of Formosa (q.v.), possibly combined with a landing on the adjacent Chinese coast, the course supported by Nimitz. The matter was not resolved until the fall, when the United States Joint Chiefs of Staff (q.v.) authorized the Luzon invasion. See also Luzon versus Formosa Debate.

PELELIU. See PALAU ISLANDS.

PERCIVAL, ARTHUR ERNEST (1887–1966). British general; general officer commanding, Malaya force, 1941–1942; prisoner of war (q.v.), 1942–1945. As the commander of British forces in Malaya, Percival led the unsuccessful defense of the Malay peninsula (q.v.) and the heavily fortified island Singapore (q.v.) against the Japanese invasion in December 1941. On February 15, 1942, he surrendered Singapore to Japan (q.v.), becoming a prisoner of the Japanese for the duration of the war. Following the Japanese surrender (q.v.), Percival was freed from a Japanese camp in Manchuria (q.v.) and participated in the formal ceremony on the battleship USS *Missouri* on September 2, 1945.

PESCADORES ISLANDS. Group of islands between Formosa (q.v.) and the coast of mainland China (q.v.); acquired by Japan (q.v.) from China in 1895. During the First Cairo Conference (q.v.) in 1943, the Allies (q.v.) agreed that China should regain control of the islands at the close of the war. Japan officially renounced claims to the Pescadores in the Japanese peace treaty (q.v.) in 1951.

PHIBUNSONGKHRAM, LUANG (1897–1964). Also called Pibul Songgram; prime minister and field marshal of Thailand, 1938–1944. Before the war, Phibunsongkhram, an army officer, helped to end the absolute monarchy in Thailand (q.v.), and as prime minister, he changed the country's name from Siam to Thailand. His regime was militaristic, ultranationalistic, and sympathetic to the Axis powers (q.v.). Trying to profit by the confusion in France (q.v.) after its surrender to Germany (q.v.) in 1940, Phibunsongkhram moved forces into French Indochina (q.v.) in an attempt to seize territory; he later accepted Japanese mediation. On December 8, 1941, Japanese troops invaded Thailand, which then signed an alliance with Japan (q.v.). Thailand later declared war on the United States and the United Kingdom (qq.v.).

During the war, Phibunsongkhram led Thai forces as field marshal until he was overthrown in 1944 by the anti-Japanese Free Thai Movement. Later he again served as premier (1948–1957) and worked against communist gains in Southeast Asia. He was ousted by a military coup and lived his last years in Japan.

PHILIPPINE ISLANDS. U.S. possession since 1898, which had been granted commonwealth status in 1935 and promised that independence would be achieved in 1945. In 1941, United States Army and Army Air Forces (qq.v.) troops and the small Asiatic Fleet (q.v.) were stationed in the Philippines, mostly at bases near the capital of Manila (q.v.) on the main island of Luzon (q.v.). According to prewar U.S. strategic plans such as War Plan Orange (q.v.), the Philippines would probably be targeted by Japan (q.v.) in the event of a U.S.-Japanese war; if the Japanese invaded, the American and Filipino armed forces on Luzon would have to withdraw to the Bataan peninsula and conduct defensive actions until reinforcements arrived several months later. Less optimistic versions of the plans projected a Japanese victory before the United States (q.v.) could send aid. In July 1941, as tensions between the United States and Japan mounted, President Franklin D. Roosevelt (q.v.) nationalized the Philippine army and recalled to active duty retired Major General Douglas MacArthur (q.v.), who had been serving in the Philippines as military adviser to the Commonwealth. In the fall of 1941, the United States sent additional aircraft to the Philippines and established the Far East Air Force under Major General Lewis H. Brereton, who arrived in Manila in November.

When the Japanese invaded the islands in 1941–1942, Philippine Commonwealth President Manuel L. Quezon and Vice President Sergio Osmeña (qq.v.) set up a government in exile in Washington, D.C., where they campaigned for a U.S. offensive to retake the Philippines. Upon Quezon's death in 1944, Osmeña assumed the presidency. In the Philippines, the Japanese established a puppet government with which many Filipinos cooperated. Their president from 1943 to 1945 was José Paciano Laurel (q.v.), who had served on the supreme court before the war. As U.S. forces returned to the Philippines in October 1944, Osmeña proclaimed the reestablishment of his government. The Philippines received its independence from the United States in 1946. *See also* Philippine Islands Campaign (1941–1942); Philippine Islands Campaign (1944–1945).

PHILIPPINE ISLANDS CAMPAIGN (1941–1942). Successful Japanese operation to seize control of the Philippines (q.v.) from the United States (q.v.) and prevent U.S. interference with Japanese expansion into Southeast Asia. On December 8, 1941, several hours after the attack on Pearl Harbor (q.v.), Japanese planes began to bomb U.S. facilities in the Philippines, especially the aircraft at Clark Field near the capital of Manila on Luzon (qq.v.). Two days later small Japanese units moved ashore in northern Luzon, followed on December 22 by the major landing at Lingayen Gulf of the Fourteenth Army under the command of Lieutenant General Masaharu Homma (q.v.). A secondary force landed

Philippine Islands

along Lamon Bay southeast of Manila. Opposing them were General Douglas MacArthur's (q.v.) United States Army forces (q.v.), including the nationalized Philippine army. As Homma's soldiers moved south toward Manila, MacArthur ordered his troops to evacuate the city and withdraw to the Bataan peninsula extending into Manila Bay. His headquarters and Filipino government officials moved to the island of Corregidor in the bay. Japanese troops controlled Manila by January 2, 1942. As the U.S. forces completed their retreat, accompanied by many civilians, the Japanese began their siege of Bataan on January 7. With inadequate supplies of food, medicinal supplies, and ammunition, the defenders were further hampered by the heavy jungles and mountainous terrain of Bataan. The Japanese naval blockade of the islands and the losses suffered by the United States at Pearl Harbor prevented the sending of U.S. assistance to the Philippines. On April 9, 1942, the troops on Bataan surrendered, malnourished and ill. The Japanese then marched their 70,000 American and Filipino prisoners of war (q.v.) more than 50 miles to a prison camp; the captives' arduous trip became known as the Bataan Death March (q.v.) for the atrocities and mistreatment suffered by the prisoners.

Before Bataan fell, MacArthur on March 11 left the Philippines for Australia (q.v.) on orders from President Franklin D. Roosevelt (q.v.), who knew the Philippines would fall and did not want the Japanese to capture such a prominent prisoner. Lieutenant General Jonathan M. Wainwright (q.v.), assigned by Washington officials to assume MacArthur's command, surrendered Corregidor on May 6, 1942, and broadcast capitulation orders to all remaining forces in the Philippines. The last organized force surrendered on June 9, although numbers of American and Filipino soldiers escaped and worked with guerrilla groups during the ensuing Japanese occupation. The campaign to capture the Philippines took much longer than planned by the Japanese Imperial General Headquarters (q.v.), which did not entrust another major command to Homma.

PHILIPPINE ISLANDS CAMPAIGN (1944–1945). Recapture of the islands by the United States (q.v.), October 1944–August 1945. In the fall of 1944, after the Luzon versus Formosa debate (q.v.), the United States Joint Chiefs of Staff (q.v.) approved the invasion of Luzon (q.v.), to be preceded by the capture of Leyte (q.v.). Earlier plans to invade the southern Philippine island of Mindanao were changed when Admiral William F. Halsey (q.v.) reported that his air raids encountered light resistance in the Philippines and recommended that Mindanao be bypassed in favor of islands farther north.

Conducted by General Douglas MacArthur's Southwest Pacific Area (SWPA) (qq.v) theater, the campaign began with an assault on Leyte in the central Philippines; its primary goal was to acquire sites for air bases to support the larger Luzon operation. Covering the landing of the U.S. Sixth Army, under Lieutenant General Walter Krueger (q.v.), were the U.S. Seventh Fleet, commanded by Vice Admiral Thomas C. Kinkaid (q.v.) and assigned to SWPA, and Halsey's U.S. Third Fleet, loaned by the Pacific Ocean Areas (POA) (q.v.) theater. The first landings on Leyte on October 20, 1944, were followed by the enormous naval Battle for Leyte Gulf (q.v.), October 23–26, which virtually ended the effectiveness of Japan's naval forces. During the Leyte operations, organized Japanese kamikazes (q.v.) attacked Allied ships for the first time. General Tomoyuki Yamashita (q.v.), in charge of the overall defense of the Philippines, sent reinforcements from Luzon to Leyte. While the Japanese forces on Leyte continued to resist strongly, the U.S. Eighth Army, commanded by Lieutenant General Robert L. Eichelberger (q.v.), relieved the Sixth Army in December 1944. Eichelberger's forces completed the capture of Leyte in May 1945 while also conducting extensive operations to liberate islands in the southern Philippines, landing on Mindanao on March 10.

On December 15, 1944, U.S. forces captured the island of Mindoro to provide air bases for the Luzon operations. The Luzon invasion, using 1,000 ships, began on January 9, 1945. Its ground forces included the Sixth Army and units of the Eighth, covered by the Seventh and Third fleets and the Fifth Air Force. The Japanese force was Yamashita's Fourteenth Area Army. Yamashita planned to yield the Central Plain and Manila (q.v.) to the invaders, while conducting his defense in the mountainous regions of Luzon. Contrary to his orders, Rear Admiral Sanji Iwabuchi's (q.v.) naval force spent a month fighting to the death in Manila, while committing numerous atrocities. During the same period, U.S. forces retook control of Manila Bay. The recapture of the island of Corregidor began with paratrooper drops and an amphibious assault (q.v.) on February 16 and lasted until March 1, when the Japanese defenders killed themselves with massive underground explosions. U.S. forces took the other islands in the bay by April 16.

Most of Luzon came under U.S. control during the campaign, but when Japan (q.v.) capitulated on August 15, 1945, Yamashita and the force he commanded personally were still fighting in the mountains of northern Luzon. He formally surrendered on September 3, 1945. Throughout the Philippine operations, guerrilla organizations made up of Americans and Filipinos contributed substantially to the defeat of the Japanese forces.

PHILIPPINE SEA, BATTLE OF. Naval action occurring during the U.S. invasion of the Mariana Islands (q.v.), June 19–20, 1944. While the assault on Saipan (q.v.) was under way, Japanese naval forces under Vice Admiral Jisaburo Ozawa (q.v.) traveled from New Guinea and the Netherlands East Indies (qq.v.) to halt the enemy action in the Marianas. U.S. Fifth Fleet commander Admiral Raymond A. Spruance (q.v.) postponed the invasion of Guam (q.v.) and sent his Fast Carrier Force (q.v.), under Vice Admiral Marc A. Mitscher (q.v.), to meet Ozawa. On June 19, waves of planes from Ozawa's carriers attacked Mitscher's force, which in a few hours shot down 350 Japanese planes in an action called the "Great Marianas Turkey Shoot." That day and the next, U.S. forces sank several Japanese carriers and other vessels. As Ozawa retreated, Spruance in a controversial decision ordered Mitscher to return to the Saipan action rather than follow the crippled fleet. U.S. losses in the naval battle were small, but Japan lost its last reserve of trained naval pilots.

PHILLIPS, TOM SPENCER VAUGHAN (1888–1941). British admiral; commander, British Eastern Fleet, 1941. After serving as the vice chief of staff in the Royal Navy, Phillips was transferred to head the small Eastern Fleet in 1941, partly because of his strategic differences with Prime Minister Winston S. Churchill (q.v.). He arrived at his fleet headquarters in Singapore (q.v.) on December 2, 1941. After the Japanese invaded the Malay peninsula (q.v.) on December 8, Phillips went to sea on board his only battleship, the *Prince of Wales,* which was sunk, along with the cruiser *Repulse,* on December 10, in a Japanese attack. Phillips died during the assault.

PLACENTIA BAY CONFERENCE. *See* ATLANTIC CONFERENCE.

PLAN DOG MEMORANDUM. Strategic document written by U.S. Admiral Harold R. Stark (q.v.) in November 1940. In it, Stark, the chief of naval operations, examined U.S. policies while considering the war in Europe and the rising tensions with Japan (q.v.) in the Pacific. He concluded that the security of the United States (q.v.)

depended on the continued existence of the United Kingdom (q.v.), which at the time was the major country opposing the Axis powers (q.v.) in Europe. He recommended that if the United States went to war, American efforts should focus on helping the British defeat Germany (q.v.) by mounting strong offensives in Europe while maintaining a defensive stance in the Pacific. After the end of the war in Europe, the United States would assume the offensive against Japan. The Plan Dog Memorandum was affirmed in the ABC-1 (q.v.) document of early 1941 and became the basis for U.S. strategy in World War II, as described in the Rainbow 5 war plan (q.v.).

POISON GAS. Produced by Japan and the Allies (qq.v.); reportedly employed by Japan against China (q.v.) during the war. By the time of its surrender, Japan had stored large quantities of poison gas in the Japanese home islands (q.v.) and in Manchuria. Neither Japan nor the Western Allies used poison gas against the other, although U.S. officials did consider its application in the Philippines, Okinawa (qq.v.), and the projected invasion of the home islands.

PONAPE. *See* CAROLINE ISLANDS.

PORT MORESBY. Site on the southern coast of Papua, New Guinea (q.v.), which remained under Allied control during the war despite several Japanese offensives to capture it. Port Moresby, a base in the Australian territory of Papua, was a major objective of the Japanese command, which wanted to use its strategic location to control supply lines to Australia (q.v.) and possibly threaten Australia itself. In the Battle of the Coral Sea (q.v.) in May 1942, a Japanese naval force moving toward Port Moresby was stopped by Allied forces. The Japanese then tried to use overland routes to capture it, which resulted in fierce battles in New Guinea in 1942–1943. In September 1942, Japanese troops reached a point 30 miles from Port Moresby before they had to withdraw. Numerous Allied ground and air installations built around Port Moresby played key roles in the later conquests of the Southwest Pacific Area (q.v.). For a time it served as General Douglas MacArthur's (q.v.) theater headquarters.

PORTAL, CHARLES FREDERICK ALGERNON (1893–1971). British Marshal of the Royal Air Force; chief of air staff, 1940–1945. Portal directed the Royal Air Force throughout the war, concentrating on the defense of the United Kingdom (q.v.) and the strategic bombing campaign against Germany and Italy (qq.v.). As a member of the British Chiefs of Staff Committee and the Combined Chiefs of Staff (qq.v.), he participated in the strategic direction of the war and attended the major Allied conferences (q.v.), where he consistently supported the policy of defeating Germany before Japan (q.v.). Portal joined U.S. General of the Army Henry H. Arnold (q.v.) in promoting the value of strategic air campaigns (q.v.). Beginning with the Second Quebec Conference (q.v.), Portal offered Royal Air Force assistance in the strategic air campaign against Japan; no firm arrangements had been made by war's end.

PORTUGAL. *See* INTELLIGENCE, ALLIED; INTELLIGENCE, JAPANESE; POTSDAM CONFERENCE; PRISONERS OF WAR HELD BY JAPAN; TIMOR.

POTSDAM CONFERENCE (TERMINAL), JULY 16–AUGUST 1, 1945. Last "Big Three" meeting, held in a suburb of Berlin, Germany (q.v.); attended by Soviet Premier Joseph V. Stalin, British Prime Minister Winston S. Churchill, and U.S. President Harry S. Truman (qq.v.), who had become president in April 1945 upon the death of Franklin D. Roosevelt (q.v.). On July 28, Churchill was succeeded by Clement R. Attlee (q.v.), whose Labour Party had defeated Churchill's government. Much of the agenda concerned political issues regarding the occupation of Germany and the aftermath of the European War. The conferees agreed to establish the Council of Foreign Ministers to draft peace treaties for the defeated countries.

The Combined Chiefs of Staff (CCS) (q.v.) reviewed the military progress in the war against Japan (q.v.) and the U.S. plans to continue the naval blockade and strategic air campaign (q.v.) while planning for invasions of the Japanese home islands (q.v.) of Kyushu and Honshu. They discussed the prospects of further British participation in the Pacific. In addition to the British Pacific Fleet (q.v.) and a strategic bomber (q.v.) force mentioned at previous conferences, the British offered to send a British Commonwealth Force, the East Indies Fleet, and a tactical air force to assist in the invasion of Honshu. The U.S. chiefs accepted the British proposals in principle. Also discussed by the CCS were proposals by France, the Netherlands (qq.v.), and Portugal to participate militarily in the defeat of Japan and to reoccupy their former territories. In preparation for future operations, the CCS decided to transfer southern French Indochina, Borneo, Java, and

Celebes (qq.v.) to the Southeast Asia Command (q.v.) from the China Theater and the Southwest Pacific Area (qq.v.). The change went into effect on September 2 and determined which theater bore the responsibility for accepting Japanese surrenders (q.v.) and occupying the transferred areas.

The United States and the Union of Soviet Socialist Republics (qq.v.), which had not yet entered the war against Japan, reached agreements regarding the Soviet collection of weather information in Asia for U.S. forces and the use of Soviet facilities for emergency repairs of U.S. ships and planes. They also set boundaries near the U.S.S.R., to which U.S. forces would adhere.

On July 26, the United States, the United Kingdom, and China (qq.v.) called for the surrender of Japan in the Potsdam Proclamation (q.v.). While at Potsdam, Truman received notification that the atomic bomb (q.v.) had been tested successfully.

POTSDAM PROCLAMATION. Allied demand for the unconditional surrender of Japan (q.v.), announced on July 26, 1945, during the Potsdam Conference (q.v.). Issued by U.S. President Harry S. Truman, Chinese Generalissimo Chiang Kai-shek (who was not present at the conference), and British Prime Minister Winston S. Churchill (qq.v.), the Potsdam Proclamation warned Japan that Allied military forces were "poised to strike the final blows upon Japan" and would cause "the inevitable and complete destruction of the Japanese armed forces and . . . the utter devastation of the Japanese homeland." The document called for "the unconditional surrender of all Japanese armed forces." Among its terms were the elimination of militarism, the occupation of Japan by Allied forces, the reduction of Japanese territory to the home islands, complete disarmament, and punishment of war criminals, "including those who have visited cruelties upon our prisoners." After the dropping of two atomic bombs (q.v.) on Japanese cities and the entry of the Union of Soviet Socialist Republics (q.v.) into the war, the Japanese accepted the Potsdam Proclamation on August 14, 1945. *See also* Japanese Peace Treaty; Japanese Surrender.

POUND, DUDLEY PICKMAN ROGERS (1877–1943). British Admiral of the Fleet; first sea lord, 1939–1943. In addition to leading the Royal Navy, Pound headed the British Chiefs of Staff Committee from 1939 until early 1942, when General Alan F. Brooke (q.v.) succeeded him as chairman. Pound attended the international Allied conferences (q.v.) from 1941 to 1943 as a member of the Combined Chiefs of Staff (CCS) (q.v.). Much of his time in office was consumed by the European War, especially the Allied response to the German submarine (q.v.) campaign. He resigned for health reasons in the fall of 1943 and died soon afterward. His successor as first sea lord was Admiral Andrew B. Cunningham (q.v.).

PRIDI PHANOMYONG (1900–1983). Also called Pridi Banomyong; Thai political leader. Before the war Pridi worked to overthrow the absolute monarchy of Thailand (q.v.), wrote the country's constitution (1932), and held several governmental positions. In 1941, he resigned as minister of finance because of Prime Minister Luang Phibunsongkhram's (q.v.) close relationship with Japan (q.v.). During the war Pridi led the underground Free Thai Movement in opposition to the Japanese and also acted as regent for the young king, who spent the wartime years in Switzerland (q.v.). After the Free Thai Movement forced Phibunsongkhram to resign in 1944, Pridi wielded enormous political power during the rest of the war. He briefly served as Thailand's first elected prime minister in 1946–1947.

PRINCE OF WALES. See BATTLESHIPS; BOMBERS; MALAY PENINSULA; PHILLIPS, TOM S. V.

PRISONERS OF WAR HELD BY ALLIES. In contrast to the large numbers of Allied troops that surrendered in the early months of the war, very few Japanese became prisoners of war (POWs). In the Pacific, the Allies (q.v.) captured only 604 Japanese prisoners from December 1941 through December 1943. Beginning with the Allied return to the Philippines (q.v.) in October 1944, the number of Japanese prisoners in the Pacific War increased significantly, with 12,000 captured in the Philippines before the war ended. Statistics for the number of POWs vary tremendously, with totals ranging up to 40,000 for Japanese prisoners held by the Allies, excluding China and the Union of Soviet Socialist Republics (qq.v.).

One important reason for the small number of POWs was the tenet of the Bushido (q.v.) code that Japanese forces should fight to the death on behalf of the emperor. If wounded or trapped, a soldier was expected to commit suicide rather than submit to the dishonor of capture. Some POWs continued their resistance to imprisonment. The largest incident occurred in the summer of 1944 at the Cowra camp in Australia (q.v.), where 1,000 Japanese POWs launched banzai (q.v.) attacks against their guards; more than 200 prisoners died before the uprising was subdued. Another factor limiting the number of POWs was the immense savagery of the war; in many battles, Allied troops took few prisoners.

In accordance with an agreement made in 1942, most Japanese seized in the Pacific were transferred to prisons in Australia and New Zealand (qq.v.), with the United States (q.v.) paying a substantial part of the costs. In the later stages of the war, camps in the Philippines and Okinawa (q.v.) also held large groups of POWs. Incarcerated in the United States were 5,400 Japanese POWs who were considered especially important for interrogation or who were captured closer to the United States than to Australia, such as the midget submarine (q.v.) pilot who participated in the attack on Pearl Harbor (q.v.). Also held in the United States were 500 Koreans (q.v.) who had served with the Japanese armed forces. Participating in the interrogation process were a number of Japanese Americans (q.v.) in the Military Intelligence Service.

In handling the POWs, the United States followed the guidelines of the Geneva Convention of 1929, hoping that Japan would reciprocate although not bound by the agreement. The International Committee of the Red Cross regularly visited prison camps and relocation centers in the United States. Spanish officials, who represented the interests of Japan (q.v.) in the United States, also inspected prison camps and addressed the concerns of Japanese prisoners. In the summer of 1945, the U.S. government began a reeducation effort to persuade its Axis (q.v.) POWs of the benefits of democracy before releasing them to their home countries.

After the war, the United States returned its Japanese POWs to Japan fairly quickly. The repatriation of Japanese prisoners from other countries was delayed by severe shipping shortages, poor living conditions and food shortages in Japan, and the Allied need for labor. The U.S.S.R., which had captured approximately 1.3 million Japanese military personnel and civilians in Asia during the last week of the war, refused to provide information about its captives and declined to return any of them to Japan until the conclusion of an Allied agreement in December 1946. Thereafter, the Soviets permitted limited repatriation, with the United States and Japan bearing the expenses; many of the prisoners allowed to return had become communists. In 1950, the Soviet Union announced that the repatriation was complete, although the Japanese government claimed that 300,000 of its citizens had not been returned.

PRISONERS OF WAR HELD BY JAPAN. During the first six months of the war with the West, Japan (q.v.) captured large groups of American, Australian, British, Canadian, Dutch, Filipino, Indian, and New Zealand (qq.v.) military personnel. The bulk of the prisoners of war (POWs) surrendered or were seized in Singapore, British Borneo, Burma, Hong Kong, the Netherlands East Indies, and the Philippines (qq.v.). Smaller numbers of prisoners were added during later campaigns. In Asia, Japan separated the Indian troops from the other POWs and urged them to join Japan's side; the prisoners who agreed formed the nucleus of the Indian National Army (q.v.). Additionally, Japan held countless numbers of Chinese prisoners.

Also taken into custody early in the war with the West were many Allied civilian internees. Limited numbers of these were repatriated through the offices of Spain, Switzerland (q.v.), Portugal, and the International Committee of the Red Cross (ICRC), but many, including children, were interned for the duration of the war. The Japanese imprisoned the top governmental officials of Hong Kong, the East Indies, the Philippines, and Singapore, and housed them with POWs holding senior military rank, who were separated from lower-ranking officers and enlisted men. In general, the Japanese treated the high-ranking civilian and military captives better than other military prisoners.

Early in the 20th century, Japan's humane handling of Russian POWs in the Russo-Japanese War had impressed other countries; such was not the case during World War II. Japan signed but declined to ratify the Geneva Convention of 1929, which set international standards for the treatment of military prisoners. Japan agreed in early 1942 to follow the convention but, instead, repeatedly violated the rules governing food, medical care, forced labor, penalties for attempted escapes, and regular inspection of POW camps by Red Cross representatives. Japanese officials severely limited ICRC visits to some camps and totally barred access to others. The prisoners received little mail and few of the Red Cross food parcels provided to Japan for distribution to POWs. Switzerland represented the British and American governments in dealing with the Japanese regarding Allied POW matters, including the payment of funds to reimburse Japan for the prisoners' care.

Allied POWs in Japanese custody died at a high rate, suffering from malnutrition, hostile climates, a host of diseases, poor medical care, overwork, and, in many cases, atrocities inflicted by the guards. Strongly influencing the harsh Japanese treatment was the Bushido (q.v.) code, which held that surrender was disgraceful and that prisoners deserved contempt. Another contributing factor was Japan's inadequate logistical system, which failed to meet the needs of both its troops and its prisoners. During the early part of the war with the West, Japanese officials were ill equipped to handle the unexpectedly large groups of captured Allied troops. As the war progressed, Allied disruption of Japanese shipping increased the food shortages for Japanese civilians and armed forces, further adversely affecting the POWs. Other prisoners died during Allied bombing raids in Japan and Manchuria (q.v.). Some of the Allied airmen shot down and captured during the strategic air campaign (q.v.) were executed.

After the war ended, Allied war crimes trials (q.v.) addressed the charges of Japanese atrocities committed against prisoners of war. The case best known to the American public was the Bataan Death March (q.v.), which occurred in April 1942 in the Philippine Islands (q.v.). Another episode in the Philippines took place in December 1944, when Japanese guards at a POW camp on Palawan mistakenly believed Allied troops were approaching; they set their American prisoners on fire and shot the survivors. Japan's requirement that most of its prisoners work led to abuses, especially in coal mines, factories, and construction projects. In the most infamous case of forced labor, Japan ordered 60,000 Allied POWs to build the Burma-Thailand Railway (q.v.) under such brutal conditions that one-fifth of the prisoners died. Japan's failure to notify the ICRC when it transferred POWs to different camps led to the drowning deaths of thousands of Allied captives on "death ships" or "hell ships," sunk by U.S. submarines (q.v.) and planes unaware of the passengers. Other POWs were subjects of Japanese medical and biological warfare (q.v.) experiments. The abrupt Japanese surrender (q.v.) in August 1945 preempted plans in some prison compounds to massacre the POWs if Allied troops tried to take the camps by force. *See also* Medicine.

PROXIMITY FUZE. Also known as the VT (variable-time) fuze; a radio proximity fuze in an artillery (q.v.) shell, bomb (q.v.), or rocket (q.v.) that detonated when it neared a target. Before the American entry into the war, the British shared their research on the fuze with the United States (q.v.), where British, Canadian, and American researchers further developed it. The Anglo-American Combined Chiefs of Staff (CCS) (q.v.) considered the fuze so important that they initially restricted its use to Pacific naval actions to preclude the enemy from finding an unexploded artillery shell and learning about the technology. The United States Navy (q.v.) first employed the fuze in January 1943 against Japanese dive bombers (q.v.) in operations in the Solomons (q.v.), where it significantly improved the accuracy of antiaircraft (q.v.) fire. The CCS first permitted the fuze's use in European ground operations in late 1944. It was then used in the Pacific during the invasion of Okinawa (q.v.) in April 1945 and the next month in operations on Luzon (q.v.). The proximity fuze enabled shells to explode above concentrations of Japanese troops, causing heavy casualties.

In February 1945, Allied planes dropped bombs equipped with proximity fuzes on Iwo Jima (q.v.). The fuze's use in aerial attacks increased quickly. During the carrier-based air attacks on the Japanese home islands (q.v.) in the summer of 1945, one-third of the bombs contained the proximity fuze.

Both Germany and Japan (qq.v.) conducted research into variations of the proximity fuze, but neither produced or employed a fuze similar to the Allied product. One of the purposes of the Alsos (q.v.) intelligence mission in Europe was to determine if the Germans had learned about the successful Allied fuze and shared it with Japan. During the war, Japanese scientists designed but did not use a photoelectric proximity fuze.

PT BOAT. *See* PATROL TORPEDO BOAT.

PU-YI, HENRY (AISIN-GIORO) (1906–1967). Chinese emperor, 1909–1911; regent and emperor of Manchukuo, 1932–1945. As a child Pu-Yi, known to Westerners as Henry, served briefly as the last Manchu emperor of China (q.v.) until dethroned by the Chinese Revolution of 1911. When the Japanese Kwantung Army (q.v.) seized control of Manchuria (q.v.) from China in 1931–1932, it proclaimed a new nation, calling it Manchukuo (q.v.) to identify it with the Manchus. At the invitation of the Kwantung Army, Pu-Yi became the nominal head of the new puppet government, holding the position until he was captured by Soviet forces in August 1945. After the war he was imprisoned by the Union of Soviet Socialist Republics (q.v.) and then by the Chinese Communists. Following his release, he worked as a gardener and historian.

PURKAYEV, MAKSIM ALEKSEEVICH (1894–1953). Soviet general of the Army; commander, Far Eastern Front, 1943–1945; commander, Second Far Eastern Front, 1945. Following service in the war against Germany (q.v.), Purkayev was transferred to head the Far Eastern Front (army group) in April 1943. As the Union of Soviet Socialist Republics (q.v.) prepared to attack Japanese forces in Manchuria in the summer of 1945, the Second Far Eastern Front was formed under Purkayev's command. In the Soviet operations beginning on August 9, 1945, the Second Far Eastern Front was ordered to support the offensives of the Trans-Baikal and First Far Eastern fronts by tying down Japanese forces in northern Manchuria. While accomplishing its mission, Purkayev's force encountered the heaviest fighting of any of the fronts in Manchuria. After the war he remained in the Far East, holding a number of posts, until 1952. *See also* Manchuria Campaign (1945).

-Q-

QUADRANT. *See* QUEBEC CONFERENCE, FIRST.

QUEBEC CONFERENCE, FIRST (QUADRANT), AUGUST 11–24, 1943. Allied meeting of British Prime Minister Winston S. Churchill, U.S. President Franklin D. Roosevelt (qq.v.), and their advisers. In a secret accord, Churchill and Roosevelt agreed to cooperate in the development of the atomic bomb (q.v.), a collaboration that had been suspended by the United States (q.v.). To direct the cooperative effort, they appointed the Combined Policy Committee, composed of representatives from the United States, the United Kingdom, and Canada (qq.v.). The main debate concerning the war in Europe involved the relative advantages of further operations in the Mediterranean and the cross-channel invasion of France (q.v.). Regarding the war against Japan, the participants created a new Allied theater: the Southeast Asia Command (q.v.), to be headed by British Admiral Louis Mountbatten (q.v.), with U.S. Lieutenant General Joseph W. Stilwell (q.v.) serving as deputy commander. The British and American military chiefs continued to disagree about operations to retake south Burma, north Sumatra, and Singapore (qq.v.), with the U.S. delegation pressing for more emphasis on Burma to open supply lines into China (q.v.).

In the Southwest Pacific Area (SWPA) (q.v.), the Combined Chiefs of Staff approved the seizure of Northeast New Guinea (q.v.) and most of the Bismarck Archipelago, with Rabaul (q.v.) to be neutralized and bypassed; SWPA forces were then to advance westward along the northern coast of New Guinea. The British chiefs suggested unsuccessfully that SWPA operations be deemphasized, with the surplus forces shifted to

Europe. In the Central Pacific, the Combined Chiefs accepted U.S. plans to assault the Gilberts, the Marshalls, Truk (qq.v.), Ponape, the Palaus, and the Marianas (qq.v.). Also discussed were U.S. plans for the Boeing B-29 (q.v.) bomber, which was expected to be available in sizable numbers in 1944 for use in the strategic air campaign (q.v.) against Japan.

QUEBEC CONFERENCE, SECOND (OCTAGON), SEPTEMBER 12–16, 1944. Allied meeting of British Prime Minister Winston S. Churchill, U.S. President Franklin D. Roosevelt (qq.v.), and their advisers. Concerning the war against Germany (q.v.), the participants discussed the progress of the Allied ground advance across Northwest Europe and plans for postwar Germany. In their deliberations regarding Asia and the Pacific, they considered operations in Burma and the Philippines (qq.v.). The British chiefs pressed for a role for their fleet in the major Pacific drive toward Japan (q.v.), which Admiral Ernest J. King (q.v.) resisted, although Roosevelt had agreed to it. The British also offered to assist in the strategic bombing of Japan; the Combined Chiefs of Staff asked the Royal Air Force to prepare a plan. In an agreement reached at Roosevelt's home in Hyde Park, New York, on September 18, Churchill and Roosevelt agreed that the United Kingdom and the United States (qq.v.) would keep the atomic bomb (q.v.) project secret and would continue to collaborate on its development after the end of the war; they also recognized the possibility that the bomb would be used against Japan.

QUEZON, MANUEL L. (1878–1944). President of the Philippine Commonwealth, 1935–1944. After the Japanese invaded the Philippine Islands (q.v.) and neared the capital of Manila (q.v.) in December 1941, Quezon moved to the island of Corregidor in Manila Bay with his government and the headquarters of General Douglas MacArthur (q.v.), commander of United States Army Forces in the Far East. In February 1942, Quezon was evacuated by submarine (q.v.) and subsequently traveled to Washington, D.C., where he set up a government in exile and pressed for the ouster of the Japanese from the Philippines. He died in 1944 and was succeeded by his vice president, Sergio Osmeña (q.v.).

-R-

RABAUL. Port on the eastern tip of the island of New Britain in the Bismarck Archipelago, northeast of New Guinea (q.v.). In late January 1942, after several days of heavy bombardment, Japanese troops

Rabaul, the Bismarck Sea, and Eastern New Guinea

moved into New Britain and captured the small Australian force at Rabaul, where Japan then built massive, heavily fortified naval and air bases. From there the Japanese conducted their operations in New Guinea and the Solomon Islands (q.v.). In 1943, the Allied high command authorized Operation Cartwheel (q.v.) with the objective of capturing Rabaul, but the United States Joint Chiefs of Staff (q.v.) decided later to isolate it instead, by capturing nearby islands and the western part of New Britain. By late 1943, Allied forces had acquired air bases close enough to begin an intense bombing campaign against Rabaul. In December 1943, U.S. troops invaded the island at Arawe and at Cape Gloucester. When Cartwheel concluded in the spring of 1944,

Rabaul had been effectively neutralized. Its surviving forces surrendered in September 1945. *See also* Imamura, Hitoshi.

RADAR. Acronym for "radio detection and ranging"; used by aircraft, naval vessels (q.v.), and ground forces. Although a number of countries had begun to develop radar in the 1930s, Allied radar during the war was vastly superior to that of Japan (q.v.), both in technology and in use. In 1940, the British Tizard Mission shared with the United States (q.v.) British discoveries regarding microwave radar, which became enormously important in the conflict with Japan. U.S. forces first began to use microwave radar sets in 1942. Extensive research during the war resulted in improvements and new applications.

Japanese scientists also conducted research on radar, with the army and navy developing rival systems. Germany's (q.v.) transfer of selected technology, especially during the latter part of the war, aided Japan's efforts, but projects such as the production of advanced radar sets to direct antiaircraft fire (q.v.) remained unfinished at the end of the war. By many accounts, Allied radar in 1945 was several years ahead of Japan's.

The Allies (q.v.) made effective use of radar much earlier in the war than did Japan, especially in naval warfare. By December 1941, the United States had equipped its carriers (q.v.), newer submarines (q.v.), and some other naval vessels with radar, adding it to the remaining American warships by the end of 1942. In contrast, Japan did not begin to install primitive radar on its surface ships until mid-1942 and did not use it extensively until late 1943. Japanese submarines finally acquired it in 1944. During the Battles of the Coral Sea and Midway (qq.v.) in 1942, the radar on U.S. carriers (q.v.) gave the United States a big advantage over the Japanese. Allied radar also helped to offset the Japanese advantages in night tactics and superior torpedoes (q.v.) during the numerous naval battles in the Solomon Islands (q.v.). During the capture of Okinawa (q.v.), the Allies established protective picket lines of radar-equipped ships to detect and intercept kamikaze (q.v.) flights.

When the United States entered the war, only a few of its aircraft in the Pacific carried radar. During the first part of the war, the Allies concentrated much effort on the development of airborne radar for spotting ships and surfaced submarines, which performed especially well against Japanese shipping. Another early focus was radar for night fighters (q.v.), primarily the Northrop P-61 Black Widow and the Bristol Beaufighter. The United States installed its most extensive radar equipment in the Boeing B-29 Superfortress (q.v.) bomber, which came into service in mid-1944. The Japanese did not use airborne radar for antisubmarine warfare until 1944, when they first installed it on flying boats (q.v.). During the Battle for Leyte Gulf (q.v.), Japanese aircraft effectively used radar to launch torpedoes, forcing Allied forces to develop special jamming measures.

At the time the Japanese attacked Pearl Harbor and the Philippines (qq.v.), the U.S. ground radar sets in Hawaii operated only on a limited basis to spot approaching aircraft, and U.S. forces on Luzon (q.v.) had only two functioning radar sets. Ground radar proved of little use to the Allies during Japan's overwhelming victories in late 1941–1942, but thereafter, it became an important advantage, especially with the development of the U.S. SCR-584 microwave radar. The Allies and Japan established ground radar stations throughout Asia and the Pacific, as well as providing infantry forces with mobile sets. Beginning in 1943, Allied planes equipped with special radar located Japanese ground sets that posed particular danger to Allied operations. The existence of Japanese radar stations on Iwo Jima (q.v.) enabled Japanese fighters to threaten the Allied strategic air campaign (q.v.) and became an important factor in the Allied decision to invade the island. *See also* Office of Scientific Research and Development; Science and Technology.

RAINBOW PLANS. U.S. contingency plans for wars in which the United States (q.v.) faced more than one enemy at the same time. In 1939, U.S. planners began to develop plans for five different war situations, some involving allies. Rainbow 5, completed by the summer of 1941, most closely resembled the strategy that the United States actually followed. According to Rainbow 5, the United States would be allied with the United Kingdom and France against Germany, Italy, and Japan (qq.v.). In addition to defending the Western Hemisphere, U.S. forces would join the Allies (q.v.) in conducting offensive operations against Germany and Italy. Until the European War was won, the United States would hold to the strategic defensive in the Pacific; it would then assume the offensive against Japan. In giving the priority to the defeat of Germany and Italy rather than Japan, Rainbow 5 followed the Plan Dog Memorandum and the ABC-1 agreement (qq.v.). *See also* War Plan Orange.

RAPE OF NANKING. *See* NANKING.

RAW MATERIALS, STRATEGIC. Among the primary reasons for the conflict between the Western Allies and Japan (qq.v.), a nation with insufficient natural resources to support its heavy industrialization and its war in China (q.v.). In September 1940, to protest the stationing of Japanese troops in northern French Indochina (q.v.), the United States (q.v.) stopped the sale of scrap iron and steel to Japan. After the Japanese move into southern Indochina (q.v.) the next year, the United States embargoed oil to Japan, which had depended heavily on such imports. Knowing that war would result, the leaders of Japan made the final decision in 1941 to expand southward with the objective of securing strategic raw materials such as oil, rubber, bauxite, timber, and tin. In addition to supplying its own needs, Japan later traded strategic materials for German (q.v.) technology.

After the Japanese successes in 1941–1942 ended Allied access to these sources, the Allies further developed their own natural resources as well as purchasing raw materials from Latin America (q.v.), Spain, Portugal, and other neutral areas. They also placed strategic materials under tight governmental controls and rationed civilian use of gasoline, rubber, tin, leather, and certain essential foods. Because the Japanese had captured most of the world's source of quinine in the East Indies (q.v.), the U.S. government produced large quantities of atabrine, an antimalarial drug. Allied scientists also produced synthetic rubber and other substitutes. *See also* Logistics.

RENNELL'S ISLAND, BATTLE OF. *See* GUADALCANAL CAMPAIGN: NAVAL BATTLES.

RIDGWAY, MATTHEW B. *See* JAPANESE OCCUPATION; SUPREME COMMANDER FOR THE ALLIED POWERS.

RIFLE. *See* SMALL ARMS.

RIO DE JANEIRO CONFERENCE, JANUARY 15–28, 1942. Meeting of the American republics, called by the United States (q.v.) to discuss the war. Representatives agreed to recommend that their countries break diplomatic relations with the Axis powers (q.v.). The U.S. desire for a stronger resolution was thwarted by the opposition of Argentina and Chile. Within a short time after the meeting, all governments had severed relations or declared war except for Chile and Argentina, which reluctantly did so later. The Rio Conference also set up the Inter-American Defense Board and initiated a number of cooperative agreements regarding strategic raw materials (q.v.), transportation, and economic development. It marked a significant step in the contributions of Latin America (q.v.) to the war effort.

ROCKET AND ROCKET LAUNCHER. Employed heavily during World War II. In the war with Japan (q.v.), the Allies (q.v.) fired rockets from the land, sea, and air. Primarily through the Office of Scientific Research and Development (q.v.), the United States focused enormous resources on the development of rockets and launchers. Beginning in late 1943, the Southwest Pacific and the South Pacific Areas (qq.v.) relied on the extensive use of rockets launched from landing craft (q.v.), amphibious vehicles, patrol torpedo boats (q.v.), and other surface vessels to assist amphibious assaults (q.v.). In April 1944, rockets effectively supported the landings at Hollandia on New Guinea (q.v.). Preceding the invasions of Leyte and Luzon in the Philippine Islands (qq.v.) in 1944 and 1945, U.S. ships hit Japanese positions with enormous numbers of rockets. The Central Pacific Area (q.v.) employed barrage rockets in a major way during the invasion of Okinawa (q.v.) in 1945. The Allied use of naval-launched rockets was still expanding when the war ended, as researchers attempted to find effective means of directing them at Japanese kamikazes (q.v.).

By early 1944, the Allies were using airborne rockets in Burma (q.v.) and the Pacific, where Allied torpedo bombers (q.v.) first directed them against Rabaul (q.v.) in February. In addition to supporting amphibious assaults, the aircraft rockets performed especially well against Japanese ships, submarines (q.v.), and groups of personnel. By the spring of 1945, an increasing number of fighter planes (q.v.) had replaced their bombs with rockets, which hit targets more precisely and with greater penetration. Under development at the end of the war were rockets guided by radar (q.v.).

Rocket launchers on the ground varied widely. Infantrymen fired a shoulder-held, recoilless rocket launcher against Japanese tanks, pillboxes, and caves. The most famous version was the bazooka, the U.S.-produced tube accommodating a rocket with a 2.36-inch diameter; after its introduction in the North African campaigns in 1942–1943, the bazooka became standard equipment in the Pacific. Ground forces also used rocket launchers mounted on tanks (q.v.), trucks, and other vehicles to attack Japanese fortifications.

Japan also employed rockets in the Pacific War, although not nearly as extensively as the Allies. Japan's first sizable use of rockets occurred in 1945 during the defense of the Philippines. Japanese forces on Luzon, and later on Okinawa, fired 20-cm and 45-cm rockets against Allied forces. Although Germany (q.v.) had given Japan technical information about its long-range rocket program, Japan did not produce such weapons during the war. In the Nomonhan (q.v.) conflict of 1939, the Union of Soviet Socialist Republics (q.v.) became the first country to use aerial rockets against Japan.

ROOSEVELT, FRANKLIN DELANO (1882–1945). U.S. president, 1933–1945. The only person elected to the presidency four times, Roosevelt's tenure included the growth of militarism and expansionism throughout the world in the 1930s, the beginning of the Sino-Japanese War in 1937, the start of the European War in 1939, and the American engagement in a global conflict in 1941. Although he believed strongly in the Anglo-American relationship and the necessity to aid the British struggle in Europe, Roosevelt also watched developments in Asia and supported China's (q.v.) resistance to Japan (q.v.). Before the United States (q.v.) entered the war, the Roosevelt administration condemned Japanese aggression, instituted embargoes on Japan, and extended lend-lease aid (q.v.) to China. In recognition of increasing strains with Japan, the president also moved the main U.S. Fleet from California to Pearl Harbor (q.v.) and recalled to duty Major General Douglas MacArthur (q.v.) to lead augmented U.S. forces in the Philippines (q.v.). After France fell to Germany (qq.v.) in the summer of 1940, Roosevelt moved to increase bipartisan support for his Democratic administration by appointing two well-regarded Republicans to his cabinet: Henry L. Stimson (q.v.) as secretary of war and Frank Knox (q.v.) as secretary of the navy.

After the Japanese attacked Pearl Harbor on December 7, 1941, Roosevelt asked Congress to go to war against Japan. Following declarations of war against the United States by Germany and Italy (q.v.), the United States reciprocated and entered the war in Europe. Throughout the conflict, Roosevelt played an active role in the formation of grand strategy, communicated frequently with British Prime Minister Winston S. Churchill (q.v.), and met with Churchill and Soviet Premier Joseph V. Stalin (q.v.) in major Allied conferences (q.v.). He worked to persuade Stalin to have the Union of Soviet Socialist Republics (q.v.) enter the war against Japan and campaigned for a postwar international organization to prevent future wars, which became the United Nations organization (q.v.). Roosevelt often sent his trusted adviser Harry R. Hopkins to represent him personally with Churchill and Stalin.

Roosevelt oversaw many aspects of the war effort and appointed Admiral William D. Leahy (q.v.) as his chief of staff and personal representative to the United States Joint Chiefs of Staff (q.v.), which Leahy chaired. In July 1944, he and Leahy traveled to Pearl Harbor to confer with Admiral Chester W. Nimitz (q.v.) and MacArthur, his theater commanders in the Pacific. In November 1944, Roosevelt was elected to a fourth presidential term. During the war period, his health declined markedly, and he died on April 12, 1945. Harry S. Truman (q.v.), his vice president since January of the same year, succeeded him in office and presided over the end of the war in Europe and the Japanese surrender (q.v.) in the Pacific.

RYUKYU ISLANDS. *See* OKINAWA.

-S-

SAIPAN. Island in the Marianas (q.v.) chain captured by U.S. forces, June 15–July 9, 1944, after which the Japanese government of Hideki Tojo (q.v.) fell. Saipan, the first of the Mariana Islands targeted by the offensive of the Central Pacific Area (CENPAC) (q.v.), had been administered as a mandate (q.v.) since World War I by Japan, which considered it Japanese home territory. The invasion of Saipan began on June 15 under the overall direction of Admiral Raymond A. Spruance's (q.v.) Fifth Fleet, with the CENPAC forces headed by Marine Lieutenant General Holland M. Smith (q.v.). Opposing them were the 30,000 men commanded by Lieutenant General Yoshigugu Saito and Vice Admiral Chichi Nagumo (q.v.).

The Japanese first tried to stop the invaders on the beaches and then fought intensely while moving inland and launching numerous banzai (q.v.) attacks on the American soldiers. The hostilities ended on July 9 with the deaths of most Japanese soldiers, including Saito and Nagumo, who committed suicide. Also dying by their own hands were hundreds of Saipan civilians who leaped to their deaths from the cliffs of Marpi Point, accompanied by Japanese soldiers. The American forces also suffered heavy casualties.

During the campaign, Holland Smith relieved from duty United States Army Major General Ralph D. Smith for the poor performance of the 27th Infantry Division, which he commanded. The relief of a United States Army general by a United States Marine (qq.v.) general resulted in an interservice feud and numerous investigations. The marine general was later promoted to head the Fleet Marine Force, which removed him from direct control of troops.

An amphibious invasion of the nearby island of Tinian (q.v.) was launched from Saipan on July 24. Bombing raids originating in Saipan formed an important part of the strategic air campaign (q.v.) against Japan.

SAKHALIN. Island in the Sea of Okhotsk, northwest of the Japanese home island (q.v.) of Hokkaido. In 1905, as a result of the Russo-Japanese War, Japan acquired the southern part of the island from Russia, which retained possession of the north. The Union of Soviet Socialist Republics (q.v.) occupied all of Sakhalin in August 1945, and after the war continued to control the southern part of the island in accordance with the Allied agreement at the Yalta Conference (q.v.). Japan renounced its claims to Sakhalin in the principal Japanese peace treaty (q.v.), which the U.S.S.R. did not sign. In later negotiations with the Soviets, the Japanese unsuccessfully sought the return of southern Sakhalin, as well as the southern Kurile Islands (q.v.).

SAN FRANCISCO CONFERENCE, 1945. Officially called the United Nations Conference on International Organization, April 25–June 26, 1945. Attended by the delegates of 50 nations, the conference resulted in the charter of the United Nations organization (UN) (q.v.), which was based in large part on decisions reached at the wartime conferences at Moscow, Dumbarton Oaks, and Yalta (qq.v.). Playing prominent roles in San Francisco were U.S. Secretary of State Edward R. Stettinius, Jr., and Foreign Ministers Anthony Eden (United Kingdom), T. V. Soong (China), and Vyacheslav M. Molotov (U.S.S.R.) (qq.v.). Australia and New Zealand (qq.v.) joined with other smaller powers in challenging the dominance of the major countries. On June 26, all 50 nations approved the charter.

SAN FRANCISCO CONFERENCE, 1951. See JAPANESE PEACE TREATY.

SANTA CRUZ, BATTLE OF. See GUADALCANAL CAMPAIGN: NAVAL BATTLES.

SARAWAK. See BORNEO.

SATO, NAOTAKE (1882–1971). Japanese diplomat; ambassador to Union of Soviet Socialist Republics (q.v.), 1942–1945. As ambassador, Sato maintained contact with Vyacheslav M. Molotov (q.v.), people's commissar for foreign affairs, throughout the war and conveyed his government's interest in maintaining and renewing its neutrality pact with the U.S.S.R. Following the Yalta Conference (q.v.) in February 1945, at which Premier Joseph V. Stalin (q.v.) had repeated his secret promise to the Allies (q.v.) to enter the war against Japan (q.v.), Molotov told Sato that the Far East had not been discussed during the meetings. In April 1945, Molotov announced that the U.S.S.R. would not extend its five-year neutrality agreement with Japan, which was due to expire in one year.

While privately urging his government to surrender to the Allies, Sato followed orders in July 1945 and attempted unsuccessfully to arrange Soviet mediation in peace negotiations that would allow the Japanese to keep their emperor. Stalin alluded to the Japanese peace contacts at the Potsdam Conference (q.v.), where the Allies demanded that Japan surrender unconditionally. On the night of August 8, Molotov informed Sato in Moscow that the U.S.S.R. was at war with Japan, effective the next day. Before the news reached Tokyo (q.v.), Soviet troops had moved into Manchuria (q.v.).

SAVO ISLAND, BATTLE OF. *See* GUADALCANAL CAMPAIGN: NAVAL BATTLES.

SAW, U (1900–1948). Prime minister of Burma (q.v.), 1940–1942. As head of the Myochit party, U Saw became prime minister of Burma, a British colony, in 1940. When the United Kingdom (q.v.) entered the war against Japan (q.v.), U Saw pressed the British for full independence, while negotiating secretly with the Japanese. Learning of his Japanese contacts, British authorities arrested him and removed him from office. After the war he was responsible for the assassination of his Burmese rival, Aung San (q.v.).

SCIENCE AND TECHNOLOGY. An area in which the resources and collaboration of the United States, United Kingdom, Canada, Australia (qq.v.), and other countries resulted in an enormous Allied advantage over Japan (q.v.). An important step in Allied cooperation, which preceded U.S. entry into the war, was the visit of the Tizard Mission to the United States in September 1940. Led by Henry T. Tizard, the group gave the United States the most advanced British-Canadian technology concerning radar (q.v.), proximity fuzes (q.v.), motorized gun turrets for bombers (q.v.), aircraft engines, explosives, depth charges, sonar, and other tools for antisubmarine warfare. During the same period, the United States and the United Kingdom agreed to exchange information about signal intelligence (q.v.) and atomic bomb (q.v.) research, although the latter arrangement underwent several changes during the war. In 1941, each country established a scientific office in the other's capital. The principal U.S. wartime agency was the Office of Scientific Research and Development (q.v.), headed by Vannevar Bush (q.v.).

In addition to intelligence and weapons research, the Allies (q.v.) made enormous advances in military medicine (q.v.), including the distribution of penicillin and the development of antimalarial programs. They used early versions of computers to assist the war effort against Japan. Beginning in early 1944, the Colossus computer deciphered German and Japanese codes at the primary British facility for signal intelligence (q.v.), Bletchley Park, which was located northwest of London. In the United States, the Mark I computer at Harvard University, completed in 1944, calculated ballistics for the navy and performed computations for the Manhattan Project (q.v.). Other areas of Allied research benefited the military effort, ranging from special paint that protected night-flying bombers (q.v.) from detection by searchlights, to infrared technology, to the development of synthetics to compensate for sources of raw materials (q.v.) captured by Japan. Allied scientists also conducted research on poison gas and biological warfare agents (qq.v.), although they employed neither during the war. One device not shared by the United States with the British was the highly valued Norden bombsight, designed to drop bombs accurately. The U.S. military protected its secrecy by removing all bombsights from planes on the ground and locking them up securely between bombing missions. Postwar studies concluded that the Norden bombsight was less precise than thought during the conflict.

In contrast to the Allies, Japan did not fully incorporate its civilian scientists into the war effort. Its Board of Technology involved civilians but had no control over the Japanese army and navy, which carried out rival programs and tended to distrust nonmilitary scientists, especially those educated abroad. In the fall of 1944, the army and navy attempted to coordinate their efforts by forming the Joint Technical Control Commission and including civilian scientists, but the new agency could not substantially change the country's unfavorable military situation. By that time, Japan's scientific program, as well as the whole country, suffered from extreme shortages of strategic raw materials in the home islands. Throughout the war, Japanese scientists tried various methods, mostly unsatisfactory, to alleviate the desperate fuel shortage by creating synthetic products from Manchurian oil shale, fish oils, pine roots, sugar, and potatoes.

Although Japan's technology was superior to the Allies' in such areas as fighter planes and torpedoes (qq.v.) in December 1941, the country was unable to maintain its advantages and to match the scope of Allied research, development, and production throughout the conflict. During the final year of the war, Japanese scientists became increasingly involved in developing kamikaze and other *tokko* (qq.v.) attack methods. Germany (q.v.) gave technology to Japan in exchange for strategic materials, but did not provide information about some of its most sophisticated projects until late in the war and withheld details of others entirely. The Germans delivered to Japan designs for advanced radar, submarines (q.v.), aircraft engines, rockets (q.v.), sonar, and artillery weapons. When the war ended, Japan was engaged in work on some of the German plans as well as its own limited research on nuclear energy and the proximity fuze. The Japanese also conducted programs in chemical and biological warfare, which involved hideous medical experiments on living enemy subjects.

SEABEES. *See* UNITED STATES NAVY.

SEXTANT. *See* CAIRO CONFERENCE, FIRST.

SHANGHAI. City on the eastern coast of central China (q.v.), site of Chinese-Japanese fighting in 1932 (January 28–May 5) and 1937 (August 8–November 8). After Japan (q.v.) invaded Manchuria (q.v.) in 1931, the Chinese declared a boycott of Japanese goods and demonstrations occurred in many areas, including Shanghai. Japan sent additional forces there, ostensibly to protect its citizens, but the stiff resistance of the Chinese Nineteenth Route Army led Japan to increase its troops to 70,000. After fighting extended to the international settlement in Shanghai, the Japanese forced the Chinese army from the city on March 3. In the truce of May 5, the Chinese ended their boycott and the Japanese withdrew their forces from the area. Japanese ultranationalists assassinated the Japanese prime minister and cabinet members a few days after the truce.

On August 8, 1937, as the Japanese advanced into China after the Marco Polo Bridge (q.v.) incident, they attempted to capture Shanghai by amphibious assault (q.v.). After heavy naval and air bombardment of the city, street-by-street fighting, and additional reinforcements, the Japanese finally took the city on November 8 and held it for the rest of the war. *See also* China, Japanese Operations in.

SHIGEMITSU, MAMORU (1887–1957). Japanese diplomat; ambassador to China (q.v.), 1941–1943; foreign minister, 1943–1945. In December 1941, after a long career in the foreign service that most recently had included the ambassadorship to the United Kingdom (q.v.), Shigemitsu was appointed ambassador to the Japanese-sponsored Chinese government in Nanking headed by Wang Ching-wei (q.v.). From 1943 until April 1945, he served as foreign minister under Hideki Tojo and Kuniaki Koiso (qq.v.) and urged that Japan (q.v.) deal with Asian nations more by economic cooperation and less by military occupation.

After the emperor announced the Japanese surrender (q.v.) and Kantaro Suzuki's (q.v.) cabinet resigned on August 15, 1945, Shigemitsu again became foreign minister, this time in the government of Naruhiko Higashikuni (q.v.). On September 2, 1945, in the ceremony on the USS *Missouri* in Tokyo Bay, Shigemitsu signed the formal surrender document on behalf of his country. He later spent seven years in prison for war crimes (q.v.) and served again as foreign minister from 1954 to 1956.

SHIKOKU. *See* JAPANESE HOME ISLANDS.

SHORT, WALTER C. *See* PEARL HARBOR, ATTACK ON.

SIAM. *See* THAILAND.

SINGAPORE. Heavily fortified British colony and one of Japan's (q.v.) main objectives in its offensives launched in December 1941. On the island of Singapore, located off the southern tip of the Malay peninsula (q.v.) and occupying an important strategic position, the British had built a massive naval base. Unlike the British colony in Hong Kong (q.v.), Singapore was considered strong enough to withstand a potential Japanese assault. Its large fixed guns were positioned to defend against an attack from the sea, but they could not be shifted to prevent an invasion from the Malay peninsula, where the difficult terrain was considered an adequate deterrent to enemy action.

Japanese forces under Lieutenant General Tomoyuki Yamashita (q.v.) landed in northern Malaya and Thailand (q.v.) on December 8, 1941, and advanced quickly down the Malay peninsula to Singapore, with the British forces of Lieutenant General Arthur Percival (q.v.) retreating ahead of them. Percival's troops finished their withdrawal to the island on January 31, 1942, and were followed by Japanese soldiers on the night of February 7. Unknown to the British, the defenders heavily outnumbered the enemy army. Nevertheless, Percival unconditionally surrendered on February 15. The remainder of the British fleet had already left the island, having lost the *Prince of Wales* and the *Repulse,* along with Admiral Tom S. V. Phillips (q.v.), to a Japanese attack in December. Percival and more than 130,000 troops became Japanese prisoners of war (q.v.).

Singapore was reoccupied by the British after the war. Admiral Louis Mountbatten (q.v.) , head of the Southeast Asia Command (q.v.), accepted the formal Japanese surrender (q.v.) on September 12, 1945.

SINO-AMERICAN COOPERATIVE ORGANIZATION (SACO). Allied group that carried out intelligence (q.v.) and guerrilla activities in China (q.v.). After the United States (q.v.) entered the war against Japan (q.v.), the United States Navy (q.v.) considered access to Chinese ports (then under Japanese control) to be vital for future American naval operations against Japan. In early 1942, Admiral Ernest J. King appointed Lieutenant Commander (later Rear Admiral) Milton E. Miles (qq.v.) to head Naval Group, China and to direct Friendship Project, which trained Chinese guerrillas, established an intelligence network, and set up weather stations. In April 1943, the arrangement was formalized as SACO. By the end of the war, SACO had trained 10,000 guerrillas.

General Tai Li, Chiang Kai-shek's (q.v.) intelligence specialist, headed the Chinese component of SACO. Miles directed the American part, which consisted of Naval Group, China, and, from September 1942 until December 1943, also the Office of Strategic Services (OSS) (q.v.) contingent in China. After the OSS removed Miles as its chief in China, both he and Tai Li continued their efforts to constrict OSS activities.

Miles reported to the Navy Department and operated independently from General Joseph W. Stilwell's China-Burma-India theater and the lend-lease program (qq.v.); in 1945 he came under the jurisdiction of

Lieutenant General Albert C. Wedemeyer's (q.v.) China theater. Deeply involved in Chinese politics, Miles formed an alliance with Major General Claire L. Chennault (q.v.), worked to undermine Stilwell, promoted the Nationalist government of Chiang Kai-shek, and vehemently opposed any U.S. cooperation with Chinese Communists, such as the Dixie Mission (q.v.). As the war with Japan ended, SACO helped the Nationalists reclaim territory from the Japanese. Critics have charged that SACO benefited the Nationalists' efforts against the Chinese Communists more than it assisted in the war against Japan.

SINO-JAPANESE WAR. *See* CHINA INCIDENT; CHINA, JAPANESE OPERATIONS IN; MARCO POLO BRIDGE.

SKIP BOMBING. Technique used by bombers (q.v.) flying at low altitudes to cause bombs to bounce across the water into the sides of enemy ships. In the Southwest Pacific Area (q.v.), Lieutenant General George C. Kenney (q.v.) trained his crews in skip bombing, which first succeeded spectacularly in destroying a large Japanese convoy in the Battle of the Bismarck Sea (q.v.) in March 1943. Thereafter, Allied bombers frequently used the same technique in attacking Japanese ships. Delayed fuzes ensured heavy damage to the enemy ships and enabled the attacking planes to avoid the explosions.

SLIM, WILLIAM JOSEPH (1891–1970). British field marshal; commander, I Burma Corps and XV Indian Corps, 1942–1943; commander, British Fourteenth Army, 1943–1945; commander in chief, Allied Land Forces in Southeast Asia Command (q.v.), 1945. After service in the Middle East, Slim was transferred to Burma (q.v.) in March 1942 but was forced two months later by the Japanese to retreat with his troops to India (q.v.). Moving to the counteroffensive in 1944, his Fourteenth Army defeated Japanese offensives at Imphal (q.v.) in India and at Arakan in Burma. Slim's force then helped to liberate Burma from the Japanese in May 1945. That summer he was appointed commander in chief, Allied Land Forces, Southeast Asia Command (q.v.). After the war he served as chief of the Imperial General Staff and governor general of Australia (q.v.).

SMALL ARMS. Employed against personnel, tanks (q.v.), and aircraft. When the United States (q.v.) entered the war, its marines and some other forces in the Pacific carried the Model 1903 Springfield rifle. By late 1942, most had received the highly regarded M1 Garand semiautomatic rifle, which became the standard individual weapon for U.S. troops during the war. Other basic weapons included the Browning automatic rifle (BAR); the M1 carbine; the Thompson submachine gun, introduced in 1943; the M3 submachine gun (known as the grease gun), first issued in 1942; the Browning light machine gun; and the Browning heavy machine gun, designed for ground targets and aircraft. During the campaigns in the Solomon Islands (q.v.), Marines used the Reising submachine gun.

Most Japanese infantrymen carried the Model 38 Arisaka rifle or the Model 38 carbine. The Type 97 semiautomatic rifle was employed against tanks. Although Japan lacked a good submachine gun, it used a number of machine guns in the Pacific, among them the Type 99 light machine gun, based on a Czechoslovakian weapon; the Type 92 heavy machine gun, an antiaircraft gun; and the Type 93 heavy machine gun, employed against tanks and aircraft. *See also* Fighter and Fighter-bomber.

SMITH, HOLLAND MCTYEIRE (1882–1967). United States Marine general; commander, V Amphibious Corps, 1943–1944; commander, Fleet Marine Force, 1944–1945. An aggressive marine nicknamed "Howlin' Mad," Smith planned and directed the Central Pacific's (q.v.) amphibious assaults (q.v.) in the Gilbert, Marshall, and Mariana Islands, and on Iwo Jima and Okinawa (qq.v.). He personally led forces in all but the last two campaigns, during which he headed the Fleet Marine Force. His most controversial action during the war was his relief of Major General Ralph C. Smith, an army officer, during the invasion of Saipan (q.v.) in 1944. Although his superiors supported him, Holland Smith became the focus of an enormous interservice debate, and he was soon transferred to the Fleet Marine Force command. In 1946, he was promoted to general and retired.

SOLOMON ISLANDS. Island chain to the east of New Guinea (q.v.) in the southern Pacific, where Allied and Japanese troops fought difficult, costly campaigns from 1942 to 1945. Among its islands are Bougainville, Buka, Choiseul, Florida, Green Islands, Guadalcanal (q.v.), Munda, New Georgia, Rendova, Russell Islands, Santa Isabel, Savo, and Tulagi. Before the war, the northernmost islands, including Bougainville, were an Australian mandate (q.v.), while the rest were under British control. Because the Solomons lay along the communication and

GREEN

BUKA
BOUGAINVILLE

**SOLOMON
ISLANDS**

CHOISEUL

VELLA LAVELLA
KOLOMBANGARA
NEW GEORGIA
RENDOVA

SANTA ISOBEL

FLORIDA

MALAITA

RUSSELL IS.
TULAGI

GUADALCANAL

SOLOMON SEA

SAN
CRISTOBAL

RENNELL

Solomon Islands

supply lines between the United States and New Zealand and Australia (qq.v.), both the Allies and Japan (qq.v.) considered their possession critical. The Japanese occupied most of the islands, beginning in 1942. The first major fighting occurred on the southern island of Guadalcanal, where both sides wanted to build airfields. *See also* Cartwheel, Operation; Guadalcanal Campaign: Naval Battles; South Pacific Area.

SOMERVELL, BREHON BURKE (1892–1955). United States Army general; head, Army Services of Supply, 1942–1943; head, Army Service Forces (ASF), 1943–1946. When Chief of Staff George C. Marshall (q.v.) reorganized the United States Army (q.v.) in March 1942, he placed Somervell, an experienced manager and engineer, in charge of the Services of Supply, later renamed the Army Service Forces. In this post, Somervell organized and supervised logistics (q.v.) for the army throughout the war, successfully overseeing a vast bureaucracy.

SOMERVILLE, JAMES FOWNES (1882–1949). British Admiral of the Fleet; commander in chief, Eastern Fleet, 1942–1944; member, British Joint Staff Mission (q.v.), 1944–1945. When the United Kingdom (q.v.) went to war with Germany (q.v.), Somerville came out of retirement. He commanded forces in Gibraltar prior to his appointment to head the Eastern Fleet in March 1942, its previous commander, Admiral Tom S. V. Phillips (q.v.), having been killed in December 1941. One of Somerville's first challenges was to defend against the Indian Ocean (q.v.) raids led by Vice Admiral Chuichi Nagumo (q.v.) in late March and early April 1942. Somerville's fleet was vastly inferior to the Japanese force, so he sent his older battleships (q.v.) to the coast of Africa to protect them from attack until Nagumo left the area. His other vessels fought several battles and sustained heavy damage, as did the naval bases and merchant ships attacked by the Japanese. Nagumo's force withdrew on April 9, 1942, and did not return to the Indian Ocean. Somerville commanded the fleet until his transfer in the summer of 1944 to head the British Admiralty Delegation in the British Joint Staff Mission (BJSM) in Washington, D.C. He remained there for the rest of the war, briefly chairing the BJSM in late 1944 after the death of Field Marshal John Dill (q.v.) and prior to the arrival of Dill's successor, Field Marshal Henry Maitland Wilson (q.v.). *See also* British Pacific Fleet.

SOONG, TSU-WEN (T. V.) (1894–1971). Chinese financier and governmental official; chairman, Central Bank, 1925–1943; minister of finance, 1925–1931; foreign minister, 1942–1945; premier, 1945–1947. Educated at Harvard University, Soong belonged to an influential Chinese family long associated with the Nationalist Party. His sister Ch'ing-ling married Sun Yat-sen; his sister Mei-Ling was Madame Chiang Kai-shek (q.v.). T. V. Soong founded the Central Bank of China to finance the Nationalist Party; he later reorganized the financial system of the Nationalist government. From 1941 to 1945, Soong served as foreign minister. Making frequent trips to the United States (q.v.), he exercised his considerable influence to promote the Nationalist government and to acquire loans and aid for China (q.v.). He lobbied repeatedly for the removal of General Joseph W. Stilwell (q.v.) as Chiang's chief of staff. Soong attended the Third Washington and the First

Quebec Conferences (qq.v.) and played a prominent role at the San Francisco Conference (q.v.) of 1945. He conducted the negotiations for the Sino-Soviet treaty concluded on August 14, 1945. After the Japanese surrender (q.v.), he served as premier in the Nationalist government from 1945 to 1947. In 1949, Soong moved to the United States.

SORGE, RICHARD (1895–1944). Soviet spy in Japan, 1933–1941. Working as a journalist for a German publication, Sorge lived in Tokyo (q.v.) from 1933 to 1941 and cultivated multiple high-level sources in the Japanese government and the German embassy. A longtime Soviet agent, Sorge relayed the information he collected to the Union of Soviet Socialist Republics (q.v.). Of particular strategic importance, he communicated Germany's (q.v.) decision to attack the U.S.S.R. in 1941 and Japan's inclination the same year to move toward Southeast Asia instead of north toward the U.S.S.R. Japanese authorities arrested Sorge in October 1941 and executed him three years later.

SOUTH AFRICA. British dominion, which declared war against Germany (q.v.) on September 6, 1939, and against Japan (q.v.) on December 8, 1941. The country's major contributions to the war against Japan were its facilities for ship repairs and its provision of food, strategic raw materials (q.v.), and manufactured goods to the Allies, particularly the United Kingdom and India (qq.v.). South African armed forces participated in the capture of Madagascar from Vichy France (qq.v.) in 1942. South African air forces were later based there and in the Southeast Asia Command (q.v.).

SOUTH PACIFIC AREA (SOPAC). Subtheater of the Allied Pacific Ocean Areas (POA) (q.v.) theater. Encompassing New Zealand (q.v.), New Caledonia (q.v.), Samoa, Fiji, and part of the Solomon Islands (q.v.), SOPAC was commanded by Vice Admiral Robert L. Ghormley (q.v.) until October 1942, when he was replaced by Vice Admiral William A. Halsey (q.v.). POA's first major offensive took place in SOPAC, when Guadalcanal (q.v.) and other islands of the southern Solomons were assaulted in August 1942. The campaign for Guadalcanal lasted until February 1943 and was accompanied by a series of costly naval battles in the Solomons. SOPAC next collaborated with the Southwest Pacific Area (SWPA) (q.v.) in Operation Cartwheel (q.v.) to neutralize the major Japanese base at Rabaul (q.v.). SOPAC's operations concentrated on the central and northern Solomons, Emirau, and the Green Islands. The subtheater was deactivated in June 1944, with its army and army air forces transferred to SWPA and most of its naval and marine forces moved to the Central Pacific Area (q.v.).

SOUTHEAST ASIA COMMAND (SEAC). Allied theater commanded by British Admiral Louis Mountbatten (q.v.), who formally established his headquarters in November 1943. At the First Quebec Conference (q.v.) in August 1943, British Prime Minister Winston S. Churchill (q.v.) proposed the formation of a new Allied theater to direct operations against the Japanese in Burma, Malaya, Singapore, and Sumatra (qq.v.), with the immediate emphasis on Burma. Also included in SEAC were Ceylon and Thailand (qq.v.). To command the new theater, which was to come under the executive responsibility of the British Chiefs of Staff (q.v.), Churchill proposed Mountbatten, with U.S. Lieutenant General Joseph W. Stilwell (q.v.) as his deputy commander. In November 1944, U.S. Lieutenant General R. A. Wheeler succeeded Stilwell in his SEAC post. Mountbatten's deputy chief of staff was U.S. Major General Albert C. Wedemeyer (q.v.), who later replaced Stilwell as chief of staff to Chiang Kai-shek (q.v.).

The SEAC headquarters, based first in Delhi, India, and then in Kandy, Ceylon, carried out most of its actions in Burma. Other operations were proposed, but the Anglo-American high command considered SEAC a low priority compared with other theaters of operation, and Mountbatten had to amend or postpone many of his plans. After driving the Japanese out of Burma, which was largely accomplished in early May 1945, Mountbatten intended to invade Malaya, but the Japanese surrender (q.v.) occurred first. At the Potsdam Conference (q.v.) in July 1945, the Combined Chiefs of Staff (q.v.) decided to move SEAC's boundaries eastward, to include Borneo, Java (qq.v.), and Celebes. Also added to Mountbatten's jurisdiction was French Indochina (q.v.) south of the 16th parallel. The changes took effect on September 2, 1945. Mountbatten accepted the formal Japanese surrender (q.v.) in Singapore on September 12, 1945.

SOUTHWEST PACIFIC AREA (SWPA). Allied theater of operations including Australia, New Guinea, the Philippine Islands (qq.v.), the Bismarck Islands, part of the Solomon Islands, and the Netherlands East Indies except for Sumatra (qq.v.). Established on March 30, 1942, it was commanded by U.S. General Douglas MacArthur (q.v.), who reported to U.S. General George C. Marshall (q.v.) as the executive agent of the United States Joint Chiefs of Staff (q.v.). Under MacArthur the Allied Land Forces commander was General Thomas A. Blamey (q.v.) of Australia, which provided the majority of troops to SWPA during the first years of the war. The theater later included also the U.S. Sixth and Eighth armies, commanded, respectively, by General Walter Krueger and Lieutenant General Robert L. Eichelberger (qq.v.). SWPA's air arm was headed by U.S. Lieutenant General George H. Brett until July 1942, when U.S. Major General George C. Kenney (q.v.) took command of the Allied Air Forces, which ultimately consisted of the U.S. Fifth and Thirteenth air forces, the 1st Marine Air Wing, and elements of the air forces of Australia, the Netherlands, and New Zealand (qq.v.). Beginning in late 1943, U.S. Vice Admiral Thomas Kinkaid (q.v.) commanded the theater's naval forces, mainly the U.S. Seventh Fleet. SWPA's operations occurred primarily in New Guinea, the Bismarcks, the Philippines, and Borneo (q.v.) from 1942 to 1945. On September 2, 1945, responsibility for Borneo, Celebes, and Java (q.v.) passed to the Southeast Asia Command (q.v.). *See also* INTELLIGENCE, ALLIED.

SOVIET UNION. *See* UNION OF SOVIET SOCIALIST REPUBLICS.

SPAATZ, CARL ANDREW (1891–1974). United States Army and Air Force general; commander, U.S. Strategic Air Forces, Pacific, 1945. From the spring of 1942 to the spring of 1945, Spaatz directed much of the American air effort against the Axis powers (q.v.) in Europe and North Africa. Beginning in January 1944, he commanded the U.S. Strategic Air Forces, Europe. With the conclusion of the war in Europe in May 1945, General of the Army Henry H. Arnold (q.v.) assigned Spaatz to head the strategic air forces in the Pacific. Under Spaatz's command, established on July 18, were the Twentieth Air Force, which included the Boeing B-29 (q.v.) bombers that operated from the Mariana Islands (q.v.), and the Eighth Air Force, which was being transferred from bases in the United Kingdom (q.v.). Soon after Spaatz arrived in the Marianas, he received word from Secretary of War Henry L. Stimson (q.v.) that President Harry S. Truman (q.v.) had ordered the use of atomic bombs (q.v.) against Japan (q.v.). Planes from Spaatz's command dropped atomic bombs on Japan on August 6 and 9. After the war, Spaatz succeeded Arnold as head of the United States Army Air Forces (q.v.) and became the first chief of staff of the United States Air Force upon its creation in 1947.

SPAIN. *See* ANTI-COMINTERN PACT; JAPANESE AMERICANS; PRISONERS OF WAR HELD BY ALLIES; PRISONERS OF WAR HELD BY JAPAN.

SPECIAL OPERATIONS EXECUTIVE (SOE). British agency formed in July 1940 to conduct subversive warfare against the Axis powers (q.v.). Originally responsible to the minister of economic warfare, the SOE reported to the British Chiefs of Staff (q.v.) after February 1942. The U.S. Office of Strategic Services (OSS) (q.v.) used the SOE as the model for some of its covert practices. The SOE operated around the world, employing its main efforts and achieving its primary successes in the war against Germany (q.v.). In the Americas, the SOE promoted Anglo-American cooperation in intelligence matters; however, SOE agents also operated in Latin America (q.v.) without U.S. permission.

SOE activities in the war against Japan (q.v.) emanated from two main headquarters: India (then Ceylon) and Australia (qq.v.). From India and Ceylon, the SOE organization, also known as Force 136, conducted operations in Burma, French Indochina, Malaya, Sumatra, and Thailand (qq.v.). The SOE was most successful in Burma, where it encouraged Aung San (q.v.) and the Burma National Army to switch from the Japanese to the Allied side. Elsewhere in Southeast Asia, differences in Anglo-American postwar goals complicated the already confused intelligence situation and often brought the SOE into conflict with the OSS. In French Indochina, where the OSS backed the anticolonial Viet Minh (q.v.), the SOE supported the interests of the Free French, who were eager to regain control after Japan's (q.v.) defeat. In Thailand also, the SOE and the OSS operated independently and sometimes in competition. The SOE provided some aid to the Malayan People's Anti-Japanese Army in Malaya but could not lessen Japanese control of the area. Many of its Sumatran operations, undertaken to gather information for possible military operations, were failures, although the SOE succeeded in the summer of 1945 in positioning special teams in Sumatra to assist prisoners of war (q.v.) and internees. The SOE also sent agents to China (q.v.), especially communist-held areas, in violation of an agreement with the OSS.

In Australia, the SOE established a branch known by the different names of Special Operations Australia (SOA), Force 137, and Z Special Unit. It participated in Allied operations behind Japanese lines in the Southwest Pacific Area (q.v.) theater. Most of the SOA's missions to the Netherlands East Indies, especially Java (qq.v.), failed, but it found more success in British Borneo (q.v.), where it conducted operations preceding Allied landings in the summer of 1945.

SPRUANCE, RAYMOND AMES (1886–1969). U.S. admiral; chief of staff, Pacific Fleet, 1942–1943; commander, Central Pacific Area (CENPAC) (q.v.) and Fifth Fleet, 1943–1945. After Rear Admiral Frank Jack Fletcher's (q.v.) flagship was crippled in the Battle of Midway (q.v.) in June 1942, Spruance assumed tactical command of the American effort, which decisively defeated the Japanese. Working closely with Admiral Chester W. Nimitz (q.v.), who delegated to him the command of the CENPAC subtheater, Spruance planned and led successful offensives in the Gilberts, Marshalls, Marianas, Iwo Jima, and Okinawa (qq.v.). He also oversaw the U.S. victory in the Battle of the Philippine Sea (q.v.).

After the war, Spruance followed Nimitz as commander of the Pacific Fleet and then served as president of the Naval War College. When the navy's final fifth star was given to Admiral William F. Halsey (q.v.) in December 1945, many senior naval officers believed that Spruance, who was much quieter and less flamboyant than Halsey, deserved the recognition instead.

STALIN, JOSEPH V. (1879–1953). General secretary, Soviet Communist party, 1922–1953; premier, Union of Soviet Socialist Republics (q.v.), 1941–1953. During the 1930s, as Germany, Italy, and Japan (qq.v.) expanded their armed forces and territories, Stalin purged his military of possible opponents, leaving him with a greatly weakened defense by 1939. That year Stalin concluded a pact with Germany; the following year, he signed a nonaggression agreement with Japan. Although the German agreement was broken by Adolf Hitler's (q.v.) invasion of the U.S.S.R. in June 1941, Stalin remained at peace with Japan until the last days of the war.

Stalin continued his authoritarian rule of the U.S.S.R. during the war and also commanded the armed forces, adding the titles of marshal (1943) and generalissimo (1945). He attended the international conferences in Teheran, Yalta, and Potsdam (qq.v.), in addition to meetings in Moscow (q.v.). Throughout most of the war, he refused Allied requests to declare war against Japan, although he pledged at the Moscow Foreign Ministers Conference (q.v.) in 1943 to enter the war in Asia after Germany was defeated. In exchange for this agreement, reaffirmed at Teheran and Yalta (qq.v.), the Allies (q.v.) promised him significant territorial concessions. Early on August 9, 1945, hours after Japanese ambassador Naotake Sato was told that the U.S.S.R. was at war with Japan, massive Soviet forces entered Manchuria and attacked Japanese positions. After the Japanese surrender (q.v.), Soviet cooperation with the West rapidly declined and ended with the intensification of the cold war. Stalin retained his firm control over the U.S.S.R. until his death in 1953.

STARK, HAROLD RAYNSFORD (1880–1972). U.S. admiral; chief of naval operations, 1939–1942; commander, U.S. Naval Forces in Europe, 1942–1945. As chief of naval operations during the period before the United States (q.v.) entered the war, Stark wrote the Plan Dog Memorandum (q.v.), an analysis of U.S. policy which became the basis for U.S. strategy in World War II. In this report of November 1940, Stark asserted the importance of the United Kingdom (q.v.) to U.S. security and recommended that the United States work to defeat Germany (q.v.) before confronting Japan's (q.v.) aggression. From January to March 1941, he participated in the secret Washington conferences between British and American officials that produced ABC-1 (q.v.), the strategic agreement that the two countries would work together to defeat the Axis powers (q.v.) and would make Europe the priority in event of war with Japan at the same time.

After the Japanese attack on Pearl Harbor (q.v.), President Franklin D. Roosevelt (q.v.) initially retained Stark as chief of naval operations while appointing Admiral Ernest J. King (q.v.) as commander in chief, U.S. Fleet, with headquarters in Washington, D.C. In the early months of the war, Stark participated in the Allied conferences (q.v.) and served as a member of the Combined Chiefs of Staff and the United States Joint Chiefs of Staff (qq.v.). In March 1942, Stark was appointed commander, U.S. Naval Forces in Europe, and spent the rest of the war in London, acting as a liaison between American and British officials. King assumed the job of chief of naval operations in addition to his other duties. Numerous military and congressional investigations of the Pearl Harbor attack examined Stark's role but reached different conclusions about his responsibility for the U.S. losses.

STATE-WAR-NAVY COORDINATING COMMITTEE. *See* JAPANESE OCCUPATION; UNITED STATES.

STETTINIUS, EDWARD R., JR. *See* HULL, CORDELL; SAN FRANCISCO CONFERENCE; UNITED STATES.

STILWELL, JOSEPH WARREN (1883–1946). United States Army general; commander, U.S. China-Burma-India (q.v.) theater, 1942–1944; chief of staff, Chiang Kai-shek (q.v.), 1942–1944; deputy commander of Southeast Asia Command (q.v.), 1943–1944; commander, United States Army Ground Forces, 1945; commander, U.S. Tenth Army, 1945. Soon after the United States (q.v.) entered the war, army plans called for Stilwell to command a future offensive in North Africa. Upon the recommendation of Army Chief of Staff George C. Marshall (q.v.), however, he was appointed in March 1942 to serve as chief of staff to Chiang Kai-shek and to head the U.S. China-Burma-India theater. Stilwell, who had served in China (q.v.) and spoke the language well, reluctantly accepted the position and arrived in Burma (q.v.) in the spring of 1942. Almost immediately he was forced by overwhelming Japanese forces to lead a retreat of his forces to India (q.v.).

From the spring of 1942 to the fall of 1944, Stilwell divided his time between Chungking (q.v.) (the capital of Chiang's government), India, and Burma, where he personally led troops fighting the Japanese and supervised the building of the Ledo Road, a key supply route later renamed the Stilwell Road (q.v.). Upon the formation of the Southeast Asia Command in the fall of 1943, Stilwell served as its deputy commander in addition to his other responsibilities, which also included the administration of lend-lease aid (q.v.) to China. His many duties and commands overlapped, a situation complicated further by his difficult relationships with Chiang, General Ho Ying-chin (q.v.), and Major General Claire L. Chennault (q.v.). The rapid Japanese advances in China during Operation Ichigo (q.v.) in 1944 added further stress to Stilwell's situation. Although he was promoted to full general in August 1944 and continued to receive Marshall's support, President Franklin D. Roosevelt (q.v.) agreed to recall him in October 1944 at Chiang's insistence.

Stilwell then headed the United States Army Ground Forces until June 1945, when he succeeded Lieutenant General Simon B. Buckner (q.v.), who had been killed in action, as commander of the U.S. Tenth Army on Okinawa (q.v.). When Japan surrendered, Stilwell's Tenth Army was under consideration for a role in the planned ground invasion of Japan (q.v.).

STILWELL ROAD. Route originally named the Ledo Road, running from Ledo in Assam, India (q.v.), to Bhamo, Burma (q.v.), where it linked up with the Burma Road (q.v.). When Japan invaded Burma and closed the

Burma Road in the spring of 1942, no overland route existed to deliver Allied military supplies into China (q.v.), where Chiang Kai-shek's (q.v.) forces were battling the Japanese. To compensate partly for the loss of the road, the United States (q.v.) began to fly large transport planes (q.v.) from bases in India over the Himalaya Mountains, or the Hump (q.v.), into China. Although the air route was successful, fewer supplies could be transferred by air than by land. In 1942, U.S. engineers, using troops and local laborers, began to construct a 500-mile road through jungles and mountains from India to a point in northern Burma where it could connect with the old Burma Road. U.S. General Joseph W. Stilwell (q.v.) was one of the strongest advocates of the project, which was completed after his recall in the fall of 1944. In January 1945, Allied troops captured the final points in northern Burma to complete the link, and convoys immediately began to travel to China. Chiang Kai-shek, who had demanded Stilwell's recall, renamed the road in his honor. *See also* Logistics.

STIMSON, HENRY LOUIS (1867–1950). U.S. secretary of war, 1940–1945. During Stimson's long career of public service, he twice served as secretary of war, from 1911 to 1913, and again from 1940 to 1945; and as secretary of state from 1929 to 1933. In the latter post, Stimson strongly protested Japanese actions in Manchuria (q.v.) in 1931 and the following year enunciated the "Stimson Doctrine," which declared that the United States (q.v.) would not recognize changes in land administration made through aggression—namely, Japanese seizure of Manchuria (or China [q.v.]). A prominent Republican, he was appointed secretary of war in 1940 by President Franklin D. Roosevelt (q.v.) as a gesture of bipartisanship. In this position, Stimson functioned as the civilian head of the War Department (the United States Army). He supported and worked harmoniously with Army Chief of Staff George C. Marshall (q.v.).

Before American entry into the war, Stimson advocated aid to the British war effort and the massive expansion of the army through peacetime conscription. From the beginning of the U.S. project to build the atomic bomb (q.v.), Stimson participated in decisions regarding its development and use, chairing the Anglo-American-Canadian Combined Policy Committee and informing President Harry S. Truman (q.v.) about the atomic program after Roosevelt's death. He supported the employment of the weapon in August 1945 and relayed Truman's order to drop the bomb. Stimson retired shortly after the close of the war.

STRATEGIC AIR CAMPAIGN. Allied bombing campaign of Japanese-held areas and the Japanese home islands (q.v.), conducted with the goal of destroying Japan's capacity and will to continue the war. From the time the United States (q.v.) entered the war, President Franklin D. Roosevelt and General Henry H. Arnold (qq.v.), head of United States Army Air Forces (q.v.), were eager to bomb Japan. With the exception of the single Doolittle raid (q.v.) in April 1942, which had a primarily psychological impact, air attacks directly against Japan had to wait until the production of a very long-range heavy bomber (q.v.) and the acquisition of air bases close enough to the targets. At the First Cairo Conference (q.v.) in December 1943, Arnold discussed the new Boeing B-29 Superfortress (q.v.) bombers, which he planned to assign to Allied airfields in India and China (qq.v.) in the spring of 1944. Used only in the war against Japan, the B-29s comprised the Twentieth Air Force, retained under the direct control of Arnold as the executive agent of the United States Joint Chiefs of Staff (q.v.) until the summer of 1945. Theater commanders who wanted the B-29s to execute specific missions had to get Arnold's permission.

The B-29s based in India and China formed the Twentieth Air Force's XX Bomber Command, which attacked Bangkok, Thailand (q.v.), in its first bombing strike on June 5, 1944. In late August, Major General Curtis E. LeMay (q.v.) became the head of the command. Targets included mostly airfields, shipyards, docks, and industrial facilities in the Japanese home islands, Manchuria and other Japanese-held parts of China, Burma, Thailand, Indochina, Malaya, and Sumatra (in a special mission staged from Ceylon) (qq.v.). In the fall of 1944, B-29s bombed Formosa (q.v.) as part of the preparation for the Allied invasion of the Philippines (q.v.). In addition to dropping bombs, B-29s also mined rivers and harbors. The air campaign was hampered by the logistical difficulties of transporting fuel and equipment over the dangerous Hump (q.v.) route from India to China, by the Japanese capture of several B-29 bases in China, such as Chengtu (q.v.), and by technical problems of the new planes, which had been rushed into production. In April 1945, the XX Bomber Command was transferred to the Mariana Islands (q.v.), where the XXI Bomber Command, also part of the Twentieth Air Force, was already stationed.

As soon as the airfields in the Marianas were completed in the fall of 1944, the XXI Bomber Command began its operations under Brigadier General Haywood S. Hansell, Jr. On November 24, 1944, the command targeted Tokyo (q.v.) in its first full-scale bombing attack. During the following months, the B-29s struggled with bad weather, the unpredictable jet stream, and Japanese fighter planes (q.v.) in attempting to carry out high-altitude, daylight precision bombing. Causing significant problems were the Japanese radar (q.v.) facilities and fighters based on Iwo Jima (q.v.), which lay in the flight path between the Marianas and Japan. In late January 1945, Arnold, angry at the XXI Bomber Command's heavy losses and poor bombing results, put LeMay in charge in the Marianas. After the Allied invasion of Iwo Jima in February removed important obstacles to the B-29 flights, LeMay experimented with incendiary weapons, such as napalm (q.v.), and instituted new bombing tactics. Beginning with a devastating attack on Tokyo on the night of March 9–10, he instructed the B-29s to fly at night and to drop incendiaries at altitudes below 7,000 feet instead of the normal 30,000 feet. In Tokyo, the bombs set off enormous firestorms that devastated the city, causing more damage than any other raid of the war. Thereafter, many B-29s used incendiaries in low-level, night operations against urban centers, while others, protected (beginning in April) by P-51 Mustang fighters based on Iwo Jima, conducted high-altitude raids by day against specific targets. At the insistence of Fleet Admiral Chester W. Nimitz (q.v.), Arnold ordered LeMay to divert some of his planes to bomb kamikaze (q.v.) airfields and to participate in Operation Starvation, the extensive mining of the waters around Japan.

By the summer of 1945, carrier (q.v.) aircraft and land-based bombers from other commands joined the B-29s in bombing the home islands, while continuing to hit other Japanese-held areas. In July, General Carl A. Spaatz (q.v.) arrived from Europe to head the U.S. Strategic Air Forces, Pacific, which would coordinate the efforts of the different commands participating in strategic bombing. Arnold also appointed Lieutenant General Nathan F. Twining (q.v.) to command the Twentieth Air Force. The Eighth Air Force was being transferred from Europe to join the strategic air campaign; its commander, Lieutenant General James H. Doolittle (q.v.), had already arrived on Okinawa when the war ended. Additional plans called for future use of the Royal Air Force in the Pacific strategic air campaign, as discussed by the Combined Chiefs of Staff during the Second Quebec Conference (q.v.) and subsequent meetings.

At Arnold's direction, several B-29s were modified to carry atomic weapons, and special crews were trained to fly the planes. On August 6 and 9, 1945, B-29s dropped atomic bombs (q.v.) on Hiroshima and

Nagasaki (qq.v.). The strategic air planners had avoided heavy conventional bombing of these cities and other potential targets, so that if an atomic bomb were dropped, its impact could be accurately measured. The strategic bombing of Japan continued until the announcement of its surrender.

From late November 1944 to August 1945, according to the U.S. Strategic Bombing Survey, Japan suffered 806,000 civilian casualties (including 330,000 deaths) from the air attacks (both conventional and atomic), with burns causing the most injuries. The bombings also destroyed 30 percent of homes in the cities. When the first B-29s attacked the home islands, Japanese fighters and antiaircraft weapons (q.v.) resisted, but the reserves were soon exhausted and could offer little protection from the devastating strikes. In suicidal attacks, some Japanese pilots rammed their planes into the B-29s. On the ground, civil defense teams created firebreaks in futile attempts to minimize the impact of the incendiary attacks; 8.5 million people evacuated the cities for the countryside. Tunnels, some quite elaborate, were constructed to house the emperor and government officials and to protect stores of munitions. *See also* Science and Technology.

SUBMARINE. Naval vessel designed to operate below the water for extended periods of time; played a significant role in the defeat of Japan (q.v.). In December 1941, Japanese submarines numbered 60. Among the Allies, the United States (q.v.) had 56 in the Pacific, the Dutch had 7 in the Netherlands East Indies (q.v.), and the United Kingdom (q.v.) had none in the Far East, having transferred its submarines to the Mediterranean the previous year.

At the start of the war, the Japanese I-class, long-range submarines were generally larger, faster, and more heavily armored than the American models. Japan's liabilities included substantial noise during submersion, the crews' crowded living conditions, and the lack of radar (q.v.) until 1944. The preeminent American submarines in late 1941 belonged to the *Tambor* class, which were quieter and more habitable, equipped with primitive radar, and aided by signal intelligence (q.v.). The average Japanese long-range submarine displaced from 1,600 to 2,200 tons, could travel on the surface at 23 knots, and had a range of 16,000 miles. The comparable American vessel displaced 1,500 tons, with a surface speed of 20 knots and a range of 10,000 miles. Near the end of the war, the Japanese built several larger submarines with a displacement of 3,500 tons and a range of 30,000 miles.

Prewar strategists of both Japan and the United States considered the principal mission of the submarine to be the destruction of warships, which would occur in conjunction with surface fleet operations. Although American doctrine changed, Japanese leaders continued to direct submarine attacks primarily against enemy warships rather than merchant vessels. As the war progressed and Allied attacks sank many of its cargo ships, Japan increasingly diverted its submarines to transport troops, supplies, oil, and other raw materials (q.v.) between the Japanese home islands (q.v.) and the widespread geographic areas under its control. Japanese submarines also traversed the Atlantic and Indian Oceans in the *Yanagi* operations—attempts to break the Allied blockade of Europe, where the vessels would exchange cargoes of gold and strategic materials for German technology. On occasion, Japanese officials in Europe traveled to Asia by submarine. A number of Japanese submarines carried small aircraft, used for reconnaissance and, in September 1942, for bombing the continental United States. (On this mission, a Japanese pilot dropped bombs on Oregon in an unsuccessful effort to cause forest fires.) Other submarines served as mother ships for midget submarines (q.v.). Beginning in 1944, the Japanese modified many submarines to carry *kaitens,* or human torpedoes, one of several suicidal, or *tokko* (q.v.) weapons deployed during the last year of the war.

In contrast to the Japanese, U.S. leaders changed the main target of American submarine attacks from warships to the Japanese lines of communication. Immediately upon entering the war, the United States declared its policy to be unrestricted submarine warfare. The campaign against Japanese merchant shipping began to achieve success in the fall of 1943, when American submarines acquired reliable torpedoes (the improved Mark 14, followed by the Mark 18 electrical torpedo) and began to operate in small groups. Newer submarines, especially the *Gato* and *Balao* classes, strengthened the American effort, which was also aided by the failure of Japanese ships to take effective defensive measures, such as traveling in convoys and using escort vessels. U.S. submarines sank more than 1,300 Japanese ships (including more than 200 warships), while U.S. losses were 52 submarines and 3,500 men. Instrumental in the American contribution to the war was Vice Admiral Charles A. Lockwood, Jr. (q.v.), who commanded submarine forces in the Southwest Pacific (1942–1943) and the Pacific Ocean Areas (1943–1945) (qq.v.). In addition to attacking enemy ships, American submarines laid mines (q.v.), evacuated people from the Philippines (q.v.) and other areas, transported forces such as Carlson's

Raiders (q.v.), conducted reconnaissance missions, maintained contacts with guerrilla and resistance groups behind enemy lines, and rescued downed airmen.

The impact of submarines during Pacific battles was mixed. Japanese submarines—both large and midget—participated in the Pearl Harbor attack (q.v.) but did not significantly help the action; they played an important role, however, in the Solomon Islands (q.v.) campaigns. Early in the war, the submarines of the U.S. Asiatic Fleet (q.v.) were ineffective in slowing the Japanese assault on the Philippines, but the improved performance of U.S. submarines was especially important in the Battles of the Philippine Sea and Leyte Gulf (qq.v.).

Also participating in the war against Japan were Dutch and British submarines. The few Dutch submarines that survived the Japanese capture of the Netherlands East Indies in early 1942 moved to Ceylon (q.v.), where they operated under British jurisdiction. Joined by several additional Dutch submarines and, beginning in late 1943, by significant numbers of British submarines, they patrolled the waters off India and Southeast Asia, attacked Japanese shipping, and delivered agents to Japanese-held areas, such as Sumatra (q.v.).

A small number of German submarines, or U-boats, also operated in the Indian Ocean, primarily from a Japanese base at Penang Island off the Malay peninsula (q.v.). Their attacks on Allied shipping achieved considerable success in late 1943 and early 1944. Upon Germany's (q.v.) surrender in May 1945, the Japanese took custody of the few U-boats still in Penang. The Germans also used large submarines to exchange strategic materials and technology with Japan, especially as Allied attacks on surface ships increased.

One major weapon employed against submerged submarines was the depth charge, dropped by naval vessels or aircraft such as flying boats (qq.v.). When the United States entered the war, its depth charges were deficient in explosive power, rate of sinking, and depth limits. Incorporating British technology, the United States produced improved depth charges with 325-pound warheads, for use by aircraft, and charges carrying 300- and 600-pound warheads, to be deployed by surface vessels. Their depth limit was 600 feet. The Japanese modified their general purpose bombs (q.v.) to produce depth charges. During the campaign for Guadalcanal (q.v.), they began to increase the number of charges carried on destroyers (q.v.) by removing minesweeping equipment. Naval mines (q.v.) also damaged or destroyed some submerged submarines. *See also* Merchant Marine.

SUBMARINE, MIDGET. Small underseas boat carried by a larger submarine (q.v.) or surface ship to waters near its targets; employed by both the Japanese and the British. Unlike the *kaiten* weapons launched by Japanese submarines in the last months of the war, midget submarines were designed to return to the mother ships following an attack. In its Pearl Harbor (q.v.) strike force, Japan included five midget submarines, which were 78 feet long, had a range of 100 miles, and carried two men and two torpedoes each. The midget subs did not contribute to the Japanese success, and all were lost, with one crew member becoming a prisoner of war (q.v.). Japan later dispatched midget submarines, carrying two- to five-man crews and armed with torpedoes and explosive charges, to the harbors of Sydney, Australia (q.v.), and Diego Suarez, Madagascar (q.v.). The small boats also operated in the Solomon, Aleutian, and Philippine Islands (qq.v.), where they inflicted damage to some enemy vessels, but were not a decisive factor. The British, having successfully used midget submarines against Germany (q.v.), sent new versions of their "X-craft" to the Far East, where the submarines sank a Japanese vessel in the harbor of Singapore (q.v.) in July 1945. *See also Tokko.*

SUKARNO, ACHMAD (1901–1970). Indonesian nationalist leader. Throughout the 1920s and 1930s, Sukarno worked for the end of Dutch control of the Netherlands East Indies (q.v.) and was imprisoned by the Dutch as a political threat. When Japan (q.v.) occupied the colony in early 1942, Sukarno headed an association of nationalist organizations that collaborated with the Japanese in exchange for independence. In 1944, Japan promised eventual independence to Indonesia, which Sukarno and Mohammad Hatta (q.v.) proclaimed on August 17, 1945, after the Japanese surrender (q.v.). Sukarno then assumed the presidency of the Republic of Indonesia, which the Netherlands (q.v.) did not recognize as independent until 1949, after a bloody four-year war.

SULTAN, DANIEL ISOM (1885–1947). United States Army general; deputy commander, U.S. China-Burma-India (CBI) (q.v.) theater, 1943–1944; commander, U.S. India-Burma (q.v.) theater, 1944–1945. Beginning in late 1943, Sultan served as deputy to Lieutenant General Joseph W. Stilwell (q.v.) in the CBI theater, supervising operations in Burma (q.v.) while acting as liaison between Stilwell and the British-dominated Southeast Asia Command (q.v.) headquarters. When

Stilwell was recalled in October 1944, the CBI theater was split into two: the India-Burma theater under Sultan and the China theater under Major General Albert C. Wedemeyer (q.v.). Sultan personally commanded his forces in Burma, which defeated the Japanese at Myitkyina (q.v.) and opened the Ledo Road, later renamed the Stilwell Road (q.v.). As the Allies (q.v.) completed the liberation of Burma in May 1945, many of Sultan's troops were transferred to the China theater while he assumed new duties in Washington, D.C.

SUMATRA. Large island in the Netherlands East Indies (q.v.), separated from the Malay peninsula and Singapore (qq.v.) by the Strait of Malacca. Invaded by Japanese forces in February 1942, Sumatra remained under Japanese control until the end of the war. Beginning in 1943, the British proposed that northern Sumatra be recaptured as part of an effort to open an Allied naval supply route through the Strait of Malacca to the coast of China (q.v.); this operation, they argued, would negate the need for the reopening of a land route through Burma (q.v.) into China. Opposing the recurring British proposals for Sumatra, the United States Joint Chiefs of Staff (q.v.) strongly backed Lieutenant General Joseph W. Stilwell's (q.v.) plans for ground operations in Burma. British Prime Minister Winston S. Churchill (q.v.) remained enthusiastic about the advantages of invading Sumatra, but the operation was not undertaken during the war. Several Allied intelligence missions to Sumatra were unsuccessful, partly because of local opposition. Beginning in June 1945, the British successfully parachuted Special Operations Executive (q.v.) teams on to the island, where they located and established contacts with prisoner of war (q.v.) and internment camps. After the Japanese surrender (q.v.), British and Indian troops occupied Sumatra, turning over control to Dutch military forces in the fall of 1946. *See also* Intelligence, Allied.

SUNDA STRAIT, BATTLE OF THE. Naval battle on the night of February 28–March 1, 1942. Two Allied cruisers (q.v.) that had fought in the Battle of the Java Sea (q.v.) tried to attack transports bringing Japanese soldiers to three landing sites in western Java (q.v.), from which they planned to capture the capital, Batavia. The badly outnumbered Allied ships sank, as did several Japanese ships, some of which were hit by their own forces. The invading forces soon captured Batavia and, joining the soldiers landing on the eastern coast, took control of the entire island.

SUPREME COMMANDER FOR THE ALLIED POWERS (SCAP).
Refers both to the person and to the command for overseeing the postwar Japanese occupation (q.v.). After obtaining Allied approval, U.S. President Harry S. Truman (q.v.) appointed General of the Army Douglas MacArthur (q.v.) to accept the Japanese surrender (q.v.) and head the occupation of the country. Using Tokyo (q.v.) as his headquarters, MacArthur served as SCAP from August 15, 1945, until April 11, 1951, when he was succeeded by Lieutenant General Matthew B. Ridgway. SCAP came to a close with the end of the occupation in April 1952.

SUPREME WAR DIRECTION COUNCIL. Japanese governmental body of political and military officials that provided strategic direction to the war, August 5, 1944–August 22, 1945. When Kuniaki Koiso succeeded Hideki Tojo (qq.v.) as prime minister in July 1944, one of his early acts was to establish the Supreme War Direction Council to coordinate political and military strategy. The council replaced the Liaison Conference between the political part of the government and Imperial General Headquarters (q.v.), the military high command that was highly independent from political control. The council's six regular members were the prime minister, the foreign minister, the navy and army ministers, and the navy and army chiefs of staff. Also included were a number of assistants representing various bureaus, who were often more militant than the basic members.

After Koiso's resignation in April 1945 and the formation of the government headed by Kantaro Suzuki (q.v.), the council's six main members increasingly met alone to engage in confidential discussions about the termination of the war. During the final months of the war, the members were Suzuki, Shigenori Togo (foreign minister), Admiral Mitsumasa Yonai (navy minister), General Korechika Anami (army minister), Admiral Soemu Toyoda (navy chief of staff), and General Yoshijiro Umezu (army chief of staff) (qq.v.). On many issues the six deadlocked, with Suzuki, Togo, and Yonai favoring peace negotiations and the other three, led by Anami, holding out for a costly defense of the Japanese home islands (q.v.). After the atomic bombs (q.v.) were dropped and the Union of Soviet Socialist Republics (q.v.) entered the war, the council again split on the question of ending the war. The decision was made after Emperor Hirohito (q.v.) expressed his wish to surrender in a meeting with the cabinet and the full council.

The Supreme War Direction Council was dissolved on August 22, 1945, in preparation for the occupation of the country. It was succeeded by the War Termination Arrangements Council, which included a minister without portfolio and the holders of the same six positions as the earlier council.

SURIBACHI, MOUNT. *See* IWO JIMA.

SURRENDER. *See* JAPANESE SURRENDER.

SUZUKI, KANTARO (1867–1948). Prime minister of Japan (q.v.), 1945. A retired admiral and president of the privy council, Suzuki served as the last wartime prime minister of Japan after Kuniaki Koiso (q.v.) resigned in April 1945. During his tenure, top officials argued about continuation of the war, peace negotiations, possible Soviet mediation, and responses to the Potsdam Proclamation (q.v.). A respected figure since his success in the Sino-Japanese War (1894–1895) and the Russo-Japanese War (1904–1905), Suzuki provided ambiguous leadership to a sharply divided government. When the Supreme War Direction Council (q.v.) and the Cabinet split on a surrender decision after the dropping of the atomic bombs (q.v.) and the entry of the Union of Soviet Socialist Republics (q.v.) into the war, Suzuki invited Emperor Hirohito (q.v.) to intervene in the discussions. Suzuki and his cabinet resigned on August 15, 1945, after the emperor broadcast the Japanese surrender (q.v.) to the Allies (q.v.).

SWEDEN. *See* INTELLIGENCE, JAPANESE; JAPANESE AMERICANS; JAPANESE SURRENDER.

SWITZERLAND. Neutral country that functioned as an international center for diplomatic, financial, intelligence (q.v.), and humanitarian activities during World War II. Diplomatically, Switzerland represented 43 countries in the nations with which they had broken relations. In Asia, for example, Switzerland guarded the interests of the United States (q.v.) in Japan, occupied China, French Indochina, and Thailand (qq.v.). Through Swiss auspices, the United States and Japan exchanged interned civilians and diplomats during the war. Japan's offer to surrender in August 1945 was transmitted to the United States and China through Swiss channels.

The base for the International Committee of the Red Cross and other relief organizations, Switzerland tried to assist internees and prisoners of war (q.v.) by inspecting their living conditions, distributing food parcels, and transmitting mail and information. These humanitarian efforts were severely limited in territories controlled by Japan. The United States and the United Kingdom (q.v.) transferred funds to Switzerland to pay Japan for the care of Allied internees and prisoners; reportedly, Japan agreed that Switzerland would retain some of the payments to satisfy Japanese debts to the Swiss.

Switzerland conducted trade, including sales of munitions, with both Allied and Axis (q.v.) nations, especially Germany (q.v.), while many belligerents used its currency and its extensive financial system. Switzerland's strategic geographic location and the presence of citizens from numerous countries contributed to its significance as a site for gathering and exchanging intelligence information.

SYMBOL. *See* CASABLANCA CONFERENCE.

-T-

TAIWAN. *See* FORMOSA.

TANK. Armored vehicle used in numerous operations in the war with Japan (q.v.). For the most part, Japanese tanks were inferior to U.S. and Soviet tanks, which were more heavily armored and equipped with better guns. In accordance with Japanese doctrine, the tank performed primarily in support of infantry troops, often in small numbers. The Japanese basically designed their tanks to fight in Manchuria and China (qq.v.), where their armor encountered very little opposition from the Chinese. At Nomonhan (q.v.) in 1939, massed Soviet tanks overwhelmed Japanese forces, but the Japanese did not substantially change their tank doctrine or design as a result. Although Japanese tanks were effective in the Malay peninsula, Burma, and Philippine campaigns (qq.v.) in 1941 and 1942, thereafter Japanese production failed to replace obsolete tanks, which could not compete with improved Allied tanks used in large numbers. In many Pacific campaigns after 1942, the Japanese used partially buried tankettes and tanks as pillboxes. Tank models completed during the last part of the war were reserved for the defense of the Japanese home islands (q.v.). When the Union of Soviet Socialist Republics (q.v.) invaded in August 1945, its armor crushed the remaining Japanese tanks in Manchuria.

Based mainly on the needs of its forces in Manchuria in the 1930s, the Japanese produced inexpensive tankettes, small, highly maneuverable, and very lightly armored vehicles. The Type 94 Tankette was manufactured in large numbers and used widely through 1942. It had a two-man crew, weighed nearly four tons, and was armed with one 7.7-mm machine gun. Its maximum speed was 25 miles per hour, and its range was 100 miles. Japan's main light tank was the Type 95 or Ha-Go, its most heavily produced tank of the war. It weighed eight tons and carried a 37-mm gun and two 7.7-mm machine guns, which were operated by a crew of three. Like other Japanese tanks, its armor was inadequate. The Type 95, powered by a diesel engine, could reach 28 miles per hour and had a 100-mile range. The major Japanese medium tanks were the Type 89 and Type 97, or Chi-Ha. Superior to other Japanese models, the Type 97 weighed nearly 15 tons, held a crew of four, and carried a 47- or 57-mm gun, as well as machine guns. It had a diesel engine, a top speed of 25 miles per hour, and a range of 150 miles.

Because of the terrain and weather, Allied tank operations against Japan were not as frequent or large as in the war against Germany and Italy (qq.v.). In many Pacific island battles, U.S. tanks proved more valuable as bulldozers and dug-in weapons platforms than as fast-moving combat vehicles. Until late in the 1930s, the United States (q.v.) placed relatively little emphasis on armor and had not developed a good medium or heavy tank. In December 1941, U.S. forces in the Pacific were equipped with the M-3 Stuart light tank, armed with one 37-mm gun, and the M-3 medium tank, which carried one 75-mm and one 37-mm gun. Called the Grant or the Lee, the M-3 medium tank was outperformed and outnumbered in the early part of the war. The following year, it began to be replaced by the M-4 Sherman medium tank, the most numerous tank produced by the United States and the most widely used in the Pacific. It weighed 30 tons, operated with a five-man crew, had a 100-mile range, and could travel at 24 miles per hour. Its main gun was the 75-mm. The M-4 was modified to carry flamethrowers, rocket launchers (q.v.), and other equipment. In the Okinawa (q.v.) campaign, U.S. forces used the M-26 Pershing heavy tank, a mobile, heavily armored vehicle with a 90-mm gun. Weighing 46 tons, it had a top speed of 30 miles per hour, a range of 91 miles, and a crew of five. The Allies (q.v.) also added armor and guns to amphibious vehicles such as the landing vehicle, tracked (LVT) for use as tanks.

Among the Soviet armor at Nomonhan in 1939 was the BT-5 tank, which outperformed Japanese forces. Weighing more than 12 tons, the BT-5 used wide tracks to travel easily across rough ground. It could achieve speeds of 45 miles per hour and had a range of 124 miles. It was armed with a 45-mm gun and carried a crew of three. The U.S.S.R. next faced Japan in Manchuria in August 1945, when Soviet armor totally overpowered the Kwantung Army (q.v.). One of the main Soviet tanks was the T-34/85 medium tank, introduced in 1943 and equipped with an 85-mm gun. Heavily armored, the tank weighed 35 tons, operated with a five-man crew, had a 224-mile range, and could travel at 34 miles per hour. By the end of the war, the most important Soviet heavy tank was the JS-2, which weighed 50 tons and bore a 122-mm gun. It had a four-man crew, a top speed of 23 miles per hour, and a maximum range of 150 miles.

Antitank weapons included rifles, antitank guns, mines (q.v.), rockets (q.v.), and flamethrowers (some mounted on tanks). On Okinawa, Japanese minefields delayed Allied tanks for days, and individual Japanese soldiers made suicidal attacks against Allied tanks. *See also* Landing Craft and Ships; Small Arms.

TARAKAN. *See* BORNEO.

TARAWA. *See* GILBERT ISLANDS.

TASK FORCE 38. *See* FAST CARRIER FORCE.

TASK FORCE 58. *See* FAST CARRIER FORCE.

TASSAFARONGA, BATTLE OF. *See* GUADALCANAL CAMPAIGN: NAVAL BATTLES.

TEHERAN CONFERENCE (EUREKA), NOVEMBER 28–DECEMBER 1, 1943. First conference of the Allied "Big Three": British Prime Minister Winston S. Churchill, U.S. President Franklin D. Roosevelt, and Soviet Premier Joseph V. Stalin (qq.v.). At the conclusion of the First Cairo Conference (q.v.), Churchill, Roosevelt, and their advisers traveled to Teheran to confer with Stalin. Most of the agenda concerned the war in Europe, the cross-channel invasion, and postwar political issues. Regarding Japan, Stalin repeated the pledge he made at the end of the Moscow Foreign Ministers Conference (q.v.) to declare war after Germany's (qq.v.) surrender. He also discussed possible territorial demands in Asia, such as a warm-water port on the Pacific. Stalin postponed a response to Roosevelt's proposal that the Union of Soviet Socialist Republics (q.v.) allow U.S. planes to use bases in Siberia.

TERAUCHI, HISAICHI (1879–1946). Japanese field marshal; army minister, 1936–1937; commander, North China Area Army, 1937–1938; commander, Southern Expeditionary Army, 1941–1945. The son of a former prime minister, Terauchi was one of Japan's most senior army officers when he was appointed to head the North China Area Army in 1937, soon after the beginning of the Sino-Japanese War. As his next assignment, in late 1941 Terauchi assumed command of the Southern Expeditionary Army to carry out Japanese expansion to the south. Beginning in December 1941, Terauchi's command invaded the Philippines, Malaya, the Netherlands East Indies, and Burma (qq.v.), swiftly conquering vast territories.

Terauchi commanded the Southern Army throughout the war, extending Japanese control and then resisting Allied attempts to recapture the seized areas. His headquarters was located in Singapore or French Indochina (q.v.), except for the period from May to November 1944, when he moved to the Philippines on Prime Minister Hideki Tojo's (q.v.) orders. After the Allies (q.v.) began their recapture of the Philippines by invading the island of Leyte (q.v.) in October 1944, Terauchi ordered General Tomoyuki Yamashita (q.v.) to mount a strong defense of Leyte instead of concentrating on the more important island of Luzon (q.v.) as Yamashita wanted. The month following the Leyte invasion, Terauchi left the islands and moved to Indochina, where he was involved in Japanese efforts to declare the independence of Southeast Asian nations from colonial powers, such as the nationalist movement in the Netherlands East Indies (q.v.). Terauchi became ill at the end of the war and died the next year.

THAILAND. Independent country in Southeast Asia, whose leaders favored the Axis powers (q.v.) throughout much of the war; also known as Siam, although its government inaugurated the name Thailand before the war. Prime Minister Luang Phibunsongkhram (q.v.) sent Thai forces to seize disputed territory from French Indochina (q.v.) on January 10, 1941, accepting Japanese mediation when the military action became stalemated. Japan (q.v.) settled the claim in favor of Thailand; the weak Vichy France (q.v.) government had no recourse.

On December 8, 1941, Japanese forces under Lieutenant General Tomoyuki Yamashita (q.v.) moved into Thailand and the Malay peninsula (q.v.). The Thai government signed a treaty with Japan (q.v.) and on January 25, 1942, declared war on the United States and the United Kingdom (qq.v.). Thailand's ambassador to the United States, Seni

Pramoj, refused to deliver the declaration of war and headed the Free Thai resistance organization in the United States. Subsequently, the United States did not regard Thailand as a belligerent, although the United Kingdom did.

The Thai government continued to ally itself with Japan, whose forces used Thailand as a base for its invasion and occupation of Burma (q.v.). To supply its troops in Burma, Japan built the Burma-Thailand Railway (q.v.) through rugged terrain in both countries. Japan allowed Thailand to seize border areas of Burma and Malaya. In 1943, Thailand sent a representative to Tokyo (q.v.) to attend the Japanese-sponsored conference of the Greater East Asia Co-Prosperity Sphere (q.v.).

The Free Thai, or Seri Thai, resistance movement received assistance from the U.S. Office of Strategic Services and the British Special Operations Executive (qq.v.). Led in Thailand by Pridi Phanomyong (q.v.), who also acted as regent for the young Thai king, the Free Thais ousted Phibunsongkhram's pro-Japanese government in 1944. Because of the intervention of the United States, Thailand was granted peace terms more generous than those proposed by the United Kingdom and France (q.v).

THEOBALD, THEODORE A. *See* NORTH PACIFIC AREA.

TIMOR. Island northwest of Australia (q.v.); before the war, the Portuguese owned the eastern part and the Dutch held the western portion, which formed part of the Netherlands East Indies (q.v.). After the Japanese began their conquests in Southeast Asia, Australia sent forces to assist the Dutch troops in Timor. This move was protested by Portugal, which hoped its neutrality would discourage a Japanese attack on eastern Timor. Japanese forces invaded on February 20, 1942, and captured most of the island within three days. Dutch, Portuguese, and Australian guerrillas carried out resistance operations until the end of the year when the remaining Australians were withdrawn. During the last year of the war, Portugal discussed with the Allies (q.v.) the reoccupation of eastern Timor by Portuguese troops, which would have to depend on Allied logistical support. No agreement had been reached when Japan (q.v.) surrendered. Portugal remained officially neutral throughout the war.

TINIAN. One of the Mariana Islands (q.v.), seized by U.S. forces, July 24–August 1, 1944. Tinian, a Japanese mandate (q.v.) since World

War I, was bombarded for more than a month and then captured in an amphibious assault (q.v.) launched from nearby Saipan (q.v.), which had been taken several weeks earlier. Its defenders had expected the invasion to occur at a different place, but they responded fiercely with banzai (q.v.) attacks. During the fight for Tinian, U.S. planes dropped napalm bombs (q.v.) in combat for the first time during the war. After the island was secured on August 1, the construction of air fields for Boeing B-29 (q.v.) bombers started immediately. Beginning in late 1944, Tinian served as one of the staging bases for the strategic air campaign (q.v.) against the Japanese home islands (q.v.). The planes that dropped the atomic bombs (q.v.) on Japan (q.v.) in August 1945 took off from the island.

TIZARD MISSION. See RADAR; SCIENCE AND TECHNOLOGY.

TOGO, SHIGENORI (1882–1950). Japanese diplomat; foreign minister, 1941–1942, 1945. After service as ambassador to Germany and the Union of Soviet Socialist Republics (qq.v.), Togo joined Hideki Tojo's (q.v.) government as foreign minister in October 1941 and oversaw the unsuccessful negotiations with the United States (q.v.) before the Pearl Harbor attack (q.v.). In September 1942, Togo resigned after Tojo's formation of the Greater East Asian Ministry, which preempted the Foreign Ministry's conduct of foreign policy with Asian nations.

In April 1945, Togo joined the cabinet of Kantaro Suzuki (q.v.) as foreign minister with the intention of seeking a peaceful end to the war. He promoted unsuccessful attempts to persuade the Soviets to mediate between Japan and the Allies (qq.v.). Following the atomic attacks on Hiroshima and Nagasaki (qq.v.), Togo supported Japan's unconditional surrender. After the war he was imprisoned for war crimes (q.v.) and died in custody.

TOJO, HIDEKI (1884–1948). Japanese army general; army minister, 1940–1944; prime minister, 1941–1944. A strong militarist and ultranationalist, Tojo advocated Japanese expansion into China (q.v.) and served as chief of staff of the Kwantung Army (q.v.) during Japan's invasion of China (qq.v.) in 1937–1938. As a cabinet member he promoted the Tripartite Pact (q.v.) and the Japanese move into French Indochina (q.v.). He became prime minister in October 1941, after the resignation of Fumimaro Konoye (q.v.), and oversaw Japan's decision to attack Pearl Harbor (q.v.) and go to war with Western countries. Tojo was an extremely strong prime minister, retaining his position as army minister and at times holding the additional posts of home minister, foreign minister, and army chief of staff. When the Allies (q.v.) captured Saipan in the Mariana Islands (qq.v.) in July 1944, Tojo was forced to resign, although he still wielded influence with the militarists and as a member of the *jushin* (q.v.). Arrested after the war, he attempted suicide but survived to be convicted of war crimes (q.v.). He was executed in 1948.

TOKKO. Suicidal "special attacks," employed as an organized strategy by the Japanese military during the last 10 months of the war. The best known and most effective of the types of *tokko* was the kamikaze (q.v.) attack in which a Japanese pilot tried to crash his plane into an Allied ship; the first such coordinated missions took place during the Leyte operations (q.v.) in October 1944. After the Japanese Combined Fleet (q.v.) failed to turn back the Allied invasion of Leyte and suffered severe losses during the Battle for Leyte Gulf (q.v.), Japanese military leaders increasingly used desperate measures, such as *tokko* warfare, to slow the Allied advances.

Another *tokko* weapon was the *oka* or Baka bomb, which was attached to the underside of a plane. When the plane was within several miles of the target, it released the *oka* and its passenger, who guided it in a glide toward an Allied ship. In a similar arrangement, the *kaiten*, a torpedo (q.v.) with a human pilot, was launched by a submarine (q.v.) and then directed by the pilot toward the objective. Also used were suicide boats, constructed from wood and loaded with explosives, to sink ships near the beaches. A number of these, 15 feet in length, attacked Allied ships during the landings on Luzon (q.v.) in January 1945. In other operations, Japanese soldiers strapped explosives to their bodies, approached Allied tanks (q.v.) on foot, and tried to blow up the tanks. To counter the strategic air campaign (q.v.) against the home islands, Japanese fighter pilots flew directly at the Boeing B-29 (q.v.) cockpits, attempting to fire at the crews or ram the planes; most of the Japanese pilots died in these attacks.

The Japanese authorities incorporated many *tokko* methods into their defensive strategy against the anticipated Allied invasion of the Japanese home islands (q.v.). They planned to arm both soldiers and civilians to carry out suicidal attacks against the invaders. Although the Allies had repeatedly attacked Japanese airfields, Japan at the time of its surrender still had 9,000 planes, more than half of which were already equipped for kamikaze missions.

TOKYO. Capital and largest city of Japan (q.v.) located on the island of Honshu. The United States (q.v.) first bombed Tokyo on April 18, 1942, when the Doolittle Raid (q.v.) had a profound psychological impact on Japan. Thereafter, Tokyo remained untouched until November 24, 1944, when Boeing B-29 (q.v.) bombers based in the Mariana Islands (q.v.) attacked the city. From then until the end of the war, Tokyo sustained repeated attacks from the strategic air campaign (q.v.). The most costly raid occurred on the night of March 9–10, 1945, when almost 300 B-29s conducted low-level incendiary attacks on Tokyo. The resulting firestorm killed 83,000 people, injured 100,000 more, demolished 250,000 buildings, and destroyed 15 square miles of the city. The final bombing strike, conducted by 1,000 B-29s, hit Tokyo on August 14, 1945.

TOKYO ROSE. Announcer for Japanese-sponsored radio programs aimed at English-speaking soldiers in the Pacific and Asia. In addition to music, the broadcasts included propaganda and misinformation designed to weaken the morale of Allied soldiers. A number of women were known collectively as "Tokyo Rose." After the war, the United States (q.v.) convicted one American citizen, Iva Ikuko Toguri D'Aquino, for her participation in the broadcasts. Released from prison in 1955, she was pardoned by U.S. President Gerald Ford in 1977.

TOLSTOY. See MOSCOW CONFERENCE, 1944.

TORPEDO. Launched from aircraft, submarines (q.v.), or surface vessels. At the time of the Pearl Harbor attack (q.v.), Japanese torpedoes were vastly superior to those of the United States (q.v.). Especially outstanding was the Type 93 Long Lance, the 24-inch, oxygen-powered torpedo that left almost no wake. Used by Japanese cruisers, destroyers (qq.v.), and other surface vessels, the Long Lance carried a 1,000-pound warhead, could travel at speeds of 49 knots, and had a range of 20 miles, three times greater than U.S. torpedoes. The Japanese equipped their submarines with the Type 95 21-inch torpedo, which was also superior to U.S. models. To counter the effectiveness of Japanese torpedoes, the United States had to depend on its advantages in radar and signal intelligence (qq.v.). During the last year of the war, the Japanese used *kaitens,* or human torpedoes, as a special *tokko* (q.v.), or suicidal, weapon.

When the United States entered the war, its submarines carried the steam-driven Mark 14 torpedo, equipped with the Mark 6 magnetic exploder. Because of the cost of the torpedo and the classified nature of the exploder, it had not undergone extensive field tests since its adoption in April 1941. After torpedoes missed numerous targets in combat, submarine commanders such as Vice Admiral Charles A. Lockwood, Jr. (q.v.) pressured the United States Navy (q.v.) to investigate the Mark 14, but its multiple defects were not entirely corrected until September 1943. The Mark 14 was 21 inches and traveled at a speed of 45 knots. In 1944, submarines began to change to the Mark 18 electric torpedo, which had a lower speed of 28 knots but left very little wake. U.S. aircraft generally carried the Mark 13 torpedo; U.S. surface vessels used the Mark 8, Mark 13, or Mark 15. *See also* Naval Vessels.

TOYODA, SOEMU (1885–1957). Japanese admiral; commander in chief, Combined Fleet, 1944–1945; navy minister, 1945. After the death of Admiral Mineichi Koga (q.v.), Toyoda assumed command of the Japanese Combined Fleet (q.v.) on May 5, 1944. During his year-long tenure, the fleet suffered disastrous losses in the Battle of the Philippine Sea (June 1944) and the Battle for Leyte Gulf (October 1944) (qq.v.). Thereafter, the fleet was unable to mount an offensive and relied increasingly on suicidal, or *tokko* (q.v.), missions to attack Allied operations. In May 1945, Toyoda became navy chief of staff. As a member of the Supreme War Direction Council (q.v.), he joined General Korechika Anami (q.v.), army minister, and General Yoshijiro Umezu (q.v.), army chief of staff, in opposing the termination of the war. During the postwar occupation, Toyoda was convicted of war crimes (q.v.) and imprisoned from 1945 to 1948.

TRANSPORT PLANE. Cargo- and troop-carrying plane, which formed an essential part of the complex logistical system of the Allies (q.v.) in the war against Japan (q.v.). Transport planes were also converted to evacuate wounded personnel and to drop paratroopers or tow gliders (q.v.). In the Southwest Pacific Area (q.v.) theater, where naval forces were often insufficient to support ground operations, General George C. Kenney (q.v.) frequently airlifted troops and supplies to the front. On the mainland of Asia, cargo planes regularly traveled the Hump (q.v.) route over the Himalaya Mountains to deliver Allied supplies to China (q.v.) after the closing of the Burma Road (q.v.). The Allies also used planes to supply the operations of the Chindits, Merrill's Marauders (qq.v.), and other groups behind Japanese lines, as well as to enable the defenders of Imphal (q.v.) to outlast the Japanese siege. The ground forces that recaptured Burma (q.v.) were heavily supported by air supply.

The primary Allied transports were versions of the Douglas DC-3, the Curtiss-Wright C-46 Commando, and the Douglas DC-4, which were produced in the United States but provided in substantial numbers to other Allies. The DC-3 began service as a commercial plane in the 1930s and was converted to military use under the names C-47 Skytrain (United States Army [q.v.]), R4D (United States Navy [q.v.]), and Dakota (Royal Air Force). Another version of the DC-3, employed to transport wounded, carry paratroopers, and tow gliders, was the C-53 Skytrooper, or Dakota II. The twin-engined DC-3 traveled at speeds up to 229 miles per hour, had a range of 1,600 to 2,000 miles, and carried 6,000 pounds. The larger C-46, adopted by the United States Marine Corps (q.v.) as R5C, had two engines, a top speed of 269 miles per hour, a range of 1,200 miles, and a capacity of 10,000 pounds. Like the DC-3, the C-46 participated in airborne operations as well as transporting cargo and personnel. The DC-3 carried up to 26 fully equipped troops, and the C-46 held 35.

Capable of a much greater range was the four-engined DC-4, which was designated C-54 Skymaster by the United States Army and R5D by the United States Navy. Used primarily to carry personnel and cargo, it could reach speeds of 265 miles per hour and travel distances of 3,900 miles, making it especially suited to the long-distance needs of the Pacific and Asian theaters. The DC-4 could handle 14,000 pounds of freight. Among the other planes used in the Pacific were two versions of the Consolidated Vultee B-24 bomber: the C-87, used primarily for transport; and the C-109, modified to perform as a tanker.

The Japanese also used transport planes, among them the Mitsubishi L3Y Tina (a version of the G3M Nell bomber), the Kawanishi H6K4-L, and the Mitsubishi Ki-57 (a version of the Ki-21 Sally bomber), as well as a type of the DC-3 produced by Showa and Nakajima in Japan. *See also* Burma Campaigns.

TRANSPORT SHIP. *See* MERCHANT MARINE.

TREASURY ISLANDS. *See* CARTWHEEL, OPERATION.

TRICOMALEE. *See* CEYLON; INDIAN OCEAN, JAPANESE RAIDS ON.

TRIDENT. *See* WASHINGTON CONFERENCE, THIRD.

TRIPARTITE PACT. Treaty signed by Japan, Germany, and Italy (qq.v.) on September 27, 1940. In a provision aimed at the United States (q.v.), the three nations agreed to aid each other if attacked by a country not already at war in Europe or Asia. Japan acknowledged the leadership in Europe of Germany and Italy, which recognized Japan's dominance in Asia. The agreement retained the existing nonaggression treaty between Germany and the Union of Soviet Socialist Republics (q.v.), which was invited to join the new pact but failed to negotiate acceptable terms with Germany. Later signers of the pact included Romania, Hungary, Slovakia, Bulgaria, Yugoslavia, and Croatia.

TROBRIAND ISLANDS. *See* CARTWHEEL, OPERATION.

TRUK. Site of major Japanese air and naval bases in the Caroline Islands (q.v.) in the west Pacific, which was neutralized by Allied forces during the war. Japan had occupied the Carolines since 1914 and had established its fleet at the deep harbor of Truk, called the "Japanese Pearl Harbor" by Americans. Its important strategic position in the Pacific was recognized by U.S. military planners, whose early plans for the Central Pacific Area (q.v.) drive included the capture of Truk. After the successful capture of the Marshall Islands (q.v.) in February 1944 and U.S. carrier (q.v.) raids on Truk the same month, Admiral Chester W. Nimitz (q.v.) recommended that Truk be bypassed. The following month the United States Joint Chiefs of Staff (q.v.) agreed, ordering Nimitz to neutralize Truk by air raids and to advance the assault date for the invasion of the Mariana Islands (q.v.). U.S. carrier attacks in March and April 1944 virtually ended Truk's effectiveness.

TRUMAN, HARRY S. (1884–1972). U.S. senator, 1935–1945; vice president, 1945; president, 1945–1953. During most of World War II, Truman represented Missouri in the U.S. Senate, aggressively chairing the influential Select Committee to Investigate the National Defense Program, or Truman Committee. In 1944 President Franklin D. Roosevelt (q.v.) chose Truman as the vice presidential candidate for his fourth term as president. Taking office as vice president in 1945, Truman had limited contact with Roosevelt and was not informed about many important developments even though the president's health was clearly declining. After Roosevelt's death on April 12,

1945, Secretary of War Henry L. Stimson (q.v.) gave Truman his first knowledge of the atomic bomb (q.v.) project.

As president, Truman presided over the conclusion of the wars in Europe and the Pacific. Already suspicious of the Union of Soviet Socialist Republics (q.v.), he participated in the last major wartime conference of the Allies (q.v.) at Potsdam (q.v.), on the outskirts of Berlin, in July 1945. While there, Truman learned of the successful detonation of an atomic bomb in New Mexico. He made the final decision to use the new weapon against Japan (q.v.).

Truman's presidency also included the occupations of Japan and Germany (q.v.), which were greatly complicated by the advent of the cold war with the Soviets. Midway through the Japanese occupation (q.v.), his administration decided to build Japan into an economically strong country to counter the expansion of communism in Asia. He was a two-war commander in chief, presiding over the U.S. and United Nations (q.v.) efforts in the Korean War until its final months.

TURNER, RICHMOND KELLY (1885–1961). U.S. admiral; director, navy War Plans Division; 1940–1942; commander, Amphibious Force, South Pacific, 1942–1943; commander, V Amphibious Force, 1943–1944; commander, Amphibious Forces, Pacific, 1944–1945. As director of the War Plans Division, Turner was responsible for the navy's planning before the Pearl Harbor attack (q.v.) and during the first few months of the war. One of his assignments was to plan the Guadalcanal invasion (q.v.), the first major amphibious assault (q.v.) made by the United States (q.v.) during the war. Admiral Ernest J. King (q.v.) then chose Turner to direct the landing, which was followed by a long series of important amphibious operations planned and led by Turner: the rest of the Solomons, the Gilberts, the Marshalls, the Marianas, Iwo Jima, and Okinawa (qq.v.). When the war ended, Turner was involved in planning for the invasion of Japan (q.v.).

TWINING, NATHAN FARRAGUT (1897–1982). United States Army and Air Force general; commander, Thirteenth Air Force, 1943; commander, Fifteenth Air Force, 1944–1945; commander, Twentieth Air Force, 1945. In mid-1942, Twining became chief of staff of Allied air forces in the South Pacific Area (q.v.). He then headed the Thirteenth Air Force in the South Pacific after its activation in January 1943, moving to the Mediterranean the next year to command the Fifteenth Air Force. During the last month of the war, he returned to the Pacific as commander of the Twentieth Air Force, the force of Boeing B-29 Superfortresses (q.v.) engaged in the strategic air campaign (q.v.) against Japan (q.v.). Twining served as chief of staff, United States Air Force, from 1953 to 1957, and as chairman of the United States Joint Chiefs of Staff (q.v.) from 1957 to 1960.

-U-

ULITHI. *See* CAROLINE ISLANDS.

ULTRA. *See* INTELLIGENCE, ALLIED SIGNAL.

UMEZU, YOSHIJIRO (1882–1949). Japanese general; commander, Kwantung Army (q.v.), and ambassador plenipotentiary to Manchukuo (q.v.), 1939–1944; army chief of staff, 1944–1945. As the commander of the China Garrison Army in Tientsin, Umezu negotiated the Ho-Umezu Agreement in 1935, in which the Chinese Nationalists made major concessions to Japan (q.v.) regarding northern China (q.v.). Already one of the most powerful generals, Umezu assumed command of the Kwantung Army in 1939 and also served as ambassador to Manchukuo (q.v.). When Hideki Tojo (q.v.) was ousted as prime minister in July 1944, Umezu was chosen to become army chief of staff, a position Tojo had also held. Umezu additionally served as a member of the Supreme War Direction Council (q.v.) and strongly opposed the Japanese surrender (q.v.) in discussions during the summer of 1945. After the capitulation to the Allies (q.v.), Umezu represented the Imperial General Headquarters (q.v.) in the surrender ceremony on the USS *Missouri* on September 2, 1945. Following the war, he was convicted of war crimes (q.v.) and died in prison.

UNION OF SOVIET SOCIALIST REPUBLICS (U.S.S.R.). Allied power (q.v.) that declared war against Japan (q.v.), effective on August 9, 1945. Throughout the war years, Premier Joseph V. Stalin (q.v.) exerted his dictatorial rule over the U.S.S.R. In 1936, Japan and Germany (q.v.) signed the Anti-Comintern Pact (q.v.), which identified the U.S.S.R. as their common enemy. Japan was consequently surprised and furious when the German-Soviet Nonaggression Pact (q.v.) was concluded in August 1939. At the time of this agreement, Japan's Kwantung Army (q.v.) had been fighting Soviet forces for several months near Nomonhan (q.v.) on the Mongolian-Manchurian border.

In addition to the Nomonhan dispute, which was settled in September, Japanese and Soviet troops had also fought in 1938 at Changkufeng (q.v.), along the Soviet-Manchurian-Korean border. Also angering Japan was the U.S.S.R.'s nonaggression pact with China (q.v.), concluded on August 21, 1937, and subsequent military aid to Japan's Chinese enemies.

In spite of the German treaty with the U.S.S.R, Japan joined Germany and Italy (q.v.) in the Tripartite Pact (q.v.) in September 1940. The following April, Japanese Foreign Minister Yosuke Matsuoka (q.v.) negotiated a neutrality agreement with the Soviets, displeasing some Japanese leaders who viewed the U.S.S.R. as a logical area for further expansion on the Asian mainland. After Germany's Adolf Hitler (q.v.) broke his agreement with Stalin and invaded the U.S.S.R. in June 1941, many Japanese officials argued that Japan should seize Soviet territory in the Far East while the Germans attacked from Europe. The Japanese strategic debate was won by those advocating instead the move south, thereby provoking war with the United States, the United Kingdom (qq.v.), and other countries.

Japan maintained its neutrality agreement with the U.S.S.R. throughout the war, as did the Soviet Union until the last weeks of the war. While participating as one of the Allies in the war against Germany and Italy, Stalin resisted heavy pressure, especially from the Americans, to enter the war against Japan at the same time. In the fall of 1943 and on later occasions, he promised to join the Pacific War within three months after Germany's defeat. Otherwise he was cautious about upsetting his agreement with Japan, as he interned American airmen who made emergency landings in the eastern U.S.S.R. and refused to help the U.S. strategic air campaign (q.v.) against Japan by granting access to Soviet territory. Throughout the war, the U.S.S.R. received large amounts of lend-lease aid (q.v.) from the United States, which hoped to keep the Soviets in the war against Germany. Part of the aid was delivered through the northern Pacific, primarily by air from Alaska or by surface ship from Portland, Oregon, to Vladivostok.

At the Yalta Conference (q.v.) in early 1945, Stalin demanded and received major territorial concessions in exchange for his firm promise to fight Japan. In April 1945, the U.S.S.R. informed Japan that it would not renew the neutrality treaty when it expired the next year. Two days after the United States dropped an atomic bomb on Hiroshima (qq.v.), the U.S.S.R. announced that it would go to war with Japan on August 9, 1945; early that morning, Soviet armies began their invasion of

Manchuria, Korea (qq.v.), and other Japanese-held areas. On August 14, 1945, the U.S.S.R. signed a treaty of friendship with Nationalist China, in which Chiang Kai-shek (q.v.) agreed to the territorial terms of the Yalta Conference (q.v.).

In the formal Japanese surrender (q.v.) ceremony on the battleship USS *Missouri* in Tokyo Bay, September 2, 1945, the U.S.S.R. was represented by Lieutenant General Kuzma N. Derevyanko, its senior officer in the ensuing Japanese occupation (q.v.). The U.S.S.R. later claimed that its proper role as one of the victors was denied by the U.S.-dominated occupation. One major controversy of the occupation was the Soviet reluctance to repatriate more than one million Japanese troops and laborers in Asia who had surrendered to Soviet authorities in August 1945. With the cold war in full swing, the U.S.S.R. declined to join the other Allies in signing a Japanese peace treaty (q.v.). Not until 1956 did the state of war between Japan and the U.S.S.R. officially end, when they normalized relations and the U.S.S.R. agreed not to block Japanese membership in the United Nations (q.v.). The two did not conclude a peace treaty. *See also* Intelligence, Soviet; Prisoners of War Held by Allies.

UNIT 731. *See* BIOLOGICAL WARFARE.

UNITED KINGDOM (U.K.). Allied country and the closest wartime partner of the United States (q.v.). The United Kingdom went to war with Germany (q.v.) on September 3, 1939, and declared war on Japan (q.v.) on December 8, 1941. During the conflict with Japan, the British prime ministers were Winston S. Churchill (1940–1945) and Clement R. Attlee (1945) (qq.v.). Serving as foreign minister under Churchill was Anthony Eden (q.v.). The British military forces were directed by the British Chiefs of Staff Committee (q.v.).

Anglo-American cooperation began before the Allied war with Japan and involved the U.S. lend-lease program (q.v.), the exchange of military observers, and policy agreements such as the ABC-1 document and the Atlantic Charter (qq.v.). In late December 1941, Churchill and President Franklin D. Roosevelt (q.v.) met to discuss cooperation in the war and formed the Combined Chiefs of Staff (q.v.) to direct the coalition's military strategy. The British Joint Staff Mission (q.v.) was stationed in Washington, D.C., to facilitate daily coordination. Among the numerous areas of collaboration were intelligence, science and technology, logistics, and the atomic bomb (qq.v.). Early in the war, the United

Kingdom established the Pacific War Council (q.v.) as an advisory group of other nations involved in the war with Japan.

Japan attacked British possessions in Asia on December 8, 1941, beginning with assaults on the Malay peninsula and Hong Kong (qq.v.) and moving during the following days against Burma, British Borneo, and the Gilbert Islands (qq.v.). After the British surrender of Singapore (q.v.) in February 1942, a Japanese naval force raided the Indian Ocean (q.v.) and forced the weak British Eastern Fleet to leave the area. By the end of May, the remaining British forces had retreated from Burma to India (q.v.), where Churchill had dispatched Richard Stafford Cripps (q.v.) in a futile effort to win the nationalists' support for the war. India and Ceylon (q.v.) served as the main British bases in Asia until the recapture of Burma in 1945.

Although Churchill and the British chiefs strongly pushed the Allied agreement to defeat Germany before taking the offensive against Japan, they participated in the unsuccessful ABDACOM (q.v.) theater in early 1942. Its head was British General Archibald P. Wavell (q.v.), who returned to India after the theater's dissolution. Acknowledging that they could spare few forces for the Pacific, the British agreed in March 1942 to declare the Pacific to be the responsibility of the United States Joint Chiefs of Staff. The British retained control of their forces in India and operations in Burma, where their chief commanders were Generals Wavell, Harold R. Alexander (q.v.), Claude J. E. Auchinleck (q.v.) and William J. Slim (q.v.). In late 1943, British Admiral Louis Mountbatten (q.v.) assumed command of the new Allied Southeast Asia Command (q.v.) and directed the reconquest of Burma. The British Eastern Fleet, reorganized as the British Pacific Fleet (q.v.) in 1944, constituted the British naval force in the war with Japan. At the time the war ended, plans for the ground invasion of Japan involved British ground and naval forces, while the air forces had offered to join the strategic air campaign (q.v.).

After the Japanese surrender (q.v.), British forces participated in the Japanese occupation (q.v.). They also reestablished control over their territories seized by Japan, although strong nationalist movements led to the later independence of most areas. The British accepted the Japanese surrenders on behalf of the French in southern Indochina and the Dutch in the Netherlands East Indies (qq.v.).

Participating in the United Kingdom's military effort against Japan were the British Commonwealth and Empire armed forces of Australia, Canada, India, New Zealand, South Africa (qq.v.), and, beginning in

1944, West Africa and East Africa. Burmese and Malay soldiers also aided the Allied effort.

UNITED NATIONS, DECLARATION OF. Joint declaration of the nations allied against the Axis powers (q.v.), announced in Washington, D.C., on January 1, 1942. The participating countries affirmed the Atlantic Charter (q.v.), pledged to work together to defeat the members of the Tripartite Pact (q.v.), and promised not to conclude a separate peace with any of the enemy powers. The document was first signed by China, the Union of Soviet Socialist Republics, the United Kingdom, and the United States (qq.v.). Twenty-two other countries soon endorsed the agreement, and 19 other nations eventually agreed to the declaration. These countries formed the nucleus of the United Nations organization (q.v.) created in 1945.

UNITED NATIONS ORGANIZATION. International institution chartered at the San Francisco Conference (q.v.), June 26, 1945. The Atlantic Charter (q.v.), adopted in August 1941 by the United Kingdom and the United States (qq.v.), formed the basis in 1942 for the Declaration of the United Nations (q.v.), affirmed by countries opposed to the Axis powers (q.v.). The "Big Four" countries of China (q.v.), the United Kingdom, the United States, and the Union of Soviet Socialist Republics (q.v.), the first signers of the declaration, reached agreements regarding the formation and structure of a postwar international organization during the Moscow Foreign Ministers Conference in 1943, the Dumbarton Oaks Conference in 1944, and the Yalta Conference in 1945 (qq.v.). Fifty countries sent delegates to the United Nations Conference on International Organization, held in San Francisco from April 25 to June 26, 1945. The conference basically developed the decisions reached during the wartime meetings; the charter provided for the General Assembly, Security Council, International Court of Justice, and other major agencies. Many of the smaller powers, led by Australia and New Zealand (qq.v.), protested the dominance of the Big Four plus France (q.v.), which would become permanent members of the Security Council with veto authority. The San Francisco Conference concluded with the adoption of the United Nations charter, which took effect on October 24, 1945. The General Assembly held its first meeting in London in January 1946 and later moved its headquarters to New York. Membership was initially restricted to countries that had opposed the Axis powers. Japan (q.v.) became a member in 1956 after the U.S.S.R. dropped its opposition.

UNITED STATES (U.S.). Allied country; headed during the war by two presidents: Franklin D. Roosevelt (1933–1945) and Harry S. Truman (1945–1953) (qq.v.). Serving as vice president were Henry A. Wallace (1941–1945) and Truman (1945). The United States formally entered the war against Japan (q.v.) on December 8, 1941, the day after the Japanese attacked American bases at Pearl Harbor (q.v.), Hawaii, and became a belligerent in the European War when Germany and Italy (qq.v.), allied with Japan (q.v.), declared war against the United States on December 11. American military strategy was directed by the United States Joint Chiefs of Staff (JCS) (q.v.), an organization created in response to the war that reported directly to the president. The United States coordinated its strategy with its closest partner, the United Kingdom (q.v.), through the Combined Chiefs of Staff (q.v.), which presided over the successful wartime command structure of the two allies.

Cordell Hull (q.v.) served as U.S. secretary of state from 1933 to 1944. He was succeeded by Edward R. Stettinius, Jr. (December 1944–June 1945) and James F. Byrnes (June 1945–January 1947) (q.v.). In 1940, Roosevelt appointed two prominent Republicans to head the War and Navy departments: Henry L. Stimson (q.v.), who served throughout the entire war, and Frank Knox (q.v.), who died in 1944. Knox's longtime deputy, James V. Forrestal, followed him as secretary of the navy. At Stimson's urging, the State-War-Navy Coordinating Committee, composed of representatives from the three departments, was formed in 1944 to provide high-level planning for the country's national security, including its participation in the postwar Japanese occupation (q.v.). The secretary of the treasury from 1934 to 1945 was Henry T. Morgenthau, Jr. Filling a number of important roles, including presidential adviser and envoy to the United Kingdom and the Union of Soviet Socialist Republics (q.v.), was Harry L. Hopkins.

UNITED STATES ARMY. Reorganized in March 1942 to include Army Air Forces, Army Ground Forces, and Army Services of Supply, renamed Army Service Forces the following year; headed by General of the Army George C. Marshall (q.v.), chief of staff from 1939 to 1945. Under Marshall, the army reached its peak strength of 8,200,000 in 1945. Commanding the Army Air Forces was General of the Army Henry H. Arnold (q.v.). The Army Ground Forces was directed by Lieutenant General Lesley J. McNair until his death in July 1944; General Joseph W. Stilwell (q.v.) held the command from January to June 1945. General Brehon B. Somervell (q.v.) headed the Army Services of Supply and

Army Service Forces. Four army generals received the five-star rank of General of the Army in December 1944: Marshall, Arnold, Douglas MacArthur (q.v.), and Dwight D. Eisenhower. Throughout the war, the civilians in charge of the War Department (the United States Army) were Secretary of War Henry L. Stimson (q.v.) and Assistant Secretary of War for Air Robert A. Lovett. Two of the agencies established within the army during the war were the Women's Army Auxiliary Corps (WAAC), created in May 1942 and renamed the Women's Army Corps (WAC) the following year; and the Manhattan Engineering District, or Manhattan Project (q.v.), headed by Major General Leslie R. Groves (q.v.) and charged with the development of an atomic bomb (q.v.).

The greatest concentration of army ground forces in the war against Japan (q.v.) was in the Southwest Pacific Area (SWPA) (q.v.) under MacArthur. U.S. forces in SWPA ultimately included the Sixth Army, commanded by General Walter Krueger (q.v.), and the Eighth Army, headed by Lieutenant General Robert L. Eichelberger (q.v.). Army forces served in the army-led China-Burma-India (CBI) theater (q.v.), a complex command headed by Stilwell from 1942 to 1944, and in its successors: the China theater (q.v.) under Lieutenant General Albert C. Wedemeyer (q.v.) and the India-Burma theater under Lieutenant General Daniel I. Sultan (q.v.). A significant proportion of the CBI forces were members of the Army Corps of Engineers. Army troops also participated in operations from Guadalcanal to Okinawa (qq.v.) in the Pacific Ocean Areas (POA) (q.v.), which was dominated by the navy. The third numerical army in the war against Japan was the Tenth Army, activated in the Central Pacific (q.v.) in 1944 under Lieutenant General Simon B. Buckner, Jr. (q.v.). Upon his death during the campaign for Okinawa (q.v.) the following year, Stilwell succeeded him.

At the time of the Japanese surrender (q.v.), the First Army under General Courtney Hodges was being transferred from Europe to assist in the invasion of the Japanese home islands (q.v.). In preparation for the anticipated invasion, the United States reorganized its commands in April 1945 and placed MacArthur in charge of United States Army Forces, Pacific, which included army forces in POA as well as SWPA. The Eighth Army served as the principal force for the postwar Japanese occupation (q.v.).

One of many branches of the army that played an important role against Japan was the Corps of Engineers. Serving in all theaters, the engineers built roads, including the lengthy Alaska Highway and Stilwell Road (qq.v.); oil pipelines; airfields; bridges; electrical and water systems; buildings ranging from barracks to hospitals; and fortifications. They also performed the vital work of mapping, frequently using aerial photographs to assist in charting areas for which the military had no maps at all. Beginning with the Philippine Islands campaign (q.v.) in 1941–1942, the engineers also served in combat, placing and defusing mines (q.v.), blowing up bridges, building infantry roads, and using explosives to destroy heavily fortified areas such as caves. *See also* Logistics; United States Army Air Forces.

UNITED STATES ARMY AIR FORCES. Created in June 1941 to succeed the Army Air Corps. From 1941 to 1945, the Army Air Forces (AAF) was headed by General of the Army Henry H. Arnold (q.v.), who reported to Army Chief of Staff George C. Marshall (q.v.). When the United States (q.v.) entered the war against Japan (q.v.), its major air force in the Pacific was the Far East Air Force in the Philippine Islands (q.v.), organized in November 1941 under Major General Lewis H. Brereton. Japanese attacks early in the war destroyed many of the American planes in the Philippines, especially on Luzon (q.v.); most of the remaining aircraft were soon transferred to bases in Australia (q.v.), while the Far East Air Force was absorbed by other commands in 1942. Also in operation in December 1941, but not under direct AAF control, was the American Volunteer Group (q.v.), or "Flying Tigers," on the Asian mainland. Although the United States held to its prewar decision to defeat Germany and Italy (qq.v.) before Japan, it steadily increased AAF resources in Asia and the Pacific throughout the war and assigned its new very long-range heavy bomber, the Boeing B-29 (q.v.), exclusively to the war against Japan.

The numerical air forces in the war against Japan were the Fifth, activated in the Southwest Pacific Area (q.v.) in September 1942; the Seventh, which was formed as the Hawaiian Air Force, was sent to Guadalcanal (q.v.) in late 1942, and supported Central Pacific (q.v.) operations beginning with the invasion of the Gilbert Islands (q.v.) in November 1943; the Tenth, which included all forces in Asia, except for China (q.v.) after March 1943; the Eleventh, stationed in Alaska and the Aleutians (q.v.); the Thirteenth, activated in the South Pacific Area (q.v.) in January 1943 and transferred to the Southwest Pacific in 1944; the Fourteenth, formerly the China Air Task Force, which became independent of the Tenth Air Force in March 1943; and the Twentieth, originated in 1944 to administer the B-29 bombers in the strategic air campaign (q.v.). In the summer of 1945, the Twentieth became part of the new U.S. Strategic Air Forces, Pacific, commanded by General Carl A. Spaatz (q.v.). One of its components, the Eighth Air Force, was being transferred from Europe to Okinawa (q.v.) when the war ended. Also in the Pacific was the Far East Air Forces, established in June 1944 under Lieutenant General George C. Kenney (q.v.) to encompass the Fifth and Thirteenth air forces in the Southwest Pacific Area and, beginning in spring 1945, additionally the Seventh Air Force. Also active in the war against Japan was the Air Transport Command. Serving with the Army Air Forces was the Women's Airforce Service Pilots (WASP) and a substantial proportion of the Women's Army Corps (WAC). *See also* Transport Plane.

UNITED STATES ARMY OBSERVER GROUP. *See* DIXIE MISSION.

UNITED STATES ASIATIC FLEET. The U.S. naval force based in the Philippine Islands (q.v.), when the United States (q.v.) entered the war. Commanded by Admiral Thomas C. Hart (q.v.), its headquarters had been located in Manila (q.v.) since October 21, 1940. The Asiatic Fleet was the smallest and weakest of the U.S. fleets, with the main naval force, the Pacific Fleet, stationed at Pearl Harbor (q.v.) in the Hawaiian Islands. According to navy plans, the Asiatic Fleet was to leave the Philippines in the event of a Japanese attack and move to a more defensible location, such as the British base at Singapore (q.v.) or a Dutch base on Java in the Netherlands East Indies (qq.v).

Japanese air attacks on the Philippines in December 1941 destroyed the Cavite Navy Yard, the major naval repair facility south of Manila, as well as most of the U.S. air defenses. Hart immediately began to send most of the fleet southward, retaining the submarines (q.v.) under his command in the Philippines. By the end of the year, with Japanese troops seizing much of the island of Luzon, Hart moved to Java and assumed command of the naval forces in the ABDACOM (q.v.) theater. The Asiatic Fleet then fought as part of ABDACOM, continuing after Hart was succeeded by Dutch Vice Admiral Conrad E. L. Helfrich on February 14, 1942. Much of the fleet was destroyed during the Japanese captures of the Netherlands East Indies and the Philippines. The remnants eventually became part of the Seventh Fleet in the Southwest Pacific Area (q.v.) theater.

UNITED STATES, ATTACKS ON WESTERN CONTINENTAL. Subject of great fears by the American public during the first part of the war, but in reality occurring only in isolated incidents. In 1942, Japanese submarines (q.v.) sank two tankers in U.S. waters and fired on oilfields near Santa Barbara, California (February 23), and on the Fort Stevens military reservation in Oregon (June 22). On September 9, a Japanese pilot flying a plane launched from a submarine dropped bombs on forests in Oregon, unsuccessfully attempting to set off large fires. Beginning in late 1944, the Japanese again tried to attack the West Coast of the United States and Canada (qq.v.) by sending balloon bombs (q.v.) across the Pacific Ocean; however, few casualties and fires resulted. Citing the potential threat of espionage, the United States, Canada, and several Latin American countries interned people of Japanese descent when the war began. *See also* Japanese Americans; Japanese Canadians; Latin America; Mexico.

UNITED STATES COAST GUARD. *See* UNITED STATES NAVY.

UNITED STATES JOINT CHIEFS OF STAFF (JCS). Organization of top military officials created in February 1942 to direct American strategy in the war, under the authority of the U.S. president. The Combined Chiefs of Staff (CCS) (q.v.), which was established at the First Washington Conference (q.v.) in December 1941–January 1942, was composed of the British Chiefs of Staff Committee (q.v.) and the JCS, which was created as a counterpart to the British organization. After the CCS designated the Pacific War (excluding Asia) as a JCS area of responsibility, the JCS formed two Allied theaters of operation: the Pacific Ocean Areas (q.v.), under Admiral Chester W. Nimitz (q.v.), and the Southwest Pacific Area (q.v.), under General Douglas MacArthur (q.v.). In the war against Japan (q.v.), the JCS also administered the U.S. China-Burma-India (CBI) (q.v.) theater, whose commander, General Joseph W. Stilwell (q.v.), held concurrent positions in Allied theaters. The Office of Strategic Services (q.v.) reported directly to the JCS.

The original members of the JCS were General George C. Marshall (q.v.), army chief of staff; Admiral Ernest J. King (q.v.), commander in chief, U.S. Fleet; Admiral Harold R. Stark (q.v.), chief of naval operations; and General Henry H. Arnold (q.v.), commanding general, United States Army Air Forces (q.v.). In March 1942, Stark left the JCS when King became chief of naval operations in addition to his other duties. The final JCS member, added in July 1942, was Admiral William D. Leahy (q.v.), a former chief of naval operations who had been serving as ambassador to Vichy France (q.v.). Upon his recall to the United States (q.v.), he assumed the new positions of chief of staff to President Franklin D. Roosevelt (q.v.) and chairman of the JCS. All four men served throughout the war and were elevated to five-star rank in December 1944.

UNITED STATES MARINE CORPS. One service under the Navy Department; headed by wartime commandants Lieutenant General Thomas Holcomb (1936–1943) and Lieutenant General A. A. Vandegrift (1944–1947) (q.v.). Upon Vandegrift's promotion to full general in 1945, he became the first active-duty Marine to hold that rank. Prior to U.S. entry into the war, the Marine Corps specialization in amphibious assaults (q.v.) led to collaboration with shipbuilder Andrew J. Higgins (q.v.) to develop landing craft and ships (q.v.). During the war the marines reached their peak strength of 485,000, including a group of women marines organized in 1943. The overwhelming majority of marines served in the Pacific War, where they were concentrated in the South and Central Pacific Areas (qq.v.). By the end of the war, six marine divisions and two amphibious corps had been formed. Prominent commanders included Lieutenant General Holland M. Smith and Lieutenant General Roy S. Geiger (qq.v.).

UNITED STATES MERCHANT MARINE. *See* MERCHANT MARINE.

UNITED STATES NAVAL GROUP, CHINA. *See* SINO-AMERICAN COOPERATIVE ORGANIZATION.

UNITED STATES NAVY. Reorganized in March 1942 to combine the positions of commander in chief, U.S. Fleet, and chief of naval operations under Admiral Ernest J. King (q.v.). At the time of the Pearl Harbor attack (q.v.), Admiral Husband E. Kimmel (q.v.) commanded the U.S. Fleet, and Admiral Harold R. Stark (q.v.) served as the chief of naval operations. Following the U.S. entry into the war, King succeeded Kimmel in December 1941 and assumed Stark's duties in March 1942. The civilian heads of the navy were Secretary of the Navy Frank Knox (1940–1944) (q.v.) and James V. Forrestal (1944–1947). In 1942, the navy formed a reserve force named Women Accepted for Volunteer Emergency Service (WAVES). The navy's top strength during the war was 3.3 million.

In December 1941, the United States Navy had three fleets: the Atlantic Fleet, engaged in the Battle of the Atlantic; the Asiatic Fleet, the smallest force, stationed in the Philippine Islands (q.v.); and the Pacific Fleet, the largest, which was based in Hawaii. In the command changes that followed the Japanese attack, Admiral Chester W. Nimitz (q.v.) became the commander of the Pacific Fleet and, within a few months, also the head of the Pacific Ocean Areas (POA) (q.v.) theater. Both in numbers and in command structure, the navy dominated POA. The theater contained both the Third Fleet, under Admiral William F. Halsey (q.v.) and the Fifth Fleet, under Admiral Raymond A. Spruance. Beginning in the summer of 1944, the fleets were combined except for their top commands, which alternated in charge of the force: when Halsey was in command, it was designated the Third Fleet; under Spruance, it became the Fifth Fleet. Japanese leaders believed the Third and Fifth to be two distinct fleets. An essential part of the fleet was the Fast Carrier Force (q.v.), headed alternately by Vice Admiral Mark A. Mitscher and Vice Admiral John S. McCain (qq.v.). Serving with the Pacific Fleet during the last part of the war were elements of the British Pacific Fleet (q.v.).

Within a few weeks of the Japanese attack, the Asiatic Fleet, commanded by Admiral Thomas C. Hart (q.v.), left the Philippines and joined the short-lived ABDACOM (q.v.) theater. Its remnants later formed the nucleus of the Seventh Fleet under Admiral Thomas C. Kinkaid (q.v.) in the Southwest Pacific Area (SWPA) (q.v.) theater.

In December 1944, the U.S. Congress created the five-star rank of Fleet Admiral for King, Nimitz, and Admiral William D. Leahy (q.v.), a former chief of naval operations who served as the president's chief of staff and chaired the United States Joint Chiefs of Staff (q.v.) throughout the war. One additional five-star slot was authorized at the same time but was not awarded until December 1945, when Halsey received the honor.

By an executive order dated November 1, 1941, President Roosevelt transferred the United States Coast Guard from the control of the Treasury Department to the United States Navy. In the Pacific War, the Coast Guard escorted convoys, conducted antisubmarine patrols, and participated in amphibious assaults (q.v.) by furnishing fire support and operating landing craft and ships (q.v.). The Coast Guard also carried out rescues, using helicopters (q.v.) in some missions. Beginning in late 1942, women joined the Coast Guard as SPARs, a name derived from the Coast Guard motto in Latin and

English. At the conclusion of the war, the Coast Guard reverted to Treasury Department control.

In January 1942, the navy created the Naval Construction Force to build advance bases in combat theaters. In the war against Japan, the "Seabees," named because of the initials of their basic unit, the construction battalion, served in SWPA and all parts of POA. They frequently worked under combat conditions, beginning with the construction of Henderson Field on Guadalcanal (qq.v.) in August 1942. Throughout the Pacific, they constructed airfields, naval bases, hospitals, housing, storage facilities, and roads, and also handled cargo. *See also* Logistics; United States Marine Corps.

UNITED STATES PACIFIC FLEET. *See* UNITED STATES NAVY.

-V-

VANDEGRIFT, ALEXANDER ARCHER (1887–1973). United States Marine general; commander, 1st Marine Division, 1942–1943; commander, I Marine Amphibious Corps, South Pacific Area, 1943; commandant, United States Marine Corps (q.v.), 1943–1947. In March 1942, Vandegrift took command of the 1st Marine Division at its training camp in the United States and shortly learned that the division would lead the invasion of Guadalcanal in the Solomon Islands (qq.v.). As the first offensive of the South Pacific Area (SOPAC) (q.v.), Vandegrift and the 1st Marine Division landed on Guadalcanal on August 7, 1942, quickly seizing the Japanese airfield under construction, which became Henderson Field (q.v.). Initially the Japanese opposition was light, but the combat escalated as both sides poured reinforcements onto the island by sea and fought fierce ground and naval battles. Tropical diseases as well as combat wounds weakened Vandegrift's men, who were relieved in early December 1942 by Major General Alexander M. Patch (q.v.) and fresh troops.

In mid-1943, Vandegrift was appointed to head the I Marine Amphibious Corps in SOPAC, and, after the invasion of Bougainville in late 1943, he returned to Washington, D.C., to become commandant of the Marine Corps in January 1944. He remained in that position through the end of 1947, overseeing operations in SOPAC and in the Central Pacific Area (q.v.) that involved extremely heavy combat for marines. In April 1945, he was promoted to general, the first man in the Marine Corps to hold that rank on active duty.

VASILEVSKY, ALEXANDER MIKHAILOVICH (1895–1977). Marshal of the Soviet Union; chief of the General Staff, 1942–1945; supreme commander, Far Eastern Command, 1945. After successfully leading operations against Germany (q.v.) and serving in the Soviet high command, Vasilevsky was appointed in June 1945 to command all Soviet forces in the Far East. By August, these numbered more than 80 divisions organized into three fronts, or army groups, including veteran troops and commanders shifted secretly from Europe during the previous three months. Early on August 9, after the Union of Soviet Socialist Republics (q.v.) declared war against Japan (q.v.), Vasilevsky's forces began massive invasions of Manchuria, where they surprised the Japanese Kwantung Army (q.v.) and advanced rapidly. General Otozo Yamada (q.v.), commander of the Japanese forces, refused the initial ceasefire order from Tokyo (q.v.) on August 14, 1945, and finally surrendered on August 20. After the war, Vasilevsky held a number of high governmental positions, among which was army minister, 1950–1953. *See also* Manchuria Campaign (1945).

VELLA GULF, BATTLE OF. *See* CARTWHEEL, OPERATION.

VELLA LAVELLA, BATTLE OF. *See* CARTWHEEL, OPERATION.

VENONA. *See* INTELLIGENCE, SOVIET.

VICHY FRANCE. *See* FRANCE, VICHY.

VIET MINH. Vietnamese nationalistic organization that conducted resistance operations against the Japanese in French Indochina (q.v.) during the war. The Viet Minh, whose full title translates as the League for the Independence of Vietnam, was founded in 1941 to achieve independence from both France and Japan (qq.v.). Its leader, Ho Chi Minh (q.v.), and the commander of its military forces, Vo Nguyen Giap (q.v.), were communists, although not all of its members were. Beginning in late 1943, the Viet Minh carried out guerrilla operations in Indochina, aided in part by the U.S. Office of Strategic Services (q.v.), and controlled areas of northern Vietnam by the end of the war. When Japan surrendered, Viet Minh forces captured Hanoi and announced the formation of the Democratic Republic of Vietnam. By late 1946, Viet Minh and French forces were engaged in war.

VIETNAM. *See* FRENCH INDOCHINA.

VO NGUYEN GIAP (1910–). Vietnamese nationalist military leader. A longtime member of the Indochinese Communist Party and promoter of Vietnamese independence, Vo Nguyen Giap (commonly referred to as "Giap" in the West), escaped to China (q.v.) in 1939. There he helped Ho Chi Minh (q.v.) and others to form the Viet Minh (q.v.) organization to drive Japan and France out of French Indochina (qq.v.). In 1944–1945, he directed guerrilla operations against the Japanese in the northern part of the country. At the end of the war Ho Chi Minh proclaimed the independence of Vietnam, in which Giap held the position of defense minister. He developed strategy and directed military operations against the French, the South Vietnamese, and the United States (q.v.) from 1946 to 1975.

VOLCANO ISLANDS. *See* IWO JIMA.

-W-

WAINWRIGHT, JONATHAN MAYHEW (1883–1953). United States Army general; commander, U.S. Philippine Division, 1940–1941; commander, North Luzon Defense Force, 1941–1942; commander, Luzon Force, 1942; commander, U.S. Forces in the Philippines, 1942; prisoner of war (q.v.), 1942–1945. When the Japanese attacked the island of Luzon in the Philippine Islands (qq.v.) on December 8, 1941, Wainwright headed the North Luzon Defense Force under General Douglas MacArthur (q.v.). On December 22, the Japanese Fourteenth Army under Lieutenant General Masaharu Homma (q.v.) landed in force on northern Luzon and moved swiftly south toward Manila (q.v.). Following War Plan Orange (q.v.), Wainwright conducted a skillful withdrawal to the peninsula of Bataan, from which U.S. and Filipino troops battled the Japanese. On March 11, 1942, MacArthur left the Philippines on the orders of President Franklin D. Roosevelt (q.v.), who expected him to form a new Allied command in Australia (q.v.).

Army Chief of Staff George C. Marshall (q.v.) appointed Wainwright to fill MacArthur's position as head of U.S. Forces in the Philippines, which was then headquartered on the island of Corregidor in Manila Bay. The Bataan forces capitulated on April 9, 1942, with Corregidor holding out until May 6. On that date Homma forced Wainwright to broadcast surrender orders to all troops in the Philippines. Wainwright spent the rest of the war as a Japanese prisoner, imprisoned last in a camp in Manchuria (q.v.). Following his release by Soviet troops, he stood with the Allied delegation during the formal Japanese surrender (q.v.) ceremony on the battleship USS *Missouri* on September 2, 1945. He received the Medal of Honor and retired in 1947.

WAKE ISLAND. Small, U.S.-held atoll in the Pacific, where military bases were under construction when the Japanese bombed it on December 7, 1941. Located 1,200 miles west of Midway Island, Wake received no reinforcements after the initial attack. Its marine contingent repelled the first invasion attempt but could not withstand the second, much larger force that landed on December 23 and overwhelmed the defenders. Throughout the rest of the war, the United States (q.v.) bombed Wake Island but did not land forces on it until September 4, 1945, after the official Japanese surrender (q.v.).

WALLACE, HENRY A. *See* MANHATTAN PROJECT; UNITED STATES.

WANG CHING-WEI (1884–1944). Chinese politician; president, Reformed government of the Republic of China, 1940–1944. A former revolutionary, Wang was alternately a colleague and rival of Chiang Kai-shek (q.v.). In November 1938, Japan (q.v.) persuaded him to defect from Chiang's Kuomintang government (q.v.) in Chungking (q.v.) and work with the Japanese occupiers in China (q.v.). Settling in Nanking (q.v.), Wang in 1940 became president of the Reformed government of the Republic of China, a puppet regime under the jurisdiction of the Japanese Central China Expeditionary Army. Under Japanese pressure, he declared war on the Allies (q.v.) in January 1943. Although his government and armed forces were allowed to administer certain areas, Wang's independence was extremely limited. Upon his death, Wang was succeeded by Chou Fu-hai.

WAR CRIMES TRIALS. Series of Allied trials held in Asia and the Pacific, 1945–1951. In accordance with the warning in the Potsdam Proclamation (q.v.) that "stern justice shall be meted out to all war criminals," the Allies (q.v.) conducted numerous trials of Japanese civilians and members of the armed forces. The 28 major Japanese defendants, including prime ministers, generals, admirals, and other high-ranking officials, were tried on charges of "crimes against peace, conventional war crimes, and crimes against humanity" by the International Military Tribunal for the Far East (IMTFE) in Tokyo (q.v.). Established in January

1946 by General of the Army Douglas MacArthur (q.v.) in his capacity as Supreme Commander for the Allied Powers (q.v.), the IMTFE was headed by an Australian and consisted of judges from 11 countries. During the trial, which lasted from May 1946 to November 1948, two defendants died and one was declared insane. The tribunal found the remaining 25 guilty, condemning 7 to death and sentencing the others to prison terms. In December 1948, the 7 men, including former Prime Minister Hideki Tojo (q.v.), were hanged. In other trials held in Japan, military commissions of the U.S. Eighth Army decided 5,100 lesser cases. Contrary to popular sentiments expressed by many Allied leaders, Emperor Hirohito (q.v.) was excluded from the war crimes trials and allowed to retain his throne.

In addition to the trials in Japan, 6,000 Japanese were tried elsewhere by Australia, China, France, the Netherlands, the Philippines, the United Kingdom, and the United States (qq.v.). These trials lasted until 1951 and resulted in 1,000 executions. In addition to atrocities occurring during battle, many charges involved the mistreatment of internees and prisoners of war (q.v.). Among the prominent men convicted by U.S. military commissions in the Philippines (q.v.) were General Tomoyuki Yamashita and Lieutenant General Masaharu Homma (qq.v.), held responsible, respectively, for crimes committed during the Battle for Manila in 1945 and the Bataan Death March (qq.v.) in 1942. After appeals to the U.S. Supreme Court, which ruled it lacked jurisdiction, both men were executed. Some of the British courts focused on the abuse of prisoners during the building of the Burma-Thailand Railway (q.v.). The Netherlands prosecuted officials for the enslavement of Dutch nationals as comfort women (q.v.). The Union of Soviet Socialist Republics (q.v.) also conducted war crimes trials, making public charges that the Japanese waged biological warfare (q.v.); no figures are available for the Soviet cases. Among their prominent prisoners was General Otozo Yamada (q.v.), commander of the Kwantung Army (q.v.) at the end of the war. *See also* Japanese Occupation; Nanking.

WAR PLAN ORANGE. U.S. contingency plan for a war involving it solely with Japan (q.v.); one of the "color" war plans for projected conflicts in which the United States (q.v.) engaged a single enemy at one time. Originated in the early 1900s, the Orange plan underwent numerous revisions, with the last version, War Plan Orange-3 (WPO-3), substantially completed in 1938. Based on the premise that the Japanese would attack without warning, WPO-3 envisioned a primarily naval war, in which the United States would mobilize its forces and then fight its way across the central Pacific by seizing the Japanese-mandated Marshall, Caroline, and Mariana Islands (qq.v.). U.S. planners assumed that Japan would assault the U.S.-owned Philippine Islands (q.v.) long before reinforcements could arrive. When attacked, the U.S.-Filipino forces in the Philippines were to defend Manila Bay on the island of Luzon (q.v.) and withdraw if necessary to the Bataan peninsula overlooking the bay, where they were to hold out as long as possible and block enemy use of Manila (q.v.) as a port. U.S. naval forces would eventually break through the Japanese blockade and relieve them. Elements of the Orange plan were incorporated into the later Rainbow war plans (q.v.).

WAR PLANS, U.S. *See* ABC-1; PLAN DOG MEMORANDUM; RAINBOW PLANS; WAR PLAN ORANGE.

WASHINGTON CONFERENCE, FIRST (ARCADIA), DECEMBER 22, 1941–JANUARY 14, 1942. First Allied strategic conference following the United States' (q.v.) entry into the war. After the Japanese attack on Pearl Harbor (q.v.) in December 1941, British Prime Minister Winston S. Churchill (q.v.) and his military chiefs traveled to Washington, D.C., to meet with U.S. President Franklin D. Roosevelt (q.v.) and his advisers. The British, fearful that public outrage would lead the United States to focus its primary military efforts against Japan (q.v.), sought successfully to reaffirm the "Europe First" policy stated in ABC-1 (q.v.) and to advance the Anglo-American partnership. To coordinate the strategic direction of the war, Roosevelt and Churchill authorized the formation of the Combined Chiefs of Staff (q.v.) and its supporting committees. Also created was ABDACOM (q.v.), the Allied theater assigned to halt the Japanese advance in the southwestern Pacific. During the conference, 26 countries signed the Declaration of the United Nations (q.v.), the foundation for Allied opposition to the Axis powers (q.v.).

WASHINGTON CONFERENCE, SECOND, JUNE 19–25, 1942. Allied meeting held in Hyde Park, New York, and in Washington, D.C., between British and American leaders. Although the participants focused on Allied offensive operations in Europe and North Africa in 1942 and 1943, they also addressed the atomic bomb (q.v.) project. On the last day of the conference, U.S. President Franklin D. Roosevelt and British Prime Minister Winston S. Churchill (qq.v.) discussed the war against Japan (q.v.) with the Pacific War Council (q.v.).

WASHINGTON CONFERENCE, THIRD (TRIDENT), MAY 12–25, 1943.

Allied conference of British Prime Minister Winston S. Churchill, U.S. President Franklin D. Roosevelt (qq.v.), and their advisers. Concerning the war against Germany and Italy (qq.v.), the Combined Chiefs of Staff (CCS) (q.v.) decided to begin operations in mainland Italy following the capture of Sicily; they also set the tentative date of May 1, 1944, for the cross-channel invasion of northern France (q.v.). Regarding the war against Japan, the CCS agreed to complete the conquest of the Solomon Islands (q.v.) and the Bismarck Archipelago; to move farther west along the northern coast of New Guinea (q.v.); to seize the Marshall and Caroline Islands (qq.v.); to oust the Japanese from the Aleutian Islands (q.v.); and to increase the emphasis on air operations in China (q.v.). This last decision was influenced by British reluctance for large-scale offensive operations in Burma (q.v.), which had been approved at the Casablanca Conference (q.v.), and the enthusiasm expressed by Major General Claire L. Chennault (q.v.), which Roosevelt and Churchill shared, for placing the priority on air, rather than ground, forces in China.

WAVELL, ARCHIBALD PERCIVAL (1883–1950).

British field marshal; commander in chief, India, 1941–1943; commander, American-British-Dutch-Australian Command (ABDACOM [q.v.]), 1942; viceroy, India, 1943–1947. After leading forces in the Middle East in 1939–1941, and facing constant pressure from Prime Minister Winston S. Churchill (q.v.), Wavell was appointed commander in chief of India (q.v.) in 1941. He headed ABDACOM during its brief existence in early 1942 with the impossible assignment of defending Southeast Asia against the overwhelming Japanese forces. After defeats on the ground and in sea battles, the command was dissolved on February 25, 1942. Wavell returned to India, where he bolstered Indian security and worked toward the defense and then liberation of Burma (q.v.). In 1943, Churchill, again critical of Wavell's progress, replaced him as commander in India with General Claude J. E. Auchinleck (q.v.). Wavell then became viceroy of India, a position he held until succeeded by Louis Mountbatten (q.v.) in 1947.

WEDEMEYER, ALBERT COADY (1897–1989).

United States Army general; member, army War Plans and Operations divisions, 1941–

1943; deputy chief of staff, Southeast Asia Command (q.v.), 1943–1944; commander, China theater (q.v.), and chief of staff to Chiang Kai-shek (q.v.), 1944–1946. As a member of the army's War Plans Division (WPD), Wedemeyer was the chief author of the Victory Program, which in September 1941 accurately projected the manpower and resources needs of the armed forces if the United States (q.v.) should enter the war. He continued in the Operations Division (successor to WPD) in the War Department through the fall of 1943 and attended many of the Allied conferences (q.v.).

In October 1943, Wedemeyer was appointed deputy chief of staff to Admiral Louis Mountbatten (q.v.), commander of the newly created Southeast Asia Command. One year later he succeeded General Joseph W. Stilwell (q.v.) as chief of staff to Chiang Kai-shek (q.v.) and headed the China theater, formerly part of the China-Burma-India (q.v.) theater. In Asia Wedemeyer worked fairly well with both Mountbatten and Chiang, although by the time of his arrival, the United States considered China (q.v.) less important strategically. He remained in China until the spring of 1946, returning later to carry out a special mission on behalf of the State Department regarding the Chinese civil war.

WILKINSON, THEODORE STARK (1888–1946). U.S. admiral; director of Naval Intelligence, 1941–1943; deputy to commander, South Pacific Area (q.v.), 1943; commander, III Amphibious Force, 1943–1945. Arriving in the South Pacific in early 1943, Wilkinson served as deputy to theater commander Admiral William F. Halsey (q.v.). He took command of the III Amphibious Force in July 1943 and participated in Operation Cartwheel (q.v.). After the deactivation of the South Pacific subtheater in mid-1944, Wilkinson moved to the Central Pacific Area (CENPAC) (q.v.) with Halsey and continued to head amphibious operations conducted by Halsey's Third Fleet. In September 1944, Wilkinson led the Joint Expeditionary Force in the invasion of the Palau Islands (q.v.). The next month, CENPAC loaned the Third Fleet for the invasion of Leyte in the Philippines (qq.v.), where Wilkinson commanded the Southern Attack Force. He headed the Lingayen Attack Force during the assault on Luzon (q.v.) in January 1945. Wilkinson then became involved in planning for the invasion of Japan (q.v.).

WILSON, HENRY MAITLAND (1881–1964). British field marshal; head, British Joint Staff Mission, 1944–1947. During most of the war, Wilson commanded forces against the European Axis powers (q.v.), rising to the position of supreme allied commander, Mediterranean theater, in early 1944. Late the same year, after the death of Field Marshal John Dill (q.v.), he was named to succeed Dill as head of the British Joint Staff Mission (q.v.) in Washington, D.C. In that capacity he represented the British Chiefs of Staff (q.v.) in the regular meetings of the Combined Chiefs of Staff (q.v.), except during the international meetings attended by the British Chiefs.

WINGATE, ORDE (1903–1944). British general; commander, Long Range Penetration Forces, Burma (q.v.), 1942–1944. An expert in guerrilla warfare, Wingate served in the Sudan and Ethiopia (1940–1941). In March 1942, General Archibald P. Wavell (q.v.) asked for his transfer to India (q.v.) and approved his plans for long-range penetration groups ("Chindits" [q.v.]) to conduct guerrilla operations in Burma. Wingate's Chindit campaign in 1943 produced heavy losses but boosted Allied morale, including that of Prime Minister Winston S. Churchill (q.v.). Wingate's proposal for a major offensive in 1944 was approved in August 1943 at the First Quebec Conference (q.v.), which he attended at Churchill's invitation. In March 1944, one month after the Chindits began their work behind enemy lines in Burma, Wingate died in a plane crash.

WOMEN ACCEPTED FOR VOLUNTEER EMERGENCY SERVICE (WAVES). *See* UNITED STATES NAVY.

WOMEN'S AIRFORCE SERVICE PILOTS (WASP). *See* UNITED STATES ARMY AIR FORCES.

WOMEN'S ARMY CORPS (WAC). *See* UNITED STATES ARMY.

-Y-

YALTA CONFERENCE (ARGONAUT), FEBRUARY 4–11, 1945. The second "Big Three" conference of British Prime Minister Winston S. Churchill, U.S. President Franklin D. Roosevelt, and Soviet Premier Joseph V. Stalin (qq.v.), held outside Livadia in the Crimean region of the Union of Soviet Socialist Republics (q.v.). The British and Americans conferred in Malta (q.v.) prior to traveling to the Crimea.

Some of the Yalta agreements were reached in private meetings between Roosevelt and Stalin and were not announced publicly for years.

The European issues on the agenda mainly concerned the postwar political situation: occupation zones, Soviet demands for reparations, and the borders of Poland. To Roosevelt's great satisfaction, the participants reached a consensus on the new United Nations organization (q.v.), resolving issues left unsettled at the Dumbarton Oaks Conference (q.v.); the Soviets accepted a compromise on the Security Council veto, and the British and Americans agreed to accept the Ukraine and Belorussia as additional member countries, in effect giving the U.S.S.R. three votes.

Stalin formally agreed to declare war against Japan (q.v.) within "two or three months" after Germany's (q.v.) defeat. In exchange for entering the war, the Soviets demanded and received assurances that they would receive the southern half of Sakhalin (q.v.), the Kurile Islands (q.v.), the preservation of the status quo in the Mongolian People's Republic, the internationalization of the port of Dairen, the lease for a Soviet naval base at Port Arthur, and special rights over Manchurian railroads. Stalin promised to form an alliance with Nationalist China (q.v.); the Sino-Soviet treaty was signed on August 14. In this accord, Chiang Kai-shek (q.v.) accepted the privileges granted at Yalta to the Soviets in Manchuria and Mongolia (qq.v.), areas claimed by China.

In discussions among the military officials, the U.S. chiefs asked for permission to use air bases in the Soviet Far East, as well as bases in Europe, during the rest of the war. Stalin told Roosevelt he approved of the cooperative efforts, but the Soviets repeatedly delayed and never allowed American usage of the airfields.

YAMADA, OTOZO (1881–1965). Japanese general; commander, 12th Division (Manchuria [q.v.]), 1937–1938; commander, Central China Expeditionary Army, 1938–1939; inspector general for military education, 1939–1941; commander, Kwantung Army (q.v.), 1944–1945. Throughout the war, the Kwantung Army in Manchuria maintained large forces to repel an invasion of the Union of Soviet Socialist Republics (q.v.), but by the summer of 1945 the army, although numerically large, had been stripped of its veteran units for other operations or for the defense of the Japanese home islands (q.v.). As Yamada assumed command of the army in 1944, Japanese strategy in Manchuria shifted to the defensive, but the system of fortifications was not completed when the U.S.S.R. entered the war. The massive Soviet attacks on August 9, 1945, totally overwhelmed the Kwantung Army and caught Yamada's high command by surprise, making an effective defense impossible. On the night of August 14, the Japanese Imperial General Headquarters (q.v.) relayed to the Kwantung Army a cease-fire order, which Yamada countermanded. The Soviets resumed their advances, as some Japanese units surrendered and others resisted. The Kwantung Army announced a cease-fire on August 20, although fighting continued in some areas. After the war, the U.S.S.R. charged Yamada with war crimes (q.v.) and imprisoned him until 1956. *See also* Manchuria Campaign (1945).

YAMAMOTO, ISORUKU (1884–1943). Japanese admiral; commander in chief, Combined Fleet (q.v.), 1939–1943. As Japan's chief naval strategist, Yamamoto originated and planned the surprise attack on Pearl Harbor (q.v.) on December 7, 1941. Although he dissented from the decision to challenge the United States (q.v.) in war, he believed that Japan had to immobilize the American fleet to win a negotiated peace. Yamamoto's assault devastated the forces at Pearl Harbor, although the American carriers (q.v.) were at sea and escaped damage. During the following months, Yamamoto was credited with many naval victories in the Pacific and Indian Oceans (q.v.), as Japan continued to extend its boundaries. In early June 1942, however, he suffered an overwhelming defeat in the Battle of Midway (q.v.), where he had intended to destroy the remainder of the U.S. Pacific Fleet but instead lost four carriers and thousands of trained pilots. The following April, American intelligence (q.v.) learned of Yamamoto's route for an inspection tour and shot down his plane in the Solomon Islands (q.v.), killing him.

YAMASHITA, TOMOYUKI (1888–1946). Japanese general; commander, Twenty-fifth Army, 1941–1942; commander, First Area Army, 1942–1944; commander, Fourteenth Area Army, 1944–1945. When Japan launched its multiple attacks on December 7–8, 1941, Yamashita's assignment was to capture the Malay peninsula and Singapore (qq.v.). On December 8, his Twenty-fifth Army landed in Thailand (q.v.) and northern Malaya and began its swift conquest of the Malay peninsula, earning Yamashita the title of "Tiger of Malaya." Reaching the southern tip of the peninsula, the outnumbered Japanese forces crossed into Singapore, which surrendered on February 15, 1942.

In part because of Yamashita's long-standing enmity with Prime Minister Hideki Tojo (q.v.), his next post was the less visible command of the First Area Army in Manchuria (q.v.), where he spent two years.

In October 1944, with Tojo out of power, Yamashita was sent to the Philippine Islands (q.v.) to head the Fourteenth Area Army and prepare for the expected Allied invasion. Soon after his arrival, U.S. forces under General Douglas MacArthur (q.v.) began their recapture of the Philippines with a landing on Leyte (q.v.) on October 20, 1944. Yamashita planned to make his major challenge to the Allies (q.v.) on Luzon (q.v.), but he was ordered by his superior, Field Marshal Hisaichi Terauchi (q.v.), to reinforce Leyte.

In spite of the diversion to Leyte, the bulk of Yamashita's army was still on Luzon when the Allies invaded it on January 9, 1945. Yamashita divided his troops into three groups to defend different areas of Luzon, with the largest group (Shobu) in the northern mountains and under his personal command. Contrary to Yamashita's orders to abandon the capital Manila (q.v.), Rear Admiral Sanji Iwabuchi (q.v.) and his naval forces instead fought a month-long battle for the city, committing atrocities against the local population. When the war ended, much of the island was under Allied control, but Yamashita and over 50,000 troops of his Shobu group were still fighting in the hills of northeastern Luzon. They surrendered on September 3, 1945. Yamashita was later found guilty of war crimes (q.v.), including responsibility for the actions of Iwabuchi's forces in Manila. He was executed in 1946.

YAMATO. Japanese superbattleship, sunk on April 7, 1945. During the war, Japan completed two *Yamato*-class battleships (q.v.), the *Yamato* and the *Musashi,* while converting a third, the *Shinano,* to an aircraft carrier (q.v.). Far larger and more heavily armed than any other contemporary warships, the superbattleships operated with crews of 2,500, were equipped with 18-inch guns, displaced 72,000 tons, and could achieve speeds of 27 knots. Completed in December 1941, the *Yamato* served as Admiral Isoruku Yamamoto's (q.v.) flagship in the Battle of Midway (q.v.) the following June. In 1944, both ships participated in the Battles of the Philippine Sea and Leyte Gulf (qq.v.); the *Musashi* was sunk in the latter action. Reflecting the desperation of Japan's military situation, its leaders expended the *Yamato* in a suicidal mission in April 1945. Carrying only enough fuel for a one-way journey, the *Yamato,* accompanied by destroyers and one cruiser (qq.v.), embarked on April 6 for Okinawa (q.v.), where the battleship was to attack the assembled Allied forces and run aground on the island, where it could continue to use its massive guns. Unprotected by

Japanese planes, the *Yamato* was attacked by U.S. carriers and sank on April 7 in the East China Sea, far from its target.

YANAGI OPERATIONS. *See* GERMANY; SUBMARINES.

YENAN. *See* DIXIE MISSION; MAO TSE-TUNG.

YONAI, MITSUMASA (1880–1948). Japanese admiral; navy minister, 1937–1939; prime minister, 1940; navy minister, 1940–1941; deputy prime minister, 1944–1945; navy minister, 1944–1945. Yonai was a moderate regarding Japanese expansion and militarism. He served as prime minister from January to June 1940, when his government fell because he opposed an alliance with Germany and Italy (qq.v.). After Prime Minister Hideki Tojo (q.v.) was forced to resign in July 1944, Yonai, who favored peace negotiations, and Kuniaki Koiso (q.v.) were asked to form a government; Yonai served as deputy prime minister and navy minister under Koiso from July 1944 to April 1945. When the Allies (q.v.) invaded Okinawa (q.v.) in April 1945, Koiso was succeeded by Admiral Kantaro Suzuki (q.v.) as prime minister, with Yonai continuing as navy minister. As a member of the Supreme War Direction Council (q.v.) and the Cabinet, Yonai supported efforts to terminate the war, first by seeking Soviet mediation and finally by accepting the Potsdam Proclamation (q.v.). When Emperor Hirohito (q.v.) broadcast Japan's (q.v.) surrender on August 15, 1945, Suzuki and his cabinet resigned. Yonai was asked to remain as navy minister under the new government of General Naruhiko Higashikuni (q.v.).

YOSHIDA, SHIGERU (1878–1967). Japanese diplomat and prime minister; ambassador to the United Kingdom (q.v.), 1936–1939; foreign minister, 1945–1946; prime minister, 1946–1954 (five different terms). A career diplomat, Yoshida attended the Paris Peace Conference after World War I, was appointed vice foreign minister, and served as ambassador to Italy (q.v.) and the United Kingdom. He retired in 1939 from the foreign ministry. Yoshida opposed the Anti-Comintern and Tripartite pacts (qq.v.) and favored a negotiated end to the war with the Allies (q.v.). From April to June 1945, he was imprisoned by the military police because of his activities.

In September 1945, Yoshida became foreign minister, and the following year he began his first of five terms as prime minister. Yoshida dominated Japanese politics during the Japanese occupation (q.v.) and worked closely with General of the Army Douglas MacArthur (q.v.), Supreme Commander for the Allied Powers (q.v.) in Japan. Yoshida negotiated the Japanese peace treaty (q.v.) that ended the occupation and signed a security pact with the United States (q.v.).

-Z-

ZERO. *See* FIGHTER.

ZHUKOV, GEORGI KONSTANTINOVICH (1896–1974). Marshal of the Soviet Union; commander, First Army Group, 1939; army chief of staff, 1941; deputy commander in chief, armed forces, 1942–1945. In the summer of 1939, Soviet Premier Joseph V. Stalin (q.v.) sent Zhukov to the Mongolian-Manchurian border to lead a counteroffensive against Japanese troops that had moved into the area. Zhukov's First Army Group, a massive, newly formed force including large numbers of tanks (q.v.) and planes, inflicted heavy casualties on the Japanese at Nomonhan (q.v.), or Khalkhin-Gol, before a cease-fire was negotiated. After his success against Japan (q.v.) he became a member of the Soviet military high command, and, thereafter, he concentrated on the defense of his country against the European Axis (q.v.) forces and on the overall strategy of the Union of Soviet Socialist Republics (q.v.). In May 1945, forces under Zhukov's command captured Berlin, where he headed the occupation during the following year.

Appendix 1

Code Names

The following list represents only a fraction of the numerous code names used during the war. All code names are Allied unless otherwise specified. On a number of occasions, Allied countries and theaters assigned more than one code name to the same plans, events, and conferences. Further complicating the situation were the varying names used for different versions or stages of plans and the existence of codes for operations that were never carried out. Excluded from this list are the personal names, such as Betty, Nell, and Val, given by the Allies to types of Japanese aircraft.

A-Go   Japanese naval plan to engage the U.S. Fleet east of the Philippine Islands

Alamo   U.S. Sixth Army when functioning as a task force in SWPA

Alsos   Intelligence mission to Europe to determine Axis progress in science and technology, especially the atomic bomb

Anakim   Plan to recapture Burma

Arcadia   First Washington Conference

Argentia   Atlantic Conference

Argonaut   Yalta Conference and the military parts of the Malta Conference

Axiom   Southeast Asia Command mission to military leaders in the United States and United Kingdom

Birdcage	Plan to announce the Japanese surrender to POWs held by Japan
Blacklist	Plan for the postsurrender occupation of Japan
Buccaneer	Plan for an amphibious assault in the Andaman Islands
Cactus	Guadalcanal, Solomon Islands
Cartwheel	Operation conducted by SOPAC and SWPA forces to isolate Japanese-held Rabaul on New Britain
Coronet	Plan to invade the Japanese island of Honshu
Cricket	Malta as a location
Culverin	Plan to capture northern Sumatra
Dixie	U.S. mission to the Chinese Communist headquarters in Yenan, China
Downfall	Plan to invade the Japanese home islands
Dukw	Amphibious 2.5-ton truck
Elkton	Plan to capture New Britain, New Guinea, and New Ireland
End Run	Task force of Merrill's Marauders in the seizure of Myitkyina, Burma
Eureka	Teheran Conference
Fat Man	Plutonium bomb dropped on Nagasaki, Kyushu, August 9, 1945
Forager	Plan to capture the Mariana Islands
Galahad	U.S. long-range penetration unit in Burma; also called Merrill's Marauders

Galvanic	Plan to capture the Gilbert Islands
Iceberg	Plan to invade Okinawa
Ichigo	Massive Japanese offensive in China, 1944–1945
Ketsu-go	Japanese plan to defend the home islands
Little Boy	Uranium bomb dropped on Hiroshima, Honshu, August 6, 1945
Magic	Signal intelligence gained from reading high-level Japanese diplomatic messages
Magneto	Yalta as a location
Manhattan Project	Program to design and construct an atomic weapon
Mastiff	Air supply and rescue of Allied prisoners held by the Japanese, following Japan's surrender
Matterhorn	Plan for the strategic bombing of Japan by Boeing B-29 planes using Chinese bases
Maud	British committee to study nuclear energy
Milepost	Provision of supplies to the Union of Soviet Socialist Republics for use against Japan when the Soviets entered the war
Oboe	Plan to seize the East Indies
Octagon	Second Quebec Conference
Olympic	Plan to invade the Japanese island of Kyushu
Orange	U.S. contingency plan for a war involving it solely with Japan
Purple	Encoded high-level Japanese diplomatic communications

Quadrant	First Quebec Conference
Rainbow	U.S. contingency plans for wars in which the United States (sometimes with Allies) faced more than one enemy at the same time
RO	Japanese reinforcement of air forces at Rabaul, New Britain
Sextant	First Cairo conference
SHO	Japanese victory plans to stop the Allied drive in the Pacific
SHO-1	Japanese plan to commit most of the Japanese Navy to destroy Allied forces invading the Philippine Islands
SHO-2	Japanese plan to protect Formosa and the Ryukyu Islands
SHO-3	Japanese plan to defend the southern and central home islands
SHO-4	Japanese plan to save the northern home islands and the Kurile Islands
S-1	Section 1 of the U.S. Office of Scientific Research and Development; also used to describe the atomic bomb project
Starvation	Massive mine-laying around Japanese home islands, executed partly by Boeing B-29 bombers
Symbol	Casablanca Conference
Ten-go	Japanese plan to stop an Allied invasion of the Ryukyu Islands and Japan
Terminal	Potsdam Conference
Tradewind	Plan to capture Morotai, Molucca Islands

Trident	Third Washington Conference
Trinity	Test of the atomic bomb near Alamogordo, New Mexico, July 16, 1945
Tube Alloys	British name for atomic energy research; frequently used in Allied conferences
U-Go	Japanese offensive toward Imphal, India
Ultra	High-level signal intelligence acquired by the Allies
Venona	U.S. operation to decipher intercepted Soviet diplomatic messages
Watchtower	Plan to capture Guadalcanal and Tulagi, Solomon Islands
Zipper	Plan to invade the Malay peninsula

Appendix 2

Selected Statistics[1]

United States

U.S. Armed Forces in all theaters, December 1941–December 31, 1946:[2]

Personnel	
Total	16,112,566
Army (including Army Air Forces)	11,260,000
Navy (excluding Marine Corps)	4,183,466
Marine Corps	669,100
Battle deaths	
Total	291,557
Army (including Army Air Forces)	234,874
Navy (excluding Marine Corps)	36,950
Marine Corps	19,733
Other deaths	113,842
Wounds, not fatal	671,846

---

[1]Statistics regarding the war with Japan vary tremendously. The figures for the U.S. and the British Commonwealth are the most reliable, although each nation and occasionally the armed services within each country kept records differently. Information about civilian casualties and deaths in Asia and the Pacific consists primarily of estimates, with widely conflicting results. The statistics selected for inclusion here provide an indication of the war's tremendous scope and losses. For a discussion of the human costs of the war, see John W. Dower, *War Without Mercy: Race and Power in the Pacific War* (New York: Pantheon, 1986), 293–301.

[2]U.S. Department of Defense, 1998.

Overseas Deployment of U.S. Forces, December 31, 1943:[3]

	War Against Japan	War Against Germany
Personnel	1,878,152	1,810,367
Army	688,711	979,310
Army Air Forces	224,231	437,175
Navy	804,800	391,400
Marine	160,410	2,482
Divisions	16+ (13 Army, 3+ Marine)	17 (all Army)
Aircraft	7,857	8,807
Army	4,254	8,237
Navy	3,603	570
Combat ships	713	515

Distribution of U.S. Forces in the war against Japan, December 31, 1943:[4]

	Pacific Ocean Areas and Southwest Pacific Area	China-Burma-India	Alaska
Army	534,471	52,624	101,616
Army Air Forces	162,376	41,936	19,919
Navy	772,800	100	31,900
Marine	159,376	0	1,034

---

[3]Maurice Matloff, *Strategic Planning for Coalition Warfare, 1943–1944,* U.S. Army in World War II (Washington, D.C.: Office of the Chief of Military History, Department of the Army, 1959), 398. Beginning in January 1944, the ground forces in the war against Germany underwent an enormous buildup in preparation for the cross-channel invasion of France. By September 1944, 40 Army divisions were deployed in Europe and the Mediterranean, while 21 Army divisions and 5 Marine divisions were in the Pacific (520).

[4]Matloff, *Strategic Planning,* 398.

U.S. casualties in the war against Japan:

Army (including Army Air Forces)[5]

Total battle casualties	169,635
Died in action or from battle wounds	45,621
(excluding prisoner deaths)	
Prisoners captured	28,256
Prisoners died in captivity	11,516

Navy (including Marine Corps)[6]

Total battle casualties	127,294
Died in action or from battle wounds	48,426
(including 1,343 who died as prisoners)	
U.S. civilians interned in Asia and the Pacific by Japan during the war[7]	12,100

British Commonwealth

United Kingdom Armed Forces in all theaters, June 1945:[8]

Peak strength	4,683,000
Serving in the war against Japan	666,000
Royal Navy	224,000
Army	315,000
Royal Air Force	127,000

---

[5]*Army Battle Casualties and Nonbattle Deaths in World War II: Final Report, 7 December 1941–31 December 1946* (Washington, D.C.: Department of the Army, 1953), 8–9.

[6]U.S. Navy Bureau of Medicine and Surgery, *The History of the Medical Department of the United States Navy in World War II,* vol. 3, *The Statistics of Diseases and Injuries* (Washington, D.C.: Government Printing Office, 1950), 84, 171–74.

[7]P. Scott Corbett, *Quiet Passages: The Exchange of Civilians between the United States and Japan during the Second World War* (Kent, Ohio: Kent State University Press, 1987), 168.

[8]W. Franklin Mellor, ed. *Casualties and Medical Statistics,* History of the Second World War: United Kingdom Medical Series (London: Her Majesty's Stationery Office, 1972), 832.

U.K. Armed Forces casualties, September 3, 1939–February 28, 1946:[9]

Total casualties in the war	755,439
Killed (including died as prisoner of war)	264,443
Missing	41,327
Wounded, nonfatal	277,077
Prisoners of war who survived	172,592
Casualties suffered in the war against Japan	90,332
Killed (including died as prisoner of war)	29,698
Missing	6,252
Wounded, nonfatal	16,529
Prisoners of war who survived	37,583
Prisoners of war captured by Japan[10]	
Total captured	50,016
Royal Navy	2,304
Army	42,610
Royal Air Force	5,102
Died while prisoner	12,433
Royal Navy	421
Army	10,298
Royal Air Force	1,714

British Commonwealth land forces in Asia, including British, Indian, Canadian, Malay, Burmese, East African (from 1944), and West African (from 1944) forces, December 7, 1941–November 1946:[11]

Total battle casualties	208,733
Killed	16,468
Wounded, nonfatal	47,821
Missing and prisoners of war	143,920
Major sites for missing and prisoner losses, which occurred mostly in 1941–1942	
Hong Kong	10,622
Malaya	112,405

---

[9]Mellor, *Casualties and Medical Statistics,* 836–37.

[10]Mellor, *Casualties and Medical Statistics,* 837.

[11]S. Woodburn Kirby, *The War Against Japan,* vol. 5, *The Surrender of Japan* (London: Her Majesty's Stationery Office, 1969), 542–44. Australian casualties are excluded.

Java and Sumatra	5,716
Borneo (including killed)	524
Burma	9,369

Australian battle casualties in the war with Japan (all services):[12]

Total casualties	45,843
Killed, died of wounds, and missing, presumed dead	9,470
Died as prisoner of war	8,031
Survived as prisoner of war	14,345
Wounded, nonfatal	13,997

New Zealand battle casualties in the war with Japan:[13]

Army	
Killed and died of wounds	97
Wounded, nonfatal	187
Navy	
Killed	494
Died as prisoner of war	9
Air Force	
Killed	256

Canadian battle casualties in the war with Japan:[14]

Total casualties	2,282
Hong Kong capture, 1941	2,272
Killed in battle	277

---

[12]Gavin Long, *The Final Campaigns,* Australia in the War of 1939–1945 (Canberra: Australian War Memorial, 1963), 623.

[13]Arthur Salusbury MacNalty and W. Franklin Mellor, eds., *Medical Services in War: The Principal Medical Lessons of the Second World War; Based on the Official Medical Histories of the United Kingdom, Canada, Australia, New Zealand and India* (London: Her Majesty's Stationery Office, 1968), 711–13.

[14]C. P. Stacey, *Six Years of War: The Army in Canada, Britain and the Pacific,* Official History of the Canadian Army in the Second World War (Ottawa: Queen's Printer and Controller of Stationery, 1957), 1:524–25.

Died as prisoner of war	277
Survived as prisoner of war	1,418
Wounded, nonfatal	300
Other parts of Asia and Pacific	10

Union of Soviet Socialist Republics

U.S.S.R. battle casualties in the war with Japan, August 1945:[15]

Total casualties	30,483
Killed	8,219
Wounded, nonfatal	22,264

China

Chinese battle casualties, July 1937–May 1945, according to the Chinese Nationalist government:[16]

Total casualties of Chinese regular troops (excluding guerrilla and local militia troops)	3,177,973
Killed	1,310,224
Wounded, nonfatal	1,752,591
Missing	115,158

Japan

Military deaths, 1937–1941[17]	1,740,955
Deaths in China, 1937–1941	185,647
Army deaths, 1941–1945	1,140,429
Navy deaths	414,879

---

[15]Kirby, *The Surrender of Japan*, 200.

[16]Chinese Ministry of Information, comp., *China Handbook, 1937–1945*, rev. ed. (New York: Macmillan, 1947), 301.

[17]Dower, *War without Mercy*, 297. Dower uses statistics of the Japanese government.

Japanese military and civilian personnel 2.3 million
    working for the military, killed in combat,
    July 1937–August 1945, according to the
    Japanese Ministry of Health and Welfare, 1956[18]

Japanese civilians not working for the military, 658,595
    killed in the home islands, Okinawa, and China[19]

Japanese civilian casualties in the home islands, November 1944–August
1945, as a result of the Allied strategic air campaign[20]

Total casualties 806,000
  Deaths 330,000

Japanese armed forces at time of surrender[21]
  Total forces 6,983,000
    Forces in the home islands 3,352,000

Japanese armed forces and civilians 6,000,000
  overseas at the time of the surrender[22]

Foreign nationals (mostly Koreans) in 1,170,000
  Japan at the time of the surrender[23]

Japanese prisoners of war (both 1,000,000 to 2,000,000
  military and civilian) captured by the
  U.S.S.R. in August–September 1945

---

[18]Saburo Ienaga, *The Pacific War: World War II and the Japanese, 1931–1945* (New York: Pantheon, 1978), 152.

[19]Ienaga, *The Pacific War,* 202.

[20]*United States Strategic Bombing Surveys: Summary Reports* (Washington, D.C.: Government Printing Office, 1945–1946; reprint, Maxwell Air Force Base, Ala.: Air University Press, 1987), 92.

[21]*Reports of General MacArthur,* vol. 1 supplement, *MacArthur in Japan: The Occupation: Military Phase* (Washington, D.C.: Department of the Army, 1966), 117.

[22]*Reports of General MacArthur,* vol. 1 supplement, 149.

[23]*Reports of General MacArthur,* vol. 1 supplement, 149, 164.

Japanese prisoners of war captured before the country's surrender

POWs held in U.S. prisons, 1941–1945[24]	5,424
POWs held in Australian prisons, August 1944[25]	2,223
POWs captured during the campaign for Luzon (Philippines), 1945[26]	9,050
POWs captured during the campaign for Okinawa, April 1–June 30, 1945[27]	7,401

[24]Arnold Krammer, "Japanese Prisoners of War in America," *Pacific Historical Review* 52 (February 1983): 67. Until the fall of 1944, the Allies captured very few Japanese prisoners in the Pacific. Most were housed in Australia or New Zealand until the last months of the war, when sizable numbers of newly captured Japanese were imprisoned in the Philippines or Okinawa (69–70).

[25]Long, *The Final Campaigns,* 623.

[26]Robert R. Smith, *Triumph in the Philippines,* U.S. Army in World War II (Washington, D.C.: Office of the Chief of Military History, Department of the Army, 1963), 694.

[27]Roy E. Appleman, et al., *Okinawa: The Last Battle,* U.S. Army in World War II (Washington, D.C.: Historical Division, Department of the Army, 1948), 489. More prisoners were captured after the end of the campaign.

Bibliographical Essay

Long before its end, World War II became the focus of a vast number of books and articles, a body of literature that continues to grow at a rapid pace. This bibliography, which by necessity is highly selective, consists primarily of books, with journal articles and dissertations chosen to supplement certain topics. It is limited to items published in English, while including translated works whenever possible. Chronologically, it focuses on the period from Japan's seizure of Manchuria in 1931 through the end of the Allied occupation of Japan in 1952. Among its subjects are the war's military, diplomatic, political, social, economic, and scientific aspects, in addition to the lives of the people who participated in and directed the war. Important to the study of the war but largely omitted from this list are collections of documents published on microfilm and such vital sources as the U.S. Department of State's multivolume *Foreign Relations of the United States* (*FRUS*).

One impediment facing many Westerners studying the war is the large number of Japanese works that have not been translated. Although selected portions of the Japanese history of the approach to war have been published in English in works edited by James W. Morley, other significant records, such as the 102-volume Japanese official history, have not. An area needing more coverage in English-language works is Japan's lengthy war with China, whose history has been further obscured by the Chinese civil war, limitations on access to Chinese archives, and the destruction of wartime documents. Among Japanese sources available in English are the extensive studies produced by the U.S. Strategic Bombing Survey (USSBS) and the Supreme Commander of the Allied Powers (SCAP), which both relied heavily on Japanese records and postwar interviews. In the SCAP publication *The Reports of General MacArthur,* edited by Charles W. Willoughby, Japanese historians writing under American supervision during the Allied occupation described in detail

Japan's conduct of the war. Although the USSBS and SCAP reports are flawed, they contribute valuable information.

In contrast to the Sino-Japanese War, the conflict between the Western Allies and Japan has been explored in numerous and varied writings. Topics that have received particularly intense attention from writers and continue to generate strong discussion are the Japanese assaults on Western territories, especially Pearl Harbor, in December 1941, and the U.S. employment of atomic weapons against Japan in August 1945. Among the many analyses of the Pearl Harbor attack are two classic works: Gordon W. Prange's *At Dawn We Slept: The Untold Story of Pearl Harbor* (1981) and Roberta Wohlstetter's *Pearl Harbor: Warning and Decision* (1962). In the fierce debate regarding the decision to drop the atomic bomb, two of the leading revisionists are Gar Alperovitz and Barton J. Bernstein. Another subject of intense, longtime scrutiny is the wartime Grand Alliance of the Soviet Union, the United Kingdom, and the United States, which deteriorated into the cold war as communism spread across postwar Asia and Europe. One significant factor that is prompting reevaluation and reconsideration of earlier World War II histories is the declassification of records relating to Allied signal intelligence, a process that began in the mid-1970s. Subsequent releases of records have made possible a number of works with fresh perceptions about the war with Japan. One final topic drawing special analysis is the wartime treatment of people of Japanese descent in the Americas.

Among the U.S. repositories housing important archives concerning the war are the National Archives, the Library of Congress Manuscript Division, the Franklin D. Roosevelt and the Harry S. Truman presidential libraries, the U.S. Army Military History Institute, the George C. Marshall Research Library, and the MacArthur Memorial Archives. In the United Kingdom, major collections are located in the Public Record Office, the Liddell Hart Centre of King's College, London, the University of Southampton, and the Churchill College Archives, Cambridge. The Australian War Memorial Research Centre holds the primary documents concerning Australia's military participation in the war.

Many of these archives, in addition to those of other museums, organizations, and government agencies, have extended access to their holdings about the war through their on-line Web sites. Especially helpful sites regarding the military facets of the U.S. effort in the Pacific War, for example, are sponsored by the U.S. Army Center of Military History, the U.S. Naval Historical Center, and the U.S. Marine Corps Historical Center.

This bibliography begins with a listing of specialized bibliographies that examine various aspects of the war against Japan. Two that provide excellent introductions are John J. Sbrega's massive *The War against Japan, 1941–1945: An Annotated Bibliography* (1989) and Loyd Lee's *World War II in Asia and the Pacific and the War's Aftermath, with General Themes: A Handbook of Literature and Research* (1998).

A number of works provide good overviews of the war. One recent, major history of the war as a whole is Gerhard L. Weinberg's *A World at Arms: A Global History of World War II* (1994). The standard work on the U.S. war against Japan is Ronald H. Spector's *Eagle against the Sun: The American War with Japan* (1985); British accounts include, among others, John Costello's *The Pacific War* (1981) and Basil Collier's *The War in the Far East, 1942–1945: A Military History* (1969). Two works focusing on Japan's perspectives are Saburo Ienaga's *The Pacific War: World War II and the Japanese, 1931–1945* (1978) and John Toland's *The Rising Sun: The Decline and Fall of the Japanese Empire, 1936–1945* (1970). Other influential studies are John W. Dower's *War without Mercy: Race and Power in the Pacific* (1986) and Akira Iriye's *Power and Culture: The Japanese-American War, 1941–1945* (1981).

Among the most basic, reliable studies of the war are the official accounts of Australia, Canada, India, New Zealand, the United Kingdom, and the United States. One British title of special interest is S. Woodburn Kirby's five-volume *The War against Japan* (1957–1969). The U.S. Navy's official history of the war is Samuel Eliot Morison's 15-volume *History of United States Naval Operations in World War II* (1947–1963). The volumes in the U.S. Army's extensive series on the war are listed individually by author under different subject headings, as are many of the Australian, Indian, and U.S. Marine volumes. Extremely important for the U.S. strategic direction of the war is Grace P. Hayes's *The History of the Joint Chiefs of Staff in World War II: The War against Japan* (1982), also an official history.

In the wealth of other books listed, two series are especially accessible to beginners and at the same time interesting to more advanced students of the war. Published by Time-Life Books (in the late 1970s and early 1980s) and Ballantine Books (1960s and early 1970s), these volumes are listed by individual authors under the appropriate subject categories. Also of general interest are a number of classic eye-witness accounts, including, among others, Clark Lee's *They Call It Pacific: An Eye-witness Story of Our War against Japan from Bataan to the Solomons* (1943), Robert Sherrod's *Tarawa: The Story of a Battle* (1954), Richard Tregaskis's *Guadalcanal Diary* (1943), and Mitsuo Fuchida and Masatake Okumiya's *Midway: The Battle That Doomed Japan* (1955).

This bibliography is arranged by subject, as shown in the following outline. References following the headings in the actual bibliography indicate closely related divisions that the reader might wish also to check. No attempt has been made to cross-reference the biographies and memoirs, which span numerous categories. Abbreviations used in the bibliography include U.S. Government Printing Office (GPO), His (or Her) Majesty's Stationery Office (HMSO), New Zealand (N.Z.), the U.S. Army Office of the Chief of Military History (OCMH), the official series The U.S. Army in World War II (USAWWII), and abbreviations for states in the United States.

Bibliography

I. General Accounts

A. BIBLIOGRAPHIES

Aster, Sidney, ed. *British Foreign Policy, 1918–1945: A Guide to Research and Research Materials.* Wilmington, Del.: Scholarly Resources, 1991.

Bayliss, Gwyn M. *Bibliographic Guide to the Two World Wars: An Annotated Survey of English-Language Reference Materials.* New York: Bowker, 1977.

Controvich, James T. *The Central Pacific Campaign, 1943–1944: A Bibliography.* Westport, Conn.: Meckler, 1990.

Croddy, Eric. *Chemical and Biological Warfare: An Annotated Bibliography.* Lanham, Md.: Scarecrow, 1997.

DeWhitt, Benjamin L. *Records Relating to Personal Participation in World War II: American Military Casualties and Burials.* Washington, D.C.: National Archives and Records Administration, 1993.

DeWhitt, Benjamin L., and Jennifer Davis Heaps, comps. *Records Relating to Personal Participation in World War II: American Prisoners of War and Civilian Internees.* Washington, D.C.: National Archives and Records Administration, 1992.

Enser, A. G. *A Subject Bibliography of the Second World War: Books in English, 1939–1974.* Boulder, Colo.: Westview, 1977.

Enser, A. G. *A Subject Bibliography of the Second World War and Aftermath: Books in English, 1975–1987.* Brookfield, Vt.: Gower, 1990.

Falk, Stanley L. "Leyte Gulf: A Bibliography of the Greatest Sea Battle." *Naval History* (Fall 1988): 60–61.

Funk, Arthur L., comp. *Fighting for Freedom, the United States in World War II: A Select Bibliography of Books in English on the Second World War* [1985–1990]. Washington, D.C.: U.S. Information Agency, 1990.

Funk, Arthur L., comp. *The Second World War: A Select Bibliography of Books in English since 1975.* Claremont, Calif.: Regina, 1985.

Funk, Arthur L., comp. *A Select Bibliography of Books on the Second World War in English Published in the United States, 1966–1975.* Gainesville, Fla.: American Committee on the History of the Second World War, 1975.

Gaetzer, Hans G., and Larry M. Browning. *The Atomic Bomb: An Annotated Bibliography.* Pasadena, Calif.: Salem, 1992.

Glantz, David M. "The Red Army at War, 1941–1945: Sources and Interpretations." *Journal of Military History* 62 (July 1998): 595–617.

Japan and Its Occupied Territories during World War II: A Guide to O.S.S./State Department Intelligence and Research Reports. Washington, D.C.: University Publications of America, 1977.

Law, Derek G. *The Royal Navy in World War Two: An Annotated Bibliography.* London: Greenhill, 1988.

Lee, Loyd E., ed. *World War II in Asia and the Pacific and the War's Aftermath, with General Themes: A Handbook of Literature and Research.* Westport, Conn.: Greenwood, 1998.

Morley, James W., ed. *Japan's Foreign Policy, 1868–1941: A Research Guide.* New York: Columbia University Press, 1974.

Rasor, Eugene. *The China-Burma-India Campaign, 1931–1945: Historiography and Annotated Bibliography.* Westport, Conn.: Greenwood, 1998.

Rasor, Eugene. *Earl Mountbatten of Burma, 1900–1979: Historiography and Annotated Bibliography*. Westport, Conn.: Greenwood, 1998.

Rasor, Eugene. *General Douglas MacArthur, 1880–1964: Historiography and Annotated Bibliography*. Westport, Conn.: Greenwood, 1994.

Rasor, Eugene L. *The Solomon Islands Campaign, Guadalcanal to Rabaul: Historiography and Annotated Bibliography*. Westport, Conn.: Greenwood, 1997.

Rasor, Eugene L. *The Southwest Pacific Campaign, 1941–1945: Historiography and Annotated Bibliography*. Westport, Conn.: Greenwood Press, 1996.

Sbrega, John J. *The War against Japan, 1941–1945: An Annotated Bibliography*. New York: Garland, 1989.

Sexton, Donal J., Jr., comp. *Signals Intelligence in World War II: A Research Guide*. Westport, Conn.: Greenwood, 1996.

Smith, Myron J., Jr. *Air War Bibliography, 1930–1945: English-Language Sources*. Manhattan, Kans.: Aerospace Historian, 1977.

Smith, Myron J., Jr. *The Battles of Coral Sea and Midway, 1942: A Selected Bibliography*. Westport, Conn.: Greenwood, 1991.

Smith, Myron J., Jr. *Battleships and Battle-cruisers, 1884–1984: A Bibliography and Chronology*. New York: Garland, 1985.

Smith, Myron J., Jr. *Pearl Harbor, 1941: A Bibliography*. Westport, Conn.: Greenwood, 1991.

Smith, Myron J., Jr. *The Secret Wars: A Guide to Sources in English*. Vol. 1: *Intelligence, Propaganda and Psychological Warfare, Resistance Movements, and Secret Operations, 1939–1945*. Santa Barbara, Calif.: ABC-Clio, 1980.

Smith, Myron J. *The Soviet Army, 1939–1980: A Guide to Sources in English*. Santa Barbara, Calif.: ABC-Clio, 1982.

Smith, Myron J., Jr. *World War II at Sea: A Bibliography of Sources in English*. 3 vols. Metuchen, N.J.: Scarecrow, 1976.

Smith, Myron J., Jr. *World War II at Sea: A Bibliography of Sources in English, 1974–1989*. Metuchen, N.J.: Scarecrow, 1990.

Tutorow, Norman E., with Karen Winnovich. *War Crimes, War Criminals, and War Crimes Trials: An Annotated Bibliography and Source Book*. New York: Greenwood, 1986.

Walker, J. Samuel. "The Decision to Use the Bomb: A Historiographical Update." *Diplomatic History* 14 (Winter 1990): 97–114.

Ward, Robert E., and Frank Joseph Shulman, eds. *The Allied Occupation of Japan, 1945–1952: An Annotated Bibliography of Western Language Materials*. Chicago: American Library Association, 1974.

World War II from an American Perspective: An Annotated Bibliography. Santa Barbara, Calif.: ABC-Clio, 1983.

Ziegler, Janet. *World War Two: A Bibliography of Books in English, 1945–1965*. Stanford, Calif.: Hoover Institution Press, 1971.

B. BIOGRAPHICAL DICTIONARIES

Ancell, R. Manning. *The Biographical Dictionary of World War II Generals and Flag Officers: The U.S. Armed Forces*. Westport, Conn.: Greenwood, 1996.

Boatner, Mark M., III. *Biographical Dictionary of World War II*. Novato, Calif.: Presidio, 1996.

Dupuy, Trevor N., Curt Johnson, and David L. Bongard. *The Harper Encyclopedia of Military Biography*. New York: HarperCollins, 1992.

Spiller, Roger J., ed. *Dictionary of American Military Biography*. 3 vols. Westport, Conn.: Greenwood, 1984.

Tunney, Christopher. *A Biographical Dictionary of World War II*. New York: St. Martin's, 1972.

C. CHRONOLOGIES AND GENERAL REFERENCE

Carter, Kit C., and Robert Mueller, comps. *The Army Air Forces in World War II: Combat Chronology, 1941–1945*. Washington, D.C.: Center for Air Force History, 1973.

Chant, Christopher. *The Encyclopedia of Codenames of World War II*. London: Routledge & Kegan Paul, 1986.

Clodfelter, Micheal. *Warfare and Armed Conflicts: A Statistical Reference to Casualty and Other Figures, 1618–1991*. Jefferson, N.C.: McFarland, 1992.

Dear, I. C. B. ed. *The Oxford Companion to World War II*. New York: Oxford University Press, 1995.

Dupuy, R. Ernest, and Trevor N. Dupuy. *The Encyclopedia of Military History from 3500 B.C. to the Present*. New York: Harper & Row, 1970.

Ellis, John. *World War II: A Statistical Survey: The Essential Facts and Figures for All the Combatants*. New York: Facts on File, 1993.

Graham, Otis L., Jr., and M. R. Wander, eds. *The Franklin D. Roosevelt Encyclopedia*. Boston: Hall, 1985.

Hammel, Eric M. *Air War Pacific: America's Air War against Japan in East Asia and the Pacific, 1941–1945: Chronology*. Pacifica, Calif.: Pacifica, 1998.

Hutchison, Kevin Don. *World War II in the North Pacific: Chronology and Fact Book*. Westport, Conn.: Greenwood, 1994.

Parrish, Thomas, ed. *The Simon and Schuster Encyclopedia of World War II*. New York: Simon & Schuster, 1978.

Perrett, Bryan, and Ian V. Hogg. *Encyclopedia of the Second World War*. Novato, Calif.: Presidio, 1989.

Polmar, Norman, and Thomas B. Allen. *World War II: The Encyclopedia of the War Years, 1941–1945*. New York: Random House, 1996.

Royal Institute of International Affairs, comp. *Chronology and Index of the Second World War, 1938–1945*. Westport, Conn.: Meckler, 1990.

Smith, Myron J., Jr. *Air War Chronology, 1939–1945*. 3 vols. Manhattan, Kans.: Military Affairs/Aerospace Historian, 1977.

Snyder, Louis. *Historical Guide to World War II*. Westport, Conn.: Greenwood, 1982.

Stanton, Shelby L. *World War II Order of Battle*. New York: Galahad, 1991.

U.S. Naval History Division. *United States Naval Chronology, World War II*. Washington, D.C.: GPO, 1955.

Wheal, Elizabeth-Anne, Stephen Pope, and James Taylor. *A Dictionary of the Second World War*. New York: Bedrick, 1990.

Williams, Mary H., comp. *Chronology, 1941–1945*. USAWWII. Washington, D.C.: OCMH, Department of the Army, 1960.

Young, Peter. *The World Almanac of World War II*. New York: World Almanac, 1986.

D. ATLASES

Esposito, Vincent J., ed. *The West Point Atlas of American Wars*. 2 vols. New York: Praeger, 1959.

Goodenough, Simon. *War Maps: World War II from September 1939 to August 1945—Air, Sea, and Land, Battle by Battle*. New York: St. Martin's, 1982.

Keegan, John, ed. *The Times Atlas of the Second World War*. New York: Harper & Row, 1989.

Messenger, Charles. *The Chronological Atlas of World War II*. New York: Macmillan, 1989.

Pimlott, John. *The Historical Atlas of World War II*. New York: Holt, 1995.

Pitt, Barrie, ed. *The Month-by-Month Atlas of the Second World War*. New York: Summit, 1989.

Smurthwaite, David. *The Pacific War Atlas, 1941–1945*. London: HMSO, 1985.

Young, Peter. *Atlas of the Second World War*. New York: Putnam, 1974.

E. GENERAL STUDIES ON WORLD WAR II

Ambrose, Stephen. *American Heritage New History of World War II*. New York: Viking, 1967.

Calvocoressi, Peter, Guy Wint, and John Pritchard. *Total War: The Causes and Courses of the Second World War*. New York: Pantheon, 1989.

Churchill, Winston S. *The Second World War*. 6 vols. Boston: Houghton Mifflin, 1948–1954.

Divine, Robert A., ed. *Causes and Consequences of World War II*. Chicago: Quadrangle, 1969.

Ellis, John. *Brute Force: Allied Strategy and Tactics in the Second World War*. New York: Viking, 1990.

Ellis, John. *The Sharp End: The Fighting Man in World War II*. New York: Scribner's, 1980.

Esposito, Vincent J., ed. *A Concise History of World War II*. New York: Praeger, 1964.

Fussell, Paul. *Wartime: Understanding and Behavior in the Second World War*. New York: Oxford University Press, 1989.

Greenfield, Kent Roberts, ed. *Command Decisions*. New York: Harcourt, Brace, 1959.

Keegan, John. *The Second World War*. New York: Viking, 1990.

Leckie, Robert. *Delivered from Evil: The Saga of World War II*. New York: Harper & Row, 1987.

Liddell Hart, B. H. *History of the Second World War*. New York: Putnam, 1970.

Milward, Alan S. *War, Economy, and Society, 1939–1945*. Berkeley: University of California Press, 1977.

Noakes, Jeremy. *The Civilian in War: The Home Front in Europe, Japan and the USA in World War II*. Exeter: University of Exeter Press, 1992.

Overy, Richard. *Why the Allies Won*. New York: Norton, 1995.

Rigge, Simon. *War in the Outposts*. Alexandria, Va.: Time-Life Books, 1980.

Stamps, Thomas D., and Vincent J. Esposito. *A Military History of World War II*. 2 vols. West Point, N.Y.: United States Military Academy, 1953.

Stokesbury, James L. *A Short History of World War II*. New York: Morrow, 1980.

Terkel, Studs. *The Good War: An Oral History of World War II*. New York: Pantheon, 1984.

Weinberg, Gerhard L. *A World at Arms: A Global History of World War II*. Cambridge: Cambridge University Press, 1994.

Willmott, H. P. *The Great Crusade*. New York: Free Press, 1990.

Young, Peter. *World War, 1939–1945: A Short History*. New York: Crowell, 1966.

F. GENERAL STUDIES ON THE WAR IN ASIA AND THE PACIFIC

Bateson, Charles. *The War with Japan: A Concise History*. East Lansing: Michigan State University Press, 1968.

Bischof, Gunter, and Robert L. Dupont, eds. *The Pacific War Revisited*. Baton Rouge: Louisiana State University, 1997.

Bradley, John H., and Jack W. Dice. *The Second World War: Asia and the Pacific*. West Point, N.Y.: U.S. Military Academy, 1980.

Collier, Basil. *The War in the Far East, 1942–1945: A Military History*. New York: Morrow, 1969.

Congdon, Don, ed. *Combat: The War with Japan*. New York: Dell, 1962.

Costello, John. *The Pacific War*. New York: Rawson, Wade, 1981.

Detwiler, Donald S., and Charles D. Burdick, eds. *War in Asia and the Pacific*. 15 vols. New York: Garland, 1980.

Dockrill, Saki, ed. *From Pearl Harbor to Hiroshima: The Second World War in Asia and the Pacific, 1941–1945*. New York: St. Martin's, 1994.

Dower, John W. *War Without Mercy: Race and Power in the Pacific War*. New York: Pantheon, 1986.

Dunnigan, James F. *Victory at Sea: World War II in the Pacific*. New York: Morrow, 1995.

Ienaga, Saburo. *The Pacific War: World War II and the Japanese, 1931–1945*. New York: Pantheon, 1978.

Iriye, Akira, and Warren Cohen, eds. *American, Chinese, and Japanese Perspectives on Wartime Asia, 1931–1949*. Wilmington, Del.: Scholarly Resources, 1990.

Iriye, Akira. *Power and Culture: The Japanese-American War, 1941–1945*. Cambridge, Mass.: Harvard University Press, 1981.

James, D. Clayton. "American and Japanese Strategies in the Pacific War," in *Makers of Modern Strategy: From Machiavelli to the Nuclear Age,* ed. Peter Paret. Princeton, N.J.: Princeton University Press, 1986.

James, David H. *The Rise and Fall of the Japanese Empire.* New York: Macmillan, 1951.

Karig, Walter, et al. *Battle Report.* 6 vols. New York: Farrar & Rinehart, 1944–52. [Vol. 1: *Pearl Harbor to Coral Sea;* vol. 3: *Pacific War: Middle Phase;* vol. 4: *The End of an Empire;* vol. 5: *Victory in the Pacific*]

Lee, Clark. *They Call It Pacific: An Eye-witness Story of Our War against Japan from Bataan to the Solomons.* New York: Viking, 1943.

Levine, Alan J. *The Pacific War: Japan versus the Allies.* Westport, Conn.: Praeger, 1995.

MacIntyre, Donald G. F. *The Battle for the Pacific.* New York: Norton, 1966.

Mason, John T., Jr. *The Pacific War Remembered: An Oral History Collection.* Annapolis, Md.: Naval Institute Press, 1989.

Rees, David. *The Defeat of Japan.* Westport, Conn.: Praeger, 1997.

Renzi, William A., and Mark D. Roehrs. *Never Look Back: A History of World War II in the Pacific.* Armonk, N.Y.: Sharpe, 1995.

Reynolds, Clark G. "Maritime Strategy of World War II: Some Implications?" *Naval War College Review* 39 (May–June 1986): 43–50.

Reynolds, Clark. *War In the Pacific.* New York: Military Press, 1990.

Spector, Ronald H. *Eagle against the Sun: The American War with Japan.* New York: Free Press, 1985.

Steinberg, Rafael. *Island Fighting.* Alexandria, Va.: Time-Life Books, 1978.

Stewart, Adrian. *The Underrated Enemy: Britain's War with Japan, December 1941–May 1942.* London: Kimber, 1987.

Thorne, Christopher. *The Issue of War: States, Societies and the Far Eastern Conflict of 1941–1945.* New York: Oxford University Press, 1985.

Toland, John. *But Not in Shame: The Six Months after Pearl Harbor.* New York: Random House, 1961.

Toland, John. *The Rising Sun: The Decline and Fall of the Japanese Empire, 1936–1945.* New York: Random House, 1970.

Willmott, H. P. *The Barrier and the Javelin: Japanese and Allied Pacific Strategies, February to June 1942.* Annapolis, Md.: Naval Institute Press, 1983.

Willmott, H. P. *Empires in the Balance: Japanese and Allied Pacific Strategies to April 1942.* Annapolis, Md.: Naval Institute Press, 1982.

Willoughby, Charles A., ed. *The Reports of General MacArthur*. 4 vols. Washington, D.C.: GPO, 1966.

Winton, John. *War in the Pacific: Pearl Harbor to Tokyo Bay*. New York: Mayflower, 1978.

Zich, Arthur. *The Rising Sun*. Alexandria, Va.: Time-Life Books, 1977.

II. Origins of the War and Approach to War with the West
[see also V.A; V.DD]

Andrews, E. M. *The Writing on the Wall: The British Commonwealth and Aggression in the East, 1931–1935*. Sydney: Allen & Unwin, 1987.

Barnhart, Michael A. *Japan Prepares for Total War: The Search for Economic Security, 1919–1941*. Ithaca, N.Y.: Cornell University Press, 1987.

Barnhart, Michael A. "The Origins of the Second World War in Asia and the Pacific: Synthesis Impossible?" *Diplomatic History* 20 (Spring 1996): 241–60.

Beard, Charles A. *President Roosevelt and the Coming of War, 1941: A Study in Appearances and Realities*. New Haven, Conn.: Yale University Press, 1948.

Ben-Zvi, Abraham. *The Illusion of Deterrence: The Roosevelt Presidency and the Origins of the Pacific War*. Boulder, Colo.: Westview, 1987.

Bergamini, David. *Japan's Imperial Conspiracy: How Emperor Hirohito Led Japan into War against the West*. New York: Morrow, 1971.

Best, Anthony. *Britain, Japan, and Pearl Harbor: Avoiding War in East Asia, 1936–1941*. New York: Routledge, 1995.

Borg, Dorothy. *The United States and the Far Eastern Crisis of 1933–1938: From the Manchurian Incident through the Initial State of the Undeclared Sino-Japanese War*. Cambridge, Mass.: Harvard University Press, 1964.

Borg, Dorothy, and Shumpei Okamoto, eds. *Pearl Harbor as History: Japanese-American Relations, 1931–1941*. New York: Columbia University Press, 1973.

Burns, Richard Dean, and Edward M. Bennett, eds. *Diplomats in Crisis: United States-Chinese-Japanese Relations, 1919–1941*. Santa Barbara, Calif.: ABC-Clio, 1974.

Butow, Robert J. C. *The John Doe Associates: Backdoor Diplomacy for Peace, 1941*. Stanford, Calif.: Stanford University Press, 1974.

Butow, Robert J. C. "Marching off to War on the Wrong Foot: The Final Note Tokyo Did Not Send to Washington." *Pacific Historical Review* 6 (February 1994): 67–79.

Butow, Robert J. C. *Tojo and the Coming of the War.* Princeton, N.J.: Princeton University Press, 1961.

Clifford, Nicholas R. *Retreat from China: British Policy in the Far East, 1937–1941.* Seattle: University of Washington, 1967.

Crowley, James B. *Japan's Quest for Autonomy: National Security and Foreign Policy, 1930–1938.* Princeton, N.J.: Princeton University Press, 1966.

Day, David. *The Great Betrayal: Britain, Australia and the Onset of the Pacific War, 1939–42.* New York: Norton, 1989.

Divine, Robert A. *The Reluctant Belligerent: American Entry into World War II.* New York: Wiley, 1979.

Doenecke, Justus D. *When the Wicked Rise: American Opinion-Makers and the Manchurian Crisis of 1931–1933.* Lewisburg, Pa.: Bucknell University Press, 1984.

Elson, Robert T. *Prelude to War.* Alexandria, Va.: Time-Life Books, 1977.

Endicott, Stephen L. *Diplomacy and Enterprise: British China Policy, 1933–1937.* Vancouver: University of British Columbia Press, 1975.

Feis, Herbert. *The Road to Pearl Harbor.* Princeton, N.J.: Princeton University Press, 1950.

Haggie, Paul. *Britannia at Bay: The Defence of the British Empire against Japan, 1931–1941.* Oxford: Clarendon, 1981.

Haslam, Jonathan. *The Soviet Union and the Threat from the East, 1933–41: Moscow, Tokyo, and the Prelude to the Pacific War.* Pittsburgh: University of Pittsburgh Press, 1992.

Heinrichs, Waldo. *Threshold of War: Franklin D. Roosevelt and American Entry into World War II.* New York: Oxford University Press, 1988.

Herzog, James H. *Closing the Open Door: American-Japanese Diplomatic Negotiations, 1936–1941.* Annapolis, Md.: Naval Institute Press, 1973.

Ike, Nobutaka, ed. *Japan's Decision for War: Records of the 1941 Policy Conferences.* Stanford, Calif.: Stanford University Press, 1967.

Iriye, Akira. *After Imperialism: The Search for a New Order in the Far East, 1921–1931.* Cambridge, Mass.: Harvard University Press, 1968.

Iriye, Akira. *The Origins of the Second World War in Asia and the Pacific.* New York: Longman, 1987.

Koginos, Manny T. *The Panay Incident: Prelude to War.* Lafayette, Ind.: Purdue University Studies, 1967.

Komatsu, Keiichiro. *Origins of the Pacific War and the Importance of "Magic."* New York: St. Martin's, 1997.

Kutakov, Leonid N. *Japanese Foreign Policy on the Eve of the Pacific War: A Soviet View.* Tallahassee, Fla.: Diplomatic Press, 1972.

Langer, William L., and S. Everett Gleason. *The Challenge to Isolation, 1937–1940.* New York: Harper, 1952.

Langer, William L., and S. Everett Gleason. *The Undeclared War, 1940–1941.* New York: Harper, 1953.

Lee, Bradford A. *Britain and the Sino-Japanese War, 1937–1939: A Study in the Dilemmas of British Decline.* Stanford, Calif.: Stanford University Press, 1973.

Liang, Hsi-Huey. *The Sino-German Connection: Alexander von Falkenhausen between China and Germany, 1900–1941.* Assen, Netherlands: Van Gorcum, 1978.

Linn, Brian McAllister. *Guardians of Empire: The U.S. Army and the Pacific, 1902–1940.* Chapel Hill: University of North Carolina Press, 1997.

Lowe, Peter. *Great Britain and the Origins of the Pacific War: A Study of British Policy in East Asia, 1937–1941.* Oxford: Clarendon, 1977.

McCormack, Gavan. *Chang Tso-lin in Northeast China, 1911–1928: China, Japan, and the Manchurian Idea.* Stanford, Calif.: Stanford University Press, 1977.

Marshall, Jonathan. *To Have and Have Not: Southeast Asian Raw Materials and the Origins of the Pacific War.* Berkeley: University of California Press, 1995.

Morley, James W., ed. *The China Quagmire: Japan's Expansion on the Asian Continent, 1933–1941; Selected Translations from* Taiheiyo Senso e no michi, kaisen gaiko shi. New York: Columbia University Press, 1983.

Morley, James W., ed. *Deterrent Diplomacy: Japan, Germany, and the U.S.S.R., 1935–1940; Selected Translations from* Taiheiyo Senso e no michi, kaisen gaiko shi. New York: Columbia University Press, 1976.

Morley, James W., ed. *The Fateful Choice: Japan's Advance into Southeast Asia, 1939–1941; Selected Translations from* Taiheiyo Senso e no michi, kaisen gaiko shi. New York: Columbia University Press, 1980.

Morley, James W., ed. *The Final Confrontation: Japan's Negotiations with the United States, 1941; Selected Translations from* Taiheiyo Senso e no michi. New York: Columbia University Press, 1994.

Morley, James W., ed. *Japan Erupts: The London Naval Conference and the Manchurian Incident, 1928–1932; Selected Translations from* Taiheiyo Senso e no michi, kaisen gaiko shi. New York: Columbia University Press, 1984.

Murray, Williamson, and Allan R. Millett, eds. *Calculations: Net Assessment and the Coming of World War II.* New York: Free Press, 1992.

Neu, Charles E. *The Troubled Encounter: The United States and Japan.* New York: Wiley, 1975.

Nish, Ian H. *Japanese Foreign Policy, 1869–1942: Kasumigaseki to Miyakezaka.* London: Routledge & Kegan Paul, 1977.

Nish, Ian. *Japan's Struggle with Internationalism: Japan, China, and the League of Nations, 1931–33.* New York: Kegan Paul International, 1992.

Ogata, Sadako N. *Defiance in Manchuria: The Making of Japanese Foreign Policy, 1931–1932.* Berkeley: University of California Press, 1964.

Ong Chit Chung. *Operation Matador: Britain's War Plans against the Japanese, 1918–1941.* Portland, Ore.: Time Academic Press, 1997.

Pelz, Stephen E. *Race to Pearl Harbor: The Failure of the Second London Naval Conference and the Onset of World War II.* Cambridge, Mass.: Harvard University Press, 1974.

Perry, Hamilton Darby. *The Panay Incident: Prelude to Pearl Harbor.* New York: Macmillan, 1969.

Russett, Bruce M. *No Clear and Present Danger: A Skeptical View of the United States Entry into World War II.* New York: Harper & Row, 1972.

Shai, Aron. *Origins of the War in the East: Britain, China and Japan 1937–39.* London: Croom Helm, 1976.

Sun, Youli. *China and the Origins of the Pacific War, 1931–1941.* New York: St. Martin's, 1993.

Tansill, Charles C. *Back Door to War: The Roosevelt Foreign Policy, 1933–1941.* Chicago: Regnery, 1952.

Tarling, Nicholas. *Britain, Southeast Asia and the Onset of the Pacific War.* New York: Cambridge University Press, 1996.

Thorne, Christopher. *The Limits of Foreign Policy: The West, the League and the Far Eastern Crisis of 1931–1933.* New York: Putnam, 1973.

Trotter, Ann. *Britain and East Asia, 1933–1937.* New York: Cambridge University Press, 1975.

Utley, Jonathan G. *Going to War with Japan, 1937–1941.* Knoxville: University of Tennessee Press, 1985.

Wheeler, G. E. *Prelude to Pearl Harbor: The United States Navy and the Far East, 1921–1931.* Columbia: University of Missouri Press, 1963.

Worth, Roland H. *No Choice But War: The United States Embargo against Japan and the Eruption of War in the Pacific.* Jefferson, N.C.: McFarland, 1995.

III. Coalitions, Strategy, and Diplomacy

A. JAPAN AND THE AXIS COALITION [SEE ALSO VIII]

Boyd, Carl. *The Extraordinary Envoy: General Hiroshi Oshima and Diplomacy in the Third Reich, 1934–1939.* Washington, D.C.: University Press of America, 1980.

Brooker, Paul. *The Faces of Fraternalism: Nazi Germany, Fascist Italy, and Imperial Japan.* New York: Oxford University Press, 1991.

Chapman, John W. M., ed. and trans. *The Price of Admiralty: The War Diary of the German Naval Attaché in Japan, 1939–1943.* Ripe, England: Saltire, 1982.

Fox, John P. *Germany and the Far Eastern Crisis, 1931–1938: A Study in Diplomacy and Ideology.* New York: Clarendon, 1982.

Iklé, Frank William. *German-Japanese Relations, 1936–1940.* New York: Bookman Associates, 1956.

Meskill, Johanna M. *Hitler and Japan: The Hollow Alliance.* New York: Atherton, 1966.

Mueller-Hillebrand, Burkhart. *Germany and Its Allies in World War II: A Record of Axis Collaboration Problems.* Frederick, Md.: University Publications of America, 1980.

Presseisen, Ernst L. *Germany and Japan: A Study in Totalitarian Diplomacy, 1933–1941.* The Hague: Nijhoff, 1958.

Schroeder, Paul W. *The Axis Alliance and Japanese-American Relations, 1941.* Ithaca, N.Y.: Cornell University Press, 1958.

Toscano, Mario. *The Origins of the Pact of Steel.* Baltimore, Md.: Johns Hopkins University Press, 1967.

B. ALLIED COALITION [SEE ALSO XIX]

1. General Diplomacy and Strategy

Beitzell, Robert. *The Uneasy Alliance: America, Britain, and Russia, 1941–1943.* New York: Knopf, 1972.

Bell, Roger J. *Unequal Allies: Australian-American Relations and the Pacific War.* Carlton: Melbourne University Press, 1977.

Bennett, Edward M. *Franklin D. Roosevelt and the Search for Victory: American-Soviet Relations, 1939–1945.* Wilmington, Del.: Scholarly Resources, 1990.

Brinkley, Douglas, and David R. Facey-Crowther, eds. *The Atlantic Charter*. New York: St. Martin's, 1994.

Conn, Stetson, and Byron Fairchild. *The Framework of Hemispheric Defense*. USAWWII. Washington, D.C.: OCMH, Department of the Army, 1960.

Dziuban, Stanley W. *United States Military Collaboration with Canada in World War II*. USAWWII. Washington, D.C.: OCMH, Department of the Army, 1954.

Edmonds, Robin. *The Big Three: Churchill, Roosevelt and Stalin in Peace and War*. New York: Norton, 1991.

Feis, Herbert. *Churchill, Roosevelt, Stalin: The War They Waged and the Peace They Sought*. Princeton, N.J.: Princeton University, 1957.

Gorodetsky, Gabriel. *Stafford Cripps' Mission to Moscow 1940–1942*. Cambridge: Cambridge University Press, 1984.

Horner, D. M. *High Command: Australia and Allied Strategy, 1939–1945*. Boston: Allen & Unwin, 1982.

Kersaudy, François. *Churchill and de Gaulle*. New York: Atheneum, 1982.

Kitchen, Martin. *British Foreign Policy toward the Soviet Union during the Second World War*. London: Macmillan, 1986.

Kolko, Gabriel. *The Politics of War: Allied Diplomacy and the World Crisis of 1943–1945*. Rev. ed. New York: Pantheon, 1990.

Kondapi, C. *Allied War Diplomacy and Strategy, 1940–45*. Madras: Woodside Books, 1994.

Lane, Ann, and Howard Temperley, eds. *The Rise and Fall of the Grand Alliance, 1941–45*. New York: St. Martin's, 1995.

Lawrey, John. *The Cross of Lorraine in the South Pacific: Australia and the Free French*. Canberra: Journal of Pacific History, 1982.

McNeill, William H. *America, Britain, and Russia: Their Co-operation and Conflict, 1941–1946*. New York: Oxford University Press, 1953.

Maga, Timothy P. "Vision and Victory: Franklin Roosevelt and the Pacific War Council, 1942–1944." *Presidential Studies Quarterly* 21 (Spring 1991): 351–63.

Maguire, G. E. *Anglo-American Policy towards the Free French*. New York: St. Martin's, 1995.

Matloff, Maurice. *Strategic Planning for Coalition Warfare, 1943–1944*. USAWWII. Washington, D.C.: OCMH, Department of the Army, 1959.

Matloff, Maurice, and Edwin M. Snell. *Strategic Planning for Coalition Warfare, 1941–1942*. USAWWII. Washington, D.C.: OCMH, Department of the Army, 1953.

Miner, Steven M. *Between Churchill and Stalin: The Soviet Union, Great Britain, and the Origins of the Grand Alliance*. Chapel Hill: University of North Carolina Press, 1988.

Neumann, William L. *After Victory: Churchill, Roosevelt, Stalin and the Making of the Peace*. New York: Harper & Row, 1967.

Perlmutter, Amos. *FDR & Stalin: A Not So Grand Alliance, 1943–1945*. Columbia: University of Missouri Press, 1993.

Ready, J. Lee. *Forgotten Allies: The Military Contribution of the Colonies, Exiled Governments, and Lesser Powers in the Allied Victory in World War II*. 2 vols. Jefferson, N.C.: McFarland, 1985.

Reynolds, David, et al., eds. *Allies at War: The Soviet, American and British Experience, 1939–1945*. New York: St. Martin's, 1994.

Richardson, Stewart, ed. *The Secret History of World War II: The Ultra-Secret Wartime Letters and Cables of Roosevelt, Stalin, and Churchill*. New York: Richardson & Steirman, 1986.

Rozek, Edward J. *Allied Wartime Diplomacy*. Boulder, Colo.: Westview, 1989.

Rzheshevsky, Oleg A., ed. *War and Diplomacy: The Making of the Grand Alliance: Documents from Stalin's Archives*. Trans. T. Sorokina. Amsterdam: Harwood Academic, 1996.

Shai, Aron. *Britain and China, 1941–1947: Imperial Momentum*. New York: St. Martin's, 1983.

Snell, John. *Illusion and Necessity: The Diplomacy of Global War 1939–1945*. Boston: Houghton Mifflin, 1963.

Viorst, Milton. *Hostile Allies: FDR and Charles de Gaulle*. New York: Macmillan, 1965.

White, Dorothy Shipley. *Seeds of Discord: De Gaulle, Free France, and the Allies*. Syracuse, N.Y.: Syracuse University Press, 1964.

2. Anglo-American Coalition

Charmley, John. *Churchill's Grand Alliance: The Anglo-American Special Relationship 1940–57*. New York: Harcourt Brace, 1995.

Cowman, Ian. *Dominion or Decline: Anglo-American Naval Relations in the Pacific, 1937–1941*. Oxford: Berg, 1996.

Dobson, Alan P. *The Politics of the Anglo-American Economic Special Relationship*. New York: St. Martin's, 1988.

Dobson, Alan P. *U.S. Wartime Aid to Britain, 1940–1946*. New York: St. Martin's, 1986.

Hough, Richard. *The Greatest Crusade: Roosevelt, Churchill, and the Naval Wars*. New York: Morrow, 1986.

Kimball, Warren F. *Churchill and Roosevelt: The Complete Correspondence*. 3 vols. Princeton, N.J.: Princeton University Press, 1984.

Kimball, Warren D. *Forged in War: Roosevelt, Churchill, and the Second World War*. New York: Morrow, 1997.

Lash, Joseph P. *Roosevelt and Churchill, 1939–1941: The Partnership that Saved the West*. New York: Norton, 1976.

Loewenheim, Francis L., et al., eds. *Roosevelt and Churchill: Their Secret Wartime Correspondence*. New York: Dutton, 1975.

Reynolds, David. *The Creation of the Anglo-American Alliance, 1937–1941: A Study in Competitive Co-operation*. Chapel Hill: University of North Carolina Press, 1981.

Rigby, David Joseph. "The Combined Chiefs of Staff and Anglo-American Strategic Coordination in World War II." Ph.D. dissertation, Brandeis University, 1997.

Sainsbury, Keith. *Churchill and Roosevelt at War: The War They Fought and the Peace They Hoped to Make*. New York: New York University Press, 1994.

Thorne, Christopher. *Allies of a Kind: The United States, Britain, and the War against Japan, 1941–1945*. New York: Oxford University Press, 1979.

Weiss, Steve. *Allies in Conflict: Anglo-American Strategic Negotiations, 1938–44*. New York: St. Martin's, 1996.

Woods, Randall Bennett. *A Changing of the Guard: Anglo-American Relations, 1941–1946*. Chapel Hill: University of North Carolina Press, 1990.

3. Allied Conferences

Armstrong, Anne. *Unconditional Surrender: The Impact of the Casablanca Policy upon World War II*. New Brunswick, N.J.: Rutgers University Press, 1961.

Beitzell, Robert, ed. *Teheran, Yalta, Potsdam: The Soviet Protocols*. Hattiesburg, Miss.: Academic International, 1970.

Buhite, Russell D. *Decisions at Yalta: An Appraisal of Summit Diplomacy*. Wilmington, Del.: Scholarly Resources, 1986.

Clemens, Diane S. *Yalta*. New York: Oxford University Press, 1970.

Eubank, Keith. *Summit at Teheran: The Untold Story*. New York: Morrow, 1985.

Feis, Herbert. *Between War and Peace: The Potsdam Conference*. Princeton, N.J.: Princeton University Press, 1960.

Gormly, James L. *From Potsdam to the Cold War: Big Three Diplomacy, 1945–1947.* Wilmington, Del.: Scholarly Resources, 1990.

Hilderbrand, Robert C. *Dumbarton Oaks: The Origins of the United Nations and the Search for Postwar Security.* Chapel Hill: University of North Carolina Press, 1990.

Hoska, Lukas E., Jr. *A Critical Analysis of the Summit Conferences of Teheran, the Crimea, and Berlin.* Cambridge, Mass.: Center for International Affairs, Harvard University, 1960.

Laloy, Jean. *Yalta: Yesterday, Today, Tomorrow.* Trans. William R. Tyler. New York: Harper & Row, 1990.

Mayle, Paul D. *Eureka Summit: Agreement in Principle and the Big Three at Tehran, 1943.* Newark: University of Delaware Press, 1987.

Mee, Charles L., Jr. *Meeting at Potsdam.* New York: Evans, 1975.

Neumann, William L. *Making the Peace, 1941–1945: The Diplomacy of the Wartime Conferences.* Washington, D.C.: Foundation for Foreign Affairs, 1950.

Sainsbury, Keith. *The Turning Point: Roosevelt, Stalin, Churchill and Chiang Kai-Shek, 1943: The Moscow, Cairo, and Teheran Conferences.* New York: Oxford University Press, 1986.

Schild, Georg. *Bretton Woods and Dumbarton Oaks: American Economic and Political Postwar Planning in the Summer of 1944.* New York: St. Martin's, 1995.

Snell, John L., ed. *The Meaning of Yalta: Big Three Diplomacy and the New Balance of Power.* Baton Rouge: Louisiana State University Press, 1956.

Stettinius, Edward R. *Roosevelt and the Russians: The Yalta Conference.* Garden City, N.Y.: Doubleday, 1949.

Theoharis, Athan. *The Yalta Myths: An Issue in U.S. Politics, 1945–1955.* Columbia: University of Missouri Press, 1970.

Wilson, Theodore A. *The First Summit: Roosevelt and Churchill at Placentia Bay, 1941.* Lawrence: University Press of Kansas, 1991.

Wilt, Alan F. "The Significance of the Casablanca Decisions, January 1943." *Journal of Military History* 55 (October 1991): 517–29.

C. OTHER RELATIONSHIPS [SEE ALSO IV.D]

Garver, John W. *Chinese-Soviet Relations, 1937–1945: The Diplomacy of Chinese Nationalism.* New York: Oxford University Press, 1988.

Lenson, George A. *The Strange Neutrality: Soviet-Japanese Relations during the Second World War 1941–1945*. Tallahassee, Fla.: Diplomatic Press, 1972.

McLane, Charles B. *Soviet Policy and the Chinese Communists, 1931–46*. New York: Columbia University Press, 1958.

Roberts, Geoffrey. *The Unholy Alliance: Stalin's Pact with Hitler*. Bloomington: Indiana University Press, 1990.

Tai Wan-chin, ed. *The 1945 Sino-Soviet Treaty of Friendship and Alliance*. Taipei: Tamkang University, 1995.

D. NEUTRAL COUNTRIES

Beaulac, Willard L. *Franco: Silent Ally in World War II*. Carbondale: Southern Illinois University Press, 1986.

Carlgren, W. M. *Swedish Foreign Policy during the Second World War*. New York: St. Martin's, 1977.

Cortada, James W. *United States-Spanish Relations, Wolfram and World War II*. Barcelona: Manuel Pareja, 1971.

Feis, Herbert. *The Spanish Story: Franco and the Nations at War*. New York: Norton, 1966.

Fodor, Denis J. *The Neutrals*. Alexandria, Va.: Time-Life Books, 1982.

Fox, Annette. *The Power of Small States: Diplomacy in World War II*. Chicago: University of Chicago Press, 1959.

Gabriel, Jürg Martin. *The American Conception of Neutrality after 1941*. New York: St. Martin's, 1988.

Garlinski, Jósef. *The Swiss Corridor: Espionage Networks in Switzerland during World War II*. London: Dent, 1981.

Meier, Heinz K. *Friendship under Stress: U.S. Swiss Relations, 1900–1950*. Bern: Lang, 1970.

Packard, Jerrold M. *Neither Friend nor Foe: The European Neutrals in World War II*. New York: Scribner's, 1992.

IV. Nations, Territories, and Other Entities Involved in the War
[see also V;VI;VII]

A. AUSTRALIA

Alcorta, Frank. *Australia's Frontline: The Northern Territory's War*. North Sydney: Allen & Unwin, 1991.

Ball, Reg A. *Torres Strait Force, 1942 to 1945: The Defence of Cape York-Torres Strait and Merauke in Dutch New Guinea*. Loftus: Australian Military History Publications, 1996.

Barker, Anthony J., and Lisa Jackson. *Fleeting Attraction: A Social History of American Servicemen in Western Australia during the Second World War*. Nedlands: University of Western Australia Press, 1996.

Beaumont, Joan, ed. *Australia's War, 1939–1945*. St. Leonards, Australia: Allen & Unwin, 1996.

Buggy, Hugh. *Pacific Victory: A Short History of Australia's Part in the War Against Japan*. Melbourne: Australian Ministry for Information, 1945.

Burns, Paul. *The Brisbane Line Controversy: Political Opportunism versus National Security, 1942–1945*. St. Leonards, Australia: Allen & Unwin, 1998.

Crawford, John G., et al. *Wartime Agriculture in Australia and New Zealand, 1939–50*. Stanford, Calif.: Stanford University Press, 1954.

Day, David. *Menzies and Churchill at War*. New York: Paragon House, 1988.

Day, David. *Reluctant Nation: Australia and the Allied Defeat of Japan, 1942–1945*. New York: Oxford University Press, 1992.

Day, David, ed. *Brave New World: Dr. H. V. Evatt and Australian Foreign Policy, 1941–1949*. St. Lucia: University of Queensland Press, 1996.

Frei, Henry P. *Japan's Southward Advance and Australia: From the Sixteenth Century to World War II*. Honolulu: University of Hawaii Press, 1991.

Hall, Robert A. *Fighters from the Fringe: Aborigines and Torres Strait Islands Recall the Second World War*. Canberra: Aboriginal Studies Press, 1995.

Hasluck, Paul. *The Government and the People*. 2 vols. Australia in the War of 1939–1945. Canberra: Australian War Memorial, 1952–1970.

Hasluck, Paul. *Diplomatic Witness: Australian Foreign Affairs, 1941–1947*. Melbourne: Melbourne University Press, 1980.

Horner, David, ed. *The Battles that Shaped Australia: The Australian's Anniversary Essays*. St. Leonards, Australia: Allen & Unwin, 1994.

Horner, David M. *Crisis of Command: Australian Generalship and the Japanese Threat, 1941–1943*. Canberra: Australian National University Press, 1978.

Horner, David M. *Inside the War Cabinet: Directing Australia's War Effort, 1939–45*. St. Leonards, Australia: Allen & Unwin, 1996.

Johnston, Mark. *At the Front Line: Experiences of Australian Soldiers in World War II*. New York: Cambridge University Press, 1996.

Long, Gavin. *The Six Years' War: A Concise History of Australia in the 1939–1945 War*. Canberra: Australian War Memorial and Australian Government Publishing Service, 1973.

McKernan, Michael. *All In! Australia during the Second World War*. Melbourne: Nelson, 1983.

McKinlay, Brian. *Australia, 1942: End of Innocence*. Sydney: Collins, 1985.

Moore, John Hammond. *Over-Sexed, Over-Paid, and Over Here: Americans in Australia, 1941–1945*. St. Lucia: University of Queensland Press, 1981.

Penglase, Joanna, and David Horner. *When the War Came to Australia: Memories of the Second World War*. St. Leonards, Australia: Allen & Unwin, 1992.

Potts, E. Daniel, and Annette Potts. *Yanks Down Under, 1941–1945: The American Impact on Australia*. New York: Oxford University Press, 1985.

Robertson, John. *Australia at War, 1939–1945*. Melbourne: Heinemann, 1981.

Robertson, John, and John McCarthy, eds. *Australian War Strategy, 1939–1945: A Documentary History*. St. Lucia: University of Queensland Press, 1985.

B. BURMA [SEE ALSO IV.I.3]

Ba Maw, U. *Breakthrough in Burma: Memoirs of a Revolutionary, 1939–1946*. New Haven, Conn.: Yale University Press, 1968.

Maung Maung, U. *Burmese Nationalist Movements: 1940–1948*. Honolulu: University of Hawaii Press, 1990.

Nu, U. *Burma Under the Japanese*. Ed., trans., J. S. Furnivall. New York: St. Martin's, 1954.

Tinker, Hugh, ed. *Burma: The Struggle for Independence, 1944–1948*. 2 vols. London: HMSO, 1983–1984.

Trager, Frank N., ed. *Burma: Japanese Military Administration*. Philadelphia: University of Pennsylvania Press, 1971.

C. CANADA

1. General

Broadfoot, Barry. *Six War Years, 1939–1945: Memories of Canadians at Home and Abroad*. Toronto: Doubleday Canada, 1974.

Douglas, W. A. B., and Brereton Greenhouse. *Out of the Shadows: Canada in the Second World War*. Toronto: Oxford University Press, 1977.

Granatstein, J. L. *Canada's War: The Politics of the Mackenzie King Government, 1939–1945*. 2d ed. Toronto: Oxford University Press, 1975.

Granatstein, J. L., and Desmond Morton. *A Nation Forged in Fire: Canadians and the Second World War, 1939–1945*. Toronto: Lester & Orpen Dennys, 1989.

McNeil, Bill. *Voices of a War Remembered: An Oral History of Canadians in World War Two*. Toronto: Doubleday Canada, 1991.

Nolan, Brian. *King's War: Mackenzie King and the Politics of War, 1939–1945*. Toronto: Random House, 1988.

Pickersgill, J. W., and Forster, Donald F. *The Mackenzie King Record*. 2 vols. Toronto: University of Toronto Press, 1960–1968.

Stacey, C. P. *Arms, Men and Governments: The War Policies of Canada 1939–1945*. Ottawa: Queen's Printer, 1970.

Stacey, Charles P. *Official History of the Canadian Army in the Second World War*. 3 vols. Ottawa: Queen's Printer, 1955–1960.

2. *Japanese Canadians [see also XIV.C.I]*

Ito, Roy. *We Went to War: The Story of the Japanese Canadians Who Served during the First and Second World Wars*. Stittsville: Canada's Wings, 1984.

D. CHINA [SEE ALSO II]

1. *General*

Bunker, Gerald E. *The Peace Conspiracy: Wang Ching-wei and the China War, 1937–1941*. Cambridge, Mass.: Harvard University Press, 1972.

Chen, Yung-fa. *Making Revolution: The Communist Movement in Eastern and Central China, 1937–1945*. Berkeley: University of California Press, 1986.

Chi, Hsi-Sheng. *Nationalist China at War: Military Defects and Political Collapse*. Ann Arbor: University of Michigan Press, 1982.

Coble, Parks M. *Facing Japan: Chinese Politics and Japanese Imperialism, 1931–1937*. Cambridge, Mass.: Harvard University Press, 1991.

Eastman, L. E. *Seeds of Destruction: Nationalist China in War and Revolution, 1937–1945*. Stanford, Calif.: Stanford University Press, 1984.

Fu, Poshek. *Passivity, Resistance, and Collaboration: Intellectual Choices in Occupied Shanghai, 1937–1945*. Stanford, Calif.: Stanford University Press, 1993.

Hooton, E. R. *The Greatest Tumult: The Chinese Civil War, 1936 – 49*. Washington, D.C.: Brassey's, 1991.

Johnson, Chalmers A. *Peasant Nationalism and Communist Power: The Emergence of Revolutionary China, 1937–1945*. Stanford, Calif.: Stanford University Press, 1979.

Jordan, Donald A. *Chinese Boycotts versus Japanese Bombs: The Failure of China's "Revolutionary Diplomacy," 1931–32*. Ann Arbor: University of Michigan Press, 1991.

Kataoka, Tetsuya. *Resistance and Revolution in China; The Communists and the Second United Front*. Berkeley: University of California Press, 1974.

Lattimore, Owen. *China Memoirs: Chiang Kai-shek and the War against Japan*. Comp. Fujiko Isono. Tokyo: University of Tokyo Press, 1990.

Lee, Chong-Sik. *Revolutionary Struggle in Manchuria: Chinese Communism and Soviet Interest, 1922–1945*. Berkeley: University of California Press, 1983.

Pu-Yi, H. *From Emperor to Citizen: The Autobiography of Aisin-Gioro Pu-Yi*. Trans. W. J. F. Jenner. New York: Oxford University Press, 1987.

Reardon-Anderson, James. *Yenan and the Great Powers: The Origins of Chinese Communist Foreign Policy, 1944–46*. New York: Columbia University Press, 1980.

Sih, Paul K. T., ed. *Nationalist China during the Sino-Japanese War, 1937–1945*. Hicksville, N.Y.: Exposition Press, 1977.

Van Slyke, Lyman P. *Enemies and Friends: The United Front in Chinese Communist History*. Stanford, Calif.: Stanford University Press, 1967.

Young, A. N. *China's Wartime Finance and Inflation, 1937–1945*. Cambridge, Mass.: Harvard University Press, 1965.

2. Relationship with the United States [see also VIII]

Barrett, David D. *Dixie Mission: The United States Army Observer Group in Yenan, 1944*. Berkeley: University of California Press, 1970.

Bland, Larry I., ed. *George C. Marshall's Mediation Mission to China, December 1945–January 1947*. Lexington, Va.: George C. Marshall Foundation, 1998.

Caldwell, Oliver J. *A Secret War: Americans in China, 1944–1945*. Carbondale: Southern Illinois University Press, 1973.

Carter, Carolle J. *Mission to Yenan: American Liaison with the Chinese Communists, 1944–1947*. Lexington: University Press of Kentucky, 1997.

Feis, Herbert. *The China Tangle: The American Effort in China from Pearl Harbor to the Marshall Mission*. Princeton, N.J.: Princeton University Press, 1953.

Liu Xiaoyuan. *A Partnership for Disorder: China, the United States, and Their Plans for the Postwar Disposition of the Japanese Empire, 1941–1945*. Cambridge: Cambridge University Press, 1996.

Miles, Milton E. *A Different Kind of War: The Little-Known Story of the Combined Guerrilla Forces Created in China by the U.S. Navy and the Chinese during World War II*. Garden City, N.Y.: Doubleday, 1967.

Peterkin, Wilbur J. *Inside China, 1943–1945: An Eyewitness Account of America's Mission in Yenan*. Baltimore, Md.: Gateway, 1992.

Schaller, Michael. *The U.S. Crusade in China, 1938–1945*. New York: Columbia University Press, 1979.

Schaller, Michael. "SACO! The United States Navy's Secret War in China." *Pacific Historical Review* 44 (November 1975): 527–53.

Tsou Tang. *America's Failure in China, 1941–1950*. Chicago: University of Chicago Press, 1963.

Varg, Paul A. *The Closing of the Door: Sino-American Relations, 1936–1946*. East Lansing: Michigan State University Press, 1973.

E. FIJI [SEE ALSO IV.N]

Howlett, Robert A. *The History of the Fiji Military Forces, 1939–1945*. London: Crown Agents for the Colonies, 1948.

F. FRANCE AND FRENCH INDOCHINA [SEE ALSO XVIII.A]

Aldrich, Robert. *France and the South Pacific since 1940*. Honolulu: University of Hawaii Press, 1993.

Auphan, Gabriel A., and Herve Cras. *The French Navy in World War II*. Annapolis, Md.: U.S. Naval Institute, 1959.

Clayton, Anthony. *Three Marshals of France: Leadership after Trauma*. London: Brassey's, 1992.

DePort, A. W. *DeGaulle's Foreign Policy, 1944–1948*. Cambridge, Mass.: Harvard University Press, 1948.

Dougherty, James J. *The Politics of Wartime Aid: American Economic Assistance to France and French Northwest Africa, 1940–1946*. Westport, Conn.: Greenwood, 1978.

Footitt, Hilary, and John Simmonds. *France, 1943–1945*. New York: Holmes & Meier, 1988.

Gardner, Lloyd C. *Approaching Vietnam: From World War II through Dienbienphu, 1941–1954*. New York: Norton, 1988.

Griffiths, Richard. *Marshal Petain*. London: Constable, 1970.

Koburger, Charles W. *Naval Expeditions: The French Return to Indochina, 1945–1946*. Westport, Conn.: Greenwood, 1997.

O'Neill, Robert J. *General Giap, Politician And Strategist*. New York: Praeger, 1969.

Roth, Andrew. *Japan Strikes South: The Story of French Indo-China Passing Under Japanese Domination*. New York: American Council, Institute of Pacific Relations, 1941.

Schulzinger, Robert D. *A Time for War: The United States and Vietnam, 1941–1975*. New York: Oxford University Press, 1997.

Thomas, Martin. "Free France, the British Government, and the Future of French Indo-China, 1940–1945," *Journal of Southeast Asian Studies* 28 (1997): 137–60.

Tønnesson, Stein. *The Vietnamese Revolution of 1945: Roosevelt, Ho Chi Minh and de Gaulle in a World at War*. Newbury Park, Calif.: PRIO/Sage, 1991.

Vigneras, Marcel. *Rearming the French*. USAWWII. Washington, D.C.: OCMH, Department of the Army, 1957.

G. HONG KONG

Endacott, G. B. *Hong Kong Eclipse*. New York: Oxford University Press, 1978.

Lindsay, Oliver. *At the Going Down of the Sun: Hong Kong and South-East Asia, 1941–1945*. London: Hamilton, 1981.

Luff, John. *The Hidden Years*. Hong Kong: South China Morning Post, 1967.

Proulx, Benjamin A. *Underground from Hongkong*. New York: Dutton, 1943.

Ride, Edwin. *BAAG: Hong Kong Resistance, 1942–1945*. New York: Oxford University Press, 1981.

H. INDIA

Brown, J. M. *Gandhi: Prisoner of Hope*. New Haven, Conn.: Yale University Press, 1989.

Bhuyan, Arun Chandra. *The Quit India Movement: The Second World War and Indian Nationalism.* New Delhi: Manas Publications, 1975.

Elliott, James Gordon. *Unfading Honour: The Story of the Indian Army, 1939–1945.* South Brunswick, N.J.: Barnes, 1966.

Fay, Peter Ward. *The Forgotten Army: India's Armed Struggle for Independence, 1942–1945.* Ann Arbor: University of Michigan Press, 1993.

Gopal, Sarvepalli. *Jawaharlal Nehru.* 3 vols. London: Cape, 1975–1984.

Gordon, Leonard A. *Brothers against the Raj: A Biography of Indian Nationalists Sarat and Subhas Chandra Bose.* New York: Columbia University Press, 1990.

Hauner, Milan. *India in Axis Strategy: Germany, Japan, and Indian Nationalists in the Second World War.* Stuttgart: Klett-Cotta, 1981.

Hess, Gary. *America Encounters India, 1941–1947.* Baltimore, Md.: Johns Hopkins University Press, 1971.

Knight, Henry. *Food Administration in India, 1939–47.* Stanford, Calif.: Stanford University Press, 1954.

Lebra, Joyce C. *Jungle Alliance: Japan and the Indian National Army.* Singapore: Donald Moore for Asia Pacific Press, 1971.

Lumby, E. W. R. *The Transfer of Power 1942–1947.* 12 vols. London: HMSO, 1970–1983.

Mangat, Gurbachan Singh. *Indian National Army: Role in India's Struggle for Freedom.* Ludhiana, India: Gangan Pub., 1991.

Mitrokhin, L. V. *Friends of the Soviet Union: India's Solidarity with the USSR during the Second World War in 1941–1945.* Bombay: Allied, 1977.

Moore, Robin J. *Churchill, Cripps, and India, 1939–1945.* New York: Oxford University Press, 1979.

Prasad, Bisheshwar. *India and the War.* New Delhi: Combined Inter-services Historical Section, India & Pakistan, 1966.

Prasad, Sri Nandan. *Expansion of the Armed Forces and Defence Organisation, 1939–45.* Delhi: Combined Inter-Services Historical Section, India & Pakistan, 1956.

Sareen, T. R. *Japan and the Indian National Army.* New Delhi: Mounto, 1996.

Toye, Hugh. *The Springing Tiger: A Study of a Revolutionary.* London: Cassell, 1959. [Subhas Chandra Bose]

Tucher, Paul H. von. *Nationalism, Case and Crisis in Missions: German Missions in British India, 1936–1946.* Erlangen, Germany: Tucher, 1980.

Voigt, Johannes H. *India in the Second World War*. New Delhi: Arnold-Heinemann, 1987.

Zaidi, A. M., ed. *Congress, Nehru, and the Second World War*. New Delhi: Indian Institute of Applied Political Research, 1985.

I. JAPAN

1. General [see also XIII]

Berger, Gordon Mark. *Parties out of Power in Japan, 1931–1941*. Princeton, N.J.: Princeton University Press, 1973.

Buruma, Ian. *Wages of Guilt: Memories of War in Germany and Japan*. New York: Farrar Straus Giroux, 1994.

Coffey, Thomas M. *Imperial Tragedy: Japan in World War II, the First Days and the Last*. New York: World, 1970.

Cohen, Jerome B. *Japan's Economy in War and Reconstruction*. Minneapolis: University of Minnesota Press, 1949.

Cook, Haruko Taya, and Theodore F. Cook. *Japan at War: An Oral History*. New York: New Press, 1992.

Dower, John. *Japan in Peace and War: Selected Essays*. New York: New Press, 1993.

Drea, Edward J. *The 1942 Japanese General Election: Political Mobilization in Wartime Japan*. Lawrence: Center for East Asia Studies, University of Kansas, 1979.

Fletcher, William Miles, III. *The Search for a New Order: Intellectuals and Fascism in Prewar Japan*. Chapel Hill: University of North Carolina Press, 1982.

Gibney, Frank, ed. *Senso: The Japanese Remember the Pacific War: Letters to the Editor of Asahi Shimbun*. Armonk, N.Y.: Sharpe, 1995.

Havens, Thomas R. H. *Valley of Darkness: The Japanese People and World War Two*. New York: Norton, 1978.

Hicks, George. *Japan's War Memories: Amnesia or Concealment?* Aldershot, England: Ashgate, 1997.

Iritani, Toshio. *Group Psychology of the Japanese in Wartime*. New York: Kegan Paul International, 1991.

Johnston, Bruce F., Mosaburo Hosoda, and Yoshio Kusumi. *Japanese Food Management in World War II*. Stanford, Calif.: Stanford University Press, 1953.

Kranzler, David. *Japanese, Nazis, and Jews: The Jewish Refugee Community of Shanghai, 1938–1945*. New York: Yeshiva University Press, 1976.

Levine, Hillel. *In Search of Sugihara: The Elusive Japanese Diplomat Who Risked His Life to Rescue 10,000 Jews from the Holocaust.* New York: Free Press, 1996.

Maxon, Yale Candee. *Control of Japanese Foreign Policy: A Study of Civil-Military Relations 1930–1945.* Berkeley: University of California Press, 1957.

Murakami, Hyoe. *Japan: The Years of Trial, 1919–52.* New York: Kodansha International, 1983.

Shillony, Ben-Ami. *Politics and Culture in Wartime Japan.* New York: Oxford University Press, 1981.

Sugihara, Seishiro. *Between Incompetence and Culpability: Assessing the Diplomacy of Japan's Foreign Ministry from Pearl Harbor to Potsdam.* Trans. Norman Hu. Lanham, Md.: University Press of America, 1997.

Time-Life Books editors. *Japan at War.* Alexandria, Va.: Time-Life Books, 1980.

Tipton, Elise K. *The Japanese Police State: The Tokko in Interwar Japan.* Honolulu: University of Hawaii Press, 1990.

Titus, David A. *Palace and Politics in Prewar Japan.* New York: Columbia University Press, 1974.

Tokayer, Marvin, and Mary Swartz. *The Fugu Plan: The Untold Story of the Japanese and the Jews during World War II.* New York: Weatherill, 1996.

Tsurumi, Shunsuke. *An Intellectual History of Wartime Japan, 1931–1945.* New York: KPI, 1986.

Women's Division of Soka Gakkai, comps. *Women against the War.* Trans. Richard L. Gage. Tokyo: Kodansha International, 1986.

2. Armed Forces

Drea, Edward J. *In the Service of the Emperor: Essays on the Imperial Japanese Army.* Lincoln: University of Nebraska Press, 1998.

Edgerton, Robert B. *Warriors of the Rising Sun: A History of the Japanese Military.* New York: Norton, 1997.

Fuller, Richard. *Shokan—Hirohito's Samurai: Leaders of the Japanese Armed Forces, 1926–1945.* London: Arms and Armour Press, 1992.

Harries, Meirion, and Susie Harries. *Soldiers of the Sun: The Rise and Fall of the Imperial Japanese Army.* New York: Random House, 1991.

Hayashi, Saburo, and A. D. Coox. *Kogun: The Japanese Army in the Pacific War.* Westport, Conn.: Greenwood, 1978.

Humphreys, Leonard A. *The Way of the Heavenly Sword: The Japanese Army in the 1920's*. Stanford, Calif.: Stanford University Press, 1995.

McLean, Donald B. *Japanese Parachute Troops*. Wickenburg, Ariz.: Normount Technical Publications, 1973.

Madej, W. Victor, ed. *Japanese Armed Forces Order of Battle, 1937–1945*. Allentown, Pa.: Game Marketing Co., 1981.

Onoda, Hiroo. *No Surrender: My Thirty-year War*. Tokyo: Kodansha International, 1974.

Saikai, Saburo, with Martin Caidin and Fred Saito. *Samurai!* New York: Dutton, 1957.

Shillony, Ben-Ami. *Revolt in Japan: The Young Officers and the February 26, 1936 Incident*. Princeton, N.J.: Princeton University Press, 1973.

Wetzler, Peter. *Hirohito and War: Imperial Tradition and Military Decision Making in Prewar Japan*. Honolulu: University of Hawaii Press, 1998.

Yoshihashi, Takehiko. *Conspiracy at Mukden: The Rise of the Japanese Military*. New Haven, Conn.: Yale University Press, 1963.

3. Empire and Occupation [see also II; IV Individual Entries]

Beasley, W. G. *Japanese Imperialism, 1894–1945*. New York: Oxford University Press, 1987.

Duus, Peter, Ramon H. Myers, and Mark R. Peattie, eds. *The Japanese Wartime Empire, 1931–1945*. Princeton, N.J.: Princeton University Press, 1996.

Elsbree, Willard H. *Japan's Role in Southeast Asian Nationalist Movements, 1940–1945*. Cambridge, Mass.: Harvard University Press, 1953.

Friend, Theodore. *The Blue-Eyed Enemy: Japan against the West in Java and Luzon, 1942–45*. Princeton, N.J.: Princeton University Press, 1988.

Goodman, Grant K., ed. *Japanese Cultural Policies in Southeast Asia during World War 2*. New York: St. Martin's, 1991.

Hicks, George. *The Comfort Women: Japan's Brutal Regime of Enforced Prostitution in the Second World War*. New York: Norton, 1995.

Jones, Francis Clifford. *Japan's New Order in East Asia: Its Rise and Fall, 1937–1945*. London: Oxford University Press, 1954.

Lebra, Joyce C. *Japanese-Trained Armies in Southeast Asia: Independence and Volunteer Forces in World War II*. New York: Columbia University Press, 1977.

Lebra, Joyce C., ed. *Japan's Greater East Asia Co-Prosperity Sphere in World War II*. New York: Oxford University Press, 1975.

McCoy, Alfred W., ed. *Southeast Asia under Japanese Occupation*. New Haven, Conn.: Yale University Southeast Asia Studies, 1980.

Myers, Ramon H., and Mark R. Peattie, eds. *The Japanese Colonial Empire, 1895–1945*. Princeton, N.J.: Princeton University Press, 1984.

Newell, William H., ed. *Japan in Asia, 1942–1945*. Singapore: Singapore University Press, 1981.

Ooi, Keat Gin. *Japanese Empire in the Tropics: Selected Documents and Reports of the Japanese Period in Sarawak, Northwest Borneo, 1941–1945*. Athens: Ohio University Center for International Studies, 1997.

Peattie, Mark R. *Nanyo: The Rise and Fall of the Japanese in Micronesia, 1885–1945*. Honolulu: University of Hawaii Press, 1988.

Ward, Robert S. *Asia for the Asiatics? The Techniques of Japanese Occupation*. Chicago: University of Chicago Press, 1945.

Yanihara, Todeo. *Pacific Islands under Japanese Mandate*. London: Oxford University Press, 1940.

Young, Louise. *Japan's Total Empire: Manchuria and the Culture of Wartime Imperialism*. Berkeley: University of California Press, 1998.

Yu, Te-jen. *The Japanese Struggle for World Empire*. New York: Vantage, 1967.

J. KOREA

Cumings, Bruce. *Child of Conflict: The Korean-American Relationship, 1943–1953*. Seattle: University of Washington Press, 1983.

Cumings, Bruce. *The Origins of the Korean War*. 2 vols. Princeton, N.J.: Princeton University Press, 1981–1990.

Kang, Wi Jo. *Religion and Politics in Korea under the Japanese Rule*. Lewiston, N.Y.: Mellen, 1987.

Matray, James I. *The Reluctant Crusade: American Foreign Policy in Korea, 1941–1950*. Honolulu: University of Hawaii Press, 1985.

Nahm, Andrew C., ed. *Korea under Japanese Colonial Rule*. Kalamazoo, Mich.: Center for Korean Studies, Western Michigan University, 1973.

Weiner, Michael. *Race and Migration in Imperial Japan*. London: Routledge, 1994.

K. LATIN AMERICA [SEE ALSO XIV.C.4]

Gellman, Irwin F. *Good Neighbor Diplomacy: United States Policies in Latin America, 1933–1945*. Baltimore, Md.: Johns Hopkins University Press, 1979.

Humphreys, R. A. *Latin America and the Second World War*. 2 vols. Atlantic Highlands, N.J.: Humanities Press, 1981–1982.

Paz, Maria Emilia. *Strategy, Security, and Spies: Mexico and the U.S. as Allies in World War II*. University Park: Pennsylvania State University Press, 1997.

L. MALAY PENINSULA AND SINGAPORE

Cross, John. *Red Jungle*. London: Hale, 1957.

Hamond, Robert. *A Fearful Freedom: The Story of One Man's Survival Behind the Lines in Japanese Occupied Malaya, 1942–45*. London: Leo Cooper, 1984.

Kennedy, Joseph. *British Civilians and the Japanese War in Malaya and Singapore, 1941–45*. Basingstoke, England: Macmillan, 1987.

Kheng, C. B. *Red Star over Malaya: Resistance and Social Conflict during and after the Japanese Occupation of Malaya, 1941–1946*. Singapore: Singapore University Press, 1983.

Kratoska, Paul H. *Malaya and Singapore during the Japanese Occupation*. Singapore: Singapore University Press, 1995.

Shinozaki, Mamoru. *Syonan, My Story: The Japanese Occupation of Singapore*. Singapore: Asia Pacific Press, 1975.

Smith, Simon C. *British Relations with the Malay Rulers from Decentralization to Malayan Independence, 1930–1957*. New York: Oxford University Press, 1995.

M. THE NETHERLANDS AND NETHERLANDS EAST INDIES [SEE ALSO XVIII.A]

Anderson, Benedict R. O'G. *Java in a Time of Revolution: Occupation and Resistance, 1944–1946*. Ithaca, N.Y.: Cornell University Press, 1972.

Benda, Harry Jindrich. *The Crescent and the Rising Sun: Indonesian Islam and the Japanese Occupation, 1942–45*. The Hague: van Hoeve, 1958.

Krancher, Jan A. *The Defining Years of the Dutch East Indies, 1942–1949: Survivors' Accounts of Japanese Invasion and Enslave-*

ment of Europeans and the Revolution That Created Free Indonesia. Jefferson, N.C.: McFarland, 1996.

Legge, J. D. *Sukarno: A Political Biography.* New York: Praeger, 1972.

Lockwood, Rupert. *Black Armada: Australia & the Struggle for Indonesian Independence, 1942–49.* Sydney: Hale & Iremonger, 1982.

Lucas, Anton, ed. *Local Opposition and Underground Resistance to the Japanese in Java, 1942–1945.* Melbourne: Monash University, 1986.

Maass, Walter B. *The Netherlands at War, 1940–1945.* New York: Abelard-Schuman, 1970.

Mook, H. J. van. *The Netherlands Indies and Japan: Their Relations, 1940–1941.* London: Allen & Unwin, 1944.

National Federation of Kenpeitai Veterans' Associations. *The Kenpeitai in Java and Sumatra.* Trans. Barbara Gifford Shimer and Guy Hobbs. Ithaca, N.Y.: Cornell University, 1986.

Notosusanto, Nugroho. *The Peta Army during the Japanese Occupation of Indonesia.* Tokyo: Waseda University Press, 1979.

Pusat Temaga Rakyat. *The Putera Reports: Problems in Indonesian-Japanese Wartime Cooperation.* Ithaca, N.Y.: Cornell University Press, 1971.

Reid, Anthony, and Oki Akira. *The Japanese Experience in Indonesia: Selected Memoirs of 1942–1945.* Athens: Center for International Studies, Ohio University, 1986.

Sato, Shigeru. *War, Nationalism, and Peasants: Java under the Japanese Occupation, 1942–1945.* Armonk, N.Y.: Sharpe, 1994.

Tantri, K'tut. *Revolt in Paradise.* New York: Harper, 1960.

Van der Post, Laurens. *The Admiral's Baby.* New York: Morrow, 1996.

N. NEW ZEALAND

Baker, John V. T. *The New Zealand People at War: War Economy.* Wellington: Historical Publications Branch, Department of Internal Affairs, 1965.

Bevan, Denys. *United States Forces in New Zealand, 1942–1945.* Alexandra, N.Z.: Macpherson, 1992.

Bioletti, Harry. *The Yanks Are Coming: The American Invasion of New Zealand, 1942–1944.* Auckland: Century Hutchinson, 1989.

Gillespie, Oliver A. *The Pacific.* Official History of New Zealand in the Second World War, 1939–45. Wellington: War History Branch, Department of Internal Affairs, 1952.

Larsen, Colin R. *Pacific Commandos: New Zealanders and Fijians in Action.* Wellington: Reed, 1946.

McGibbon, I. C. *Blue-Water Rationale: The Naval Defence of New Zealand, 1914–1942*. Wellington: Government Printer, 1981.

Rogers, Anna, ed. *The War Years: New Zealanders Remember, 1939–1945*. Wellington: Platform, 1989.

Taylor, Nancy. *The New Zealand People at War: The Home Front*. 2 vols. Wellington: Historical Publications Branch, 1986.

Trotter, Ann. *New Zealand and Japan, 1945–1952: The Occupation and the Peace Treaty*. Highlands, N.J.: Humanities, 1990.

Wood, F. L. W. *The New Zealand People at War: Political and External Affairs*. Wellington: War History Branch, Department of Internal Affairs, 1958.

O. PHILIPPINE ISLANDS

Baclagon, Uldarico S. *Filipino Heroes of World War II*. Manila: Argo, 1980.

Baclagon, Uldarico S. *The Philippine Resistance Movement against Japan, 10 December 1941–14 June 1945*. Manila: Munoz, 1966.

Hernandez, Juan B. *Not the Sword: A True Story of the Courageous People of the Philippines during the Japanese Occupation in World War II*. New York: Greenwich, 1959.

Kawashima, Midori. "The Records of the Former Japanese Army Concerning the Japanese Occupation of the Philippines." *Journal of Southeast Asian Studies* 27 (March 1996): 124–31.

Lear, Elmer. *The Japanese Occupation of the Philippines: Leyte, 1941–1945*. Ithaca, N.Y.: Cornell University, 1961.

Steinberg, David Joel. *Philippine Collaboration in World War II*. Ann Arbor: University of Michigan Press, 1967.

Syjuco, Ma. Felisa A. *The Kempei Tai in the Philippines, 1941–1945*. Quezon City, Philippines: New Day, 1988.

Volckmann, Russell W. *We Remained: Three Years Behind the Enemy Lines in the Philippines*. New York: Norton, 1954.

Willoughby, Charles A. *The Guerrilla Resistance Movement in the Philippines, 1941–1945*. New York: Vantage, 1972.

P. THAILAND

Aldrich, Richard J. *The Key to the South: Britain, the United States and Thailand during the Approach of the Pacific War, 1929–1942*. New York: Oxford University Press, 1993.

Brailey, Nigel J. *Thailand and the Fall of Singapore: A Frustrated Asian Revolution*. Boulder, Colo.: Westview, 1986.

Direk Chaiyanam. *Siam and World War II*. Ed. Jane Godfrey Keyes. Bangkok: Social Science Association of Thailand Press, 1978.

Haseman, John B. *The Thai Resistance Movement during the Second World War*. De Kalb: Center for Southeast Asian Studies, Northern Illinois University, 1978.

Reynolds, E. Bruce. *Thailand and Japan's Southern Advance, 1940–1945*. New York: St. Martin's, 1994.

Suwannathat-Pian, Kobkua. "Thai Wartime Leadership Reconsidered: Phibun and Pridi." *Journal of Southeast Asian Studies* 27 (March 1996): 166–78.

Wimon Wiriyawit. *Free Thai*. Bangkok: White Lotus, 1997.

Q. UNION OF SOVIET SOCIALIST REPUBLICS
[SEE ALSO III.B; XIX]

Beloff, Max. *Soviet Policy in the Far East, 1944–1951*. New York: Oxford University Press, 1953.

Conner, Albert Z., and Robert G. Poirier. *The Red Army Order of Battle in the Great Patriotic War*. Novato, Calif.: Presidio, 1985.

Fischer, Louis. *The Road to Yalta: Soviet Foreign Relations, 1941–1945*. New York: Harper & Row, 1972.

Glantz, David M. *Soviet Military Deception in the Second World War*. London: Cass, 1989.

Harrison, Mark. *Soviet Planning in Peace and War, 1938–1945*. New York: Cambridge University Press, 1985.

Larionov, V., et al. *World War II: Decisive Battles of the Soviet Army*. Trans. William Biley. Moscow: Progress, 1984.

Shtemenko, Sergei M. *The Soviet General Staff at War, 1941–1945*. Trans. Robert Daglish. Moscow: Progress, 1974.

Werth, Alexander. *Russia at War, 1941–1945*. New York: Dutton, 1964.

R. UNITED KINGDOM

Butler, James R. M., ed. *Grand Strategy*. 6 vols. History of the Second World War. London: HMSO, 1956–1976.

Donnison, F. S. V. *British Military Administration in the Far East, 1943–46*. History of the Second World War. London: HMSO, 1956.

Jefferys, Kevin. *The Churchill Coalition and Wartime Politics, 1940–45*. Manchester: Manchester University Press, 1991.

Kirby, S. Woodburn, ed. *The War Against Japan*. 5 vols. History of the Second World War. London: HMSO, 1957–1969. [Vol. 1: *The Loss of Singapore;* vol. 2: *India's Most Dangerous Hour;* vol. 3: *The Decisive Battles;* vol. 4: *The Reconquest of Burma;* vol. 5: *The Surrender of Japan*.]

Lewin, Ronald, ed. *The War on Land: The British Army in World War II*. New York: Morrow, 1970.

Nish, Ian, ed. *Anglo-Japanese Alienation, 1919–1952: Papers of the Anglo-Japanese Conference on the History of the Second World War*. New York: Cambridge University Press, 1982.

Smurthwaite, David, ed. *The Forgotten War: The British Army in the Far East*. London: National Army Museum, 1992.

Woodward, E. L. *British Foreign Policy in the Second World War*. 5 vols. London: HMSO, 1970–1976.

S. UNITED STATES [SEE ALSO IV.D.2]

1. General

Hess, Gary. *The United States' Emergence as a Southeast Asian Power, 1940–1950*. New York: Columbia University, 1987.

James, D. Clayton, and Anne Sharp Wells. *From Pearl Harbor to V-J Day: The American Armed Forces in World War II*. Chicago: Dee, 1995.

Kennett, Lee. *G.I.: The American Soldier in World War II*. New York: Scribner's, 1987.

Kimball, Warren. *America Unbound: World War II and the Making of a Super Power*. New York: St. Martin's, 1992.

Linderman, Gerald F. *The World Within War: America's Combat Experience in World War II*. New York: Free Press, 1997.

Maddox, Robert James. *The United States and World War II*. Boulder, Colo.: Westview, 1992.

Marshall, George C., et al. *The War Reports of General of the Army George C. Marshall, Chief of Staff; General of the Army Henry H. Arnold. Commanding General, Army Air Forces; and Fleet Admiral Ernest J. King, Commander-in-Chief, United States Fleet and Chief of Naval Operations*. Philadelphia: Lippincott, 1947.

O'Neill, William L. *A Democracy at War: America's Fight at Home and Abroad in World War II*. New York: Free Press, 1993.

Perret, Geoffrey. *There's a War to be Won: The United States Army in World War II*. New York: Random House, 1991.

2. Strategy and Planning

Brower, Charles F. "The Joint Chiefs of Staff and National Policy: American Strategy and the War with Japan, 1943–1945." Ph.D. dissertation, University of Pennsylvania, 1987.

Cline, Ray S. *Washington Command Post: The Operations Division.* USAWWII. Washington, D.C.: OCMH, Department of the Army, 1951.

Greenfield, Kent Roberts. *American Strategy in World War II: A Reconsideration.* Baltimore, Md.: Johns Hopkins University Press, 1963.

Hayes, Grace Person. *The History of the Joint Chiefs of Staff in World War II: The War against Japan.* Annapolis, Md.: Naval Institute Press, 1982.

Kirkpatrick, Charles E. *An Unknown Future and a Doubtful Present: Writing the Victory Plan of 1941.* Washington, D.C.: U.S. Army Center of Military History, 1990.

Lowenthal, Mark W. *Leadership and Indecision: American War Planning and Policy Process, 1937–1942.* 2 vols. New York: Garland, 1987.

Miller, Edward S. *War Plan Orange: The U.S. Strategy to Defeat Japan, 1897–1945.* Annapolis, Md.: Naval Institute Press, 1991.

Morgan, H. G. *Planning the Defeat of Japan.* Washington, D.C.: OCMH, Department of the Army, 1961.

Morison, Samuel Eliot. *Strategy and Compromise.* Boston: Little, Brown, 1958.

Morton, Louis. *Strategy and Command: The First Two Years.* USAWWII. Washington, D.C.: OCMH, Department of the Army, 1962.

Ross, Steven T. *American War Plans, 1941–1945: The Test of Battle.* Portland, Ore.: Frank Cass, 1997.

Ross, Steven T. *American War Plans, 1945–1950.* Portland, Ore.: Frank Cass, 1996.

Sherry, Michael S. *Preparing for the Next War: American Plans for Postwar Defense, 1941–1945.* New Haven, Conn.: Yale University Press, 1977.

Stoler, Mark A. "The 'Pacific First' Alternative in American World War II Strategy." *International History Review* 2 (July 1980): 432–52.

3. Foreign Relations

Cole, Wayne S. *Determinism and American Foreign Relations during the Franklin D. Roosevelt Era.* Lanham, Md.: University Press of America, 1995.

Cole, Wayne S. *America First: The Battle Against Intervention, 1940–1941.* Madison: University of Wisconsin Press, 1953.

Cole, Wayne S. *Roosevelt and the Isolationists, 1932–1945.* Lincoln: University of Nebraska Press, 1983.

Cole, Wayne S. *Charles A. Lindbergh and the Battle against American Intervention in World War II.* New York: Harcourt Brace Jovanovich, 1974.

Dallek, Robert. *Franklin D. Roosevelt and American Foreign Policy, 1932–1945.* New York: Oxford University Press, 1979.

Friedman, Donald J. *The Road from Isolation: The Campaign of the American Committee for Non-Participation in Japanese Aggression, 1938–1941.* Cambridge, Mass.: East Asian Research Center, Harvard University Press, 1968.

O'Connor, Raymond G. *Diplomacy for Victory: FDR and Unconditional Surrender.* New York: Norton, 1971.

Smith, Gaddis. *American Diplomacy during the Second World War, 1941–1945.* 2d ed. New York: Knopf, 1985.

4. Lend-Lease

Jones, Robert H. *The Roads to Russia: United States Lend-Lease to the Soviet Union.* Norman: University of Oklahoma Press, 1969.

Kimball, Warren. *The Most Unsordid Act: Lend Lease, 1939–1941.* Baltimore, Md.: Johns Hopkins University Press, 1969.

Stettinius, Edward R., Jr. *Lend-Lease: Weapon for Victory.* New York: Macmillan, 1944.

5. Economic and Manpower Mobilization

Clifford, J. Garry, and Samuel R. Spencer, Jr. *The First Peacetime Draft.* Lawrence: University Press of Kansas, 1986.

Flynn, George Q. *The Mess in Washington: Manpower Mobilization in World War II.* Westport, Conn.: Greenwood, 1979.

Foster, Mark S. *Henry J. Kaiser: Builder in the Modern American West.* Austin: University of Texas Press, 1989.

Hooks, Gregory. *Forging the Military-Industrial Complex: World War II's Battle of the Potomac.* Urbana: University of Illinois Press, 1991.

Lane, F. C. *Ships for Victory: A History of Shipbuilding under the United States Maritime Commission during World War II.* Baltimore, Md.: Johns Hopkins University Press, 1951.

Lichtenstein, Nelson. *Labor's War at Home: The CIO in World War II*. New York: Cambridge University Press, 1982.

Nelson, Donald. *Arsenal of Democracy: The Story of American War Production*. New York: Harcourt, Brace, 1946.

Sligh, Robert B. *The National Guard and National Defense: The Mobilization of the Guard in World War II*. Westport, Conn.: Praeger, 1992.

Vatter, Harold G. *The U.S. Economy in World War II*. New York: Columbia University Press, 1985.

White, Gerald T. *Billions for Defense: Government Financing by the Defense Plant Corporation during World War II*. University of Alabama Press, 1980.

Wrynn, V. Dennis. *Detroit Goes to War: The American Auto Industry in World War II*. Oceola, Wis.: Motorbooks International, 1993.

6. Home Front

Bailey, Ronald H. *The Home Front: U.S.A.* Alexandria, Va.: Time-Life Books, 1977.

Bennett, Michael. *When Dreams Came True: The GI Bill and the Making of Modern America*. Washington, D.C.: Brassey's, 1996.

Blum, John M. *V for Victory: Politics and American Culture during World War II*. New York: Harcourt Brace Jovanovich, 1976.

Brinkley, David. *Washington Goes to War*. New York: Knopf, 1988.

Hess, Gary R. *The United States at War, 1941–1945*. Arlington Heights, Ill.: Harlan Davidson, 1986.

Jeffries, John W. *Wartime America: The World War II Home Front*. Chicago: Dee, 1996.

Lingeman, Richard R. *Don't You Know There's a War On? The American Front, 1941–1945*. New York: Putnam, 1970.

Mix, Ann Bennett, and Susan Johnson Hadler, comp. *Lost in the Victory: Reflections of American War Orphans of World War II*. Denton: University of North Texas Press, 1998.

Perret, Geoffrey. *Days of Sadness, Years of Triumph: The American People, 1939–1945*. Madison: University of Wisconsin Press, 1985.

Polenberg, Richard. *War and Society: The United States, 1941–1945*. Philadelphia: Lippincott, 1972.

Winkler, Allan M. *Home Front USA: America during World War II*. Arlington Heights, Ill.: Harlan Davidson, 1986.

7. Hawaii

Allen, Gwenfread E. *Hawaii's War Years, 1941–1945*. Honolulu: University of Hawaii Press, 1950.

Anthony, J. Garner. *Hawaii Under Army Rule*. Stanford, Calif.: Stanford University Press, 1955.

Bailey, Beth L., and David Farber. *The First Strange Place: Race and Sex in World War II Hawaii*. Baltimore, Md.: Johns Hopkins University Press, 1994.

Miyamoto, Kazuo. *Hawaii: End of the Rainbow*. Japan: Bridgeway, 1964.

Ogawa, Dennis. Kodomo No Tame Ni: *For the Sake of the Children: The Japanese American Experience in Hawaii*. Honolulu: University of Hawaii Press, 1978.

Rodriggs, Lawrence R. *We Remember Pearl Harbor: Honolulu Civilians Recall the War Years, 1941–1945*. Newark, Calif.: Communications Concepts, 1991.

Stephan, John J. *Hawaii under the Rising Sun: Japan's Plans for Conquest after Pearl Harbor*. Honolulu: University of Hawaii Press, 1984.

8. Alaska and the Aleutian Islands [see also IX]

Chandonnet, Fern. *Alaska at War, 1941–1945: The Forgotten War Remembered*. Anchorage: Alaska at War Committee, 1995.

Kirtland, John C., and David F. Coffin, Jr. *The Relocation and Internment of the Aleuts during World War II*. Anchorage, Alaska: Aleutian/Pribilof Islands Association, 1981.

Kohlhoff, Dean. *When the Wind Was a River: Aleut Evacuation in World War II*. Seattle: University of Washington Press, 1995.

Marston, Muktuk. *Men of the Tundra: Eskimos at War*. New York: October House, 1969.

9. African Americans

Buchanan, A. Russell. *Black Americans in World War II*. Santa Barbara, Calif.: Clio, 1977.

Lee, Ulysses. *The Employment of Negro Troops*. USAWWII. Washington, D.C.: U.S. Army Center of Military History, 1966.

MacGregor, Morris J., Jr. *Integration of the Armed Forces, 1940–1965*. Washington, D.C.: U.S. Army Center of Military History, 1981.

McGuire, Phillip, ed. *Taps for a Jim Crow Army: Letters from Black Soldiers in World War II.* Lexington: University Press of Kentucky, 1993.

Motley, Mary Penick, ed. *The Invisible Soldier: The Experience of the Black Soldier, World War II.* Detroit, Mich.: Wayne State University Press, 1975.

Nalty, Bernard C. *Strength for the Fight: A History of Black Americans in the Military.* New York: Free Press, 1986.

Osur, Alan M. *Blacks in the Army Air Forces during World War II: The Problem of Race Relations.* Washington, D.C.: Office of Air Force History, 1977.

Putney, Martha S. *When the Nation Was in Need: Blacks in the Women's Army Corps during World War II.* Metuchen, N.J.: Scarecrow, 1992.

10. Japanese Americans [see also IV.S.7; VIII.E; XIV]

Crost, Lyn. *Honor by Fire: Japanese Americans at War in Europe and the Pacific.* Novato, Calif.: Presidio, 1994.

Wakamatsu, Jack K. *Silent Warriors: A Memoir of America's 442nd Regimental Combat Team.* New York: Vantage, 1995.

11. Native Americans [see also IV.S.8; VIII.D]

Bernstein, Alison R. *American Indians and World War II.* Norman: University of Oklahoma, 1991.

Franco, Jere. "Patriotism on Trial: Native Americans in World War II." Ph.D. dissertation, University of Arizona, 1990.

V. Military Battles, Operations, and Campaigns [see also VI; VII]

A. BEGINNING OF THE WAR WITH THE WEST

Beekman, Allan. *Crisis: The Japanese Attack on Pearl Harbor and Southeast Asia.* Honolulu: Heritage Press of Pacific, 1992.

Weintraub, Stanley. *Long Day's Journey into War: December 7, 1941.* New York: Dutton, 1991.

Wigmore, Lionel. *The Japanese Thrust.* Australia in the War of 1939–1945. Canberra: Australian War Memorial, 1957.

Young, Donald J. *First 24 Hours of War in the Pacific.* Shippensburg, Pa.: Burd Street, 1998.

B. ALEUTIAN ISLANDS AND NORTH PACIFIC

Bradley, Charles C. *Aleutian Echoes*. Fairbanks: University of Alaska Press, 1994.

Garfield, Brian. *The Thousand-Mile War: World War II in Alaska and the Aleutians*. Fairbanks: University of Alaska Press, 1995.

Gilman, William. *Our Hidden Front*. New York: Reynal & Hitchcock, 1944.

Lorelli, John A. *The Battle of the Komandorski Islands, March 1943*. Annapolis, Md.: Naval Institute Press, 1984.

Perras, Galen R. "Canada as a Military Partner: Alliance Politics and the Campaign to Recapture the Aleutian Island of Kiska." *Journal of Military History* 56 (July 1992): 423–54.

Rourke, Norman Edward. *War Comes to Alaska: The Dutch Harbor Attack, June 3–4, 1942*. Shippensburg, Pa.: Burd Street, 1997.

U.S. Naval Historical Center. *The Aleutians Campaign, June 1942–August 1943*. Washington, D.C.: Naval Historical Center, Department of the Navy, 1993.

U.S. Naval Historical Center. *U.S. Naval Experience in the North Pacific during World War II: Selected Documents*. Washington, D.C.: Naval Historical Center, Department of the Navy, 1989.

U.S. War Department. *The Capture of Attu: As Told by the Men Who Fought There*. Washington, D.C.: Infantry Journal, 1944.

C. ASIA: GENERAL [SEE ALSO IX]

Bhargava, Krishna Dayal, and Kasi N. Venkatasubba Sastri. *Campaigns in South-east Asia, 1941–42*. Delhi: Combined Inter-services Historical Section, India & Pakistan, 1960.

Fischer, Edward. *The Chancy War: Winning in China, Burma, and India in World War II*. New York: Crown, 1991.

Hager, Alice R. *Wings for the Dragon: The Air War in Asia*. New York: Dodd, Mead, 1945.

Moser, Don. *China-Burma-India*. Alexandria, Va.: Time-Life Books, 1978.

Romanus, Charles F., and Riley Sunderland. *Stilwell's Command Problems*. USAWWII. Washington, D.C.: OCMH, Department of the Army, 1956.

Romanus, Charles F., and Riley Sunderland. *Stilwell's Mission to China*. USAWWII. Washington, D.C.: OCMH, Department of the Army, 1953.

Romanus, Charles F., and Riley Sunderland. *Time Runs Out in CBI*. USAWWII. Washington, D.C.: OCMH, Department of the Army, 1959.

Sunderland, Riley, and Charles F. Romanus, eds. *Stilwell's Personal File–China, Burma, India, 1942–1944*. Wilmington, Del.: Scholarly Resources, 1976.

D. AUSTRALIA

Connaughton, R. M. *Shrouded Secrets: Japan's War on Mainland Australia, 1942–1944*. Washington, D.C.: Brassey's, 1994.

Hall, Timothy. *Darwin 1942: Australia's Darkest Hour*. Sydney: Methuen, 1980.

Jenkins, David. *Battle Surface: Japan's Submarine War against Australia 1942–44*. Sydney: Random House Australia, 1992.

Lind, Lew. *The Midget Submarine Attack on Sydney*. Garden Island, Australia: Bellrope, 1990.

Lind, Lew. *Toku-tai: Japanese Submarine Operations in Australian Waters*. Kenthurst, Australia: Kangaroo, 1992.

Lockwood, Douglas. *Australia's Pearl Harbour: Darwin, 1942*. Melbourne: Cassell Australia, 1966.

E. BISMARCK SEA, BATTLE OF

Cortesi, Lawrence. *Operation Bismarck Sea*. Canoga Park, Calif.: Major Books, 1977.

Graham, Burton. *None Shall Survive: The Graphic Story of the Annihilation of the Japanese Armada in the Bismarck Sea Battle*. Sydney: Johnston, 1946.

McAulay, Lex. *Battle of the Bismarck Sea*. New York: St. Martin's, 1991.

Tracy, Michael, Jeff Isaacs, and Irene Coombes. *The Battle of the Bismarck Sea: 50th Anniversary Commemoration*. Canberra: Australian Defence Force Journal, 1993.

F. BURMA AND INDIA [SEE ALSO V.C]

Allen, Louis. *Burma: The Longest War 1941–1945*. New York: St. Martin's, 1984.

Bidwell, Shelford. *The Chindit War: Stilwell, Wingate, and the Campaign in Burma, 1944*. New York: Macmillan, 1980.

Bjorge, Gary J. *Merrill's Marauders: Combined Operations in Northern Burma in 1944*. Fort Leavenworth, Kans.: Combat Studies Institute, U.S. Army and Command General Staff College, 1996.

Callahan, Raymond A. *Burma 1942–1945*. Newark: University of Delaware Press, 1979.

Campbell, Arthur F. *The Siege: A Story from Kohima*. London: Allen & Unwin, 1956.

Carew, Tim. *The Longest Retreat: The Burma Campaign, 1942*. London: Hamilton, 1969.

Carfrae, Charles. *Chindit Column*. London: Kimber, 1985.

Chandra, Anil. *Indian Army Triumphant in Burma: The Burmese Campaign, 1941–45*. Delhi: Atma Ram, 1984.

Colvin, John. *Not Ordinary Men: The Story of the Battle of Kohima*. London: Cooper, 1994.

Evans, Geoffrey C., and Antony Brett-James. *Imphal: A Flower on Lofty Heights*. New York: St. Martin's, 1962.

Fellowes-Gordon, Ian. *The Battle for Naw Seng's Kingdom: The Magic War; The Battle for North Burma*. New York: Scribner's, 1971.

Fergusson, Bernard. *Beyond the Chindwin*. London: Collins, 1945.

Franks, Norman L. R. *Hurricanes over the Arakan*. Wellingborough, England: Stephens, 1989.

James, Harold. *Across the Threshold of Battle: Behind Japanese Lines with Wingate's Chindits: Burma, 1943*. Sussex: Book Guild, 1993.

Lunt, James. *The Retreat from Burma: 1941–1942*. Newton Abbot, England: David & Charles, 1989.

Madan, N. N., and Bisheshwar Prasad *The Arakan Operations, 1942–1945*. Delhi: Combined Inter-Services Historical Section, India & Pakistan, 1954.

Matthews, Geoffrey F. *The Re-Conquest of Burma, 1943–1945*. Aldershot: Gale & Polden, 1966.

Ogburn, Charlton. *The Marauders*. New York: Harper, 1959.

Peers, William R., and Dean Brelis. *Behind the Burma Road: The Story of America's Most Successful Guerrilla Force*. Boston: Little, Brown, 1963.

Perrett, Bryan. *Tank Tracks to Rangoon: The Story of British Armour in Burma*. London: Hale, 1978.

Phillips, C. E. Lucas. *The Raiders of Arakan*. London: Heinemann, 1971.

Prasad, Sri Nandan, et al. *The Reconquest of Burma*. 2 vols. Calcutta: Combined Inter-Services Historical Section, India & Pakistan, 1958–1959.

Prasad, Bisheshwar, ed. *The Retreat from Burma, 1941–1942*. Delhi: Combined Inter-Services Historical Section, India & Pakistan, 1952.

Rooney, David. *Burma Victory: Imphal, Kohima, and the Chindit Issue, March 1944 to May 1945*. London: Arms & Armour, 1992.

Russell, Wilfrid W. *Forgotten Skies: The Story of the Air Forces in India and Burma*. London: Hutchinson, 1946.

Smith, E. D. *Battle for Burma*. New York: Holmes & Meier, 1979.

Swinson, Arthur. *The Battle of Kohima*. New York: Stein & Day, 1967.

Turnbull, Patrick. *The Battle of the Box*. London: Allan, 1979.

G. CENTRAL PACIFIC: GENERAL

Alexander, Joseph H. *Storm Landings: Epic Amphibious Battles in the Central Pacific*. Annapolis, Md.: Naval Institute Press, 1997.

Denfeld, D. Colt. *Japanese Fortifications and Other Military Structures in the Central Pacific*. Saipan: Division of Historic Preservation, 1992.

Sherrod, Robert. *On to Westward: War in the Central Pacific*. New York: Duell, Sloan & Pearce, 1945.

Sledge, E. B. *With the Old Breed, at Peleliu and Okinawa*. Novato, Calif.: Presidio, 1981.

Wheeler, Keith. *The Road to Tokyo*. Alexandria, Va.: Time-Life Books, 1979.

H. CHANGKUFENG

Coox, Alvin D. *The Anatomy of a Small War: The Soviet-Japanese Struggle for Changkufeng-Khasan, 1938*. Westport, Conn.: Greenwood, 1977.

Kikuoka, Michael T. *The Changkufeng Incident: A Study in Soviet-Japanese Conflict, 1938*. Lanham, Md.: University Press of America, 1988.

I. CHINA [SEE ALSO V.C; V.V]

Boyle, John H. *China and Japan at War 1937–1945: The Politics of Collaboration*. Stanford, Calif.: Stanford University Press, 1972.

Chang, Iris. *The Rape of Nanking: The Forgotten Holocaust of World War II*. New York: Basic Books, 1997.

Cornelius, Wanda, and Thayne Short. *Ding Hao: America's Air War in China, 1937–1945*. Gretna, La.: Pelican, 1980.

Dorn, Frank. *The Sino-Japanese War, 1937–41: From Marco Polo Bridge to Pearl Harbor*. New York: Macmillan, 1974.

Ford, Daniel. *Flying Tigers: Claire Chennault and the American Volunteer Group*. Washington, D.C.: Smithsonian, 1991.

Hotz, Robert B. *With General Chennault: the Story of the Flying Tigers*. New York: Coward-McCann, 1943.

Hsiung, James C., and Steven I. Levine, eds. *China's Bitter Victory: The War with Japan, 1937–1945*. Armonk, N.Y.: Sharpe, 1992.

Hsu Long-Hsuen and Chang Ming-Kai, comps. *History of the Sino-Japanese War, 1937–1945*. Taipei: Chung Wu, 1985.

Hu Pu-Yu. *A Brief History of the Sino-Japanese War (1937–1945)*. Taipei, Taiwan: Chung Wu, 1974.

Li, Lincoln. *The Japanese Army in North China, 1937–1941: Problems of Political and Economic Control*. New York: Oxford University Press, 1975.

Lindsay, Michael. *The Unknown War: North China, 1937–1945*. London: Bergstrom & Boyle Books, 1975.

Liu, F. F. *A Military History of Modern China, 1924–1949*. Princeton, N.J.: Princeton University Press, 1956.

White, John Alexander. *The United States Marines in North China*. Millbrae, Calif.: White, 1974.

Wilson, Dick. *When Tigers Fight: The Story of the Sino-Japanese War, 1937–1945*. New York: Viking, 1982.

J. CORAL SEA, BATTLE OF

Australian National Maritime Museum. *The Battle of the Coral Sea 1942: Conference Proceedings, 7–10 May 1992*. Sydney: The Museum, 1993.

Johnston, Stanley. *Queen of the Flat-tops: the U.S.S. Lexington and the Coral Sea Battle*. New York: Dutton, 1942.

Millot, Bernard. *The Battle of the Coral Sea*. Trans. S. V. Whitley. Annapolis, Md.: Naval Institute Press, 1974.

K. DOOLITTLE RAID ON TOKYO

Glines, Carroll V. *Doolittle's Tokyo Raiders*. Princeton, N.J.: Van Nostrand, 1964.

Merrill, James M. *Target Tokyo: The Halsey-Doolittle Raid*. Chicago: Rand-McNally, 1964.

Schultz, Duane P. *The Doolittle Raid*. New York: St. Martin's, 1988.

L. EAST INDIES

Frei, Henry. "Japan's Reluctant Decision to Occupy Portuguese Timor, 1 January 1942–20 February 1942." *Australian Historical Studies* 108 (April 1997): 281–302.

Jacobs, G. F. *Prelude to the Monsoon: Assignment in Sumatra.* Philadelphia: University of Pennsylvania Press, 1982.

Kelly, Terence. *Battle for Palembang.* London: Hale, 1985.

Schultz, Duane. *The Last Battle Station: The Story of the U.S.S. Houston.* New York: St. Martin's, 1985.

Stanley, Peter. *Tarakan: An Australian Tragedy.* St. Leonards, Australia: Allen & Unwin, 1997.

Tarling, Nicholas. "Britain, Portugal and East Timor in 1941." *Journal of Southeast Asian Studies* 27 (March 1996): 132–38.

Thomas, David A. *Battle of the Java Sea.* New York: Stein & Day, 1968.

Van Oosten, F. C. *The Battle of the Java Sea.* Annapolis, Md.: Naval Institute Press, 1976.

Waters, Gary. *Oboe: Air Operations over Borneo, 1945.* Canberra: Air Power Studies Centre, 1995.

Winslow, Walter G. *The Ghost That Died at Sunda Strait.* Annapolis, Md.: Naval Institute Press, 1984.

M. GILBERT ISLANDS

Alexander, Joseph H. *Utmost Savagery: The Three Days of Tarawa.* Annapolis, Md.: Naval Institute Press, 1995.

Crowl, Philip A., and Edmund G. Love. *Seizure of the Gilberts and Marshalls.* USAWWII. Washington, D.C.: OCMH, Department of the Army, 1955.

Russ, Martin. *Line of Departure: Tarawa.* Garden City, N.Y.: Doubleday, 1975.

Shaw, Henry I., Jr. *Tarawa: A Legend Is Born.* New York: Ballantine, 1968.

Sherrod, Robert. *Tarawa: The Story of a Battle.* New York: Duell, Sloan, & Pearce, 1954.

Stockman, James R. *The Battle for Tarawa.* Washington, D.C.: Marine Corps Historical Section, 1947.

N. HONG KONG

Brown, Wenzell. *Hong Kong Aftermath.* New York: Smith & Durrell, 1943.

Carew, Tim. *Fall of Hong Kong.* London: Blond, 1960.

Ferguson, Ted. *Desperate Siege: The Battle of Hong Kong.* Garden City, N.Y.: Doubleday, 1980.

Vincent, Carl. *No Reason Why: The Canadian Hong Kong Tragedy, an Examination.* Stittsville: Canada's Wings, 1981.

O. INDIAN OCEAN [SEE ALSO V.T]

Leasor, James. *Boarding Party.* Boston: Houghton Mifflin, 1979.

Skidmore, Ian. *Escape from Singapore, 1942: The Story of an Incredible Voyage through Enemy Waters.* New York: Scribner's, 1974.

Tomlinson, Michael. *The Most Dangerous Moment.* London: Kimber, 1976.

Turner, Leonard D. F. *War in the Southern Oceans, 1939–1945.* Cape Town: Oxford University Press, 1961.

Winton, John. *Sink the Haguro! The Last Destroyer Action of the Second World War.* London: Seeley, 1979.

P. *INDIANAPOLIS,* SINKING OF

Helm, Thomas. *Ordeal by Sea: The Tragedy of the U.S.S. Indianapolis.* New York: Dodd, Mead, 1963.

Kurzman, Dan. *Fatal Voyage: The Sinking of the U.S.S. Indianapolis.* New York: Atheneum, 1990.

Newcomb, Richard F. *Abandon Ship! Death of the U.S.S. Indianapolis.* Bloomington: Indiana University Press, 1976.

Q. IWO JIMA

Albee, Bishop Parker, Jr., and Keller Cushing Freeman. *Shadow of Suribachi: Raising the Flags on Iwo Jima.* Westport, Conn.: Praeger, 1995.

Bartley, Whitman S. *Iwo Jima: Amphibious Epic.* Washington, D.C.: Marine Corps Historical Branch, 1954.

Marling, Karal A., and John Wetenhall. *Iwo Jima: Monuments, Memories, and the American Hero.* Cambridge, Mass.: Harvard University Press, 1991.

Morehouse, Clifford P. *The Iwo Jima Operation.* Washington, D.C.: Marine Corps Historical Division, 1946.

Newcomb, Richard F. *Iwo Jima.* New York: Holt, Rinehart & Winston, 1965.

Ross, Bill D. *Iwo Jima: Legacy of Valor.* New York: Vanguard, 1985.

Wheeler, Richard. *Iwo*. New York: Lippincott & Crowell, 1980.

R. KURILE ISLANDS

Gallicchio, Marc. "The Kuriles Controversy: U.S. Diplomacy in the Soviet-Japan Border Dispute, 1941–1956." *Pacific Historical Review* 60 (February 1991): 69–101.

Perras, Galen Roger. "Eyes on the Northern Route to Japan: Plans for Canadian Participation in an Invasion of the Kurile Islands—A Study in Coalition Warfare and Civil-Military Relationship." *War and Society* 8 (May 1990): 100–17.

Rees, David. *The Soviet Seizure of the Kuriles*. New York: Praeger, 1985.

Stephan, John. *The Kuril Islands: Russo-Japanese Frontier in the Pacific*. Oxford: Clarendon, 1974.

S. LEYTE GULF, BATTLE FOR [SEE ALSO V.FF]

Cutler, Thomas J. *The Battle of Leyte Gulf, 23–26 October 1944*. New York: HarperCollins, 1994.

Field, James A. *The Japanese at Leyte Gulf: The Sho-Operation*. Princeton, N.J.: Princeton University Press, 1947.

Solberg, Carl. *Decision and Dissent: With Halsey at Leyte Gulf*. Annapolis, Md.: Naval Institute Press, 1995.

Stewart, Adrian. *The Battle of Leyte Gulf*. New York: Scribner's, 1980.

Woodward, C. Van. *The Battle for Leyte Gulf*. New York: Macmillan, 1947.

Yoshimura, Akira. *Build the Musashi!: The Birth and Death of the World's Greatest Battleship*. New York: Kodansha International, 1991.

T. MADAGASCAR

Buckley, Christopher. *Five Ventures: Iraq, Syria, Persia, Madagascar, Dodecanese*. London: HMSO, 1954.

Brown, James Ambrose. *Eagles Strike: The Campaigns of the South African Air Force in Egypt, Cyrenaica, Libya, Tunisia, Tripolitania and Madagascar, 1941–1943*. Cape Town: Purnell, 1974.

Croft-Cooke, Rupert. *The Blood-red Island*. London: Staples, 1953.

Gandar Dower, Kenneth Cecil. *Into Madagascar*. New York: Penguin, 1943.

Rosenthal, Eric. *Japan's Bid for Africa, Including the Story of the Madagascar Campaign*. Johannesburg: Central News Agency, 1944.

Shores, Christopher F. *Dust Clouds in the Middle East: The Air War for East Africa, Iraq, Syria, Iran, and Madagascar, 1940–42*. London: Grub Street, 1996.

U. MALAY PENINSULA AND SINGAPORE

Allen, Louis. *Singapore 1941–1942*. Newark: University of Delaware Press, 1979.

Attiwill, Kenneth. *Fortress: The Story of the Siege and Fall of Singapore*. Garden City, N.Y.: Doubleday, 1960.

Barber, Noel A. *Sinister Twilight: The Fall of Singapore, 1942*. Boston: Houghton Mifflin, 1968.

Callahan, Raymond A. *The Worst Disaster: The Fall of Singapore*. Cranbury, N.J.: University of Delaware Press, 1977.

Chapman, F. Spencer. *The Jungle is Neutral*. New York: Norton, 1949.

Elphick, Peter. *Singapore: The Pregnable Fortress: A Study in Deception, Discord and Desertion*. London: Hodder & Stoughton, 1995.

Falk, Stanley L. *Seventy Days to Singapore: The Malayan Campaign, 1941–1942*. New York: Putnam, 1975.

Glover, Edwin M. *In 70 Days: The Story of the Japanese Campaign in British Malaya*. London: Muller, 1949.

Grenfell, Russell. *Main Fleet to Singapore*. London: Faber & Faber, 1951.

Hall, Timothy. *The Fall of Singapore*. North Ryde: Methuen Australia, 1983.

Kennedy, Joseph. *When Singapore Fell: Evacuations and Escapes, 1941–42*. New York: St. Martin's, 1989.

Keogh, E. G. *Malaya, 1941–1942*. Melbourne: Directorate of Military Training, 1961.

Kinvig, Clifford. *Scapegoat: General Percival of Singapore*. Washington, D.C.: Brassey's, 1996.

Kirby, S. Woodburn. *Singapore: The Chain of Disaster*. New York: Macmillan, 1971.

Leasor, James. *Singapore: The Battle That Changed the World*. Garden City, N.Y.: Doubleday, 1968.

MacIntyre, W. David. *The Rise and Fall of the Singapore Naval Base 1919–1942*. Hamden, Conn.: Archon, 1979.

Middlebrook, Martin, and Patrick Mahoney. *Battleship: The Sinking of the Prince of Wales and the Repulse*. New York: Scribner's, 1977.

Neidpath, James. *The Singapore Naval Base and the Defence of Britain's Eastern Empire, 1919–1941*. New York: Oxford University Press, 1981.

Simson, Ivan. *Singapore: Too Little, Too Late; Some Aspects of the Malayan Disaster in 1942*. London: Cooper, 1970.

Smyth, John. *Percival and the Tragedy of Singapore*. London: Macdonald, 1971.

Swinson, Arthur. *Defeat in Malaya and the Fall of Singapore*. New York: Ballantine, 1970.

Tsuji, Masanobu. *Singapore, 1941–1942: The Japanese Version*. New York: St. Martin's, 1961.

Uhr, Janet. *Against the Sun: The AIF in Malaya, 1941–1942*. St. Leonards, Australia: Allen & Unwin, 1998.

V. MANCHURIA, 1945

Drea, Edward J. "Missing Intentions: Japanese Intelligence and the Soviet Invasion of Manchuria, 1945." *Military Affairs* 48 (April 1984): 66–73.

Dzirkals, Lilita I. *"Lightning War" in Manchuria: Soviet Military Analysis of the 1945 Far East Campaign*. Santa Monica, Calif.: Rand, 1976.

Garthoff, Raymond L. "Soviet Operations in the War with Japan, August 1945." *U.S. Naval Institute Proceedings* 92 (May 1966): 50–63.

Glantz, David M. *August Storm: Soviet Tactical and Operational Combat in Manchuria, 1945*. Fort Leavenworth, Kans.: Combat Studies Institute, U.S. Army Command and General Staff College, 1983.

Glantz, David M. *August Storm: The Soviet 1945 Strategic Offensive in Manchuria*. Fort Leavenworth, Kans.: Combat Studies Institute, U.S. Army Command and General Staff College, 1983.

W. MARIANA ISLANDS

Crowl, Philip A. *Campaign in the Marianas*. USAWWII. Washington, D.C.: OCMH, Department of the Army, 1960.

Denfeld, D. Colt. *Hold the Marianas: The Japanese Defense of the Mariana Islands*. Shippensburg, Pa.: White Mane, 1996.

Gailey, Harry. *Howlin' Mad vs. the Army: Conflict in Command, Saipan, 1944*. Novato, Calif.: Presidio, 1986.

Gailey, Harry. *The Liberation of Guam, 21 July–19 August 1944*. Novato, Calif.: Presidio, 1988.

Hoffman, Carl W. *Saipan: The Beginning of the End.* Washington, D.C.: Marine Corps Historical Division, 1950.

Hoffman, Carl W. *The Seizure of Tinian.* Washington, D.C.: Marine Corps Historical Division, 1951.

Hoyt, Edwin P. *To the Marianas.* New York: Van Nostrand Reinhold, 1980.

Lodge, Orlan Robert. *The Recapture of Guam.* Washington, D.C.: Marine Corps Historical Branch, 1954.

X. MARSHALL ISLANDS [SEE ALSO V.M]

Bailey, Dan E. *WWII Wrecks of the Kwajalein and Truk Lagoons.* Redding, Calif.: North Valley Diver Publications, 1982.

Heinl, Robert D., Jr., and John A. Crown. *The Marshalls: Increasing the Tempo.* Washington, D.C.: Marine Corps Historical Branch, 1954.

Y. MIDWAY, BATTLE OF

Barker, A. J. *Midway: The Turning Point.* New York: Ballantine, 1971.

Fuchida, Mitsuo, and Masatake Okumiya. *Midway: The Battle That Doomed Japan.* Annapolis, Md.: U.S. Naval Institute, 1955.

Gay, George H. *Sole Survivor: The Battle of Midway and Its Effects on His Life.* Naples, Fla.: Midway, 1980.

Hough, Richard. *The Battle of Midway.* New York: Macmillan, 1970.

Lord, Walter. *Incredible Victory.* New York: Harper & Row, 1967.

Prange, Gordon W., Donald M. Goldstein, and Katherine V. Dillon. *Miracle at Midway.* New York, McGraw-Hill, 1982.

Smith, William W. *Midway: Turning Point of the Pacific.* New York: Crowell, 1966.

Tuleja, Thaddeus. *Climax at Midway.* New York: Norton, 1960.

Z. NEW GUINEA [SEE ALSO V.II]

Baker, Clive. *Milne Bay 1942.* Loftus, Australia: Baker-Knight, 1991.

Brune, Peter. *The Spell Broken: Exploding the Myth of Japanese Invincibility: Milne Bay to Buna-Sanananda, 1942–1943.* St. Leonards, Australia: Allen & Unwin, 1998.

Dexter, David. *The New Guinea Offensives.* Australia in the War of 1939–1945. Canberra: Australian War Memorial, 1961.

Drea, Edward J. *Defending the Driniumor: Covering Force Operations in New Guinea, 1944.* Fort Leavenworth, Kans.: Combat Studies Institute, U.S. Army Command and General Staff College, 1984.

Graham, Burton, and Frank Smyth. *A Nation Grew Wings: The Graphic Story of the Australian-Built Beauforts of the Royal Australian Air Force in New Guinea.* Melbourne: Winterset House, 1946.

Hall, Timothy. *New Guinea, 1942–44.* Sydney: Methuen, 1981.

McAulay, Lex. *To the Bitter End: The Japanese Defeat at Buna and Gona, 1942–43.* Milsons Point: Random House Australia, 1992.

McCarthy, Dudley. *South-West Pacific Area—First Year: Kokoda to Wau.* Australia in the War of 1939–1945. Canberra: Australian War Memorial, 1959.

Mayo, Lida. *Bloody Buna: The Campaign that Halted the Japanese Invasion of Australia.* Garden City, N.Y.: Doubleday, 1974.

Milner, Samuel. *Victory in Papua.* USAWWII. Washington, D.C.: OCMH, Department of the Army, 1957.

Paull, Raymond. *Retreat from Kokoda: The Australian Campaign in New Guinea.* London: Heinemann, 1958.

Riegelman, Harold. *The Caves of Biak.* New York: Dial, 1955.

Taaffe, Stephen R. *MacArthur's Jungle War: The 1944 New Guinea Campaign.* Lawrence: University Press of Kansas, 1998.

Tanaka, Kengoro. *Operations of the Imperial Japanese Armed Forces in Papua New Guinea Theater during World War II.* Tokyo: Japan-Papua New Guinea Goodwill Society, 1980.

AA. NOMONHAN

Coox, Alvin D. *Nomonhan: Japan against Russia, 1939.* 2 vols. Stanford, Calif.: Stanford University Press, 1985.

Drea, Edward J. *Nomonhan: Japanese-Soviet Tactical Combat, 1939.* Fort Leavenworth, Kans.: Combat Studies Institute, U.S. Army Command and General Staff College, 1981.

BB. OKINAWA [SEE ALSO V.LL]

Appleman, Roy E., et al. *Okinawa: The Last Battle.* USAWWII. Washington, D.C.: Historical Division, Department of the Army, 1948.

Astor, Gerald. *Operation Iceberg: The Invasion and Conquest of Okinawa in World War II.* New York: Fine, 1995.

Belote, James, and William Belote. *Typhoon of Steel: The Battle for Okinawa.* New York: Harper & Row, 1970.

Feifer, George. *Tennozan: The Battle of Okinawa and the Atomic Bomb.* New York: Ticknor & Fields, 1992.

Foster, Simon. *Okinawa 1945: Final Assault on the Empire.* London: Arms & Armour, 1994.

Frank, Benis. *Okinawa*. New York: Elsevier-Dutton, 1978.

Gow, Ian T. *Okinawa 1945: Gateway to Japan*. Garden City, N.Y.: Doubleday, 1985.

Hallas, James H. *Killing Ground on Okinawa: The Battle for Sugar Loaf Hill*. Westport, Conn.: Praeger, 1996.

Huber, Thomas M. *Japan's Battle of Okinawa, April–June 1945*. Fort Leavenworth, Kans.: Combat Studies Institute, U.S. Army Command and General Staff College, 1991.

Leckie, Robert. *Okinawa: The Last Battle of World War II*. New York: Viking, 1995.

Nichols, Charles S., and Henry I. Shaw. *Okinawa: Victory in the Pacific*. Washington, D.C.: Marine Corps Historical Branch, 1955.

Thurman, Paul. *Picket Ships at Okinawa*. New York: Carlton, 1996.

Yahara, Hiromichi. *The Battle for Okinawa*. Trans. Roger Pineau and Masatoshi Uehara. New York: Wiley, 1995.

CC. PALAU ISLANDS

Denfeld, H. Colt. *Peleliu Revisited: An Historical and Archaelogical Survey of World War II Sites on Peleliu Island*. Saipan: Micronesian Archaelogical Survey, 1988.

Falk, Stanley L. *Bloodiest Victory: Palaus*. New York: Ballantine, 1974.

Funasaka, Hiroshi. *Falling Blossoms*. Trans. Hiroshi Funasaka and Jeffery D. Rubin. Singapore: Times Books International, 1986.

Gailey, Harry. *Peleliu 1944*. Annapolis, Md.: Nautical & Aviation Pub. Co. of America, 1983.

Hallas, James H. *The Devil's Anvil: The Assault on Peleliu*. Westport, Conn.: Praeger, 1994.

Hough, Frank O. *The Assault on Peleliu*. Washington, D.C.: Marine Corps Historical Division, 1950.

Ross, Bill D. *Peleliu: Tragic Triumph*. New York: Random House, 1991.

DD. PEARL HARBOR [SEE ALSO II; V.A; VIII]

Albright, Harry. *Pearl Harbor: Japan's Fatal Blunder: The True Story Behind Japan's Attack on December 7, 1941*. New York: Hippocrene, 1988.

Beekman, Allan. *The Niihau Incident: The True Story of the Japanese Fighter Pilot Who, after the Pearl Harbor Attack, Crash-Landed on the Hawaiian Island of Niihau and Terrorized the Residents*. Honolulu: Heritage Press of Pacific, 1982.

Clarke, Thurston. *Pearl Harbor Ghosts.* New York: Morrow, 1991.

Clausen, Henry C., and Bruce Lee. *Pearl Harbor: Final Judgement.* New York: Crown, 1992.

Conroy, Hilary, and Harry Wray, eds. *Pearl Harbor Reexamined: Prologue to the Pacific War.* Honolulu: University of Hawaii Press, 1990.

Costello, John. *Days of Infamy: MacArthur, Roosevelt, Churchill, The Shocking Truth Revealed: How Their Secret Deals and Strategic Blunders Caused Disasters at Pearl Harbor and the Philippines.* New York: Pocket, 1994.

Goldstein, Donald, and Katherine Dillon, eds. *The Pearl Harbor Papers: Inside the Japanese Plans.* Washington, D.C.: Brassey's, 1993.

Honan, William H. *Visions of Infamy: The Untold Story of How Journalist Hector C. Bywater Devised the Plans that Led to Pearl Harbor.* New York: St. Martin's, 1991.

Kahn, David. "The Intelligence Failure of Pearl Harbor." *Foreign Affairs* 70 (Winter 1991–1992): 138–52.

Kahn, David. "Why Weren't We Warned?" *MHQ: The Quarterly Journal of Military History* 4 (Autumn 1991): 50–59.

La Forte, Robert S., and Ronald E. Marcello, eds. *Remembering Pearl Harbor: Eyewitness Accounts by U.S. Military Men and Women.* Wilmington, Del.: Scholarly Resources, 1991.

Lord, Walter. *Day of Infamy.* New York: Holt, 1957.

Melosi, Martin V. *The Shadow of Pearl Harbor: Political Controversy Over the Surprise Attack, 1941–1946.* College Station: Texas A&M University Press, 1977.

Millis, Walter. *This Is Pearl!* New York: Morrow, 1947.

Prange, Gordon W. *At Dawn We Slept: The Untold Story of Pearl Harbor.* New York: McGraw-Hill, 1981.

Prange, Gordon W. *God's Samurai: Lead Pilot at Pearl Harbor.* Washington, D.C.: Brassey's, 1990.

Prange, Gordon W. *Pearl Harbor: The Verdict of History.* New York: McGraw-Hill, 1986.

Raymer, Edward C. *Descent into Darkness: Pearl Harbor, 1941.* Novato, Calif.: Presidio, 1996.

Rusbridger, James, and Eric Nave. *Betrayal at Pearl Harbor: How Churchill Lured Roosevelt into World War II.* New York: Summit, 1991.

Sakamaki, Kazuo, and Toru Matsumoto. *I Attacked Pearl Harbor.* New York: Association Press, 1949.

Smith, Stanley H., comp. *Investigations of the Attack on Pearl Harbor: Index to Government Hearings*. Westport, Conn.: Greenwood, 1990.

Stillwell, Paul. *Battleship Arizona: An Illustrated History*. Annapolis, Md.: Naval Institute Press, 1991.

Toland, John. *Infamy: Pearl Harbor and Its Aftermath*. Garden City, N.Y.: Doubleday, 1982.

Wallin, Homer N. *Pearl Harbor: Why, How, Fleet Salvage and Final Appraisal*. Washington, D.C.: Naval Historical Division, 1968.

Wohlstetter, Roberta. *Pearl Harbor: Warning and Decision*. Stanford, Calif.: Stanford University, 1962.

EE. PHILIPPINE ISLANDS, 1941–1942

Bartsch, William H. *Doomed at the Start: American Pursuit Pilots in the Philippines, 1941–1942*. College Station: Texas A&M University Press, 1992.

Beck, John Jacob. *MacArthur and Wainwright: Sacrifice of the Philippines*. Albuquerque: University of New Mexico Press, 1974.

Belote, James H., and William M. Belote. *Corregidor: The Saga of a Fortress*. New York: Harper & Row, 1967.

Ind, Allison. *Bataan: The Judgment Seat: The Saga of the Philippines Command and the U.S. Army Air Forces, May 1941 to May 1942*. New York: Macmillan, 1944.

Morris, Eric. *Corregidor: The End of the Line*. New York: Stein, 1982.

Morton, Louis. *The Fall of the Philippines*. USAWWII. Washington, D.C.: OCMH, Department of the Army, 1953.

Underbrink, Robert L. *Destination Corregidor*. Annapolis, Md.: Naval Institute Press, 1971.

Whitman, John W. *Bataan: Our Last Ditch: The Bataan Campaign, 1942*. New York: Hippocrene, 1990.

Young, Donald J. *The Battle of Bataan: A History of the 90 Day Siege and Eventual Surrender of 75,000 Filipino and United States Troops to the Japanese in World War II*. Jefferson, N.C.: McFarland, 1992.

FF. PHILIPPINE ISLANDS, 1944-1945 [SEE ALSO V.S]

Cannon, M. Hamlin. *Leyte: The Return to the Philippines*. USAWWII. Washington, D.C.: OCMH, Department of the Army, 1954.

Connaughton, R. M., John Pimlott, and Duncan Anderson. *The Battle for Manila*. Novato, Calif.: Presidio, 1995.

Falk, Stanley L. *Decision at Leyte*. New York: Norton, 1966.

Flanagan, E. M., Jr. *Corregidor: The Rock Force Assault, 1945*. Novato, Calif.: Presidio, 1988.

Ogawa, Tetsuro. *Terraced Hell: A Japanese Memoir of Defeat & Death in Northern Luzon, Philippines*. Rutland, Vt.: Tuttle, 1972.

Owens, William A. *Eye-Deep in Hell: A Memoir of the Liberation of the Philippines, 1944–1945*. College Station: Texas A&M University Press, 1989.

Smith, Robert R. *The Approach to the Philippines*. USAWWII. Washington, D.C.: OCMH, Department of the Army, 1953.

Smith, Robert R. *Triumph in the Philippines*. USAWWII. Washington, D.C.: OCMH, Department of the Army, 1963.

Steinberg, Rafael. *Return to the Philippines*. Alexandria, Va.: Time-Life Books, 1979.

GG. PHILIPPINE SEA, BATTLE OF

Dickson, W. D. *The Battle of the Philippine Sea, June 1944*. London: Allan, 1975.

Lockwood, Charles A., and Hans C. Adamson. *Battles of the Philippine Sea*. New York: Crowell, 1967.

Y'Blood, William T. *Red Sun Setting: The Battle of the Philippine Sea*. Annapolis, Md.: Naval Institute Press, 1980.

HH. SOLOMON ISLANDS (INCLUDING GUADALCANAL)
   [SEE ALSO V.II; VIII.C]

Ballard, Robert D. *The Lost Ships of Guadalcanal*. New York: Warner/Madison, 1993.

Coggins, Jack. *The Campaign for Guadalcanal*. Garden City, N.Y.: Doubleday, 1972.

Cook, Charles. *The Battle of Cape Esperance: Strategic Encounter at Guadalcanal*. New York: Crowell, 1968.

Coombe, Jack D. *Derailing the Tokyo Express: The Naval Battles for the Solomon Islands That Sealed Japan's Fate*. Harrisburg, Pa.: Stackpole, 1991.

Frank, Richard B. *Guadalcanal*. New York: Random House, 1990.

Gailey, Harry A. *Bougainville: The Forgotten Campaign, 1943–1945*. Lexington: University Press of Kentucky, 1991.

Gamble, Bruce D. *The Black Sheep: The Definitive Account of Marine Fighting Squadron 214 in World War II*. Novato, Calif.: Presidio, 1998.

Griffith, Samuel B. *The Battle for Guadalcanal*. Philadelphia: Lippincott, 1963.

Hammel, Eric M. *Guadalcanal: The Carrier Battles: Carrier Operations in the Solomons, August–October 1942*. New York: Crown, 1987.

Hammel, Eric M. *Guadalcanal: Decision at Sea: The Naval Battle of Guadalcanal, November 13–15, 1942*. New York: Crown, 1998.

Hammel, Eric M. *Munda Trail: The New Georgia Campaign*. New York: Orion, 1989.

Horton, D. C. *New Georgia: Pattern for Victory*. New York: Ballantine, 1971.

Kent, Graeme. *Guadalcanal: Island Ordeal*. New York: Ballantine, 1971.

Koburger, Charles W. *Pacific Turning Point: the Solomons Campaign, 1942–1943*. Westport, Conn.: Praeger, 1995.

Leckie, Robert. *Challenge for the Pacific: Guadalcanal, the Turning Point of the War*. Garden City, N.Y.: Doubleday, 1965.

Lundstrom, John B. *The First Team and the Guadalcanal Campaign: Naval Fighter Combat from August to November 1942*. Annapolis, Md.: Naval Institute Press, 1994.

Medcalf, Peter. *War in the Shadows: Bougainville, 1944–45*. Sydney: Collins Australia, 1989.

Miller, John, Jr. *Guadalcanal: The First Offensive*. USAWWII. Washington, D.C.: Historical Division, Department of the Army, 1949.

Miller, Thomas G. *The Cactus Air Force*. New York: Harper & Row, 1969.

Newcomb, Richard F. *Savo: The Incredible Naval Debacle Off Guadalcanal*. New York: Holt, Rinehart, Winston, 1961.

Piper, Robert K. "The Royal Australian Air Force at Guadalcanal." *Defence Force Journal* 87 (March–April 1991): 27–34.

Rentz, John N. *Bougainville and the Northern Solomons*. Washington, D.C.: Marine Corps Historical Branch, 1948.

Rentz, John N. *Marines in the Central Solomons*. Washington, D.C.: Marine Corps Historical Branch, 1952.

Stewart, Adrian. *Guadalcanal: World War II's Fiercest Naval Campaign*. London: Kimber, 1985.

Tregaskis, Richard. *Guadalcanal Diary*. New York: Random House, 1943.

Twining, Merrill B. *No Bended Knee: The Battle for Guadalcanal*. Novato, Calif.: Presidio, 1996.

Walton, Frank E. *Once They Were Eagles: The Men of the Black Sheep Squadron*. Lexington: University Press of Kentucky, 1986.

Warner, Denis, and Peggy Warner. *Disaster in the Pacific: New Light on the Battle of Savo Island*. Annapolis, Md.: Naval Institute Press, 1992.

Zimmerman, John L. *The Guadalcanal Campaign*. Washington, D.C.: Marine Corps Historical Division, 1949.

II. SOUTH AND SOUTHWEST PACIFIC: GENERAL

Adams, Bruce. *Rust in Peace: South Pacific Battlegrounds Revisited*. Sydney: Antipodean, 1975.

Bergerud, Eric. *Touched with Fire: Land War in the South Pacific*. New York: Viking, 1966.

Charlton, Peter. *The Unnecessary War: Island Campaigns of the South-West Pacific, 1944–45*. South Melbourne: Macmillan, 1983.

Edmonds, Walter D. *They Fought with What They Had: The Story of the Army Air Forces in the Southwest Pacific, 1941–1942*. Boston: Little, Brown, 1951.

Gilmore, Allison B. *You Can't Fight Tanks with Bayonets: Psychological Warfare against the Japanese Army in the Southwest Pacific*. Lincoln: University of Nebraska Press, 1998.

Hough, Frank O., and John A. Crown. *The Campaign on New Britain*. Washington, D.C.: Marine Corps Historical Division, 1952.

Keogh, E. G. *South West Pacific 1941–45*. Melbourne: Grayflower, 1965.

Kenney, George C. *The Saga of Pappy Gunn*. New York: Duell, Sloan & Pearce, 1959.

Long, Gavin. *The Final Campaigns*. Australia in the War of 1939–1945. Canberra: Australian War Memorial, 1963.

Lundstrom, John B. *The First South Pacific Campaign: Pacific Fleet Strategy, December, 1941–June 1942*. Annapolis, Md.: Naval Institute Press, 1976.

Miller, John, Jr. *The War in the Pacific: Cartwheel: The Reduction of Rabaul*. USAWWII. Washington, D.C.: OCMH, Department of the Army, 1959.

JJ. WAKE ISLAND

Cressman, Robert J. *"A Magnificent Fight": The Battle for Wake Island*. Annapolis, Md.: Naval Institute Press, 1995.

Cunningham, Winfield S. *Wake Island Command*. Boston: Little, Brown, 1961.

Devereux, James P. S. *The Story of Wake Island*. Philadelphia: Lippincott, 1947.

Heinl, Robert. *Defense at Wake*. Washington, D.C.: Marine Corps Historical Section, 1952.

Kinney, John F. *Wake Island Pilot: A World War II Memoir*. Washington, D.C.: Brassey's, 1995.

Schultz, Duane. *Wake Island: The Heroic Gallant Fight*. New York: St. Martin's, 1978.

Urwin, Gregory J. W. *Facing Fearful Odds: The Siege of Wake Island*. Lincoln: University of Nebraska Press, 1997.

KK. UNITED STATES MAINLAND [SEE ALSO XII.C]

Reynolds, Clark G. "Submarine Attacks on the Pacific Coast, 1942." *Pacific Historical Review* 33 (May 1964): 183–93.

Webber, Bert. *Retaliation: Japanese Attacks and Allied Countermeasures on the Pacific Coast in World War II*. Corvallis: Oregon State University Press, 1975.

Webber, Bert. *Silent Siege: Japanese Attacks against North America in World War II*. Fairfield, Wash.: Ye Galleon Press, 1984.

LL. *YAMATO,* SINKING OF [SEE ALSO V.BB]

Spurr, Russell. *A Glorious Way to Die: The Kamikaze Mission of the Battleship* Yamato, *April 1945*. New York: New Market Press, 1981.

Yoshida, Mitsuru. *Requiem for Battleship* Yamato. Trans. Richard H. Minear. Seattle: University of Washington Press, 1985.

VI. Air War [see also V; VII.C; IX.B]

A. GENERAL

Charlton, Lionel E. O. *Britain at War: The Royal Air Force and U.S.A.A.F.* 5 vols. London: Hutchinson, n.d.

Lundstrom, John B. *The First Team: Pacific Air Combat from Pearl Harbor to Midway*. Annapolis, Md.: Naval Institute Press, 1984.

McFarland, Stephen L. *America's Pursuit of Precision Bombing, 1910–1945*. Washington, D.C.: Smithsonian, 1995.

Morrison, Wilbur H. *Above and Beyond, 1941–1945*. New York: St. Martin's, 1983.

Murphy, James T., with A. B. Feuer. *Skip Bombing*. Westport, Conn.: Praeger, 1993.

B. NATIONAL AIR FORCES

1. Australia

Balfe, J. D. *War Without Glory: Australians in the Air War With Japan, 1941–45.* Melbourne: Macmillan, 1984.

Hall, E. R. *Glory in Chaos: The RAAF in the Far East in 1940–1942.* West Coburg, Australia: Sembawang Association, 1989.

Odgers, George. *Air War against Japan, 1943–45.* Australia in the War of 1939–1945. Canberra: Australian War Memorial, 1957.

Pearson, Ross A. *Australians at War in the Air, 1939–1945.* Kenthurst, Australia: Kangaroo, 1995.

The RAAF in the Southwest Pacific Area, 1942–1945. Canberra: Royal Australian Air Force Air Power Studies Centre, 1993.

2. United States

Craven, Wesley Frank, and James Lea Cate, eds. *The Army Air Forces in World War II.* 7 vols. Chicago: University of Chicago Press, 1953–1958. [Vol. 1: *Plans and Early Operations, January 1939 to August 1942;* vol. 4: *The Pacific: Guadalcanal to Saipan, August 1942 to July 1944;* vol. 5: *The Pacific: Matterhorn to Nagasaki, June 1944 to August 1945;* vol. 6: *Men and Planes;* vol. 7: *Services Around the World.*]

Mondey, David, and Lewis Nalls. *USAAF at War in the Pacific.* New York: Scribner's, 1980.

Perret, Geoffrey. *Winged Victory: The Army Air Forces in World War II.* New York: Random House, 1993.

Sherrod, Robert. *History of Marine Corps Aviation in World War II.* Washington, D.C.: Combat Forces Press, 1952.

Terry, Michael R. *Historical Dictionary of the United States Air Force and Its Antecedents.* Lanham, Md.: Scarecrow, 1999.

3. Other

Gupta, S. C. *History of the Indian Air Force, 1933–45.* Ed. Bisheshwar Prasad. Delhi: Combined Inter-services Historical Section, India & Pakistan, 1961.

Melnyk, T. W. *Canadian Flying Operations in South East Asia, 1941–1945.* Ottawa: Minister of National Defence, 1976.

Probert, Henry. *The Forgotten Air Force: The Royal Air Force in the War against Japan, 1941–1945.* Washington, D.C.: Brassey's, 1995.

C. STRATEGIC AIR CAMPAIGN AGAINST JAPAN
[SEE ALSO XVII.C]

Birdsall, Steve. *Saga of the Superfortress: The Dramatic History of the B-29 and the Twentieth Air Force*. Garden City, N.Y.: Doubleday, 1980.

Caidin, Martin. *A Torch to the Enemy: The Fire Raid on Tokyo*. New York: Ballantine, 1960.

Crane, Conrad C. *Bombs, Cities, and Civilians: American Airpower Strategy in World War II*. Lawrence: University Press of Kansas, 1993.

Edoin, Hoito. *The Night Tokyo Burned*. New York: St. Martin's, 1987.

Hansell, H. S., Jr. *The Strategic Air War Against Japan*. Maxwell Air Force Base, Ala.: Air War College, 1983.

Herbert, Kevin. *Maximum Effort: The B-29's against Japan*. Manhattan, Kans.: Sunflower University Press, 1984.

Kennett, Lee. *A History of Strategic Bombing*. New York: Scribner's, 1982.

Kerr, E. Bartlett. *Flames Over Tokyo: The U.S. Army Air Forces' Incendiary Campaign against Japan, 1944–1945*. New York: Fine, 1991.

LeMay, Curtis E., and Bill Yenne. *Superfortress: The Story of the B-29 and American Air Power*. New York: McGraw-Hill, 1988.

MacIsaac, David. *Strategic Bombing in World War II: The Story of the United States Bombing Survey*. New York: Garland, 1976.

Morrison, Wilbur H. *Hellbirds: The Story of the B-29s in Combat*. New York: Duell, Sloan & Pearce, 1960.

Morrison, Wilbur H. *Point of No Return: The Story of the Twentieth Air Force*. New York: Times Books, 1979.

Schaffer, Ronald. *Wings of Judgment: American Bombing in World War II*. New York: Oxford University Press, 1985.

Sherry, Michael S. *The Rise of American Air Power: The Creation of Armageddon*. New Haven, Conn.: Yale University Press, 1987.

U.S. Strategic Bombing Survey. *Air Campaigns of the Pacific War*. Washington, D.C.: GPO, 1947.

U.S. Strategic Bombing Survey. *The Campaigns of the Pacific War*. Washington, D.C.: GPO, 1946.

U.S. Strategic Bombing Survey. *Interrogations of Japanese Officials*. 2 vols. Washington, D.C.: GPO, 1946.

Werrell, Kenneth P. *Blankets of Fire: U.S. Bombers over Japan during World War II*. Washington, D.C.: Smithsonian, 1996.

Wheeler, Keith. *Bombers over Japan*. Alexandria, Va.: Time-Life Books, 1982.

D. AIRCRAFT

Berger, Carl. *B-29: The Superfortress.* New York: Ballantine, 1970.

Bridgman, Leonard, ed. *Jane's Fighting Aircraft of World War II.* London: Jane's, 1946.

Collier, Basil. *Japanese Aircraft of World War II.* New York: Mayflower, 1979.

Francillon, R. J. *Japanese Aircraft of the Pacific War.* New York: Funk & Wagnalls, 1970.

Freeman, Roger A. *B-17 Fortress at War.* London: Allan, 1977.

Gunston, Bill. *An Illustrated Guide to Bombers of World War II.* New York: Prentice Hall, 1986.

Horikoshi, Jiro. *Eagles of Mitsubishi: The Story of the Zero Fighter.* Seattle: University of Washington Press, 1981.

Jablonski, Edward. *Flying Fortress: The Illustrated Biography of the B-17s and the Men Who Flew Them.* Garden City, N.Y.: Doubleday, 1965.

Mikesh, Robert C. *Japanese Aircraft: Code Names and Designations.* Atglen, Pa.: Schiffer, 1993.

Mikesh, Robert C. *Zero.* Osceola, Wis.: Motorbooks International, 1994.

Mondey, David, comp. *Concise Guide to Axis Aircraft of World War II.* Feltham, England: Temple, 1984.

Okumiya, Masatake, and Jiro Horikoshi, with Martin Caidin. *Zero!* New York: Dutton, 1956.

Reardon, Jim. *Koga's Zero: The Fighter that Changed World War II.* Missoula, Mont.: Pictorial Histories, 1995.

Tillman, Barrett. *The Dauntless Dive Bomber of World War II.* Annapolis, Md.: Naval Institute Press, 1976.

Tillman, Barrett. *Hellcat: The F6F in World War II.* Annapolis, Md.: Naval Institute Press, 1979.

Vander Meulen, Jacob A. *Building the B-29.* Washington, D.C.: Smithsonian, 1995.

VII. Naval and Amphibious War [see also V; VI; IX.C]

A. GENERAL

Boyne, Walter J. *Clash of Titans: World War II at Sea.* New York: Simon & Schuster, 1995.

Creswell, John. *Sea Warfare, 1939–1945.* Berkeley: University of California Press, 1967.

Miller, Nathan. *War at Sea: A Naval History of World War II.* New York: Oxford University Press, 1995.

Van der Vat, Dan. *The Pacific Campaign, World War II: The U.S.-Japanese Naval War, 1941–1945.* New York: Simon & Schuster, 1991.

B. NATIONAL NAVIES

1. Australia

Campbell, Hugh. *Notable Service to the Empire: Australian Corvettes and the British Pacific Fleet, 1944–45.* Garden Island: Naval Historical Society of Australia, 1995.

Gill, G. Hermon. *Royal Australian Navy.* 2 vols. Australia in the War of 1939–1945. Canberra: Australian War Memorial, 1957.

Stevens, David, ed. *Royal Australian Navy in World War II.* St. Leonards, Australia: Allen & Unwin, 1996.

2. Japan

Andrieu d'Albas, Emmanuel M. A. *Death of a Navy: Japanese Naval Action in World War II.* Trans. Anthony Rippon. New York: Devin-Adair, 1957.

Dull, Paul S. *A Battle History of the Imperial Japanese Navy (1941–1945).* Annapolis, Md.: Naval Institute Press, 1978.

Enright, Joseph F., with James W. Ryan. *Shinano!: The Sinking of Japan's Secret Supership.* New York: St. Martin's, 1987.

Evans, David C., ed. and trans. *The Japanese Navy in World War II: In the Words of Former Japanese Naval Officers.* 2d. ed. Annapolis, Md.: Naval Institute Press, 1990.

Evans, David C., and Mark R. Peattie. *Kaigun: Strategy, Tactics, and Technology in the Imperial Japanese Navy, 1887–1941.* Annapolis, Md.: Naval Institute Press, 1997.

Hata, Ikuhiko, and Yashuo Izawa. *Japanese Naval Aces and Fighter Units in World War II.* Trans. Don Cyril Gorham. Annapolis, Md.: Naval Institute Press, 1989.

Hirama, Yoichi. "Japanese Naval Preparations for World War II." *Naval War College Review* 44 (Spring 1991): 63–81.

Howarth, Stephen. *The Fighting Ships of the Rising Sun: The Drama of the Imperial Japanese Navy, 1895–1945.* New York: Atheneum, 1983.

Ito, Masanori, and Roger Pineau. *The End of the Imperial Japanese Navy.* Trans. Andrew Y. Kuroda and Roger Pineau. New York: Norton, 1962.

Thomas, David A. *Japan's War at Sea: Pearl Harbor to the Coral Sea.* London: Deutsch, 1978.

Watts, Anthony J., and Brian G. Gordon. *The Imperial Japanese Navy.* Garden City, N.Y.: Doubleday, 1971.

3. United Kingdom

Barnett, Correlli. *Engage the Enemy More Closely: The Royal Navy in the Second World War.* New York: Norton, 1991.

Jackson, Robert. *The Royal Navy in World War II.* Annapolis, Md.: Naval Institute Press, 1997.

Marder, Arthur J., Mark Jacobsen, and John Horsfield. *Old Friends, New Enemies: The Royal Navy and the Imperial Japanese Navy.* 2 vols. New York: Oxford University Press, 1981–1990.

Roskill, Stephen W. *The War at Sea, 1939–1945.* 3 vols. London: HMSO, 1954–1961.

Smith, P. C. *Task Force 57: The British Pacific Fleet, 1944–1945.* London: Kimber, 1969.

Willmott, H. P. *Grave of a Dozen Schemes: British Naval Planning and the War against Japan, 1943–1945.* Annapolis, Md.: Naval Institute Press, 1996.

Winton, John. *The Forgotten Fleet: The British Navy in the Pacific, 1944–1945.* New York: Coward-McCann, 1970.

4. United States

Adamson, Hans C., and George F. Kosco. *Halsey's Typhoons, A First-hand Account of How Two Typhoons, More Powerful than the Japanese, Dealt Death and Destruction to Admiral Halsey's Third Fleet.* New York: Crown, 1967.

Calhoun, C. Raymond. *Typhoon, the Other Enemy: The Third Fleet and the Pacific Storm of December 1944.* Annapolis, Md.: Naval Institute Press, 1981.

Morison, Samuel Eliot. *History of United States Naval Operations in World War II.* 15 vols. Boston: Little, Brown, 1947–1962. [Vol. 3: *The Rising Sun in the Pacific, 1931–April 1942;* vol. 4: *Coral Sea, Midway, and Submarine Actions, May 1942–August 1942;* vol. 5: *The Struggle for Guadalcanal, August 1942–February 1943;* vol. 6: *Breaking the Bismarcks Barrier, 22 July 1942–1 May 1944;* vol. 7: *Aleutians, Gilberts, and Marshalls, June 1942–April 1944;* vol. 8: *New Guinea and the Marianas, March 1944–August 1944;* vol. 12: *Leyte, June 1944–January 1945;* vol. 13: *The Liberation of the Philippines;* vol. 14: *Victory in the Pacific, 1945;* vol. 15: *Supplement and general index.*]

Morison, Samuel Eliot. *The Two Ocean War: A Short History of the United States Navy in the Second World War.* Boston: Little, Brown, 1963.

Morris, Edward H., and Patricia M. Kearns. *Historical Dictionary of the United States Navy.* Lanham, Md.: Scarecrow, 1998.

Parkin, Robert S. *Blood on the Sea: American Destroyers Lost in World War II.* New York: Sarpedon, 1995.

Potter, E. B., and Chester W. Nimitz, eds. *Triumph in the Pacific: The Navy's Struggle against Japan.* Upper Saddle River, N.J.: Prentice Hall, 1963.

Roscoe, Theodore. *United States Destroyer Operations in World War II.* Annapolis, Md.: U.S. Naval Institute, 1953.

Smith, S. E., ed. *The United States Navy in World War II.* New York: Random House, 1966.

Willoughby, Malcolm F. *The U.S. Coast Guard in World War II.* Annapolis, Md.: Naval Institute Press, 1957.

Winslow, W. G. *The Fleet the Gods Forgot: The U.S. Asiatic Fleet in World War II.* Annapolis, Md.: Naval Institute Press, 1982.

5. Other

Collins, D. J. E. *The Royal Indian Navy, 1939–45.* Delhi: Combined Inter-services Historical Section, India & Pakistan, 1964.

Kroese, A. *The Dutch Navy at War.* London: Allen & Unwin, 1945.

Waters, Sydney D. *The Royal New Zealand Navy.* Wellington: War History Branch, Department of Internal Affairs, 1956.

C. CARRIER WAR [SEE ALSO VI]

Belote, James, and William Belote. *Titans of the Seas: The Development and Operations of Japanese and American Carrier Forces during World War II.* New York: Harper & Row, 1975.

Brown, David. *Carrier Operations in World War II.* Vol. 2. London: Allan, 1974.

Condon, John Pomeroy. *Corsairs and Flattops: Marine Carrier Air Warfare, 1944–1945.* Annapolis, Md.: Naval Institute Press, 1998.

Friedman, Norman. *British Carrier Aviation: The Evolution of the Ships and Their Aircraft*. Annapolis, Md.: Naval Institute Press, 1988.

Kilduff, Peter. *US Carriers at War*. Harrisburg, Pa.: Stackpole, 1981.

Lindley, John M. *Carrier Victory: The Air War in the Pacific*. New York: Elsevier-Dutton, 1978.

MacIntyre, Donald. *Aircraft Carrier: The Majestic Weapon*. New York: Ballantine, 1968.

Miller, Nathan. *The Naval Air War, 1939–1945*. Annapolis, Md.: Nautical & Aviation, 1980.

Polmar, Norman. *Aircraft Carriers: A Graphic History of Carrier Aviation and Its Influence on World Events*. Garden City, N.Y.: Doubleday, 1969.

Reynolds, Clark G. *The Fast Carriers: The Forging of an Air Navy*. Annapolis, Md.: Naval Institute Press, 1992.

Sherman, Frederick C. *Combat Command: The American Aircraft Carriers in the Pacific War*. New York: Dutton, 1950.

Wooldridge, E. T., ed. *Carrier Warfare in the Pacific: An Oral History Collection*. Washington, D.C.: Smithsonian, 1993.

Y'Blood, William T. *The Little Giants: U.S. Escort Carriers against Japan*. Annapolis, Md.: Naval Institute Press, 1987.

D. SUBMARINES

Alden, John D. *The Fleet Submarine in the U.S. Navy*. Annapolis, Md.: Naval Institute Press, 1979.

Alden, John D. *U.S. Submarine Attacks during World War II: Including Allied Submarine Attacks in the Pacific Theater*. Annapolis, Md.: Naval Institute Press, 1989.

Blair, Clay, Jr. *Silent Victory: The U.S. Submarine War against Japan*. New York: Harper & Row, 1975.

Boyd, Carl, and Akihiko Yoshida. *The Japanese Submarine Force and World War II*. Annapolis, Md.: Naval Institute Press, 1995.

Hashimoto, Mochitsura. *Sunk: The Story of the Japanese Submarine Fleet, 1941–1945*. Trans. E. H. M. Colegrave. New York: Holt, 1954.

Holmes, Wilfred J. *Undersea Victory: The Influence of Submarine Operations on the War in the Pacific*. Garden City, N.Y.: Doubleday, 1966.

Lockwood, Charles A. *Down to the Sea in Subs*. New York: Norton, 1967.

Lockwood, Charles A. *Sink 'em All: Submarine Warfare in the Pacific*. New York: Dutton, 1951.

Polmar, Norman, and Dorr Carpenter. *Submarines of the Imperial Japanese Navy*. Annapolis, Md.: Naval Institute Press, 1986.

Roscoe, Theodore. *United States Submarine Operations in World War II*. Annapolis, Md.: U.S. Naval Institute, 1949.

Saville, Allison W. "German Submarines in the Far East." *United States Naval Institute Proceedings* 87 (August 1961): 80–92.

Stevens, David. *U-boat Far from Home: The Epic Voyage of U 862 to Australia and New Zealand*. St. Leonards, Australia: Allen & Unwin, 1997.

U.S. Naval History Division. *United States Submarine Losses, World War II, Reissued with an Appendix of Axis Submarine Losses*. Washington, D.C.: GPO, 1964.

Waldron, Thomas J., and James J. Gleeson. *Midget Submarine*. New York: Ballantine, 1975.

Warner, Peggy. *The Coffin Boats: Japanese Midget Submarine Operations in the Second World War*. London: Cooper, 1986.

Warren, Charles E. T., and James Benson. *Above Us the Waves: The Story of Midget Submarines and Human Torpedoes*. London: Harrap, 1953.

Wheeler, Keith. *War Under the Pacific*. Alexandria, Va.: Time-Life Books, 1980.

E. NAVAL VESSELS

1. General

Jane's Fighting Ships of World War II. New York: Military Press, 1989.

Hodges, Peter, and Norman Friedman. *Destroyer Weapons of World War II*. Annapolis, Md.: Naval Institute Press, 1979.

2. Allies

Allied Landing Craft of World War Two. Annapolis, Md.: Naval Institute Press, 1985.

Breuer, William B. *Devil Boats: The PT War against Japan*. Novato, Calif.: Presidio, 1987.

Bulkley, Robert J. *At Close Quarters: PT Boats in the U.S. Navy*. Washington, D.C.: Naval History Division, 1962.

Bunker, John G. *Liberty Ships: The Ugly Ducklings of World War II*. Annapolis, Md.: Naval Institute Press, 1972.

Dulin, Robert O., Jr., and William H. Garzke, Jr. *Battleships: United States Battleships in World War II*. Annapolis, Md.: Naval Institute Press, 1976.

Elliott, Peter. *Allied Escort Ships of World War II: A Complete Survey.* Annapolis, Md.: Naval Institute Press, 1977.

Friedman, Norman. *Battleship Design and Development, 1905–1945.* New York: Mayflower, 1978.

Garzke, William H., Jr., and Robert O. Dulin, Jr. *Allied Battleships of World War II.* Annapolis, Md.: Naval Institute Press, 1980.

Lenton, H. T. *British and Empire Warships of the Second World War.* Annapolis, Md.: Naval Institute Press, 1998.

Raven, Alan, and John Roberts. *British Battleships of World War Two: The Development and Technical History of the Royal Navy's Battleships and Battlecruisers from 1911 to 1946.* Annapolis, Md.: Naval Institute Press, 1976.

Sawyer, L. A., and W. H. Mitchell. *The Liberty Ships.* Newton Abbot, England: David & Charles, 1970.

Scheina, Robert L. *U.S. Coast Guard Cutters & Craft of World War II.* Annapolis, Md.: Naval Institute Press, 1982.

Silverstone, Paul H. *U.S. Warships of World War II.* Annapolis, Md.: Naval Institute Press, 1989.

Smith, Peter. *The Great Ships Pass: British Battleships at War, 1939–1945.* London: Kimber, 1977.

Strahan, Jerry E. *Andrew Jackson Higgins and the Boats That Won World War II.* Baton Rouge: Louisiana State University Press, 1994.

Terzibaschitsch, Stefan. *Battleships of the U.S. Navy in World War II.* Trans. Heinz O. Vetters and Richard Cox. London: Brassey's, 1977.

3. Japan

Brice, Martin. *Axis Blockade Runners of World War II.* Annapolis, Md.: Naval Institute Press, 1981.

Fukui, Shizuo. *Japanese Naval Vessels at the End of World War II.* Annapolis, Md.: Naval Institute Press, 1991.

Garzke, William H., Jr., and Robert O. Dulin, Jr. *Battleships: Axis and Neutral Battleships in World War II.* Annapolis, Md.: Naval Institute Press, 1985.

Japanese Naval Vessels of World War Two as Seen by U.S. Naval Intelligence. Annapolis, Md.: Naval Institute Press, 1987.

Jentschura, Hansgeorg, et al. *Warships of the Imperial Japanese Navy, 1869–1945.* Annapolis, Md.: Naval Institute Press, 1977.

Lacroix, Eric. *Japanese Cruisers of the Pacific War.* Annapolis, Md.: Naval Institute Press, 1997.

Watts, Anthony J. *Japanese Warships of World War II*. Garden City, N.Y.: Doubleday, 1967.

F. AMPHIBIOUS WARFARE

1. General

Ladd, James D. *Assault from the Sea, 1939–45: The Craft, the Landings, the Men*. New York: Hippocrene, 1976.
Lorelli, John. *To Foreign Shores: U.S. Amphibious Operations in World War II*. Annapolis, Md.: Naval Institute Press, 1994.

2. U.S. Marine Corps

Cameron, Craig M. *American Samurai: Myth, Imagination and the Conduct of Battle in the First Marine Division, 1941–1951*. New York: Cambridge University Press, 1994.
Gailey, Harry A. *Historical Dictionary of the United States Marine Corps*. Lanham, Md.: Scarecrow, 1998.
Isely, Jeter A., and Philip A. Crowl. *The U.S. Marines in Amphibious Warfare: Its Theory, and Its Practice in the Pacific*. Princeton, N.J.: Princeton University, 1951.
Leckie, Robert. *Strong Men Armed: The United States Marines against Japan*. New York: Random House, 1962.
McMillan, George. *The Old Breed: A History of the First Marine Division in World War II*. Washington, D.C.: Infantry Journal Press, 1949.
Moskin, J. Robert. *The U.S. Marine Corps Story*. New York: McGraw-Hill, 1977.
O'Sheel, Patrick. *Semper Fidelis: The U.S. Marines in the Pacific, 1942–1945*. New York: William Sloane Associates, 1947.
Pratt, Fletcher. *The Marines' War: An Account of the Struggle for the Pacific from both American and Japanese Sources*. New York: William Sloane Associates, 1948.
U.S. Marine Corps Historical Branch. *History of U.S. Marine Corps Operations in World War II*. 5 vols. Washington, D.C.: U.S. Marine Corps Historical Branch, 1958–1968. [Vol. 1: *Pearl Harbor to Guadalcanal*, by F. O. Hough, V. E. Ludwig, and H. I. Shaw, Jr.; vol. 2: *Isolation of Rabaul*, by H. I. Shaw, Jr., and D. T. Kane; *Central Pacific Drive*, by H. I. Shaw, Jr., B. C. Nalty, and E. T. Turnbladh; vol. 4: *Western Pacific Operations*, by G. W. Garand and T. R. Stro-

bridge; vol. 5: *Victory and Occupation,* by B. M. Frank and H. I. Shaw, Jr.]

Wheeler, Richard. *A Special Valor: The U.S. Marines and the Pacific War.* New York: Harper & Row, 1983.

VIII. Intelligence [see also II; V. DD.]

A. GENERAL

Ballard, Geoffrey. *On ULTRA Active Service: The Story of Australia's Signal Intelligence Operations during World War II.* Richmond, Australia: Spectrum, 1990.

Beesly, Patrick. *Very Special Intelligence: The Story of the Admiralty's Operational Intelligence Centre, 1939–1945.* Garden City, N.Y.: Doubleday, 1977.

Benson, Robert Louis. *A History of U.S. Communications Intelligence during World War II: Policy and Administration.* Fort George G. Meade, Md.: Center for Cryptologic History, 1997.

Benson, Robert Louis, and Michael Warner, eds. *Venona: Soviet Espionage and the American Response, 1939–1957.* Washington, D.C.: National Security Agency, Central Intelligence Agency, 1996.

Bleakley, Jack. *The Eavesdroppers.* Canberra: AGPS Press, 1991.

Boyd, Carl. *Hitler's Japanese Confidant: General Oshima Hiroshi and Magic Intelligence, 1941– 1945.* Lawrence: University of Kansas Press, 1993.

Breuer, William B. *MacArthur's Undercover War: Spies, Saboteurs, Guerrillas, and Secret Missions.* New York: Wiley, 1995.

Brown, Anthony Cave. *"C": The Secret Life of Sir Stewart Graham Menzies, Spymaster to Winston Churchill.* New York: Macmillan, 1987.

Bryden, John. *Best Kept Secret: Canadian Secret Intelligence in the Second World War.* Toronto: Lester, 1993.

Chalou, George C., ed. *The Secrets War: The Office of Strategic Services in World War II.* Washington, D.C.: National Archives and Records Administration, 1992.

Clark, Ronald. *The Man Who Broke Purple: The Life of Colonel William F. Friedman, Who Deciphered the Japanese Code in World War II.* Boston: Little, Brown, 1977.

Courtney, G. B. *Silent Feet: The History of "Z" Special Operations, 1942–1945.* McCrae, Australia: R.J. and S.P. Austin, 1993.

Cruickshank, Charles. *SOE in the Far East*. New York: Oxford University Press, 1983.

Deakin, F. W., and G. R. Storry. *The Case of Richard Sorge*. New York: Harper & Row, 1966.

Dillard, James E., and Walter T. Hitchcock, ed. *The Intelligence Revolution and Modern Warfare*. Chicago: Imprint, 1996.

Dorwart, Jeffery M. *Conflict of Duty: The U.S. Navy's Intelligence Dilemma 1919–1945*. Annapolis, Md.: Naval Institute Press, 1983.

Drea, Edward J. *MacArthur's ULTRA: Codebreaking and the War against Japan, 1942–1945*. Lawrence: University Press of Kansas, 1992.

Dunlop, Richard. *Behind Japanese Lines: With the OSS in Burma*. Chicago: Rand McNally, 1979.

Dunlop, Richard. *Donovan: America's Master Spy*. Chicago: Rand McNally, 1982.

Edwards, Duval A. *Spy Catchers of the U.S. Army in the War with Japan: The Unfinished Story of the Counter Intelligence Corps*. Gig Harbor, Wash.: Red Apple, 1994.

Farago, Ladislas. *The Broken Seal: The Story of "Operation Magic" and the Pearl Harbor Disaster*. New York: Random House, 1967.

Feuer, A. B. *Commando! The M/Z Unit's Secret War against Japan*. Westport, Conn.: Praeger, 1996.

Foot, M. R. D. *SOE: An Outline History of the Special Operations Executive, 1940–1946*. Frederick, Md.: University Publications of America, 1985.

Gilbert, James L., and John P. Finnegan. *U.S. Army Signals Intelligence in World War II: A Documentary History*. USAWWII. Washington, D.C.: U.S. Army Center of Military History, 1993.

Gilchrist, Andrew. *Bangkok Top Secret: Being the Experiences of a British Officer in the Siam Country Section of Force 136*. London: Hutchinson, 1970.

Glantz, David M. *The Role of Intelligence in Soviet Military Strategy in World War II*. Novato, Calif.: Presidio, 1990.

Goren, Dina. "Communication Intelligence and the Freedom of the Press: The *Chicago Tribune's* Battle of Midway Dispatch and the Breaking of the Japanese Naval Code." *Journal of Contemporary History* 16 (1981): 663–90.

Goudsmit, Samuel A. *Alsos*. New York: Schuman, 1947.

Gough, Richard. *SOE Singapore, 1941–42*. London: Kimber, 1985.

Harris, Ruth R. "The 'Magic' Leak of 1941 and Japanese-American Relations." *Pacific Historical Review* 50 (February 1981): 77–96.

Hilsman, Roger. *American Guerrilla: My War Behind Japanese Lines.* Washington, D.C.: Brassey's, 1990.

Hinsley, F. H., et al. *British Intelligence in the Second World War.* 5 vols. New York: Cambridge University Press, 1979–1990.

Hogan, David W. *U.S. Army Special Operations in World War II.* US-AWWII. Washington, D.C.: U.S. Army Center of Military History, 1992.

Holmes, W. J. *Double-Edged Secrets: U.S. Naval Intelligence Operations in the Pacific during World War II.* Annapolis, Md.: Naval Institute Press, 1979.

Hyde, H. Montgomery. *The Atom Bomb Spies.* New York: Ballantine, 1981.

Ind, Allison. *Allied Intelligence Bureau: Our Secret Weapon in the War against Japan.* New York: McKay, 1958.

Johnson, Chalmers. *An Instance of Treason: Ozaki Hotsumi and the Sorge Spy Ring.* Expanded ed. Stanford, Calif.: Stanford University Press, 1990.

Kahn, David. *The Code-Breakers: The Story of Secret Writing.* New York: Scribner's, 1996.

Katz, Barry M. *Foreign Intelligence: Research and Analysis in the Office of Strategic Services, 1942–1945.* Cambridge, Mass.: Harvard University Press, 1989.

Kreis, John F., ed. *Piercing the Fog: Intelligence and Army Air Forces Operations in World War II.* Washington, D.C.: Air Force History and Museums Program, 1996.

Ladd, James D., et al. *Clandestine Warfare: Weapons and Equipment of the SOE and OSS.* London: Blandford, 1988.

Layton, Edwin T., with Roger Pineau and John Costello. *"And I Was There": Pearl Harbor and Midway–Breaking the Secrets.* New York: Morrow, 1985.

Lee, Bruce. *Marching Orders: The Untold Story of World War II.* New York: Crown, 1995.

Lewin, Ronald. *The American Magic: Codes, Ciphers and the Defeat of Japan.* New York: Farrar, Straus, Giroux, 1982.

Lewin, Ronald. *Ultra Goes to War: The First Account of World War II's Greatest Secret.* New York: McGraw-Hill, 1978.

Mahl, Thomas E. *Desperate Deception: British Covert Operations in the United States, 1939–44.* Washington, D.C.: Brassey's, 1997.

Maochun Yu. *OSS in China: Prelude to Cold War.* New Haven, Conn.: Yale University Press, 1996.

May, Ernest R., ed. *Knowing One's Enemies: Intelligence Assessment before the Two World Wars*. Princeton, N.J.: Princeton University Press, 1984.

Miller, Russell. *The Commandos*. Alexandria, Va.: Time-Life Books, 1981.

O'Brien, Terence. *The Moonlight War: The Story of Clandestine Operations in South-east Asia, 1944–45*. London: Collins, 1987.

Pash, Boris T. *The Alsos Mission*. New York: Award House, 1969.

Powell, Alan. *War by Stealth: Australians and the Allied Intelligence Bureau, 1942–1945*. Carlton South: Melbourne University Press, 1996.

Prados, John. *Combined Fleet Decoded: The Secret History of American Intelligence and the Japanese Navy in World War II*. New York: Random House, 1995.

Prange, Gordon W., Donald M. Goldstein, and Katherine V. Dillon. *Target Tokyo: The Story of the Sorge Spy Ring*. New York: McGraw-Hill, 1984.

Russell, Francis. *The Secret War*. Alexandria, Va.: Time-Life Books, 1981.

Smith, Bradley F. *The Shadow Warriors: OSS and the Origins of the CIA*. Novato, Calif.: Presidio, 1993.

Smith, Bradley F. *Sharing Secrets with Stalin: How the Allies Traded Intelligence, 1941–1945*. Lawrence: University Press of Kansas, 1996.

Smith, Bradley F. *The Ultra-Magic Deals and the Most Secret Relationship, 1940–1946*. Novato, Calif.: Presidio, 1993.

Smith, Nicol, and Thomas B. Clark. *Into Siam, Underground Kingdom*. Indianapolis: Bobbs-Merrill, 1946.

Smith, R. Harris, *OSS: The Secret History of America's First Central Intelligence Agency*. Berkeley: University of California, 1972.

Spector, Ronald H., ed. *Listening to the Enemy: Key Documents on the Role of Communications Intelligence in the War with Japan*. Wilmington, Del.: Scholarly Resources, 1987.

Stanley, Roy M. *World War II Photo Intelligence*. New York: Scribner's, 1981.

Stripp, Alan. *Codebreaker in the Far East*. London: Frank Cass, 1989.

Thorpe, Elliott R. *East Wind, Rain: The Intimate Account of an Intelligence Officer in the Pacific, 1939–1949*. Boston: Gambit, 1969.

Trenowden, Ian. *Operations Most Secret: SOE–Malayan Theatre*. London: Kimber, 1978.

Troy, Thomas R. *Wild Bill and Intrepid: Donovan, Stephenson, and the Origin of the CIA*. New Haven, Conn.: Yale University Press, 1996.

U.S. Department of Defense. 5 vols. *The "Magic" Background of Pearl Harbor*. Washington, D.C.: U.S. Department of Defense, 1978.

Van der Rhoer, Edward. *Deadly Magic: A Personal Account of Communications Intelligence in World War II in the Pacific*. New York: Scribner's, 1978.

Wallace, David, comp. *The MAGIC Documents: Summaries and Transcripts of the Top-Secret Diplomatic Communications of Japan, 1938–1945*. Frederick, Md.: University Publications of America, 1982.

Williams, Robert C. *Klaus Fuchs, Atom Spy*. Cambridge, Mass.: Harvard University Press, 1987.

Willoughby, Charles A. *Shanghai Conspiracy: The Sorge Spy Ring*. New York: Dutton, 1952.

Winbon, Byron R. *Wen Bon: A Naval Air Intelligence Officer behind Japanese Lines in China*. Denton: University of North Texas Press, 1994.

Winks, Robin W. *Cloak and Gown: Scholars in the Secret War, 1939–1961*. New York: Morrow, 1987.

Winton, John. *Ultra in the Pacific: How Breaking Japanese Codes & Cyphers Affected Naval Operations against Japan, 1941–45*. Annapolis, Md.: Naval Institute Press, 1993.

Wise, William. *Secret Mission to the Philippines: The Story of "Spyron" and the American-Filipino Guerrillas of World War II*. New York: Dutton, 1968.

Yardley, Herbert O. *The Chinese Black Chamber*. Boston: Houghton Mifflin, 1983.

Zacharias, Ellis M. *Secret Missions: The Story of an Intelligence Officer*. New York: Putnam, 1947.

B. JAPAN

Allen, Louis. "Japanese Intelligence Systems." *Journal of Contemporary History* 22 (Oct. 1987): 547–62.

Bennett, J. W., et al. *Intelligence and Cryptanalytic Activities of the Japanese during World War II*. Laguna Hills, Calif.: Aegean Park Press, 1986.

Chapman, John W. M. "Signals Intelligence Collaboration among the Tripartite Pact States on the Eve of Pearl Harbor." *Japan Forum* 3 (1991): 231–56.

Deacon, Richard. *Kempei Tai: A History of the Japanese Secret Service*. New York: Beaufort, 1983.

Fujiwara, Iwaichi. *F Kikan! Japanese Army Intelligence in Southeast Asia during World War II*. London: Heinemann Educational, 1983.

Matthews, Tony. *Shadows Dancing: Japanese Espionage against the West, 1939–1945*. New York: St. Martin's, 1994.

C. COASTWATCHERS

Feldt, Eric A. *The Coastwatchers*. New York: Oxford University Press, 1946.

Feuer, A. B., ed. *Coast Watching in the Solomon Islands: The Bougainville Reports, December 1941–July 1943*. New York: Praeger, 1992.

Horton, D. C. *Fire over the Islands: The Coast Watchers of the Solomons*. Sydney: Reed, 1970.

Lord, Walter. *Lonely Vigil: Coastwatchers of the Solomons*. New York: Viking, 1977.

Wright, Malcolm. *If I Die: Coastwatching and Guerrilla Warfare Behind Japanese Lines*. Melbourne: Lansdowne, 1965.

D. NAVAJO CODE TALKERS [SEE ALSO IV.S.11]

Bixler, Margaret T. *Winds of Freedom: The Story of the Navajo Code Talkers of World War II*. Darien, Conn.: Two Bytes, 1992.

Kawano, Kenji. *Warriors: Navajo Code Talkers*. Flagstaff, Ariz.: Northland, 1990.

McClain, S. *Navajo Weapon*. Boulder, Colo.: Books Beyond Borders, 1994.

Paul, Doris A. *Navajo Code Talkers*. Philadelphia: Dorrance, 1973.

E. JAPANESE AMERICANS [SEE ALSO IV.S.10; XIV]

Falk, Stanley, and Warren M. Tsuneishi, eds. *MIS in the War against Japan: Personal Experiences Related at the 1993 MIS Capital Reunion, "The Nisei Veteran: An American Patriot."* Vienna, Va.: Japanese American Veterans Association of Washington, D.C., 1995. [Military Intelligence Service]

Harrington, Joseph D. *Yankee Samurai: The Secret Role of Nisei in America's Pacific Victory*. Detroit: Pettigrew, 1979.

Kiyosaki, Wayne S. *A Spy in Their Midst: The World War II Struggle of a Japanese-American Hero: The Story of Richard Sakakida*. Lanham, Md.: Madison, 1995.

IX. Logistics [see also IV.S.4,5]

A. GENERAL

Anders, Leslie. *The Ledo Road: General Joseph W. Stilwell's Highway to China*. Norman: University of Oklahoma Press, 1965.

Ballantine, Duncan S. *U.S. Naval Logistics in the Second World War*. Princeton, N.J.: Princeton University Press, 1947.

Carter, Worrall Reed. *Beans, Bullets, and Black Oil: The Story of Fleet Logistics Afloat in the Pacific during World War II*. Washington, D.C.: Department of the Navy, 1953.

Castillo, Edmund L. *The Seabees of World War II*. New York: Random House, 1963.

Coakley, Robert W., and Richard M. Leighton. *Global Logistics and Strategy, 1943–1945*. USAWWII. Washington, D.C.: OCMH, Department of the Army, 1968.

Coates, K. S., and W. R. Morrison. *The Alaska Highway in World War II: The U.S. Army of Occupation in Canada's Northwest*. Norman: University of Oklahoma Press, 1992.

Dod, Karl C. *The Corps of Engineers: The War against Japan*. USAWWII. Washington, D.C.: OCMH, Department of the Army, 1966.

Goralski, Robert. *Oil and War: How the Deadly Struggle for Fuel in World War II Meant Victory or Defeat*. New York: Morrow, 1987.

Heavey, William F. *Down Ramp! The Story of the Army Amphibian Engineers*. Washington, D.C.: Infantry Journal Press, 1947.

Hurstfield, Joel. *The Control of Raw Materials*. History of the Second World War. London: HMSO, 1953.

Leighton, Richard M., and Robert W. Coakley. *Global Logistics and Strategy, 1940–1943*. USAWWII. Washington, D.C.: OCMH, Department of the Army, 1955.

Millet, John D. *The Organization and Role of the Army Service Forces*. USAWWII. Washington, D.C.: OCMH, Department of the Army, 1954.

Ohl, John Kennedy. *Supplying the Troops: General Somervell and American Logistics in WWII*. DeKalb: Northern Illinois University Press, 1994.

Petrov, Vladimir. *Money and Conquest: Allied Occupation Currencies in World War II*. Baltimore, Md.: Johns Hopkins University Press, 1967.

Remley, David A. *Crooked Road: The Story of the Alaska Highway*. New York: McGraw-Hill, 1976.

Rundell, Walter, Jr. *Military Money: A Fiscal History of the U.S. Army Overseas in World War II*. College Station: Texas A & M University Press, 1980.

Schwan, C. Frederick, and Joseph E. Boling. *World War II Military Currency*. Port Clinton, Ohio: BNR, 1980.

Smith, Kevin. *Conflict over Convoys: Anglo-American Logistics Diplomacy in the Second World War*. New York: Cambridge University Press, 1996.

Stoff, Michael B. *Oil, War, and American Security: The Search for a National Policy on Foreign Oil, 1941–1947*. New Haven, Conn.: Yale University Press, 1980.

U.S. Strategic Bombing Survey. *Oil in Japan's War*. San Francisco: U.S. Strategic Bombing Survey, 1946.

Van Creveld, Martin. *Supplying War*. Cambridge: Cambridge University Press, 1977.

B. AIR TRANSPORT

Cleveland, Reginald M. *Air Transport at War*. New York: Harper, 1946.

Hays, Otis, Jr. *The Alaska-Siberia Connection: The World War II Air Route*. College Station: Texas A&M University Press, 1996.

Martin, John G. *It Began at Imphal: The Combat Cargo Story*. Manhattan, Kans.: Sunflower University Press, 1988.

Spencer, Otha C. *Flying the Hump: Memories of an Air War*. College Station: Texas A&M University Press, 1992.

Thorne, Bliss K. *The Hump: The Great Military Airlift of World War II*. Philadelphia: Lippincott, 1965.

Tunner, William H. *Over the Hump*. New York: Duell, Sloan, & Pearce, 1964.

C. MERCHANT MARINE

Behrens, C. B. A. *Merchant Shipping and the Demands of War*. London: HMSO, 1955.

Browning, Robert M., Jr. *U.S. Merchant Vessel War Casualties of World War II*. Annapolis, Md.: Naval Institute Press, 1996.

Bunker, John. *Heroes in Dungarees: The Story of the American Merchant Marine in World War II*. Annapolis, Md.: Naval Institute Press, 1995.

Carse, Robert. *The Long Haul: The United States Merchant Service in World War II*. New York: Norton, 1965.

Edwards, Bernard. *The Merchant Navy Goes to War*. London: Hale, 1990.

Moore, Arthur R. *"A Careless Word—A Needless Sinking": A History of the Staggering Losses Suffered by the U.S. Merchant Marine, Both in Ships and Personnel during World War II*. Kings Point, N.Y.: American Merchant Marine Museum, 1983.

Parillo, Mark P. *The Japanese Merchant Marine in World War II*. Annapolis, Md.: Naval Institute Press, 1993.

Riesenberg, Felix. *Sea War: The Story of the U.S. Merchant Marine in World War II*. New York: Rinehart, 1956.

Slader, John. *The Red Duster at War: A History of the Merchant Navy during the Second World War*. London: Kimber, 1988.

X. Medicine and Casualties

Adams, David P. *"The Greatest Good to the Greatest Number": Penicillin Rationing on the Home Front, 1940–1945*. New York, 1991.

Condon-Rall, Mary Ellen. "U.S. Army Medical Preparations and the Outbreak of War: The Philippines, 1941–6 May 1942." *Journal of Military History* 56 (Jan. 1992): 35–56.

Cowdrey, Albert E. *Fighting for Life: American Military Medicine in World War II*. New York: Free Press, 1994.

Green, F. H. K., and Gordon Covell, eds. *Medical Research: Medical History of the Second World War*. London: HMSO, 1953.

Herman, Jan K. *Battle Station Sick Bay: Navy Medicine in World War II*. Annapolis, Md.: Naval Institute Press, 1997.

Krivosheev, G. F, ed. *Soviet Casualties and Combat Losses in the Twentieth Century*. Trans. Christine Barnard. London: Greenhill, 1997.

MacNalty, Arthur Salusbury, and W. Franklin Mellor, eds. *Medical Service in War: The Principal Medical Lessons of the Second World War; Based on the Official Medical Histories of the United Kingdom, Canada, Australia, New Zealand and India*. London: HMSO, 1968.

Mellor, W. Franklin, ed. *Casualties and Medical Statistics*. History of the Second World War. London: HMSO, 1972.

Raina, B. L. *World War II: Medical Services, India*. New Delhi: Commonwealth, 1990.

Reister, Frank A., ed. *Medical Statistics in World War II*. USAWWII. Washington, D.C.: Office of the Surgeon General, Department of the Army, 1975.

Stone, James H., ed. *Crisis Fleeting: Original Reports on Military Medicine in India and Burma in the Second World War*. Washington, D.C.: Office of the Surgeon General, U.S. Army, 1969.

Stout, Thomas D. M. *Medical Services in New Zealand and the Pacific in Royal New Zealand Navy, Royal New Zealand Air Force and with Prisoners of War*. Wellington: War History Branch, Department of Internal Affairs, 1958.

U.S. Department of the Army, Office of the Adjutant General. *Army Battle Casualties and Nonbattle Deaths in World War II: Final Report, 7 December 1941–31 December 1946*. Washington, D.C.: Department of the Army, 1953.

U.S. Navy Department Bureau of Medicine and Surgery. *The History of the Medical Department of the United States Navy in World War II*. 3 vols. Washington, D.C.: GPO, 1950–1953.

Vedder, James S. *Surgeon on Iwo: Up Front with the 27th Marines*. Novato, Calif.: Presidio, 1984.

Walker, Allan S. *The Island Campaigns*. Australia in the War of 1939–1945. Canberra: Australian War Memorial, 1957.

XI. Science and Technology [see also X; XII]

Baxter, James Phinney. *Scientists against Time*. Boston: Little, Brown, 1946.

Clark, Ronald W. *Tizard*. Cambridge, Mass.: MIT Press, 1965.

Conant, James B. *My Several Lives: Memoirs of a Social Inventor*. New York: Harper & Row, 1970.

Hartcup, Guy. *The Challenge of War: British Scientific and Engineering Contributions to World War II*. New York: Taplinger, 1970.

Jones, Reginald V. *The Wizard War: British Scientific Intelligence, 1939–1945*. New York: Coward, McCann & Geoghegan, 1978.

Lindsey, George, ed. *No Day Long Enough: Canadian Science in World War II*. Toronto: Canadian Institute of Strategic Studies, 1997.

Mellor, D. P. *The Role of Science and Industry*. Australia in the War of 1939–1945. Canberra: Australian War Memorial, 1958.

Stewart, Irvin. *Organizing Scientific Research for War: The Administrative History of the Office of Scientific Research and Development*. Boston: Little, Brown, 1948.

Thiesmeyer, Lincoln R., and John E. Burchard. *Combat Scientists*. Science in World War II. Office of Scientific Research and Development. Boston: Little, Brown, 1947.

Zimmerman, David. *Top Secret Exchange: The Tizard Mission and the Scientific War*. Buffalo, N.Y.: McGill-Queen's University Press, 1996.

XII. Weapons [see also VI.D; VII.E; XI]

A. GENERAL

Baldwin, Ralph B. *The Deadly Fuze: The Secret Weapon of World War II*. Novato, Calif.: Presidio, 1980.

Butler, Howard K. "The Army Ground Forces and the Helicopter, 1941–1945." *United States Army Aviation Digest* 3 (May–June 1990): 8–13.

Campbell, John. *Naval Weapons of World War Two*. Annapolis, Md.: Naval Institute Press, 1985.

Couffer, Jack. *Bat Bomb: World War II's Other Secret Weapon*. Austin: University of Texas Press, 1992.

Devereux, Tony. *Messenger Gods of Battle — Radio, Radar, Sonar: The Story of Electronics in War*. London: Brassey's, 1991.

Fitzpatrick, Jim. *The Bicycle in Wartime*. Washington, D.C.: Brassey's, 1998.

Feist, Joe Michael. "Bats Away." *American Heritage* 33 (April–May 1982): 93–96.

Gannon, Robert. *Hellions of the Deep: The Development of American Torpedoes in World War II*. University Park: Pennsylvania State University Press, 1996.

Grove, Eric. *The Military Hardware of World War II: Tanks, Aircraft, and Naval Vessels*. New York: Military Press, 1984.

Hogg, Ian V. *The Encyclopedia of Infantry Weapons of World War II*. London: Arms & Armour, 1977.

Markham, George. *Japanese Infantry Weapons of World War Two*. New York: Hippocrene, 1976.

Mayer, Sydney L., ed. *The Rise and Fall of Imperial Japan*. New York: Military Press, 1984.

Reit, Seymour. *Masquerade: The Amazing Camouflage Deceptions of World War II*. London: Hale, 1979.

Stanton, Shelby. *U.S. Army Uniforms of World War II*. Harrisburg, Pa.: Stackpole, 1991.

Weeks, John. *World War II Small Arms*. London: Orbis, 1979.

Willinger, Kurt, and Jean Guerney. *The American Jeep: In War and Peace*. New York: Crown, 1983.

B. ATOMIC BOMB DEVELOPMENT [SEE ALSO VIII; XVII.C]

Brooks, Geoffrey. *Hitler's Nuclear Weapons*. London: Cooper, 1992.

Clark, Ronald W. *The Birth of the Bomb: The Untold Story of Britain's Part in the Weapon That Changed the World*. London: Phoenix House, 1961.

Davis, Nuel Pharr. *Lawrence & Oppenheimer*. New York: Simon & Schuster, 1968.

Ehrman, John. *The Atomic Bomb: An Account of British Policy in the Second World War*. London: Cabinet Office, 1953.

Fermi, Laura. *The Story of Atomic Energy*. New York: Random House, 1961.

Gowing, Margaret. *Britain and Atomic Energy, 1939–1945*. New York: St. Martin's, 1964.

Groueff, Stephane. *Manhattan Project: The Untold Story of the Making of the Atomic Bomb*. Boston: Little, Brown, 1967.

Groves, Leslie R. *Now It Can Be Told: The Story of the Manhattan Project*. New York: Harper & Row, 1962.

Hershberg, James G. *James B. Conant: Harvard to Hiroshima and the Making of the Nuclear Age*. New York: Knopf, 1993.

Hewlett, Richard G., and Oscar E. Anderson, Jr. *A History of the United States Atomic Energy Commission*. Vol. 1: *The New World, 1939–1946*. University Park: Pennsylvania State University Press, 1962.

Holloway, David. *Stalin and the Bomb: The Soviet Union and Atomic Energy, 1939–1956*. New Haven, Conn.: Yale University Press, 1994.

Johnson, Charles W., and Charles O. Jackson. *City Behind a Fence: Oak Ridge, Tennessee, 1942–1946*. Knoxville: University of Tennessee Press, 1981.

Jones, Vincent C. *Manhattan: The Army and the Atomic Bomb*. USAWWII. Washington, D.C.: Center of Military History, Department of the Army, 1985.

Kurzman, Dan. *Blood and Water: Sabotaging Hitler's Bomb*. New York: Holt, 1997.

Lamont, Lansing. *The Day of Trinity*. New York: Atheneum, 1965.

Laurence, William L. *Dawn Over Zero: The Story of the Atomic Bomb*. New York: Knopf, 1946.

MacPherson, Malcolm M. *Time Bomb: Fermi, Heisenberg, and the Race for the Atomic Bomb*. New York: Dutton, 1986.

Meigs, Montgomery Cunningham. "Managing Uncertainty: Vannevar Bush, James B. Conant and the Development of the Atomic Bomb, 1940–1945." Ph.D. dissertation, University of Wisconsin–Madison, 1982.

Powers, Thomas. *Heisenberg's War: The Secret History of the German Bomb*. New York: Knopf, 1993.

Purcell, John F. *The Best-kept Secret: The Story of the Atomic Bomb*. New York: Vanguard, 1963.

Rhodes, Richard. *The Making of the Atomic Bomb*. New York: Simon & Schuster, 1986.

Rose, Paul Lawrence. *Heisenberg and the Nazi Atomic Bomb Project*. Berkeley: University of California Press, 1998.

Smyth, Henry DeWolf. *Atomic Energy for Military Purposes: The Official Report on the Development of the Atomic Bomb under the Auspices of the U.S. Government, 1940–1945*. Princeton, N.J.: Princeton University Press, 1945.

Stoff, Michael B., ed. *The Manhattan Project: A Documentary Introduction to the Atomic Age*. Philadelphia: Temple University Press, 1991.

Szasz, Ferenc M. *British Scientists and the Manhattan Project: The Los Alamos Years*. New York: St. Martin's, 1992.

Szasz, Ferenc M. *The Day the Sun Rose Twice: The Story of the Trinity Site Nuclear Explosion, July 16, 1945*. Albuquerque: University of New Mexico Press, 1984.

Walker, Mark. *Nazi Science: Myth, Truth, and the German Atomic Bomb*. New York: Plenum, 1995.

Wilcox, Robert K. *Japan's Secret War*. New York: Morrow, 1985.

Wyden, Peter. *Day One: Before Hiroshima and After*. New York: Simon & Schuster, 1984.

Zachary, G. Pascal. *Endless Frontier: Vannevar Bush, Engineer of the American Century*. New York: Free Press, 1997.

C. BALLOON BOMBS [SEE ALSO V.KK]

Conley, Cornelius W. "The Great Japanese Balloon Offensive." *Air University Review* 19 (January–February 1968): 68–83.

Hidagi, Yasushi. "Attack against the U.S. Heartland." *Aerospace Historian* 27 (June 1981): 87–93.

Mikesh, Robert C. *Japan's World War II Balloon Bomb Attacks on North America*. Washington, D.C.: Smithsonian, 1973.

Prioli, Carmine A. "The FU-GO Project." *American Heritage* 33 (April–May 1982): 89–92.

Reynolds, Clark G. "Attack of the Paper Balloons." *Airpower History* 12 (April 1965): 51–55.

D. CHEMICAL AND BIOLOGICAL WEAPONS

Bernstein, Barton J. "Why We Didn't Use Poison Gas in World War II." *American Heritage* 36 (August–September 1985): 40–46.

Bryden, John. *Deadly Allies: Canada's Secret War, 1937–1947.* Toronto: McClelland & Stewart, 1989.

Gold, Hal. *Unit 731: Testimony.* Tokyo: Yenbooks, 1996.

Gomer, Robert, John W. Powell, and Bert V. A. Roling. "Japan's Biological Weapons, 1930–1945." *Bulletin of the Atomic Scientists* 37 (October 1981): 43–53.

Harris, Robert, and Jeremy Paxman. *A Higher Form of Killing: The Secret Story of Gas and Germ Warfare.* London: Chatto & Windus, 1982.

Harris, Sheldon H. *Factories of Death: Japanese Biological Warfare 1932–1945 and the American Cover-up.* London: Routledge, 1994.

"Japan's Biological Weapons: 1930–1945 — An Update." *Bulletin of the Atomic Scientists* 38 (October 1982): 62.

Kleber, Brooks E., and Dale Birdsall. *The Chemical Warfare Service: Chemicals in Action.* USAWWII. Washington, D.C.: OCMH, Department of the Army, 1966.

Moon, John Ellis Van Courtland. "Chemical Weapons and Deterrence: The World War II Experience." *International Security* 8 (Spring 1984): 3–35.

Powell, John W. "Japan's Biological Weapons, 1930–1945: A Hidden Chapter in History." *Bulletin of the Atomic Scientists* 37 (October 1981): 44–52.

Williams, Peter. *Unit 731: Japan's Secret Biological Warfare in World War II.* New York: Free Press, 1989.

Yamada, Otozo. *Materials of the Trial of Former Servicemen of the Japanese Army Charged with Manufacturing and Employing Bacteriological Weapons.* Moscow: Foreign Languages Publishing House, 1950.

E. KAMIKAZES AND OTHER *TOKKO* WEAPONS

Inoguchi, Rikihei, Tadashi Nakajima, and Roger Pineau. *Divine Wind: Japan's Kamikaze Force in World War II.* Annapolis, Md.: Naval Institute Press, 1958.

Larteguy, Jean, ed. *The Sun Goes Down: Last Letters from Japanese Suicide-Pilots and Soldiers.* Trans. Nora Wydenbruck. London: Kimber, 1956.

Millot, Bernard. *Divine Thunder: The Life and Death of Kamikazes.* Trans. Lowell Blair. New York: McCall, 1971.

Naito, Hatsuho. *Thunder Gods: The Kamikaze Pilots Tell Their Story.* New York: Kodansha International, 1989.

O'Neill, Richard. *Suicide Squads, World War II: Axis and Allied Special Attack Weapons of World War II; Their Development and Their Missions.* New York: St. Martin's, 1981.

Nagatsuka, Ryuji. *I Was a Kamikaze: The Knights of the Divine Wind.* Trans. Nina Rootes. London: Abelard-Schuman, 1973.

Warner, Denis, and Peggy Warner, with Sadao Seno. *The Sacred Warriors: Japan's Suicide Legions.* New York: Van Nostrand Reinhold, 1982.

Yokoi, Toshiyuki, with Roger Pineau. "Kamikazes and the Okinawa Campaign." *United States Naval Institute Proceedings* 80 (May 1954): 505–13.

Yokota, Yutaka, and Joseph D. Harrington. *The Kaiten Weapon.* New York: Ballantine, 1962.

F. MINES

Elliott, Peter. *Allied Minesweeping in World War 2.* Annapolis, Md.: Naval Institute Press, 1979.

Johnson, Ellis A., and David A. Katcher. *Mines against Japan.* Silver Spring, Md.: Naval Ordnance Laboratory, 1973.

Lott, Arnold S. *Most Dangerous Sea: A History of Mine Warfare and an Account of U.S. Navy Mine Warfare Operations in World War II and Korea.* Annapolis, Md.: U.S. Naval Institute, 1959.

G. RADAR

Buderi, Robert. *The Invention That Changed the World: How a Small Group of Radar Pioneers Won the Second World War and Launched a Technological Revolution.* New York: Simon & Schuster, 1996.

Burns, Russell W., ed. *Radar Development to 1945.* London: Peter Peregrinus, 1988.

Fisher, David E. *A Race on the Edge of Time: Radar–the Decisive Weapon of World War II.* New York: McGraw-Hill, 1988.

Guerlac, Henry E. *Radar in World War II.* 2 vols. New York: American Institute of Physics, 1987.

H. TANKS

Berndt, Thomas. *American Tanks of World War II*. Osceola, Wis.: Motorbooks International, 1994.

Chamberlain, Peter, and Cris Ellis. *British and American Tanks of World War II*. New York: Arco, 1969.

Crow, Duncan. *Tanks of World War II*. Windsor, England: Profile, 1979.

Gabel, Christopher R. *Seek, Strike, and Destroy: U.S. Army Tank Destroyer Doctrine in World War II*. Fort Leavenworth, Kans.: Combat Studies Institute, U.S. Army Command and General Staff College, 1986.

Hunnicutt, R. P. *Sherman: A History of the American Medium Tank*. Novato, Calif.: Presidio, 1989.

McLean, Donald B. *Japanese Tanks, Tactics, & Antitank Weapons*. Wickenburg, Ariz.: Normount Technical Publications, 1973.

Zaloga, Steven J., and James Grandsen. *Soviet Tanks and Combat Vehicles of World War Two*. London: Arms & Armour, 1984.

XIII. Media, Propaganda, and Censorship

A. JOURNALISM AND PHOTOGRAPHY

Collier, Richard. *Fighting Words: The War Correspondents of World War II*. New York: St. Martin's, 1990.

Maslowski, Peter. *Armed with Cameras: The American Military Photographers of World War II*. New York: Free Press, 1993.

Reporting World War II. 2 vols. New York: Library of America, 1995.

Sowinski, Larry. *Action in the Pacific: As Seen by U.S. Navy Photographers during World War 2*. Annapolis, Md.: Naval Institute Press, 1981.

Stenbuck, Jack, ed. *Typewriter Battalion: Dramatic Front-Line Dispatches from World War II*. New York: Morrow, 1995.

B. PROPAGANDA AND CENSORSHIP

Brewer, Susan A. *To Win the Peace: British Propaganda in the United States during World War II*. Ithaca, N.Y.: Cornell University Press, 1997.

Cull, Nicholas John. *Selling War: The British Propaganda against American "Neutrality" in World War II*. New York: Oxford University Press, 1995.

Hilvert, John. *Blue Pencil Warriors: Censorship and Propaganda in World War II*. St. Lucia: University of Queensland Press, 1984.

Howe, Russell Warren. *The Hunt for "Tokyo Rose."* Lanham, Md.: Madison, 1990.

Kasza, Gregory J. *The State and the Mass Media in Japan, 1918–1945*. Berkeley: University of California Press, 1987.

Meo, L. D. *Japan's Radio War on Australia, 1941–1945*. New York: Melbourne University Press, 1968.

Mitchell, Richard H. *Censorship in Imperial Japan*. Princeton, N.J.: Princeton University Press, 1983.

Roeder, George H., Jr. *The Censored War: American Visual Experience during World War II*. New Haven, Conn.: Yale University Press, 1993.

Shulman, Holly Cowan. *The Voice of America: Propaganda and Democracy, 1941–1945*. Madison: University of Wisconsin Press, 1990.

Winkler, Allan M. *The Politics of Propaganda: The Office of War Information, 1942–1945*. New Haven, Conn.: Yale University Press, 1978.

C. FILM

Aldgate, Anthony, and Jeffrey Richards. *Britain Can Take It: The British Cinema in the Second World War*. Oxford: Blackwell, 1986.

Basinger, Janine. *The World War II Combat Film: Anatomy of a Genre*. New York: Columbia University Press, 1986.

Chambers, John Whiteclay, II, and David Culbert. *World War II, Film, and History*. New York: Oxford University Press, 1996.

Coultass, Clive. *Images for Battle: British Film and the Second World War, 1939–1945*. London: Routledge, 1989.

Dick, Bernard F. *The Star-Spangled Screen: The American World War II Film*. Lexington: University of Kentucky Press, 1985.

Koppes, Clayton R., and Gregory D. Black. *Hollywood Goes to War: How Politics, Profits, and Propaganda Shaped World War II Movies*. New York: Free Press, 1987.

Manvell, Roger. *Films and the Second World War*. South Brunswick, N.J.: Barnes, 1974.

Nornes, Abe Mark, and Fukushima Yukio, eds. *The Japan/America Film Wars: World War II Propaganda and Its Cultural Context*. Philadelphia: Harwood Academic, 1994.

Shindler, Colin. *Hollywood Goes to War: Films and American Society, 1939–1952*. London: Routledge, 1979.

Short, K. R. M. *Film and Radio Propaganda in World War II: A Global Perspective.* Knoxville: University of Tennessee Press, 1983.

Suid, Lawrence. *Guts and Glory: Great American War Movies.* Reading, Mass.: Addison-Wesley, 1978.

XIV. Prisoners of War and Internees [see also XVIII.B]

A. GENERAL

Bailey, Ronald H. *Prisoners of War.* Alexandria, Va.: Time-Life Books, 1981.

Christgau, John. *"Enemies": World War II Alien Internment.* Ames: Iowa State University Press, 1985.

Corbett, P. Scott. *Quiet Passages: The Exchange of Civilians Between the United States and Japan during the Second World War.* Kent, Ohio: Kent State University Press, 1987.

Dingman, Roger. *Ghost of War: The Sinking of the Awa Maru and Japanese-American Relations, 1945–1995.* Annapolis, Md.: Naval Institute Press, 1997.

Moore, Bob, and Kent Fedorowich, eds. *Prisoners of War and Their Captors in World War II.* Washington, D.C.: Berg, 1996.

B. HELD BY JAPAN

1. General

Waterford, Van. *Prisoners of the Japanese in World War II: Statistical History, Personal Narratives and Memorials Concerning POWs in Camps and on Hellships, Civilian Internees, Asian Slave Laborers and Others Captured in the Pacific Theater.* Jefferson, N.C.: McFarland, 1994.

2. Military

Arthur, Anthony. *Deliverance at Los Baños.* New York: St. Martin's, 1985.

Berry, William A. *Prisoner of the Rising Sun.* Norman: University of Oklahoma Press, 1993.

Bird, Tom. *American POWs of World War II: Forgotten Men Tell Their Stories.* Westport, Conn.: Praeger, 1992.

Blair, Joan, and Clay Blair, Jr. *Return From the River Kwai*. New York: Simon & Schuster, 1979.

Brougher, William Edward. *South to Bataan, North to Mukden: The Prison Diary of Brigadier General W. E. Brougher*. Ed. D. Clayton James. Athens: University of Georgia Press, 1971.

Clarke, Hugh V. *Twilight Liberation: Australian Prisoners of War Between Hiroshima and Home*. Sydney: Allen & Unwin, 1985.

Clarke, Hugh V., and Colin Burgess. *Barbed Wire and Bamboo: Australian POWs in Europe, North Africa, Singapore, Thailand and Japan*. St. Leonards, Australia: Allen & Unwin, 1992.

Cohen, Bernard M., and Maurice Z. Cooper. *A Follow-up Study of World War II Prisoners of War*. Washington, D.C.: GPO, 1954.

Dancocks, Daniel G. *In Enemy Hands: Canadian Prisoners of War*. Edmonton, Alberta: Hurtig, 1983.

Davies, Peter N. *The Man Behind the Bridge: Colonel Toosey and the River Kwai*. Atlantic Highlands, N.J.: Humanities Press, 1991.

Daws, Gavan. *Prisoners of the Japanese: POWs of World War II in the Pacific*. New York: Morrow, 1994.

Dunlop, E. E. *The War Diaries of Weary Dunlop: Java and the Burma-Thailand Railway, 1942–1945*. Melbourne: Nelson, 1986.

Dyess, William E. *The Dyess Story: The Eyewitness Account of the Death March from Bataan and the Narrative of Experiences in Japanese Prison Camps and of Eventual Escape*. New York: Putnam, 1944.

Falk, Stanley. *Bataan: The March of Death*. New York: Norton, 1962.

Flanagan, Edward M., Jr. *The Los Baños Raid: The 11th Airborne Jumps at Dawn*. Novato, Calif.: Presidio, 1986.

Fujita, Frank. *Foo, a Japanese-American Prisoner of the Rising Sun: The Secret Prison Diary of Frank "Foo" Fujita*. Denton: University of North Texas Press, 1993.

Jones, Betty B. *The December Ship: A Story of Lt. Colonel Arden R. Boellner's Capture in the Philippines, Imprisonment, and Death on a World War II Japanese Hellship*. Jefferson, N.C.: McFarland, 1992.

Kenny, Catherine. *Australian Army Nurses in Japanese Prison Camps*. St. Lucia: University of Queensland Press, 1986.

Kerr, E. Bartlett. *Surrender and Survival: The Experience of American POWs in the Pacific, 1941–1945*. New York: Morrow, 1985.

Kinvig, Clifford. *River Kwai Railway: The Story of the Burma-Siam Railroad*. Washington, D.C.: Brassey's,1992.

Knox, Donald. *Death March: The Survivors of Bataan*. New York: Harcourt Brace Jovanovich, 1981.

La Forte, Robert S., and Ronald E. Marcello, eds. *Building the Death Railway: The Ordeal of American POWs in Burma, 1942–1945*. Wilmington, Del.: Scholarly Resources, 1993.

La Forte, Robert S., Ronald E. Marcello, and Richard L. Himmel, eds. *With Only the Will to Live: Accounts of Americans in Japanese Prison Camps, 1941–1945*. Wilmington, Del.: SR Books, 1994.

. Lawton, Manny. *Some Survived: An Epic Account of Japanese Captivity during World War II*. Chapel Hill, N.C.: Algonquin, 1984.

Lomax, Eric. *The Railway Man: A POW's Searing Account of War, Brutality and Forgiveness*. New York: Norton, 1995.

McCormack, Gavan, and Hank Nelson, eds. *The Burma-Thailand Railway: Memory and History*. St. Leonards, Australia: Allen & Unwin, 1993.

McIntosh, Dave. *Hell on Earth: Aging Faster, Dying Sooner: Canadian Prisoners of the Japanese during World War II*. Toronto: McGraw-Hill Ryerson, 1997.

Martin, Adrian R. *Brothers from Bataan: POWs, 1942–1945*. Manhattan, Kans.: Sunflower University Press, 1992.

Mason, W. Wynne. *Prisoners of War*. Official History of New Zealand in the Second World War, 1939–45. Wellington: War History Branch, Department of Internal Affairs, 1954.

Searle, Ronald. *To the Kwai–and Back: War Drawings, 1939–1945*. London: Collins, 1986.

Simons, Jessie Elizabeth. *While History Passed*. Melbourne: Heinemann, 1954.

Wright, John M. *Captured on Corregidor: Diary of an American P.O.W. in World War II*. Jefferson, N.C.: McFarland, 1988.

3. Civilian [see also IV Individual Entries]

Allan, Sheila. *Diary of a Girl in Changi, 1941–45*. Kenthurst, Australia: Kangaroo, 1994.

Bonga, Dieuwke Wendelaar. *Eight Prison Camps: A Dutch Family in Japanese Java*. Athens: Ohio University Center for International Studies, 1996.

Colijn, Helen. *Song of Survival: Women Interned*. Ashland, Ore.: White Cloud, 1997.

Crouter, Natalie. *Forbidden Diary: A Record of Wartime Internment, 1941–1945*. Ed. Lynn Z. Bloom. New York: Franklin, 1980.

Gilkey, Langdon. *Shantung Compound: The Story of Men and Women Under Pressure*. New York: Harper & Row, 1966.

Keith, Agnes Newton. *Three Came Home*. Boston: Little, Brown, 1974.

Mathers, Jean. *Twisting the Tail of the Dragon*. Sussex, England: Book Guild, 1994.

Montgomery, Brian. *Shenton of Singapore: Governor and Prisoner of War*. London: Cooper, 1984.

Onorato, Michael P. *Forgotten Heroes: Japan's Imprisonment of American Civilians in the Philippines, 1942–1945; An Oral History*. Westport, Conn.: Greenwood, 1989.

Sams, Margaret. *Forbidden Family: A Wartime Memoir of the Philippines, 1941–1945*. Madison: University Press of Wisconsin, 1989.

Stevens, Frederick. *Santo Tomas Internment Camp, 1942–1945*. New York: Stratford, 1946.

Van der Post, Laurens. *The Prisoner and the Bomb*. New York: Morrow, 1971.

Van Sickle, Emily. *The Iron Gates of Santo Tomas: The Firsthand Account of an American Couple Interned by the Japanese in Manila, 1942–45*. Chicago: Academy Chicago, 1992.

Vaughan, Elizabeth. *Community under Stress: An Internment Culture*. Princeton, N.J.: Princeton University Press, 1949.

Vaughan, Elizabeth. *The Ordeal of Elizabeth Vaughan: A Wartime Diary of the Philippines*. Ed. Carol M. Petillo. Athens: University of Georgia Press, 1985.

Warner, Lavinia, and John Sandilands. *Women Beyond the Wire: A Story of Prisoners of the Japanese, 1942–1945*. London: Joseph, 1982.

C. HELD BY THE ALLIES (EXCLUDING THE UNION OF SOVIET SOCIALIST REPUBLICS)

1. General

Aida, Yuji. *Prisoner of the British: A Japanese Soldier's Experiences in Burma*. London: Cresset, 1966.

Bevege, Margaret. *Behind Barbed Wire: Internment in Australia during World War II*. St. Lucia: University of Queensland Press, 1993.

Carr-Gregg, Charlotte. *Japanese Prisoners of War in Revolt: The Outbreaks at Featherston and Cowra during World War II*. New York: St. Martin's, 1978.

Gordon, Harry. *Voyage from Shame: The Cowra Breakout and Afterwards*. St. Lucia: University of Queensland Press, 1994.

Krammer, Arnold. "Japanese Prisoners of War in America." *Pacific Historical Review* 52 (February 1983): 67–91.

Nagata, Yuriko. *Unwanted Aliens: Japanese Internment in Australia.* St. Lucia: University of Queensland Press, 1996.

2. Japanese Americans [see also IV.S.10; VIII.E]

Bosworth, Allan R. *America's Concentration Camps.* New York: Norton, 1967.

Collins, Donald E. *Native American Aliens: Disloyalty and the Renunciation of Citizenship by Japanese Americans during World War II.* Westport, Conn.: Greenwood, 1985.

Daniels, Roger, ed.. *American Concentration Camps: A Documentary History.* 9 vols. New York: Garland, 1989.

Daniels, Roger. *Concentration Camps U.S.A.: Japanese Americans and World War II.* New York: Holt, Rinehart & Winston, 1971.

Daniels, Roger, Sandra C. Taylor, and Harry H. L. Kitano, eds. *Japanese Americans: From Relocation to Redress.* Salt Lake City: University of Utah Press, 1986.

DeWitt, John D. *Final Report: Japanese Evacuation from the West Coast, 1942.* Washington, D.C.: GPO, 1943.

Drinnon, Richard. *Keeper of Concentration Camps: Dillon S. Myer and American Racism.* Berkeley: University of California Press, 1987.

Girdner, Audrie, and Anne Loftis. *The Great Betrayal: The Evacuation of the Japanese-Americans during World War II.* New York: Macmillan, 1969.

Grodzins, Morton. *Americans Betrayed: Politics and the Japanese Evacuation.* Chicago: University of Chicago Press, 1949.

Hane, Mikiso. "Wartime Internment." *Journal of American History* 77 (September 1990): 569–75.

Hansen, Arthur A., ed. *Japanese American World War II Evacuation Oral History Project.* 2 vols. Westport, Conn.: Meckler, 1991.

Ichihashi, Yamato. *Morning Glory, Evening Shadow: Yamato Ichihashi and his Internment Writings, 1942–1945.* Stanford, Calif.: Stanford University Press, 1997.

Irons, Peter. *Justice at War: The Story of the Japanese-American Internment Cases.* New York: Oxford University Press, 1983.

Myer, Dillon S. *Uprooted Americans: The Japanese Americans and the War Relocation Authority during World War II.* Tucson: University of Arizona Press, 1971.

Nishimoto, Richard S. *Inside an American Concentration Camp: Japanese-American Resistance at Poston, Arizona.* Ed. Lane Ryo Hirabayashi. Tucson: University of Arizona Press, 1995.

Smith, Page. *Democracy on Trial: The Japanese American Evacuation and Relocation in World War II.* New York: Simon & Schuster, 1995.

Tateishi, John, comp. *And Justice for All: An Oral History of the Japanese American Detention Camps.* New York: Random House, 1984.

Weglyn, Michi. *Years of Infamy: The Untold Story of America's Concentration Camps.* New York: Morrow, 1976.

3. Japanese Canadians [see also IV.C.2]

Adachi, Ken. *The Enemy That Never Was: A History of the Japanese Canadians.* Buffalo, N.Y.: Books Canada, 1976.

Broadfoot, Barry. *Years of Sorrow, Years of Shame: The Story of the Japanese Canadians in World War II.* Garden City, N.Y.: Doubleday, 1977.

Carter, David John. *Behind Canadian Barbed Wire: Alien, Refugee, and Prisoner of War Camps in Canada, 1914–1946.* Calgary: Tumbleweed, 1980.

Daniels, Roger. "Chinese and Japanese in North America: The Canadian and American Experiences Compared." *Canadian Review of American Studies* 17 (Summer 1986): 173–87.

LaViolette, Forrest E. *The Canadian Japanese and World War II.* Toronto: University of Toronto Press, 1948.

Nakano, Takeo Ujo. *Within the Barbed Wire Fence: A Japanese Man's Account of His Internment in Canada.* Toronto: University of Toronto Press, 1980.

Roy, Patricia E., et al. *Mutual Hostages: Canadians and Japanese during the Second World War.* Toronto: University of Toronto Press, 1990.

4. Latin American Japanese [see also IV.K]

Barnhart, Edward N. "Japanese Internees from Peru." *Pacific Historical Review* 31 (May 1962): 169–78.

Connell, Thomas. "The Internment of Latin-American Japanese in the U.S. during WWII: Peruvian Japanese Experience." Ph.D. dissertation, Florida State University, 1995.

Emmerson, John K. "Japanese and Americans in Peru, 1942–1943." *Foreign Service Journal* 54 (May 1977): 40–47, 56.

Gardiner, C. Harvey. *Pawns in a Triangle of Hate: The Peruvian Japanese and the United States.* Seattle: University of Washington Press, 1981.

D. HELD BY THE UNION OF SOVIET SOCIALIST REPUBLICS

Fehling, Helmut M., and Charles R. Joy. *One Great Prison: The Story Behind Russia's Unreleased POW's*. Boston: Beacon, 1951.

Hays, Otis, Jr. *Home From Siberia: The Secret Odysseys of Interned American Airmen in World War II*. College Station: Texas A&M University Press, 1990.

Nimmo, William F. *Behind a Curtain of Silence: Japanese in Soviet Custody, 1945–1946*. New York: Greenwood, 1988.

Sano, Iwao Peter. *One Thousand Days in Siberia: The Odyssey of a Japanese-American POW*. Lincoln: University of Nebraska Press, 1997.

Yamamoto, Tomomi. *Four Years in Hell: I Was a Prisoner behind the Iron Curtain*. Tokyo: Asian, 1952.

XV. Women [see also XIV]

Alsmeyer, Marie Bennet. *The Way of Waves: Women in the Navy*. Conway, Ark.: Hamba, 1982.

Anderson, Karen. *Wartime Women: Sex Roles, Family Relations, and the Status of Women in World War II*. Westport, Conn.: Greenwood, 1981.

Campbell, D'Ann. *Women at War with America: Private Lives in a Patriotic Era*. Cambridge, Mass.: Harvard University Press, 1984.

Campbell, D'Ann. "Women in Combat: The World War II Experience in the United States, Great Britain, Germany, and the Soviet Union." *Journal of Military History* 57 (April 1993): 301–23.

Cole, Jean Hascall. *Women Pilots of World War II*. Salt Lake City: University of Utah Press, 1992.

Edmund, Lauris, ed., with Carolyn Milward. *Women in Wartime: New Zealand Women Tell Their Story*. Wellington: Government Printing Office, 1986.

Fessler, Diane Burke. *No Time for Fear: Voices of American Military Nurses in World War II*. East Lansing: Michigan State University Press, 1996.

Gluck, Sherna B. *Rosie the Riveter Revisited: Women, the War, and Social Change*. Boston: Twayne, 1987.

Gossage, Carolyn. *Greatcoats and Glamour Boots: Canadian Women at War, 1939–1945*. Toronto: Dundurn Press, 1991.

Hamblet, Julia E. *Women Marines: The World War II Era*. Westport, Conn.: Praeger, 1992.

Holm, Jeanne M., and Judith Bellafaire. *In Defense of a Nation: Service-women in World War II*. Washington, D.C.: Military Women's Press, 1998.

Hoyt, Olga Gruhzit. *They Also Served: American Women in World War II*. New York: Birch Lane, 1995.

Kesselman, Amy Vita. *Women Shipyard Workers in Portland and Vancouver during World War II and Reconversion*. Ithaca, N.Y.: Cornell University Press, 1985.

Litoff, Judy Barrett, and David C. Smith. *We're In This War, Too: World War II Letters from American Women in Uniform*. New York: Oxford University Press, 1994.

Merryman, Molly. *Clipped Wings: The Rise and Fall of the Women Airforce Service Pilots (WASPs) of World War II*. New York: New York University Press, 1997.

Meyer, Leisa D. *Creating GI Jane: Sexuality and Power in the Women's Army Corps during World War II*. New York: Columbia University Press, 1996.

Saywell, Shelley. *Women in War*. New York: Viking, 1985.

Scott, Jean. *Girls with Grit: Memories of the Australian Women's Land Army*. Sydney: Allen & Unwin, 1986.

Soderbergh, Peter A. *Women Marines: The World War II Era*. Westport, Conn.: Praeger, 1992.

Taylor, Eric. *Women Who Went to War, 1938–46*. London: Hale, 1988.

Thomson, Joyce A. *The WAAAF in Wartime Australia*. Carlton: Melbourne University Press, 1991.

Tomblin, Barbara Brooks. *G.I. Nightingales: The Army Nurse Corps in World War II*. Lexington: University Press of Kentucky, 1996.

Treadwell, Mattie E. *The Women's Army Corps*. USAWWII. Washington, D.C.: OCMH, Department of the Army, 1954.

Weatherford, Doris. *American Women and World War II*. New York: Facts on File, 1990.

XVI. Biographies and Memoirs of Leaders

A. COLLECTIVE

Bialer, Seweryn, comp. *Stalin and His Generals: Soviet Military Memoirs of World War II*. New York: Pegasus, 1969.

Carver, Michael, ed. *The War Lords: Military Commanders of the Twentieth Century*. Boston: Little, Brown, 1976.

Howarth, Stephen, ed. *Men of War: Great Naval Captains of World War II*. New York: St. Martin's, 1993.

James, D. Clayton, with Anne Sharp Wells, *A Time for Giants: Politics of the American High Command in World War II*. New York: Franklin Watts, 1987.

Keegan, John, ed. *Churchill's Generals*. New York: Grove Weidenfeld, 1991.

Larrabee, Eric. *Commander in Chief: Franklin Delano Roosevelt, His Lieutenants, and Their War*. New York: Harper & Row, 1987.

Leary, William M., ed. *We Shall Return! MacArthur's Commanders and the Defeat of Japan, 1942–1945*. Lexington: University Press of Kentucky, 1988.

Pitt, Barrie. *Churchill and the Generals: Their Finest Hour*. Newton Abbot, England: David & Charles, 1988.

Reynolds, Clark G. *Famous American Admirals*. New York: Van Nostrand Reinhold, 1978.

Roskill, Stephen. *Churchill and the Admirals*. New York: Simon & Schuster, 1974.

Shukman, Harold, ed. *Stalin's Generals*. New York: Grove, 1993.

Stephen, Martin. *The Fighting Admirals: British Admirals of the Second World War*. Annapolis, Md.: Naval Institute Press, 1991.

B. JAPAN

Agawa, Hiroyuki. *The Reluctant Admiral: Yamamoto and the Imperial Navy*. Trans. John Bester. Tokyo: Kodansha International, 1979.

Barker, A. J. *Yamashita*. New York: Ballantine, 1973.

Behr, Edward. *Hirohito: Behind the Myth*. New York: Villard Books, 1989.

Browne, Courtney. *Tojo: The Last Banzai*. New York: Holt, Rinehart & Winston, 1967.

Coox, Alvin D. *Tojo*. New York: Ballantine, 1975.

Dower, John W. *Empire and Aftermath: Yoshida Shigeru and the Japanese Experience, 1878–1954*. Cambridge, Mass.: Council on East Asian Studies, Harvard University, 1979.

Glines, Carroll V. *Attack on Yamamoto*. New York: Orion, 1990.

Gluck, Carol, and Stephen Graubard, eds. *Showa: The Japan of Hirohito*. New York: Norton, 1992.

Hall, R. Cargill, ed. *Lightning Over Bougainville: The Yamamoto Mission Reconsidered*. Washington, D.C.: Smithsonian, 1991.

Hoyt, Edwin P. *The Last Kamikaze: The Story of Admiral Matome Ugaki.* Westport, Conn.: Praeger, 1993.

Hoyt, Edwin Palmer. *Three Military Leaders: Heihachiro Togo, Isoruku Yamamoto, Tomoyuki Yamashita.* New York: Kodansha International, 1993.

Hoyt, Edwin P. *Yamamoto: The Man Who Planned Pearl Harbor.* New York: McGraw-Hill, 1990.

Irokawa, Daikichi. *The Age of Hirohito: In Search of Modern Japan.* Trans. Mikiso Hane and John Urda. New York: Free Press, 1995.

Kanroji, Osanaga. *Hirohito: An Intimate Portrait of the Japanese Emperor.* Los Angeles: Gateway, 1975.

Kawahara, Toshiaki. *Hirohito and His Times: A Japanese Perspective.* New York: Kodansha International, 1990.

Kido, Koichi. *The Diary of Marquis Kido, 1931–1945: Selected Translations into English.* Frederick, Md.: University Publications of America, 1984.

Large, Stephen S. *Emperor Hirohito and Showa Japan: A Political Biography.* New York: Routledge, 1992.

Manning, Paul. *Hirohito: The War Years.* New York: Dodd, Mead, 1986.

Nakamura, Masanori. *The Japanese Monarchy: Ambassador Joseph Grew and the Making of the "Symbol Emperor System," 1931–1991.* Armonk, N.Y.: Sharpe, 1992.

Oka, Yoshitake. *Konoe Fumimaro: A Political Biography.* Trans. Shumpei Okamoto and Patricia Murray. Lanham, Md.: Madison Books, 1983.

Potter, John Deane. *Yamamoto: The Man Who Menaced America.* New York: Viking Press, 1965.

Shigemitsu, Mamoru. *Japan and Her Destiny: My Struggle for Peace.* Ed. S. G. Piggott. Trans. Oswald White. New York: Dutton, 1958.

Swinson, Arthur. *Four Samurai: A Quartet of Japanese Army Commanders in the Second World War.* London: Hutchinson, 1968.

Togo, Shigenori. *The Cause of Japan.* Trans., ed. Togo Fumihiko and Ben B. Blakeney. New York: Simon and Schuster, 1956.

Ugaki, Matome. *Fading Victory: The Diary of Admiral Matome Ugaki, 1941–1945.* Trans. Masataka Chihaya, with Donald M. Goldstein and Katherine V. Dillon. Pittsburgh: University of Pittsburgh Press, 1991.

Yoshida, Shigeru. *The Yoshida Memoirs: The Story of Japan in Crisis.* Trans. Kenichi Yoshida. Boston: Houghton Mifflin, 1962.

C. ALLIES

1. Civilian

Barker, Elisabeth. *Churchill and Eden at War*. London: Macmillan, 1978.

Burns, James MacGregor. *Roosevelt: The Soldier of Freedom 1940–1945*. New York: Harcourt Brace Jovanovich, 1970.

Byrnes, James F. *Speaking Frankly*. New York: Harper, 1947.

Churchill, Randolph S., and Martin Gilbert. *Winston S. Churchill*. 8 vols. Boston: Houghton Mifflin, 1966–1988. [Vol. 6: *Finest Hour, 1939–1941;* vol. 7: *Road to Victory, 1941–1945;* both by Martin Gilbert.]

Crozier, Bryan. *The Man Who Lost China: The First Full Biography of Chiang Kai-shek*. New York: Scribner's, 1976.

Donovan, Robert J. *Conflict and Crisis: The Presidency of Harry S. Truman, 1945–1948*. New York: Norton, 1977.

Ferrell, Robert H. *The Dying President: Franklin D. Roosevelt, 1944–1945*. Columbia: University of Missouri Press, 1998.

Freidel, Frank. *Franklin Delano Roosevelt: A Rendezvous with Destiny*. Boston: Little Brown, 1990.

Gilbert, Martin. *Churchill: A Life*. New York: Holt, 1991.

Goodwin, Doris Kearns. *No Ordinary Time: Franklin and Eleanor Roosevelt: The Home Front in World War II*. New York: Simon & Schuster, 1994.

Grew, Joseph C. *Ten Years in Japan*. New York: Simon & Schuster, 1944.

Harriman, W. Averell, and Elie Abel. *Special Envoy to Churchill and Stalin, 1941–1946*. New York: Random House, 1975.

Heinrichs, Waldo H. *American Ambassador: Joseph C. Grew and the Development of the United States Diplomatic Tradition*. Boston: Little, Brown, 1966.

Hodgson, Godfrey. *The Colonel: The Life and Wars of Henry Stimson, 1867–1950*. New York: Knopf, 1990.

Hull, Cordell. *The Memoirs of Cordell Hull*. 2 vols. New York: Macmillan, 1948.

Kimball, Warren F. *The Juggler: Franklin Roosevelt as Wartime Statesman*. Princeton, N.J.: Princeton University Press, 1991.

Lamb, Richard. *Churchill as War Leader*. New York: Carroll & Graf, 1993.

Laqueur, Walter. *Stalin: The Glasnost Revelations*. New York: Scribner's, 1990.

McCullough, David. *Truman*. New York: Simon & Schuster, 1992.

McJimsey, George T. *Harry Hopkins: Ally of the Poor and Defender of Democracy*. Cambridge, Mass.: Harvard University Press, 1987.

McNeal, Robert H. *Stalin: Man and Ruler*. New York: New York University Press, 1988.

Parrish, Thomas. *Roosevelt and Marshall: Partners in Politics and War*. New York: Morrow, 1989.

Radzinsky, Edvard. *Stalin*. Trans. H. T. Willets. New York: Doubleday, 1996.

Rappaport, Armin. *Henry L. Stimson and Japan, 1931–1933*. Chicago: University of Chicago Press, 1963.

Ross, Lloyd M. *John Curtin: A Biography*. Melbourne: Macmillan, 1977.

Schoenfeld, Maxwell P. *The War Ministry of Winston Churchill*. Ames: Iowa State University Press, 1972.

Seaton, Albert. *Stalin as Military Commander*. New York: Praeger, 1976.

Sherwood, Robert E. *Roosevelt and Hopkins: An Intimate History*. New York: Harper & Brothers, 1948.

Stettinius, Edward R., Jr. *The Diaries of Edward Stettinius, Jr., 1943–46*. New York: New Viewpoints, 1975.

Stimson, Henry L., and McGeorge Bundy. *On Active Service in Peace and War*. New York: Harper & Brothers, 1947.

Truman, Harry S. *Memoirs*. Vol. 1: *Year of Decision, 1945*. New York: Doubleday, 1955.

Volkogonov, Dmitri. *Stalin: Triumph and Tragedy*. Ed. and trans. Harold Shukman. New York: Grove & Weidenfeld, 1991.

2. Military

Adams, Henry H. *Witness to Power: The Life of Fleet Admiral William D. Leahy*. Annapolis, Md.: Naval Institute Press, 1985.

Alexander, Harold R. L. G. *The Alexander Memoirs, 1940–1945*. Ed. John North. London: Cassell, 1962.

Arnold, Henry H. *Global Mission*. New York: Harper, 1949.

Barbey, Daniel D. *MacArthur's Amphibious Navy: Seventh Amphibious Force Operations, 1943–45*. Annapolis, Md.: Naval Institute Press, 1969.

Beldon, Jack. *Retreat with Stilwell.* New York: Knopf, 1943.

Boyington, Gregory. *Baa Baa Black Sheep.* New York: Putnam, 1958.

Brereton, Lewis H. *The Brereton Diaries: The War in the Air in the Pacific, Middle East and Europe, 3 October 1941–8 May 1945.* New York: Morrow, 1946.

Bryant, Arthur. *Triumph in the West: a History of the War Years Based on the Diaries of Field-Marshal Lord Alanbrooke, Chief of the Imperial General Staff.* Garden City, N.Y.: Doubleday, 1959.

Bryant, Arthur. *The Turn of the Tide: a History of the War Years Based on the Diaries of Field-Marshal Lord Alanbrooke, Chief of the Imperial General Staff.* Garden City, N.Y.: Doubleday, 1957.

Buell, Thomas. *Master of Seapower: A Biography of Fleet Admiral Ernest J. King.* Boston: Little, Brown, 1980.

Buell, Thomas. *The Quiet Warrior: A Biography of Admiral Raymond A. Spruance.* Boston: Little, Brown, 1974.

Byrd, Martha. *Chennault: Giving Wings to the Tiger.* Tuscaloosa: University of Alabama Press, 1987.

Carton de Wiart, Adrian. *Happy Odyssey.* London: Cape, 1950.

Chaney, Otto P. *Zhukov.* Rev. ed. Norman: University of Oklahoma Press, 1996.

Chennault, Claire L. *Way of a Fighter: The Memoirs of Claire Lee Chennault.* Ed. Robert B. Hotz. New York: Putnam, 1949.

Chwialkowski, Paul. *In Caesar's Shadow: The Life of General Robert Eichelberger.* Westport, Conn.: Greenwood, 1993.

Clark, J. J., with Clark G. Reynolds. *Carrier Admiral.* New York: McKay, 1967.

Coffey, Thomas M. *Hap: The Story of the U.S. Air Force and the Man Who Built It, General Henry H. "Hap" Arnold.* New York: Viking, 1982.

Coffey, Thomas M. *Iron Eagle: The Turbulent Life of General Curtis E. LeMay.* New York: Crown, 1986.

Collins, J. Lawton. *Lightning Joe: An Autobiography.* Baton Rouge: Louisiana State University Press, 1979

Connell, John. *Wavell: the Supreme Commander, 1941–1943.* London: Collins, 1969.

Cray, Ed. *General of the Army: George C. Marshall: Soldier and Statesman.* New York: Norton, 1990.

Danchev, Alexander. *Very Special Relationship: Field Marshal Sir John Dill and the Anglo-American Alliance, 1941–1944.* London: Brassey's, 1986.

Deane, John R. *The Strange Alliance: The Story of American Efforts at Wartime Co-operation with Russia*. New York: Viking, 1947.

Donovan, Robert J. *PT 109: John F. Kennedy in World War II*. New York: McGraw-Hill, 1961.

Doolittle, James H., with Carroll V. Glines. *I Could Never Be So Lucky Again: The Memoirs of General James H. "Jimmy" Doolittle*. New York: Bantam, 1991.

Dorn, Frank. *Walkout with Stilwell in Burma*. New York: Crowell, 1971.

Dyer, George C. *The Amphibians Came to Conquer: The Story of Admiral Richmond Kelly Turner*. 2 vols. Washington, D.C.: Department of the Navy, 1972.

Dyer, George C., ed. *On the Treadmill to Pearl Harbor: The Memoirs of Admiral James O. Richardson*. Washington, D.C.: Naval History Division, 1973.

Eichelberger, Robert L. *Dear Miss Em: General Eichelberger's War in the Pacific, 1942–1945*. Ed. Jay Luvaas. Westport, Conn.: Greenwood, 1972.

Eichelberger, Robert L. *Our Jungle Road to Tokyo*. New York: Viking, 1950.

Forrestel, E. P. *Admiral Raymond A. Spruance, USN: A Study in Command*. Washington, D.C.: Department of the Navy, 1966.

Frank, Benis M. *Halsey*. New York: Ballantine, 1974.

Fraser, David. *Alanbrooke*. New York: Atheneum, 1982.

Halsey, William F., and Joseph Bryan III. *Admiral Halsey's Story*. New York: Whittlesey House, 1947.

Hetherington, John A. *Blamey: The Biography of Field-Marshal Sir Thomas Blamey*. Melbourne: Cheshire, 1954.

Hough, Richard A. *Mountbatten*. New York: Random House, 1981.

Huff, Sid, with Joe Alex Morris. *My Fifteen Years with General MacArthur*. New York: Curtis, 1951.

Humble, Richard. *Fraser of North Cape*. London: Routledge, 1983.

Ismay, Hastings L. *The Memoirs of General Lord Ismay*. New York: Viking, 1960.

James, D. Clayton. *The Years of MacArthur*. 3 vols. Boston: Houghton Mifflin, 1970–1985.

Jones, Ken, and Hubert Kelley, Jr. *Admiral Arleigh (31-Knot) Burke, the Story of a Fighting Sailor*. Philadelphia: Chilton, 1962.

Kenney, George C. *General Kenney Reports: A Personal History of the Pacific War*. New York: Duell, Sloan & Pearce, 1949.

Kenney, George C. *The MacArthur I Know*. New York: Duell, Sloan & Pearce, 1951.

Kimmel, Husband E. *Admiral Kimmel's Story*. Chicago: Regnery, 1954.

King, Ernest J., and Walter Muir Whitehall. *Fleet Admiral King: A Naval Record*. New York: Norton, 1952.

Krueger, Walter. *From Down Under to Nippon: The Story of Sixth Army in World War II*. Washington, D.C.: Combat Forces Press, 1953.

Leahy, William D. *I Was There: The Personal Story of the Chief of Staff to Presidents Roosevelt and Truman, Based on His Notes and Diaries Made at the Time*. New York: Whittlesey House, 1950.

LeMay, Curtis E., and MacKinlay Kantor. *Mission with LeMay: My Story*. Garden City, N.Y.: Doubleday, 1965.

Leutze, James. *A Different Kind of Victory: A Biography of Admiral Thomas C. Hart*. Annapolis, Md.: Naval Institute Press, 1981.

Lewin, Ronald. *The Chief: Field Marshal Lord Wavell, Commander-in-Chief and Viceroy, 1939–47*. New York: Farrar, Straus, Giroux, 1980.

Lewin, Ronald. *Slim: The Standard Bearer*. Hamden, Conn.: Archon, 1976.

Long, Gavin. *MacArthur as Military Commander*. London: Batsford, 1969.

MacArthur, Douglas. *Reminiscences*. New York: McGraw-Hill, 1964.

MacIntyre, Donald. *Fighting Admiral*. London: Evans, 1961. [James F. Somerville]

Marshall, George C. *The Papers of George Catlett Marshall*. Eds. Larry I. Bland and Sharon Ritenour Stevens. 4 vols. to date. Baltimore, Md.: Johns Hopkins University Press, 1981– .

Merrill, James M. *A Sailor's Admiral: A Biography of William F. Halsey*. New York: Crowell, 1976.

Mets, David R. *A Master of Air Power: General Carl A. Spaatz*. Novato, Calif.: Presidio, 1988.

Mountbatten, Louis. *Personal Diary of Admiral The Lord Louis Mountbatten, Supreme Allied Commander, South-east Asia, 1943–1947*. Ed. Philip Ziegler. London: Collins, 1988.

Nicolson, Nigel. *Alex: the Life of Field Marshal Earl Alexander of Tunis*. New York: Harcourt, Brace & World, 1973.

Percival, Arthur E. *The War in Malaya*. London: Eyre & Spottiswoode, 1949.

Petillo, Carol Morris. *Douglas MacArthur: The Philippine Years*. Bloomington: Indiana University Press, 1981.

Pogue, Forrest C. *George C. Marshall*. 4 vols. New York: Viking, 1964–1985.

Potter, E. B. *Admiral Arleigh Burke: A Biography*. New York: Random House, 1990.

Potter, E. B. *Bull Halsey*. Annapolis, Md.: Naval Institute Press, 1985.

Potter, E. B. *Nimitz*. Annapolis, Md.: Naval Institute Press, 1976.

Regan, Stephen D. *In Bitter Tempest: The Biography of Admiral Frank Jack Fletcher*. Ames: Iowa State University Press, 1994.

Reynolds, Clark G. *Admiral John H. Towers: The Struggle for Naval Air Supremacy*. Annapolis, Md.: Naval Institute Press, 1991.

Richards, Denis. *Portal of Hungerford*. New York: Holmes & Meier, 1977.

Robertson, John H. *Auchinleck: A Biography of Field-Marshal Sir Claude Auchinleck*. London: Cassell, 1959.

Royle, Trevor. *Orde Wingate: Irregular Soldier*. London: Weidenfeld & Nicolson, 1995.

Schaller, Michael. *Douglas MacArthur: The Far Eastern General*. New York: Oxford University Press, 1985.

Schultz, Duane P. *Hero of Bataan: The Story of General Jonathan M. Wainwright*. New York: St. Martin's, 1981.

Shortal, John Francis. *Forged by Fire: Robert L. Eichelberger and the Pacific War*. Columbia: University of South Carolina Press, 1987.

Simpson, B. Mitchell. *Admiral Harold R. Stark: Architect of Victory, 1939–1945*. Columbia: University of South Carolina Press, 1989.

Slim, William. *Defeat into Victory*. London: Cassell, 1956.

Slim, William. *Unofficial History*. New York: McKay, 1962.

Smith, Holland M. *Coral and Brass*. New York: Scribner's, 1949.

Somerville, James. *The Somerville Papers*. Ed. Michael Simpson. Brookfield, Vt.: Ashgate, 1995.

Stilwell, Joseph W. *The Stilwell Papers*. Ed. Theodore H. White. New York: William Sloane Associates, 1948.

Sykes, Christopher. *Orde Wingate*. Cleveland: World, 1959.

Taylor, Theodore. *The Magnificent Mitscher*. New York: Norton, 1954.

Terraine, John. *The Life and Times of Lord Mountbatten*. New York: Holt, Rinehart & Winston, 1980.

Thomas, Lowell, and Edward Jablonski. *Doolittle: A Biography*. Garden City, N.Y.: Doubleday, 1976.

Tilloch, Derek. *Wingate: In Peace and War*. London: MacDonald, 1972.

Tuchman, Barbara W. *Stilwell and the American Experience in China, 1911–1945*. New York: Macmillan, 1970.

Vandegrift, A. A., with Robert Asprey. *Once a Marine: The Memoirs of General A. A. Vandegrift, U.S. Marine Corps*. New York: Norton, 1964.

Wainwright, Jonathan M. *General Wainwright's Story*. Ed. Robert Considine. Garden City, N.Y.: Doubleday, 1946.

Wavell, Archibald P. *Wavell: the Viceroy's Journal*. Ed. Penderel Moon. London: Oxford, 1973.

Wedemeyer, Albert C. *Wedemeyer Reports!* New York: Holt, 1958.

Wheeler, Gerald E. *Kinkaid of the Seventh Fleet: A Biography of Admiral Thomas C. Kinkaid, U.S. Navy*. Annapolis, Md.: Naval Institute Press, 1996.

Willoughby, Charles A., and John Chamberlain. *MacArthur, 1941–1945: Victory in the Pacific*. New York: McGraw-Hill, 1954.

Wilson, Henry Maitland. *Eight Years Overseas, 1939–1947*. London: Hutchinson, 1950.

Wingate, Ronald. *Lord Ismay: A Biography*. London: Hutchinson, 1970.

Wyant, William K. *Sandy Patch: A Biography of Lt. Gen. Alexander M. Patch*. New York: Praeger, 1991.

Zhukov, G. K. *Memoirs*. New York: Delacourt, 1971.

Ziegler, Philip. *Mountbatten*. New York: Harper & Row, 1985.

XVII. Close of the War

A. GENERAL

Allen, Louis. *The End of the War in Asia*. London: Hart-Davis MacGibbon, 1976.

Coox, Alvin D. *Japan: The Final Agony*. New York: Ballantine, 1970.

McCune, Shannon. *Intelligence on the Economic Collapse of Japan in 1945*. Lanham, Md.: University Press of America, 1989.

Moskin, J. Robert. *Mr. Truman's War: The Final Victories of World War II and the Birth of the Postwar World*. New York: Random House, 1996.

Sigal, Leon V. *Fighting to a Finish: The Politics of War Termination in the United States and Japan, 1945*. Ithaca, N.Y.: Cornell University Press, 1988.

Wheeler, Keith. *The Fall of Japan*. Alexandria, Va.: Time-Life Books, 1983.

B. PLANNED INVASION OF JAPAN

Allen, Thomas B., and Norman Polmar. *Codename Downfall: The Secret Plan to Invade Japan–and Why Truman Dropped the Bomb*. New York: Simon & Schuster, 1995.

Chappell, John D. *Before the Bomb: How America Approached the End of the Pacific War*. Lexington: University Press of Kentucky, 1997.

Giangreco, D. M. "Casualty Projections for the U.S. Invasions of Japan, 1945–1946: Planning and Policy Implications." *Journal of Military History* 61 (July 1997): 521–81.

Huber, Thomas M. *Pastel: Deception in the Invasion of Japan.* Fort Leavenworth, Kans.: Combat Studies Institute, U.S. Army Command and General Staff College, 1988.

Skates, John Ray. *The Invasion of Japan: Alternative to the Bomb.* Columbia: University of South Carolina Press, 1994.

Yoder, H. S., Jr. *Planned Invasion of Japan, 1945: The Siberian Weather Advantage.* Philadelphia: American Philosophical Society, 1997.

C. ATOMIC BOMB DECISION AND USE
   [SEE ALSO XII.B; XVII.B]

Alperovitz, Gar. *Atomic Diplomacy: Hiroshima, and Potsdam: The Use of the Atomic Bomb and the American Confrontation with Soviet Power.* New York: Simon & Schuster, 1965.

Alperovitz, Gar. *The Decision to Use the Atomic Bomb and the Architecture of an American Myth.* New York: Knopf, 1995.

Amrine, Michael. *The Great Decision: The Secret History of the Atomic Bomb.* New York: Putnam, 1959.

Bernstein, Barton J. *The Atomic Bomb: The Critical Issues.* Boston: Little, Brown, 1976.

Bernstein, Barton J. "Eclipsed by Hiroshima and Nagasaki: Early Thinking About Tactical Nuclear Weapons." *International Security* 15 (Spring 1991): 149–73.

Bernstein, Barton J. "A Postwar Myth: 500,000 Lives Saved." *Bulletin of the Atomic Scientists* 42 (June–July 1986): 38–40.

Bernstein, Barton J. "Truman and the A-Bomb: Targeting Noncombatants, Using the Bomb, and Defending the 'Decision.'" *Journal of Military History* 62 (July 1998): 547–70.

Bungei, Shunju. *The Day Man Lost.* Tokyo: Kodansha, 1972.

Chinnock, Frank W. *Nagasaki: The Forgotten Bomb.* New York: World, 1969.

Drea, Edward J. "Previews of Hell: Intelligence, the Bomb, and the Invasion of Japan." *MHQ* 7 (Spring 1995): 74–81.

Feis, Herbert. *Japan Subdued: The Atomic Bomb and the End of the War in the Pacific.* Princeton, N.J.: Princeton University Press, 1961.

Fussell, Paul. "Hiroshima: A Soldier's View." *New Republic* 185 (August 22, 29, 1981): 26–30.

Gallicchio, Marc. "After Nagasaki: General Marshall's Plan for Tactical Nuclear Weapons in Japan." *Prologue* 23 (Winter 1991): 396–404.

Giovannitti, Len, and Fred Freed. *The Decision to Drop the Bomb*. New York: Coward-McCann, 1965.

Goldstein, Donald, Katherine Dillon, and J. Michael Wenger. *Rain of Ruin: A Photographic History of Hiroshima and Nagasaki*. Washington, D.C.: Brassey's, 1995.

Hachkya, Michihiko. *Hiroshima Diary: The Journal of a Japanese Physician, August 6–September 30, 1945*. Chapel Hill: University of North Carolina Press, 1955.

Herken, Gregg. *The Winning Weapon: The Atomic Bomb in the Cold War, 1945–1950*. New York: Knopf, 1980.

Hersey, John. *Hiroshima*. New York: Modern Library, 1946.

Ibuse, Masuji. *Black Rain*. Trans. John Bester. New York: Bantam, 1985.

Kurzman, Dan. *Day of the Bomb: Countdown to Hiroshima*. New York: McGraw-Hill, 1986.

Lifton, Robert Jay, and Greg Mitchell. *Hiroshima in America: Fifty Years of Denial*. New York: Putnam, 1995.

Marx, Joseph Lawrence. *Nagasaki: The Necessary Bomb?* New York: Macmillan, 1971.

Messer, Robert L. "New Evidence on Truman's Decision." *Bulletin of the Atomic Scientists* 41 (August 1985): 50–56.

Minear, Richard H., ed. and trans. *Hiroshima: Three Witnesses*. Princeton, N.J.: Princeton University Press, 1990.

Nagai, Takashi. *The Bells of Nagasaki*. Tokyo: Kodansha International, 1984.

Newman, Robert P. *Truman and the Hiroshima Cult*. East Lansing: Michigan State University Press, 1995.

Ogura, Toyofumi. *Letters from the End of the World: A Firsthand Account of the Bombing of Hiroshima*. Tokyo: Kodansha International, 1997.

Osada, Arata. *Children of the A-bomb*. New York: Putnam, 1963.

Sherwin, Martin J. *A World Destroyed: The Atomic Bomb and the Grand Alliance*. New York: Knopf, 1975.

Stimson, Henry L. "The Decision to Use the Bomb." *Harper's Magazine* 197 (Feb. 1947): 97–107.

Takaki, Ronald T. *Hiroshima: Why America Dropped the Atomic Bomb*. Boston: Little, Brown, 1995.

Thomas, Gordon, and Max M. Witts. *Enola Gay*. New York: Stein & Day, 1977.

Tibbets, Paul W., with Clair Stebbins and Harry Franken. *The Tibbets Story.* New York: Stein & Day, 1978.

Wainstock, Dennis D. *The Decision to Drop the Atomic Bomb.* Westport, Conn.: Praeger, 1996.

Walker, J. Samuel. *Prompt and Utter Destruction: Truman and the Use of Atomic Bombs against Japan.* Chapel Hill: University of North Carolina Press, 1997.

D. JAPANESE SURRENDER

Brooks, Lester. *Behind Japan's Surrender: The Secret Struggle that Ended an Empire.* New York: McGraw-Hill, 1967.

Butow, Robert J. C. *Japan's Decision to Surrender.* Stanford, Calif.: Stanford University Press, 1954.

Coox, Alvin D. "The *Enola Gay* and Japan's Decision to Surrender." *Journal of American-East Asian Relations* 4 (Summer 1995): 161–67.

Kase, Toshikazu. *Journey to the Missouri.* New Haven, Conn.: Yale University Press, 1950.

Oya, Soichi, ed. *Japan's Longest Day.* Tokyo: Kodansha, 1965.

Quigley, Martin S. *Peace without Hiroshima: Secret Action at the Vatican in the Spring of 1945.* Lanham, Md.: Madison, 1991.

Sbrega, John J. "The Japanese Surrender: Some Unintended Consequences in Southeast Asia." *Asian Affairs* 7 (September–October 1979): 45–63.

XVIII. Postwar

A. DEMOBILIZATION AND DECOLONIZATION
[SEE ALSO IV INDIVIDUAL ENTRIES]

Ballard, Jack Stokes. *The Shock of Peace: Military and Economic Demobilization After World War II.* Lanham, Md.: University Press of America, 1983.

Dennis, Peter. *Troubled Days of Peace: Mountbatten and South East Asia Command, 1945–1946.* New York: St. Martin's, 1987.

Grimal, Henri. *Decolonization: The British, Dutch, and Belgian Empires, 1919–1963.* Trans. Stephan De Vos. London: Routledge & Kegan Paul, 1978.

Latourette, Kenneth S. *The American Record in the Far East, 1945–1951.* New York: Macmillan, 1952.

Louis, William Roger. *Imperialism at Bay: The United States and the Decolonization of the British Empire, 1941–1945.* New York: Oxford University Press, 1978.

McMahon, Robert I. *Colonialism and Cold War: The United States and the Struggle for Indonesian Independence, 1945–1949.* Ithaca, N.Y.: Cornell University Press, 1981.

Sbrega, John J. *Anglo-American Relations and Colonialism in East Asia, 1941–1945.* New York: Garland, 1983.

Smith, Tony, ed. *The End of the European Empire: Decolonization after World War II.* Lexington, Mass.: Heath, 1975.

Sundhaussen, Ulf. *The Road to Power: Indonesian Military Politics, 1945–1967.* New York: Oxford University Press, 1982.

Time-Life Books editors. *The Aftermath: Asia.* Alexandria, Va.: Time-Life Books, 1983.

B. WAR CRIMES TRIALS [SEE ALSO XIV]

Brackman, Arnold C. *The Other Nuremberg: The Untold Story of the Tokyo War Crimes Trials.* New York: Morrow, 1987.

Brode, Patrick. *Casual Slaughters and Accidental Judgments: Canadian War Crimes Prosecutions, 1944–1948.* Toronto: University of Toronto Press, 1997.

Goodwin, Michael J. *Shobun: A Forgotten War Crime in the Pacific.* Mechanicsburg, Pa.: Stackpole, 1995.

Hosoya, Chihiro, et al., eds. *The Tokyo War Crimes Trial: An International Symposium.* Tokyo: Kodansha, 1986.

Lael, Richard L. *The Yamashita Precedent: War Crimes and Command Responsibility.* Wilmington, Del.: Scholarly Resources, 1982.

Minear, R. H. *Victors' Justice: The Tokyo War Crimes Trial.* Princeton, N.J.: Princeton University Press, 1971.

Piccigallo, Phillip R. *The Japanese on Trial: Allied War Crimes Operations in the East, 1945–1951.* Austin: University of Texas Press, 1979.

Potter, John Deane. *A Soldier Must Hang: The Biography of an Oriental General.* London: Muller, 1963.

Pritchard, R. J., and S. M. Zaide, eds. *The Tokyo War Crimes Trial: The Complete Transcripts of the Proceedings of the International Miltiary Tribunal for the Far East.* 22 vols. New York: Garland, 1981.

Reel, A. Frank. *The Case of General Yamashita.* Chicago: University of Chicago Press, 1949.

Roling, B. V. V., and Antonio Cassese. *The Tokyo Trial and Beyond: Reflections of a Peacemonger.* Cambridge: Polity, 1993.

Russell, Edward F. L. *The Knights of Bushido: The Shocking History of Japanese War Atrocities.* New York: Dutton, 1958.

Shiroyama, Saburo. *War Criminal: The Life and Death of Hirota Koki.* Trans. John Bester. New York: Kodansha International, 1977.

Tanaka, Yuki. *Hidden Horrors: Japanese War Crimes in World War II.* Boulder, Colo.: Westview, 1996.

Taylor, Lawrence. *A Trial of Generals: Homma, Yamashita, MacArthur.* South Bend, Ind.: Icarus, 1981.

C. ALLIED OCCUPATION OF JAPAN

Baerwald, Hans H. *The Purge of Japanese Leaders Under the Occupation.* Westport, Conn.: Greenwood, 1977.

Braw, Monica. *The Atomic Bomb Suppressed: American Censorship in Occupied Japan.* Armonk, N.Y.: Sharpe, 1991.

Buckley, Roger J. *Occupation Diplomacy: Britain, the United States and Japan, 1945–1952.* New York: Cambridge University Press, 1982.

Burkman, Thomas W., ed. *The Occupation of Japan: Arts and Culture.* Norfolk, Va.: MacArthur Memorial, 1988.

Burkman, Thomas W., ed. *The Occupation of Japan: The International Context.* Norfolk, Va.: MacArthur Memorial, 1984.

Cohen, Theodore. *Remaking Japan: The American Occupation as New Deal.* New York: Free Press, 1987.

Finn, Richard B. *Winners in Peace: MacArthur, Yoshida, and Postwar Japan.* Berkeley: University of California Press, 1992.

Harries, Meirion, and Susie Harries. *Sheathing the Sword: The Demilitarisation of Japan.* New York: Macmillan, 1987.

Kawai, Kazuo. *Japan's American Interlude.* Chicago: University Press of Chicago, 1960.

Nishi, Toshio. *Unconditional Democracy: Education and Politics in Occupied Japan, 1945–1952.* Stanford, Calif.: Hoover Institution, 1982.

Oppler, Alfred C. *Legal Reform in Occupied Japan: A Participant Looks Back.* Princeton, N.J.: Princeton University Press, 1976.

Perry, John Curtis. *Beneath the Eagle's Wings: Americans in Occupied Japan.* New York: Dodd, Mead, 1980.

Redford, L.H., ed. *The Occupation of Japan: Economic Policy and Reform.* Norfolk, Va.: MacArthur Memorial, 1980.

Redford, L. H., ed. *The Occupation of Japan: Impact of Legal Reform.* Norfolk, Va.: MacArthur Memorial, 1978.

Schaller, Michael. *The American Occupation of Japan: The Origins of the Cold War in Asia.* New York: Oxford University Press, 1985.

Schonberger, Howard B. *Aftermath of War: Americans and the Remaking of Japan, 1945–1952.* Kent, Ohio: Kent State University Press, 1989.

Sebald, William J. *With MacArthur in Japan: A Personal History of the Occupation.* New York: Norton, 1965.

Ward, Robert W., and Sadamoto Yoshikazu. *Democratizing Japan: The Allied Occupation.* Honolulu: University of Hawaii Press, 1987.

Wildes, Harry E. *Typhoon in Tokyo: The Occupation and Its Aftermath.* New York: Macmillan, 1954.

Williams, Justin. *Japan's Political Revolution under MacArthur: A Participant's Account.* Athens: University of George Press, 1979.

Wolfe, Robert, ed. *Americans as Proconsuls: United States Military Government in Germany and Japan, 1944–1952.* Carbondale: Southern Illinois University Press, 1984.

D. PEACE TREATY

Cohen, Bernard C. *The Political Process and Foreign Policy: The Making of the Japanese Peace Settlement.* Princeton, N.J.: Princeton University Press, 1957.

Dunn, Frederick S. *Peace-Making and the Settlement with Japan.* Princeton, N.J.: Princeton University Press, 1963.

Yoshitsu, Michael M. *Japan and the San Francisco Peace Settlement.* New York: Columbia University Press, 1983.

E. UNITED NATIONS [SEE ALSO III.B.3.]

Campbell, Thomas M. *Masquerade Peace: America's UN Policy, 1944–1945.* Tallahassee: Florida State University Press, 1973.

Holburn, Louise W. *War and Peace Aims of the United Nations.* 2 vols. Boston: World Peace Foundation, 1943–1948.

Hoopes, Townsend, and Douglas Brinkley. *FDR and the Creation of the U.N.* New Haven, Conn.: Yale University Press, 1997.

Meisler, Stanley. *United Nations: The First Fifty Years.* New York: Atlantic Monthly Press, 1995.

Russell, Ruth B. *A History of the United Nations Charter: The Role of the United States, 1940–1945.* Washington, D.C.: Brookings Institution, 1958.

XIX. Beginning of the Cold War [see also III.B.]

Anderson, Terry H. *The United States, Great Britain, and the Cold War, 1944–1947*. Columbia: University of Missouri Press, 1981.

Buhite, Russell D. *Soviet-American Relations in Asia, 1945–1954*. Norman: University of Oklahoma Press, 1981.

Gaddis, John Lewis. *The United States and the Origins of the Cold War, 1941–1947*. New York: Columbia University Press, 1972.

Gallicchio, Mark S. *The Cold War Begins in Asia: American East Asian Policy and the Fall of the Japanese Empire*. New York: Columbia University Press, 1988.

Gormly, James L. *The Collapse of the Grand Alliance, 1945–1948*. Baton Rouge: Louisiana State University Press, 1987.

Herring, George C. *Aid to Russia, 1941–1946: Strategy, Diplomacy, and the Origins of the Cold War*. New York: Columbia University Press, 1973.

Mastny, Vojtech. *Russia's Road to the Cold War: Diplomacy, Warfare, and the Politics of Communism, 1941–1945*. New York: Columbia University Press, 1979.

Messer, Robert L. *The End of an Alliance: James F. Byrnes, Roosevelt, Truman, and the Origins of the Cold War*. Chapel Hill: University of North Carolina Press, 1982.

Nagai, Yonosuke, and Akira Iriye, eds. *The Origins of the Cold War in Asia*. New York: Columbia University Press, 1977.

Rothwell, Victor. *Britain and the Cold War, 1941–1947*. London: Cape, 1982.

Siracusa, Joseph M., ed. *The American Diplomatic Revolution: A Documentary History of the Cold War, 1941–1947*. New York: Holt, Rinehart and Winston, 1976.

Westad, Odd Arne. *Cold War and Revolution: Soviet-American Rivalry and the Origins of the Chinese Civil War*. New York: Columbia University Press, 1993.

About the Author

Anne Sharp Wells (M.L.S., University of Alabama; M.A., Mississippi State University) is a member of the staff of the George C. Marshall Foundation and the assistant editor of the *Journal of Military History*. She previously served on the faculties of the Virginia Military Institute and Mississippi State University. In addition to teaching a college course on the United States and World War II, she has edited the *Newsletter of the World War Two Studies Association,* participated in the Douglas MacArthur Biographical Project, and coauthored two books about the war with D. Clayton James: *From Pearl Harbor to VJ Day: The American Armed Forces in World War II* (1995) and *A Time for Giants: Politics of the American High Command in World War II* (1987). She has written two other books with James: *America and the Great War, 1914–1920* (1998) and *Refighting the Last War: Command and Crisis in Korea, 1950–1953* (1992).